The Seattle School of Theology & Psychology
2501 Elliott Ave.
Seattle, WA 98121
theseattleschool.edu

Loving to Know

"This book is a *tour de force* of clarity, depth, and compelling wisdom. Esther Meek argues that we become what we love and that if we love truth then we must love to engage in the interpersonal dialogue of seeing the world well through the prism of another's heart. Her premise is lived out through dialogue with a range of authors that makes my head spin. She seizes their wisdom and yet pursues it further to the person of Christ than any I have read. This is an epistemologically therapeutic embrace of how to live well in the world of divergent thought that nevertheless longs to reveal Jesus as the center of all true wisdom. It is a breathtaking and beautiful labor."

—Dan B. Allender
Professor of Counseling Psychology and Founding President
Mars Hill Graduate School

"*Loving to Know* is a marvelous follow-up to Meek's *Longing to Know*. Like her earlier work, this is clearly the work of a masterful, compassionate teacher inviting a wide audience to reflect on the nature of knowledge. Here is epistemology for the people, so to speak. In the process, through a rich set of conversation partners, Meek puts her own stamp on a Reformed epistemology that makes love and covenant central to our account of knowing. An excellent achievement."

—James K. A. Smith
Professor of Philosophy
Calvin College

Loving to Know

Introducing Covenant Epistemology

Esther Lightcap Meek

CASCADE *Books* · Eugene, Oregon

LOVING TO KNOW
Introducing Covenant Epistemology

Portions of chapter 6 are taken from "Speaking the Truth in Love" by John Hughes
ed. ISBN 978-1-59638-164-3 article titled "Servant Thinking; The Polanyian
Workings of the Framean Triad" pg 611–27. P&R Publishing Co., P.O. Box 817,
Phillipsburg N.J. 08865.
www.prpbooks.com

An earlier version of Texture 5 appeared as "Making the Most of College: Learning
With Friends" in *Comment* magazine, the opinion journal of CARDUS:
www.cardus.ca/comment

Cascade Books
An Imprint of Wipf and Stock Publishers
199 W. 8th Ave., Suite 3
Eugene, OR 97401

www. wipfandstock.com

ISBN 13: 978-1-60899-928-6

Cataloging-in-Publication data

Meek, Esther L., 1953–.

Loving to know : introducing covenant epistemology / Esther Lightcap Meek.

xviii + 518 p. ; 23 cm. —Includes bibliographical references and indices.

ISBN 13: 978-1-60899-928-6

1. Knowledge, Theory of (Religion). 2. Christianity—Philosophy. I. Title.

BT50 M44 2011

In memory of Russell Louden

CONTENTS

Acknowledgments / xi

Introduction / xiii

PART ONE: On the Way

1 The Need for "Epistemological Therapy": Our Defective "Default" in Knowing / 3

    Texture 1: Rekindling the Longing to Know / 31

2 Another Kind of Knowing: Suggestive Preliminary Conversations and Proposal / 35

3 What Covenant Epistemology Offers / 49

PART TWO: Transformation

4 Knowing as Subsidiary-Focal Integration: Conversation with Michael Polanyi / 67

    Texture 2: Body Knowledge: Forays into the Subsidiary / 104

5 Knowing as Transformation: Conversation with James Loder / 123

    Texture 3: Knowing as Transformation, Not Information: Implications for Academic and Theological Curriculum, Education, and Pedagogy / 131

PART THREE: Covenant

6 Knowing as Stewardship: Conversation with John Frame / 145

    Texture 4: Anticipative Knowing and Common Grace / 184

7 Knowing as Unfolding Covenant Relationship: Conversation with Mike Williams / 193

PART FOUR: Interpersonhood

8   Knowing as Interpersonal: Conversation with John
    Macmurray / 215

9   Knowing as I-You Encounter: Conversation with Martin
    Buber / 248

   *Texture 5: Friendship and Learning: All Knowing is Knowing
    With / 264*

10 Knowing Before the Face of the Holy: Second Conversation
    with James Loder / 272

   Texture 6: A Sense of Personal Beauty / 298

11 Knowing and Healthy Interpersonhood: Conversation with
    David Schnarch / 310

12 Knowing as Dance: Conversation with Colin Gunton / 327

   Texture 7: Dance as Metaphysical Therapy / 360

13 Reality as Gift: Conversation with Philip Rolnick / 365

   *Texture 8: Stopping Short of Personhood: Inadvertent Insights
    from Marjorie Grene / 383*

PART FIVE: Covenant Epistemology

14 Contours of Covenant Epistemology / 395

15 Inviting the Real: An Epistemological Etiquette / 425

16 Knowing for Shalom / 469

    Bibliography / 481
    Subject Index / 489
    Name Index / 515

Acknowledgments

THIS BOOK IS DEDICATED to the memory of my friend, Dr. (and Rev.) Russell Louden who, in the wake of the publication of *Longing to Know*, was one of a handful of readers who walked into my life and told me what I knew that I didn't know I knew (which is why we need a nuanced epistemology of knowing on the way!). Russell artlessly lived covenant epistemology. A couple weeks before he died of cancer in August of 2008, I told him that I had realized that he *was* this book. He lived *semper transformanda*, continually, joyously, indwelling and disseminating the vision of God. He was always present in the present. Russell thought everybody needed to know knowing in order to know God—and vice versa. To know Russell was to be known by him, loved into joy and wholeness. I have seen this in the countenances of his congregation, Emmanuel Presbyterian Church in Wildwood, Missouri (Russell called them "his Emmanuelites"!) even as I have known it in my own life and work.

Dr. Robert Frazier, my friend and colleague in philosophy at Geneva College, is the one with whom I am currently blessed to know. He is my first reader, whose insightful comments and assuring assessment helps birth my work. He invests countless hours in this ministration, yet acts continually as if it is the thing he most delights to do. There is no decent gauge for the value of this personal and professional gift.

I am grateful to Geneva College for continuous support for my summers of writing. Specifically, I thank Dr. David Guthrie, former Academic Dean, for his undying passion "to start a project" with and for the faculty at Geneva. I am grateful to have the opportunity to teach this book at Geneva, engaging continually with eager (and unsuspecting!) students in these conversations. The *Christian Understanding of Life* classes, over the years, have shaped me and the conversation that is this book. Special thanks to the students in Fall 2009, who first read a complete version of the manuscript, helpfully reflecting it back to me. Special thanks back over the years to the Covenant Theological Seminary class, *Epistemology*, Spring 2002, in which Dr. Mike Williams and I and class members began to forge the idea of covenant epistemology. I also thank others who read and offered comments, great ideas, and text corrections, including Starr Meek, Andrew Colbert, and Dr. R. J. Snell. Thank you to Mary Speckhard and Garrett Sipes, who helped prepare the manuscript for publication. Thanks to Dr. Robin Parry of Cascade Books for his editorial work, counsel, and encouragement. And thanks to Trinity Evangelical Divinity School, Westminster Seminary in Southern California, and Erskine Seminary, for inviting me to present on covenant epistemology. These special opportunities inspired my ongoing work.

Finally, deep thanks to readers of *Longing to Know*—students, professionals, amateurs (i.e., lovers) extraordinary knowers all—who have entered and continued with me in conversation. May this book contribute to widening and deepening that stream.

Introduction

THIS IS A BOOK about how we know. Knowing is something we all do all the time. Most of us think we are pretty good at knowing throughout our experience. So it asks a lot of the reader to accept that a tome on this subject is worth reading.

Further, this book claims that something has infected our knowing that thwarts it, yet it is something people generally do not recognize. So to prove its value, the book first has to convince you of the reality of the need. To do this it must move upstream in a strong current of a certain popular savvy about knowing.

Quite possibly to reduce the appeal even further, some would say this discussion has to be philosophical. How we know what we know is a philosophical question, and the topic is called epistemology. This book represents my own creative epistemological proposal.

I am one of those odd people who think that epistemology is almost the most important and practical thing everybody needs to consider. This calling compels me always to try to acquaint everybody with philosophy, and to talk about these hard-to-express matters in a way that invites everybody to indwell and be shaped by them. On the other hand, I have every confidence that plenty of ordinary people are odd, if I am, in feeling that epistemology matters. Even if we haven't known that it is epistemology, we have realized many times that something related to knowing is gumming up the works of our lives. Because we haven't known what it is nor had the tools to begin to cope with it, the problems have continued to plague us. Epistemology is important to all of us.

Professional, in-house, philosophy inadvertently locks up its treasures rather than winsomely adapting them for the rest of us. The onus placed on guild language means that philosophers seeking to speak with the uninitiated have to revoke the guild. So be it; while I respect the value of formal philosophical exchange, I feel no lockstep loyalty to guild language. If all people actually live responses to philosophical questions such as how we know, then philosophical proposals should be expressed for ordinary people as their audience.

But then, for people with no previous philosophical awareness raising, which, sadly, is the vast majority in the United States, tackling a popular philosophy book like *Loving to Know* means exercising courage to enter into some discussions in which they feel the discomfort of half-understanding. Hospitably welcoming beginning philosophy students is something I love to do. But I repeatedly tell them: "You have to learn to be okay with half-understanding. Thicken your skin! Hear my encouragement! Philosophy is difficult, and it isn't that you lack the capacity or the need to study it. It tackles life's most fundamental orientations, the commitments that shape our very language and rationality; so, of course, it is difficult. But it is also deeply valuable and practical. It has widespread personal and cultural impact. I once thought proficiency in the discipline would eliminate my own half-understanding; instead, I learned to thicken my skin. And once you get acquainted with my epistemological proposals, you will see why I am confident that half-understanding is nevertheless productive."

I believe that the separation between guild and street in philosophy is itself, in part, a result of the very problem this book labors to identify and heal. To write a guild-approved epistemology is to perpetuate the problem rather than offer the subverting cure. So I take an approach that invites in the uninitiated as its primary audience. And though we have philosophical discussions in this book, and though I believe them to be expert philosophy critically valuable for the guild, the conversation stays ordinary: kitchen table philosophy.

Professional philosophers may well find this disappointing. I hope they will see that the book's approach reflects its epistemological proposal. It should not be seen as sub-par so much as creatively subversive. But to see that involves personal investment, formation, in this epistemology. Consonant with the epistemology it commends, this book offers a case that is intrinsically practical. So, again on the other hand, I am confident that for this very reason this book offers philosophers, and scholars generally, a critical contribution to the professional conversation and to academic training.

This book proposes that we take as a paradigm, of all acts of knowing, the unfolding, covenantally constituted, interpersonal relationship. The book itself is the journal of my own unfolding coming to know, my search for "the face that will not go away." I have tried to reflect both of these things in the structure of the book itself: it unfolds, conversation by conversation, foray by foray. I do this both for integrity's sake, to prompt readers' feel of the thing, and to invite you into the conversation.

So I have taken some creative liberties with the expected timeless linearity of books and arguments. Most noticeably, I characterize my engagement of others' work as successive conversations. Conversations are interpersonal exchanges typified by deep, indwelling listening, and then by a response in which the thoughtful participant creatively melds insights gleaned with others previously acquired. And by conversation I do not mean noncommittal, information-passing chit-chat; I have in mind conversations in which the participants assume the posture of mutual submission with a loved and trusted friend whom each invites to speak into their lives.

My argument unfolds conversation by conversation, the way a group of close friends on a lengthy walking tour venture might walk for awhile next to this one or that one of the group. Then, as those hikers might take stock together around a campfire at the end of the day's journey, so at chapters' ends I interweave the gleanings of each fresh conversation with the ones before.

I see my personal understanding as a growing string of such conversations. I have moved from one to the next to mature my lived orientation to life. *Loving to Know*, in a significant way, just is my intellectual autobiography. I want to model the actual practice of it as the coming to know that this epistemology commends. And while these particular conversants may not be the most acclaimed philosophers or theologians, and they may not be widely known, in presenting my own learning with them, I am intentionally modeling the delightful particularity of any thoughtful person's "being on the way" to knowing. I am showing, as Ludwig Wittgenstein said memorably, "how to go on." Indeed, this being on the way with friends is the essence of my epistemological proposal.

In addition to the main conversations, I have invented "textures," and interwoven them with the text. A texture is an excursus, a foray; it goes at the matter from a different direction, or from it to venture in a fresh direction. I want there to be interweaving, but not so tightly as to create a homogeneously smooth product. Like handmade paper or a roughly woven tapestry, the gritty pieces add earthy reality to the thing.

Both of these strategies are meant to subvert the very defective approach to knowing that this epistemic proposal hopes to challenge and heal.[1] The textures also offer sabbathlike, rhythmical interludes to break the intensity of sustained argument. Long journeys require rests and side excursions.

Adding to the variegated nature of this odd book on epistemology is the fact that its culminating chapter is "an epistemological etiquette" that compends concrete ways that we, in our efforts to know, "invite the real." As text, the etiquette is distinctive because it is at once a meditation and a catechesis to form aspiring covenantal knowers.

So readers will do well to pattern their reading of the book on the book's own structure. It perhaps may be best read episodically over a period of time. It is, of course, best read in conjunction with the reader's own coming to know, and in concert with the reader's own friends in learning. I have supplied questions for discussion of each chapter and texture.

Readers of my former book, *Longing to Know,* will find *Loving to Know* different and similar. This book represents the further development of my covenant epistemology, promised in a footnote in that one. It takes the epistemic proposal that drives *Longing to Know* and advances it into the personal—the interpersoned, as I will call it. Knowing works the way I have described it in that book because its telltale features are fraught with the interpersoned.

Plus, the focus of this book is different: written for people considering Christianity and struggling with questions about knowing, *Longing to Know* addressed the specific question, "Can we know God?," by talking about how we know anything at all. I argued that knowing God is like knowing your auto mechanic: it is an ordinary act of knowing (distinct for its life-transforming impact!). Knowing knowing makes better sense of knowing God, along with knowing anything at all.

Loving to Know, by contrast, is written for anybody wanting think more deeply about knowing—for whatever reason, from living well and

---

1. Some great works of fiction are stories of journeys toward a great quest, into which particular adventures and story-telling is embedded. J. R. R. Tolkien's *Lord of the Rings* and C. S. Lewis's *Chronicles of Narnia* are well-known recent ones; Homer's *Odyssey* and *Iliad* are ancient ones. Another that comes to mind is Richard Adams' *Watership Down.* Rabbit legend stories such as "Rowsby Woof and the Fairy Wog-Dog" interweave with the larger narrative. *Loving to Know* mirrors this time-honored episodic unfolding. Its distinction is that it does so as epistemology, and as essential to epistemology.

Christian discipleship, to professional excellence, and academic and philosophical scholarship. I try to speak in a way that welcomes all and excludes none. I am hoping that you will sense that this conversation is with you, along with others.

Longing to Know applied a general approach to knowing to a very specific question. Many readers also saw that the general approach to knowing applies in every corner of their lives—that is part of the way the very specific question is dealt with. This book expounds the general approach to knowing in its further developed version, suggests the wide range of its applications and implications, and shapes the reader to pursue implementing it wherever knowing happens.

Longing to Know has its own contrived structure; *Loving to Know* has a different one. And where the first book's chapters were short— bathroom reading, as I thought of them at the time—this book's chapters are the length of a seminar reading assignment. Taken as a whole, *Loving to Know* constitutes the bulk of a single course's reading list. In fact, it is my text in my course, *Christian Understanding of Life*.

Playing off the driving analogy of the last book, that knowing God is like knowing your auto mechanic, I argue that knowing your auto mechanic is like knowing God. I want to say that the kind of transformative interpersoned, face-to-face encounter and communion that all of us experience in the richest moments of our lives affords us the best paradigm of *all* knowing. For Christian believers, it is knowing Christ in communion that best captures the dynamism of knowing well in every corner of our lives and pursuits. I tap into a biblical theological vision; but for the best theological reasons, along with other sorts of reasons, I insist that covenant epistemology describes knowing for, and is commendably employed by, both people who know God and people who don't see themselves that way.

One spring I inherited the care of a wild bird from one of my students. Bandit, a cedar waxwing, fallen from his nest, had been rescued by my student and his family. Soon after, a well-meaning housesitter had clipped his wings. At the point that Bandit took up with me, his one wing looked virtually non-existent, and he could not fly. He looked simply horrible.

His former family, I noted in the exchange, would pick him up in their cupped hands to carry him around, and playfully called his fluttering struggle "break-dancing." Early in my time with Bandit, I did the same. I was quickly smitten with this bird; in fact, the love began when that student first told me of Bandit, before that student or I realized that I should inherit him.

I attended carefully to that little bird. In so doing, I figured out what he loved and what he hated. I discovered that he wanted always to see my face (waxwings are group birds; I was Bandit's group!). I learned, through close proximity, that he abhorred loud machine noises. I discovered that he ate, not seeds, but fruit (80 percent) and bugs (20 percent). Never was he so happy as when I made fruit salad! And I figured out that he was happiest to be carried around on a stick, rather than in my cupped hands. All I needed to do to "recover" him from wherever he happened to be was to stick out the stick, and he hopped on to it jauntily, with no "break-dancing." I figured out that, if you are a bird, having your flying feathers touched or petted is definitely not a good thing. It would be like bending the wings of a jet, or cutting the veins of a human. I learned what he was saying in the rich variety of his chirps. I lived life on his terms, scavenging my neighborhood for wild berries, throwing a diaper over my shoulder so I could keep him near. A few people thought I was crazy. But I was also somehow finding myself reflected in his gaze, and actually understanding God better.

Over that summer on the stick, and on my shoulder, Bandit re-grew his rich chestnut feathers (I fell in love with the color brown), including his crest, and the signature yellow tips and red "wax drop" that gives the species its name. One day in September, after twenty minutes on my shoulder as I sat on my deck, when I was not expecting it, Bandit took off and flew, straight and true, to the woods behind my house. Not only Bandit had changed; I had changed as well. It had been a mutual healing.

That is covenant knowing; thus it offers a concrete example of what I want to describe and recommend in this book. You may think that you need no book guidance to know a wild bird. Why you do is the question with which this book begins.

 PART ONE

On the Way

The Need for "Epistemological Therapy"

Our Defective "Default" in Knowing

*E*PISTEMOLOGY IS A WORD that many people have never heard, find intimidating. Many think that epistemology must be a field of study that is inscrutable, impractical, and not relevant to real life. Many people think the subject would be way over their heads, and painful to engage. This widespread perception has some truth to it: the formal philosophical study of epistemology has often deserved these epithets. But *epistemology* is the study of how we know what we know. It concerns knowing, and knowing is something that we *all* do *all* the time. It is neither optional nor avoidable. And we spend life seeking to know well. Growing grapes and making wine involves knowing. Working with computers involves knowing. Cancer research involves knowing. Seeking God involves knowing. Artistry of any sort involves knowing. Marketing involves knowing. Counseling involves knowing. Athletics involves knowing.

Knowing, like any semi-automatic aptitude, can be misdirected, or, with practice, can become a fine-tuned skill. A person aspiring to be an expert runner, or simply physically fit, can benefit from being coached how to breathe. Such coaching may feel odd, difficult, unnecessary, and for a time even unnatural. But the result will be better breathing and running. Similarly, what I am doing in this book is coaching readers to replace faulty habits of knowing with healthy ones.

In this book I want to talk about how we know what we know—epistemology—in such a way that everybody who reads it will benefit from it in every area of life that involves knowing—which is every area of life.

Everyone, in their knowing, is making some assumptions, probably not even consciously, about what knowing is. When my children were younger, we read a series of books about Amelia Bedelia, an enthusiastic, well-intended house servant, who always managed to misunderstand the directions she had been given.[1] The misunderstanding always had to do with the oddities of our English language. For example, once Amelia Bedelia was sent to prune the bushes. What she did was to stick prunes all over the bushes, when what she was supposed to have done was to cut back their branches. Just as Amelia Bedelia's doing the task involved a tacit assumption about what the task was, so knowing involves tacit assumption about what knowing is.

Whereas most of us get it right about pruning the bushes, I want to argue that most of us get it wrong about what knowing is. And while sticking prunes on the bushes isn't perhaps the end of the world, getting it wrong about knowing—as a culture, over centuries, and as individual participants in that culture—turns out to be damaging to ourselves, our world, and our knowing in any endeavor. So while it may be a bit uncomfortable at first, exposing what is defective in our ideas about what knowing is, and reworking it, will make a great difference, and also become more natural, as we go.[2]

I am passionate about the importance of this book on epistemology. It endeavors to correct a defective outlook we all have without even knowing we have it, and one that issues in damage in all corners of our lives. My sister has a disease so rare that doctors don't even know what its symptoms are. This means that my sister can have something wrong, in just about any bodily process, and nobody recognizes it as the disease it is. This describes aptly the situation in epistemology: unhealth crops up in every discipline, and often is not even recognized. Healing this disease will have widespread positive impact—perhaps even cultural change.

Education guru Parker Palmer underscores the critical importance of epistemology to all of life.

> What is the nature of the knower? What is the nature of the known? And what is the nature of the relation between the two? These questions belong to a discipline called *epistemology*. It is an abstract and sometimes even esoteric inquiry into the dynamics of knowing. Its six-syllable name does not leap to our lips in normal conversation, and its insights appear remote from daily

---

1. Peggy and Herman Parish. Amelia Bedelia Series, multiple publishers.

2. To name just a couple factors that make studying knowing especially odd: what I am about to say is that there is something we haven't known about our knowing; and, in talking about how we know, we are doing it, practicing knowing, in the very act.

life . . . But now I understand that the patterns of epistemology can help us decipher the patterns of our lives. Its images of the knower, the known, and their relationship are formative in the way an educated person not only thinks but acts. The shape of our knowledge becomes the shape of our living; the relation of the knower to the known becomes the relation of the living self to the larger world.[3]

In his work, Palmer argues that the single key to the rehabilitation of pedagogy is challenging and replacing the reigning epistemological vision that has produced damaging practical effects for education, for persons, and for the world. As we talk about epistemology, we will come to understand this.

So this is a book for people who may never have heard of epistemology but who are involved in knowing all the time. It is also a book for people like me who have studied epistemology professionally for decades. I offer the proposals of this book as both common-sensically therapeutic, but also as philosophically worthwhile, a philosophical conversation that I hope many will enter and forward. But of the two groups, I put the "ordinary" knowers first—because we are all, after all, ordinary knowers.

OUR "SUBCUTANEOUS EPISTEMOLOGICAL LAYER," AND OUR "DEFAULT MODE"

In this book I want to offer a fresh, transformative understanding of what knowing is. But before I talk about this, we need first to see how what we think knowing is adversely impacts what we are doing in knowing, and why all this matters so very much. So in this opening chapter we start with that.

Our outlook on what knowing is shapes all our knowing, whether we are aware of it or not. We can be operating, without knowing it, from defective or disordered presumptions about knowing. To make the point graphically, we all have acquired "a subcutaneous epistemological layer"—something operating from "under the skin" of our knowing. I also think of it as a default mode or setting—a way we (to compare ourselves to a computer) are preset to function. This default needs to be reset. I want to help us identify that subcutaneous layer, to expose that default mode to the light of day. "Epistemological therapy" is what I call

---

3. Palmer, *To Know as We are Known*, 21.

my personal effort to help people reform their default epistemological settings in a way that brings health, hope, and productivity.

I do not mean to insinuate that a person could adopt an epistemological stance the way he/she might select a ripe tomato. Epistemological commitments are so much a part of us that they are more like our body, portions of which we may view "objectively" only with the help of a mirror, a video camera, or another person or group. And when we stop and look at our body or our epistemic commitments, it feels awkward; it bears little resemblance to our lived bodily experience. Usually we simply live out of an implicitly held epistemological vision. So scrutinizing and reforming our epistemological vision involves an allusive, complex, and possibly invasive process, rather than a calculating or arbitrary choice. But we do need to begin by identifying the commitments of which we haven't been conscious, bringing them to the surface for a time, so that we can assess and adjust them. The ultimate goal is not to put an end to tacitly indwelling epistemic commitments, but to reform them, and then indwell them with intentionality and virtuosity. In fact, this book argues that knowing is more about transformation than it is about information. What I expect and intend is for this book itself itself to be the therapy that reshapes your epistemological stance as you read.

Since knowing is integral to everything humans do, our epistemic default impacts how we live and everything we do. It can adversely impact every kind of work. It impacts education, for example: since teachers teach knowledge, faulty and hidden assumptions can shape the process. Teaching is just one practice which stands to be made more effective and intentional if we do some "epistemological therapy." Business, engineering, and library cataloguing are a few others. Others are theological studies, and living as a Christian. Any area where knowing is involved is adversely impacted by the default that we don't name and reform. It is both responsible and advantageous to uncover that subcutaneous epistemological layer and diagnose its health.

I believe that the source of the defective default setting is the Western tradition of ideas and culture.[4] We acquire this default epistemic

---

4. By this I refer to the last couple millennia of culture and thought, especially dating from the Athenian civilization of Plato's time; Plato, known as the father of Western philosophy, lived around 400 BCE. The other equally formative intellectual stream in western civilization is the Judeo-Christian one, dating back to Abraham in the third millennium BCE, and transformed by Jesus the Messiah around the turn from BCE to CE—the very designations of which indicate his influence.

setting, we may say, with our mother's milk, because it is embedded in the Western cultural tradition. The legacy of the Western philosophical tradition continues to issue to children and grown-ups a default setting concerning knowledge.

This defective default epistemic setting we inherit actually goes against the grain of our humanness. What I will propose in this book as a replacement will restore us to the grain of our humanness. So there is a second sense in which I do not mean to insinuate that we can choose an epistemic outlook as we would choose a ripe tomato. For one outlook rather than another can align more favorably, healthfully, productively, with who we are as humans. Perhaps we may say that there is a deeper, truer, default.

The default we have inherited is a distortion that leads us to think that knowing is something other than what it is. The default means that even when we are going about knowing humanly, what we have been trained to see blinds us to what we are actually doing, which is actually working. It leads us to deemphasize the most important parts of the knowing event, rather than cultivate them. All this will become clearer as the book unfolds.

So what is this acquired epistemic default, and in what way is it defective? What do most people think that knowledge is?[5] For starters, when we think of knowledge, we tend to picture it as *information, facts, statements, and proofs.* Knowledge *consists exclusively of* statements, pieces of information, facts. The best (and only) specimens of knowledge are those adequately justified by other statements that offer rational support, reasons, for the claim in question. Knowledge is statements and proofs. Knowledge is facts. I sometimes use the word, "factoids," for its slight connotation of disconnected bits whose meaning isn't particularly connected to the grand scheme of things. This is how we tend to picture what knowledge is.

---

5. In constructing this diagnostic tool, I do not draw on particular formal discussions but rather address what people generally commonly exhibit, whether they have studied it or not, and whether it is true or not. However, much formal philosophical discourse from the nineteenth century on takes umbrage at these binary oppositions. Notable voices are Friedrich Nietzsche, Martin Heidegger and the Continental phenomenological tradition, Michael Polanyi, and Francois Lyotard. Currently, some scholars in virtually every field of study and practice, including theology and Christian thought, work to identify these and challenge them, as I am doing in this book.

People just assume that knowledge is information. To suggest that this is an epistemic outlook that could be revised can sound ridiculous to novice ears. Having a stance about knowledge being about information is like having an opinion about breathing. That's why this book is going to be a tough sell. You will have to make a decision in the half-dark about buying it.

A "DAISY OF DICHOTOMIES"

Knowledge, thought of in this way, involves some sharp distinctions. This feature of our default setting becomes apparent when we start to think about what people generally contrast knowledge *to*. I am about to list a series of dichotomies. If you are visual, like I am, you can sketch the daisy as we go. For every pair, the first one goes on the yellow middle, and the second is a white petal. Put knowledge and its associates at the center of the daisy, and cast all their counterparts to the outside as petals, and you have it. I mean this as a diagnostic tool that helps us get a sense of our epistemic default.

Here's how people generally think of knowledge:

- *Knowledge* gets contrasted to *belief.*

- Knowledge is identified with *facts*; facts stand over against *opinions* and *interpretation*, as well as against *values* and *morals.*

- Knowledge and facts are identified with *reason*; reason is opposed to *faith*, also to *emotion.*

- Knowledge, facts, and reason are identified with *theory*; theory, everyone thinks, is distinct from *application*, and distinct from *action.*

- Knowledge, facts, reason, and theory are epitomized by *science*; people oppose science to *art*, to *imagination*, and they oppose it to *religion*, and also to *authority.*

- Knowledge, facts, reason, theory, and science are *objective*; anything *subjective* should be set to the side, a contaminant to be minimized.

- Knowledge, facts, reason, theory, science, and the objective get aligned with *the neutral public sphere*; all outside of this isn't knowledge, and should be kept *private.* Public is what we can agree on and discuss; private is and should be different from person to person.

- Knowledge, facts, reason, theory, science, objectivity, and the neutral public sphere align with *mind*; mind is divorced from *body*. Also, mind is, when you get right down to it, divorced from the *world*, from *reality*.

- Knowledge, facts, reason, theory, science, objectivity, the neutral public sphere, and mind align with *the way things are (reality),* to be distinguished from *the way things appear (appearance).*

Let's add one more that I feel is frequently implicitly countenanced by both genders:

- Knowledge, facts, reason, theory, science, objectivity, the neutral public sphere, and mind are *male*; male is set over against *female.*

Let's think about some possible implications of this daisy of dichotomies, these "binary oppositions,"[6] in our default mode. Whatever is on the petals is *not* in the sphere of knowledge: belief, opinion, values, morals, faith, religion, emotion, art, body, practical application, imagination, authority, femaleness. These are sizeable, critical, portions of who we are! Where on the daisy, for example, does exercise go, or other body care? Or indifference to them, for that matter? That's on a petal. It has nothing to do with knowledge, according to a subtly operating default mode.

What's in the center of the daisy, we think, is what matters most. It has value; the petals, by contrast, appear to have less value, and also to threaten the "purity" of the center. We can think of the center as a core, which we peel away the petals to attain.

Is knowledge to be had only in the absence of emotion? Of passion? Might we not expect, then, that learners should be disengaged, bored? What happens to childlike wonder? If knowledge is to be found in science, what is going on in literary fiction—in stories? Something that isn't knowledge, our default can imply.

If knowledge is facts and identified with theory, over against application, if knowledge is information, where would something called wisdom be located? What would it be? Could it be that this deeply en-

---

6. A phrase I associate with philosopher Jacques Derrida.

grained default setting has led to the assessment of twenty-first-century young people as "note sensitive and melody deaf"?[7]

Many people think of interpretation as something that must be kept out of the fact picture as much as possible. Interpretation stands in the way of facts. We see training in interpretation as important for getting beyond bias to facts. If interpretation were to be part of knowledge, knowledge would no longer be knowledge, people think. Nowadays it is widely held that everybody "has a perspective." But what is generally concluded is that this means there is no untainted knowledge. This is the dichotomous epistemic default at work.

Do we tend to associate some of the petals with one other? Since art is not knowledge, is it therefore female? Similarly, is religion effeminate? Also, since art is not knowledge, in the academic world do the humanities take a second seat to the sciences? And what about athletes? Can they be expected to be intelligent? Is emotion appearance and not reality? Is religion emotional? Is it a matter of appearance and not reality? Are emotion and religion private and not to be admitted to the public domain, unlike science? You can see that this is a default setting dominant in our culture.

It is commonplace for men and women both to think that men are more rational, and women are more emotional, despite a plethora of evidence that points in the opposite direction, if it points at all. Men, as a result, can think it unmanly to cry; women, as a result, can think it unwomanly or unattractive (and we presume that women are to attract— body, not mind) to be expert mathematicians. We all feel the pressure of stereotypes shaped by a defective epistemic default.

The default setting affects our common view of various disciplines of academic study, to take one instance. "Hard sciences," as we valuatively term them, continue to dominate our ideal of knowledge. Life science and the social sciences struggle to vindicate themselves as science by playing up their similarity to hard sciences. Theology, in some quarters, attempts this also. So does education. Art, by contrast to the other disciplines, resists and flaunts its difference from the ideal; it has never succumbed to the temptation to turn itself into a science. Classes across the curriculum often display pedagogy and student expectation shaped by the unquestioned conviction that knowledge is about information.

---

7. I no longer recall the origin of this comment. I first heard it from my former colleague, Dr. Donald Guthrie, a higher education specialist.

Then there is the very live question whether the daisy has any middle at all. Is truth, knowledge, even to be had? No facts, just opinions? No public, just private? No reality, just appearance? Or are there just the disparate petals, scattered to the four winds, fought over by selfish people wanting to top the pile of power? Small wonder that the western mind's default setting inclines people to a more skeptical version: knowledge isn't possible; or if it is, it is merely the function of our cranial activity, or the individual knower's personal fabrication. But this default inclination gains no ground toward resolving the disconnects. On the contrary, it continues to concede those very disconnects.

Where would the default mode I am sketching incline people who are not believers to locate Christianity, or other religious stances? If they locate it on the petal, would they not, therefore, hear Christian witness to the gospel as requiring them to jettison their minds? Where do Christians themselves locate Christianity? Is it reason or is it faith? Is theology, reason, and my relationship with Jesus, faith? And then, how do Christians perceive what they do at church? Is the sermon and Bible study the main event at church? Is this because it is about information? Is revelation perceived as divine information?

Among Christian believers, as well as in the West in general, I think that the mind-body distinction is especially severe. We tend to hear the word, *spiritual,* and associate it immediately with "immaterial." We don't know what to do with our bodies, because we also associate the immaterial with what alone is of value. But everybody in general is inclined to think of their body as an object, something that we "have," rather than "are." The "real me," we can think, is not my body. And we can have little feel of our body's felt involvement in knowing. Yes, we are growing by leaps and bounds in probing the brain's involvement in knowing; but that research treats the body as an object, not as a lived knower. We fear that the brain research, coupled with the invention of ever smarter robots, implies that there is no mind.

Again, many Christians espouse a specific, powerful, version of the dichotomy. There is "absolute" truth, or there is no truth. Absolute truth consists of a complete set of rational propositions about everything. "Absolute" truth's only alternative is relativism, subjectivism, or skepticism, Christians often think. Many Christians are convinced that if you do not believe in "absolute" truth, you cannot be a Christian. These

Christians do not see their own subcutaneous epistemic layer, and nevertheless have equated it with Christianity.[8]

Taking a look at the entire daisy, don't you come off feeling . . . fragmented? Which part of it is the real you? Which part of it is the real world—the center or the petals? But how can my emotions and my body not matter? And what does all this mean about my ability to connect with the world? Am I not divorced from it? Divorced from myself? Divorced from others? Divorced from God?

I have raised several matters here; I hope that they have prompted you to think of other places in life where our hidden presumptions about knowing come into play and make things problematic. The point of the daisy exercise is to draw attention to the existence of people's subcutaneous epistemological layer, to suggest its widespread impact, and to suggest that it is operating actively but unhealthily. Even if you do not fully agree with the way I have sketched the default mode here, the exercise effectively draws attention to the fact that people have a subcutaneous epistemological layer—hidden yet influential presumptions about what knowledge is. And this default setting, on examination, slices whole portions of our humanness from what is deemed knowledge. Unaware of these operative dichotomies, we nevertheless remain tormented by their implications. They actually impede us from following through on positive, human, healthy, effective approaches to knowing.

DEADENING THE LONGING TO KNOW:
BOREDOM, HOPELESSNESS, BETRAYAL

This default setting has generated a few common and predictable responses to the prospect of knowing, things that deaden what I believe should be a very human longing to know. One response is boredom. If we think that knowledge is information, on the one hand, we rightly deem that it is readily available and plenteous, delivered instantly via our internet. But on the other hand, it has been ingrained in us that we

---

8. This book will show that there is a biblically consonant positive alternative understanding of knowing that challenges the false dichotomy of "absolute" and relative truth. The choices are not between, "I believe in absolute truth," and "there is no such thing as absolute truth," both of which are logically problematic statements that reflect an underlying defective epistemic default. The alternative might be expressed like this: "I responsibly profess truth with universal intent." (Michael Polanyi developed this approach in his *Personal Knowledge*.) This book will help this to be understood.

should keep our emotions, our selves, out of the information, as you would strive to keep contaminants out of a water supply. Small wonder that people are bored, when personal commitment and passion are "subjective" items we must check at the door. Small wonder that we are bored, when we presume that information is ever only dispassionately derived or held to be true. Dispassionately gleaned information, dispassionately conveyed and dispassionately apprehended, spells boredom. It suggests that knowledge has little to do with what is meaningful in life.

Another response to the prospect of knowing is hopelessness. People can think that knowledge, to be knowledge, would be information and facts, statements and proofs, but such knowledge can't really be had. We can't really know anything at all. To say it another way, whatever we think we know is really just opinion—petal, not daisy center. The receding hope of certainty, it has been said, lives on as disillusionment, in our skepticism. It is widely held that there is no "way things really are," that truth is (only) relative to an individual's perspective, or socially constructed; that what is knowledge is integrally connected to who is in power. Nor is it socially acceptable or morally acceptable to deny this. This approach may be held in the name of honesty or tolerance, but it offers the holder little hope of future success, let alone a lively interest, in knowing.

These newer perspectives about knowledge as societally constructed, perspectival or power-shaped are not totally mistaken. But our proclivity to dichotomies leads us to think it is "all or nothing." As "all," these perspectives engender hopelessness. Skepticism is a hopelessness unsuited to humanness and to the abundant world in which we live.

But the newer perspectives suggest that something is really wrong with the western default setting. Important things are being disparaged or dismissed: the legitimate and critical involvement of knowers, their perspectives, their passions, their communities, and their clout, in knowledge. Also, as knowledge itself has been exalted, other more important things have been marginalized damagingly: people, relationships, justice, environmental care, to name a few very large matters.

People and relationships matter deeply; this prompts a third factor that deadens a longing to know: betrayal. Who can care about truth when trust has been violated? The more pressing and painful matter is not, what is true, but, whom can I trust to care for me? It is my belief that the premier importance of trust and betrayal actually reveals more about the contours of human knowing than the default setting has allowed us to acknowledge. What if, at its heart, knowing is *about* trust?

KNOWN, AND KNOWER, AS IMPERSONAL

Epistemology, and knowing of any sort, involves the knower, the known, and the knowing. This is language we will use a lot in this book. If people working from such a default mode unthinkingly cast knowledge as factoids, information, statements and proofs, how does this also shape how they implicitly see reality? The default mode generally casts "reality" as impersonal, mindless, soulless, impassive, facts or states of affairs. The world is impersonal. There's nobody home, we might say. If the facts are soulless, the world is soulless, too. Or maybe reality simply isn't "there." Whether that is worse or better than seeing it as impersonal is debatable.

The legacy of modern science is that many people think of the truly true, the really real, either as mathematical equations or as inert, random, chaos. Equations are the bare-boned structure of the universe. But most people also regard mathematical equations as about as impersonal and lifeless as it gets: dead, disembodied, to most of us inscrutable, hieroglyphics scrawled across a blackboard in the highest seats of learning. Actually, some think that the equations aren't really "there"; the equations are just convenient summaries of how things appear. But if equations are dead, or if they are merely useful summaries, why have scientists been so excited about discovering them?—we might well ask. Or is it rather that our default mode has predisposed us to this actually unwarranted supposition?

If "nobody has been home" in the world outside of us, often there has been nobody allowed to be at home within us as knowers, either. Our default mode casts sense perception as a passive registering of the world, and our knowledge judgments as involving us as minimally as possible in a linear aligning of this data. We have been summoned to objectivity—meaning that we are expected not to inject personal bias into this procedure. The more like computers we can be, the better will be the results of our efforts to register the world. The known we see as passive and impersonal; the knower we would cast as passive and minimally personal also. Like my little digital camera, we simply record what we see. And we record it by looking at it, and what we think we see is disparate and uninterpreted data. In our knowing of it we need to stick as closely to disparate and uninterpreted data as we are able, lest we contaminate it.

We have already noted an uneasy ambivalence in the default. What if the daisy really has no center? Yes that's what knowledge is, but it can't be had. The meaningless data are just what I make of them, and I may connect the dots however I choose. It's less like a camera and more like a random scribble drawing I make up. As over against seeing the knower as nobly passive; people can also incline to the opposite extreme of thinking that the knower creates reality. The knower becomes all. Knowing is no longer about accessing the world but about formulating constructs. Rhetoric and interpretation come to replace epistemology. And realism, the belief that in knowing we connect with a world that is objectively there, independent of my knowing it, falls by the wayside. We can see in this a kind of self-absorption about knowing: it's all about me. Or we can read a hopelessness in this outlook.

But whether the knower is passive, or active, in this default mode, whether the knowing is merely descriptive or excessively creative, the known—reality—has remained passive and impersonal, or nonexistent. The known is at best ours to bend to our purposes, as opposed to respecting it. It is brutish grist to our utilitarian mill; or we just mill away without it.

Perhaps we think of reality as impersonal because we think of knowing as impersonal. Perhaps the fault lies with our almost precritical commitment to knowing, itself, as impersonal and detached. The paradigm of knowing has shaped our fundamental sense of what it is we are knowing. I think this is correct. If so, the point of entry for us, if we want to address this lackluster situation is to take heed first to our responsibility as knowers; we may well find that it reshapes how we perceive the reality we aspire to know. This is why I write a book on epistemology.

DEADENING, NOT JUST THE LONGING, BUT THE KNOWING: CLUELESSNESS

One more very important thing: if people generally think that knowledge is factoids, strung together like popcorn and cranberries for a Christmas tree, this might account for the diagnosis I mentioned earlier of people today being "note sensitive and melody deaf." If knowledge is information, what is wisdom or understanding? And how might one attain it? How might one arrive at anything profound or new or transformative? We may not simply be bored, hopeless, or betrayed; we may also be clueless. And I am suggesting that our preconceived notion of what knowledge is may be a big part of the problem. Could it be, if we had a different understanding of what knowledge is that we might be better at it? Perhaps it is not just the longing that needs rekindling, but the knowing itself.

Consider the following example. Businesses and corporations often produce technical manuals of their procedures. Entry into the company requires reading the manual. But the question is: is the manual all there is to the kind of knowledge that drives that business? Does it even resemble knowledge? Businesses run into real problems, as their executives retire, finding people qualified to replace them. Why is this, if everyone has to read the manual? They also run into problems finding people who reliably produce new and good ideas. Could this be because people presume you follow an explicit procedure to come up with a new idea? Revising one's epistemology, then, holds the prospect of very concretely impacting the bottom line.

I must qualify the generality of my claims about this diagnostic daisy in two respects. One is that in many quarters its compartmentalizing reductivism has, in fact, been explicitly and helpfully challenged. While widely influential philosophical ideas have distorted our default mode, in the last centuries there have also been powerful philosophical challenges and alternatives to the distortion.[9] In fact, a philosophical distortion could only be countered, not by deserting philosophy (which I think is impossible anyway), but by doing excellent philosophy. In addition to philosophy, such disciplines as education and psychotherapy contain theorists whose work challenges the still prevailing default mode.[10] I see my own effort in this book as one such challenge, one that is philosophical, but also interdisciplinary.

But secondly, I believe that most people actually live and know well in at least some arenas of their lives. Healthy and effective knowing is hampered, but nevertheless occurs, though our default blinds us to

9. One can name Hegel, Nietzsche, Kierkegaard, the existentialists, the phenomenologists, Wittgenstein, the pragmatists, Polanyi—the list goes on.

10. To name just one effort: Harris's and Sansom's pamphlet, *Discerning is More Than Counting: Higher Education and Assessment*, in which the first chapter is entitled, "Numbers Cannot Tell the Whole Story." The whole move in assessment to accredit qualitative research in addition to quantitative research evidences an appropriate sensitivity to a more holistic understanding of knowledge. See Booth, et al., *Craft of Research*.

the fact that our best capacities for engaging the world do not actually conform to the epistemic paradigm we believe we hold. People can do knowing well and yet, when you ask them what they are doing, the way they describe it reflects the default and fails to accredit what they are doing well. Both of these qualifications to my diagnosis actually underscore it as well as the therapy this book offers.

DIAGNOSIS: WESTERN PHILOSOPHY AND ITS CULTURAL FALLOUT

Where did these destructive dichotomies come from? One answer is that they came from Greek philosophy, starting with Plato, the father of western philosophy.[11]

I am a philosopher, and I passionately believe that all great philosophers are worth exploring. In fact, in line with what I feel to be our God-given obligation and privilege to image God in earth-development and care, we are to cull and steward the truth which abounds in a broken world of which God is nevertheless Lord. We have much to learn from great philosophers. It's also important to understand powerful philosophical errors, both in the original and in subsequent adaptations of thought, which have shaped whole cultures, as well as our own outlook, without our knowing it. I want to be clear that the problem that this book diagnoses and labors to address is not the original claims of great philosophers in the Western tradition, but rather the philosophical and cultural fallout that continues to distort the outlook of ordinary people, our own inherited, operative, defective default. Often the defect has resulted not from the original philosophers, but more from the students of the philosophers, or from the distorted popularization of their ideas.[12]

11. In this book I attend exclusively to the western philosophical and cultural tradition. While I do not here devote the kind of attention to eastern thought that it deserves, I believe that it evidences a defective epistemic default of a different sort, to which covenant epistemology could helpfully be applied as well. More than one of *Loving to Know*'s conversation partners himself engages eastern thought, arguing for the superiority of his own approach, that which I fold into covenant epistemology. In particular, James Loder, Martin Buber, and Colin Gunton argue for an ultimate *personed* Other, with whom the knower's goal is, not absorption, but communion, things not characteristic of eastern approaches. See chs. 10, 9, and 12, respectively.

12. I must further qualify my continued negative assessment of the western philosophical and especially the Cartesian tradition in the following ways. It's not as if, had western philosophy developed otherwise, we would have been full-bodied, responsible knowers. Humans tend to duck responsibility, to distort the truth in the name of per-

Finally, where defective philosophical ideas thwart our understanding, the answer can never be to avoid philosophy. This is impossible. The answer is to draw widely on the understanding of others to do excellent philosophy.

We can trace the dichotomies of our defective default to the Platonic tradition. Most real was the unified, eternal, unchanging, non-material, rational dimension of reality; and this dimension is also the standard of goodness and beauty. Less real—and sharply distinguished from the rational—was the tangible, the material. Matter was ever changing, not unified, not rational, and inferior in goodness and beauty. Of course, any sort of religion and salvation involved seeking the former and flee-ing (or moving beyond) the latter. Platonism's influence on Christians' understanding of Christianity, down through the centuries even to the present, is marked. Case in point: we confess "the resurrection of the body," but our default tends to expect a disembodied immortality of the soul. Christians continue to struggle to value anything material—despite professing the doctrines that God created the world and that Jesus be-came flesh.

We can trace the modern exacerbation of the dichotomous default to Descartes, the father of modern philosophy. A Christian, Descartes nevertheless sowed seeds of atheism as, in search of certainty in knowl-edge, he exalted the individual "I"—the disembodied mind—to the su-preme position in knowing. This is the philosopher whose thought I most associate with my own early defective default mode. Descartes took the already extant penchant in western philosophy, inherited from Plato, to divide reality into "the intelligible" and "the sensible," that is, that which is known by the intellect or reason, and that which is apprehended via the senses. Descartes then drew the lines even more starkly: mind and body. Mind is unextended thought; body is unminded physical extension. The knower must, as such, be in the unextended thought category. That puts the known—even if it is the knower's hands capably dipping pen in ink and inscribing powerful philosophical proposals on parchment—in the

---

sonal ease and self-aggrandizement, and to mess up interpersonal relationships out of fear and self-protection, not to mention foolhardiness, self-deception, and plain old hatred. While we were made to love the good, the true, and the beautiful, our efforts so often are warped and thwarted. We need no help from Descartes, per se. For all that, if we know how to fix it, we need to take steps in the direction of doing so, especially when it is something so foundational as our epistemology. Knowing requires responsibility; so does knowing knowing.

category of unminded extension. Descartes, a mathematician, was trying to make all of knowledge as certain as he perceived mathematical knowledge to be.[13] But in the process, all that was outside the individual mind was/is mindless, only worth measuring. Measurement gets old. My point is that as a result of this outlook, we tend to think of the world, the real, as mindless—like nobody is home.

Also, consider the chasm Descartes' radical separation causes between knower and known. Mind is intrinsically interesting and meaningful; the world is intrinsically neither. It compels us to ask how we ever thought that such a knower could access such a known, let alone why we would want to. Small wonder that many here among the flotsam and jetsam of modern philosophy, both in professional philosophy as well as on the streets, have concluded that we can't. (I also think, small wonder some people struggle with eating disorders or other body abuse.)

Philosophers from the 1800s to this day have been blowing the whistle on Descartes' *cogito*, as it is called. Some really wonderful philosophical forays have transpired as a result. However, the default mode is still operative—I have only to think of the eighteen-year-olds that show up in my classroom in the fall. Also, it is widely documented that the disease of philosophical modernism, as it is often called, has especially infected the Protestant evangelical church in the global North.[14] The fact that Protestant Christians since the nineteenth century have avoided the study of philosophy (often in the name of spirituality) has especially rendered us vulnerable to this chronic condition.

I need look no further than myself to document the default setting. This is the story of my own mental furniture. I remember asking the question of myself, with great anxiety, as a middle-schooler: how can I be sure that there is a material world outside my mind? Nor has my own lived experience of my body even been something I could name, until recently. It was only within the last decade that I have felt that my body and mind reconnected in a "conversion" from Cartesianism. Also, growing up as a Protestant Christian, I presumed the dichotomies, and thus struggled, as many people considering Christianity do, to figure out

13. See Marjorie Grene's wonderful argument that Descartes, when he was doing mathematics, failed to follow the very rules that he prescribed for all knowledge. See *Knower and the Known*, ch. 3. This shows that a person, even a great mind, can be mistaken about her/his own operative epistemic endeavors (thankfully!).

14. See, for example, Noll, *Scandal of the Evangelical Mind*.

whether my faith is rational or not, certain or not, and which of these is in fact preferable. I struggled with the effects of the default that still characterizes Christian churches: is theology, or even Scripture, propositions, over against my personal relationship with God, which is—what? And if this is a struggle for people in the church, how can we expect it to be anything other for people outside it?

These are hard words; I hope they are a wake-up call. Philosophy is for everybody, because everybody practices it. We can live out a philosophical stance in ignorance. Or we can steward the cleanup, and live out a healthy philosophical stance with responsible intentionality. The payoff is better living, better knowing, better teaching, and, for those alive to the ultimate personal of reality, better enjoyment of God.

DIAGNOSIS: CERTAINTY

Another way we can recognize the power of our default epistemological orientation is to identify a few common fundamental commitments: certainty, objectivism, the ocular metaphor, and substantivalism. Let us start with certainty.

In our knowing, we westerners have generally aspired to the ideal of certainty. Knowledge, to be knowledge, must be true, accurately representing the way things are, and it *must not prove to be mistaken*—or else we could not consider it knowledge. The justification that we insist on and strive to uncover is one that will insure against defective products. To this end, we have gradually restricted the domain and the character of knowledge. We have restricted the domain of knowledge to the visually apprehended. We have restricted its character to the articulable and exhaustively justified. Knowledge must be restricted to propositions—statements and proofs. We have excluded other forms of awareness. We have excluded the apparently defective personal contribution of the knower and the apparently defective mysteriously uncategorizable of the known. Like Lake Woebegone's 5 & 10—if they don't have it, you probably didn't need it anyway—knowledge is limited to what keeps within these stipulations.

Why have we sought certainty? One might respond that it simply seems obvious. Certainty is epistemic purity. But I suggest that a possible motivation for this commitment to the certainty of propositions can be the less laudable one of avoiding personal responsibility, avoiding risk of failure, in knowing. If we must be perfectly certain of something to accept it, then we ourselves need take no risks, nor need we be held personally responsible for our lack of commitment. Certainty conveniently opens the back door to escape to irresponsibility.

It always strikes me, by contrast, how un-American our stipulation of risk-free knowing is. We Americans like risks, don't we? We like risk in our snowboarding, our bike riding, our rollercoasters, in our *Survivor* challenges. Why not in our epistemology? But another thing that strikes me is that, in actual fact, there is plenty of risk in our knowing—too much for comfort. Anyone facing medical or financial choices knows this, not to mention cultivating and maintaining relationships. Why, then, do we not acknowledge this in our epistemology? On the other hand, relativism and skepticism, apparent opposites of certainty, also sidestep personal epistemic responsibility. Relativism and skepticism are forms of "Certainty, or bust." So they continue to concede certainty, and thus can involve a kind of irresponsibility.

There is a far more laudable motivation for commitment to certainty, which, I believe, stems from a particular conception of truth and reality, one that I believe is unnecessary and unwarranted. We have tended since the time of Plato to think that truth to be truth had to be unchanging. We have added the stipulations, necessary and universal, as well. The idea of truth as changing appears oxymoronic. That means, we think, that objective reality must be unchanging as well. To accommodate this requirement, I think we have figured that to believe in objective truth, we must conceive of such truth and reality as impersonal, as there being nobody home.

It could be, finally, that our commitment to certainty is our longing for transcendence. It might be seen as our longing for personal conquest or control. I have occasionally observed a close connection of the passion for certainty with obsessive-compulsive disorder. But it may also be seen as our longing, not for a *what*, but for a *who*. I believe that this is legitimate, but as such, it points beyond certainty to a better way of construing knowing.

The ideal of certainty is illusory, however. Michael Polanyi made the case that, for every truth claim to which we are giving our attention at a certain time, there are several truth claims which we cannot even specify and yet must rely on in trust. It is not possible to doubt or question all our commitments simultaneously and offer foolproof justification for the lot. All knowing, he said was either wholly, or at its roots, subsidiary, tacit, and anticipative.[15] We will explore this more fully in chapter 3.

The impossibility of certainty does not, as our common presumption leads us to think, entail that knowledge is not to be had. It isn't "certainty or bust." Nor does it entail, as we will see, that we must settle for probability. These implications grow out of the damaging disconnects of our epistemic default. They show the power that the ideal of certainty continues to exercise in people's subcutaneous epistemic layer.

The false ideal of certainty itself leads us to approach reality in a certain way, and to see reality in a certain way. It leads us to see reality as impersonal objects or disembodied rationality, and to see knowing as a passive, dispassionate, registering of data. So the ideal of certainty leads to the other epistemic ideals I name here.

DIAGNOSIS: OBJECTIVISM

Objectivism can refer to two interrelated aspects of knowing I just mentioned: what we take the world to be, and how we go about apprehending it. Objectivism renders the world as composed of impersonal objects. Objectivism is also the conviction that nothing can be allowed to bias our knowing. It shouldn't take too much effort to see that objectivism is a conviction against conviction, a bias against bias. It thus indicates both the presence and the defectiveness of our epistemic default.

Objectivism would rule out of court my claim that we have an epistemic default; or it would claim that if we do, the point is to eliminate it. It fails to see that it exercises the default itself. It fails to admit that having a default is unavoidable. And it has no idea that this is not necessarily a bad thing; what needs to happen is not that it be eliminated, but that it be healed.

Palmer, to whose work in education I have already appealed and will continue to do so, challenges the objectivist paradigm as that which has wrought havoc both in our world and in our educational practice. In search of certainty, he says, we have determined that "if we can know only what is available to our senses and our logic, then reality is reduced to those narrow terms . . . the self creates the world by forcing it into the limits of our own capacity to know."[16]

---

15. Polanyi, *Personal Knowledge*, ch. 9: "The Critique of Doubt."

16. Palmer, *To Know as We are Known*, 12.

He describes his own youthful and unquestioned embrace of the objectivist paradigm: "we have been schooled in a way of knowing that treats the world as an object to be dissected and manipulated, a way of knowing that gives us power over the world . . . my [inherited] theory of knowing helped form (or deform) my sense of who I was and how I was related to the world . . . The ultimate outcome for me was growing weariness, withdrawal, and cynicism. What else could result from a way of knowing and living driven mainly by the need for power and deficient in the capacity to love?"[17]

Objectivism leads to weariness, withdrawal, and cynicism in the knower—responses I have suggested in connection with our dichotomous default setting. It also leads to a distorted self-image, a knower immune to the potentially transformative impact of the real. But most condemningly, Palmer argues that reducing the world to mute and inert objects that cannot fight back, that cannot assert their own selfhood, actually creates the most subjective of worlds. Palmer himself, as we will see, recommends that we instead understand truth to be personal, the world to be personal, arguing that seeing the world as personal is, not subjective, but rather more obviously objective.[18]

Michael Polanyi's major work, *Personal Knowledge,* comprises his all-out challenge to "the false ideal of objectivity."[19] This is a critique of objectivism as a method of apprehending the world. Polanyi argues that the actual demeanor of scientists in pursuit of discovery is never, as is commonly upheld as the objectivist ideal, dispassionate or uninvested, with the scientist ready at any moment to reject his/her proposals at the first empirical counter evidence. Polanyi argues that scientists, to do their work well, must accredit intellectual passions and responsible personal commitment, the fiduciary (faith-like) roots of all knowing and the scientist's own tradition-cultivated, expert skill and artistry in identifying good problems and pursuing them to discovery. Polanyi calls us to a far richer understanding of objectivity both in our epistemic approach, and in our understanding of the world.

So objectivism, in line with the western default epistemic stance, has been first misconstrued, and then either pursued as knowledge or

17. Ibid., 2, 4.

18. Ibid., 56.

19. Polanyi, *Personal Knowledge,* ch. 1, passim. Polanyi's epistemology forms a critical strand of my covenant epistemology (see ch. 4).

rejecting the possibility of objective knowledge altogether—both of which are impossible and destructive.

DIAGNOSIS: THE OCULAR METAPHOR

Why have we thought of knowledge as impersonal? Another, closely intertwined, sort of answer is offered by Colin Gunton in his assessment of modern Western philosophy.[20] He proposes that in this tradition we have overdone the human sense of seeing and underdone the other senses, such as touch. For as long as there has been western philosophy, the visual sense has seemed especially suited as a metaphor for knowing and knowledge. Plato's allegories of the Sun and the Cave in *The Republic* both applied the visual metaphor in the service of things epistemic. Probably the last time someone explained something to you, and you understood it, you replied, "I *see*." We talk of understanding as "enlightenment," which picks up the ocular metaphor. We have said, "Seeing is believing," to such an extent that we have needed to be persuaded of the point that believing is seeing.[21]

With our presumptions about seeing as passive registering of objects, the world is reduced accordingly. In fact, I believe, we have caricatured seeing itself so that it involves us in a looking at the exterior of something, as opposed to any sensitive indwelling of it. Seeing has led us, not to empathy, but to criticism. Seeing empathetically has been virtually nonexistent as a feature of our prevailing epistemology. At least it has been nonexistent *as seeing*. We might have called it pity, or intuition—but not seeing, or knowing. Seeing has turned into, not *in*sight, but objectification.

Gunton contrasts Polanyi's work with that of the modern empiricist, John Locke, widely remembered for his idea that the mind, prior to sense perception, is a *tabula rasa*, a blank tablet. Polanyi began his analysis of perception with a blind man working his probing stick. The sense that Polanyi's metaphor foregrounds is precisely not vision, but rather, touch. Says Gunton: "Locke thought the mind to be white paper,

---

20. Gunton, *Enlightenment and Alienation*, pt. 1. I engage Gunton in ch. 12. Snell, in *Through a Glass Darkly*, also addresses the ocular metaphor. His contention in that work is that neopragmatist Richard Rorty is right to identify the ocular metaphor as problematic in the western understanding of knowing, but mistaken in concluding that therefore knowledge of objective reality, as such, is not possible.

21. Barash, "Believing is Seeing."

on which the world mechanically wrote. Polanyi in this example visualizes it as being more like a white stick. The change of metaphor gives rise to a very different understanding of what happens when we perceive the world."[22] Gunton believes that sight is the most problematic of senses. In sight "we are essentially at a distance from the objects we are perceiving, whereas in touch we are actually in direct contact with them."[23]

What if we replace the ocular metaphor with the tactile metaphor, attempting to make it epistemically paradigmatic? Elizabeth Moltmann-Wendel notes that "our senses, above all our tactile senses, have long been stifled in a verbal culture . . . touching grasps, stimulates, changes our bodies. Words, too, can have something of the same effect. But they can also resound ineffectively. One cannot miss a touch. The body notices being touched."[24] She says that what makes the skin unique as compared with all other organs is that it communicates in both directions. It can communicate what is inside outwards, and what is outside inwards. It can do that, presumably in a single act, especially if that which is being touched and touching is another person. Sensuality, she affirms, is bodily presence. "And that means two things. The environment can be felt where we are, and at the same time we disseminate an atmosphere."[25] Moltmann-Wendel believes that what touches us shapes us memorably, and that "from the first to the last day, touch is experienced as assurance, confirmation of the self and healing."[26] She exults in "the network, interrelatedness—those are the magic words which promise our power and our helplessness, our interdependence and our autonomy. That is how blessing can come and develop."[27] But, she concludes, "we have little practice or tradition here."

One may begin to imagine how, by the time we are finished, we might recast knowing in such a way as to envision it as being therapeutic. Physical touch, whether that of the blind man's probe, the violin maker, or the mother-newborn relationship, more obviously displays the reciprocity of knowing than does our conventional understanding

22. Gunton, *Enlightenment and Alienation*, 38.

23. Ibid., 36.

24. Moltmann-Wendel, *I Am My Body*, 60. I turn repeatedly to her work throughout this book (see for example textures 2 and 6, and ch. 15).

25. Ibid., 86.

26. Ibid., 62.

27. Ibid., 4.

of visual perception. Reciprocity is to be found at the locus of bodily presence. In touch, communication goes both ways. This is not passive communication of information; it is mutual change.

I believe that seeing, as a human activity, actually can be and must be redeemed, recast so that it is thought of as a sort of visual touch, one that evokes mutuality and reciprocity. For there is a kind of seeing that distances us from the object; there is a kind of seeing that moves beyond objectifying and allows us to see from the inside out. (Think of the word, *insight*.) There is also a kind of seeing which we rightly call vision, in which we sense possibilities and significances hitherto overlooked.[28] We will return in later chapters to consider all of these matters more fully.

So Gunton's assessment is perceptive (!), that disconnected seeing has dominated our default epistemic. His point is that this has contributed to the alienation which is our legacy of the Enlightenment, as it has obscured the empathetic reciprocity between human knower and known.

DIAGNOSIS: SUBSTANTIVALISM

Gunton identifies substantivalism as yet another fundamental yet operative commitment in our default setting, also something philosophical deeply engrained in our western approach. It has to do with what we think it is to be human or to be anything—with what it means to *be*. What does this mean? A substantival understanding of being, or substance ontology,[29] would be one in which saying "Man is a rational animal," as the ancient Greek philosopher, Aristotle, did, makes sense. Things are substances (Aristotle's word for things, or individuals) and they have attributes and qualities. So a man is an animal whose distinguishing attribute is that he is rational.[30] Similarly, a chair is a piece of furniture made for people to sit in or on. A chair might be a swivel chair or a bar stool, a ladderback chair or a recliner or a folding beach chair. Each chair is a

---

28. Consider these comments from Maurice Merleau-Ponty, in his work on the artist, Cezanne ("Cezanne's Doubt," 69–85). "The artist is the one who arrests the spectacle in which most men take part without really seeing it and who makes it visible to the most 'human' among them." And this: "Expressing what exists is an endless task." We will engage these tantalizing matters later on in *Loving to Know*.

29. Twentieth-century Continental philosopher Martin Heidegger's work, *Being and Time*, also challenges substance ontology.

30. The gender specificity of this comment is deliberate.

substance with certain essential, defining, attributes that make it a chair. Those attributes or qualities are contained within the thing.

In this approach, any *relation* of the thing to other things is, by contrast, downplayed; it is perceived as only accidental to the thing's essential nature. It is accidental to the chair that I happen to be sitting in it. What is essential is what matters. When it comes to what it is to be human, we think that essential humanness is self-contained: it does not depend on any "exterior" relation to something or someone else. We add on to this the idea that it is noble for individuals to know themselves well (strong personal identity), to become themselves more fully (self-actualization) and be inner-directed, as opposed to other-directed. Being other-directed would be a bad thing, the sort of thing that happens in middle school, when peer pressure wins and a person allows others' values and commitments to drive him or her.[31]

Substantivalism fosters the daisy of dichotomies. To conceive ourselves as rational animals also implies that I "have" rationality as an essential attribute. We tend to think of rationality the way we think, in our default mode, of knowledge: rationality involves the capacity to offer reasons or proofs for our statements. A worldview that separates the rational from the tangible, and opposes the one to the other, issues inevitably in a divorce between theory and practice. Rationality has to do with thinking. Thinking is opposed to physicality. Practice has to do with action and physicality. And then one wonders how it is possible to think about physical things. Any thought of the world would by definition not connect with the world. The "egocentric predicament," the legacy of Descartes, quickly becomes a sore reality.[32]

31. In this, I will argue in ch. 11, I believe the popular understanding of David Riesman's terminology in the mid-twentieth century classic, has been widely misconstrued, bent to conform to an underlying substantivalism.

32. Here in western Pennsylvania, I attend the annual San Rocco Festa, an eighty-year-old gathering of area Italians in Aliquippa. In light of the experience, I facetiously yet confidently assert that the egocentric predicament could never have originated in Italy! The San Rocco parade begins at church with the celebration of Mass, strolls and plays its way from house to house through the neighborhood, stopping to eat and to drink, and to greet neighbors with kisses and hugs. Rosatis and Rizzos and Grazianos and Mancinis stand close and gaze directly into the eyes of those with whom they converse, maintaining a presence palpable enough to cut with scissors. From the vantage point of my own more disconnected, transplanted, individualist Protestant tradition, that these people have lived together through three generations and still enjoy each other's company, young and old, at first simply amazed me. Descartes simply couldn't

The idea of a human as a rational animal obviously has some validity: Animality is what I share with my dog, Miles. It would seem that rationality distinguishes me, and so makes me what I am, answering the question of identity. But the rational-animal, substance-attribute, approach has always been problematic. How does it account for my identity? Neither my rationality nor my animality set me off from others uniquely. Plus, one or the other may be defective. I may be a quadriplegic, or I may have acne. Or I may flunk Logic class. Or unmitigated grief or desperate emotional survival may preempt my thinking. We are generally uncomfortable with, on those grounds, discounting the identity or personhood or value of the individual.

A substantival approach offers little support for our common experience of shaping and being shaped by interpersonal connection, including the impact it has on our acting and knowing. I now believe that a substantival approach does not accredit and thus overlooks critical interpersonal features of epistemic acts, and thus adjusting this will make us better knowers and make the world a better place.

Gunton and others draw attention to the need to identify and challenge our default substantival understanding of being, and being human, and replace it with a relational one.[33] John Zizioulas believes that "being a person is basically different from being an individual or 'personality' in that the person cannot be conceived in itself as a static entity, but only as it *relates to*. Thus personhood implies the 'openness of being,' and even more than that, the *ek-stasis* of being, i.e., a movement towards communion which leads to a transcendence of the boundaries of the

---

have been an Italian. It's possible that Martin Luther couldn't have been, either. For the Italians of Aliquippa, it appears, being is most assuredly being-in-communion, and personhood is persons-in-relation—speaking Italian, kissing each other and shouting *Viva San Rocco!* "I think, therefore, I am"? Who do you think you are, anyway?! Whose family are you from—*that* is the question.

I believe also that the Aristotelian/Thomistic understanding of things as informed rationally and grasped both sensibly and rationally by embodied knowers, although exalting the rational, nevertheless effectively sidesteps the divorce of reason and action: the human knower and the known share a kinship of rationality, so that the knower may truly understand the known from the inside out. Contrast Aquinas' efficient cause (always acting for the sake of an end) to the opaque externality of a mechanistic "eight-ball in the side-pocket" of the modern understanding of causality. But then—Aquinas was an Italian.

33. Gunton, *One, the Three and the Many*; Zizioulas, "Human Capacity and Incapacity."

'self' and thus to *freedom*."[34] He continues: "it is not in its 'self-existence' but in *communion* that this being is *itself* and thus *is at all*. Thus communion does not threaten personal particularity; it is constitutive of it."[35] Gunton summarizes by saying "that we live in a perichoretic universe . . . Everything may be what it is and not another thing, but it is also what it uniquely is by virtue of its relation to everything else."[36]

I will be engaging these ideas in later chapters. But let us note the point at hand. A substantival understanding of persons and things has maintained a stranglehold on the Western outlook. Gunton, Zizioulas, and others argue that it must be challenged and replaced by a *relational* understanding: to be is *to be in communion*, in relationship. Our view of knowledge under the reign of substantivalism dismisses relational aspects, including reciprocity, as insignificant epistemically, whereas on a model of personhood and thinghood that is founded on relationship, human knowing and being would honor and leverage them.

This book endeavors to develop such a model. But here what we see, with regard to the common default setting regarding knowledge, is that an underlying commitment to certainty, objectivism, the ocular metaphor, and substantivalism is widespread, powerful, and also problematic. Looking at them leads us to dispute them, and to hope to revise them.

So here in this first chapter we see and feel the need for epistemological therapy. Even if we have not been conscious of it, a defective epistemic default, or a subcutaneous epistemic layer, has been operative. Everyone brings notions of what knowledge is, and what it isn't, to all their knowing. Those presumptions are significantly shaped culturally. They can be distorted and thus adversely affect our knowing. In fact, I have argued, our default is both distorted and damaging. I have named a number of its proclivities, ones easily identifiable once we know what

---

34. Zizioulas, "Human Capacity and Incapacity," 408. As Trinitarian theologians, Zizioulas and Gunton argue that, because of this substantival definition, Christian theology has been sub-biblical, especially when it comes to doctrines such as the Trinity. As a result, Christian theology has failed to offer the positive influence it should have on western culture. See ch. 12 of this volume. Ch. 12 n. 10 contains a short summary of Zizioulas' theses.

35. Zizioulas, "Human Capacity and Incapacity," 409.

36. Gunton, *One, the Three and the Many*, 173. *Perichoresis*, a term developed to express the interworkings of the members of the divine Trinity, suggests dynamic, mutual interpenetration, communion and activity. See ch. 12 of this volume.

to look for. We have seen that they adversely impact our understanding of knower, known, and knowing, all three. It is reasonable to surmise that we are less effective knowers as a result, that we are less than whole as persons, and that the world is damaged in the knowing. This book, it is my conviction, administers just the epistemological therapy that the default desperately needs.

QUESTIONS FOR DISCUSSION

1. In what areas of your life do you see the defective default, the daisy of dichotomies, operative?

2. What are some other adverse consequences of it in your life, work, and Christian discipleship?

3. Start a list of philosophical terms you need to know more about. As you read on, and you grow to understand them, write a short definition. Or you may jumpstart this helpfully by looking them up on reputable online philosophical glossaries.

4. Discuss: in what ways do you think it will help you to study epistemology?

REKINDLING THE LONGING TO KNOW

L ET'S STEP ASIDE TO take a backward and a forward glance from a different angle. The default setting has engendered boredom, indifference. But let's ask the question, why care about knowing? Because not to care is to be dead. Indifference to one's surroundings is a telltale sign of sickness, of impending death. You only have to think of the last time you were deathly ill. A sure sign that you were convalescing was that you started to care again about things—like how in need of a shower and shampoo you were, and how cluttered the room around you was. It is human to care. Boredom, absence of wonder, is a sign of sickness. If our outlook on knowledge is such that it leads to boredom, then something is amiss in our outlook on knowledge.

To be human is to care. To be a human is to be situated in a world and oriented toward it, ever reaching beyond where we are, made to care for it. To be human is to long to know, to knock persistently on the door of the world in which we find ourselves, to beg entrance and receive far more than we anticipate.

I am convinced that even where the default mode is fully operative, and boredom, disillusionment, and cynicism reign, in every person is some dimension of their lives and knowing that does not conform to that defective default. There always remains a witness to their humanness, something pointing beyond the disordered default. There is a place where that person cares.

Why care to know? Why pick out chords on a guitar? Why get to know that quiet young woman who works on the third floor? Why yearn to go to West Africa, or seek peace in the Middle East? Why long to design a more environment-friendly automobile, or find a cure for cancer? Why seek God?

Caring is the vector that carries us into the world. To care is to move toward the unknown in hope. Caring—coping, longing—is what thrusts us or pulls us into the world. This documentably human dynamic intrigues me because it shows that the way we have thought of knowledge and truth, and the ensuing hopelessness and boredom concerning truth, has been wrongheaded.

It is possible to rework our own default by blowing on the coals of our care. Or if a friend you care for is dying epistemically, you can blow on the coals of his/her care. We can serve others (and they serve us) by noticing the place in their lives where they do, in fact, care about knowing, and blowing on those coals. This is a way to rekindle the longing to know. Pay attention, not to the factoids, but to the longing. Start, not with what you think you know, but with what you long to know. Let longing shape what you think knowing is, and let it draw you into it. Longing, I believe, is part of knowing. Embrace your care and ride its wave crest to knowing. Care,

by the way, is not just human, it may also be divine.

You can cultivate wonder (something in you). You can look for something that beckons (something beyond you) and allow yourself to be beckoned to. You can start to own the search. You have to take responsibility regarding the value of what you pursue and don't know; this is like investing in a person, or a company. By definition, you can't wait for an airtight rationale to justify your involvement, because you can't yet name what you are searching for. If you wait for an airtight rationale, you will never plunge in and you will never discover. Longing for what we do not yet know opens us up to that as yet unknown reality. It exposes our flank. We incur risk. Please notice that there is nothing about this that bears kinship to an alternative of dispassionate reckoning of probability. We *long* to know.

What does this longing suggest about knowing? It says that knowing begins from the before-words, palpably felt, sense of our situatedness in the world. It starts with somebody home. Knowing is embodied, already in the world, poised as cat before a leap, both to martial resources at hand and to gauge uncharted terrain beyond.

It means that we do not yet know fully what it is we long for. We pursue an as-yet undiscovered reality—another intriguing commonplace of human experience. How do we do that? If we do not know it, why do we desire it? Our caring affirms the reality that we have yet to discover.

Even if we do not fully know the thing we long for, we must also begin to live our lives on its terms. We show respect for it and submit to it. We can sustain such longing over moments, or over years. It requires that we comport ourselves with patience and humility. We must wait, and risk the wait's issuing in nothing. We pledge ourselves to the yet-to-be-known. Examples abound—taking a math class, learning to fly, learning a language. We must show our readiness to obey it, to live in light of its only partially revealed reality. We pay attention. We scrabble to understand what it feels like from the inside. Living life on the terms of the longed-for reality calls for an attentiveness on our part that is far less like dispassionate cataloguing

of information and more like passionate indwelling of that half-hidden object of our care. To practice blowing on the coals of our care is to start to overhaul the defective default setting we have belabored in this chapter, and to replace it a healthier epistemology.

We will see as this book unfolds that caring invites the real, and reality responds to our overtures with the gift of surprising self-disclosure. If knowing is care at its core, caring leads to knowing. To know is to love; to love will be to know. We will speak of the covenantal character of real things, and of the relationship between knower and known. There will be about the relationship between knower and known the mutual deference of covenant partners. We need to think of the knowing relationship—knower and known are in this together. Coming to know will turn into coming to be known. It should be mutually transforming, and healing. All this somehow suggests, implicitly anticipates, knowing and being known . . . by God.

Human knowing, like beautiful wood shot through with the fine grain of its origin, bears the telltale markings of covenant relationship, and ultimately of our life-defining connection with God. Knowing is interpersonal, reciprocal, and most effective when pursued in covenant faithfulness of the knower to the known. To affirm this will be to breathe restorative life into our epistemic stance. It will rekindle the longing to know.

QUESTIONS FOR DISCUSSION

1. Rate your own level of boredom/longing, using a scale of 1 to 5.

2. Rate that of your close friends.

3. How does it help to consider that the boredom may in part be due to a defective epistemic default?

4. What will it look like for you to "blow on the coals of the care" of yourself or your friends?

ANOTHER KIND OF KNOWING

Suggestive Preliminary Conversations and Proposal

I HAVE STARTED TO signpost a fresh approach to knowing, one which I call covenant epistemology. In chapter 1 I identified symptomatic features of a prevailing default outlook concerning knowing, noting also that it is unhealthy. In key ways, the epistemic unhealth points beyond itself to the prospect of rehabilitation. It is a kind of negative contour of covenant epistemology.

Before sketching my proposal for covenant epistemology in this chapter, I present glimpses of three people's ideas which prompted me in the direction of covenant epistemology: Annie Dillard, Lesslie Newbigin, and Parker Palmer. All three offer hope of another way to conceive knowing, and they indicate the direction to look.

CONVERSATIONS ON THE WAY TO KNOWING

I am one who navigates by conversations. My understanding moves forward as I move from one conversation to the next. Both people I talk with and books I engage count as conversations. A conversation is no mere gossip or can-you-top-this repartee. Nor is it a dispassionate debate. It is a deep, meditative listening, which indwells the authoritative guidance of the other, an encounter intensified by a passionate readiness to understand and be changed. I come away from each conversation with another piece of a whole picture that I am trying to apprehend and flesh out. Also, once I can think in the vein of the one to whom I have been listening, I honor that vein sometimes by moving beyond it.[1] The progress is not linear as much as it is repeatedly unfolding and transforming.

---

1. This is another unique insight of Polanyi, who restored to twentieth-century western thought an epistemological accreditation of the role of tradition. A good tradition is one in which the apprentice is formed, to the end of moving beyond her or his master's

Although this is my personal penchant, I do not think this is just a random eccentricity. I think that this is the way all knowing unfolds, that it is the way knowing *should* be seen to unfold, and that it holds a clue to the heart of what knowing is about. So this approach to knowing is not just one that suits me personally. It also accords with the epistemological vision I write to commend. Thus I hope the conversations in this book will have the feel of listening deeply and then of creatively building insights apprehended into a whole, allusively three-dimensional pattern that becomes our orientation to the world.

To know is to "be on the way"—a phrase I take from Lesslie Newbigin.[2] I will argue that knowing has centrally definitive features that are more effectively seen as involving persons together in communion— hence in conversations. A good picture of conversation is "starbucking," a term I coined: being present in communion and conversation with a close friend over coffee.

So the book's layout intentionally reflects this practice of navigating by conversations. The book will unfold its proposals by engaging the work of one person after another, thus modeling and hopefully effecting the epistemology it commends. The reader also is joining this conversation on the way to knowing.

In this first section, then, I am relating three of the earliest conversations that prompted my thinking about covenant epistemology.

KNOWING AS COVENANTAL:
CONVERSATION WITH ANNIE DILLARD

Annie Dillard's prize-winning meditation on nature, *Pilgrim at Tinker Creek*, first prompted me to conceive of knowing as having covenantal, hence relational, features.[3] I had already been immersed in Polanyi's work, and before that in John Frame's, and I had already linked the two as complementary. I had become conversant with Mike Williams' understanding of covenant as shaping the story of Scripture. All these are

---

to greater and surprising insights. Copernicus would have turned over in his grave to know that Kepler deemed the planetary orbits elliptical. It's like this because reality is like this. Indeterminate future manifestations confirm that we have made contact with the real. Polanyi, *Personal Knowledge*, 5, 53–54.

2. Newbigin, *Proper Confidence*, 10. I also use his phrase in this chapter's title.

3. This realization of mine, and the seeds of this current book, can be found in ch. 22 of Meek, *Longing to Know*.

the conversations of later chapters. Dillard, however, prompted me to notice covenantal behavior in her effort to know . . . muskrats! I began to consider that covenantal self-binding operates in all human knowing.

She describes how she goes about seeing a muskrat appear in the stream.

> In summer, I stalk. The creatures I seek have several senses and free will; it becomes apparent that they do not wish to be seen. When I stalk this way I take my stand on a bridge and wait, emptied . . . It used to bother me . . . I just could not bear to lose so much dignity that I would completely alter my whole way of being for a muskrat. So I would move or look around or scratch my nose, and no muskrats would show, leaving me alone with my dignity for days on end, until I decided that it was worth my while to learn—from the muskrats themselves—how to stalk.[4]

Stalking muskrats can only be done by the "via negativa"—meaning that you must compose yourself to do nothing but wait, still enough, long enough, so that, if you are lucky, the muskrat will come. You must do it on the muskrat's terms, not on your terms. If indeed you are lucky, even if you get only a wee glimpse, you sense the glory of this condescension. Dillard likens it to Moses getting a wee glimpse of Yahweh, and Heisenberg uncovering the Uncertainty Principle.

Note that it is not the knower who is in the driver's seat, but rather the yet-to-be-discovered reality. The real discloses itself, in its own time and way. And when it does, it is grace.

Dillard disputes the notion, deeply engrained in our default outlook: that reality is such that you can clear away all the "surface" appearances to get to a lucid core of the thing's "true" nature and thus have gleaned complete understanding: "Nature is a fan-dancer and the fans come attached"—there is mystery all the way down, not some "inner core under the externals." Its gracious self-disclosure never strips the real of mystery.

But it makes a difference how the would-be knower behaves. In this I recognized two things: first, knowing is covenantal, second, that therefore there are better and worse ways of going about it. Knowing is perhaps a bit like a marriage. First you bind yourself with promises to love, honor, and obey. Only then does reality unfold itself to you. If you do, and you're favored, it will. Dillard notes that she learned from the

4. Dillard, *Pilgrim at Tinker Creek*, ch. 11.

muskrats themselves how to stalk. Also, if you don't comport yourself sensitively, reality won't unfold. If you don't comport yourself honorably and you force the real into disclosure, perhaps what you have is less like marriage and more like rape. Such an approach would distort the thing that we were trying to know. It is objectifying, rather than personifying. We would not know it as it is. Or we may not know it at all.

So then, how may we comport ourselves honorably, and in so doing, "invite the real"? When I wrote *Longing to Know*, working from the muskrat text I identified commitment, patience, respect, and humility as virtues requisite to unlocking and engaging the real. We should put ourselves in the way of knowing—on the bridge, waiting for a muskrat. You have to start to live life on the terms of the yet-to-be-known to have any hope of accessing it. I started to develop the idea of an "epistemological etiquette" by which we may invite the real. Later we will explore this rich catalog of behaviors that invite the real.[5] Inviting the real, as an apt description of how responsible knowers comport themselves, also recasts the dynamic of knowing as an unfolding courtship between knower and known, overture, response, something akin to dance. And in this vision, knower and known are also rehabilitated as personal.

RELATIONAL KNOWING:
CONVERSATION WITH LESSLIE NEWBIGIN

But is such an approach merely the fanciful result of an overactive literary imagination? Is it perhaps too great of a leap from tracking muskrats to all knowing? There were other people in other fields calling for "another kind of knowing."

Missiologist Lesslie Newbigin summons knowers to embrace a personalist paradigm in knowing. He does so to the end of helping Christendom move beyond the enervating predilection to objectivism towards embracing a robust practice of discipleship. Newbigin writes:

> But there is another kind of knowing which, in many languages, is designated by a different word. It is the kind of knowing that we seek in our relations with other people. In this kind of knowing we are not in full control. We may ask questions, but we must also answer the questions put by the other. We can only come to know others in the measure in which they are willing to share.

5. See ch. 15.

The resulting knowledge is not simply our own achievement; it is also the gift of others.[6]

The impersonalist, objectivist, paradigm has dominated the Western philosophical tradition, he argues. In its quest for certainty, it has led only to nihilism and skepticism. It is impossible for Christian discipleship responsibly to be approximated in an epistemological paradigm that espouses objectivism in religion—such as, Newbigin believes, does Christian fundamentalism—nor one that rejects it—as does liberalism in Christianity. Fundamentalism reduces knowing to facts and thus cannot account for much of the rich personal dynamism of discipleship, reality, or truth. Liberalism, in rejecting objectivism, rejects objectivity in truth. Both presume the same faulty either-or of the defective epistemic default we identified in chapter 1.

Personal knowing, by contrast, is the kind of knowing that is the knowing by one person of another. In contrast to both fundamentalism and liberalism, it profoundly suits the message of the gospel. This is because the gospel turns the tables of truth with finality by the incarnation of Jesus Christ: Jesus, the Word made flesh, is the new fact that changes everything about how we see the world. If it does not, then we have failed to grasp it. It is obvious to Newbigin, the Christian missionary, that what is at the heart of the gospel of Jesus Christ is not truth as a mere proposition so much as Truth as a personed event: God "walks into the room." Think, he says, how the conversation shifts radically when the person you have been talking about enters the room. Newbigin argues that we must understand that this fact of Jesus Christ's coming, this event, does not need to be fit into other plausibility structures. Rather, we must see that it is the plausibility structure in light of which all others must be assessed.

Newbigin is saying that Jesus the Truth must challenge and reshape our epistemological vision. To say that Jesus is the Truth should not depersonalize Jesus; it should "person" truth. Our understanding of what knowing is must come around to align with the Truth. Otherwise, our understanding of knowing will distort the Truth. It will prevent it from being heard, damaging self, others, world, church, and society in the

---

6. Newbigin, *Proper Confidence*, 10. My comments here summarize his message throughout his work, both in *Proper Confidence*, but also in *Foolishness to the Greeks* and *Gospel in a Pluralist Society*.

process. My work to develop covenant epistemology can be seen as a response to Newbigin's summons.

To the end of reforming epistemology, Newbigin says, let's think of another kind of knowing—interpersonal knowing. Let's take that as our paradigm or model. We move from third to second person, from objectifying, informational pronouncements to person-to-person conversation that asks, listens, and receives discovery as grace. Of the two kinds of knowing, which would you say is more basic a form of knowing? Or which can dwell with and support the other, and which can't? Newbigin, and others, as we will see, make the case that personal knowing is both prior and supportive.

This other kind of knowing has obvious application to Christian discipleship. Discipleship and religious formation are far better understood as a "being on the way to knowing." But I believe that it pertains, as a model of knowing, to all human efforts to know anything at all.

TRUTH AS TROTH:
CONVERSATION WITH PARKER PALMER

Parker Palmer, for the sake of effectiveness in pedagogy as well as the healing of humans and the world, argues for a replacement of the impersonal paradigm of knowing with a personal paradigm: "The myth of objectivity, which depends on a radical separation of the knower from the known, has been declared bankrupt. We now see that to know something is to have a living relationship with it—influencing and being influenced by the object known."[7]

In his effort to stimulate a personalist epistemology, Palmer appeals to the etymology of the word, *truth*: it descends from *troth*. *Troth* is an old word for *pledge*. Palmer recommends that we resuscitate that connection.

> To know something or someone in truth is to enter troth with the known, to rejoin with new knowing what our minds have put asunder. To know is to become betrothed, to engage the known with one's whole self, an engagement one enters with attentiveness, care, and good will. To know in truth is to allow one's self to be known as well, to be vulnerable to the challenges and changes any true relationship brings. To know in truth is to enter into the life of that which we know and to allow it to enter

7. Palmer, *To Know as We are Known*, xv.

into ours. Truthful knowing weds the knower and the known; even in separation, the two become part of each other's life and fate . . . [T]ruth involves entering a relationship with someone or something genuinely other than us, but with whom we are intimately bound . . . Truth requires the knower to become interdependent with the known. Both parties have their own integrity and otherness, and one party cannot be collapsed into the other . . . We find truth by pledging our troth, and knowing becomes a reunion of separated beings whose primary bond is not of logic but of love.[8]

Palmer represents the known as person-like, and human knowing as interpersonal and covenantal. We can see that he uses covenantal language as he commends troth as a paradigm. It obviously suggests the metaphor of marriage ("I pledge you my troth," as the old service of marriage says), of an intimate and mutually discovering and nourishing, pledged relationship. Knower and known are two persons in relationship. We can hear in Palmer's work the language of "epistemological etiquette" in inviting the real. Covenantally binding ourselves (behaving!) includes commitment to the as-yet undiscovered reality, love, patience, humility, listening beyond our previously conceived categories, personal openness, and embracing with hope the half-understood promise of the real, to the end of communion and . . . friendship. All knowing is, at least paradigmatically, knowing *whom*.

The way the knower views him/herself as knower, and the way he/she views the world, are intimately connected, says Palmer. The more expansive and reverent paradigm of knowing as interpersonal covenant relationship allows for better knowing, knowing that is fuller-orbed and mutually person-enhancing and therapeutic. Palmer reflects on the old word, adequation, which traditionally had designated that quality of a truth claim that makes it knowledge, or the process of suiting the knowing to the real:

we know not just with senses or reason but with everything we have got as one unity, and this as a person in relationship. If you truncate the knower, you truncate the known . . . We find all of this, but ultimately we find a self whose nature is not simply to know, but to know in relationship, as a means to relationship. The self is greater than the sum of its parts, and its greatness is in its ability to move beyond perception in any mode—beyond

8. Ibid., 31–32.

the isolation of the observer—into relationship with the world to be known . . . The relationships of the self require not only sensory evidence of the other; not only logical linkages of cause and effect; they also require inner understanding of the other, which comes from empathy; a sense of the other's value, which comes from love; a feel for its origins and ends, which comes from faith; and a respect for its integrity and selfhood, which comes from respecting our own. The most expansive *adaequatio* between ourselves and the world—one that does not narrow and impoverish reality—is found in our capacity for relationship. In relating to the other we find ourselves drawing on "instruments" the observer role never evokes. As our relatedness is called out, we find ourselves knowing reality more deeply and roundly than the observer ever can. The structure of reality is not exhausted by the principles of empiricism and rationality. Reality's ultimate structure is that of an organic, interrelated, mutually responsive community of being. Relationships—not facts and reasons—are the key to reality; as we enter those relationships, knowledge of reality is unlocked.[9]

Palmer is saying that knowing involves our whole selves wholly with the world, a kind of inner understanding that consists of empathy, respect, love, and the truthful imagining of one another's destinies.[10] These are fundamentally the distinctive behaviors of healthy interpersonal relationship. They reflect covenantal behavior. Interpersonal attentiveness is far richer and more truth-bearing than mere observation; and there is far more to the world than an impersonal approach could ever uncover.

The tenor of true knowing is love, interpersonal resonance, interpenetration, rather than impersonal description. The former connects; the latter separates.

In personal knowing, the relation of the knower and the known does not conform to the stiff protocol of observer and observed. It is more like the resonance of two persons. When we know something truly and well, that which we know does not feel like a separate object to be manipulated and mastered. Instead, we feel inwardly related to it; knowing it means that we have somehow entered into its life, and it into ours. Such knowledge is a relationship of personal care and fidelity, grounded in troth. In

9. Ibid., 52.

10. My last phrase here picks up on philosopher Caroline Simon's definition of love, as imagining someone's destiny truly, in Simon, *Disciplined Heart*.

the words of Abraham Joshua Heschel (another Jew who, like Buber, has a profound understanding of personal truth), "It is impossible to find Truth without being in love." In the words of St. Gregory, "Love itself is knowledge; the more one loves the more one knows."[11]

This is not to dismiss or minimize the value and role of reasoned justification or data collection. It is instead to resist its quasi-successful but radically damaging divorce from its personal context. Much of our epistemic effort goes forward despite our prevailing misimpression that knowledge is solely impersonal in character. We have habituated a blindness to its personal context. That personal context nevertheless still functions, while exiled, to render knowing effective. Human knowing regularly triumphs over the blinders, by our surreptitious employment of action more truthfully described as "trust and obedience." I propose this paradigm of covenant epistemology because I am convinced that acting intentionally and with integrity with respect to the personal will make us better knowers of everything.

A NOTE ABOUT SOURCES

A final comment before I turn to the proposal proper. In developing covenant epistemology, I have often looked to sources other than the traditional philosophical ones. Dillard is a writer, lover, and seer of nature. Newbigin was a renowned missiologist and long-term missionary in India. Palmer is an educator. Other people whose work I engage are not philosophers, let alone foremost philosophers. These particular encounters shaped my own intellectual development; *Loving to Know* is my personal journey. What is to be said about the credibility of this approach?

We can already see that, given the way fundamental outlooks on knowing operate, traditional approaches themselves are significantly imbued with the very epistemic stance that we want to reform. How will philosophical discussions conducted under the unquestioned presumption that knowledge is all about impersonal, propositional statements and proof, help to reshape the paradigm? How will philosophy and other disciplines, compartmentalized as they are from Christian theology, ever have ears that can pick up an interpersonal paradigm for all reality and

11. Palmer, *To Know as We are Known*, 57.

knowing? And since much Christian theology itself operates from a primarily impersonal epistemic paradigm, not to mention a philosophically unattuned one, how is it in a position to contribute to reshaping an epistemological vision? We must look elsewhere for guidance to move us beyond what has come to be a stranglehold of epistemological "orthodoxy."

On the other hand, once epistemology is redrawn in the personal medium, I believe that even the most apparently impersonal forays stand to gain. Also, once the approach is delineated, we will find that it resonates with several important initiatives in contemporary philosophy. Covenant epistemology, as a paradigm shaped to accord with Jesus the personed Truth, also unleashes Christian discipleship to the full-orbed epistemic centrality it deserves. It also suggests a fresh way forward for Christian scholarship and any rapprochement between Christian theology and philosophical thought. Even as the personal hosts the impersonal, but not vice versa, we can make better sense of those important insights than perhaps those insights, working from or attempting to challenge an impersonal paradigm, have been able to do.

PROPOSING COVENANT EPISTEMOLOGY

Chapter 1 and the first part of chapter 2 have been setting the stage, raising awareness, and commending a reorientation of our fundamental epistemic outlook to a covenant epistemological one. Now we begin to work out the contours that constitute this epistemic stance.

Covenant epistemology, then, is my proposal that we take as our paradigm of all knowing the interpersonal, covenantally constituted relationship. Covenant epistemology intertwines three strands of theses: Polanyian epistemology augmented to a profounder "personal" than Polanyi articulated in his work, a theological motif and vision of biblical covenant as relationship, and a cluster of theses I refer to as "interpersonhood."[12]

I will show how covenant epistemology makes sense, why it is beneficial, and how to put this fresh outlook to work. I will show how covenant epistemology makes sense in the following way. I accept from the outset that Michael Polanyi's proposals regarding how knowing works make profound sense of how we actually know. His is thus a "phenom-

12. See parts 2, 3, and 4.

enological" description, as opposed to a theoretical statement of what counts as knowledge.[13] I present these in an early chapter.

I move further to argue that knowing, on a Polanyian construal, is *fraught with intimations of the personed—actually, of the interpersoned.* "Fraught with intimations" is a characteristic phrase of Polanyi himself. "Fraught" is a wonderful word meaning shot through with, full of, permeated by, imbued with. "Intimations" are hints, clues, signposts, of something yet to be revealed or to come clear. "Personed" and "interpersoned" are my own concocted words. The word, "personal," has so many applications; perhaps because of overuse the adjective seems bland or at least vague. "Personal" doesn't quite mean that a person is *there,* the way "person" clearly does. I want to say that knowing displays telltale features that could only be present if *a person, or persons in relationship, is, or are, in the vicinity.* All knowing holds clues or pointers that suggest the pattern of interpersonhood covenantally constituted. From them we may glimpse contours of something profoundly richer, the way we might start to glimpse the shadowed contours of a person in the vicinity, or start to pick out the contours of a surpassingly profound pattern.

I argue that interpersonal relationship is itself covenantally constituted, no matter how casual or intimate the relationship. I incorporate a notion of covenant *as* relationship. Covenanted interpersonhood is the larger context in which knowing on a Polanyian construal is itself embedded and to which it points. From the point of view of human knowing, we may discern the contours of that larger pattern. These make sense of the personlike dimensions of human knowing. I am proposing that we take as a paradigm of all knowing the interpersoned, covenantally constituted relationship.

The shape of my argument is itself distinctly Polanyian. The relationship of knowing to covenant interpersonhood is, in my thinking, much like the relationship of subsidiaries to focal pattern in Polanyi's view of knowing, something I will explain in an early chapter.[14] This means that the logical relationship between the clues and the pattern—in this case

13. I do not mean to suggest that it is possible or desirable to step outside one's interpretive theoretical framework or pretheoretical opening on the world to examine brute experience. Yet it remains true that I am most interested in how knowing works—what we are involved in in the process.

14. In ch. 4 I will explain the meaning of several of the phrases I use in these sentences here that will be unfamiliar to readers yet to be acquainted with Polanyi's epistemology.

between knowing itself and the interpersoned pattern which I am commending—is not, cannot be, need not be, either necessary or sufficient.
To embrace it involves *responsible risk in judgments*. Nevertheless, the
pattern is compellingly warranted, as I hope to show. In fact, the warrant
for this interpersoned pattern is just the sort of warrant that characterizes any ordinary act of knowing, according to Polanyi. The pattern's
coherence, its transformative connectedness linking world and knower,
and its intimations of future possibilities qualitatively exceed the very
clues that evidently comprise it, much as the countenance of someone
we love and recognize qualitatively exceeds, and then transforms, its actual facial components—this, one of Polanyi's own powerful examples.
So the shape of my argument for the interpersoned contours of knowing
is itself both Polanyian and interpersoned.

You will find that I delight in connecting pieces creatively. This
seems to characterize my whole approach to life, as well as being consonant with the Polanyian pattern-seeking approach. I proceed by
exploring the world for pieces of a pattern. I find the pieces in this and
that conversation. I look for resonances, things that are profound and
that seem to align with each other. But I expect that the pattern will
outdistance and transform the very pieces I think are significant. I do
not engage, particularly, in confrontational, reasoned critique, except
where apparent conflicts must be creatively adjudicated or set to the
side. And even at these points I follow the Polanyian corollary that
apparently conflicting claims can yet be integratively aligned in the
yet-to-be-discovered pattern—an approach that is helpfully irenic.
And then my rationale for it is that the pattern that emerges has a winsomely compelling viability; it makes sense—transformative sense—
of the entire human epistemic project.

Like so many overhead projector overlays (remember those?), subsequent chapters layer onto the base motif of Polanyian subsidiary-focal
integration, the Framean triad, the Williamsian covenant relationship,
Macmurray's form of the personal, Buber's I-Thou, Loder's four-fold
dimensions of humanness, Schnarch's differentiation, and Gunton's *perichoresis*. Taken together, these help us glimpse contours of the personed
in the knower, the known, and the knowing. I do not intend to reduce
any of these motifs to any of the others, but rather to note their resonant
alignments, to see how one elucidates the other. Retaining their distinc-

tiveness as well as their relatedness brings about an artful, richly allusive, layering that accords with life.

So my proposal of covenant epistemology is a rough sketch, a vision. In Polanyian language, there is an integrative pattern which I see and which I commend to you; and to prompt the reader in the direction of apprehending it, here I am describing telling features. I am asking, do you see what I see? Detail, linear reasoning, and airtight cases, are thus neither the argument's long suit nor its priority. In part that is due to the inadequate and flawed understanding of its author. However, it reflects the nature of the epistemic position being propounded—the way that human knowing, I believe, actually works. Either way, flaws and lacunae may be taken as themselves invitations for the reader to contribute to the conversation.

I will show, secondly, that understanding and accrediting this larger interpersoned context is beneficial to all our knowing. It enables us to name and challenge a prevailing but defective, and personally and culturally damaging, approach to knowing. It offers a viable, exciting, productive alternative. It allows us to cash in on the hints of the interpersoned with which knowing is fraught. In being intentional about viewing knowing in its interpersoned context, we become better knowers. We become better knowers in multiple senses: our understanding of the world will be richer, the world will be blessed healingly, and we ourselves will be transformed toward wholeness and healing.

Finally, I will show how to put this model to work. I will suggest strategies for effective knowing that this vision implies. The covenant epistemology project models the very approach to knowing that it recommends, making it possible to learn its ways both from its argument and from its example. *Loving to Know* is a work of epistemic formation. It is meant to be embraced and furthered by others—in interpersoned covenant relationship. We are people together covenantally on the way to the communion that is knowing. All knowing involves conversations—thus more than one person in intimate mutuality—on the way.

QUESTIONS FOR DISCUSSION

1. Come up with other examples of coming to know similar to Annie Dillard's waiting for muskrats.

2. Note what similarities your examples share with her story. In particular, where do you notice covenantal self-binding for the sake of the yet-to-be-known?

3. If we shift to "another kind of knowing"—an interpersonal paradigm—what dimensions of our lives will make better sense?

4. What are your initial thoughts about the covenant epistemology thesis?

3

What Covenant Epistemology Offers

SINCE THE DEFECTIVE OUTLOOK that shapes our knowing adversely impacts all of life, covenant epistemology targets three overlapping groups: ordinary knowers, professional philosophical conversants, and thoughtful Christian believers and scholars. In this chapter I will sketch some specific contributions it makes to each.

I always put the ordinary knowers first—it is my calling to do so, as well as my intent in writing this book. I also offer covenant epistemology as a responsibly viable philosophical contribution. But a key part of the case is that it makes healing sense of ordinary knowing in all quarters. This is what confirms covenant epistemology for me. This is another reason why I privilege the wider audience. Depending on your personal situation, you may find that you want to dip selectively into this chapter and perhaps return to it after later chapters give you more of the feel of covenant epistemology.

In general, covenant epistemology offers a developed account of and rationale for viewing knowing as relationally interpersoned. There are plenty of places in our lives where knowing construed as impersonal information gathering just isn't a fit. And if we have been led to privilege information, we have suffered as a result. To name the obvious one—knowing other persons. Whether in religion, psychology, pedagogy, business, jazz, or day-to-day life, we will find that covenant epistemology more adequately accords with and accredits actual practice. I think it accords better with knowing nonpersons as well. In turn, having found a way to articulate what we actually practice epistemically, we will find that we practice it better and with deeper delight. We will find that covenant epistemology will open the door to an indefinite range of possible implications in thought and action.

WHAT COVENANT EPISTEMOLOGY OFFERS
ORDINARY KNOWERS—WHICH WE ALL ARE

Much professional philosophy seems to offer little accessible help to people in the streets "below" the philosophical "ivory tower." In-house discussions conducted in inscrutable terminology can seem to have little potential to impact the wider culture. Plus, I am arguing that the commitment of the profession itself to an epistemic stance of knowledge as explicit statements and proofs means that there is something critically important that the guild fails to contribute to the wider culture. Covenant epistemology and my presentation of it in the book, it is my earnest hope, moves beyond both of these to offer "com-fort"—strength alongside—to ordinary people. Covenant epistemology offers ordinary knowers the liberation to be and know and do, fully, freely, effectively. This paradigm elucidates all efforts to know.

It reincorporates into the knowing act dimensions of our lives which have predominantly been excluded, unleashing underappreciated resources humans possess to unlock and engage the world. Sadly, the reigning paradigm of knowing has failed to accredit this knowhow as epistemically legitimate, nor has it been able offer an account of wisdom. But covenant epistemology reinstates this *sine qua non*, freeing us to employ with intentionality what we have probably only covertly relied on.

The paradigm of knowing as covenantally interpersonal, and of knower and known fraught with the interpersoned, suggests ways we may comport ourselves as knowers that will invite the real to disclose itself to us. Wise people have been deemed wise precisely because they have developed this skilled knack of inviting the real.

Knowing goes on humanly, in some sense, despite the hegemony of a defective epistemic paradigm. This is because the excluded dimensions can function tacitly even when mislabeled, ignored, or misunderstood. But it should make a positive difference to accredit them rather than to continue to let them atrophy. There should indeed be a pay-off for straightening out our epistemology and bringing it more in line with humanness and reality. We should be better knowers for knowing knowing.

Covenant epistemology offers insight not simply into knowing but more broadly into what it is to be human and what humans do in the world. It resonates with our humanness, restoring us to ourselves even as it amplifies our effectiveness in all that we do. It is an epistemology as large as life, a strategy for living, which forms us in its practice as we grasp it.

Knowing should bless not just the knower, but also the known. Not only should knowing knowing help us know better, it should also move the object of our knowing toward health. Knowing was meant to be therapeutic. The act ought to bring shalom, not just to the knower, but also to the known. Contrast this with a default-ridden outlook which suspects the existence of the real, doubting and thus dishonoring its initiative in surprising but faithful self-disclosure.

This confirms the viability of covenant epistemology: knowing healingly is what humans were made to do. We have been called in our earth stewarding to promote shalom; the picture of knowing as covenantally interpersonal fulfills our calling to steward the earth and therein promote shalom.[1] *Shalom* is blessed, fulfilled well-being in harmony with all else. A healthy act of knowing leaves neither knower nor known where it was, but constitutes an intersection of trajectories down the road from where each began. And down the road, with good prospect, in the direction of shalom.

In preparing this book, I myself have been inviting the real with respect to human knowing: listening attentively to several voices for clues to this marvelous act of knowingly engaging the real. I want its text to describe, to embody, and to effect interpersonal knowing. May it invite you more deeply into the dance, and into shalom.

WHAT COVENANT EPISTEMOLOGY OFFERS
THE PHILOSOPHICAL CONVERSATION
AND SCHOLARSHIP GENERALLY

To philosophical and scholarly discussions, covenant epistemology offers a fresh line of inquiry. It corroborates and improves on some great insights of contemporary philosophy. It challenges some of its problematic positions, providing a helpful alternative. It does so primarily because covenant epistemology embraces and works from the epistemological insights of Michael Polanyi. What Polanyi proposes, and how that suggests covenant epistemology, I will present in the next chapter. For those

---

1. I will develop this idea in the conversation with John Frame (ch. 6), as well as in the final chapter.

as yet unfamiliar with Polanyi's work, some of what I say here will make fuller sense at that point in the discussion.[2]

For a number of possible reasons, Polanyi's work went largely unheeded by the mainstream philosophical traditions in the mid-twentieth century. Polanyi wasn't trained originally as a philosopher, but rather as a top-notch scientist. His writing displays neither the language nor the preoccupation with certain debates typical to analytic philosophy. Instead, crashing the guild from outside, he proposed epistemological claims which radically undercut the prevailing philosophical discussions by calling into question their fundamental commitments. Philosophers who blindly embraced objectivism could only hear Polanyi's proposals as subjectivism. His work was dismissed, I and other Polanyi scholars believe, because it was before its time.[3]

Another reason for its obscurity may be that Polanyi's work is difficult to tie to a single discipline. Polanyi's personal scholarly approach was interdisciplinary and collaborative. It grew out of both his practice as a scientist, and his penchant as a polymath. His epistemological proposals invite—even require—a return to interdisciplinary coherence. In both its content and its style, his work challenges the insular compartmentalization and individualism that continues to dominate professional scholarship. But this also makes Polanyi difficult to categorize: in which courses and majors in college would professors teach his work? Science? Philosophy? Economics? Political theory? Religion? The fact is that he contributed brilliantly to all of these. But it often means he is not well-known in any of them. The very compartmentalization that his work challenges also prevents his work from being appropriated.

Another factor is that some thinkers, at the present time better known than Polanyi, evidently were exposed to and significantly influenced by his work without their debt being generally acknowledged. Thomas Kuhn is one, Alasdair MacIntyre, and Charles Taylor are others.[4]

---

2. See ch. 4.

3. Scott and Moleski, *Michael Polanyi*; also the Mars Hill Audio Report, *Tacit Knowing, Truthful Knowing*.

4. Polanyi himself expressed ambivalence regarding his professional relationship with Thomas Kuhn. It is a matter of ongoing debate whether Kuhn inappropriately appropriated Polanyi's insights. The concern is made more complex because if Kuhn did so, he only took half of them, and thus popularized a fundamental and damaging misconstrual of Polanyi's more sophisticated thought. The entire vol. XXXIII no. 2 (2006–7) issue of *Tradition and Discovery: The Polanyi Society Periodical* is devoted to this matter. Also, see John Apczynski's paper, "Relevance of Personal Knowledge."

My own hypothesis about this oversight is that the fundamental shape of Polanyi's epistemology and of his personal practice to encourage "a society of explorers," meant that he expected his ideas to be shared and adapted. Based on my own experience with his ideas, and that of my readers, I believe there is something so humbly self-liberating intrinsic to his thought that the one restored to her- or himself is therein inclined to forget whose thought occasioned the liberation.[5] But on the other hand, it is not right or helpful for an important influence to not receive due recognition.

This is especially grievous because I do not know any other source in the entire history of western philosophy for the idea of the knowing as subsidiary-focal integration. Renowned historian of philosophy Marjorie Grene rightly dubbed this unique contribution of Polanyi's, "grounds for a revolution in philosophy."[6] She concurred with Polanyi, for example, that nobody had ever resolved the dilemma Plato set forth in the *Meno*: how does anyone ever come to know? For either you don't know what you need to know, in which case you do not begin to look for it; or you do, in which case you do not need to. She believed that Polanyi is the only one who does resolve it.

Especially from the twentieth century onward various philosophers have developed wonderful insights that get a piece of what Polanyi offers a better account for. One may note a resonance between Polanyi's ideas and those of Martin Heidegger, Ludwig Wittgenstein's later work, and Maurice Merleau-Ponty. I believe that Polanyi's epistemic proposal actually makes better and more usable sense of important insights of these philosophers. Professional philosophy would benefit from considering Polanyi's contribution. Since covenant epistemology appropriates this unique Polanyian insight as a *sine qua non,* it, too, will prove critically valuable to the philosophical conversation.

There are some specific philosophical discussions to which covenant epistemology, with its Polanyian core, contributes a fresh, superior, stance. Even before I address these in later chapters, the ordinary reader can sense that they involve the professional version of the daisy of di-

5. Here I reflect ongoing informal conversations in the Polanyi Society. However, now fifty years out from the publication of Polanyi's *Personal Knowledge,* we are tremendously encouraged to witness a growth in the breadth and depth of Polanyi studies. See http://www.missouriwestern.edu/orgs/polanyi/, the official website of the Polanyi Society.

6. Grene, "Tacit Knowing," 164.

chotomies in chapter 1. They call for, not a compromise, but a positive and viable third way. Polanyi's subsidiary-focal integration offers this to the dispute between correspondence and coherence approaches to truth, as well as to the closely related realism vs. antirealism debates, and between foundationalist and non-foundationalist epistemologies.[7] Polanyi is not a foundationalist, but he is nevertheless an unflinching epistemic realist—an unheard-of combination, precisely because Polanyi's unique contribution has remained relatively unknown.

Briefly: the correspondence theory of truth proposes that the truthfulness of a claim involves its correspondence with reality. The coherence theory of truth proposes that, since it is impossible to determine correspondence, the truthfulness of a claim involves its consistency with all the other claims we take to be true. Foundationalism is a proposal about the nature of knowledge, proposing that we must have knowledge of two kinds: one is an all-important foundation of self-evidently certain claims, the other, all claims that can be derived from the foundation. Generally, foundationalists are also correspondence theorists, and they often argue that one must be both of these things in order to be epistemic realists. Epistemic realism avers that knowledge is knowledge of objective reality, rather than a mental or social construct or convention. This latter understanding would be known as anti-realism. Subsidiary-focal integration cuts the Gordian knot and offers a positive epistemic alternative.

There are other disputes related to these, such as the debate between modernism and postmodernism as it is popularly construed. Another is the debate between the epistemic naturalists and those who maintain that a non-physical dimension of humans must be acknowledged. There is the dispute, in epistemology studies, of internalism vs. externalism. To all these Polanyi's epistemological insights offer a fresh alternative that may profitably reshape the dynamic of the discussions.

In scholarship in all disciplines, recent thought has exposed the epistemically formative role of historical, sociological, and hermeneutical factors, language, and texts, as well as moral and epistemic virtues. The absence of a positive third alternative to objectivism and subjectivism has perpetuated ambivalence and misunderstanding of these fac-

---

7. As. R. J. Snell says, in reference to a Christian version of this dispute: the debate will go on forever because they are asking the wrong question. Snell, "Following Tiresias."

tors. Covenant epistemology's Polanyian contour positively accredits these and makes deeper sense of them. It shows how they may be countenanced in a profounder submission to reality.

Covenant epistemology draws another distinctive contour from a recent tradition of thought that considers the person as central to being and knowing. This notion has profound and allusive implications which have remained unnoticed in mainstream philosophical discussions. We can guess reasons for this. Personhood is difficult to articulate. It defies reduction to explicit propositions. And where philosophy restricts itself to working with propositions—a definitive feature, not only of the predominant analytic philosophical tradition, but of much of western thought—the notion of person will be exiled. Where is personhood on our daisy, for example? It isn't even the daisy. Or if it is, our default compartmentalization has rendered personhood less than who we are. Another reason that philosophy bypasses motifs of interpersonhood is that they allude quite naturally to a transcendent Person. Atheistic proclivities in modern philosophy would obviously resist this inclination. However, I believe that scholarly discussion stands to gain from covenant epistemology's contour of what I call interpersonhood.

Human knowing and being, quite broadly, stand to gain from it. Because this is so, I believe that covenant epistemology could well act as an agent for cultural change. This is a grand claim. But it is not as if the contours which comprise covenant epistemology are entirely new. In fact, I believe that the proposal accords with some of the best insights of our times, and with the general direction of current thought. Voices have been converging into a wave, we may say. Covenant epistemology contributes a creative refocusing to that wave, moving it farther along. It gathers and renames the voices in a way that is both new and recognizable. This itself is a signature feature of the act of coming to know that this book's proposal will allow us to accredit.

Covenant epistemology also offers a philosophically sophisticated epistemic model that scholarship in other disciplines may appropriate helpfully. Psychology and therapy, pedagogy, the arts and literature, and professional training and athletics, not to mention science, will find that that it makes good sense of what they do. Here is a philosophical resource that these other disciplines may collaboratively tap.

It also offers a way to rapprochement among the disciplines, and thus has much to offer higher education, especially Christian higher

education. The Western legacy has yielded academic training that is in-
dividualistic and academic disciplines that are stubbornly competitive.
The sciences and humanities compete regarding comparative superiority. It is widely believed that knowing in the sciences and knowing in the
humanities are two different things. The liberal arts, both sciences and
humanities, continually lose ground to the pragmatic and lucrative. But
covenant epistemology offers an account of knowing that is inherently
interdisciplinary by virtue of its three-dimensionality and also because
it describes how knowing works in every discipline.[8]

WHAT COVENANT EPISTEMOLOGY
OFFERS CHRISTIAN SCHOLARSHIP

Finally, covenant epistemology adds to discussions already taking place
in Christian scholarship a fresh alternative avenue of inquiry, and one I
commend as superior in some respects. The following is a rough survey
of several loci of discussion in contemporary Christian thought, in order
to locate covenant epistemology with respect to them.[9]

Modest Foundationalism and Evidentialist Apologetics—Philosopher J. P.
Moreland and some associates at Talbot School of Theology argue that
biblical Christianity requires a modest foundationalist epistemology:
that knowledge has a bedrock of modest, explicit, certainties that correspond truly to the world.[10] In their work they adopt the argumentative
style of twentieth-century philosophical analysis, and thus some of its
definitive tacit commitments. Evidentialist apologetics is an approach to
defending the gospel that does so by commending evidence to make the
case to the unbeliever for the truth and reasonableness of Christianity.
Since neither evidentialism nor foundationalism emphasizes the role
of pretheoretical commitments in knowing, they are natural bedfel-
lows. This group is committed to realism, the idea that our knowledge

8. For my discussion of this, see textures 3 and 4.

9. In this quick survey I depend in part on the expertise and gracious collaboration
of my colleague, Robert M. Frazier. See Frazier, "Considering the Tie That Binds." In
response to his paper, see my "Proposing Covenant Epistemology."

10. J. P. Moreland, William Lane Craig, R. Scott Smith, and Douglas Geivett share
this stance and dominate the discussion. See all issues of *Philosophia Christi*, the journal
of the Evangelical Philosophical Society. In Penner, ed. *Christianity and the Postmodern
Turn*, the contributors together display range of the loci I sketch here. This is true also
of Cowan, ed., *Five Views on Apologetics*.

accesses an objective reality, and thus rejects nonfoundationalist efforts as anti-realist and anti-Christian. Covenant epistemology incorporates Polanyi's unique, realist, third alternative to both foundationalism and nonfoundationalism.

Dutch Neo-Calvinian Philosophy—Growing out of the Dutch Reformed embracing of the Diltheyan idea of worldviews in the nineteenth Century is the Christian philosophy of Hermann Dooyeweerd.[11] This approach considers Dooyeweerdianism the one true Christian philosophy. Philosophical anthropology anchors this speculative philosophy; the human heart's disposition toward or away from God is the fundamental shaper of all human effort. It offers an account of human society in terms of overlapping spheres (government, church, family, school) each with its own distinctive character and sovereignty. Dooyeweerdianism, along with the influential thought of Abraham Kuyper,[12] continues to generate much fruitful scholarship. Dutch neo-Calvinian philosophy can feel, however, as if the Bible and the implications of its claim to authority have been set aside as no longer central. Covenant epistemology, while not pretending to be the final word in Christian epistemology, is an account of all human knowing that makes sense of the authoritative function of Scripture as God's self-disclosure, and of divine initiative in creation and redemption as formative and central to the account.

Van Tillianism, Presuppositional Apologetics—Cornelius Van Til spearheaded an innovative account of apologetics that shares the Dutch Calvinian emphasis on the role of presuppositions—pre-theoretical commitments—in knowing, honoring the pivotal role of fundamental belief commitments and the disposition of "the heart" in all knowing, especially that of unbelievers considering Christianity. However, Scripture and the knowledge of God are central.[13] It often is perceived as being fideist (that is, commending truth claims in the absence of reasons for them). Talk of presuppositions can feel arbitrary. Also, the position has often led to making the rather hard-to-believe claim that the unbeliever knows nothing. Van Til's students have developed his work in divergent directions. John Frame, whose work I interweave in a later chapter, has

11. Dooyeweerd's *Twilight of Western Thought* is a one-volume introduction to his work.

12. Kuyper, *Lectures on Calvinism*.

13. Van Til, *Defense of the Faith*; Frame, *Cornelius Van Til*.

modified Van Til's central insights in a more irenic and usable direction.[14] Covenant epistemology both draws from this tradition and contributes a concrete epistemological justification.

Reformed Epistemology—This refers to the work of Alvin Plantinga and Nicholas Wolterstorff, beginning in the 1980s, who have mastered the contemporary analytic philosophical technique and debate to practice scholarship from a Christian perspective.[15] Reformed epistemology thus shares an analytic philosophical style with modest foundationalists, but they reject a foundationalism of explicit certainties, offering a responsibly philosophical account of presuppositions as "control beliefs." They have advanced the cause of Christians and Christian studies in philosophy immeasurably by making a compelling case for the rationality of religious belief. And they have identified and pursue fruitful philosophical research programs that their Calvinist commitments have suggested— for example, taking seriously Calvin's indication that all people have an innate sense of deity, developing and exploring its implications for epistemology. One can feel, as with the modest foundationalists, that the methodically detailed rigor of even the most readable analytic philosophy puts people off, believers or unbelievers. Also one may justifiably suspect that analytic philosophy itself harbors hidden commitments concerning what knowledge is that need to be challenged head-on. Covenant epistemology, I believe, by reason of its proposals, is more accessible to ordinary knowers. Most importantly, it challenges the covert assumption of analytic philosophy that knowledge is restricted to articulated statements, rendering them the presumptive starting point of analysis.[16]

Postmodernism, Postliberal Philosophical Thought, and Radical Orthodoxy—There is a wide and variegated conversation that generally involves espousing some of the best insights of postmodern thought as liberating Christian thought and practice from the failed yet hegemonous Enlightenment project and allowing a creative retrieval of premodern Christian practice, as well as of premodern philosophy. James K. A. (Jamie) Smith exemplifies this, working from a Dutch neo-Calvinian base to tap the philosophical work of the Continental philosophers in

14. Meek, "Servant Thinking."

15. Sennett, ed., *The Analytic Theist*; Wolterstorff, *Reason within the Bounds of Religion*.

16. Meek, "Polanyi and Plantinga."

the Heideggerean tradition, as well as theologians ancient (Augustine) and contemporary (Radical Orthodoxy) to mine postmodernity for Christian theology.[17] They are doing a great service in modeling a positive and productive interface between Christian thought and the current philosophical trends. The "radical" in Radical Orthodoxy, as well as Smith's proposal of "unapologetics," rightfully challenges the popular presumption that religious ideas need to be checked at the door, so that public and neutral conversation can take place.[18] Smith argues that such neutrality is an impossible and misguided ideal. Instead, we should view scholarship as conversation from a plurality of contestable viewpoints, of which Christianity is one. Christian scholarship should be expected, as with other viewpoints, to make a case for its viability by devising proposals and research programs that contribute helpfully to public understanding. Covenant epistemology accords with Smith's unapologetics in this respect. Polanyian epistemology offers a more concrete and accessible understanding of human knowing than does continental philosophy. Also, one can feel that the postmodern approach inclines toward anti-realism. Polanyi's innovative realist stance contributes a formative piece of covenant epistemology. Both these features render covenant epistemology a positive alternative.

The Primacy of Scripture and Its Drama of Redemption—In the Reformed theological tradition, in particular, there are many who see themselves primarily as theologians and not philosophers, who accordingly affirm the primacy of Scripture, and who have in recent decades, in sympathy with the shift in prevailing philosophical outlook, come to emphasize a storied approach to their understanding of Scripture. I have in mind Michael Horton and Kevin Vanhoozer, as well as Michael Williams, whose work I develop in a later chapter.[19] These theologians would reject any attempt of philosophers to do philosophy that sidelines Scripture as authoritative. On the other hand, some in this tradition can practice their theology without giving due attention to its implicit philosophical commitments. In the English Reformed tradition, one can even feel that philosophy as a discipline remains under suspicion, perhaps justifiably,

17. Smith, *Fall of Interpretation*; Smith, *Radical Orthodoxy*; Smith, *Desiring the Kingdom*.

18. Smith, "Biblical Studies across the Disciplines."

19. Vanhoozer, *Drama of Doctrine*; Horton, *God of Promise*. See ch. 7 in this book.

given its excessive ascendancy in the Dutch Reformed tradition. Covenant epistemology offers a helpful philosophical awareness to Christian theologians and a helpful theological awareness to philosophers. It therefore offers a *rapprochement*, and a positive rationale for continuing together along the scholarly way. The recent Scripture and Hermeneutics series is an important ongoing conversation that involves philosophers and theologians together.[20] The conversation partners in this series deeply engage philosophical hermeneutics, using it to move over the same ground that covenant epistemology treats as epistemology. Covenant epistemology resonates profoundly with the overall commitments of this discussion and is well-qualified to make a unique contribution to it.

Catholic Philosophy—Philosophy has been practiced with surpassing excellence by Christians in the Catholic tradition for centuries. Here I have in mind the vast riches particularly of St. Thomas Aquinas and the Thomist tradition that has been rediscovered by Protestant philosophers and Christians generally, occasioned partially by the efforts of reformed epistemologists that restored credibility to the idea that religious belief is rational.[21] But only in part: for this is something the Catholics have maintained all along. Protestant thinkers have only recently rediscovered the tradition. This is due to the gulf induced by the heavy impact of modernism on the Protestant tradition, and a related withdrawal to anti-intellectualism in reaction to the challenges of modern science. When Protestants returned to intellectual engagement, important leaders of the movement, such as Francis Schaeffer, dismissed Aquinas as less than biblical in his stance concerning the effect of human sin on knowing, and influenced many others in this. But now the tides are turning. One young philosopher I locate in the contemporary Catholic tradition is R. J. Snell, whose serious development of Bernard Lonergan's Thomistic epistemology compares favorably with Polanyi's work and with the vision of covenant epistemology.[22] Indeed, the opening pages of Lonergan's *Insight* read like an introduction to *Loving to Know*, for Lonergan's insight just is the transformatively understood act of coming to know. And Martin Moleski's *Personal Catholicism*, in which he

---

20. Bartholomew, et al., eds., Scripture and Hermeneutics Seminar, 8 vols.

21. Eleonore Stump and other Thomist and medieval scholars are regular contributors to *Faith and Philosophy*, the journal of the Society of Christian Philosophers.

22. Snell, *Through a Glass Darkly*.

demonstrates the resonance between John Henry Newman's illative sense (rational intuition, insight) and Polanyi's understanding of knowing serves as an important confirmation of the resonance of Polanyian proposals with Catholic epistemology.[23] There is good prospect for fruitful collaboration.

I believe that covenant epistemology adds a fresh, viable, complementary alternative to these current approaches in Christian scholarship. It offers another avenue of inquiry and conversation. It is non-foundationalist but realist; presuppositional but emphasizing what is known as common grace rather than antithesis; it does philosophy without ascendancy, emphasizing centrally, but in a philosophically attuned way, the unfolding drama of Scripture, positively showing how Scripture and the knower's relationship to God is central to knowing.

Several of these loci are epistemological developments in the reformational, Calvinian, tradition. The reformational tradition has never consciously bought in to the default mode, as these loci indicate. But I do not believe that the tradition reflected Calvin's, or Christianity's, epistemological richness. All the contributions by Reformed scholars mentioned above are important, but I believe they fall short of the mark. I contend that covenant epistemology more profoundly resonates with John Calvin's own heart, theology, and the epistemic practice implicit in his work.[24] One evidence of this is that, although the reformational tradition all along has positively challenged the defective evangelical default mode, this default mode—evangelical and otherwise—nevertheless persists. In contrast to these, covenant epistemology actively effects the still-desperately needed epistemic reform that was implicit in Calvin's works well in advance of the ascendancy and shipwreck of modernism, along with the backlash of subjectivism and relativism, and what may be considered a twenty-first-century persistence or reentrenchment of modernism.

WHAT COVENANT EPISTEMOLOGY OFFERS
THOUGHTFUL CHRISTIAN BELIEVERS

The damaging epistemic default has especially influenced Protestant Christianity. I believe it has both thwarted and castrated biblical Chris-

---

23. Moleski, *Personal Catholicism*.

24 Calvin, *Institutes*; Meek, "Covenant Epistemology for the 21st Century."

tianity. In addition to the mind-body divorce that pervades our grasp of spirituality, which we noted in chapter 1, the following is evidence that the defective epistemic default operates, often unquestioned, in the many circles of committed Christians. Reason has been opposed to faith. And where this opposition prevails, Christians have felt the pressure to choose: some have felt that, of the two, what matters is faith, and have surrendered reason; others have defended a rational, "propositional," Christianity. Further, Christians think of truth as God's information, implicitly assuming that there is a circumscribed body of it which often receives the adjective, "absolute." It must be defended against challenges of what is perceived to be the single alternative: relativism. Third, many Christians assume that *first* you get the information, *then* you apply it. The sermon, in a Protestant worship service, occupies a central role as the information that we then apply to our lives. Protestants often see their role in worship as a passively receptive one. They often see the sacraments as recalling information, and dismiss liturgy as rote repetition.

Most telling is the fact that ordinary Christians display a disconnect between truth as propositions and a "personal relationship with Jesus Christ." Christians distinguish studying information about God (sermon or seminary) as over against their personal relationship with Jesus. Christian believers know that the relationship is the most important thing. But the default prevents people from seeing how that relationship can be central to what we think knowing is—how knowing and being known by Christ could be central *epistemically*. Not that information about God, even mistakenly so-conceived, isn't good for the soul, rather, it is that Christians' all-important relationship with Jesus isn't considered knowledge, because it isn't information. It is thus effectively left untapped for their epistemology, let alone accorded centrality.

Other not-exactly-propositional dimensions of Christianity are doctrinal profession, liturgical practice, and discipleship. Christian believers can follow the default in thinking that theory and application are distinct. Thus, discipleship has to be, not truth, but the *application* of truth. And what of liturgical practice—what is that? It is commonly deemed rote repetition. And what, even, is profession of faith, other than saying, I believe certain statements are true? It is not that no branch of Protestant Christianity has challenged this Christian version of the dichotomous default. But the default, as we saw in chapter 1, persists, especially pervasively in Protestant Christianity. Help is needed at the subcutaneous level—help which both names the change needed and effects it. Covenant epistemology offers such help to Christian believers.

Covenant epistemology directly addresses these problematic construals. It takes on the defective default mode that induces them. It installs the believer's relationship with God as the central paradigm of all knowing. This gives rich confirmation of Jesus' saying, I *am* the Truth (John 14:6). It makes the case, therefore, that a vibrant relationship with God is central to effective knowing of any sort. Knowing God is profoundly epistemic.

Knowing, I will argue, is *not information* so much as it is *transformation*. This makes sense if knowing Christ the Truth—having been known by Christ the Truth—is central epistemically. It isn't about mere information, but about being *transformatively known*. If knowing is transformation, then sacramental and liturgical practice, and faithful Christian discipleship both make sense and shed light on knowing. They involve inviting that transformation and being formed in truth.[25] "Application" is a paltry descriptor for what occurs. And if *all* truth is profession rather than proposition, doctrinal profession is of a piece with all truth claims.

Covenant epistemology accords the good news of Jesus Christ the centrality it is due. It is an epistemic approach profoundly consonant with the Christian Scripture and Christian practice. And in interpersonal covenant epistemology, where vibrant communion with God is the central paradigm of all knowing, communing is also the most effective epistemological thing you can do.

Covenant epistemology hopes to form those who indwell it as better knowers, generally speaking, but particularly as better Christian believers. By "better," I mean, more in accord with what Scripture had in mind, more attuned to joyous delight in the experience, and more effective as humans and workers and lovers and play-ers, as a result.

Also, covenant epistemology unleashes philosophy to thoughtful Christian believers, and recovers theology for philosophically sensitive ones. It does this by bringing scholarship in line with the profound insight of any believer in Christ: that her or his living communion with God is central to life, worship, the church, and the world. Neither philosophers nor theologians have typically seen that this epistemological retooling to relationship is desperately needed. But it takes a more nuanced epistemology than we typically articulate, as well as one more

25. My editor, Robin Parry comments: "A different kind of in-formation, eh? Like it."

accessibly articulated, to understand and capitalize on interpersonal relationship as a central philosophical commitment, and to start to move
beyond the gospel-castrating dichotomies of the our inherited epistemic
default so that we can.

The covenant epistemology vision of knowing thus makes an
important contribution to philosophical conversation as well as to
Christian theology and scholarship, even as it is meant for everybody
who, in knowing, seeks to engage the world—in other words, all of us.
May it draw us afresh to delight in knowing and to do it well.

QUESTIONS FOR DISCUSSION

1. Locate yourself in one or more of the audiences described in this
   chapter—ordinary knower, philosopher, scholar, Christian scholar,
   thoughtful Christian believer.

2. If you locate yourself as a Christian scholar, which, if any, of the traditions the chapter names describes your approach? If none, write a
   brief description of your tradition.

3. Say a little more to describe yourself and the audience in which you
   have located yourself as hearers of *Loving to Know*.

4. What promises does the chapter make to you and your audience?
   What questions and hopes do these promises evoke? Are there other
   possible pay-offs of covenant epistemology? If so, what are they?

5. From the perspective of your chosen audience, what will you be looking for as you read *Loving to Know*?

PART TWO

Transformation

$$4$$

KNOWING AS SUBSIDIARY-FOCAL INTEGRATION

Conversation with Michael Polanyi

I HAVE SHOWN THAT we need epistemological therapy, and we have begun to explore an alternative vision of knowing that would supply that therapy. I have sketched a proposal, and suggested what it offers to everyday knowers and professional disciplines. I have thus laid the groundwork to launch the central project of developing covenant epistemology. Three intertwining strands of theses, or contours, comprise it. The first is Polanyian epistemology.

Michael Polanyi's thought contributes to the project the central mechanism of knowing. All knowing has as its structure and dynamic the subsidiary-focal integrative feat as identified by Polanyi. By itself, apart from my further developments of it in covenant epistemology, it effectively addresses the dichotomies of the defective epistemic default, transformatively superseding them. I will show how. Within covenant epistemology, his account remains the distinctive, innovative, phenomenological backbone.

I developed my adaptation of his proposals in *Longing to Know*: "All knowing is the profoundly human struggle to rely on clues to focus on a pattern that we then submit to as a token of reality."[1] Here I want to take a fresh look at Polanyian epistemology as it informs covenant epistemology, paying special attention to some of its unique dimensions and their implications, and identifying that about it which implicitly signposts reciprocity and the personal in knowing. These suggest the pattern of covenantally constituted interpersonhood as the paradigm of all human knowing.

---

1. This sentence is the composite of *Longing to Know*'s section titles. Readers of *Longing to Know* will find the next section a review. But it will also move the discussion toward covenant epistemology.

If you are new to Polanyi's description of how we know what we know, you will find that it applies widely in your own life experience. Subsidiary-focal integration, which I will expound here, makes profound sense of all human knowing. This is an epistemology that restores you to yourself and to confidence in your knowing.

SUBSIDIARY-FOCAL INTEGRATION IN A MEEKIAN MODE

In my life and philosophical work I have appropriated the epistemological insights of twentieth-century public intellectual, Michael Polanyi, a prominent research scientist who later turned his efforts to crafting an epistemology consonant with his professional experience.[2] After all these years of personally indwelling his insightful work, I have melded his central proposals into my own adaptation.[3] In what follows I present my version, as I did also in *Longing to Know*. But I believe it truthfully and helpfully represents his profound central epistemic insights.[4]

Acts of Coming to Know

Polanyi began by arguing that epistemology should focus its efforts, not on accounting for knowledge that we have already achieved by offering adequate rational justification for our claims (as western philosophy has done predominantly), but on accounting for acts of coming to know—discoveries.[5] Knowing should be construed, Polanyi began by arguing, *contra* the still prevailing paradigm in science, not on the model of explanation, but rather on the model of discovery. This is because an explanatory paradigm offers no help for understanding discovery. But the opposite would be helpful for both. Discovery—the first knowing, when we are moving from unknowing to knowing—rather than explanation

2. See his *magnum opus, Personal Knowledge,* as well as several essays, some of which have been collected in Grene, ed., *Knowing and Being.* I have worked with his thought in Meek, *Contact With Reality,* as well as in Meek, *Longing to Know,* and several articles and unpublished papers. See www.longingtoknow.com.

3. There are a few portions of his thought that I find problematic and choose to set to the side. His theses regarding emergence, a parallel structure of knowing and being, and his views on religion, for example, do not appear to me to conform entirely to or be essential to his fundamental insights regarding knowing.

4. Key points of the following summary are to be found throughout his work. As perhaps the best entrée into his thought, I follow Marjorie Grene in recommending "Tacit Knowing," the first lecture of three in Polanyi, *Tacit Dimension.*

5. Polanyi, *Tacit Dimension,* 24–25.

is the more appropriate setting in which to find characteristic features of knowing, Polanyi believed. So it is appropriate to begin by speaking of acts of *coming* to know. It helps the discussion of knowing to begin in a different place from the idea of knowledge as statements.

Even so simple a decision as whether to attend to explanation or discovery has profound implications. The decision has been skewed by an overweening commitment to certainty. Complete lucidity has been the *sine qua non* of what it is to be knowledge. This affects what we choose to count as *bona fide* examples of knowledge. A common suggestion is, 2 + 2 = 4. Qualified examples are restricted in a manner that then distorts our perception of our perceiving. It's only a repeated, already attained, claim that, along with the reasons we martial in retrospect to support its rightness, looks to us to be knowledge. And even for these restricted examples, tacitly complying with the epistemic paradigm of certainty, we refuse to accredit, let alone notice the personal commitment and the tacit, lived, involvement by which we sustain them as true. By shifting our focus to first acts of coming to know, we notice features that characterize even the most confident holding of claims. These features are distinctively human, and very much something we often delight in and rely on joyfully.

But we can identify many experiences of coming to know: things we have learned, or learned to do, puzzles we have solved, problems we have untangled, sudden or gradual moments of insight, "aha" moments. Attending to these will bring these distinctive features to our notice.

Knowing as Subsidiary-Focal Integration

Here is a brief description and an example; I will then go over the ground more slowly. On the basis of his own research experience, Polanyi concluded that knowing is the active shaping of clues to form a pattern, to which we submit as a token of reality. This very human action he called *integration*.[6] Integration is a risky, responsible struggle, a skilled groping toward the not-yet-known. It involves shifting from looking *at* puzzling and apparently unrelated particulars to relating to them differently: relying on them, or attending *through* them or *from* them, to comprehend a deeper pattern. The shift to identifying a coherent pattern is a moment of insight, what I called, in *Longing to Know*, the "Oh! I see it!" moment. I

6. Polanyi, *Personal Knowledge*, vii; Polanyi, *Tacit Dimension*, xviii, 6.

often use Magic Eye 3-D puzzles to illustrate the key facets of Polanyian integration. In the "Oh! I see it!" moment, the person struggling for understanding integrates particulars into a pattern. The pattern becomes *focal*: we focus on it.

Prior to our successful integration to a focal pattern, we began to attend to and be puzzled by random, apparently meaningless, opaque, and personally external particulars. In the integrative feat, these particulars, both the ones we noted and even more that we didn't or couldn't, shift to become *subsidiary* clues. That means that we shift to rely on them and attend from them in our focus on the pattern. (In the act of integration, as we shift from *to* to *from* with respect to the particulars of world, words and body, we come to indwell or interiorize them all.) Particulars-turned-clues are thereby endowed with a transformed appearance, joint meaningfulness, and for the knower, a sense of incorporation into oneself. Thus we develop a lived bodiliness, a felt sense, with respect to all that we rely on in an epistemic act.

All acts of coming to know are integrative and transformative, rather than deductive and linear. They evidence this from-to, subsidiary-focal structure. So do all truth claims that we continue to hold. The knower affirms the pattern of the claim responsibly on the grounds of the clues now indwelt subsidiarily in accordance with the way the pattern has transformed their appearance and meaning. All human knowledge is wholly, or in the case of explicit knowledge, at its roots, subsidiary and tacit.[7]

A wonderful example of this is learning to read. At some point in your past, you looked at such letters as I am typing now, and saw configurations of lines on a piece of paper. Your teacher made you copy them. He/she taught you to recognize them and say them, connecting them with certain sounds. But there came a moment when you looked and saw something new: *meaning*. C-A-T became cat, and attached suddenly to the feline who hissed when you pulled its tail. Having learned to read, you have moved, with respect to the words on the page, from Point A to Point B. Now you read so well that you might be tempted to say that you hardly see the words on the page. But those marks are there, must be there, for you to be reading. You have shifted your manner of relating to them. You now *rely* on them rather than *focus* on them. The marks, the particulars, which had been your focus, have become what Polanyi calls

7. Polanyi, *Personal Knowledge*, 95.

subsidiary. You attend, not *to* them, but *from* them. No longer *particulars,* they are *clues.* Thus you rely on clues to focus integratively on a pattern.

Point A

Let us go over this ground of this Polanyian epistemology more slowly, considering how it works and what it implies. For any one of your acts of coming to know, you can remember a "Point A" when you were staring at an apparently unrelated and senseless array of particular pieces. They didn't connect with each other, with you, or with the world in the way you have now come to grasp them. Nor at Point A did you know how to proceed or in what direction. Yet despite your ignorance, you "bit"—you started pursuing what you did not know. Perhaps someone was coaching your efforts. At Point A, even this person's guiding words were opaquely meaningless.

My father taught me to ride a bicycle by dint of putting me on a two-wheeler at the top of a grassy hill and pushing me. I was skeptical; I was terrified. To make matters worse, he yelled, "Balance!"—as if I could understand what that meant!—as if that would be helpful! At the top of that hill, I was at Point A. My dad's plan, I think, was that by the time I reached the bottom of it, I would be at Point B.

At Point A, you nevertheless tried to climb into those directions to make sense of them. Quite possibly you felt as if something was tantalizing you, beckoning you. You may have felt that something inside you was aching for something it had yet to understand. This struggle to know is the driving dynamic of knowing. It characterizes anything from pursuing a cure for cancer to finding where you left your car keys; from following directions to a new location to creating a work of art; from statistical analysis to riding a bike; knowing a cat to knowing God; a decision to pull up roots to pursue one's dream in another place or a decision to try a new recipe. Integration achieved rides the crest of *longing* to know and propels you forward into the unknown

At Point A, as we stare at apparently random particulars, we actually have a choice whether to believe that there is something beyond what we see that makes sense of it. We might choose not to believe that there is anything to it, to believe instead that there is no deeper pattern. If we do not think there is something to pursue, we turn away from the apparent puzzle.

But suppose we bite. In doing so, we commit ourselves to the presence of an as-yet-undiscovered reality. We pledge that there is something there to be discovered, even at the point that we have no idea what the "it" is that is there. This choice is the stuff of risk and responsibility. We put our hand to a plough whose furrow is at that point unknown. We turn from looking over our shoulder to probing forward into darkness.

The multifarious "its" that you and I might each pursue accord often with our personal natural proclivities. I once scanned a book edited by a cook, for example, who described her lifelong pursuit of cookbooks and delight in old recipes and the forms of life they evoke. I thought to myself that cookbooks and recipes never tantalize me personally. But for her, each recipe was a doorway to imagining. Each of us is drawn by something. A key to understanding a person is knowing what he or she longs for. Part of the genius of communal learning is letting others complement our own proclivities by blessing us through theirs. Others may—must—help us see and sense what, left to ourselves, we would not.

From Point A to Point B: Integration

The dynamic transformation that moves us from Point A to Point B is integration. Integration is the creative, responsible, shaping of clues into a coherent pattern that betokens reality. Polanyi describes how moving toward integration involves two activities of the knower: creative intuition and creative imagination. Creative intuition constantly gauges the direction in which lies the thing we want to find, as well as our proximity to it. Its empty focus guides our search. Creative imagination is our active scrabbling, subsidiarily, in the direction toward which the intuition is pointing.[8]

The goal of the struggle, we sometimes say, is to connect the dots—or to make sense of experience. We are struggling to find a pattern that relates the particulars. We're struggling to understand, to see what is there, to "get it." The struggle can take any length of time, from seconds to years. Integration is always an effort to move from where we are to something beyond us, in a certain direction. I sometimes call this *vectoring* because it begins with and moves out from us—or moves us out

---

8. Polanyi, "Creative Imagination," 85.

from where we were—toward something only hinted at, in a certain direction.

There is no guarantee that we will be successful because no necessity links focal pattern to the particulars of Point A. If and when we find ourselves at Point B, we usually feel that the insight was in some way given to us from outside us. The central epistemic act of integration cannot be given a linear and fully explicit account. It is not possible to attain the focal pattern simply by setting the original particulars in a row. In fact, we find we cannot say how we got to the pattern. It's more like the pattern reached back and took hold of us. Its achievement has retroactively transformed the clues. Integration has a backwards feel to it, as if the conclusion somehow must precede the premises.[9] We lurch into knowing.

The central thrust of knowing is neither linear nor deductive, although later it is often possible to construct a partial account of it that is. A step-by-step articulated procedure may be one of the tools we offer other people to help them to the pattern.[10] Linearity in presentation is helpful, not because it constitutes learning, but because it prompts it. But if we take this linear procedure to be identical with knowledge or knowing, we commit a tempting, but massively damaging, mistake. In our penchant for the security of epistemic certainty, this mistake produces a defective epistemological vision of knowledge as statements and proofs. The human act of knowing is more aptly understood as an amazing feat of skill, much like learning to keep one's balance on a bike.

The struggle, integration, is profoundly human; it lies at the heart of what it means to be human. We are personal beings inserted in a world "toward which" we care and in which we cope. To be human is to care, to long to know. We saw this in the first texture; we will explore it more deeply in the next one.

Point B

The struggle toward an as yet undiscovered pattern will eventually shift us from Point A to Point B. If Point A is staring at unrelated particulars, Point B is looking through them to perceive a further pattern. We must

9. The young Polanyi shocked his supervisor with this confidently uttered claim that the conclusion precedes the premises. Scott and Moleski, *Michael Polanyi*.

10. Polanyi encourages us to think of these as maxims, more than as proofs or strict methods (Polanyi, *Personal Knowledge*, 30).

shift our manner of relating to the disconnected particulars of Point A to attain Point B.

At Point B, what we now focus on is the pattern, a coherent pattern that makes sense of things. When we use the expression, connecting the dots, we actually mean that the result is richer than a two-dimensional, step-by-step, move from number to number. Integrating to a pattern means getting hold of something so three-dimensional that we sense it has horizons we have yet to explore. In the moment of insight, we understand that we do not yet fully understand the full import of what we have grasped. But we recognize immediately that the disconnected particulars that we had identified at Point A (there will have been more that we had not even identified) from the vantage point of B have connected to each other, in a surprising yet recognizable way, to form a profoundly rich, coherent whole. They are fraught with richer meaning; they even look different.[11] Again, as an example, you have only to think of learning to read.

It is important to realize that at Point B, even as we may sustain Point B for the rest of our lives, we never leave the subsidiary behind. All sustained "knowledge" has two levels of awareness, we might say: the focal and the subsidiary. All sustained knowledge means a sustained integrative feat. All sustained knowledge involves our personal, responsible profession and disposing of ourselves to uphold it. In this we recognize another damaging oversight or omission that the false ideal of explicit knowledge commits: it privileges the focal and blinds us to the ever-present, ever-palpable, ever-unspecifiable subsidiary awareness which alone allows us to sustain knowledge. The ideal privileges explicit knowledge and blinds us to the fact that apart from its ongoing rootedness in the subsidiary, it will self-destruct. Wrest my book from my hands, and I am no longer reading.

Contact with Reality

Human knowing, the profoundly human struggle, the vectoring from and through particulars of world and word and body to shape a pattern, a coherent whole, is just that which connects us to the world. Once we achieve a pattern, we submit to it as a token of something objectively

---

11. These are Polanyi's phenomenal and semantic aspects of tacit knowing. Polanyi, *Tacit Dimension*, 11–13.

real, there, beyond us. We *submit* to its reality, for all our active agency in having uncovered it. To submit to something is to acknowledge its weightier presence, to treat its presence as weighty. We find ourselves in the presence of something which has already won our respect, and which has already changed us. And, far from the integration having so exhausted the known that nothing remains to intrigue us, we find ourselves beckoned farther beyond ourselves to future possibilities.

The most intriguing part of Polanyi's epistemological insights, for me, has always been his epistemic realism. The knowing event issues in a sense that we have "made contact with reality." We accredit our insight as having contacted the real because we have "a sense of the possibility of indeterminate future manifestations."[12]

We find this exemplified especially in knowing persons. The hidden horizons of the person we encounter can testify more effectively to her or his reality than what we perceive already. Note the curiousness of a statement we frequently make: "I want to get to know her better!" How is it that any of us makes such a statement? How would we know that we want to get to someone better? What we are doing is sensing the possibility of further dimensions and eventualities that we cannot yet name. Polanyi once described this as a real thing's being "pregnant with unforeseen intimations."

Every integration to a pattern calls us yet again beyond ourselves. With the integrative feat, the shift from Point A to Point B, we have come to extend ourselves into, or to indwell the particulars turned clues. But having attained a fresh focal pattern, we are drawn on by the tantalizing possibilities of it to an as-yet-undiscovered reality. This is the never-ending adventure of coming to know.

All knowing "bears indeterminately on reality," Polanyi said. Our very sense of the truth of a claim draws both on unspecifiable clues and also on unspecifiable hints of future possibilities.[13] The things an impersonal and detached paradigm views as facts, pieces of knowledge, say more than they explicitly claim. It is more apt to see them as contacting and intimating a richly surprising reality, rather than passively, exhaustively, mirroring it.

---

12. Sentences and phrases such as this can be found throughout his entire work. See one instance at Polanyi, *Personal Knowledge*, vii–viii.

13. Ibid., 147–50.

Our tacit skill enables us tacitly to sense such intimations and navigate in light of them. Doing this is neither irrational nor mystical nor an arbitrary fabrication, though it is by no means foolproof. Relying on unspecifiable clues and hints has a palpably lived feel. This is something we do in any skilled action, as our example of reading shows.

Our lives are a tapestry of such acts of coming to know. And the distinctive features of subsidiary-focal integration also hint at dimensions of covenant epistemology.

Three Dimensions of Knowing

I believe that the wide array of once disparate particulars that integration transforms into a pattern, in an act of coming to know, always comprise three sorts. I call these sectors of clues, the world, the lived body, and the directions or normative word. This just is the "perspectival" triad of John Frame, whose work I engage in a later chapter.[14] These three each have a distinct nature, and thus contribute differently to the act of knowing. But they pervade one another entirely. You never have one without the other two, and it is impossible to distinguish them strictly. The achieved integration will possess all three dimensions inseparably.

At Point A, the particulars of world, body and word make no sense.[15] Known feels exterior to knower, alien, opaque. My very own body feels like it belongs to somebody else. Directions that someone is giving me sound like a foreign language. Successful integration to Point B noticeably shifts opacity to transparency, exteriority to a sense of its connection with me. I feel an internalized familiarity with what I understand. In the process of coming to know, in each of these sectors integration transforms the clues as they come to be internalized, indwelled, and second nature.

World

World clues are those contributed by the situation or circumstances we seek to make sense of. They include the once puzzling and apparently unrelated pieces that first drew our attention. They include more than

---

14. Frame, *Doctrine of the Knowledge of God*, pt. 1. I first made this application of the triad to the Polanyian clues as I laid out pt. 2 of Meek, *Longing to Know*.

15. This is not to say they are meaningless; it is to say they don't connect meaningfully.

these, more than we can specify, which will come to shape both back-ground and foreground in our integration.

The shift from Point A to Point B impacts the world clues. Integration renders them transparent. It changes the way the world appears, as it connects me more intimately with it. It moves from seeming opaque to being wonderfully transparent. In the purview of our fresh integration, the world makes sense. It has meaning. Far from screening us from the world, our feats of knowing unlock the world to us. In the transforma-tion I come to find myself rooted deeply in the world that I understand.

Far from our integration representing the world in a way that ex-haustively confirms our predictions, it surprises us, and we find we must relate to it on its terms, not only on mine. And I have a sense of horizons, possibilities, hints of future manifestations, which lie beyond my pres-ent grasp. This is what makes reality—the known I grasp now—seem so profound.

Lived Body

The second dimension of particulars-turned-subsidiaries is the lived body.[16] This is our experience of our body as an instrument in use in the achievement of some task. In typing on a keyboard, we know our fingers in their use to record letters and words on the screen. We attend from a complex array of interpreted body sensations to the writing task. I do not focus on or attend to my fingers or their sensations in themselves; were you to ask me what motions I use to type the word, "word," I would have difficulty naming them without literally moving my fingers. I know, feel, live my fingers as the tools I employ to effect this concatenation of markings. Polanyi helps us see—and this is his distinctive but generally unknown contribution to epistemology—that the way we relate to our bodies in our knowing is subsidiary.

Often when we think of our bodies, what comes to mind is our body as object—what the doctor examines, what breaks down when we are sick. Our traditional Cartesian approach of mind divorced from body has only allowed us to treat mind as subject, and body only ever as object. But in fact our predominating awareness of our body is of our

16. This is Maurice Merleau-Ponty's term (Merleau-Ponty, *Phenomenology of Per-ception*). I have argued elsewhere that what he designates by it is the body subsidiarily experienced as understood by Polanyi (Meek, *Contact With Reality*, pt. 4). I do not be-lieve that Merleau-Ponty's profound work contains within it the idea of subsidiary-focal integration.

body as subject, as lived subsidiarily in its bearing on the world. Polanyi noted that our bodies are the one set of physical particulars which we generally know only subsidiarily rather than focally. All knowing, even the most explicit, is rooted in the lived body.[17] It is intriguing to start to tap this idea of body as subject, something I attempt in texture 2.

All knowing is skilled knowing. There is a lived body knack to the most abstract "mental" pursuits. To research the implications of a chemical equation, for example, one must know in one's body the ways of test tubes and titrations and chemicals and safety, as well as the ways of the lab and its coworkers. Lived body knowing often is a communal enterprise—in fact, it just about always is a communal enterprise. Jazz combo improvisation, or any musical ensemble work, for example, consists of individual musicians connecting, and the lived body as larger than one's own. Humans do this sort of thing as a matter of course.

Before we learned, or as we were learning, a new skill, we might have said, "I am all thumbs!"—signaling the opacity we felt, exteriority to our own bodies. Our bodies felt clueless about what to do, devoid of the proper feel of it. The idea of keeping one's balance on a bike, for example, prior to the achievement, is inscrutable.

While along the trajectory of learning, a knower might temporarily focus on her or his body, to practice a certain technique. On returning to the activity, the knower returns to rely on, climb back into, the bodily feel of it, setting her or his focus once again in the direction of the feat yet to be achieved. The learner moves back and forth in this way repeatedly.

In integration, a lived meaning dawns in our body. We are in our body knowingly, and we, our body, is knowingly in the world. Once you have gained a skill, you may press yourself toward riskier exploits, throwing your body into them with growing confidence and delight.

In the integrative shift from Point A to Point B, body sensations-turned-lived body clues extend or enrich our lived body awareness. The act of knowing transforms me, the knower, also. I am myself in a deeper way. Also, whenever we develop the use of a tool, our lived awareness of that tool in our use of it extends our lived body.

---

17. Polanyi, *Tacit Dimension*, 15–16. Polanyi notes that he concurs with Merleau-Ponty in affirming the bodily roots of all thought.

Directions: The Normative

Another dimension of clues is the normative, which guides our struggle to know, and conceptually shapes it once held. Often it is the words of people who authoritatively name and guide the knowing. This dimension includes everything from our parents' earliest wording of our world and our societally and historically shaped worldview, to the maxims of the expert or coach with whom we are working in this specific venture, and the methodology we appropriate for the task at hand, and the very words we ourselves utter in the knowing event. I believe it also includes the ideals and goals which inspire us.

Transformation from opacity to transparency, in the normative dimension, is what makes the marks on a page or the voiced language of a teacher meaningful to us as we come to indwell those words. When a novice first hears the directions, she or he only half understands them. Somehow, the novice must "climb into" the words—indwell them. Having learned the meaning of them, the knower uses the same words knowingly, normatively, shapingly, to describe the now skilled effort.

The normative is a much overlooked but essential feature of any act of knowing. Without it, no knowing can occur. Even the simplest perception—we may speak of it as *noticing*—is constituted normatively by applying our gaze to pick out some features of the world and not others. On the other end of the spectrum, our most fundamental commitments function criterially not only to shape our view of the world but to designate what counts as rationality and evidence for and within it. In fact, I believe that the very act of knowing, on the Polanyian scheme, involves a normative shaping. To see a pattern involves assigning value to particulars: this is foreground, this is background, for example. I do not mean that this is a moral valuing; but it is normative.

Every act of knowing requires normative guidance, both from worldview commitments and working maxims. But they also involve, most fundamentally, I believe, authoritative guidance from other persons. Serious athletes require a coach. Fighter pilots and radiologists only acquire their expert skill by means of authoritative guides. Michael Polanyi challenged the individualism of western epistemology by underscoring the critical role of tradition and apprenticeship for scientific research and discovery.[18] Authoritative guides do not fabricate or teach us to fab-

---

18. Polanyi, *Personal Knowledge*, ch. 4, sec. 3.

ricate the real, rather, they teach us to see what is there.[19] Without human teaching, humans do not learn to talk and thus do not learn their world. Covenant epistemology will move further to the implied interpersoned context that knowing requires—and not just knowing, but human being as well.

The normative dimension is bound up with words, though articulation is only one form in which the normative comes to expression. But words just by themselves function normatively, never merely descriptively. According to Marjorie Grene, concepts are standards: *cat* also includes what-it-is-to-be-a-cat.[20] The idea of words and concepts as standards is, of course, as old as Plato, but it often gets forgotten. Whenever we identify something or utter a statement concerning it, both the concepts employed and the relation articulated also similarly involve evaluation. In fact, we couldn't make statements, and we couldn't know, unless we operated evaluatively. In more recent work, Grene argues that more basic than language is *symboling*.[21] Symboling is according significance in the most fundamental way to things around you. We do this just as part of being and living. But there is something uniquely human, artificial (in a good sense) and normative about symboling.

There is a distinctively human joy in naming the world into being. Walker Percy has named this well: humans are "cocelebrants of what is."[22] The baby learns to name the ball in addition to throwing it. And the naming has the exuberance of a game about it, as if the word itself were a tasty piece of candy—"Ball!" this future hall-of-famer announces. It's just fun to say the word knowingly. And we always say it *for another*, for another human, who listens and celebrates with us. Wording is a uniquely human form of play. Dogs, for example, may understand and respond to the word, ball; but they don't enjoy the word *per se*. All this hints of the interpersonal and covenantal, to which we will return.

The language game concept developed by the later Wittgenstein underscores the necessary role of the normative. Before a baby can understand that her caregiver is putting names on objects, the baby must also understand and be able to employ the rules of the naming game.[23]

19. Meek, "Learning to See," 38–49.

20. Grene, *Knower and the Known*, 159, 164, 169.

21. Grene, *Philosophical Testament*, ch. 8. More on this later, in texture 8.

22. Percy, "Naming and Being," 133.

23. Wittgenstein, *Philosophical Investigations*, passim.

Language games are clusters of rule-governed social behavior, such as naming, telling a story, or apologizing. Prescriptive must precede descriptive, and the prescriptive involves social rules of behavior.

This normative dimension of knowing, precisely because it is normative in character, lends to human knowing the sense that it is anchored, not below, but above. I have in mind two roller coasters at Six Flags Amusement Park west of St. Louis, Missouri: the Ninja, and the Batman. The Ninja's cars ride a track below them; the Batman's cars are suspended. Part of the thrill of the Batman is that the riders' feet dangle helplessly in the air, giving the sense that nothing anchors them. For all that, the Batman is the better, smoother, safer ride. All knowing, in one sense, has its anchorage in the lived body, in another sense, in the world. But here we see that knowing is also anchored above, in some sense, critically, in the normative. Knowing is anchored, or grounded, in the subsidiaries of all three dimensions, differently.

I credit John Frame with helping me identify and start to work with the normative dimension, with which I quickly saw that Polanyi and Grene concurred. It is arguably the dimension which I develop in covenant epistemology. Covenant epistemology takes seriously the operative presence of this normative dimension in all knowing, proposing that the normative dimension of knowing proves to be covenantal.

Covenant, I will argue, is to interpersonal relationships what rules are to a game, or to a Wittgensteinian language game. It prescriptively, normatively, constitutes the relationship. The presence of normativity presupposes and grows out of a context of two or more persons relating interpersonally. Picking up on the cadence of the familiar, "ought" implies "can," we may say more properly that "ought" implies "for and with whom." It is only in the context of relationship that oughtness comes to be. The normative dimension of knowing thus implies a more fundamental context: interpersonhood.

"Triangulating"

I believe that an act of coming to know may be inaugurated in any of the three segments. A student who walks into a required calculus class, and is confronted with inscrutably cryptic statements, is beginning the trajectory of learning in the normative dimension. A person whose sudden turn of circumstances compels a revised understanding is starting in the world dimension. It is also common for the vector of knowing to begin in the lived body—a feeling of restlessness or of something being out of kilter.

But wherever the vector of coming to know begins, it moves rhythmically from one corner of the triad to another, implicating each in an unfolding, recurring way. I co-opt the term, "triangulating," to refer to this. I have in mind how a bat, or a submarine, navigates by bouncing sound off successive points of orientation. This rough picture underscores something that our defective default mode can prevent us from even noticing—that knowing unfolds, and can be seen to do so in an artful, dance-like way. This idea helps us to approximate the actual complexity of human knowing.

We hear a new claim of a candidate authoritative guide. We want to come to understand or make sense of it. We do that by attempting the bodily indwelling of what is being recommended, so far as we understand it. We also gropingly explore how that accords with or opens the world. We go back to the words of the authoritative guide again and again to lay them alongside what we are trying to do. And when we do make sense of it, in some kind of integrative and transformative shift, we have come to indwell and espouse confidently the very words the guide pronounced as we make sense of how our body lives them in connecting us with and opening the world.

Thus, ordinary acts of knowing display the dynamics of subsidiary-focal integration, three interlocking sectors of clues, and the knower's unfolding triangulation among them. Why is it important to identify the triad of subsidiary clues, and the way we triangulate when we rely on them? Many people who try to make sense of how we know well ask, where does knowing *start*? Empiricists say you start with sense perception. Rationalists say you start with reason. Theologians say you start with God. Subjectivists say you start (and end) with the self. Identifying these three dimensions of any act of knowing helps us see that we can start in *any one* of these sectors, and that in some sense we start in all three. But what "start" means must be adjusted to reflect the nature and function of each sector. The sectors don't reduce to each other; knowing requires the plurality, and occurs at their intersection. Specific trajectories of coming to know may emphasize one sector over the other.

Philosophers and ordinary people have sometimes associated knowledge with one of these sectors in a way that has blinded them to the others. They might say that knowledge just has to do with "the way things are," overlooking what I bring to it and how I tell. Other people have overdone the "what I bring to it," to the exclusion of what is there. Still others have thought knowledge was just about the text, or the Scriptures, leading them to overlook and discredit the world and body that even in their own efforts they could not help but rely on. Capable and effective knowing requires intentional (not necessarily explicit) employment of all three dimensions.

Learning to Drive

The following illustrates this triangulating and three-dimensional transformation. A few years ago, I taught my daughter to drive a standard automobile. Prior to this, she had little experience even as a passenger in a stick-shift, and none to which she was attending as a prospective driver. As we sat in the school parking lot, I began with some preliminary comments: "You have to let out the clutch to the sweet spot, then start giving the car a little gas . . ."

The parking lot was her Point A. Until she made her first attempt and stalled, Steph knew the words but had no inside feel of what my words meant. Now her confident demeanor registered a bit of self-doubt and puzzlement. But then she began to try to make her body do what my words said. Eventually she got the hang of it and thereby entered the world of driving a standard gear-shift car.

As an authoritative guide, I had worded her world, and set to her the challenge of growing into my words. Her feet had to figure out what my words meant. At the outset, she had not climbed into those words. Once she learned to shift, she so embodied the words that they now named her own experience, and she expressed them with confidence. Reality flowed into the words much as wind fills boats' sails—both her body reality and the car's reality. The words normed both into being.

The words normed and called forth her own body. My words coached her to see and feel what was already there to which she had been blind and unfeeling. Prior to her own personal experience, she had to trust my opaque words blindly, or she never would have connected with the world.

The words evoked the world. They "carred" the world. When I am using a car or any tool, reality floods to me along the lines of that medium or tool. As Steph's shifting began to improve, we started to look beyond the school parking lot. We both began assessing roads in terms of their topography, as well as their proximity and traffic. The world came to us as so many road possibilities. For any act of coming to know, there is a normed medium which we come to embody knowingly and in terms of which reality unfolds to meet us. Words function in this way, as do statements, proofs, lectures, and also poetry and metaphor.[24]

This, then, is Polanyian epistemology. It is his subsidiary-focal integration, to which I have added the further developments of a triad of clues and the knower's triangulating among them. The act of knowing moves from subsidiary but indwelt clues of our embodied situatedness, not as something we focus on or articulate, but as a lived awareness from which we orient outward to make sense of the world. It proceeds *via* the norming guidance of verbal pronouncements of authoritative guides with whom we sustain a covenant-constituting interpersonal relationship. And it vectors toward the surprising externality of a systematically inexhaustive real. In an act of coming to know, the moment we succeed at making sense of the world will simultaneously be a moment when we are personally transformed; the world we have come to know changes us in the knowing. It changes us quantitatively and qualitatively, both extending and transforming our lived body awareness.

Covenant epistemology embraces these features, as we will see. You can also see that this sort of movement is how the vision of covenant epistemology itself unfolded in my life, and what I seek to replicate and model in my unfolding argument here in *Loving to Know*.

Advantageous Distinctives of Polanyian Epistemology

What is it about Polanyian epistemology that makes it so distinct, so strategically helpful for life and for thought? What is it about it that suits it to this project of covenant epistemology? I have already noted all the following, but want to amplify their significance. Covenant epistemology honors Polanyi's contribution by incorporating it and its positive effects into its vision.

---

24. Marjorie Grene describes animals' perceiving as "raising invariants to the level of affordances": squirrels see the world as so many nut sources and caches, for example. Humans have no single set of perceptual proclivities; we may focus on any number of them. But as we do, we see the world in light of them. What I am saying here is amenable to her account. Grene, *Philosophical Testament*, ch. 7.

Tacit Knowledge Named and Unleashed

It is distinctive to Polanyian epistemology to identify and accredit *tacit* knowledge, and further to insist that it is epistemically foundational. No knowledge is wholly focal, Marjorie Grene argues.[25] It is widely typical of the western tradition that knowledge be restricted to lucid, articulated statements—as Grene puts it, "pieces of information immediately present to the mind and impersonally transferable from one mind to another."[26] Tacit powers, tacit foreknowledge, tacit subsidiary knowledge, tacit commitments have commonly been designated as not knowledge. Beginning in the nineteenth century, people began to acknowledge, as operative forces shaping knowing, pretheoretical commitments, traditions, communities, prescriptive features such as rules, power, narratives emotions, virtues, metaphors, values. But many people still believe that these features operate from outside the realm of knowledge, and thus are detrimental to knowledge. Polanyi's work shows that these features are *integral* to knowing. His concrete epistemic account lends impetus to further discussion of these matters, as well as to the real prospect of making us better knowers.

Anticipative Knowledge Accredited

Polanyi believes, and Grene concurs, that this account alone successfully solves the Meno dilemma about how coming to know is possible.[27] It gives an account of anticipative knowledge, of being on the way to knowing. We can half-know something, or almost know something, or implicitly know something. And we can do these without explicitly knowing *that* we do, or knowing *what* we know correctly about it. Clues are the primary example. Something is a clue and operates as such only in advance of our accurate grasp of its import, and of its confirmation as integral to the solution. Polanyi shows how, to avail ourselves of clues, we tacitly, subsidiarily, shift to interpret the clue from the standpoint, the rationality, of the as-yet-unidentified reality, in anticipation of what we do not yet know. This is a common, yet uncommon experience. For Polanyi the research scientist, this alone allows any scientific discovery to occur. Western philosophy, he perceived, had never furnished the req-

25. Grene, *Knower and the Known*, 85.

26. Ibid., 31.

27. Ibid., ch. 1, "Legacy of the *Meno*"; See ch. 3 in this volume.

uisite account. Polanyi's rich account of tacit knowing as both subsidiary and anticipative uniquely makes sense of it.

Confirmation of Ordinary Knowing and Knowers

Polanyian epistemology, more than any other epistemic proposal I know, fits and helpfully unleashes ordinary human experiences of knowing. I lived this out in my own life: the privileges and obligations of family life drove me from the halls of Academe. But Polanyi's thought adapted easily to ordinary life. It made sense of life in the kitchen and garden, of growing my children and participating in community and church life. As the author of *Longing to Know,* I have heard numerous testimonials of its relevance to FBI investigation, corporate engineering, recording engineering, art, Christian apologetics, and teaching dermatological surgery, to name a few. I trust that this chapter's account yet again conveys how accessible and applicable it is.

The Polanyian account is a kind of trump card. It describes what we do when we are knowing, whether we know it or not, and even though the prevailing paradigm functions to blind us to this. That is why people who begin to work with this approach experience personal liberation, as well as greater effectiveness in their work.

Subsidiary-Focal Integration:
The Heartbeat of Human Knowing, Identified

No other epistemology identifies the subsidiary-focal integrative nature of all human knowing. Widespread oversight of this has produced skewed epistemic approaches, both formal and everyday, including the pervasive daisy of dichotomies. The dichotomies are perpetuated on the mistaken presumption that knowledge is only focal and explicit. Polanyi's positive challenge to this presumption enables us to circumvent the false dichotomies themselves. Subsidiary-focal integration offers the positive reorientation that rehabilitates the default we have inherited in the western tradition. I have a penchant for piling on metaphors—I apologize for this tackiness: it allows us to redraw the playing field, and torpedo the daisy of dichotomies. Covenant epistemology utilizes subsidiary-focal integration to this end, as will be explained in the next section.

The Richness of Reality Restored

And Polanyi's account helps us see how two-dimensionalizing and depersonalizing knowledge has led us to a paltry and disrespectful misrepresentation of the richness of the real. Instead, it is our privilege to invite the real respectfully, with solid hope of its surprising self-disclosure.

This, in turn, also gives rise to covenant epistemology's central claim, that there are even hints of interpersonal reciprocity in the knower-known relationship, hints we should explore, accredit, and employ with intentionality for greater good.

WEAVING POLANYI'S INSIGHTS
INTO COVENANT EPISTEMOLOGY

Toward the end of each conversation in this book, I endeavor to interweave the insights I have selected into an unfolding vision of covenant epistemology. Polanyi's is first. His contribution is foundational to the vision. Covenant epistemology grows out of it and incorporates it as one of its three major strands.

This interweaving has two loci, both of which I have just named and now want to pursue further. The first shows how subsidiary-focal integration enables covenant epistemology to torpedo the daisy of dichotomies. Secondly, I explore the curious hints of interpersonal reciprocity, implicit in Polanyian epistemology, which led me to develop the covenant epistemology thesis.

Polanyi Contra the Daisy of Dichotomies

Where the daisy of dichotomies is in play, people generally presume the pairs we have named, privilege one member of the pair, and discredit or devalue the other. We expressed this graphically by locating the privileged partners together in the daisy center. Reason over emotion is an example. In a situation that involves emotion, people have felt that reason is threatened or minimized by it. If people think emotion is in the forefront, they might still concede the dichotomy by concluding that reason doesn't exist. Or they think they must settle for a less-than-ideal compromise, a hodge-podge, never considering that something might be wrong with the either-or itself. The same dynamic plays out for each pair.

The realization that we indwell clues subsidiarily—our bodies, our interpretative frameworks, our anticipative sense of the world—creatively reconnects pairs that the default divorced. Everything in the center of the daisy of dichotomies: knowledge, fact, science, theory, and so forth, is thrivingly rooted in, contexted and contextualized by, and outrun by what we, on the default setting, took to be extraneous—"petals," understood as subsidiarily indwelt. Indeed, things central to the daisy, often focal, hint of further prospects to which they themselves might be subsidiary.

Understanding knowing as a dynamic, transformative integration restores adventure, emotion, the responsible commitment of belief to all knowing. In this it reunites science and art, science and religion. Responsible belief is the epistemic act. And this approach reshapes how we think of facts and truth: these are things we affirm and understand to bear indeterminately on reality only as we commit to indwell them. It restores an understanding of theory as insight, for which application or practice is indwelling stewardship.

Covenant epistemology makes a distinctive contribution to the generally Polanyian challenge to the defective default. In life and in an epistemic account, there is something about interpersonal knowing that helps us past the two-dimensionality of the epistemic default. Knowing a close family member person to person seems to transcend the either-ors, or merge them, or transform them. One need only consider the way we would approach the matter of knowledge in interpersonal relationship. It is not certainty so much as confidence. There is plenty of indeterminacy in truly understanding another person. To believe otherwise is the height of obnoxious presumption. But such knowing is palpable. Covenant epistemology will explore all this. But it also brings interpersonhood to bear on the reorientation of our defective epistemic default.

There is a cluster of related philosophical issues which are more systematic manifestations of the daisy. In what follows, I sketch how subsidiary-focal integration resolves some issues by providing a positive, third alternative.

Epistemic Naturalism

Epistemic naturalism is the proposal that all knowing reduces to the physical, either to physical behavior, or to brain activity. Gilbert Ryle's *Concept of Mind*, and W. V. O. Quine's, "Epistemology Naturalized," argue that we determine mind and knowledge from human behavior and thus may reduce knowledge to it. This is a pragmatic behaviorism.[28] Naturalism or physicalism is the commitment that everything reduces to the physical. Far more widely popular now is the belief that all "mental events," and thus all "knowledge" reduce to brain activity. This suggests the philosophical stance known as cognitive science.[29] Voluminous and ever growing research on brain activity demonstrates how it is integrally involved in all that we have deemed mental and even religious. The additional, philosophical, claim is that philosophy of mind reduces to study of brain activity.

Both the pragmatic, behavioristic sort and the brain activity sort of naturalism reject Cartesian dualism which postulates a sharp distinction between unminded body, and disembodied mind. It does so by rejecting mind, and replacing it with body. Dualism becomes monism. There are logical flaws in this approach, and you should be able to see that it continues tacitly to presume the dichotomy of mind and body. In philosophical anthropology, this either-or of reductive naturalism or behaviorism, on the one hand, and mind-body dualism, on the other, continues to hold sway.

Polanyian epistemology offers a third alternative that sidesteps the dichotomy itself. We live the body as subsidiary; we do not experience it primarily as an object. The best brain studies are only ever able to view the body as object. On the other hand, human consciousness is rooted in the body in the way that the focal is rooted in, moves from, and integratively transcends the subsidiary. The Polanyian idea of body knowledge as subsidiary offers a conciliatory and promising approach, but unlike the other alternatives, it does honor the mystery of personhood over impersonal lucidity. This makes possible an approach that benefits immensely from scientific discoveries about the brain without committing the damaging philosophical *non sequitur* of reducing epistemology to it.

Modernism and Postmodernism

Polanyian epistemology offers a viable third alternative to modernism and postmodernism. It unites the best insights of each in a fresh, ro-

28. Ryle, *Concept of Mind*; Quine, "Epistemology Naturalized."

29. Goldman, *Philosophical Applications*.

bustly coherent, model, as opposed to merely attempting a compromise with no undergirding epistemological vision.[30]

Modernism and postmodernism are popular terms and difficult to define. They are cultural *zeitgeists* more than philosophical positions. Modernism designates a philosophical and cultural approach associated with the Enlightenment ascendancy of reason. It is what I am representing in my defective default analogy. *Postmodernism* is popularly associated with relativism or skepticism or subjectivism. To connect this popular understanding to my daisy: postmodernism rejects the center of the daisy as impossible. I believe, however, that what postmodern philosophers are *actually* doing is not eliminating the daisy center but rather challenging the underlying dichotomous structure, as I am.

Subsidiary-focal integration shows us how to reconceive knowing in such a way that we accredit the knower's active contribution to knowing, while doing the same for the active contribution of the known—that is, the real. Subsidiary-focal integration creatively elucidates the relationship of knowledge and interpretation, for example. All knowledge is interpretation. But you must see interpretation as subsidiary and knowledge as focal (thereby more deeply open to the world). Interpretation is our window on the world. Of *course* interpretation can be skewed or biased. But *good* interpretation engages the world, it is our indwelt beachhead in the world.

The distinctive asymmetry of subsidiary and focal renders the subsidiary for the sake of the focal. Thus the knower's active contribution, as subsidiary, submits to the active contribution of the known. Polanyian epistemology supports a dynamically robust epistemic realism—we unlock and engage, we are transformed and submit.

Subsidiary-focal integration thus positively addresses the needs and weaknesses of a modernist approach. It may be argued that postmodernism is distinguished from modernism not by its exaltation of the self, as in subjectivism, but by its eradication of the self. The self is a constructed text like every other cultural artifact. Deconstruction unearths and celebrates layers of artificiality in a way that does effectively call into question modernism's dichotomies. But assessing the effort from

---

30. This latter expresses my sense upon reading Brian MacLaren's *New Kind of Christian*, a beautifully written and persuasive book that recommends that we be postmodern Christians. It indicates that all our problems would thereby be fixed but offers no thoughtful philosophical shaping of the problem and of the proposed solution.

the perspective of Polanyian categories: deconstruction, I suggest, renders all particulars focal. In this, postmodernism persists in a modernist commitment. However, postmodernism, in its truthful consistency on this point, sacrifices meaning. You have only to think of the last time you moved to a new home or job. In my experience, the new setting was distressingly overwhelming precisely because everything was equally urgently focal—from my new phone number to my new course preps. I needed to acquire the subsidiary grasp of my new place that would lend it meaning. My inference is that it takes the figure-ground of focal-subsidiary to produce meaning as well as to apprehend the real. This, in turn, suggests to me what I will argue at chapter's end: that subsidiary-focal integration betokens the personed.

Realism vs. Anti-realism

Is our cognitive effort actually knowledge of an extramental world, or is it merely a summary of our outlook? That is the question at issue in the realist vs. anti-realist debate. The form it takes in philosophy of science is the question whether theoretical "discoveries" of scientists are real, or whether they are simply helpful summaries of data. This is a centuries-old debate: the question was asked, "Is Copernicus' proposals merely a more convenient summary of the data?" The legacy of the Cartesian ideal of certainty is the concern that if knowledge aligns with mind and must involve certainty, perhaps we knowers are cut off entirely from the world. How can we say what is actually there? So it is more responsible to say that our "knowledge" is really a summary of "data." *Positivism* was the nineteenth century term for this position. As far as Polanyi was concerned, positivism was Enemy number one. From the point of view of an epistemologically savvy research scientist, the idea of discoveries being inventions or convenient summaries of data was as ludicrous as it was philosophically naïve.[31] Yet the realism vs. anti-realism debate continues to thrive, bolstered by a late-twentieth-century alignment with concerns over modernism and postmodernism, including other epistemological matters such as hermeneutics (interpretation) and foundationalism.

Subsidiary-focal integration, by reconstruing knowing and knowledge, shows a way to move beyond the debate. Human knowing on even the most sophisticated level is embedded in the logically and actually unspecifiable, shot through with subsidiary but responsible commit-

31. Polanyi, "Science and Reality," 177–96.

ment, and evokes a more-than-specifiable real. The indeterminacy of it is just what testifies to its contact with objective reality. "Convenient summary," or even "probability," are concepts inappropriate for describing what humans do in knowing. Knowledge, at the moment we obtain it, as yet only partially comprehended by us, is achieved and justified by its transformative and allusive qualities.

It isn't confirmation so much as intimation of confirmation, Marjorie Grene says, that testifies at the outset to the reality of our findings.[32]

Foundationalism vs. Coherentisim

At issue in this debate is the structure of knowledge. Foundationalists picture knowledge as being anchored by a foundation of self-evident, indubitable, and, by implication, explicit truths.[33] All "upper-level" truths receive justification by being reputably derived from these foundational truths. Modest foundationalism is often deemed a more viable option to a stringent foundationalism. Modest foundationalism construes knowledge as founded on statements that are self-justifying, and uses such statements as the ultimate justification for all other truth claims, but it settles for these being less than certain and infallible. In this, however, the ideal of certainty is still is honored in the breech, just as it was in the attempt to attain it—why else would this stance be called "modest"? The weakness of foundationalism always is the difficulty of identifying any truths which qualify universally as foundational.

The coherentist vision of knowledge is of truth claims justified, not with reference to a foundation, a view coherentists rightly see to be unworkable, but through mutual consistency. As Ernest Sosa has popularly characterized these, if foundationalism is a pyramid, coherentism is a raft.[34] Coherentism's weak spot is that it has no way to tell if any internally coherent system of statements is, in fact, true or entirely false.

But the subsidiary root or anchor of all knowing, once identified, effectively ends the attraction of both foundationalism and of coherentism. Our beliefs are indeed rooted, but the "foundation" is subsidiary.

32. Grene, "Knowledge, Belief, and Perception," in Grene, *Philosophical Testament*, 9–27. See also Meek, "'Recalled to Life,'" sec. 8; and Meek, *Contact with Reality*, ch. 9.

33. The debate over foundationalism is widespread in philosophical literature in the twentieth century. One standard discussion of the topic was Roderick Chisholm's *Theory of Knowledge*.

34. Sosa, "Raft and the Pyramid."

The subsidiary clue base of an act of knowing necessarily contains more knowledge and know-how than we can specify. In fact, by virtue of its supportive role, the clue base is logically unspecifiable. This means that the major and operative anchor of any act of knowing is tacit (not articulated or explicit). The foundation is not certain, it is lived. The alternative to certainty is neither skepticism nor probability. It is lived confidence that roots us in a world and inspires us to responsible risk and profession of truth. Polanyian epistemology changes the whole dynamic of both knowing and of epistemology, including the means by which we justify a truth claim. Justification of knowledge, primarily but not exclusively, resembles a skillful, risky, reliance on intuition and experience more three-dimensional than a methodical procedure.[35]

The subsidiary anchor of all knowledge also renders the shortcomings of coherentism apparent. While, in fact, we do gauge the merit of truth claims, at least in part, by their fit with other claims, coherentism does not have the resources to recognize, much less accredit, the fact that we do so working tacitly from subsidiary awareness beyond and beneath the explicit claims we are considering. This is how we gauge coherence, or any claim, tacitly in light of lived experience of the world. For Polanyian epistemology, while the possibility of being mistaken is real, so is the possibility of being right, the possibility of one's beliefs according favorably and fruitfully with oneself and the world.

In response to the well-known pyramid and raft characterizations, Polanyian commentator Lady Drusilla Scott has characterized the subsidiary anchor of knowledge as a swamp![36] The picture is unfortunate if it suggests a common misinterpretation of Polanyian epistemology: that since certain knowledge is not to be had, we have to make do with less than certain knowledge, with probability. No—this misinterpretation only partially conceals its own concession to the other models with their defective epistemic default. Polanyi's "swamp" is about confidence, not certainty. All knowledge is rooted in unspecifiable and logically unspecifiable subsidiaries—body, world, and directions—that thus provide leverage to connect more deeply with reality.

---

35. This fact has been readily obscured by the fact that we do try to codify our intuitive grasp, and the codification then can mask our utter dependence on the tacitly subsidiary even in the codification.

36. Scott, *Everyman Revived*, 59–61.

Religion and Science

From the time of Polanyi's earliest efforts, Christian theologians have welcomed them as offering a rapprochement between religion and "knowledge." The presumed rigors of modernism had marginalized religion. Polanyi offered religion a way back into the accredited domain of viable knowledge.

It was not a concession, but rather a radical revamping of all knowing so as to locate religious dimensions at its core. According to Polanyi, I remember noting early on in my work with his thought, *commitment* is "a manner of disposing ourselves" toward the as-yet-unknown reality. This just is the dynamic that Christian believers call "faith." There is no better solution to the *ad nauseam* dispute between religion and science than to show the inherent religiousness of effective scientific discovery. But it is not just about quelling wrongheaded disputations. Polanyian epistemology, in recasting science and religion as fundamentally similar, resuscitates and transforms the practice of both.

My own work is only one example of many creative efforts to re-think, in Polanyian terms, Christian theology, worship, practice, mission, and scholarship, and from this, to offer a vision that heals both church and culture.[37] My earlier book, *Longing to Know,* tackles the specific dichotomy of faith and reason. It shows that knowledge can't be a matter of either reason or faith, of reason over faith, of faith over reason, or of reason alone. As long as the divorce stands, both reason and faith self-destruct. We need to see knowledge as something transformatively more than mere information or statements. Areas we have typically thought of as reason and not faith, and vice versa, are each fraught with the other as part of a larger dynamic. As a result, knowing God and knowing a cure for cancer display the same dynamic. I tried to show in *Longing to Know* that the question of knowing God becomes a more accessible question once you realize that knowing anything, science in particular, involves subsidiary-focal integration.

All these formal discussions that I have sketched here display telltale marks of the defective epistemic default that everyone shares in our western cultural heritage. There are others I have not raised, and, of course,

---

37. Lesslie Newbigin, Thomas F. Torrance, Charles McCoy, William Poteat, Richard Gelwick, Andy Sanders, Martin Moleski, and Tony Clark are names that quickly spring to mind of scholars who have engaged Polanyi's work to draw its implications for scientific and theological accord and healing.

for the ones I have raised I have offered the barest of sketches. But my purpose is accomplished by showing that subsidiary-focal integration targets and helpfully realigns the defective epistemic default. Polanyi helps us rethink human knowing—actually, it restores us to knowing as fully engaged humans. This is why it is critical that subsidiary-focal integration anchors the vision of covenant epistemology.

Hints of Interpersonal Reciprocity

Years of indwelling Polanyi's thought, and viewing my own experiences in knowing in light of it, has led me to the claim that the knowing event seems to involve a reciprocity between knower and known. In the knowing event, not only is the knower active, but the known seems to comport itself in a personlike way. And there is something interpersoned about the event itself. Knowing, on a Polanyian construal, displays hints of the interpersonal that invite the covenant epistemology vision. Here, I will note features of the Polanyian model that first suggested this, leading me to postulate covenant epistemology. But in light of the covenant epistemology thesis, I want to focus these hints in such a way that we start to see contours of a person in the knower, contours of a person in the known, and contours of an interpersoned relationship in the knowing.

Knower

Polanyian epistemology reinstates the person in the epistemic process. This is what Polanyi himself wrote to achieve, and what he felt was essential to rescue epistemology and science from conceptual death. The "personal" in *Personal Knowledge* identified the risky and responsible commitment that is an essential ingredient in knowing; the necessary reliance upon informal, tacit, skilled, hunches to orient and navigate toward an impending discovery; the traditioned and communal nature of apprenticeship and conviviality, a "society of explorers."[38] While sophisticated awareness operates in animals generally, Polanyi argued, only human persons pursue and embrace truth responsibly with universal intent, in submission to self-set standards—all concepts that Polanyi develops and propounds. Polanyian epistemology thus more than makes room for the person; it requires and accredits the person. It suggests and encourages further inquiry into the personal paradigm, the exploration

---

38. Polanyi, *Science, Faith and Society*; Polanyi, "Society of Explorers," lec. 3 in *Tacit Dimension*.

of yet uncharted dimensions and profitable applications. This book is one such foray it has inspired and directed.

But I would like to add that knowing has these characteristic features precisely because it is persons who are knowers. Only a person is a reality rich enough to make a sense-full blend of these features. That may seem a silly thing to say. But I feel the need, with respect to my own hearing of the word, "knower," to counter an undertow pulling toward the impersonal. Our epistemic default has glorified the impersonal rather than appreciating how truncated it is. It should be freeing, encouraging, and restorative to many of us to find that we don't have to be automatons to be the best sort of knower.

Additionally, for a long while I have felt that recognizing and accrediting subsidiary awareness should pay off practically. We ought to be able to tap into or be intentional about the subsidiary. Of course, specifying the unspecifiable subsidiary is likely to be a bit of a challenge. But I believe that casting the subsidiary as distinctively personed helps along in this endeavor. In texture 2, just after this chapter, I attempt a few forays into the subsidiary.

Polanyian epistemology centrally affirms the personal in knowing. It also suggests that we may tap the knower's full personhood epistemically.

Known

On the Polanyian model, I think it is intriguing to note, knowing stretches from indeterminacy to indeterminacy. It is subsidiarily rooted in the more than articulable, as has been amply demonstrated; and it reaches out beyond the focal integrative achievement to the more than specifiable hints of future possibilities. Both sorts of indeterminacies, precisely because of their indeterminacy, root us in the world and move us to accredit our focal achievement as true and real. Also, I believe, as such they have about them the distinctive quality of the personal. This discussion concerns the indeterminacy that is at the other end of the trajectory of coming to know.

When I first read Polanyi's work, I was tantalized by his often-repeated statements concerning reality as *that which we may expect to manifest itself indeterminately in the future*.[39] I grew up a good little Cartesian. The

39. For a complete catalog of Polanyi's "reality" statements, see Meek, *Contact With Reality*, ch. 5.

modernist default setting held such sway in my own outlook that my desperate adolescent question was, "How do I know that there is a material world outside my disembodied mind?" To me, then, this sentence of Polanyi's was the scent of an oasis in a very parched desert. Polanyi said that when a person makes a scientific discovery, or achieves any sort of focal integrations, the achievement possesses "an ontological aspect."[40] In a discovery, the knower experiences an accompanying sense of the possibility of indeterminate future manifestations. For this I coined the acronym, IFM Effect. The discovery is pregnant with future prospects. The IFMs point us beyond an integrative achievement to hidden dimensions, horizons, aspects, that we can sense but not name. These hints of rich but at that point wholly unspecifiable, future, possibilities, confirms to us knowers that that we have made contact with reality—that the discovery has indeed connected us to the real.[41]

As I expressed it in *Longing to Know,* when the discovery is achieved, it is more as if it explodes, rather than explains, the knower's questions. Apprehending the real can feel more as if in the knowing, the knower is the one being known. We can feel about our encounters, less like they "answered our questions," and more like they made us answer theirs, or like they are quietly drawing us into a relationship that is well beyond our ability to stipulate and control. We can also feel the grace of reality's self-disclosure—that it was not my wizardry, but its generous choice, to grant insight. Along with my questions, I too am changed. The encountered real is less like sentences on a page, and more like—well, *people.* As with a three-dimensional person, reality is known to be real almost more by the hidden horizons than by the features we notice.[42] Thus it is heavy with reality and objectivity—so very *there.*

The same dynamic is what leads us on to knowing in the first place. It is not as if the unknown that intrigues us is a random panoply of logical possibilities. It could not be, for it gives us the sense that there is something there, waiting to be discovered. What we experience as there is, rather, an unknowing fraught with significance, a center of reality.

---

40. Polanyi, *Tacit Dimension*, 13.

41. I opted to write my dissertation on this phrase. Meek, *Contact With Reality*, ch. 6.

42. Parker Palmer argues that the knowledge of another person is the most "objective" knowledge there is (cf. our common thought that the impersonal is more objective!), because a person is so obviously never reducible to your own epistemic contribution. Palmer, *To Know As We Are Known*, 56, 101.

Consider these experiences and examples. I step out the front door, and I lay eyes on the copperhead curled up by the front step.[43] I see that he is looking back. Every fiber in my being somehow comes to attention. He doesn't move anywhere. He keeps looking. He wins the staring contest. I go back in the house. I contemplate what to do with him. I warn my guests as they come to the door. I squeal in protest when one of them wants to poke at the copperhead. The next morning, first thing as I leave the house, I search the ground for him. He isn't there—this is the actualization of what had been at first an indeterminate future manifestation—*now what do I do?* It was one thing when I could see him; now I don't see him. *He could be anywhere,* I think. *Look around. Watch where you step. Go out; come home, check for him . . .* All this Esther-copperhead interaction! There is a distinctive unfolding reciprocity of mutual self-disclosure to it.

Returning to the story of teaching my daughter to drive a standard stick-shift: Steph seats herself behind the wheel of our new little Ford Focus that idles in the school parking lot. Mom lectures her about shifting gears. She already knows how it feels to put her foot on the gas pedal and have the car respond. She is clueless concerning the dance of left-right, feet and hands, that is driving a standard car. That is what she is about to learn. And indeed, she does, and now drives the car quite capably. She stumbled through the initial opacities to a lived sense of herself becoming part of the car, like a partner in a dance drawing and twirling in time with a musicked reality larger than the pair. She works her feet, and the car responds, first chokingly, later smoothly. Harmony comes to reign.

I return to another favorite example of mine: the movie, *The Hunt for Red October.* I recall a wonderfully portrayed moment when Captain Ramius is peering through the periscope and reads a message Morse-coded to him that confirms to him that its sender accurately comprehends his own hitherto secret intentions. He falls backward, stunned, from the periscope, slapping up its arms. His look of rapid mental processing is appropriate response to the unanticipated but very real rationality reaching back to him from the mystery beyond. He gathers himself slowly, then out loud directs a response of, "One ping only!" Reciprocity at sea.

43. Readers may be interested to know that this is a *second* copperhead story. It occurred during the early stages of writing this book. Ahhh, those Missouri woods!

We all know this experience in the context of coming to know persons. We talked about how we say, "I want to get to know her better." We say this sort of thing precisely because we experience a sense of the possibility of indeterminate future manifestations. We know a little; we sense that there are intriguing dimensions to go on exploring for a long while. This is what we have in mind when we talk of a person (or fictional character) being three-dimensional. It is almost what we *don't know* about a person that confirms his or her reality to us, more than what we *know*. All this only makes sense, please recall, if we allow, in our account of knowing, that it is possible to know more than we can say, and navigate in light of that unspecifiable awareness.[44] This is just what Polanyian epistemology alone does.

In each of these and in myriads of our daily knowings, we see overture and response, further overture, further response. Once we have noticed it, it is mind-boggling that we could have thought either that the world was passive, or that it was non-existent. How do we know we have made contact with reality? Somebody contacts back.

Parents sometimes feel compelled to remind their children to say thank you. The child says thank you. When does a recipient feel effectively thanked for a gift? When do parents feel that they have succeeded as parents? Only when the child offers an unsolicited thank you. Similarly, we gauge the response to our efforts to engage the world in knowing. And while on some occasions we have to conclude that we have only read reality in light of our own wishes, most definitely there are other occasions when we simply cannot conclude that. These are occasions on which the response three-dimensionally supersedes what we anticipated.

Our efforts at knowing elicit response. Sometimes our efforts at knowing produce a product. Sometimes it is a statement, or a question. Sometimes it is a cultural artifact. Some of my efforts to know came to expression in the published work, *Longing to Know*. The production of this cultural artifact in turn initiated new conversations and states of affairs—indeterminate future manifestations.

Overture, response. Further overture; further response. Reciprocity in the knowing between knower and known. The obvious implication is that where there is reciprocity, there is "somebody home" on both ends of the exchange, giving the exchange the feel of a relationship. In fact, it

44. Polanyi's little aphorism was, "We know more than we can tell." Polanyi, *Tacit Dimension*, 4.

could be argued that in this overture-response pattern, the partner making the overture is not the knower but rather the known. As I suggested in concluding *Longing to Know*, our acts of coming to know often prove to have been acts of coming to *be known*. We are not the ones in the driver's seat. It is the yet-to-be-discovered reality, and upon discovery, discovery self-disclosed.

Another implication is this: if this is what we observe in our characteristic acts of knowing, then our epistemology would do well to take reciprocity seriously, and in our efforts at knowing we should be intentional about it. It thus makes a difference how the would-be knower behaves. This widely experienced reciprocity of knower and known suggests an interpersoned paradigm of knowing that makes sense of these features of our epistemic experiences.

Knowing

The knowing event itself is living. We may favorably compare the unfolding event, in its reciprocity, to a dance: overture, response, overture, response. It is a rhythmical reciprocity of growing understanding and involvement.[45] Our participating involves our subsidiarily sensing our own personhood and in some sense that of the other, and comporting ourselves in a way that enhances these in tandem. We ourselves will be better knowers if our epistemic efforts more fully conform to the dynamics of a healthy interpersonal relationship. The process of coming to know in some way transforms knower and known.

The paradigm, of course, applies well to knowing people. I believe it applies well to knowing muskrats and cures for cancer, also. And if it feels a bit strange to think of knowing, say, trees or car motors interpersonally, let me offer a deal. For centuries we have construed all knowledge on an impersonal paradigm, and, in the process, we have damagingly depersonalized people and known defectively. Let's try it the other way for a while. After developing several motifs to aid our analysis, I will eventually return to the question of the specific respect in which the real is fraught with the personed.[46]

Subsidiary-focal integration itself hints at a larger pattern of interpersonal reciprocity. Polanyi averred that there is a logical gap between

---

45. I allude to the Cappadocian Fathers' idea of *perichoresis*, "dancing around," which I will develop more fully in my conversation with Colin Gunton, ch. 12, and texture 7.

46. See ch. 13.

subsidiaries and focal pattern. The relationship of each to the other is neither necessary nor sufficient. There is more to the focal than the subsidiary can account for, and there is more to the subsidiary than the focal can account for. The connection is mutually transformative, and it is dynamic. I suggest we invent a "transformative" condition to name this relationship. For the focal pattern transforms the particulars it presses into clues. And the subsidiary clues lend their distinctive timbre to the focal pattern. Also, the focal pattern itself may adjust and grow as understanding deepens. It is pregnant with future prospects which themselves may transform us and our grasp of the real. So the integrative structure displays a rich sort of connection between subsidiary and focal.

Take, as a hypothetical example, the focal pattern of operating a vehicle in an extreme terrain situation, either literally or virtually. I imagine that the driver has his focus on the goal of effective negotiation of the terrain. But at any point there is nothing formulaic about the combination and succession of actions he takes—foot on clutch, foot on gas, hand on gear shift, hand on steering wheel. One may be doing all those things and fail at the achievement. One may lose usage of one and compensate with the others. If the only kind of logical conditions we have to work with are necessary or sufficient, I do not feel that we can satisfactorily account for the way human knowing works.

Similarly, I have heard that the great Impressionist painter, Renoir, after his forearm had to be surgically removed, strapped the paintbrush to the stub and continued to paint with no noticeable alteration of his capacity or style. If fingers and a forearm are not necessary to painting an artistic work, I don't know what is. A human body? A human in her/ his surrounding world? Of course some version of this is necessary. But a specific, specified, set of particulars and a single method? No. On the subsidiary level, humans are widely creative in their world coping.

This transformative dynamism seems to me to be characteristic of persons, especially of the way persons are related to their bodies. It is notoriously difficult to say just what a person is, or what a person is with respect even to something so obvious as that person's body. Body parts, taken separately or taken as a whole, do not seem to be either necessary or sufficient for there to be a person present. And the person present transforms the body even as he or she does not act as either a necessary or a sufficient condition for that body. Yet body and person are nevertheless integrally, mysteriously, transformatively related. This is one way that human death is so awful, as well as so complex, for example.

I believe that the transformative relation of clues and pattern in integration itself hints of the interpersonal. Knowing itself is in some way interpersoned. This signposts and suggests the covenant epistemology thesis.

Covenant epistemology, I believe, is thus anticipated by and further leverages Polanyian epistemology, as well as my expression of it in *Longing to Know.* It positively identifies as personal the characteristic indeterminacy at both ends of the trajectory of knowing, and identifies the knowing relationship as covenantally interpersoned.

Knowing, on a Polanyian construal, is *fraught with intimations of the personed—actually, of the interpersoned.* I want to say that knowing displays telltale features that could only be present if *a person, or persons in relationship, is, or are, in the vicinity.* Here's a story of a playful event that displays what I have in mind by "persons in the vicinity." This past Mother's Day I received perhaps the best gift ever—a surprise week-end visit from all three of my daughters. This was a big surprise, because two of them live several hundred miles away. When I rose from my exam grading to answer the doorbell midday on that Friday, I was greeted with the sight of a swaying mylar balloon attached to a tray of marigolds. Also attached was a slightly perturbed young black cat that I quickly surmised must be my new "grandcat" I had yet to meet. My reaction was to stand there and shriek repeatedly, "What's going on?" I could hardly take in its overwhelming implications: certain, deeply loved *persons must be in the vicinity.* The clues, the pointers, were telltale. In a few moments my girls all came running around from the side of the house to envelop me in a group hug that was desire fulfilled.

All knowing holds clues or pointers that suggest the pattern of interpersonhood covenantally constituted. From them we may glimpse contours of something profoundly richer, the way we might start to glimpse the shadowed contours of a person in the vicinity, or start to pick out the contours of a surpassingly profound pattern.

Lesslie Newbigin and Parker Palmer are scholars who have tapped Polanyi's thought to further purposes—thus in keeping with the surprising future prospects Polanyi himself averred characterizes all true knowing. They have also expressed that Polanyi's subsidiary-focal integration intrinsically points beyond itself, beyond its explicit claims, to the personal. Palmer writes:

For Polanyi, too, knowing proceeds by a kind of love . . . Polanyi's insights are obviously allied to the view that truth is personal. But . . . we must go one step further—and it is a critical step. Not only do I invest my own personhood in truth and the quest for truth, but truth invests itself personally in me and the quest from me. "Truth is personal" means not only that the knower's person becomes part of the equation, but that the personhood of the known enters the relation as well. The known seeks to know me even as I seek to know it; such is the logic of love.[47]

Similarly, Lesslie Newbigin comments

Polanyi used the phrase "personal knowledge" to define an understanding of human knowing that transcends the false dichotomy of subjective and objective . . . We must recognize our knowing as personal knowledge in a further sense: . . . our knowing of reality will be defective if it does not recognize that this reality is only fully explicable by reference to a personal being.[48]

Both Newbigin and Palmer explicitly move beyond Polanyi, but in a manner they feel to be consonant with his work, to affirm that reality is personal, fully explicable only by reference to a personal being. Thus they set the challenge for covenant epistemology. The task in this book is to offer an account of knowing that does justice to the telltale interpersoned features of knowing.

QUESTIONS FOR DISCUSSION

1. If possible spend some time playing with Magic Eye 3D pictures to get on board with "Point A" and "Point B" and the integrative feat.

2. Name and discuss skills you have. Identify and describe their Point A and Point B.

3. Give examples of knowing experiences that subsidiary-focal integration makes sense of.

4. Discuss how this account of how we know favorably impacts our practice of knowing.

5. Share any experiences you have of your knowing hinting of the personal.

---

47. Palmer, *To Know as We Are Known*, 58.

48. Newbigin, *Proper Confidence*, 58.

Texture 2

BODY KNOWLEDGE

Forays into the Subsidiary

IN ALL OUR KNOWING we responsibly integrate from relied-on clues, from which we attend, to a coherent focal pattern, to which we attend. When we recognize and embrace this dynamic, there is much to be gained in wisdom and effectiveness. I think there should be a way that we may capitalize on the fact that subsidiary awareness anchors knowing.

I have distinguished three sectors of clues: the surface features of the world, the lived body, and the directions. In other work I have expanded my account of the third one of these.[1] Here I want to consider the lived bodily subsidiaries, or body knowledge. I am intrigued to understand this better. My forays are only a feeble beginning, but one to which I trust that other people will contribute. How do we sense, and how do we employ, subsidiary knowledge of our bodies? How may we more intentionally avail ourselves of its resources? On the reasonable assumption that the Cartesian divorce between mind and body has held damaging implications for self-perception, self-awareness, and any contributions these might hold for effective knowing, how may an understanding of subsidiary knowledge rehabilitate our body epistemically?

This question, and the things I talk about here, intrigue me intensely. At the same time, I feel not only that it is difficult to articulate the inarticulable in a manner that successfully conveys it. I feel as well my own personal lack of expertise in tapping body knowledge. Others, and you may be one of them, are far better at it— wiser, I think. You will hear my efforts as baby lisping, perhaps. Yet I trust you will make out

1. Meek, "Learning to See."

what I say and in your wisdom make some mileage of it.

In this texture, I identify three areas that involve body knowledge: embodiment, presence, and virtuosity. Each is a sort of knowing that has been discredited on the pervasive model of knowledge as information-focused, precisely because it does not reduce to articulable statements. But in light of Polanyian epistemology, we may identify and accredit them. We can gain fresh appreciation and a way to be more intentional about them. These forays, additionally, lend support to the covenant epistemology thesis. For they reveal body knowledge to be uniquely personed: far from being unminded lumps of clay, our bodies are, for us and for others, highly interpreted as personed and personal.

Besides body knowledge, it has already been apparent, there are plenty of topics of thought to which the concept of subsidiary knowledge adds a great deal of insight. The idea of the subsidiary transforms any discussion of pretheoretical components of knowledge, or of personal, active contributions to knowing. For it affirms the active personal nature of the contribution, but reconstrues it as subsidiary. The effect is to take what is often deemed a matter of arbitrary convention and revitalize it as lived artistry.[2] Specifically, it removes arbitrariness by connecting the subsidiary integrally with the lived body.[3]

When we designate it in its body-as-subsidiary, lived, experience, we can begin to make sense of the body's contribution to knowing. Focus on body action and parts is important to knowing. When we are learning a skill, we focus temporarily on body action and body parts. Also it is important to study brain activity as it bears on human knowing. But if the knower does not subsidiarily embody her or his body, it is impossible for her or him even

2. One is the role of social construction in knowledge. Another is the currently prominent discussion of hermeneutics. Another topic is the rich idea of place. While the Continental phenomenological tradition has riches to mine in this discussion, again I believe that the idea of the subsidiary adds a strategic amplification, a helpful way to interpret and make more concrete the notion of "being there." For a quick entrée of a Polanyian cast, see Marjorie Grene's "Being-in-the-World," in Grene, *Philosophical Testament*, ch. 4.

3. I argued this in my critical response to David Naugle's *Worldview*; Meek, "Working Implications."

to achieve the knowing event. So while the prevailing default has successfully tempted us to reduce knowledge to focal particulars or mindless physical activity, human knowing and action, thus, are actually never in danger of being so reduced to physical components. The physical components are critical, but the determining factor in epistemic success is the manner in which we relate to them: we must live or indwell them subsidiarily with respect to the focal pattern.

We are easily familiar with our lived-body feel in the performance of any skill. It is *from*-knowledge. In the performance, we focus from the felt sense to the achievement. Here is one such example: some years ago I accompanied my sister to a sonogram of her kidneys. Seated in that half darkened room beside my sister, I watched the test. A medical resident focused on the computer monitor as with one hand she moved the sensor on my sister's abdomen. With the other hand, she continually keyed adjustments to the picture on the screen, gradually improving the digitized picture of the kidney. This subsidiary scrabbling is what Polanyi called creative imagination.[4] At one point (what must have been) the resident's supervisor stepped into the room. He observed her work; then he put his hands over hers, moving her hands on both the sensor and the keyboard, to achieve an even better picture (I presumed). The resident was relying on subsidiaries, and subsidiarily scrabbling to achieve a focus. The supervisor was doing this as well, simultaneously, as authoritative guide, training the student's bodily efforts.

Granted, in the act of knowing, the focal pattern is what gives transformative meaning to the particulars-turned-clues it incorporates. The pattern transforms the clues. But this does not mean that the clues themselves have no intrinsic value even though embedded in their focus. Beginner's luck doesn't last precisely because an effortless unskilled success at integration cannot be sustained. We forget the subsidiaries to our peril, as I said in *Longing to Know*. Rather, a dynamic reciprocity exists between clues and pattern, a kind of sharing of meaning and value. Reverential cultivation of the subsidiaries, even in gener-

4. See ch. 4.

al, not merely *ad hoc*, enriches the integrative feat. Because of this, the subsidiaries, in being valued and interpreted in the direction of an anticipated coherence, actually anticipate and prompt the coherence.[5]

However, the powerful dynamism of *from* to *to* in integration can incline us to underattend to the subsidiaries, to fail to give them their due as lived. This proclivity sustains the defective epistemic default. In the words of Maurice Merleau-Ponty (from whom I have taken the language of "body-as-subject") we must work "to reawaken perception and foil its trick of allowing us to forget it as a fact and as perception in the interest of the object which it presents to us and of the rational tradition to which it gives rise."[6] Merleau-

Ponty challenges modern empiricism when he says, "the system of experience is not arrayed before me as if I were God, it is lived by me from a certain point of view; I am not the spectator, I am involved. "[7] We subsidiarily live experience from a certain point of view. How may we attend to and heighten that involved, lived, experience?

The problem is this: how do you articulate, let along go to the bank on, what is by definition unspecifiable? Yet it seems that we should be able to do this, and doing it is just what would make the Polanyian model pay off in our efforts to know.

Subsidiary knowledge is unspecifiable in two respects.[8] One is that plenty of what we happen to be relying as we integrate to a particular focal pattern is knowledge that we do not even realize is involved. But all subsidiary knowledge is logically unspecifiable: even if particular clues can be verbalized when we focus on them, they cannot be verbalized or specified as they are within our

---

5. Thus, Polanyi argues, for the scientist to make the discovery, she or he must already tacitly and anticipatively have shifted to fundamental "premises of science" or plausibility structures that are consistent with the impending discovery (Polanyi, *Personal Knowledge*, ch. 6).

6. Meek, *Contact With Reality*, 251 (orig. ref. Merleau-Ponty, *Phenomenology of Perception*, 57). I devoted the last section of my dissertation to a productive comparison of Polanyi's and Merleau-Ponty's claims, showing that Merleau's "perception," aligns with Polanyian subsidiary awareness.

7. Meek, *Contact With Reality*, 253 (orig. ref. Merleau-Ponty, *Phenomenology of Perception*, 129–30).

8. Polanyi, *Personal Knowledge*, ch. 4.

relying on them to focus on something else.

Destructive analysis, as Polanyi called it, is the valuable exercise of reverting temporarily to focus on what is usually subsidiary, as a slumping batter studies slow-motion video of previous swings. Destructive analysis, therefore, is one way we attend to the subsidiary. But not only is it meant to be temporary, it does not involve attending to the subsidiary *as* subsidiary—that is, as it bears on the focus. Is it possible to do *this*? And if possible, is it beneficial? I think the answer must be yes to both. I believe that my three forays here do just that.

VIRTUOSITY

Expert knowing involves an intentionality in attentiveness from the clues. It is appropriate that I designate this *virtuosity*. I want to say that this is just what virtuosity involves. Sometimes you have "beginner's luck": you achieve a coherent pattern with little sense of what you did right with respect to the clues to achieve it. But as you become more skillful, you develop virtuosity with respect to the clues. Virtuosity can't be a focusing on them. Focusing on what should be subsidiary prevents or puts an end to the integrated achievement. Virtuosity is rather a kind of skilled intentionality in our use of them. It involves knowing the clues expertly, artfully, creatively, in our employment of them. We can employ them, we say, with finesse.

In any bodily achievement, virtuosity results from practice, although practice never guarantees virtuosity. Singing is a great example. The majority of us can sing, whether or not we have had training. People don't need training to get to the point of karaoke. Some people, never having had a lesson, have a natural knack for doing it well, even if untrained. But to be an expert singer takes training. A naturally talented singer, while she or he may for a time view voice lessons as a setback, will find that thorough training greatly expands any latent capacity, great or small.

A trained singer, while focusing on conveying to an audience a musical composition, is attending from the subsidiaries with a depth of intentionality born of practice. The performance displays the singer's virtuosity, her or his subsidiary finesse that enriches excellent performance. The singer sensitively and knowingly, expertly, yet subsidiarily, identifies, selects valuatively, and relies on lived experience of diaphragm, vocal chords, mouth shape, breath, body stance, and feel, in the act of musical production. (And these are just the *bodily* clues, not the world nor the coach nor the music itself! One works virtuoso-ishly with these other subsidiaries as well.)

This happens as much in science as it does in music or athletics: scientific studies always require labs alongside experts. Labs are only partly about information; they are partly about learning one's way about skillfully with equipment, developing requisite sensitivity and expertise in execution and interpretation, bodily apprenticeship to experienced members of the scientific tradition. [9]

Virtuosity, then, is a common way that knowers tap subisidiary knowledge to the end of greater effectiveness in knowing and action. It is an intentional artistry with respect to their fromness.

EMBODIMENT

What I mean by embodiment is the palpable sense that we possess that our bodies are ourselves. Our bodies are the only object of which we ordinarily have exclusively subsidiary awareness, and this is just what makes us feel them to be our own. Can we expand our understanding of this a bit farther? I think there is a wrong way to go at it, and a right way, and it will prove valuable to pursue the right way.

The wrong way of going about it is to explore body knowledge while retaining the ideal that such knowledge is of the body-as-object, rather than realizing that it must be of the body-as-subject. Focal knowledge of the body does not get at what embodiment is about.

9. Polanyi the scientist made the point graphically about his own discipline: "The popular conception of science teaches that science is a collection of observable facts, which anybody can verify for himself. We have seen that this is not true in the case of expert knowledge, as in diagnosing a disease. But it is not true either in the physical sciences. In the first place, you cannot possibly get hold of the equipment for testing, for example, a statement of astronomy or of chemistry. And supposing you could somehow get the use of an observatory or a chemical laboratory, you would probably damage their instruments beyond repair before you ever made an observation. And even if you should succeed in carrying out an observation to check upon a statement of science and you found a result which contradicted it, you would rightly assume that you had made a mistake" (Polanyi, *Tacit Dimension*, 63–64).

Subsidiary knowledge is knowledge of the body-as-subject. This is an important, almost uniquely Polanyian, distinction, but one that is not widely recognized. So while there is much talk about embodiment in current discussions, usually when embodiment is given serious treatment in epistemology it is relegated to epistemic naturalism, neural science, or some such.[10]

Take, for example, the well-known work of George Lakoff and Mark Johnson.[11] The Lakoff-Johnson thesis, in an effort to do "empirically responsible" philosophy, rejects the Cartesian divorce of mind and reason from body. It argues that we can identify primary metaphors, basic spatial pictures, with which we conflate meaning, e.g., quantity and verticality. Neural brain processes which are linked to sensory-motor activity, Lakoff and Johnson suggest, may also explain primary metaphors. "May," in the text, is then promptly promoted to "does." All of philosophy is thereby reduced to body processes.

It is laudable that Lakoff and Johnson reject Cartesian dualism and aspire to reintegrate the body into knowing. The metaphors they identify suggest the connectedness of human thought to our bodies and through them to the world. Their reductivism doesn't prevent their own tacit human valuation and interpretation of body. The problem is not with the evidence they amass nor with the thesis of primary metaphors; the problem is with the non sequitur that in this all human intelligent activity reduces to body processes. This conclusion does follow if all we have to work with is the notion of body-as-object.

Lakoff and Johnson fail to distinguish the body-as-object from the body-as-subject. Thus they actually perpetuate the Cartesian divorce; while they eliminate mind, they allow body to remain extended, mindless, substance.[12] Reducing mind to brain processes, even in the name of embodiment, thwarts rather than advances our understanding of human embodiment and body knowing.

For example, according to Lakoff and Johnson, the hu-

10. See ch. 4.

11. Lakoff and Johnson, *Philosophy in the Flesh*, especially chs. 1–5.

12. Marjorie Grene concurs: Grene, *Philosophical Testament*, 136. Grene would also probably join me in finding it surprising that they credit Maurice Merleau-Ponty with inspiring their work. See Grene, *Philosophical Testament*, ch. 6.

man idea of affection reduces to physical closeness, as if the ultimate category were mere touch, or that affection "is a function of touch." Covenant epistemology, as will be seen when we talk about personhood, wants to stand this the other end up. I will show that affection affords the context for human touch rather than vice versa.[13] Touch signifies affection because it is a function of affection. Affection is logically, and bodily, prior. For what we are first is persons in relationship. Our connectedness as persons is fraught with relationship, and with care. This we convey prethetically (before subject-predicate statements), preverbally, by tender physical touch, apart from which we would hardly be human.[14] My body does not explain or eliminate my personhood. My body bodies forth my personhood. This is not unconscious, but it is preconceptual. It is highly valuative, deeply investing the human body with significance, and it is absolutely essential to all knowing. It is the beginning, not the end, of philosophy. For all knowledge proceeds by value assignment—assigning value, significance, to the clues. Our bodies are fraught with personed value, subsidiarily lived.[15]

Our deeply entrenched intellectual penchant to dualism and then to reductivism is difficult to see, let alone overcome. It needs to be overcome, not only in our thinking; it needs far more, somehow, to be overcome in our bodies. Only if we ourselves harbor an embodied Cartesianism (an obviously ironic state of affairs!) do we not take this seriously. The important distinction can be understood only in light of Polanyian subsidiary-focal integration. Embodiment is not about how our thought reduces to our bodies. It is about how we feel our bodies, how

13. See ch. 8.

14. Tender physical touch wombs the child, then births the child, then nurses the child. The act of breast-feeding—constantly repeated, face-to-face intimacy—nourishes body in the prior context of interpersonhood. My friend, Gideon Strauss, editor of *Comment* magazine, has commissioned me to write an essay on the epistemology of breastfeeding. This point will be central to it. See further ch. 8.

15. Wendell Berry's *Remembering* poignantly portrays the intense significance of losing a body part—a hand. In my estimation, all of Berry's work demonstrates his profound working understanding of knowing as covenant epistemology understands it. *Remembering* could well be the novel version of *Loving to Know.*

we feel them as our bodies. But having understood this, how may we feel it and be healed bodily, and how may we then put that body sense to work?

Elizabeth Moltmann-Wendel offers richly sensitive insight into body-as-subject. She would have us say, not, I *have* a body, but rather, I *am* my body. In no way does she mean this to express a reductivism. The body must be regarded as highly significant, highly interpreted, the bearer of meanings. "In so far as, when I reflect on the essence of subjectivity, I find it bound up with that of the body and that of the world, this is because my existence as subjectivity is merely one with my existence as a body and with the existence of the world, and because the subject that I am, when taken concretely, is inseparable from this body and this world."[16] Moltmann-Wendel states that our society continues to be disembodied. It expresses hatred of the body and devalues it, making it a scientific object. I believe that Lakoff and Johnson's approach, though well intended, continue to perpetrate this disembodiment. Moltmann-Wendel ex-

presses this powerfully: many bodies are still haunted, she says, by Descartes' remark, *Cogito, ergo sum*. But, she states baldly, "Disembodiment is lovelessness."[17] But even with Cartesianism as a dominating paradigm, bodily truth in some situations is able to break through. Her remark is eye-opening: "the need to live in today's world creates islands of dance, physical work, experiences of the body which explode theory."[18] There are moments and activities which put us back together, and which thus belie the defective default mode.

Moltmann-Wendel argues that we need to reawaken our bodies to the interpersoned touch with which they began. "Life begins as life together; the person in relationship rather than the individual should be the starting point of our thought and action."[19]

If our bodies awaken from the passivity attributed to them, our senses will again become our own. Just as waking up is not a transition to mere activ-

17. Ibid., 104.
18. Ibid., 13.

16. Moltmann-Wendel, *I Am My Body*, 261.

19. Ibid., 43. We will take up this powerful insight in Part 4.

ity and domination, so too the awakening of our sense of self is defined by its receptive activity or active receptiveness, which gives birth, participates, allows to grow, shares, and represents the opposite relationship to the world from that of ruling and manipulating . . . French writer and educator Fenelon remarks, "When you are perceptibly touched, the scales will fall from your eyes and with the penetrating eyes of love you will recognize what your other eyes will never see."[20]

Such a reviving of the sense of one's own person, while it opens up broad ways through which one can learn to live more intensively, is an effort that takes time and practice. She quotes from another author: "For feelings in particular one needs time, not for ideas. Ideas are like lightning; feeling is a ray from a very far distant star. For feeling one needs leisure; it cannot live with anxiety."[21] Opening up this sense takes time, she says; "but at any time it can make us timelessly happy."[22] And,

"those who keep alive their bodies, their feeling, their skin, as levels of communication will find it difficult to fall victim to abstract grasping but will constantly retain bodily thought."[23]

In these tantalizing comments we may discern the contours of covenant epistemology. Moltmann-Wendel is describing a sense of self that can grow within, and that cultivates a relational rather than manipulative engagement with the world. It involves love, a special kind of seeing, and timeless happiness. It takes feeling your body in a certain way. This is itself a kind of knowing. The result is both personal wholeness, better knowing, and a better world.

Embodiment is felt sense, richly personed meaning throughout our bodies. It gives life together vast reaches of color as well as complexity. Embodiment soaks up the peculiarities of family, place, skill sets, culture, nationality, ethnicity, religion, and philosophy; in turn, it imbues them. Embodiment is subsidiarily felt. Moltmann-Wendel is arguing that honoring it intentionally is critical to full humanness as well as effectiveness. Thus

20. Ibid., 94.
21. Marija Belkina, in ibid., 96.
22. Ibid., 96.

23. Ibid., 62.

embodiment represents a key way that we may tap the reality of subsidiary awareness for knowing and being.

PRESENCE

A third phenomenon that taps subsidiary knowledge is presence. Presence is a kind of self-awareness, a sense of being present to oneself, being centered, being "there," or being "at home." Like embodiment, presence is personally felt, a personal achievement. I myself sense that I do not yet grasp it fully. Yet I know enough to know it is important for me and everyone to do so. And my point here is that in it we may tap subsidiary awareness as such.

I am hard-pressed to distinguish presence from embodiment. I feel confident that they are integrally linked. My conjecture is that presence is the highest expression of embodiment. Perhaps we may blend all three forays by defining presence as virtuoso embodiment. Not sure! For virtuosity seems artful; presence seems artless.

While presence is difficult to specify, we find ourselves able to identify people who are in accord with, connected with, *there* in, their bodies, and others who definitely aren't. Consider, for example, how Wendell Berry, writing in *Jayber Crow*, describes the character, Mattie Chatham.

> I knew Mattie Chatham a long time, and I never knew her to falsify or misrepresent herself. Whatever she gave you—a look, a question, an answer—was honest. She didn't tell you everything she knew or thought. She never made reference even by silence to anything she suffered. But in herself she was present. She was present in her dealings with other people. She was right there . . .
>
> I knew well the work and worry she had pending at home, and yet in that moment she was as free with the children as if she had been a child herself—as free as a child, but with a generosity and watchfulness that were anything but childish. She was just perfectly there with them in her pleasure . . .
>
> What moved me so toward Mattie was the sense that she withheld nothing; she was not a woman of defenses or devices. Though she might be divided in her affection and loyalty, within herself she was whole and clear.

She would be wholly present within her presence.[24]

Presence is being at home—there—in one's body. Presence is a kind of authentic alignment and identity between oneself and one's body—or, somehow, between oneself and oneself. This latter involves the quality of authenticity. I think for some people, it may be natural; for others, it may have been honed through family or experience. For all of us at one time or another, it involves resolve. The resolve is to be who we are, and to be who we are in this time and place—to be *here*.

The fact that we could ever *not* be present is something that could only be true of human persons. My dog, in contrast, never has the problem of authenticity! But we humans can be somehow disconnected from our bodies. We can be inclined to the distant future, to future projects. We can view our mind or reason as being disembodied, and see ourselves cultivating it as over against our bodies. We can actually be overly attentive to other people, or to projects, and entirely forget ourselves. Body therapist Roger Weinerth comments that "some people are so busy connecting with you that there is nobody home in their bodies for you to connect back to," a comment which, at the time I heard it, I found painfully self-revealing.[25] What results is that authentic communion, between me and other persons and objects of my attention, is precluded, because I am not "at home."

Presence is closely linked to a sense of personal beauty or significance. I believe that beauty is a gracious, naturally alluring, responsibly self-giving, presence. I will talk more about the sense of personal beauty. I will argue that it is a kind of self-knowing that comes to be in the respectful and loving gaze of another person.[26] I think that is true of presence also: it may be that presence is honed in the noticing regard of others. It may thus be—and these are all topics I will develop later on, that what presence involves is not resolve (except when un-

24. Berry, *Jayber Crow*, 189, 191, 193. See also 241. *Jayber Crow* is also a book very much about being at home, a gracious gift that binds you in a place.

25. Roger Weinerth, oral presentation to the organization, Businesspersons Between Jobs, Claymont Presbyterian Church, Chesterfield, Missouri, Fall 2003.

26. Texture 6.

der threat) so much as consent to one's own being. It involves inward shalom or accord.

It is not as if presence could happen accidentally. In fact, it seems more the gift of grace, the way Berry's Jayber Crow sees the reflection on the river as a metaphor of the sense of home. I believe that presence must develop. It involves others, for it is a kind of holding on to yourself while maintaining connection with others. Additionally, this self-valuing consents not only to oneself but to others.

You can compare all this with the act of giving a gift— another kind of "present"—the allusion should not be lost. For an action of giving a gift to be constituted as such, there must be a self-awareness: it is I who give the gift to you. Apart from that sense of the ceremony, it doesn't count as giving a gift. You can see that in that context, the self-awareness must be subsidiary: if it were focal, that would undercut the gift giving also. I believe that presence, like virtuosity and embodiment involves "intentional fromness."

Let's pick up the allusions before we move on from the effort to understand presence.

Presence is being *here*; but it is also being *now*, in the present. And it has the aura of gracious gift—present—both received and given.

Although it is difficult to pinpoint presence, I feel it is critical to knowing. We can anticipate that, if effective knowing involves something reciprocal, not being at home in one's body would quite likely deter it. The way we are living our bodies can inhibit or enhance our interaction with the world. If, as I mean to argue, knowing consists of interpersonal communion, personal presence will prove a *sine qua non*.

In discussing presence, I am arguing, we are probing subsidiary awareness. If possessing presence contributes to knowing, then this supports my claim that tapping subsidiary awareness is a great resource.

CULTIVATING BODY KNOWLEDGE

How might a person, especially a person hopelessly shaped on a Cartesian paradigm (as I seem to have been), ever begin to cultivate such an awareness? It is itself a telling challenge to Cartesianism that this is such a difficult question, even though it concerns our own body and our body's knowledge! Part of the problem is the defective epistemic default. But part is just that even if we embrace Polanyi's account, we are trying to access the realm of the subsidiary. I believe that even half-understood, groping attempts will pay off.

But there are some identifiable strategies to cultivate lived body knowledge. Each person's own body is unique among all physical beings in that it is an incomparably rich nexus of physicality and significance. The lived body is so much more than a physical sensing mechanism. It is—we are—human. The body as subject is humanly interpreted through and through. I have a meaning-laden manner of living my body. All of our integrated commitments come to expression in and through our bodies. This state of affairs is what enables us to read a person in his/her face and body.

We know our body, primarily, entirely subsidiarily as it bears on other foci. Now add to this the obvious implication that the body holds that subsidiary significance for every single one of the myriads of integrative coherent achievements of knowing and world engagement we undertake, from knitting to doing philosophy, from starting a business to discovering a cure for cancer. Our living, our educations and experiences, good and bad, have built into our lived bodies layer after layer of significance. In an act of coming to know, the moment we succeed at making sense of the world will simultaneously be a moment when we are personally transformed; the world we have come to know changes us in the knowing. It changes us quantitatively and qualitatively, both extending and transforming our lived body awareness. So simply going on living and knowing continues to cultivate this rich nexus of body knowledge.

However, I believe we may profit by cultivating it intentionally. We can do this specifically—with respect to a specific achievement, task, or act of coming to know. And we can do it generally—with respect to no one specific achievement.

Cultivating body knowledge to a specific end involves engaging in what you know to be subsidiary activity, or honing certain identified subsidiaries to expert perfection. This can be done anticipatively, thus inviting the longed-for focal pattern. One way this comes to expression is that we all know the importance of putting oneself into the mode of behavior that we surmise can prompt the desired achievement. The author, Forester, in the movie, *Finding Forester,* counsels his pupil to sit down at the typewriter and start typing. I know of no basketball player who does not dribble the ball prior to shooting a basket (also documented in that movie!). As a skier waxes her or his skis or a marksman oils his or her gun— lovingly, I might add—a knower in anticipation of the knowing cultivates and primes the pump of body subsidiaries. Dribbling or typing or waxing primes the pump of a single act. Practice equips us in a specific skill. Dribbling anticipates shooting a basket, but in a different way from how practicing shooting

baskets does. Both involve cultivating body knowledge in anticipation of knowing.

We may cultivate body knowledge in general, with respect to no specifically anticipated focus. Given the richness of body knowledge, and given that we cannot for any particular integrative knowing event specify exactly which particulars the integration presses into service, nor how, we can and should exercise a caring nurture of that entire category of subsidiaries more broadly. Much specific cultivation is transferrable: marching band documentably improves math skill. Crawling improves reading skill. Simone Weil exhorts us to "the right use of school studies with a view to the love of God."[27]

I believe that general body care counts as cultivating body knowledge. It can be seen as cultivating a felt sense of personal presence and beauty or wholeness. Both genders practice this, in different forms. Body care includes healthy diet, exercise and sleep, work and play, decisions about clothing, haircuts, manicures, and massages. It involves these things especially *understood as such.*

27. Weil, *Waiting for God*, 57–65.

Spiritual and physical practices—meditation or dance, for example—can enhance a person's presence, his/her accord with and being in his/her body. It involves *being* touched, often, in the process. We may pursue them precisely because we understand the body-as-subject benefits of doing so.[28]

Quite commonly matters of the human body are reduced to being about the body as object. People identify personal beauty with this and see it as vain focus on "personal appearance." Some people argue we "deserve" it. Others boycott it because we don't. We can helpfully move beyond this discussion, and suit our outlook more adequately to our humanity, if we recast it in terms of subsidiary awareness, the body as subject. Doing so reveals that it is not so much that "outward" beauty reflects "inner" beauty, but that personal beauty is a subsidiary virtuosity of the lived body. It does not divorce inward from outward, and does not oppose them—the way "appearance" is commonly discussed. Cultivated in appropriate body care, it comes to expression in the many mutual human acts that comprise a life well-lived.

Body care and cultivating personal beauty involve a valuing of the body, and that additionally anticipates and invites coherent achievements like knowing or understanding. They value the actual physical components for the dignity of richness they possess as skillfully lived subsidiaries to bear on a rich reality. These do not fixate or focus on the bodily components, but rather cultivate intentionality in the sensitive and skilled subsidiary living of them. Nurturing this intentional subsidiary valuing and skilled use anticipates and thereby catalyzes coherent epistemic achievement. One need not have a specific achievement in view for exercising a general valuing and care to signal a kind of readiness that anticipates and invites it.

Cultivating body knowledge invites insight. It is a being in the way of knowing. I will return to this topic of beauty later in the book in connection with two discussions. It can be listed among the activities that invite the real.[29] I want additionally to argue that a sense of personal beauty is itself a kind of self-

28. Further discussion of this may be found in texture 6.

29. See ch. 15.

knowing that develops within the gaze of another person.[30]

Quite often in life, not only do we not have the leisure for personal bodily care, but we are prevented from it by adverse and painful circumstances. But experience suggests, and Moltmann-Wendel confirms, that pain and suffering themselves offer the opportunity to develop presence.[31] Marjorie Grene, in *Philosophical Testament*, considers *authenticity* as a special quality that not all people have acquired. The few people whom she has met and felt to be authentic, she reports, are those who have weathered unimaginable suffering.[32] Of course, we should not choose pain. But we do not need to; it happens. Pain connects us to our bodies. It becomes impossible to presume to deny this. We can choose how to respond to the pain. In this lies pain's opportunity for us to cultivate presence.

RESOURCING BODY KNOWLEDGE

All knowledge is, at its roots, embodied; its roots are lived bodily. Accrediting tacit, implicit, anticipative knowledge as integral in Polanyian epistemology leads us to affirm that some truths, and some dimensions of all knowledge, may be known in the sense of felt/lived, and not yet "known" in the sense of articulated. The human body is rich with such in the sense of felt/lived knowledge.

Eugene Gendlin is a psychotherapist who has endeavored to tap this Polanyian insight. He has developed a technique he calls "focusing."[33] Focusing is a concrete method of unlocking body knowledge, a way of attending so as to let body knowledge surface and be articulated. The process, which can be performed singly or in the presence of an active listener, involves quiet attending to the felt body sense, suggesting potential one-word descriptors of the sense, and waiting to sense a body shift that confirms that the descriptor is apt. Our bodies tell us what is true, Gendlin is saying, if we only listen to them. Focusing is a strat-

30. Texture 6.

31. Moltmann-Wendel, *I Am My Body*, 24.

32. Grene, *Philosophical Testament*, 184–89. For more on Grene's account of what makes human animals persons, see texture 8.

33. Gendlin, *Focusing*.

egy to get beneath the kind of self-deception we so often perpetrate on ourselves so as to spawn real change.

I believe that Gendlin's focusing is essentially the same dynamic that just is the act of coming to know. New Zealand dancer and choreographer Michael Parmenter concurs; he affirms also that this just is the creative act as well.[34] Focusing exemplifies the productive exploration that is warranted on the assumption of subsidiary knowledge. A host of evidence may be added as well if we surmise, quite reasonably, that subsidiary body knowledge accounts for the examples of rapid cognition Malcolm Gladwell documents in his book, *Blink: The Power of Thinking Without Thinking*.[35] But Gendlin, I believe, is distinctive in offering a practical strategy for accessing and capitalizing on implicit body knowledge.

The lived body contributes critically to knowing as a finely tuned sensor. We sometimes use the crass term, *gut*, to designate it. There are situations in which we might say, "I have a bad (or a good) feeling about this!" Far more than just registering sense impressions, the lived body is how we intuit intimations that guide our pursuit, and how we sense the aptness of a judgment. A truth claim has to accord, not just with my sense of the world, but also with my sense of me. Or perhaps better: I gauge truth by sensing an all-round resonance between the claim and my bodily felt sense, and the claim and the world. Wisdom can be considered the art of disciplining, hearing, and being guided by one's gut. This in no way makes truth a private matter.

The picture I have in mind is an auditory one: tuning the strings of a guitar or the pitches of a vocal ensemble. When different pitches are out of tune with each other, it is as if they are in conflict—there are "beats," and no overtones occur. You know you are in tune, however, when the beats cease, and rich and receding reaches of overtones occur and fill out the sound. Just as we would sense that, I think our body senses a resonance that confirms the claim.

34. Personal conversation. Michael Parmenter, lecture on the creation of his piece, *Empty Chairs*. Polanyi Conference, Loyola University, June 2000. Parmenter's website: http://michaelparmenter.inza.co.nz/.

35. Gladwell, *Blink*.

One thing that I have always found especially apt about the Polanyian account of subsidiary body knowledge, which makes it superior to foundationalist efforts in this aspect: we can affirm what we know to be the case from our experience, namely, that our subsidiary body knowledge can be mistaken. It is not fool-proof. But on the other hand, neither is it to be dismissed or dealt out of the epistemic picture. Like any instrument, skilled use of it improves with proper identification and retraining.

In conclusion: We can identify common personal practices of which an account of subsidiary knowledge makes better sense, and which exemplify how we may effectively tap subsidiary awareness. We ought to be able to be intentional about cultivating and resourcing subsidiary knowledge. Doing so will make us better knowers and address therapeutically the defective epistemic default that remains embedded, precisely, in our body knowledge. And just the richness of the realm of the subsidiary, and its integrally personal nature—how our subsidiary body knowledge is fraught with our personhood—signposts the vision of covenant epistemology.

QUESTIONS FOR DISCUSSION

1. Give some examples of virtuosity. Together express them in terms of intentional and artful reliance on subsidiary clues.

2. Discuss further the notion of body as subject. How does this notion make better sense of our being, doing, and knowing?

3. Can you supply a fuller description of presence? (If so, email me!)

4. Share your thoughts about cultivating and resourcing body knowledge. What are some other ways we do this? How does this improve your knowing practices?

5

KNOWING AS TRANSFORMATION

Conversation with James Loder

I HAVE SHOWN THAT Polanyi's work points beyond itself to an interpersoned reciprocity that covenant epistemology attempts to elucidate. Over the years, I have searched for proposals which would help me make sense of this. James Loder's work has proven immensely valuable in that it supplies important insights to this vision. I and my students have been personally transformed by Loder's work. It offers an account of transformation; but far more importantly, it evokes it.

Loder, a Princeton professor (recently deceased) with expertise in theology, psychology, and education, has written *The Transforming Moment*, a dense interdisciplinary account of "convictional knowing"—existential experiences the Christian believer has of God. Loder begins his richly layered argument with an account of ordinary human knowing which patently aligns with subsidiary-focal integration. He moves on to argue that human knowing has the integrative dynamism that it does, and unfolds the way it does, first, because it taps into our humanness (for which he offers an account), and second, because it is rooted in human development (which he explains as well). It does so, third, because human knowing prototypes, anticipates, and actually *is*, we may come to see, an instance of our being graciously known by the personal God of Holy Scripture (a third account). In this chapter, I want to show how Loder's opening sketch of human knowing confirms and further elucidates subsidiary-focal integration in the direction of covenant epistemology. Chapter 10 of this work considers the rest of Loder's great discussions, drawing from them to build the contours of what I call interpersonhood.

At this point in my unfolding argument, I have already appropriated two key words/concepts from Loder: knowing as *transformation*, and knowing as *event*. I believe that they are implicit in subsidiary-focal integration, if not explicit. So the terms amplify Polanyian epistemology, contributing their shape to my work. This chapter will show why.

THE KNOWING EVENT AS TRANSFORMATION

Loder's account of human knowing is so evidently Polanyi's, even though he offers a distinct analysis of it. Taken together, these two facts offer strong confirmation of subsidiary-focal integration as the mechanism that characterizes knowing.

Human knowing exhibits "the logic of transformation." Loder says that it involves a five-step sequence. The knowing event begins with *conflict in context*, "an apparent rupture in the knowing context." The knowing context refers to the knower as situated in her or his surroundings or world. Prior to the rupture, an equilibrium of coherence has prevailed between knower and her or his situation. We have been amiably making sense of things. Then we run into a fresh challenge that ruptures into conflict in context. In chapter 4, I talked about how a trajectory of coming to know can be inaugurated in any one of the three sectors of clues— the world, the lived body, or the normative dimension. In retrospect we can see that Loder's conflict in context is describing this inauguration.

The knower responds to conflict in context by urgently seeking to achieve a deeper coherence that will restore equilibrium. The more one cares about the conflict, the more powerful the knowing event will be, Loder says. In fact, one cannot come to know what one does not care about.[1] So Loder is linking knowing and caring integrally, as I have earlier. We will see later that Loder, the philosopher of religion and psychologist, will elaborate concretely why we long to know.

The next stage in the knowing event is an *interlude for scanning*. We start to "indwell the conflicted situation with empathy for the problem," to search methodically through its pieces for a clue to its resolution. This interlude may last seconds or years. Loder's interlude for scanning compares favorably to Polanyi's account of the creative imagination, which scrabbles and gropes toward a solution.[2] Polanyi talked of creative imagination working in tandem with intuition, which guides the knower by giving a sense of increasing proximity to the solution. Loder's five-fold

1. Loder, *Transforming Moment*, 37.
2. Polanyi, "Creative Imagination."

sequence includes no specific component to parallel Polanyi's sense of increasing proximity to the solution, but taken as a whole Loder's analysis casts knowing as an anticipative prototype of longing for the face of the Other, as we will see. This notion expresses the intuitive anticipation that guides the knowing event. Also, Loder here speaks of our indwelling the conflicted situation with empathy. He thus affirms the intimacy of indwelling that distinguishes a Polanyian approach. As I have expressed it, we seek to climb inside the clues.

Where, in *Longing to Know*, I have relied on the Magic Eye as an example, Loder employs a little puzzle that features nine dots laid out as on the Nine Domino. The task is to draw four continuous straight lines, without lifting pencil from paper, that connect all the dots. Stage three of the knowing event, which he calls a constructive act of the imagination, *an insight felt with intuitive force*, involves, he says, "a constructive resolution that reconstellates the elements of the incoherence and creates a new, more comprehensive context of meaning."[3] In the example of the dots, one must come, in one's seeing, to let the lines be the context for the dots rather than the dots the context for the lines, a figure-ground reversal. At one point he calls this an imaginative leap to certainty.

This is clearly what Polanyi has in mind by the integrative feat. Says Loder: "It is by this central act that the elements of the ruptured situation are *transformed*, and a new perception, perspective, or world view is bestowed on the knower."[4]

Stage four is a *release of energy and repatterning*, an "aha." This is *Longing to Know's* "Oh! I See It!" moment. It releases the energy that has been bound up in sustaining the conflict. I think that this aligns also with Gendlin's account, in his method of focusing, of a "felt body shift."[5] This, the knower's response, is the opening of her- or himself up to the resolution. The knower now contemplates, as I may suggest that Loder is describing, what Polanyi calls indeterminate future manifestations: "a wave of related new associations, carrying the implications further than

---

3. Loder, *Transforming Moment*, 3–4, 38. At this point Loder footnotes Arthur Koestler, *Creative Act*. Polanyi and Koestler were friends and colleagues. Citing Koestler's "bisociation," Loder says that the crux of the event is "two habitually incompatible frames of reference converging, usually with surprising suddenness, to compose a meaningful unity."

4. Ibid., 38.

5. See texture 2.

the original conflict suggested and thereby immersing the knower more richly and deeply than ever in his or her [new] assumptional world."[6]

The transformative nature of this repatterning is evident in Loder's description here. It underscores all that I have said about the nonlinearity of Point B with respect to Point A, with the sense of having been invaded, inspired, from beyond the efforts of which I myself have been capable. It is this phenomenon that, for Loder, calls for grounding in an account of a deeper dynamism as central to human knowing. Why is knowing like this?—repatterning begs that we engage this question. At this early point in his argument, Loder states that the generative human spirit is "the uninvited guest in every meaningful knowing event" and the dynamic that unobstrusively and dynamically shapes them all.

The fifth step of Loder's knowing event is *interpretation*. By this he means working with the new vision to relate it back to the original conflict and to gain its acceptance with the public. Since the vision has been transformative of both the knower and of reality as he/she knows it, the knower is compelled passionately to do this. This is partly because the knower has been changed, and partly because it is part of working through to regain coherence. This account matches Polanyi's reflections regarding the persuasive passions in scientific discovery, the heated debate that we should expect in the immediate wake of fresh claims.[7]

THE EIKONIC ECLIPSE

Loder calls this five-fold knowing event the logic of transformation.[8] He demonstrates that this transformational logic characterizes all kinds of human knowing. In particular, he argues that it typifies scientific knowing, aesthetic knowing, and therapeutic knowing. In his account of therapeutic knowing he confirms something I will claim: that know-

---

6. Loder, *Transforming Moment*, 38–39.

7. Polanyi, *Personal Knowledge*, ch. 6.

8. Loder comments that, despite the discontinuity of transformation, the knowing event has continuity in the sense that the knower's longing for resolution carries him/her through to its finish: this is true intentionality. *Contra* the phenomenologists, intentionality does not stay within, but rather carries us beyond, consciousness; it cuts across the boundary between conscious and unconscious, driving toward the continuity of the event for the whole person. I think that this aptly expresses the way in which Polanyi "helps" phenomenological studies, moving the account of human epistemic acts to reach both beneath and beyond "consciousness." Loder, *Transforming Moment*, 40.

ing as transformational is also healing.[9] In his discussion of scientific knowing, he directly challenges the widely known Deweyan scientific method to demonstrate its inadequacy to account for what scientists actually do.[10] Here again Loder concurs with Polanyi, in addition to actually drawing on Polanyi's work. He shows that prevailing "canons of reason"—induction, deduction, and objectivity (in the sense of absence of personal involvement)—either self-destruct or devolve to the critical contribution of the knower's imagination. Loder states that his purpose is not to eliminate rational processes but rather to relegate them to a subordinate role, "having more to do with ordering, examining, and communicating truth than bringing it to being or discovering it in the first place." For, Loder says, "rational processes can add no knowledge that is not first imagined."[11]

Loder argues that the "eikonic eclipse" that continues to dominate our society—in which so-called reason refuses to acknowledge the role of the imagination and of the personal in knowing—only continues to wreak havoc by thwarting real knowing and true humanness. The rationalistic eclipse of the image is "a fundamental error of thought" that "eventually cuts off reason from its substance." "[E]clipsing rationalists thereby lose their perspective on themselves and whatever they know."[12]

Loder concludes: "In summary, knowing . . . is first, foremost, and fundamentally an event. At the center of an event is a nonrational intrusion of a convincing insight . . . This is the central common feature that makes every convictional event an act of knowing and every act of knowing an event."[13] From this conclusion we may glimpse his overall plan in the book to link convictional knowing with everyday knowing. But for my purpose here, what is central is that this logic of transformation is what makes every act of knowing an event. Knowing is transformation.

---

9. He writes: "Therapeutic knowing makes it evident that what is known in the event may indeed be oneself. Such self-knowing often comes through an eikonic awareness; that is, a spontaneous coalescence of many personal, often repressed developmental, fragments . . . the surest sign that healing has occurred in therapeutic knowing is the freedom of the "I" to choose for the self and against patterns of self-destruction . . ." (Loder, *Transforming Moment*, 63).

10. Ibid., 44.

11. Ibid., 33.

12. Ibid., 27.

13. Ibid., 33.

So Loder identifies and challenges the ascendancy of a two-dimensional account of rationality, arguing that it covers over the transformative dynamism that is only possible in connection with the imagination. This is Loder's equivalent to my effort to combat the defective epistemic default through the therapy of covenant epistemology. Polanyi took up the same challenge out of a concern to make better scientists, in fact, to save science as we know it from cultural death. Loder takes it up as the critical beginning step in an account of convictional knowing. But he is also making the case, in this opening step, that understanding what happens when we know is an urgently needed, fundamental epistemic reform for every area of knowing across the board—from science, to therapy, to art.

MUTUALITY AND RECIPROCITY IN KNOWING

Throughout the opening chapters of his argument, Loder repeatedly affirms the personlike reciprocity of the knowing event between knower and known. The core drive, the generativity of the human spirit, is a coherent pattern of knowing that shapes all cognition, and its passion is not so much Dionysian as it is akin to "the intuitive and affective ways we know each other in acts of love and compassion."[14] He explicates the biblical Greek words, *gnosis*—as an imaginative coming together of things in a convincing way—and *aletheia*—as the truth as a matter or state of affairs that had been latent but has now been disclosed in a way that takes possession of the knower to bring it across to conviction. "Taken together, the two words *gnosis* and *aletheia* imply a mutual indwelling of the knower and the known," Loder says.[15]

Knowing involves mutual indwelling both before and after the imaginative crux of the event. Before it, "it winds the mainspring of the imaginative leap in which subjective involvements and objective provocation combine to constitute a spontaneous image." And after, "it is by indwelling the new imaginative reality that one becomes informed by it, and it, in turn, enters history." "Knowing *anything*," says Loder, "is to indwell it and to reconstruct it in one's own terms without losing the

14. Ibid., 3.

15. Ibid., 25–26. Loder adds that this is especially significant where the truth to be known is the reality of Christ's presence. *Loving to Know* will argue that this is especially significant *because* the truth to be known is, paradigmatically, the reality of Christ's presence.

essence of what is being indwelt."[16] In the mutual indwelling of subject and object lies true objectivity.[17]

The knowing event has a dyadic and cooperative aspect, which is especially evident in instances of therapeutic knowing: knower and known "mutually create each other," and do so in "face to face relationships."[18] The reciprocity is not heavy-handed or controlling: Loder notes that the character of being, or reality, is the inherently dynamic "letting flourish." Also, the knower comes to know him- or herself "in the face of the other." He suggests that the knowing event, in which the knower is more fully her- or himself than ever before, also compels the knower to "reopen the whole question of reality."[19]

These intriguing phrases receive development and support in Loder's ensuing discussions; we will engage them in a later chapter. But at this juncture we mark that Loder explicitly confirms the mutuality and reciprocity I have sensed to be implicit in epistemic acts. Where Polanyi talks of indwelling, Loder describes indwelling as mutual, between knower and known. Loder speaks of being as dynamic "letting flourish," and of the knower's core drive as being akin to ways we know each other in love. He speaks of knower and known mutually creating one another, and the knower coming to know him or herself in the face of the other. The prevailing paradigm of knowledge as impersonal is just what leads us to overlook these personal, interpersonal dimensions of knowing. But once we start to identify them and take them seriously, we must be led to reconsider the paradigm. That is the agenda of covenant epistemology.

So in conclusion, I offer this brief chapter on Loder's account of human knowing to underscore Polanyian epistemology, to shape it emphatically in the direction of transformative event, and to offer additional confirmation of the need for a vision of knowing that has as its contours persons in covenant relationship.

16. Ibid., 25. This complex claim is one that Martin Buber makes also. See ch. 9.
17. Loder, *Transforming Moment*, 30.
18. Ibid., 63.
19. Ibid., ch. 1.

QUESTIONS FOR DISCUSSION

1. Compare and contrast Loder's account of knowing with Polanyi's subsidiary-focal integration.

2. How does it help your insight into knowing to see it as transformation?

3. Discuss Loder's eikonic eclipse. What evidence can you add of its pervasive effect in western culture? Do you think his assessment is warranted?

4. How might it change culture to see knowing as transformation?

Knowing as Transformation, Not Information

Implications for Academic and Theological Curriculum, Education, and Pedagogy

Knowing is transformation, not mere information. This insight generates an array of helpful implications for Academe and pedagogy. Covenant epistemology offers healing, hope, and a strategy to the academy. This can only be accomplished at the fundamental level of epistemology; and it's going to take covenant epistemology to do it.

Covenant epistemology challenges the default epistemic mode, re-forms students and teachers to seek transformation, and offers a positive account of wisdom as the goal of study. Its model of knowing, shared as it is by all disciplines, reunites the sciences and the humanities. For Christian liberal arts institutions, it offers the way also to integrate biblical studies at the center of the curriculum, tapping the biblical message for the very paradigm of transformative knowing. The allusively interpersonal character of knowing on the covenant epistemology paradigm offers positive epistemic warrant for mutual personal involvement in teaching and learning, and it encourages interpersonal, interdisciplinary, collegiality. Covenant epistemology solidly supports a view of the classroom as hospitable space for indwelling a subject together in mutual submission. Finally, its openness to personed transcendence implies that we may appropriately context all study in a setting of worship and relational communion. In particular, it makes it strategically suited also to center theological and pastoral curricula, and to shape theological method.

CHALLENGING THE DEFECTIVE DEFAULT

As we have talked about knowing, first as subsidiary-focal integration, now as imagination-catalyzed, transformative event, I trust that you have also seen that this epistemology confirms chapter 1's diagnosis of the widespread default setting that casts knowledge as information, and offer a way to subvert it. As a college professor who teaches first-year students, I can confirm that, in fact, many students enter college with this defective default intact and unexamined. If knowledge is information, then education should involve the passive transfer of content. Education is generally mistakenly presumed to consist of success replicating information on exams. Indeed, students and teachers often embrace this model, possibly because it means that all involved can manageably curtail what they are responsible for, and can exhaustively document and assess their performance.

Challenging the widespread defective epistemic default is of primary importance to learning. It should happen among the faculty, for the incoming students, and recurrently throughout their courses of study. It should happen in a way that accomplishes epistemological therapy.

To the extent that university and college curricula fall short of diagnosing and actively addressing this, and to the extent that they omit positive epistemic re-formation of their students, I believe that they default on their obligation to train and produce educated people. A college seriously interested in transforming students to serve the world, apart from reshaping students' epistemological paradigm, will nevertheless find their best efforts to fall short. To allow to stand unchallenged the belief that knowledge is information is to castrate what we are attempting to do. Knowledge as information engenders passivity, indifference, inaction, skepticism, compartmentalization, depersonalization, and cluelessness. I would argue that it inclines toward godlessness, as well.

Replacing lecture with discussion formats in classes, service learning, and experiential learning are strategies which have been embraced to address the felt but often undiagnosed inadequacy of the defective epistemic model. But where students are not re-formed in a positive alternative epistemology that challenges the theory-application dichotomy, these strategies will continue to be appropriated as "application" and thus opposed to "theory," thus perpetuating the default in the university and in the lives of its graduates.

The theory-application divorce comes to an additional expression at Christian colleges. Not only is theory divorced from practical application; it is also divorced from spirituality and Christian service. In my experience, apart from a positive and thorough epistemic re-formation, students tacitly feel pressured to delegitimate class learning and privilege out-of-class "faith activities" and "ministry"—as if these were opposed to the classroom. This undercuts the classroom, and prevents students from whole-hearted academic pursuit. It is self-defeating, for it produces Christians trained to discredit thoughtful engagement, and thus unable to tap it for world care.

MAKING EPISTEMIC SENSE OF WISDOM

An implicit commitment to knowledge as explicit information denies to the educational venture a positive account of wisdom, and thus of producing students and graduates who are more than, as the saying goes, note-sensitive and melody-deaf. Wisdom requires that knowing be understood to be transformative insight, and to involve responsible and artful reliance on more-than-specifiable clues. Covenant epistemology will say further that knowing involves at its core an interpersoned relationship with a transcendent Other. Wisdom, we may easily surmise, is always relational. So again, for Christian institutions, this lack is especially grievous. The default model of knowledge as information discredits Scripture's repeated claim that the fear of the Lord is the beginning of wisdom.

FOSTERING INTERDISCIPLINARY RAPPROCHEMENT

An unexamined defective approach to knowledge perpetuates the common opposition between disciplines such as the sciences and the humanities,

134

and between both of these and the professions, and between all of these and theology. It continues to feed the competitive insularity rampant in academia. As long as such institutions persist in the eikonic eclipse Loder describes, curricula will persist in compartmentalization.

Loder argues that the eikonic eclipse obscures the fundamental transformative dynamic that characterizes all sorts of coming to know. I have elsewhere likened the eikonic eclipse to wearing a pair of two-dimensional glasses—as opposed to those three-dimensional glasses issued for 3-D movies.[1] The two-dimensional glasses (the epistemic default) flatten our view of knowing: information is two-dimensional; transformation is three-dimensional. The two-dimensional glasses hide from view what nevertheless operates wherever knowing occurs: creative imagination, risky, responsible, personal integrative shaping, to say nothing of the massive subterranean region of the subsidiaries and hinted future prospects that fruitfully anchor all explicit claims.

1. Meek, "Knowledge as Information Transformation"; also Meek, "Take Off Your Two-Dimensional Glasses."

Where knowledge is restricted to propositional statements and their proofs, we are kept from accrediting the transformative as knowledge, or even recognizing that it is there. Yet I believe that uncovering the transformative root of all knowing is the very thing that holds prospect to challenge this situation in academics. If we take to heart what Polanyi and Loder are saying, knowing can be seen to have the same contours no matter the discipline. Subsidiary-focal transformative integration characterizes all knowing, whether in the sciences or the humanities or professional disciplines such as business or engineering. "Subject matter" does not comprise knowing; so knowing is not different in different subject matters. Each subject has distinctive data and standards, but live knowing in each field involves the same creative integrative dynamism.

Were we to accomplish a profound epistemological reorientation, revamping our outlook from knowledge as information to knowledge as transformation, institutions of higher learning could effectively supersede their compartmentalization. They could successfully espouse a multi-faceted liberal arts education for all students. For students learning the art of transformation that is effectively the same in multiple fields enrich their expert knowing in any one field. This also unleashes them to whole personhood and mature contribution to society.

CENTERING AND RESOURCING THE GOSPEL EPISTEMICALLY; RELIGIOUS STUDIES AT THE CORE OF THE CURRICULUM

In colleges that seriously endeavor to cast learning in the context of a biblical worldview, Bible and religious studies nevertheless remain as marginalized as they are in society. This is not because of that marginalization, but because of a defective epistemology that casts both knowledge in general and knowledge of God as passive comprehension of information. The default has uniquely infected evangelical Protestantism.[2] At a time when Christian institutions of higher learning have returned to take seriously their engagement with scholarship, to "practice scholarship in Christian perspective," the latent default persists in thwarting this laudable enterprise.[3] Simply requiring Bible courses of its students, apart from radically revamping the epistemic paradigm, only deepens the grain of the default. Regarding biblical studies as "content" is the ultimate castrating irony, at a Christian college. The inherently transformative message of the Christian gospel, covenant epistemology will claim, should be apprehended as centrally epistemic, the paradigmatic example of knowing. But apart from epistemological therapy both among faculty, as reflected in the curriculum and in assessment, and as administered to form the student, that message is prevented from having this effect. The gospel is also prevented from being itself.

Missiologist Lesslie Newbigin maintained for similar reasons that the gospel is not even heard in western culture; this led him to call for preevangelistic assault on what I have called the western subcutaneous epistemological layer.[4] My point here is related: not only

2. Noll, *Scandal of the Evangelical Mind*; also Spencer, "Between Faith and Criticism," 378–79.

3. Nicholas Wolterstorff's phrase, in Wolterstorff, "Mission of the Christian College," 30.

4. Newbigin, *Foolishness to the Greeks.*

136

can the gospel not be heard as the gospel; neither can the gospel centrally and positively anchor and revive human learning and knowing as it should. But in Christian colleges where epistemological reorientation is accomplished and practiced, the intended-to-transform Word could, as transformatively apprehended, once again model the dynamism central not only to life but to learning.

We must find ways to challenge the default setting regarding knowledge if true knowing is effectively to occur. We must shift our emphases to be more intentional about our practices that ensconce transformation as central to knowing. We must, in our teaching, not see ourselves as passing on information, but rather intentionally, artfully, transformatively replicating ourselves to catalyze transformation in the student and their ongoing knowing for shalom.[5]

THE EPISTEMICALLY UNSUNG TRIUMPH OF THE INTERPERSONAL IN PEDAGOGY

We will see, in later chapters of this work, that what most effectively catalyzes transformation is personal relationship. Knowing is transformative precisely because its dynamic is interpersonal, I will argue. So personal relationship transforms epistemically. Thus it is that, even in institutions where the defective default is well-ensconced, where "content," "data," the scientific method, and all epistemic two-dimensionality are privileged, teachers' personal passion for the subject, noticing regard of the student, and distinctive signature in professional activity, move students memorably. In this teachers nevertheless effectively catalyze transformation and subvert a two-dimensional epistemic paradigm. Similarly, students themselves have a powerful and positive effect on classmates and faculty, to say nothing of their future places of service, if they themselves become *semper transformanda*, as I will aphorize it.[6] But it takes revamping our epistemology so

5. See ch. 16.

6. See ch. 16.

that we can see this, accredit it, and capitalize on it in what we are concerned to achieve in the university and through it in the world.

Abraham Joshua Heschel suggested that unlike the Greeks, who learn in order to comprehend, the Hebrews learn in order to be apprehended.[7] This aphoristic comparison expresses the shift in outlook that colleges and universities, especially Christian ones, need proactively to cultivate both in the faculty and in the classroom. And it is highly suggestive of the possibility that what transforms us, in our knowing, is not a what but a who. This, I am saying, is at least partly the teacher. But it suggests personed features of the yet-to-be-known. Students may be apprenticed to bend their demeanor to that which invites the personlike real.

PEDAGOGY AS HOSPITALITY

Covenant epistemology clearly indicates a distinctive pedagogical practice. It offers positive epistemic warrant for mutual personal involvement, teacher and student and classmates together in formation, skill development and wisdom, and in inviting, pursuit of the yet-to-be-known.

Teachers don't teach information; they teach themselves. As authoritative guides, with humble intentionality they replicate themselves in forming their students. For learning involves tacit indwelling of the embodied clues of the master, subsidiaries that even the master cannot name. One need only think of how little boys mimic the actions of the basketball players or rap artists they aspire to be. Covenant epistemology thus solidly supports a view of the classroom as hospitable space for indwelling a subject together in mutual submission.[8] To do this, teachers hospitably open themselves to be indwelt by their learners.

Another way covenant epistemology supports such hospitality is by offering an account of anticipative knowing—knowing on the way—thus enjoining patience in our half-understanding. Apart from

7. This is my colleague Bob Frazier's paraphrase of Heschel's outlook. Personal conversation.

8. Anyone familiar with Parker Palmer will recognize this as his philosophy of teaching. Palmer, *To Know As We Are Known*, and Palmer, *Courage to Teach*.

this view and this posture of patience in advance of knowing, quite frankly, learning is stunted, warped, or entirely impeded. But good teachers exercise the covenantal patience that looks long down the road to mark anticipative knowing.

But more than enjoining patience, covenant epistemology induces excitement and confidence in the learning process. It puts the adventure back into learning, rekindling the longing to know. For not only does it affirm being on the way to knowing, in subsidiary-focal integration it offers an account of how it works that frees its adherents from the stultifying bondage of information and certainty and instead accredits responsible risk. It administers confidence in the students'—and one's own—eventual insight. And covenant epistemology's joyous realism incites us with hope of unspecifiable future prospects.

Good teachers teach to kindle the fire of ongoing transformation. They look for transformative knowing events from time to time in the hours spent covenantally alongside their students on the journey. They humbly expect all such events to prototype the descent of God, as we will soon see.

CENTERING THEOLOGICAL STUDY FOR PASTORAL SERVICE

Covenant epistemology shows that it is profoundly appropriate to situate study in a setting of worship and relational communion, and to offer its epistemologically therapeutic retooling in the curricular core. This is strategically so for theological study for pastoral service.

While I argue that covenant epistemology helps any human knowing flourish, there is a special aptness to Christian study being intentional about knowing as covenantally interpersonal—and a sorer irony when it is not. Students entering graduate seminary, especially in the Protestant tradition, can be marked deeply by the West's defective default. So can the seminary's curriculum and practice be as well. Epistemological therapy administered upon entry would profoundly reorient what students bring to their learning. And it would reshape theological study itself in a way that brings it back in line with its goal.

In Christian discipleship, where the dichotomous default has silently spread its destruction, passion and faith have been linked to relationship, and theology has been linked to knowledge. People have fallen in love with Christ, and thus felt the pull to training in Christian scholarship and ministry. But that training has been "knowledge," as opposed to passion, worship, and relationship. This is radically abetted by the subtext in all Ph.D. training; thus professors are inadvertently deeply inclined to the default. Where this defective default has persisted, the posture assumed in theological study has been at best the critical scholar, at worst, the criticizing theological information-gatherer and doctrinal impurity police. But if knowing is covenantally interpersonal, most effective when it invites the real, this default-contorted posture inhibits knowing and damages reality. And in Christian scholarship, theology, and ministry—where knowing God involves covenantal response in relationship, entering and living out the biblical story—the defective posture is sharply incongruous. It tacitly tattles of a life and epistemic approach still clueless regarding the radical implications of the redemptive gospel. I think it is fair to say that it fails to keep in step with the Spirit.

Fixation on—as opposed to artfully indwelt attendance from—Scripture, doctrine, theology, and religious information or content, is what yields this incongruity. This is the difference between legalism and obedience, also. And it is the difference between knowledge and wisdom.

But the posture of the servant of Christ, the one loved by him, and transformatively delivered to "sit at his feet, clothed and in his right mind," is the epistemic posture of a great learner and a great saint. Heschel's comment about the Hebrews, mentioned above, displays this posture. This is the most effective learner, especially the Christian disciple and theologian/pastor in training.

Covenant epistemology returns to the theological/pastoral curriculum a profound accord between studies and prior motivating experience of the grace of Christ, on the one hand, and between studies and subsequent vocational, especially ecclesial, service, on the other. All knowing, for those who have been known by Christ, is knowing God. The whole thing is of a piece. What people need, what the church needs, and thus what its training institutions need, is truth lived together, caringly shared and administered in covenant friendship. Especially where what is being studied for is Christian ministry, this dynamic is essential. It is essential because it embodies the Christian gospel, and reflects the Holy Trinity. Apart from it, the best seminary curriculum leaves a vacuum-full disconnect between classroom and future practice of both word and deed. What I am saying is that this healing and integrity must begin by intentionally shifting to embrace a fundamental epistemic reorientation.

POST-ENLIGHTENMENT THEOLOGICAL METHOD

Finally, an allusive comment about the value of covenant epistemology for theological method. This is in addition to its explicating the proper posture of the theologian as one transformed, who walks in the way of the Lord. Post-Enlightenment epistemology has rung changes on the idea that there is more to knowledge than knowledge, more to truth than truth—an exteriority rather than an interiority to truth. Proposals have included history, worldviews, social convention, power, language games and speech acts, hermeneutics, texts, presuppositions, cybernetics, and, actually, a curious insubstantiality (I have in mind here the sort of thing that deconstruction endeavors to root up.) A few have spoken of the personal and the interpersonal, but their voices have not been widely heard. Theological method over this time period, unless it has remained married to knowledge as propositions, certainty building on certainty, has tried all of these on for size. These efforts have been productive, but to the extent that they have left intact the dichotomous default—"certainty or bust"—they have been hampered by mutually contentious misunderstanding.

I would like to lobby for covenant epistemology offering a fruitful theological methodological approach which elucidates the "more" of knowledge and truth as of three mutually implicated sorts: the subsidiary, the covenantal, and the interpersonal.

Polanyian subsidiary knowledge affords a nonfoundational foundation, a curious insubstantiality, a fruitful account of brain activity, along with all embodiment, as lived indwellingly. The sophistication of the subsidiary as it supports the focal makes epistemic sense of historical and geographical place, of languages and tradition, of liturgical practices of formation, of submission to authoritative guides, of how these all concretely shape our knowing, all the while avoiding the commonly held assumption that knowing must be reduced to these.

Further on in *Loving to Know* it will become clear that all that is prescriptive about knowing can be fruitfully developed along the lines of covenant. I argue that reality itself must be normatively worded into existence—the game-making language of "let there be." Language itself is arguably, at its heart, promissory, covenantal. Language games just are the prescriptive rules that shape discourse and bind us together concretely in forms of life. Authoritative guides and the learner's submission to them, interpretive frameworks, worldviews, fundamental belief commitments, are meant to function normatively to unlock the world to us. Human knowledge is such that the normative, the authoritative, is always a constituting component.

All of this and more, I believe, will be most helpfully elucidated and accessed in light of the personal and interpersonal that cores and contexts human knowing. There is more to power, to prescription, to tradition, to embodiment, to promise, and to insubstantiality, than these things indicate. That more is the personal and interpersonal. We will understand them and their role in human knowing better when we embed them in the interpersonal. And to do so, we will see, is to bring all human knowing into encounter with God.

As we proceed to sketch the contours of covenant epistemology, I believe that its power to effect a critical reorientation in Academe will become more obvious. My hope is that many of us who long to see students not merely informed, but transformed to serve the world, may continue the conversation together to flesh the vision out further.

QUESTIONS FOR DISCUSSION

1. Draw on your experience as a student or as a teacher to reflect on this chapter's claims. In what ways do you feel that covenant epistemology offers a helpful approach?

2. How might this approach positively impact teaching and the academy?

3. What hurdles would have to be addressed, and how?

4. What are some concrete changes we can make to re-form students, teachers, and classrooms, in a covenant-epistemological orientation to learning?

PART THREE

Covenant

~~6

KNOWING AS STEWARDSHIP

Conversation with John Frame

S O FAR WE HAVE developed two contours of covenant epistemology. In part 1 we traced a negative contour—namely, the sore need to address a widely held, widely unrecognized, damagingly defective epistemology that covenant epistemology promises to suit directly. Part 2 articulated the subsidiary-focal integrative dynamism, the transformative knowing event, which is the heart of human knowing. You now comprehend this description, I trust. A wonderful single word for it is *insight.*[1]

In this third part, I develop the second strand of covenant epistemology, its covenantal contour. I offer my appropriated notions of knowing as implicitly knowing God, and of the idea of covenant as relationship. The first I derive from the work of theologian and former professor of mine, John Frame, and second from that of theologian and former colleague of mine, Mike Williams. These theologians supply the "covenant" in covenant epistemology, as well as theological parameters and resonances that shape the covenant epistemological vision.

The motif of covenant will make sense of the normative dimension of knowing. On a Meekian construal, we say, Polanyian subsidiaries include the normative as one of three sectors. If we are to make full-orbed and effective sense of knowing, subverting the defective default, we must incorporate an account of it integrally into our epistemology. And this is important enough for me to title my epistemic proposal, covenant epistemology.

I encountered the work of reformed theologian John Frame around the time I was embarking on formal philosophical study, starting to engage Polanyi's thought, and continuing to make responsible sense of my

---

1. This is Bernard Lonergan's term, and book title: *Insight.* As I noted previously, there is considerable overlap between the agenda of his masterful work and of *Loving to Know.*

own Christian belief.[2] Frame's thoroughly developed account of human knowledge of God contributed a fundamental guide and orientation for my understanding, one which, along with Polanyi's work, I have returned to time and again over decades of working things out intellectually.[3]

You may find Frame's ideas challenging. That is true for me as well. One reason I have returned to Frame's work is that each time around I hope to grasp it more deeply. But Polanyian epistemology accredits half-understanding and actually reverences the allusive that may bear indeterminately on reality. That means not only that we have to bear with half-understanding, but also that we may delight in the fruitful discomfort it engenders. Such discomfort can give way to the sense that we are "on to something," as we say.

In this chapter I will show the ways in which Frame's work has marked the long incubation of my vision of covenant epistemology. Although its influence on me, not to mention the profundity of the work itself, exceeds categorization, I distill it into five loci.

First, Frame's work is the particular articulation of the Calvinian biblical theology with which I came to be most familiar, and which I took to be a credible formalization of the fundamental claims, about God and humanity, of the Christian Scriptures—the one I have striven to navigate by personally. Since in my development of covenant epistemology I want to offer a vision that makes sense of knowing while at the same time being biblically consonant (and thus that much more on target generally), this is a key parameter.

Second, Frame has been a student of philosophy as well as doing theology. I found in his work a philosophical awareness of the sort that is critical to responsible theological work. But I also found his work to be a late-twentieth-century version of the longstanding challenge and corrective that Calvinism brings to philosophical modernism. Modernism is a still-vibrant popular philosophical outlook that is replete with the dichotomies of our daisy and their fallout. Frame's work directly addresses the twentieth-century version of modernism: a most arid objectivism.

2. The adjective, "reformed," or "reformational," is generally taken to refer to the particular branch of Protestant theology, thought, and culture shaped by the tradition of John Calvin.

3. Recently Dr. Frame has retired from teaching. This chapter shares some overlap with Meek, "Servant Thinking," my contribution to a newly released festschrift in honor of his thought and life, Hughes, ed., Speaking the Truth in Love.

Calvinist thought has long offered a powerful critique of modernism, well in advance of what has been popularly identified as the postmodern critique, and one with more positive and therapeutic content than some postmodern proposals. But Frame's work and my exposure to it transpired at a time that rendered it, for me, a promise of hope and wholeness in a desert of analytic philosophical practices and commitments. Not that I "got it," entirely, then. Covenant epistemology, I believe, a full three decades later, is that wholeness come to fruition—and not in an exhaustive elucidation, but in a vision.

Third: I felt from the outset that Polanyi's account of human knowing showed me how Frame's "servant thinking" actually works and what it looks like. What Frame supplies to Polanyi's work is an enhanced insight into the nature of the interpersonal in knowing. The resonant interface between the two confirms a fundamental accord of Polanyi's work with the Christian Scripture's claims about God, the world, and humanity in the world. Also, the works of the two thinkers share a fundamental commitment to the need to challenge the objectivism of western philosophy, and to the role of the personal and of the normative in all human knowing. Melding Frame and Polanyi helped me, additionally, to begin to make sense of what I call anticipative knowing. This idea is reflected in my talking about "being on the way" to knowing.

Fourth: the specific feature of Frame's thought to which I continually return is his triad of the situational, the existential, and the normative. We have already seen it surface in chapter 3's account of the loci of subsidiary clues which integratively support a focal pattern: the surface features of the world, the lived body, and the directions, or word of authoritative guides. In this chapter I will offer a brief description and analysis of that Framean triad. I argue that the triad widely pertains in human action in the world, because it is rooted integrally in the interpersonal. I will also suggest that the triad connects integrally with the larger interpersonal overtones that the covenant epistemology project seeks to showcase and tap.

Finally, all that I come to say, in a full-orbed development of covenant epistemology, of interpersonal, face-to-face communion, is prefigured in Frame. I mean, it was prefigured for *me*, and for my covenant epistemology: knowing as communion is briefly stated but fully explicit in Frame's thought, as we will see. The blend of Frame and Polanyi in *Longing to Know* was an earlier prototype of covenant epistemology, one that was pregnant with what now comes to full expression in *Loving to Know*.

This chapter will develop these loci, on the way to fleshing out covenant epistemology. While this is an engagement of a theologian's work, what I take away from it elucidates human knowing for all humans, believers and unbelievers. I believe that these Christian dimensions actually accord with and thus enhance everybody's knowing of everything, not just believers' knowing of God.

ADMITTING THEOLOGICAL THEMES TO THE TABLE?

Often the riches of biblical and theological themes and motifs remain locked within parochial (in the good sense) ecclesial enterprises (churches and seminaries) and within the topical confines of religion. Often people outside those structures, rejecting the structures, preclude the possibility of profiting from concepts originating from within them. On the other side, often religious people do not know how to identify and mine the epistemological riches of their own commitments.

I want to subvert all of these tendencies. I borrow the motif of *covenant* because I find it well-suited for elucidating a full-orbed vision of human knowing. Also, I think it is responsible to develop an account of knowing that does not presumptively preclude knowing God. Admittedly, the obvious implication of taking God into account is that, by very nature of being God, he impacts human knowing. I cannot hide the fact that openness to an ultimate Person shapes, as it should if he is God, and permeates the covenant epistemology vision. However, what I contend is that taking this ultimate personal context into account in epistemology makes radical and healing sense of how we actually go about knowing when we are knowing well, whether we know him explicitly or not.[4]

Thus, I engage these theological proposals philosophically because I believe doing so contributes integrally to a responsible epistemic vision such as I am attempting in this book. The reader's profitable engage-

---

4. I have always loved that throwaway comment of J. R. R. Tolkein in *The Hobbit*, made when the dwarves and Bilbo are debating entering the Mountain: "It does not do to leave a live dragon out of your calculations, if you live near him" (Tolkein, *The Hobbit*, 217). This is a playfully understated reminder much needed by all of us whenever we forget God!

ment of the matter, however, does not in itself require her or him to be a Christian believer.

Beginning in the 1980s, philosophers Alvin Plantinga and Nicholas Wolterstorff spearheaded what came to be known as reformed episte-mology.[5] It was actually a theology-inspired philosophical proposal, yet it was one which could be, and has been, widely engaged and applied. Their effort also raised awareness widely that such an approach can be rationally and helpfully taken. It does not require participants to embrace Christianity in order to understand and reap the benefits of its epistemic implications. And this claim is one which itself is supported by Christian theology, something, we will see, that Frame's approach implies.

The interface between philosophy and Christian theology has been a hot topic ever since there was Christian theology. The church fathers wrestled with it. Tertullian's rhetorical "What has Athens to do with Jerusalem?" has been taken to represent the rationale of Christians who eschew philosophical engagement (as if it were possible to avoid it). Others, most notably St. Augustine and St. Thomas Aquinas, are as re-spected today as philosophers as they are as theologians. Doing the one to do the other was natural and necessary. But even the most preliminary question of how to define theology and philosophy, and specify their relation to each other, is perennially problematic.

Sad to say, there are some Christian seminaries and colleges which fail to appreciate the critical importance of philosophical awareness to the theological enterprise, or the defectiveness of their own under-standing of scholarship if they think otherwise. Expert theology, like expert anything—science, education, art, history, business, psycholo-gy—requires a philosophical stance developed responsibly. At the other extreme, some Christians have argued for "a Christian philosophy."[6] I myself cannot bring myself to countenance the idea. I do not see my own

---

5. Plantinga and Wolterstorff, eds. *Faith and Rationality*. This book of essays opened the philosophical research program known as reformed epistemology. The theological notion which spurred the development of reformed epistemology is closely related to matters I consider in this chapter: it is the belief that humans, believers and unbelievers alike, are intimately acquainted with God. Calvin's sense of deity, *sensus divinitatis*, is a kind of inward acquaintance knowledge, such that apart from proof, belief in God must nevertheless be rational. (See earlier, ch. 3, n.16.) I have elsewhere utilized the *sensus* as a touchpoint for Polanyi's proposals: Meek, "A Polanyian Interpretation."

6. See, for example, the work of Herman Dooyeweerd and his followers. See earlier, ch. 3, n.14.

work as such, preferring rather to talk of it as philosophical proposals that accord with Scripture. What is to be feared and avoided, I believe, is a kind of Christian baptizing of a single set of philosophical proposals. On the one side, this appears to be a violation of the biblical injunction not to add to Scripture, a kind of idolatry; on the other side, it seems an arbitrary termination of philosophical inquiry. It isn't healthy, and it isn't necessary.

But Frame's thought offers a most appropriate philosophical engagement of the distinctive claims of the Christian Scriptures. Frame takes philosophy seriously, and he takes Christian theology seriously. He hears the philosophical implications of Scripture's claims, and he hears the theological implications of philosophical claims.[7] This is a responsible and gracious interface, one I aspire to in my own thinking. I think that the grace of it also has to do with his triadic approach to knowing, as we shall see: it means that one may draw from insights outside of Scripture to unpack Scripture, and vice versa. Also, if all knowing is knowing God, as he will say, then the interface between epistemology and theology is more than just a casual diversion.

John Frame strives to identify the implications for human knowing that the biblically central conviction that God is Lord naturally indicates. He is primarily concerned with human knowledge of God,[8] but that will prove to be integrally related to all human knowing. Given the specific nature of what he is saying, although Frame's agenda is to offer an account of human knowledge of God, that account is also one of human knowledge in general. He also has, in the process, identified some key features of knowing that the western philosophical tradition, down through its expression in the Enlightenment's model of knowledge, have persistently discredited and overlooked, to its own jeopardy. These insights I embed and develop in covenant epistemology.

---

7. Throughout Frame's work his profitable engagement, in particular, with the work of the later Wittgenstein is evident.

8. I am not conversant with the whole corpus of Frame's theological work. But I feel that the part of it that I engage, his doctrine of the knowledge of God, is so profound that I have explored and reexplored it, and can keep re-exploring it for a lifetime. Also, my presentation in this chapter bears the stamp of the joint reflection of me and my former colleague, theologian Mike Williams, the conversant of the next chapter. Mike and I taught and talked over Frame's work. We agreed that we felt that it, as over against the developments of Plantinga and Wolterstorff (not meaning to minimize their contribution), deserved the title, reformed epistemology.

THE CREATOR-CREATURE DISTINCTION

I want to preface my engagement of Frame with a brief exposition and analysis of the most fundamental claims of a biblical (in the Calvinian tradition) view of God and reality. This sets a shaping backdrop both for *Loving to Know* in general, but also for Frame's distinctive contributions. Frame has worked in the tradition of his teacher, reformational theologian and apologist Cornelius Van Til, moving beyond Van Til to offer a more accessible as well as more sophisticated account. By beginning briefly where Van Til begins, we may more fully understand Frame.

A Christian tenet of foremost importance philosophically is what is known as the Creator-creature distinction.[9] "In the beginning, God created the heavens and the earth," is the opening pronouncement of the Bible. Whatever may or may not be implied concerning *how* this came about, *philosophically* the Creator-creature distinction is both evident and predominant. Scripture affirms at the outset that reality comes in two sorts: God, who is ontologically (meaning, as far as being or reality is concerned) independent, and creation, which is ontologically dependent on God.

God, according to Scripture, is the infinite Person.[10] Speaking philosophically, not in the language of Scripture, he is *sui generis* (one-of-a-kind) and self-contained—meaning that he needs no point of reference beyond himself. Scripture indicates also that he is triune—God in three persons. For Van Til, the doctrine of the Trinity is what makes it that God is self-contained: no discrediting external reference is necessary. Thus, it is because God is triune that the Creator-creature distinction is

9. Van Til's book, *Defense of the Faith*, was a primary text in Frame's course. See also Frame's *Cornelius Van Til*. Van Til's fundamental claims, the couple most central that I briefly describe here, are evident throughout his work.

10. I do not in this work intend to entertain debates on this claim, nor on the unity and authority of Scripture, nor the legitimacy of the doctrine of the Trinity, nor the Apostles' Creed as the historic expression of Christianity. I well understand that many scholars are predisposed to find this an offensive oversight. I do not at all mean it either as offensive or as an oversight. I do not engage it, because others, far better qualified than I, have done so expertly and extensively. See for example, the work of John Frame and Cornelius Van Til, themselves theologians and philosophers. See also, for example, Herman Ridderbos' helpful little book, *Redemptive History*. For additional insight on this debate, see Newbigin, *Proper Confidence*, esp. ch. 6. Newbigin makes it evident that the entire debate itself rests on epistemological assumptions of the very sort that Polanyi and covenant epistemology mean to call into question. This offers positive philosophical warrant for my decision, in *Loving to Know*, to leave the debate for others.

possible. Or we may say it the other way round: the only way the Creator-creature distinction is possible is if God is triune. God as three-in-one also uniquely solves the philosophical problem of the one and the many (unity and plurality thereby being coeternal, equally ultimate), without which, Van Til reasoned, no human knowledge is even possible.[11]

Let's consider this. The Creator-creature distinction means that all reality is either God or his creation. Human thought needs to take this distinction seriously, not just in connection with redemption, but in every corner of life. No dimension of creation should ever be confused with, fused with, or exalted as God. This claim has both metaphysical (about reality) and epistemological implications. Metaphysically, it rules out pantheism or animism. It also rules out conceiving of God as impersonal. It means that we have to take seriously and explore what it is for our reality to exist as dependent. It means that every molecule of creation, in its very existing, is God's revelation—it is his speech, and it speaks of him. This is what is meant by *general*, or *natural, revelation*.

I think we also have to take seriously the nature of God's creative act. I am not referring to the question of origins in the scientific sense. That is a question of *how*; this is the separate, prior, philosophical, question of *what*. I believe that the question of the world's evolving, and the conviction that God spoke it into existence, are logically separate. Neither necessarily implies or rules out the other. Whatever the mechanism of its transpiring at the outset and moment by moment, God prescribes it covenantally. In fact, I think the latter, philosophical, claim is more obvious than any particular claim about the mechanism of it.[12]

I contend that we may say that the act of creation, as God's "Let there be"s, indicates that he constitutes creation by normative, covenantal, prescription. "Let there be" is prescriptive language—what I have used the many times that I have invented a new party game or a new philosophy course. It is not description; rather, it norms or interprets something into existence. On the assumption of creation as ontologically dependent, every moment of its existence constitutes God's ongoing "let there be"-ing. This is what Scripture identifies as God's covenant

11. The fact that it is possible conversely implies the existence of the Trinity, according to Van Til.

12. This perception bears affinity to Aquinas' Third Way, the argument for God's existence from the existence of possible or contingent being: for it to exist, something must exist which is not contingent but necessary.

faithfulness, or "steadfast love."[13] Everything that we call created reality exists and is what it is because of the normative and formative word of God prescribing it into existence and sustaining that existence in his steadfast covenant relationship. Everything exists by virtue of a covenant relationship to the Lord of all.

So whatever may be the case about the how of creation, the creative act requires the worded, "let there be." Created entities have distinctive characters, "ways they are supposed to be." A thing's character is what is definitive about it, that which is maintained as long as it is itself, that in virtue of which various specimens of the thing may be gauged as excellent or subpar. All this seems *normative* to me. By *normative*, I mean, involving a rule, standard, or pattern. Rules prescribe things into existence—again, like a game, which is constituted by the rules. For creation to be comprised of real things, it seems evident to me that they were worded, interpreted, prescriptively, covenantally, into existence. I think that their normative, covenanted, aspect implies an infinite Person covenanting. This metaphysical insight bears on our account of human knowing.

Likewise, in our epistemology, our account of how humans know, we should take the Creator-creature distinction seriously. This leads Frame to talk about and try to explicate what he calls "servant thinking," or creaturely knowing, which we turn to explore here.

GOD AS COVENANT LORD

Reformed theologians, especially with the help of recent scholarship concerning covenants in the ancient Near East, have made the case that the language of Scripture, from creation onward, is covenant language.[14] We will engage Williams' expression of this in the next chapter. However, Frame's work also employs the notion of covenant centrally and from the outset. Frame's expression of the central Van Tillian insight, the Creator-

---

13. Scripture references for God's covenant love, or lovingkindness, in the abridged concordance at the back of the NIV Study Bible span six columns. Well-known psalms such as Pss 23 and 100 both employ the phrase.

14. Fresh impetus for this project, as I understand, came from the work of Meredith Kline, in the twentieth century. To name just one of his works: Klein, *By Oath Consigned*.

creature distinction, therefore, is as follows: The most important fact about reality is that God is the Covenant Lord, the Covenant head.[15]

Frame begins his account of "the knowledge of God" with the obvious but profound claim that to know God is to know him as Lord. If God is Lord, then he is only known as such. Lordship is a covenantal concept. The Creator-creature distinction is thus, from the outset in Frame's work, cast more appropriately as a relationship. The fact of the distinction has to do with transcendence, but there is more to that transcendence than the mere distinction. The fact of the relationship concerns immanence. Covenant expresses the person-like way in which God the Lord is both transcendent and immanent. Covenant shows how these two apparent opposites coexist in a personal relationship, namely, one that is like the relationship of a parent with her or his child. God the Lord, as Lord, has authority and control. Frame avers that these characteristics reflect God's transcendence. But also as Lord, he is intimately present with his creation in what Frame calls covenant solidarity. Covenant thus expresses the character of the sort of relationship that displays how transcendence and immanence tie together integrally only in a worldview in which God, the ultimate Person, is Lord.[16]

I think that the fact that Frame begins his extended formal development of the knowledge of God, which will include his triad, with this notion of God as covenant Lord, is stunning. The notion is, of course, centrally biblical, in a way that much philosophical theological language, even Van Til's Creator-creature distinction, is not. It captures the heart of Christian discipleship—relationship with God the Lord—and locates it centrally. And since this is about knowledge of God as Lord, it is going to have obvious implications for all knowing. Thus it points in the direction of covenant epistemology. The heart of it all is knowing God as Lord, knowing the covenant Lord, being in covenant with the Lord of all. Frame says, memorably, that the goal of knowing God is *friendship*.

God the covenant Lord, as such, is the partner in the covenant that definitively shapes the covenant. He is the initiator, creation, as creation, is response. God's creative act, as well as created reality's existing, and

15. Frame, *Doctrine of the Knowledge of God*. I work primarily from the first hundred pages or so of this text.

16. Frame argues that apart from a context of God as Lord, conceptions of transcendence and immanence are irrational, and throughout philosophy they have proven to self-destruct. Ibid., 13ff.

human action and knowing, all have about them the structure of pledge or promise—the one initiates, the other responds. Everything created is, in its very existence, covenant response.

All human action and knowing is covenant response. It is a signature feature of Calvinian theology to see that the relationship of creature to Creator is intimate, unmediated. Covenant intimacy and solidarity with his creation is God's immanent Lordship as presence. Creaturely covenantal response takes the form simply expressed in the old hymn: trust, and obedience. Intimacy characterizes his people's relationship with God. The response of unbelievers to God, it can commonly be observed, displays the anger that only comes in the context of intimate relationship gone awry. Sin is Scripture's word for covenant rebellion.[17] The point here is that Frame follows in the Calvinian tradition of saying all people in some sense know God intimately.

All of life is about knowing God as Lord. On this approach, this is literally true! For everything that exists, from least to greatest, exists by virtue of being covenantally known, and thus constituted as real, by God. That is what the covenantal Lordship of God entails. All that is known into existence by him is thereby dependent on him, existing for his praise, before his gaze, in interpersonal relationship with one who both transcends (in authority and power) and is near (in intimate solidarity)—as the best sort of father-child relationship, the best sort of king-subject relationship.

Created reality just is this covenant relationship with the Lord. Creation knows God as Lord, or it doesn't exist. Human knowing, on any reckoning of what knowing is, but even as covenant response, is reasonably only part of that reality-encompassing relationship. Submissive action (obedience) is obviously part of it, and so is interpersonal communion. In fact, what starts to appear is a triad of aspects that together constitute a dynamic interpersonal covenantal relationship. I think that the Framean triad, which we are about to consider, has as its powerful, life-giving root the fact that it is the signature, "interaspectivally" allusive, multi-dimensionality of interpersonal relationship. The triad recurs

---

17. It is important to be clear that the reality of human sin has not abrogated the covenant. Scripture indicates that even after human rebellion, God maintains covenantal relationship, and calls humans to do the same (Genesis 9). This resoundingly demonstrates both his initiative and his covenant love. It also means that we can continue to view our lives as covenantal response, and offer a covenantal account of knowing.

in reality because reality is shot through with the interpersonhood of covenant relationship.

SERVANT THINKING

There is a related Calvinian conviction that is important to my out-look—one that Frame espouses, but that he does not directly address at this point in his exposition. Humans occupy within creation a two-way representative role. Humans represent God within creation, and also represent creation before God. Humans are created, and thus of a piece with the rest of creation; but they also image God—meaning, they represent him, carrying out his mission in creation. Scripture indicates that humans have this representative role as their definitive character and mission.[18] Humans are called to steward the earth, caring for it and developing it, as God's representatives. Theologians call this the cultural mandate. Humans reflect God by carrying out, in a derivative way, car-ing, normative verbal creation and preservation.[19] Humans are stewards in God's house of creation.

Human knowing, on this scheme, is humans fulfilling the cultural mandate so as derivatively to preserve and develop God's world. Human knowing is stewardly, covenant response. While Frame wants to argue that a responsible account of human knowing should be called "servant thinking," in view of creation's covenantally constituting relationship with God the Lord, the representative role Scripture accords to humans warrants our further specifying knowing as itself stewardship—hence my title for this chapter.

Humans come to the epistemic enterprise in a manner fundamen-tally distinct from whatever God does that may be called divine know-ing. It is not appropriate to say that God *has* the truth, but rather, that he *is* the truth. God designates truth, we might say—think what we have already noted about his creative activity. Humans know, by contrast,

18. The classic text here, widely referred to as the cultural mandate, is Gen 1:26–27.

19. Meek, "Learning to See." Not only does Scripture designate humans as stewards, I argue that humans are hard-wired to be this. A human can never blend in, in a forest, the way a fox can. Humans can't leave the forest untouched, even if they decide to pre-serve it. A human can save endangered species of flora and fauna. The flora and fauna can't return the favor. Yes, humans can and do desecrate the nonhuman world; but they also are the ones to bless it. Often in talks on this subject I have shown clips from the Disney film, *Lion King*: the bad king scars the earth, the good king restores it. But this is just what Scripture indicates.

somehow derivatively. But also, the larger dynamic of servant thinking is not "getting it right," but being in communion with the Lord. This is truth in the sense of covenant faithfulness, or troth. What else would one do with someone who is Lord?

We have to find a way to envision human knowing that observes the biblically expressed parameters of human knowing consonant with God's covenant Lordship. One thing that this entails is that the human knower may not be cast as the ultimate arbiter or criterion or supreme anchor in the epistemic endeavor. In our epistemology we may not absolutize anything about human knowing—not our knowledge of the Absolute Lord (our theology), nor a certain set of propositions (again as in our theology, our confessioned interpretation of Scripture), nor a certain foundation (as in foundationalism), nor the individual disembodied self as arbiter of truth (as in Cartesian modernism), nor the antirealist private interpretation as truth (as in hypermodern subjectivism)—I could go on, but you get the drift, I feel sure.[20]

But the fact that we may not absolutize anything about human knowing does not land us in skepticism, subjectivism, or relativism. To think that it might results from allowing to stand uncontested the damaging daisy of dichotomies we articulated in chapter 1. The proper alternative is to take seriously human knowing as the covenant response of the covenant servant, as the creaturely stewardship of God's creation. It is appropriate to see all knowledge as profession or confession, something that integrally requires a stance of belief. But in this, knowledge of God is no different from knowledge of anything, except, perhaps, that it

20. Well-intended Christians often strive to defend "Absolute Truth." The word, *absolute*, is neither an adjective that Scripture employs about human knowledge, nor a concept deemed particularly useful in philosophy—see the entry in Blackburn's *Oxford Dictionary of Philosophy*. Historically it has been associated with the philosophy of Hegel, where it designated an ultimate reality that merged God and the world in a manner inconsistent with the Creator-creature distinction. In the postmodern milieu, it has been warrantably associated with the repressive totalizing sleight-of-hand of the Enlightenment project's rationalistic objectivism. The implied (and false) presumption to a universal knowledge that has no presuppositional commitments, in addition to being confirmed by history to be deadly, is shabby scholarship that masks the truth—not to mention just the sort of thing that has inappropriately marginalized and discredited Christianity. See Lyotard, *Postmodern Condition*. See also Smith, "A Little Story About Metanarratives." But it should also be apparent that covenant epistemology, in administering epistemological therapy, will be challenging the very dichotomy that underlies the concern, and superseding it with something even more objectively real, as persons in relation are objectively real.

voices the profession rather than the more concrete applications of that profession.

So then, how are we to construe an epistemology that constitutes servant thinking? That is what Frame is attempting in his laborious development of a tri-perspectival account of the knowledge of God. I believe that Frame's account gives us, not the parameters of human knowing in the sense of restrictions, but the core dynamic of human knowing that effectively challenges our damaged epistemic default and restores us as humans and knowers to wholeness.

FRAME'S TRIAD

One of Frame's distinctive contributions is his move, as we saw, to unpack the notion of God as covenant head or Lord, and then to explore Lordship. Frame claims that God's Lordship consists of his control, his authority, and his presence. God has authority: he has the right to be Lord. God controls all things, and so is Lord. And God is everywhere present, and thus is Lord. To know God the covenant Lord, then, is to know his authority (expressed in his law), his control (in his works, i.e., the world), and his presence (in ourselves as knowers).

Frame diagrams these aspects using a triangle. The angle related to authority he terms the normative; the one related to control, the situational; the one related to presence, the existential. I follow him in this; although I have realized after some years that mine is a left-handed triangle! The triangle sits on one of its sides. The left base angle I label the existential, the right, the situational. The top angle is the normative. Since I have often thought of subsidiary-focal integration as a vector, I suggest the alignment of Polanyi and Frame by adding a vector that begins at the existential angle and arcs to bisect the line between the situational and the normative.

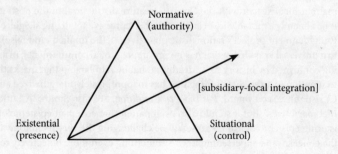

The triad of these three expressions of Lordship evocatively aligns with other triads. It aligns with other common ones in Scripture—prophet, priest, and king. A prophetic role is about authority; a priestly one is about presence; a kingly one is about control. God the Lord is all three. There is also an obvious correspondence between these and the three Persons of the Trinity: the Father, authority (the Father gives the Law); the Son, control (his incarnation brings him into the world, among us); the Holy Spirit, presence (his ministry is God within us). God's ongoing creative act involves him in all three ways: he words interpretively the world into existence, he thus controls all of it, and he is present with it in sustaining it. Humans as image bearers live out all three similarly but derivatively. That means that all human cultural productions and products involve the three. The study of ethics, for example, involves an account of goal, motive, and standard of human action.[21] The study of epistemology involves an account of criteria and justification (normative), objects of knowledge (situational), and act, experience, methods, conviction, and virtues (existential) of knowing. Ethic and epistemology are two of the three, triadic, branches of philosophy, the third being metaphysics. You can see that this triangle is both evocative and complex.

The threefold nature of God's Lordship leads Frame to identify the normative, the situational, and the existential. Frame calls these perspectives and talks of his approach as perspectivalism. A perspective is not a part, but the whole seen from a certain perspective. They are interrelated, coextensive, foci or aspects. In the spirit of Wittgenstein's, "all seeing is seeing-as," which Frame has taken to heart, each one is a seeing-as.[22] You can see all of whatever it is you are considering from the perspective of, say, the normative. In his book, *The Doctrine of the Knowledge of God*, the triad furnishes its author a systematic outline for developing the objects, justification, and methods of knowledge of God.

What this means for epistemology is that knowing as servant thinking always involves all three dimensions. Every epistemic act has all three. The dimensions are distinguishable but never separable. Every epistemic act involves a knower. Frame's designating it *existential*, to my Polanyian-formed ears, signifies that that knower must be viewed, not as an arbitrary point of subjectivity, but as a lived, embodied, situated being. Adding a Polanyian gloss, the existential can be viewed as subsidiar-

21. See Jones, *Biblical Christian Ethics*.
22. Frame, *Doctrine of the Knowledge of God*, 156–58.

ily felt. Every act of knowing vectors, from subsidiary to focal, toward the world. And the world is not an opaque object so much as the world in which I find myself. Every act of knowing involves the normative word. Everything from authoritative guides to textbooks to my own naming of things functions normatively as well as descriptively.

Not only does knowing have three dimensions; it is itself one of three dimensions. The other two are being and doing—the real, and the good and right. Frame's innovative triad suggests that these may be seen as the same thing from different perspectives, that they meld, even as they must be distinguished. One thing that this means is that you cannot do epistemology without also doing ontology and ethics. Yet you may never reduce the one to the other.

Frame's triad roundly challenges the approach to knowing that the defective default shapes. It challenges a vision of knowledge as passive reception of indifferent information. It indicates that there is more to knowing than knower and known. That more-than is the normative. All knowing has a normative dimension. The default has opposed fact to value; the triad says that fact requires value. It opposes fact to interpretation; the triad says that fact requires interpretation. Frame's theology of Lordship indicates that interpretation is what we humans were made to do as part of our situated engaging of the world.

Frame proposes this approach, I feel confident, because it is superior to any attempt to make the one perspective prior to the other or to induce a truncated, sequential linearity. It is his innovative way of staying clear of misplaced absolutism in an epistemology of creaturely knowers. And it is his way to take seriously, again with a view to our creatureliness, the undeniable (but not therefore to be viewed as defective) role of interpretation, embodiment, situatedness in time and space and community, in human knowing, even in knowing God.[23] I believe that it is his direct attempt to challenge the defective epistemological default mode of western culture, and to offer epistemological therapy.

Frame identifies three "correlativities" in knowing, which together suggest this triadic approach. The first is that, since God is covenant Lord, there is no place, no thing, in the universe that you can know without also knowing God. *Knowing the world is correlative with knowing God.* To

---

23. This courageous act of Frame's part was, I believe, misunderstood and ill-received by some Christians who, in the absence of philosophical awareness, have felt him to be surrendering "absolute" truth. Their concern evidences a defective default.

know the one is in some way to know the other. This is to take seriously that created reality reveals God. Frame calls it "generic Calvinism" to affirm that the world reveals God as authoritatively as Scripture does.

The second has to do with the intrinsically prophetic or interpretive dimension of all knowing, divine (primordially) or human (derivatively). *Knowing the world is correlative with knowing the self, as well as with knowing a standard.* All knowing of the world, Frame says, in some way is knowing the self. And it is also knowing in reference to a standard. In fact, Frame says of all knowledge that it involves a subject who knows an object according to some standard or criterion (law).[24] Knowledge is an ethically responsible orientation of the person to his experience.[25] So knowing, by definition, involves the three aspects.

Following in the reformed and Van Tillian tradition, Frame stated repeatedly, there are no "brute facts." If you are going to talk of "what God knows," and of what "the truth" is, what it is is God's preinterpreted "facts." Anything that exists does so because God "let there be"'d it into reality, as I have expressed it. All human truth claims are also interpreted. In fact, it is precisely as interpretations that they unlock and access the world, even as they develop it. All truth claims reflect the fundamental interpretive stances, the presuppositions, the heart orientations of their proponents. This is not a situation that knowledge must be cleansed of to be legitimate. It is, however, what makes knowledge a normative enterprise. To align the self with the world is the interpretive enterprise. This means that knowing is intrinsically covenantal.

That all knowing is covenantal addresses the "problem of interpretation." It challenges the data-interpretation dichotomy entrenched along with others in our default western approach to knowing. The problem of interpretation was "resolved," in modernism, by eschewing interpretation; and in the postmodern era by eschewing data. The fact that God created covenantally means that he "interpreted" to create. Humans, as servant thinkers, interpret to know and create as well. Thus, there is no "brute" data, on the one hand; on the other, precisely because of this, we know and have a world to know. Yes, interpretation can be done poorly, and that's a bad thing. But what is good is not, *no* interpretation, but *good* interpretation. This matches beautifully what Scripture says about

24. Frame, *Doctrine of the Knowledge of God*, 107.

25. Ibid., 149. I note here a fundamental alignment between Frame's understanding of knowing and Polanyi's.

humans in the world. We are called to bless the world. It may turn out that we curse the world instead. But we must do one or the other.

From the Protestant Reformer John Calvin comes the third, and in many ways exemplary, correlativity: *knowing God is correlative to knowing oneself.* Calvin opened his famous *Institutes of the Christian Religion* by saying this.[26] It makes no difference where you start, nor where he would start his *Institutes*: to pursue the one is to find the other. Thus, Frame says, to know oneself is, in some sense, to know God, and vice versa.

These three correlativities in human knowing thus suggest Frame's perspectival triad. All knowing is knowing God's word or law, knowing self, and knowing world.[27] All knowing has three correlative aspects or perspectives: the existential, the normative, and the situational.[28] He talks of these avenues of knowing as being "perspectivally related."[29] Each is the same "content," seen from a different perspective. He even says they are identical.[30] Frame wants to hold the perspectives together even as he distinguishes between them. They are not so identical that it isn't critically important to see that no one of them reduces to another. If knowing is through and through normative, it is also through and through about the world, and through and through about me. He is explicit: it doesn't matter where you "start" on the triad. He maintains that the perspectives are equally ultimate, equally important, and equally mutually dependent: each needs the other two to be what it itself is.[31] This is what

26. Calvin, *Institutes*, I, 1, 1, *et passim*.

27. Knowing God's law need not be the only way to construe the normative with respect to knowing God. It may be, and has been so widely in the Christian church throughout the ages and the world, knowing the definitive story. Old Testament saints' profession of faith was to tell a story: it began, "My father was a wandering Aramean . . ." (Deut 26:5–10). New Testament saints do the same; see, for example, Stephen's last words at his martyrdom (Acts 6). Saints in the Christian church through the centuries have not only borne witness to the story, but are formed in the story in Christian liturgy. In all these ways it is evident that the narrative or story of God's unfolding covenant relationship with his people, which is Scripture, is functioning normatively. Williams, we will see, emphasizes story in a way that Frame, writing earlier and thus reflecting a more static and substantival approach to theology and to Scripture, did not. For all that, the dynamism latent in Frame's tri-perspectival approach is breathtaking and fresh.

28. Aspect vs. perspective. See Meek, "Servant Thinking."

29. Frame, *Doctrine of the Knowledge of God*, 89.

30. Ibid., 71.

31. Ibid., 163.

it looks like to take seriously that God, the covenant Lord, is Creator, and we and the world are his creation.

To say that all knowing is servant thinking is, I believe, also to say that it is situated: historically, geographically, culturally, bodily. While Frame did not voice this specifically, I feel confident that his innovative perspectivalism anticipates what is a more current understanding of the implications of the biblical doctrine of creation. The situatedness of human knowing is not a flaw or shortcoming, it is what it is to be human. We are by nature rooted in world, (derivatively) interpreting it and unfolding it as we go.

Knowing for humans involves starting from my embodied, historied, situated, divinely accompanied, person, with knee bowed before my heavenly Father—that is, a submissive, heart commitment. This is what John Frame means by a *presupposition*.

He helpfully contrasts it to epistemic foundationalism—the still-popular idea that, for there to be knowledge, there must be a foundation of certain truths; and to epistemic conventionalism—the still-popular alternative idea that a presupposition or worldview is a postulate that we arbitrarily adopt.[32]

The implications of this shed light on Scripture, on what we understand theology to be, and on Christian practice. Frame is compelling a more modest and epistemologically sophisticated understanding of what theologians, and Christians in general, are doing when they work with Scripture and see themselves as knowing God. This parallels a more modest and nuanced understanding of what humans do when they know: they are servant thinkers.

Frame's insight that human knowing is triadic is innovative not just within Christian thought, but also, I believe, in philosophy. It offers a level of sensible sophistication, much as Polanyi's proposals do, to the effort to understand the complexities of human knowing, as well as to move us beyond the absolute truth vs. no truth debates often known as modernism vs. postmodernism.

Yet some of Frame's proposals can sound impossibly grand and irreconcilable—to say, for example, that all knowing is knowing God, or that all knowing is knowing oneself. As I will show, it was the later discovery of Polanyi's work that aided me in trying to make ordinary sense of this. But it also must be said that the approach germinates complexity.

32. Ibid., 68, 128, 125.

Any attempt at a linear, verbal, presentation, either falls short or goes on endlessly, or both. It is better to see one's apprehension of it as getting a lived feel of the thing—itself a Polanyian insight. Every perspective, for example, always involves the others. That means that you can always attend *to* one perspective *from* another, or to one aspect of another. It helps to hear in this the language of subsidiary and focal.

WEAVING FRAME'S INSIGHTS
INTO COVENANT EPISTEMOLOGY

Melding Frame and Polanyi

From the outset, when I was first encountering Polanyi's work soon after my first exposure to Frame, I sensed that Polanyi helped make sense of what Frame was trying to say. Here I note several aspects of this helpful interface, which now also shape my covenant epistemology.

Knowing is Personal and Normative

First, both thinkers situate human knowing in the personal, though neither of them particularly develops or explores that insight. But the thought of both is ripe with an open-endedness, a richness, and plenty of telling signposts, that invoke the personal context. I believe that covenant epistemology now articulates the personal implicit in both Frame and Polanyi. I have to say, though, that it is only in recent years that I have explicitly identified the personal in both, as will be made evident in Part 3. But early on, no doubt, it factored in to my unnameable sense of the resonance of these two approaches—which leads me to the next aspects.

Frame shares Polanyi's conviction that the normative plays a critical role in human knowing. I have always found the presence of the normative dimension in the Framean triad to be an especially significant feature. Frame said, memorably, that epistemology is a subset of ethics.[33] At the time that I first heard him say it, in the heyday of mid-twentieth-century analytic philosophy—a time fraught with the assumptions of our daisy—the claim was astounding. It made sense theologically, but his saying it made me begin a search to make sense of it philosophically.

At the time, I thought that *truth*—by which, in those days, I meant, all the propositions about reality—was the ultimate thing to seek, the

33. Ibid., 62–64, 108.

ultimate "box" in which we find ourselves. Frame subsumed truth under *oughtness*. This meant to me that there was a logically larger box in which truth is embedded. Over time I came to believe that where there is oughtness, there is covenant—so *covenant* is a yet larger "box" in which we find ourselves. But now I have come to realize that where there is covenant, there are persons in communion. *Persons in communion* is, indeed, the largest "box." This accords profoundly with Scripture. The integral connection between the normative, the covenantal, and interpersonal communion, while it is there in short form in Frame, has only come to the fore in my own thinking with the development of the covenant epistemological vision.

Now I am able to see what then I only sensed, that Frame himself, with his perspectival triad, was doing epistemological therapy,

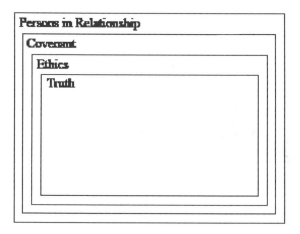

unpacking the implications of the Lordship of God (in the Calvinian tradition), in direct challenge to objectivism—not so much in critique of philosophy as in rehabilitation of it. The normative, I believe, as with all three aspects, is a *sine qua non* of knowledge, and one that signposts the personal. Objectivism has had no place for the normative, and it has diminished the self to a dot and, as a result, the world it once exalted, to a question mark.[34]

34. The postmodern critique of modernism can be interpreted using the Framean triad also: it rightly called into question the extremely damaging arrogance of claiming to be presuppositionless, attempting to deny the normative and diminish the existential. The postmodern reaction has often been to deny the situational and exalt the normative (not the existential, as people mistakenly think; that would be subjectivism, which is not

Polanyi, like Frame, was offering a frontal challenge to objectivism. He was not doing it in the name of theology; he was doing it in preservation of science.[35] The 1958 publication of his Gifford Lectures, *Personal Knowledge*, showcases the responsible and impassioned commitment of the knower, without which "knowledge" is not knowledge. He crafts an account of how we know that requires that we responsibly assign value to clues in order to shape a pattern. He thrusts back into the discussion the critical role of authoritative guides and texts, and of apprenticeship within traditions. Thus he underscores the personal presupposition and the normative dimensions of all human knowing. I felt that this radically aligned with Frame's project. This led to my distinctive melding of their proposals in my epistemology.

Making Earthy Sense of Presuppositions

What occurred to me first was that Polanyi's approach made sense of "presuppositionalism." Frame and many others affirm the determinative role that a person's presuppositions play in her or his overall views. This was an insight that thinkers in the Dutch Reformed tradition adapted from Dilthey and others in the nineteenth century.[36] Frame specifically makes clear that, in contrast to others, by presupposition he has in mind the stance of the human heart toward or away from God. Everybody "gets religious" about their own presuppositions, that is, they hold them so intimately that they are a part of themselves, and they are in no way "objective" about them.

When I encountered presuppositionalism, I felt convinced that it was undeniable philosophically.[37] It had seemed to me that the main act in any philosophical debate was always of a presuppositional nature; that

so much postmodern as modernism's extreme. Though of course there is plenty of that around, too).

35. In the 1930s Michael Polanyi encountered and was dismayed by the growing popularity in Britain and the U.S.S.R of socialized science. In an effort to dispute it, he searched the history of philosophy for an account of what he knew to be operative in scientific discovery. He found that philosophy offered no rationale for scientific discovery; that if the standard epistemology of certainty were correct, no scientific discovery could ever take place. He believed that faulty epistemology had led to the destruction of his Europe at the beginning of the twentieth century. He set about to offer an alternative epistemology, to save science, and to save culture. Scott and Moleski, *Michael Polanyi*, as well as the opening pages of Polanyi's *Tacit Dimension*.

36. Naugle, *Worldview*.

37. The following paragraphs reflect my analysis in Meek, "Working Implications."

is what had attracted me to philosophy in the first place. It seemed valuable in a debate to identify the ultimate presuppositions of each position. Frame's work countenanced this.

But I felt uneasy about how presuppositions seemed so arbitrary. It seemed a laudable and responsible exercise to articulate one's own presuppositions and bring one's other beliefs into harmony with them. And it was consoling to me as a Christian to realize that everybody, not just Christians, has faith commitments. But when I was looking at my presuppositions, I felt myself saying, "But that isn't what makes me a Christian!" They seemed exterior to me, and not at all like a living relationship with the triune God. And having reached the point of uncovering such commitments, I felt strongly the incommensurability of my own and an opponent's presuppositions, and the apparent absence of a court of appeal that did not presume one over the other.[38]

At the time that I first encountered these two thinkers and began to juxtapose them, it appeared to me that, if Frame offered the parameters of human knowing in the context of biblical Lordship, then Polanyi showed me how it worked. Polanyi showed me that presuppositions work like other tools, like hammers; we indwell them subsidiarily, extending our body to interiorize them: "[W]hen we accept a certain set of pre-suppositions and use them as our interpretative framework, we may be said to dwell in them as we do in our own body. Their uncritical acceptance for the time being consists in a process of assimilation by which we identify ourselves with them. They are not asserted and cannot be asserted, for assertion can be made only *within* a framework with which we have identified ourselves for the time being; as they are themselves our ultimate framework, they are essentially inarticulable."[39] We can relate to certain statements by articulating them, or we can relate to even the same statements by relying on them subsidiarily to focus beyond them. If we are doing this latter, we feel them from the inside as we do our own bodies. And when this is happening, at that point they are not articulable.

---

38. This is where Thomas Kuhn (*Structure of Scientific Revolutions*) leaves us, having only embraced half of Polanyi's thought. I do not remember whether I had read Kuhn before I had reached my own pre- and sub-Polanyian conclusion in this matter.

39. Polanyi, *Personal Knowledge*, 60. Naugle quotes this text in his capable representation of Polanyi's contribution to the worldview concept (Naugle, *Worldview*, 193). His copy editor failed to catch an important and comical misstatement, I may note for the next edition: what Polanyi feels "called upon to search for truth and state" are not his "feelings," but his "findings." Compare Polanyi, *Personal Knowledge*, 299.

If you feel that this makes presuppositions subjective or irrational, it's only because you need to think more about how it feels to live your body, to hammer skillfully, or to balance as you ride a bike. This tacit, body sense that is our engagement with the world at every moment of our lives is hardly arbitrary or irrational—unless, of course, you thought that Descartes was right to sever mind from body. Or rather—unless, of course, your body thought that Descartes was right.

So Polanyi helped me start to get the feel of presuppositionalism—not something most theologians, or scholars of any stripe for that matter, typically supply. He gave me the mechanism so that I could make three-dimensional and hence rational sense of it. Of course it is the case, when I examine and articulate presuppositions, that they feel arbitrary to me. That's just how I feel if I think about what my hand is doing with the hammer. Polanyi noted that although we typically indwell our presuppositions, there is pedagogical value in temporary *destructive analysis*, or temporarily focusing back on and articulating subsidiaries. It compares favorably to a pianist carefully practicing fingering in her scales, or a Bible student mastering Greek at seminary. But the point is that you do that to make you better in the performance or in the proclamation, when you reintegrate to the focus.

Thus, the central dynamic of Polanyi's epistemology is a most helpful tool for understanding, appreciating, and working with presuppositions or, as they are otherwise known, worldviews. Also, his approach shows the way to viewing these as not just mental, but bodily rooted and shaped by our context. A healthy worldview grows seamlessly out of our lived body experience. It is our interpreted, worded, storied, felt embodiment and engagement of the world. Polanyi's proposal makes sense of what Frame feels it important to say about the heart nature of presuppositions, but also shows the way to being even more biblical about presuppositions: for those who hear "heart" as disembodied, it helps us see how to honor the embodied situatedness of human creation.

Finally, and this always mattered utmost to me, Polanyi's approach shows the way that we can honor our subsidiaried commitments and also honor realism—to maintain that knowing contacts the real. Again, I believe that for biblical Christianity this is a *sine qua non*. Wedding Polanyian epistemology to the matter of presuppositions and how they function in knowing shows concrete ways we may helpfully steward them.[40]

At the outset of my juxtaposition of Frame and Polanyi, I did not see what I have only lately come to understand; that this sort of commitment is profoundly interpersonal in character, rather than aridly arbitrary. To trust and love another person is immensely risky, but it isn't arbitrary, and it isn't a working hypothesis. I now develop this interpersonal dimension in *Loving to Know*. But when I look with enlightened eyes at Frame's work, I find that was there all along.

Polanyian Epistemology Offers an Account of Knowing as Stewardship

Putting Frame and Polanyi together helps us see that Polanyi's active, personal, shaping of the pattern and thus of the world, which is knowing, also just is the fulfillment of the cultural mandate. Viewing Polanyi from Frame, we can see that the responsibility and the active shaping that is essential to human knowing is the exercise of the prophetic, interpretive, normative, role. We can see the lived body feel of the subsidiary as the existential, and indeterminate future manifestations as the situational. We can see indwelling, for example, as practicing the existential in the situational. Frame's perspectivalism underscores Polanyi's evenly balanced honoring of the knower's responsibility, active shaping, and submission to the real.

Making Sense of Commitment and Faith

Additionally, at the outset Polanyi's proposals gave me a way to make ordinary human sense of faith and commitment. These had been, for me, "religious" terms that I didn't know how to unpack epistemically, whose opacity threatened to render my whole Christianity suspect. Commitment figures large in Polanyi's "fiduciary programme."[41] It involves the knower's exercising responsibility to own the truth he or she claims, not as over against reality, but in deference to it. Luther's ringing "Here I stand; I cannot do otherwise" Polanyi cites as expressing the act of upholding any truth claim by exercising great personal responsibility, yet simultaneously being compelled by submission to reality. Polanyi's

---

40. See further in Meek, "Working Implications."

41. Polanyi, *Personal Knowledge*, ch. 4, sec. 8, and ch. 8, sec. 12, for example.

alternative vision of knowing daringly espouses the normative and existential dimensions of knowing, thus according profoundly with Frame.

But Polanyi makes it clear that what commitment refers to is our "manner of disposing ourselves," our personal assimilation whereby we press a tool or a framework into subsidiary service, indwelling it to extend ourselves in pursuit of the yet-to-be-known.

He writes: "This reliance [on a tool or construct] is a personal commitment which is involved in all acts of intelligence by which we integrate some things subsidiarily to the centre of our focal attention. Every act of personal assimilation by which we make a thing form an extension of ourselves through our subsidiary awareness of it, is a commitment of ourselves; a manner of disposing of ourselves."[42] Commitment refers to the clues we indwell subsidiarily in pursuit of a focal pattern. In other words, faith is of a piece with keeping your balance on a bike, and thus quite ordinary. Faith just is what we do in knowing. Belief is the epistemic act. But it is a lived body feel of a tool or framework indwelt with confidence. If *commitment* isn't an apt term for relying on something, I don't know what is.

I felt that understanding this made all the difference regarding understanding my Christianity, justifying it to myself, and reconciling it to all human enterprises. Polanyi shows how commitment always involves my lived body. And since, for Polanyi, commitment, as indwelling subsidiaries, is essential to all knowing, it is part and parcel of "reason," rather than opposed to it. My indwelling Scripture to understand God and the world certainly fits this description. All this also challenged my own defective default understanding of human knowing by making commitment, faith, palpable as subsidiarily embodied.

There's something else in Polanyi's proposals that also deserves to be called faith or commitment. He paints a graphic and indisputable picture of the scientist in pursuit of the as-yet undiscovered reality. Polanyi raises the philosophically awkward matter of the ancient Meno Dilemma, which we have considered already. Posed millennia ago by Plato, in a dialogue by that name, it has never satisfactorily been answered in the western tradition. How do you come to know? For either you do or you don't know something. If you don't know it, you cannot begin to move toward knowing it; and if you do know it, you don't need to move toward knowing it. Plato used this to set up his suggestion that all learning is re-

42. Polanyi, *Personal Knowledge*, 61.

calling. But this did not really resolve the dilemma. Aristotle sidestepped the dilemma by concentrating, not on coming to know (discovery), but on explanation. Most of western philosophy has tried to make do with these less than satisfying alternatives. It is a wonder, really, not to mention a radical challenge to philosophy, that scientific discovery has actually nevertheless taken place at a great rate.

Making Subsidiary-focal Sense of the Triad

Additionally, Polanyi's subsidiary-focal integrative structure of knowing accords with and elucidates the Framean triad. Frame calls the normative, the situational, and the existential, *perspectives*. A perspective is *a view from a certain point*. In Pittsburgh, John Frame's hometown and now my regional home, we are especially proud of the view from Mt. Washington. People say it is the second most popular evening view in the U.S. (the first one being the Grand Canyon). If you stand on Mt. Washington, just south of the confluence of the Allegheny and the Monongahela that forms the Ohio River, and that defines Pittsburgh's Golden Triangle, you get a spectacular view of the city. Of course, you could also view the city from the North Shore, from the upper stands of the Pirates' PNC Park, for example. Or you could see it from the east from the University of Pittsburgh's towering Cathedral of Learning. The view from the Cathedral, of the World Series in the old Forbes Field, was memorialized famously in a Life Magazine photograph. It is not as if the view from Mt. Washington is more Pittsburgh than the view from the Cathedral of Learning. Neither is it that somehow a perspective is not the thing itself: if you come to visit me and I want to show you Pittsburgh as it really is, I am going to take you to Mt. Washington for the view.

Frame's writing suggests that he thinks of perspectives as views-from-which: you stand at the one point and look toward the other. The word, "perspective," can refer to the point from which you look, the act of looking, or the looked-at. I think that the looked-at could perhaps be distinguished as an *aspect*, rather than a perspective, and I have been using this word also, in this discussion. But the act of looking, the connecting from the one to the other—that strategy of positioning oneself at one point and looking from it toward the other—is a critical feature of what Frame has in mind by perspective as well.

But Polanyi helps, as I said. For *all* knowing is perspectival, in the sense that all knowing involves orienting from one point in the direction of another. And the nature of that orientation involves relying on a subsidiary indwelling of the proximal from which we attend to focus outward on the other.

Consider this comment of Polanyi's: "This structure [of tacit knowing] shows that all thought contains components of which we are subsidiarily aware in the focal content of our thinking, and that all thought dwells in its subsidiaries, as if they were parts of our body. Hence thinking is not only necessarily intentional, as Brentano has taught; it is also necessarily fraught with the roots that it embodies. It has a *from-to* structure."[43] I myself tend to revert to thinking of a perspective as a mathematical *point*, as in *point from which*, as we have been saying. This quotation contains a critically important corrective. The vectorial directedness of all knowing from subsidiary to focal never leaves the subsidiary behind or minimizes it to a mathematical point. The subsidiary awareness that supports the act of knowing profoundly imbues its focus. Mt. Washington is no mathematical point. Traces of coal and steel industry, a legacy of devilishly hard work, life tenaciously clung to together amidst difficult circumstances the way the two remaining incline railways hug the hillside and steadily climb upward, horizons formerly aflame and smoke-filled from belching Bessemers, now green in both senses of the word, the palpable quiet of being high up in the air, the closeness of the Pittsburgh clouds, memories of the sky filled with displays of Zambelli fireworks over a massive summer regatta or blazing stadiums . . . the Mt. Washington view of Pittsburgh is fraught with its foreground.[44]

In Frame's triad, we may position ourselves at the normative and view the existential.[45] Or we may position ourselves at the situational

43. Polanyi, *Tacit Dimension*, xviii.

44. We might say that this is an existential perspective on the situational. I can imagine another hillside view that is, for me, a normative perspective on the situational. Here in my hometown of Aliquippa, downstream on the Ohio a bit from Pittsburgh, I can stand up in Plan Six, where the Jones and Laughlin Steel Mill upper crust had their homes, and gaze down on a now-empty, pollutant-buried, seven-mile stretch of shore where the mill used to be, which for decades now has been an abandoned eyesore. This *should* not be. It testifies to the abandonment of this town, that now, in God's working, is being addressed by some exciting and innovative Christian ministries of which I am a part.

45. Grene, in her *Philosophical Testament*, more than once references a helpful term of Helmuth Plessner's—"eccentric positionality" (ibid., 67). Humans are the only animals who can and do place themselves outside their bodies. I have this in mind as I talk here of using the triad.

and view the normative from there. Polanyi helps us retain the important sense of how the view is fraught with the view-from-which.[46] And he shows how we always hold the two together in subsidiary-focal integration. That this makes sense of what Frame is trying to do is corroborated by the persistent penchant, he notes, of Van Til to speak of revelation of God from nature, of God from man, of man from God, of man from nature, of nature from God, of nature from man: the *orienting* from the view-from-which in the direction of the view is perhaps the main thing. And to delineate it you need an ordered pair of coordinates, so to speak. But for Polanyi, that is just how all human knowing is: from-to.

Take, for example, the interpreting humans do as part and parcel of all our knowing, living, and fulfilling of our stewardly roles. Interpretation is the existential's perspective on the situational. Or you can be talking about interpretation as the normative aspect of the existential. Either way, it really takes specifying the two coordinates, one with respect to, or with a view to, the other, to get at what is of interest. Interpretation is an example of one or two coordinate pairs for which we actually have a term.

So it helps to see that the way the Framean perspectives interrelate in our use of them involves, as all knowing does, orienting from the one that is "near," subsidiarily relying on it in such a way that it imbues our focus, to focus on the one that is "far."

Making Triadic Sense of Subsidiary-focal Integration

I noted, in my development of Polanyi's subsidiary-focal integrative mechanism for all knowing, that Frame's triad had suggested three sorts, or sectors, of subsidiary clues. The triad also suggested that these sets be seen as equal in status, and to permeate one another as from the three angles of an equilateral triangle, thus adding, I believe, a helpful way of seeing Polanyi's shared commitments to the role of the personal and of the normative in knowing. I said also that I believe an act of coming to know may be seen to be inaugurated by "an issue" in one dimension or

46. In fact, I believe this suggests an important corrective to Frame's language of "the same content, from different directions." The idea of content (think of Pittsburgh, for example) is an abstracted concept. Such an abstraction is fine, so long as it does not blind you damagingly to the dynamic and concrete involvement of the view-from-which, or the subsidiary, and thus lead you to misconstrue and truncate what you are doing when you know. I think this corrective actually brings more integrity to Frame's own position, for it speaks in a manner consistent with Frame's idea of presupposition.

another, and then we, in our unfolding knowing, dance from one sector to another and back again. So, in this way, Frame's triad has helped me unlock subsidiary-focal integration.

I do not know how exactly to align or overlay the triad and subsidiary-focal integration. For some years, I and my students have diagrammed the interface of these two thinker's motifs by an equilateral triangle, with a vector superimposed that begins from the existential corner and moves, arrow-on-bow-like, across the line between the situational and the normative.[47] There is some kind of resonance or alignment between subsidiary-focal-integration, and existential-situational-normative. Or it may be between subsidiary-focal-integration and existential/situational-normative-dynamism. I link knower-known-knowing to the triad. It is unclear to me how to be exact in this matter. This just seems to me to be part of the allusive richness of the Framean triad, of Polanyian epistemology, and thus of my attempt to meld them. But you should know that in my mind I continue to lay both out, for exploratory purposes, as that vectored triad. And I continue to try to link other insights we will explore to one or the other of the aspects of the Framean triad.

What I see covenant epistemology contributing to that overlay is the expansion of it to incorporate the explicitly personal. How I see this occurring will become evident as we move through the next parts of this book. In particular, I locate the personal, specifically the personal as covenantally constituted interpersonal relationship, either in reference to the normative dimension, or as the context for the entire triad—actually, both. Seeing the entire triad as embedded in an overarching interpersoned relationship would make sense of dimensions of the personed that we can identify not only in knowing, but also in knower and known.

Making Sense of All People Knowing God; Anticipative Knowledge and Common Grace

For Polanyi, the Meno problem confirmed that there must be more to our knowing than we are able to articulate. There must be "anticipative" knowledge, as I call it. "The kind of tacit knowledge that solves the paradox of the *Meno* consists in the intimation of something hidden, which we may yet discover . . . we can have a tacit foreknowledge of yet undiscovered things." In fact, whenever we take a claim to be true, he said, "we commit ourselves to a belief in all these as yet undisclosed,

47. See figure on p. 158.

perhaps as yet unthinkable, consequences."[48] Polanyi concludes that the paradigmatic case of scientific knowledge is the knowledge of an approaching discovery. *Approaching!*—this has always astounded me! "To hold such knowledge is an act deeply committed to the conviction that there is something there to be discovered . . . The discoverer is filled with a compelling sense of responsibility for the pursuit of a hidden truth, which demands his services for revealing it."[49] Polanyi testified that the scientist navigates by "groping or scrabbling," guided by a "sense of increasing proximity to the solution."[50]

Commitment to a half-understood, as yet not fully discovered reality? This too makes earthy sense of what we mean by faith. For me, and for scores of my students now, Polanyi's work also has helped me to align my knowing God with every other kind of knowing, including the most elegant scientific discovery, and the most creative artistic achievement. It brings all human knowing together.

Also because of this, I felt that Polanyi's proposals made sense of what Frame was trying to say by providing the possibility of implicit knowledge, unfolding knowledge, and anticipative knowledge. Knowing, on a Polanyian scheme, has a more gracious prospect: you can be on the way to knowing something. You have to be on the way to knowing things if you are ever going to make discoveries. Our "sense of increasing proximity to the solution" guides us even as it justifies our efforts. He repeatedly identified as significant the sense of the possibility of indeterminate future manifestations that accompany and accredit our discovery. He made the case that a person can actually make a discovery and yet not know what he or she has actually discovered; it may take years, and generations, to find that out. All this makes sense of how we can know and not know at the same time, both with regard to a discovery, and also with regard to our subsidiary awareness.

This allows us to make sense of how all knowing can be, as Frame avers, knowing God, and how that can be the case even before we "know God." It makes sense of how a Christian can both know God and not yet

48. Polanyi, *Tacit Dimension*, 22–23.

49. Ibid., 25. Polanyi's realism, expressed repeatedly in tantalizing statements such as this one, drew me like the waters of an oasis in a dry desert, to write a dissertation on it. Only years later did Newbigin help me make the connection that what so drew me in Polanyi was . . . God. See ch. 16.

50. Polanyi, "Creative Imagination," 85–93.

know God, and of how an unbeliever can not know God, yet know him. It makes sense of how, in coming to know God (or anything), you can experience surprising recognition and find yourself having been the one known. It makes sense of what we will explore in covenant epistemology, that the act of knowing prototypes the act of knowing God.

Additionally, it becomes possible to say that all truthful human knowing of the world is knowing God. Catholic mystic Simone Weil has an essay titled, "Forms of the Implicit Love of God."[51] She reasons that there must be some kind of love of God going on in people before they come to realize they are loving God (sound familiar?). She identifies true friendship, love of beauty, care of neighbor, and love of religion, as such forms. I would like to suggest that every act of knowing is also such a form of the implicit love of God.

Thus, once again, Polanyi showed me the way to make sense of, reconcile, and amplify, key components of the reformed tradition, John Frame in particular.

Covenant Epistemology for Everyone

It is precisely because of this last way in which "Polanyi helps Frame" that I feel that an epistemic proposal that features the idea of covenant in the context of knowing God may be favorably applied to all human knowing. If all knowing is knowing God, occurring, like everything, in the covenantally constituted context of God's Lordship, we should be able to look at what we do when we know and find aspects that conform to this. And Framean insights may be unleashed to amplify our understanding of all knowing—hence, my appropriation of the three dimensions.

In offering covenant epistemology, I am arguing that identifying covenantally interpersoned facets makes better sense of any act of knowing, no matter who is doing the knowing, no matter what is being known. I look at how knowing actually works, and I find the dimensions that a Christian theological vision, specifically, Frame's account of knowing God as Lord, suggests might exist. Thus, for example, it was Annie Dillard and the muskrats that strategically prompted me to consider covenant epistemology. This approach, yet again, is affirmed by the equanimity of the Framean triad: if this world is God's world, and the Lord reveals himself in my thinking, my interpreting it and its self-

51. Weil, *Waiting for God*, 83–142.

disclosure can be expected to align with each other and also count as my understanding of him.[52] You can "start" anywhere on the triad.

I can well imagine that a self-described atheist has a real problem with my saying that all knowing is knowing God. I do not at all mean not to take their profession seriously when I draw out the Calvinian and Framean implications of the Polanyian claim that there is more to what we know than what we say, more to what we say than what we know, more to what we know than what we ourselves know, more to what there is than what we think we have discovered. Drawing on the insight of philosopher Caroline Simon, who defines and expounds love as "imagining someone's destiny truly"—do not our best friends see us truly in terms of possibilities more profound than sometimes even we ourselves are able to see?[53] At the same time I am well aware that at all times I "profess"—meaning that I speak from my presuppositions; I may be mistaken, but I hold my claims, as Polanyi expressed it, responsibly and with universal intent.

As a result of my epistemology, I tend not to make the matter of whether a person is a Christian believer or not into a determinative divide with respect to knowing. I think that the foregoing amply justifies this approach. Yes, the redemption by Christ of creation is the answer, the beginning and *sine qua non* for ultimately and thoroughly getting knowing right. But at this point in history we cannot, with respect to any person knowing a particular thing, conclude with finality, on the one hand, that if he or she is unbelieving, he or she does not know the thing in good measure, or does not to that extent know God. Neither can we conclude, on the other, that in successfully knowing that thing that he or she is a believer, or that being a believer will automatically afford him or her superior insight into that thing.

Knowing as Personed Covenant Response

Let's go back now to Frame's use of the idea of covenant. The relationship between Creator and creature, between Lord and servant, is covenantal. We saw that it richly blends transcendence and immanence along the lines of the relationship of parent and child. It is interpersonal, and it is intimate. Knowing is the covenantally human response to the covenant-

52. In saying this, I do not mean at all to baptize even my mistaken thought, nor blame it on God.

53. Simon, *Disciplined Heart.*

ing initiative of God the Lord, in the context of which all is what it is and does what it does and knows what it knows. Because it is an intimate relationship between persons, the covenant response that is knowing in effect can be seen to be a form of loving trust and obedience. Knowing, Frame says, ultimately is friendship, communion with God.

I am proposing that it is the normative dimension of Frame's triad, the normative dimension of every epistemic act, which in particular reflects the covenantal nature of knowing. It is not difficult to see why. But I will argue that the normative implies the covenantal. How does one explain oughtness? It involves covenant-keeping. But where there is covenant, there are persons covenanting together. So the presence of the normative in the triad signposts the larger context of the covenantal and thus of interpersonal relationship. The presence of the normative is a telltale marker of an embracing interpersonal relationship.

Compare Frame's triadic approach with, for example, the insights author Walker Percy draws from Charles Sanders Peirce, that what humans do is triadic, as opposed to dyadic—thus, as a signature facet, always involving what philosopher Marjorie Grene terms, symboling.[54] Symboling is wider and deeper than verbalizing. It includes the distinctively human artificial, such as ceremonies, rituals, and institutions. Humans, in order to do anything at all, including knowing, assign value. To see a deer in the field, I assign varying significance to the colors and patterns I see. That is the normative dimension in action. I personally have for a long while contemplated the essential reflective "artificiality" that characterizes human action—ever since I got a dog, actually! Case in point: ceremonies, funerals, and parties—commemorative events: their value is simply lost on my dog, Miles. But they are what humans do as we reflect on and value what we do, in fact, value things into existence. All this supplies additional warrant for my proposal that knowing is tri-dimensional because it is what persons do.

This is difficult to express. As a fish has no conception of life outside water, and so perhaps does not appreciate the water, it is possible that we struggle to imagine what is actually impossible to do without. It may actually be impossible that knowing could be anything other than inter-personed, three-dimensioned, covenant response. Especially under the influence of the western default mode, we tend to depersonalize know-

54. Percy, *Lost In The Cosmos*, 85–126; Grene, *Philosophical Testament*, ch. 8. See my discussion in texture 8.

ing, to overlook telltale signs that knowing could only be, even in truncated form, interpersonal covenant response. What *Loving to Know* is trying to do is to catalog those telltale signs—to show how some features of human knowing make startlingly profound sense when construed personally, and to suggest, in light of this, that being intentional about the personal and covenantal aspects of knowing will prove profitable and healing. For example: if knowing is about covenant response, would it be more effective to practice efforts to know that look like trust and obedience? What happens when we think of knowing as . . . friendship?

This directly challenges the theory-practice dichotomy of the default mode. Traditionally, we think that theory is what matters, and theory must precede practice. Justification must, for our efforts to be responsible, precede obedient compliance. It is morally culpable not to maintain "a critical stance."[55] This connects with our attraction to the idea of there being self-evident, foundational truths. What, then, can it be to reverse this, to say that obedience precedes knowledge? To locate knowledge in the context of trust? One thing to say is—and this is Polanyi's claim—that we already do place knowledge in the context of trust; we just haven't been allowed by the prevailing paradigm to see and accredit it. Another is to say that this is what Jesus said: the one who obeys will know.[56] Third is to note that Newbigin underscores this, in reference to both Polanyi and to Jesus.[57] This is what covenant epistemology means to espouse.

Frame's theological and epistemological work serves to challenge our damagingly defective epistemological default in such a way that suggests the interpersonal as an embracing context. Plus, there is something about the way Frame goes about his triad that suggests that we may use the word, "is," and have something more complex in mind than simply identity. In developing covenant epistemology, I am going to need such complexity. For I am going to want to say that knowing is loving, that it is interpersonal covenantal relationship. But I am not going to want that to be a reductive claim. Knowing isn't only loving, and only relationship. The way that Frame talks about something being the same thing seen from different perspectives offers a strategy.

---

55. So stated, the irony of the stance is glaring: is it immoral to include morals in knowing?

56. John 7:17.

57. Newbigin, *Proper Confidence*, 105.

I would like to develop a concept that I hope will make sense of this and that we will carry forward throughout the discussion. When I was much younger, in the hippie era, we sometimes referred to our cars as our "wheels." This is what is known as metonymy. It is a reference to a part that is effectively a reference to the whole. As such, it is a truncated reference, and one that only makes sense if we interact with it with a view to the whole. Were you to focus on the wheels, you wouldn't get anywhere. But the wheels signpost or reference the larger whole. You can't reduce the metonym to the larger context without stopping the fun. Nor can you reduce the embracing context to the metonym. The metonymy only works as it is imbued with the shape of the whole. Metonymy is a literary device that adds zest to life and conversation. It is at root a metaphor, and as such it has a built-in allusiveness and mystery. But the metonymous relationship, like any good metaphor, is enough to keep them apart while imbuing the part with the whole. The metonymy joins wheels and car, while keeping them distinct.

I would like to say that the normative as covenantal metonymously references its larger personal context. In looking at the normative we are seeing part of something larger. In looking at knowing, we are seeing something embracing that imbues it. I will want to say, that knowing *is* loving. But I won't want to say it in such a way that knowing is only loving. As with Frame's triad and its perspectival "identities," it is important not to let the one collapse into the other. There are several points in the conversations that comprise covenant epistemology where I will find this idea of metonym pertains.

Our penchant to depersonalize knowing—itself, I would suggest, the effect of ethical rebellion on human knowing—leads us at every turn, it seems, to cast things impersonally. Thus, here in the discussion of three dimensions, and even in the discussion of covenant, my mind tends to revert to the impersonal and abstract—*the* existential, *the* covenant. Thus I ask myself—have I depersonalized the Framean triad? Has he? The better question may be, not whether we are culpable, but how may we counteract the tendency and work to construe covenant and dimensions as fully personal? How may we see the normative, the existential, and the situational as fully personal, or pursue it against a backdrop of the interpersonal? May we see the situational as "All knowing is know-

ing *whom*"?[58]—The normative as "All knowing is knowing *with whom*"?[59]
—The existential as more vibrantly, holistically, fully-personed?[60] All
knowing as my covenantally constituted interpersonal response? This
is what I hope that the reflections that comprise covenant epistemology
will do.

In conclusion: John Frame confirms the normative dimension of
knowing that in turn suggests the covenantal. Thus his work furnishes
an important preliminary component of covenant epistemology. Both in
its theological vision and in its innovative triad, it suggests the covenant
epistemology vision that knowing is paradigmatically a covenantally
constituted, interpersoned relationship. Frame's theological proposal, if
true, of course, holds implications for human knowing. Human knowing
must be servant thinking, and it must be stewardship. All knowing is
covenant response. Knowing involves three dimensions, but specifically
a normative dimension that requires the context of interpersonal relationship, with the goal of friendship. The known, in this biblical vision, is
God the Lord and his palatial "effects." But then we must quickly add: the
known, insofar as we are referring in that designation to God the Lord,
is never the known without first having been the one who knows us into
existence originally.

Overlaying subsidiary-focal integration with Frame's triad enriches
both. It allows me to start to make sense of the person-like way that the
real responds to the covenantal self-binding of the aspiring knower. The
overlay corroborates the normative and the personal dimension Polanyi
finds in knowing.

While these, I believe, are implicit or briefly stated in Frame's work,
there are two aspects that covenant epistemology expands to deeper
significance in its vision of human knowing. One is the link between
the triad, particularly the normative, and interpersonal relationship. The
normative implies the wider and defining context of the covenantal; the
covenantal, in turn, implies the wider and defining context of interpersoned relationship. I believe that the normative should be transposed
into the notion of storied, unfolding, covenant relationship—the subject
of the next chapter. Or alternatively we need to see the entire triad as em-

58. See pt. 4.

59. See texture 5.

60. I identify our earlier discussion of virtuosity, embodiment and presence as an
intentional exploration of the personed dimensions of the existential. See texture 2.

bedded in the larger context of a covenantally constituted interpersonal relationship.

The second aspect I expand is this. I think that Frame's framework does not voice an important fundamental dynamism. Because he has a different agenda, Frame doesn't really talk about how a human ordinarily comes to know.[61] But I think there is more than a matter of difference of agendas going on. I have already suggested that a knower triangulates back and forth among the triad's corners in the unfolding trajectory of coming to know, thus already adding a dynamism to the Framean triad. If we contrast "the normative" with "storied, unfolding, relationship," as I did in the previous paragraph, we start to get a sense of the importance of that living dynamism. This dynamism was evident in Polanyi and Loder, and it will be evident in Williams. It will receive concrete specification in our conversation with Gunton. The dynamism will prove important as a critical, definitive, feature of covenantally constituted interpersoned relationship, and thus, I feel confident, to the covenant epistemology vision.

QUESTIONS FOR DISCUSSION

1. Share your assessment of Frame's claims about what biblical Christianity is about. Do his claims match the way you have understood it? How do they amplify your understanding of the Christian religion?

2. What does biblical Christianity entail for the enterprise of knowing? Is it helpful to see knowing as stewardship, and as servant thinking?

3. How have you thought about the relationship between theology and philosophy? How does this chapter revise your outlook? What do you think about this from the perspective of a nonbeliever?

4. Draw a picture of Frame's triad, and label the corners. You can put the existential on the lower left (or lower right—I think what suits you is related to whether you are left- or right-handed); the situational on the lower right, and the normative at the top. Add some of the other trios I mention in the text.

61. Frame, as a Christian theologian, of course, would profess that the knower comes to know God only through the work of God the Holy Spirit. I also take this theological profession for granted, not only for knowing God, but in some difficult-to-specify way, for all knowing. But this claim doesn't necessarily issue in a dynamism, in theistic epistemology, even though it should.

5. Together pick an example of knowing and talk about the way each of the aspects is present and interfaces with the others.

6. Consider further the normative dimension. How does recognizing its presence make better sense of our understanding knowing?

7. What things strike you about how Frame and Polanyi fit together?

ANTICIPATIVE KNOWING AND COMMON GRACE

POLANYI'S SOPHISTICATED AC-
COUNT OF human knowing
has enabled me to make sense
of John Frame's claim that all
knowing is knowing God. The
Polanyian core of covenant
epistemology offers an account of anticipative knowing,
being "on the way" to knowing. As a result, covenant epistemology offers a gracious way
to approach the thought of
people who are "on the way"
to knowing, and "on the way"
to knowing God. This has valuable implications for scholarship, as well as for any other
kind of human collaboration. It
gives a great example of how
covenant epistemology has the
resources to form our orientation to the world and make us
better knowers.

In the Van Tillian tradition,
in which Frame has worked, is
an obvious implication which,
sadly, has been underempha-
sized by many of his students.
It is known as *common grace*.
The tradition, in honoring

the Lordship of God in every
corner of the universe and
the radical heart nature of
covenant submission or rebellion and its impact on human
knowing, tends to maintain
a stance that is known as *antithesis*. Antithesis refers to
the fact that humans can't be
indifferent to God, but rather
are either in submission to or
in rebellion against God. Since
that orientation takes place
at the core of who we are, it
impacts everything we are
and do, including our knowing. So unbelievers' thought
and purposes and cultural
products can be expected to
be antithetical to those of believers. So it is common in the
tradition to infer that the unbeliever cannot know anything
at all, let alone know God, and
to debate "what the unbe-
liever can know." Christians in
education, for example, often
debate the extent to which
the rebellious stance of unbelievers inappropriately skews

their conclusions, in order to exclude God's Lordship, thus making them false.

As I have said before, I think that understanding the role of fundamental belief commitments in all scholarship is critical to excellence in scholarship.[1] We should expect there to be divergence between scholarly proposals that stem from diverging presuppositions. This characterizes not just Christian scholarship over other traditions; it characterized every single scholarly tradition. This is what Frame and others have in mind by combating the idea that facts are "neutral," or that neutrality of any sort is possible. To perpetrate the claim of "neutrality" is to commit the sin of modernity and metanarrative, as Francois Lyotard and others describe it: it is surreptitiously to attempt to hide one's own fundamental belief commitments by passing them off as the epitome of universal rationality.[2] So we can expect the philosophical counterpart of antithesis throughout scholarship—hence the need to be trained philosophically as part of any professional training.

But there is, necessarily I believe, another side to the Lordship of God. This other side is the stance of *common grace.* Common grace is like seeing the glass half-full rather than half-empty. I reason that, if God is Lord of all, then it is not possible for any human in rebellion against God to be completely successful at rebelling. If it were, then God would not be Lord of all. Also, if it were, assuming that the Lordship of God is what constitutes and sustains every atom of reality, that human wouldn't exist.

Some people, I believe, hold excessively rigorously to antithesis. People big on antithesis understandably don't relate well to unbelievers or their cultural products; they tacitly convey an off-putting superiority. Yet many cultural and epistemic productions of unbelievers nevertheless glorify God and advance his purposes in the world. In these God is restraining the inevitable evil of the ungodly by exercising his common grace.[3]

1. Nicholas Wolterstorff's account of control beliefs, in his *Reason within the Bounds of Religion,* as well as his aphoristic expression, "practicing scholarship from a Christian perspective," (texture 3, n. 2) is emblematic.

2. See ch. 6, n.17.

3. See Kuyper, *Lectures on Calvinism*; and Mouw, *He Shines In All That's Fair.*

Of the two theological stances, antithesis and common grace, which is more basic or pervasive? I believe it is common grace. For if you take antithesis to be ultimate, it implies that something escapes, and thereby nullifies, God's Lordship. Since he is Lord, you can expect to find diamonds of truth everywhere, commingled with perversities from which it is the Christian's joy and obligation to extract them.

Here is a helpful way to think about it. If you picture God as magnetic north, and a human life and its projects as the compass' arrow, the divine plan is that the arrow points to magnetic north. Rebellion means that the arrow pulls itself away from magnetic north to try to orient in another direction. The Lordship of God means that the rebellious effort is only partly successful. The Christ-anchored redemption of God means that, in time, "every knee will bow" before the Lord.[4] But this side of that time, even the most determined rebel inadvertently, partially, signposts God. What that gives us, following through on the picture, is a bunch of bent arrows! Humans, believers and unbelievers alike, actually, are, this side of the renewal of all things, bent arrows. Part of us points to God; part doesn't. The fact that part of us points to God is common grace.

So an unbeliever may explicitly deny God yet implicitly signpost him. Or, a believer can explicitly profess God, and implicitly do anything but. Christians rightly affirm that the redemptive work of Christ is the first and central act of God's redemption and renewal of all things. An obvious implication is that having been redeemed by Christ is the first and central component of truthful knowing. But the Bible is clear about "the already-not yet" state of affairs in which we find ourselves. Christians' redemption is very much an on-the-way affair.

Especially in a cultural tradition thwarted by the dichotomous epistemic default we here address, the centrality of that redemption to knowing has been poorly understood. In a key way, covenant epistemology strives to correct this. The dichotomous misunderstanding comes to expression in an erratic ambivalence between maintaining that our relationship to Christ has nothing to

4. Phil 2:10–11.

do with knowledge, and maintaining that nothing besides our relationship to Christ has anything to do with knowledge—hence the claim that unbelievers do not know anything at all. I trust that you can see that this ambivalence radically thwarts Christian scholarship, as it thwarts Christian cultural engagement of any sort. It also is offensive to not-yet believers, counterproductive, and unfortunate given that it results from truncating the Lordship of God and the vast respect-worthy dimensions of any creature of God's.

However, once again we are stumbling on a concrete manifestation of the widespread defective epistemic default. That default is just what Polanyian epistemology targets and supersedes by offering a positive account of human knowing that accords with what we actually do. As we have seen, that account admirably makes sense of the complex nuances of human knowing—how we can know and not know, be on the way to knowing, possess anticipative knowledge, etc.

Human knowing is more complex than either simple knowing or ignorance. A moralistic poem read to us in grade school asserts that some people know not and know not that they know not, some know not and know that they know not, some know and know not that they know, and some know and know that they know! If any of us, believer or no, considers the state of our own understanding, we will humbly admit this complexity.[5]

This complexity, however, is not originally the result of human rebellion, nor is it a bad thing. It is human, creaturely, stewardly—and, as I am arguing, it is just what it should be if we construe knowing as relationally, interpersonally, contexted and cored. We have already hinted that the living dynamism of it is a good thing. So also is its situatedness and its concrete particularity: *my* knowing, from this vantage point and time, from the rich concreteness of my lived being, strategically unlocks the world, as does yours, and as we may do together in conversations along the way. Covenant epistemology enables us to affirm that human knowing

5. Meek, *Longing to Know.* One such experience of mine has been that reader friends have helped me know what I "knew" in writing the book!

is more complex than either simple knowing or ignorance. It includes knowing that we cannot tell, on which we rely and which we anticipate, and telling that we have not yet and may never fully comprehend. It honors the immense richness of a reality that reflects the God who covenants it.

The Polanyian account, as I have already argued, actually helps Christian theologians such as John Frame make better sense of their theological commitments. Specifically, subsidiary-focal integration shows the way to honor the stewardly nature of human knowing and the goodness of creation. Both of these endure despite the distortions wrought by human rebellion, and which will continue to endure when the distortions are redemptively, wholly, reoriented. Human rebellion is not to be understood theologically or epistemologically to be the sole cause of an "evil" particularity that we should seek to eliminate.[6] Although human knowing is frustratingly distorted due to the noetic effects of human rebellion, according to reformed theologians, its signature complexity stems from

its human creatureliness, and is no flaw but rather its asset.

Subsidiary-focal integration, and thus also covenant epistemology, shows the way to make sense of common grace, because it combats the defective default and makes positive sense of all knowing. If we add to the bent arrow picture the Polanyian insight that part of our knowing is explicit and part implicit, and how it is so, then we can make sense of common grace as we live out a healthy, sophisticated, epistemology. This resoundingly justifies creative and selective collaboration with unbelieving scholarship and all human societal and cultural endeavors. Believers and yet-to-be-believers may exercise mutual respect and collaboration in all cultural engagement, including scholarship.

Especially, but not exclusively, this side of what Jesus termed "the renewal of all things," this means that any knower or community of knowers, like the proverbial blind men and the elephant, grasp aspects of reality and partly understand it. We can be saying something wrong yet living it right, or vice versa. We may be on the way to knowing rather

6. This is Smith's thesis in *Fall of Interpretation*.

than fully there. Having arrived at knowing, we may find ourselves and our pasts transformed, and sense unforeseen future prospects. Others who listen well often know us and know what we know better than we do; hence, conviviality is essential to knowing. The redemption of Christ, which is central to the redemption of human knowing, may or may not at some point be issuing in redeemed thought in the believer's life and work, while the not-yet-redeemed who nevertheless image God and dwell in his reality may succeed comparably well in accessing the real and expressing truth.

Christians can expect to encounter actions of unbelievers that, no matter their intention, recognizably image the glory and righteousness of the Lord. We may honor the unbeliever and employ her/his work, because it resembles the Father, valuing both initiation and product as good, without countenancing epistemic "neutrality." This applies both to believers' attitudes toward the work of unbelievers, and also to believers' attitudes to that of other believers, with whom we are fellow travelers at different stages on the

way to knowing. We may—we must—comport ourselves with care, grace, patience, and respect toward all knowers and their epistemic efforts, simply because of the complexity of human knowing. Obviously, how we comport ourselves in these matters has much to do with how we go about scholarship, teaching, and collegiality. It means that we may work together graciously and productively with others who are at different stages on the trajectory of faith, knowing, and integration.

The realization that Christians and yet-to-be Christians can be about on a par with each other, when it comes to the stewardliness and effectiveness of their knowing, this side of Christ's renewal of all things, should be very humbling to believers. It should induce us to be far more gracious in our comportment with people we view as not-yet-believers. In our societal intercourse, we may collaborate by appealing to the commonalities that point toward God. We may agree to recycle trash to save the environment or, as we do in Western Pennsylvania, award "Mancinis" for best actors and actresses in the spring's slate of local high school musicals. We may combat injustice together. And in our efforts to know, we may creatively collaborate, ferreting out the diamonds and integratively stringing them into a necklace that transformatively supersedes what anybody originally had in mind. This, by the way, is the approach to which I aspire in my case for the vision of covenant epistemology. I call it, diamond mining.

But, if you accept my bent-arrow analogy, in our intercourse with everyone we have a choice whether to appeal to the part of their arrow that points away from God, or to the part that points toward him. In some cases it is important to challenge the part that points away from God. My point, however, is that common grace and the Lordship of God calls us not to overlook the part of that arrow that points toward God, but rather to affirm it, connect with it, and collaborate in light of it.

Here is a little story which, I believe, helps us to see what common grace is like and how we may cooperate with it.[7] Some years ago, when my be-

loved rabbit died in my arms, I buried him in a huge shoe box in the woods behind my house. Soon thereafter, a young family who had moved on from our area was back in town and stopped by for a brief visit.

Her parents must have told three-year-old Evelyn about Grady: when we opened the door to them, she burst in with a volley of urgent questions. "Where's your rabbit?" she demanded. "Why is he dead?" "Where did he go?"—all this over the polite protestations of her parents. I answered her questions seriously, and they led to more: "Where is the box?" "What is he doing in the ground?" "Show me!" In three minutes Evelyn and I were in the woods, discussing matters over Grady's wee gravestone. Eventually she seemed satisfied, and only then was I released to visit with the rest of her family.

When they were leaving, we continued chatting as her parents buckled Evelyn into her child seat and climbed into the front. I leaned in to wish Evelyn good-bye. That deliciously self-important tiny human, golden curls gently bobbing as she nodded, wrinkled her brow and pooched her lip a little as

---

7. I developed this story originally in Meek, "Common Grace."

she said, "I'm sorry about your rabbit!"

I was disarmed and amused—and comforted. She was acting out the behavior of her gracious parents. It was too grown-up to be original. But she had initiated it and it was good.

Evelyn's pronouncement was an act both her own and not her own. It imaged her parents, though she was too young to be capable of the act of being self-consciously authentic. For all that, she initiated it. For all that, the act was good: I was comforted in my grieving.

This little example shows how a human act can indicate more than was intended. It shows how it can display a likeness to something larger, particularly to persons and the interpersoned in the vicinity. It shows how it can signpost these things. These are dimensions of human knowing that I am calling us, in covenant epistemology, to identify, take seriously, and optimize strategically. But the example also displays how we may relate to people and scholarship different from our own in irenic ways. We can expect to encounter actions of unbelievers that, no matter their intention, recognizably image the glory and righteousness of the Lord. We may honor the unbeliever and employ her/his work, because it resembles the Father, valuing both initiation and product as good, without ever conceding a philosophically naive notion of neutrality, or doing anything but affirming the Lordship of God. And while it should not be our simplistic intention, our Christlike response may also gently subvert heart rebellion and incline the unbeliever to Christ.

QUESTIONS FOR DISCUSSION

1. The motifs of antithesis and common grace may be new to you. Briefly describe each position in your own words.

2. You can imagine a spectrum stretching between antithetical approaches and common grace approaches. Where have you been located on the spectrum? How has this come to expression in your life?

3. In what ways does this texture lead you to revise your outlook?

4. Do you agree that covenant epistemology responsibly justifies an irenic, common-grace approach? Why or why not?

5. How is this a way that covenant epistemology prompts epistemic healing?

7

Knowing as Unfolding Covenant Relationship

Conversation with Mike Williams

ALL KNOWLEDGE AND KNOWING, covenant epistemology proposes, is in some way covenantally interpersonal. I believe that covenantal interpersonhood, as a paradigm of knowing, fleshes out a Polanyian epistemology. And I believe that, since this paradigm makes sense of key features of our everyday knowing, our knowing will be better for intentionally living out this paradigm. In this chapter I develop what I have in mind by the "covenant" in covenant epistemology.

John Frame, as we saw, offers his theological and epistemic proposals as the implications of the Lordship—the covenant headship—of God. He doesn't really talk about the covenant itself, or develop it epistemologically as I mean to do here. Theologian Michael Williams' work shares a fundamental accord with Frame's in that covenant relationship with God as Lord is the most important thing. But as we shall see, Williams offers an understanding of biblical covenant as dynamic and storied. Granted, the two address different projects: Frame is intentional in developing an epistemology—an account of knowing—on the way to his theological account of human knowledge of God. Williams' passion lies in offering the Christian believer both an accessibly coherent grasp of Scripture and an encouragement to place her- or himself in it for spiritual blessing.[1] The different emphases of these two in part reflect evolving emphases in theology over the last decades. It is Williams' idea

---

1. "My Father, My People, My Story" is the foreword I proposed for Williams' book, *Far as the Curse is Found*, which I revised for publication. It saw the light of day in Meek, "My Father, My People, My Story." Also, while Williams is philosophically sensitive, it is always his agenda to distance himself from the substantivalism that has damagingly hampered philosophical approaches and adversely impacted western culture (the defective default of ch. 1), including, most offensively, theological and biblical studies.

of covenant as unfolding relationship that we engage in this chapter, and that I draw on as a contour of covenant epistemology.[2]

But here is the important link that I discern between Frame and Williams for the argument I am forging. Frame expounded the normative dimension of all knowing. Williams shows the way for me to link the normative to covenant. Williams shows the way to understand covenant as dynamically unfolding interpersonal relationship. So the link enables a connection between the normative dimension and interpersonal relationship. Covenant as interpersonal relationship makes sense of oughtness, specifically of the normative dimension of knowing. This linkage starts to make sense of the hints of the interpersonal that we find in knowing.

Thus, following Williams, from the Christian Scriptures I cull the motif of covenant, mining it profitably for our paradigmatic understanding of knowing. While many theologians identify covenant as a helpful way to describe thematically what is going on in Scripture between people and the triune God, many of them specify "covenant" as a formal treaty, especially that between a conquering suzerain and a vassal.[3] In contrast, Williams takes covenant to refer to the unfolding relationship between persons, such as in a covenant of friendship or of marriage.

I will then widen Williams' idea of covenant to refer to the parameters that intangibly but normatively constitute any interpersonal relationship, according to the particular level and nature of the involvement. Covenants constitute interpersonal relationships the way rules constitute a game. Covenant and relationship require each other mutually. In a later section I will show how this widened account shapes covenant epistemology.

I work with Williams' notion of covenant because his approach, after several years of his and my friendship and collegiality, is implicitly my own. It brings forward the important context of relationship that covenant integrally involves, making possible the wonderful alignment between relationship, covenant, and knowing. It was in the

2. In some ways, my own project may be more akin to Frame's in that I am interested in epistemology—human knowing in general. But in contrast to both, while the theological context and motifs are critical, they are not my focus. My focus is simply human knowing. However, Frame and Williams would both agree that understanding human knowing as stewardly or creaturely has a critical pay-off for doing excellent theology (or excellent anything), for spiritual formation, and for the enjoyment of God.

3. Williams references Mendenhall, "Covenant Forms."

context of our many conversations and team-teaching that together we began to formulate the idea of covenant epistemology that I develop in this book.[4]

WILLIAMS' EXPOSITION OF COVENANT

According to Williams, twentieth-century archaeological research has discovered that *berith*, covenant, was a typical way, in the ancient Near East, of describing a relationship typified by promises and obligations, especially a political or economic one.[5] In Scripture the word occurs 286 times, never having been given a formal definition. Scripture's first readers must have been conversant with the term.

Interpersonal Relationship

As it is used in Scripture, however, it becomes apparent that covenant, specifically the covenant between Yahweh, the sovereign Lord, and his sovereignly chosen people, is no mere economic contract. What Scripture indicates is that covenant is first and foremost a relationship between persons. "A covenant is nothing less than a historical relationship between persons . . . God works in history, which is to say that he works covenantally. God enters into relationship with his people, which is to say that he calls them into covenant."[6] To enter into relationship is to call into covenant. Covenants could only exist between persons.

When Williams thinks of covenant, he generally pictures, as a prime analogy, a marriage relationship. Indeed Scripture appropriates the metaphor first: it calls God's people his bride. He makes the point that such a relationship is constituted by a pledge and also unfolds over time. Frame's usage also evidenced understanding of covenant describing an intimate familial relationship.

Also, Williams argues that the concept is justifiably and helpfully employed to describe the entire biblical story: "the Christian religion is . . . the historical unfolding of God's covenantal involvement in the world, the acme of which is God's coming into the world in the person

---

4. The name of the seminary, Covenant Theological Seminary, in St. Louis, Missouri—the context in which we collaborated—also afforded a good rationale for the choice of descriptor.

5. Williams, *Far as the Curse is Found*, 45.

6. Ibid., 36, 60, 62.

of Jesus Christ."[7] "The biblical drama displays the fundamental, unfolding continuity of a personal relationship."[8] Thus, Williams utilizes this concept of covenant to characterize, unify, and make accessible sense of the Scripture-wide "drama of redemption." Scripture, taken as a whole, can be seen as itself God's unfolding and covenantal self-disclosure to his loved people.

Mutuality: Initiative and Response

A covenant, as an interpersonal relationship, is characterized by mutuality. There is interplay of personal initiative, answered by personal response. This back and forth interplay is the pattern of covenant. In the covenant God initiates with humankind, his initiative is sovereign and gracious (not earned), a relationship approximated in ancient Near Eastern suzerain-vassal covenants. God's initiative precedes and thereby creates relationship. Parity covenants, by contrast, occur between partners of comparable status.[9] But sovereignty in the case of Yahweh, the covenant Lord, does not efface the mutuality of relationship expressed in initiative and response.

Historical

A covenant relationship is integrally historical. Historical action and context is important to the covenant relationship.[10] A covenant relationship, mutual and reciprocal as it is, is historically organic. It deepens and undergoes change even as it maintains continuity. A relationship retains the past as it develops.[11] Covenant always unfolds historically, and comes to apt expression, therefore, in story. A covenant is a historical relationship between persons. Scripture portrays and embodies—as covenant document—Yahweh working covenantally in history. The covenant document of Scripture is not an epistemology textbook, but rather it is, itself, a knowing, Williams would say. It is a specimen of the paradigmat-

---

7. Ibid., xiii. Not all covenant theologians concur with Williams' expression of it, nor are all Christian theologians covenant theologians.

8. Ibid., xii.

9. Ibid., 139.

10. Ibid., 143.

11. Ibid., 46.

ic, ultimate ontological context; the interpersonal relationship between Yahweh, the covenant Lord, and his creation and his people.

Promises and Obligations and Their Relationship

A covenant is an interpersonal relationship typified by promises and obligations—promises of loyalty and love, fulfillment of obligations—mutually.[12] It is important to see that even the sovereign covenant Lord, Yahweh, pledges loyalty and fulfills obligation. God binds himself in covenant.

Specifying the relationship between the promise of loyalty and the obligations enjoined is important to grasping the nature of covenant, setting it off in contrast to contract and law. Williams underscores repeatedly that in biblical covenant, love and loyalty precede law and obligation.[13] A covenant is an intimate relationship; it can't be reduced to formal obligations. The obligatory serves the relational. Covenant relationship is not conditioned on obligation; rather, obligation proceeds from and in response to divine initiative. Sovereign initiative (grace) precedes human responsibility. Law, so prominent in Scripture, is not to be understood as creating relationship. Rather, law nourishes relationship. Williams notes how, while fatherly love of a son is unconditional, the son's flagrant disobedience would damage rather than nourish the relationship. He notes that Torah, a term for a portion of the Hebrew Old Testament, means fatherly instruction, in compliance with which is found security and blessing and shalom. Relationship is the context of the normative; not vice versa.

This is a critical point that many well-meaning Christian believers miss or struggle to hold in view. It comes to expression as the question of law vs. grace. One of the key reasons Williams writes is to show that God as portrayed in the Old Testament is no different from the God portrayed in the New. What God does in Jesus Christ and the gospel is of a piece with his covenantal initiative from the outset. It is profoundly mistaken and personally damaging to misconstrue the Old Testament, as over against the New, as being "about law." As will be seen, I feel that this point has profound implications for epistemology and ontology.

---

12. Ibid., 46–47.
13. Ibid., 147, 211, 212–13, 62, 135, 151–52.

Not a Contract

While in common parlance the word *berith* may have signified mere political and economic treaties, *biblical* covenant is no mere contract.[14] Scripture brims with familial language: father (sometimes mother) and son (or daughter), husband and wife, to be specific. Covenant is about love and intimacy in relationship. While obligatory action is enjoined, this simply never should be thought of legalistically or contractually. Williams notes that while the breaking of a contract might be precisely designated, determining whether a covenant had been broken would be more difficult and ambiguous.

For that matter, this interpersonal intimacy is such that the term, *covenant*, resists definition. Williams quotes O. Palmer Robertson: "Asking for a definition of 'covenant' is something like asking for a definition of 'mother.'"[15] This quip implies both that it is ridiculous, and that it is ridiculous because it's your mother—a living, intimately close, person, and one who defines you more than you define her or the relationship. One does not define relationships or persons, which is what covenant integrally involves.[16]

The Goal: Friendship

The goal of covenant is intimacy, friendship, communion, the richest of interpersonal relationships, in which persons are persons to the full, as is the communion between them.[17] Here, of course, Williams' articulation accords fully with Frame's. It is, I believe, easier to see friendship as the goal in the context of Williams' formulation.

Why should covenant characterize divine dealings with human beings? Because God as triune is already three Persons in relationship.[18] God's own character is fundamentally relational. He created humans for companionship, and to image him in relationship. We'll talk more about this is in a later conversation.

14. Ibid., 145, 146, 212.

15. Ibid., 45.

16. Consider how couples moving from friendship to romance laughingly talk about DTR talks—define-the-relationship talks. In these what is occurring is a shift in the nature of the covenantal loyalty and obligations that constitute the relationship. These shifts can be frustrating and difficult—and wonderful—or not.

17. Ibid., 116.

18. Ibid., 60.

THE WORLD AS COVENANTAL

Williams argues that not only is the relationship of Yahweh to his people covenantal. The language of Scripture concerning the creation of world also displays covenantal features.[19] Thus, covenant is "a totalizing relationship," says Williams. All created things, not just humans, are bound covenantally to God. They are, as I have suggested, covenanted into existence. I noted earlier that "Let there be . . . " is the kind of language the maker of a game or a fantasy world might employ.

Frame's account meshes with Williams' elucidation of creation existing by virtue of divine covenant. Everything exists by virtue of a covenant relationship to the Lord of all. The perfectly consistent character of the objects in our world reflects the utter faithfulness of God's character in keeping to his word. An important corollary of this is that, as I noted before, were God not the covenant Lord, there would be no created reality, and no human knowers, and no knowledge. All human enterprise and objective reality exists and exists only by virtue of God being the covenant Lord he describes himself to be in Scripture. In this respect, creation, too—the known, like human knowing—is like a marriage, in that it is quite literally constituted by the pledge.

The Human as Covenant Mediator

Another feature of covenants, according to Williams, is that commonly a certain party is named to serve representatively with respect to the covenant, responsible before one party for embodying and bringing covenant promises and obligations to fruition.[20] The biblical covenant of creation designates humans to care for the rest of the created order, and to cultivate and voice its praise of him. Williams' work implies that human engagement with the world involves "transcribing God's character" in it.[21] This suggests that human engagement, including knowing, has something distinctly normative about it. All human action should be seen in this light. And since human action involves human knowing as a necessary component, human knowing is most appropriately un-

19. Ibid., 47–49.

20. Ibid., 50–52.

21. This beautiful phrase, which Williams uses in the title of ch. 9, he derives from James M. Grier, my college mentor, to whom I dedicated *Longing to Know*. Williams completed a degree at Grand Rapids Baptist Seminary, where Jim served for years as Academic Dean, and is now *emeritus*.

derstood in the context of covenantal, mediatorial, human care for God's world. When we talked about Frame's work in the context of a wider reformational worldview, we noted this important biblical vision regarding human calling. Since human knowing is part of the way humans as image-bearers engage the world, I called Frame's contribution, knowing as stewardship.

Jesus is God himself providing a perfect covenant mediator. Scripture says that humankind, represented by the first Adam, as a result of his rebellion, fell far short of fulfilling this covenant obligation. Jesus is "the second Adam" whom God provides for the sake of his own covenant. Since creation and human culture, including human knowing, has been radically bent by human sin, Jesus' atonement, thus, is central to the renewal of all things (Jesus' term for it).[22] In this way, Williams shows, the gospel of Christ fits (and then becomes) the biblical pattern of redemption, in the context of God's identifiably covenantal dealing with all creation, and specifically humankind.

Not Ascent but Descent

One final feature. Contrary to common understandings of most of the world's religious practice, including that of many well-meaning Christians, the "motion," or trajectory of the biblical covenant is not first the motion of ascent—the knower/worshipper ascending to God. It is, instead, descent—the descent of God to humans. Williams states: "If we think that the biblical story is about how we can ascend to God, we have it completely wrong. God is the one who comes to his people to enter into intimate covenant relationship with them and to be with them forever . . . The biblical hope is not the ascent of man, but the descent of God."[23]

God descends to covenant creation into existence, and to sustain it, every atom in every moment. God descends to covenant with his people—to dwell with them. God descends in the Incarnation. God descends in the renewal of all things. The pattern of redemption, and the initiative of covenant relationship, is the descent of God.

22. Matt 19:28.
23. Williams, *Far as the Curse is Found*, 281–82.

WEAVING WILLIAMS' INSIGHTS
INTO COVENANT EPISTEMOLOGY

Having sketched the idea of covenant that Williams finds to be central in the story of Scripture, we are in a position to think through its implications for human knowing and for the covenant epistemology proposal.

Theological Warrant for Covenantal Dimensions to Being and Knowing

If you grant this theological vision, it leads us to anticipate finding covenantal dimensions of both reality and knowing. It suggests that reality is strategically amenable to covenantal behavior in knowing, and knowing as covenant behavior.

It implies an ontology (an understanding of reality) in which a Person, interpersonal relationship, and covenant, are the fundamental and formative categories. God covenanted it into existence. All God's dealing with and in the universe is covenantal. The world reflects his utterly faithful character. The world is optimally reliable and also knowable, both Frame and Williams maintain, because it is in covenant relationship with him.

Real things, as covenanted into existence, display features of covenant relationship: unfolding continuity of character, responsiveness to covenant relationship. Things require a promise of fidelity prior to responsive personal disclosure, the knower's pledge of faithfulness in the face of future surprising revelations. They require submission. Knowing and growing a rose bush requires submitting to the normativity of the world, attending to the stipulations of its covenanted character and responding honorably.

The known, thus, includes both God and his personalized handiwork. And, given the relational context of covenantal action, we may say that God makes himself known—self-disclosure, self-revelation—in his Word and works, and wants to be known by his people.

This makes sense, in light of our common experience. The composer of a musical work—whether Mozart or U2—is quickly identifiable to regular listeners. Serious students of such a composer or composers listen deeply to the handiwork in order to indwell its maker. The same is true of a work of visual or literary art. Anything we create is infused by our personality.

Scripture attests that God himself wants to be known·by us from creation. Paul the apostle once addressed philosophers gathered in Athens' Areopagus. Referencing a statue "To an Unknown God," standing among the myriads of idols in the city, Paul spoke to them of the God "who made the world and everything in it" who is "Lord of heaven and earth and does not live in temples built by hands." He told them that that God created the world and history "so that men would seek him and perhaps reach out for him and find him, though he is not far from each one of us. For in him we live and move and have our being."[24] God desiring relationship, beyond that of the Trinity, perhaps because of the joys of Trinitarian communion, is back of all of reality.

Humans are covenant mediators. That means that in responding covenantally to a rose bush, for example, the gardener is also both responding covenantally to God, and mediating God's covenant of creation in preserving and developing it.

The Relationship between Relationship and Covenant

Thinking more deeply about the idea of covenant as relationship, we can see that the converse is implied: relationship is covenantal. Any relationship, no matter how minimal, has covenantal, pledge-like features. We are quite familiar with the idea of there being "levels of commitment"; but we may perhaps have never linked the word, commitment, to the word, covenant. Some may perhaps want to reserve the word, covenant, for the most comprehensive sorts of relationship. This would be a matter of term usage. My point stands, that all levels of relationship are just the levels that they are because of the implied covenantal terms (in the other sense) that constitute the relationship.

Thus, when I use the word, covenantal, I have in mind the prescriptive or normative dimensions of a relationship: its constitutive boundaries, character of commitment, substance or character, status. These are the boundaries and tacit agreements which partners in the covenant have to abide by in order to maintain the relationship.

In saying this, I do not in any way mean to oppose what Williams is saying. Williams as a theologian is challenging a long-term tendency in Christian scholarship and practice to see covenant as a contract, and to

24. Acts 17:22–28. Thanks to my former student, Andrew Colbert, for pointing out to me both the similarity of knowing a composer from his music, as well as this Scriptural corroboration. The latter is also a point made by Newbigin; see ch. 15.

be more forensic than relational, therefore, in the view of what is going on in Scripture, than Scripture itself intimates. I realize that what I am saying here may sound as if I am aligning covenant more with law than with relationship. But Williams' point about law is not that it is not involved, and not that relationship opposes it. His point is that relationship *precedes* and provides the *context for* it—always. In a relationship of love and obligation, love precedes, law nourishes.

What motivates the relationship, he wants to underscore, is not conditional stipulations—else we have misrepresented what Scripture describes and embodies regarding God's sovereign and steadfast (covenant) love. Williams would agree that all relationships have stipulative constitution, as opposed to stipulative motivation. What motivates God, we may say, is not desire for law-keeping, but desire for relationship—in other words, love of the beloved.

It's helpful to think about friendship, then, as covenantal. It is a pledge, just as marriage is a pledge, but it is usually implicit and *sans* ceremony.[25] There are levels of covenanting that match our levels of friendship: from airplane seat neighbor to acquaintance to classmate to neighbor to teammate to family, lifelong friends and a marriage partner.

Covenantal bonds are often tacit, but nevertheless palpably real. If something looks amiss at my neighbor's house when I know she is out of town, I check it out. I rescue her trash can when it has blown into the way of oncoming traffic. We trade services, each caring for the other's pets, free of charge, while the other is away. We bind ourselves to faithfulness of a certain sort or level.

Friendship is one the richest covenants, and rare. Deep friendship is intimate covenant love.[26] Deep friendship requires unconditional regard for the other's dignity and good. Part of the self-binding that friendship requires is to the end of preserving evenly free consent. "Friendship is the miracle by which a person consents to view from a certain distance, and without coming any nearer, the very being who is necessary to

25. Consider, however, the ceremonial dimensions of the pact of friendship between David and Jonathan (1 Samuel 20).

26. It is important to realize that intimacy does not require sexual relations. Intimacy, as a friend of mine defines it, is "in-to-me-see"—fundamentally, being present to one another. It is not, in all relationships, diminished by the absence of sexual relations. In fact sexual relations, if inappropriately focused on the body, can diminish intimacy.

him as food," says Simone Weil.[27] She is emphatic that if free consent is jeopardized, the term, friendship, no longer can be said to pertain. What you have instead is some form of abuse or other sub-par, sub-personal relationship.

Intimacy, or communion, takes place in friendship. Intimacy is a mutual self-disclosing, a being present to one-another. I have in mind what I have called "starbucking"—openly, mutually present communion in conversation over coffee. As Williams emphasizes, friendship should always be seen as a mutual reciprocity unfolding dynamically through time; thus, starbucking moments are not sustained unremittingly. Rather, the relation resembles the reciprocity of a dance, in which partners rhythmically and complementarily move together and move apart.

The covenantal nature of relationship is most painfully apparent when the covenant is broken. Contrasted to a contractual agreement, covenantal bonds are more subtle: it can be very difficult to say whether a covenant has been violated. Whether it has or not can be disputed by one of its partners. And if abuse has been a factor, the one being abused may actually refuse to admit even (especially!) to her or himself that a covenantal abrogation has occurred. But attack, abandonment, betrayal— these words are duly loaded with the most intense psychological pain. Violation of covenant may be technically subtle, but is more palpably felt. Its impact on a person is lifelong.[28]

My point here is that relationship is constituted by prescriptive, normative, covenantal, pledge-like dimensions. If those dimensions do not pertain, there is no relationship. But the relationship is just what makes them covenantal. This is the picture, with all its rich implications, that we take from Williams into covenant epistemology. To say "interpersonal covenant relationship" is to be a bit redundant, as the two adjectives imply one another. However, we must honor both aspects with intentionality when we bring it to understanding human knowing.

Because relationship is covenantal, covenantal features reference the interpersonal. Williams' proper gripe with an understanding

27. Weil, *Waiting for God.* 135. Weil offers profound insight into friendship in this passage.

28. Allender, *Healing Path.* Additionally, Allender makes the point that dealing with the hurt is the path to healing, and the prospect of a signature feature in one's story. He furthers this theme in Allender, *To Be Told.* Allender's thesis accords with (in fact, shapes) my claim regarding covenant epistemology that knowing, as a coming to know self and other, displays an actively healing quality.

of biblical covenant along the lines of the contractual is that biblical covenant inherently references a more intimate relationship. Covenant is not opposed to the personal; it implies the larger, intimately interpersonal relationship. Where there is covenant, there are persons in the vicinity—persons in relationship. Knowing, I am arguing, betokens the interpersonal, partly by virtue of its normative dimension and of the way it involves the knower in covenantal self-binding. It also betokens the interpersonal in the way the real self-discloses surprisingly and graciously. Williams' notion of covenant resonates with all this. Thus, it offers a critical piece of the vision that is covenant epistemology.

Knowing as Creationally Situated

Williams, in his account of covenant as historically unfolding relationship, is endeavoring to treat with integrity its situated character. Where Frame speaks of servant thinking, Williams speaks of creaturely knowing. Williams says, "We need to pay due attention to the particularity of our rootedness in time and space, both as designated by God as our starting point and as the object of our stewardship."[29] He draws the implication, as does Frame, that, methodologically, it is legitimate and requisite to explore how humans know, how knowing works, as a proximal starting point in knowing God. Having attended to the way knowing works, and the way the world works, we can return to Scripture and find that Scripture is doing the same thing. "It's okay to ransack an Egyptian," Mike quips, referring to the biblical story of the exodus of the nation of Israel from its slavery in Egypt, in which the departing Hebrews took with them the Egyptians' treasure when they left (actually, the Egyptians begged them to take it!). St. Augustine spoke of "plundering the Egyptians" as making use of unbelievers' conceptual innovations. This is just what seeing knowing as creationally situated enjoins us to do. This idea also gets referred to in connection with affirming common grace, of which we have already spoken. One may start from our situation without blindly sanctioning it, however: it is nevertheless revisable and transformable in light of subsequent insight, and in particular, in responsible, self-aware submission to authoritative guides.

Our situatedness involves what Polanyi had in mind by the bodily rootedness of all thought. It includes our embeddedness in a culture, a

29. Meek and Williams, "Covenant Epistemology."

language, a community, and a history. It requires us to depend intentionally on authoritative guides, to navigate orienting by guiding stars, maxims and persons outside ourselves who know us better than we know ourselves and teach us to see what is there. We need to see our rootedness not as inhibiting us in knowing, but rather as situating us strategically for its further advance. We only move forward from a beachhead.

Christian approaches differ widely in how they value physical creation and human culture. This is what Richard Niebuhr categorized in his famous and helpful little book, *Christ and Culture*.[30] There is a Christian version of the default mode, also: a street theology, if you will. Most Christians untaught in their beliefs (or taught but unhearing!) incline to outlooks stemming from—you guessed it—western philosophy: that the disembodied soul is what matters to God, and that physical matter is intrinsically sub-par, evil, of no interest and value to God, that salvation is of the soul not the body, and "this world is not my home." These views can only be sustained, I feel, where the Bible has not been heard and taken to heart. Williams, Frame, myself, and others in the reformational tradition, by contrast, affirm what is known as "a strong doctrine of creation": creation has value because made by God, and once human rebellion induces a curse, it becomes the object of God's redemptive concern. Jesus is incarnated, Jesus is raised bodily, and the *eschaton*—the last state—is one of "the renewal of all things." A strong doctrine of creation naturally entails an epistemological approach that honors situatedness, not absolutizing it, nor exonerating it, but treating it with integrity in the knowing process.

We have learned to identify and be intentional about seeing our rootedness as something we live, indwell, subsidiarily. I think that subsidiary knowledge is an immensely insightful way to honor, as well as profitably elucidate, the creational situatedness the biblical vision enjoins us to accredit. This is yet another resonance between Polanyian epistemology and the work of Frame and Williams that I have felt is telling.

Indeed, human knowers are situated. The rich multi-faceted conceptual frameworks of both Polanyi and Frame allow us to note that knowing is situated not just in creational rootedness but also more deeply in interpersonal covenantal relationship. The fundamental situation in which we find ourselves is, covenant epistemology is concerned to argue, an interpersonal relationship. This is another way in which the biblical

---

30. Niebuhr, *Christ and Culture*.

vision of covenant as unfolding relationship profoundly contexts, and thus situates, human knowing.

Covenantal Care and Pledge

The biblical thematic vision of covenant thus intrinsically supports the project of drawing on these resources to identify and exercise with intentionality covenantal dimensions of knowing. This is just the project of covenant epistemology. Here are some features that to me are especially telling, resonant, and significant.

Human knowing, viewed either theologically or viewed phenomenologically—meaning, viewing what actually happens when we know—involves the knower in pledge, self-binding, responsible risk and commitment, and normatively active shaping of patterns. Covenantal dimensions of knowing just are what Polanyi designated as responsible commitment and what Frame designated as the normative. Viewed theologically, the human knower, in knowing, just is stewarding the earth, fulfilling the cultural mandate, and exercising his/her covenant mediatorial role in God's creation.

Covenantal self-binding consists of commitment to the as-yet-undiscovered reality. Belief, as described in John and in Hebrews, just is the epistemic act: personal and risky submission to the reality of the known. It involves hours of investment in training to put oneself in the way of apprehending the world's disclosure. And it is the respect, humility, patience, and perseverance (often for a long time in the dark!) which brings us to a moment of insight. This is covenantal behavior that invites the real, as we will say later. Knowing takes a form not unlike trust and obedience, the language of relational surrender. Allegiance and obligation are prior to understanding and to justification. Obedience is lived truth; obedience precedes knowing/accessing truth. The truths we hold are reflected in our behavior (contra hypocrisy). Williams adds that in the knowing relationship of humans to God, the opposite of knowing is not ignorance, but rebellion.

Knowing as Unfolding Relationship

We should think of human knowing as an unfolding covenant relationship. It is highly appropriate to cast human knowing as "being on the way." In our knowing we are, as some have put it, in the middle of the story.[31] We are on the near side of knowing. That means that knowing involves risk and hope. All knowing is a coming to know, an act in process over time. Its impetus is longing, desire, for future insight, and his/her anticipation of it. It is the apprenticeship it takes to make us trained and properly positioned knowers, and the time it takes for charactered centers to unfold themselves to us. It is the knower's reaching beyond his/her current situation, vectoring from herself/himself toward the world. It is moving from situated roots in space and time toward the world. You can see that in these phrases I interweave aspects I have drawn from Polanyi, Williams, others, and life.

It involves us in what I call surprising recognition: reality's self-disclosures continually surprise us, yet we often feel that we recognize them. I have in mind Polanyi's constant reminder that the indeterminate future manifestations of the real are both inexhaustive and systematic, and to see our sense of this as indicating that we have indeed made contact. I noted this elsewhere: Williams would say that in Scripture, prophecy works like this, as does what he calls the pattern of redemption. Prophecy is not prediction, but rather, promise. There is no way that Isaiah, writing chapter 53, could have predicted Jesus of Nazareth and his crucifixion. But having known Jesus and his crucifixion, a disciple such as those on the road to Emmaus would experience deeply surprising recognition, and Isaiah 53 could no longer be understood except as fulfilled by Jesus. Knowing unfolds transformatively: we anticipate it, yet when it comes it seems to be both what we anticipated, as well as something far richer than we ever imagined. Williams' understanding of unfolding relationship aligns with this.

Descent and Realism

With regard to the real that we are coming to know, I believe we may helpfully allow our sense of the matter to be shaped by biblical covenant. Covenant epistemology rejects the idea that human knowing is one-way, that an inert known is either uncovered or constituted in a linear, methodical way by the knower. Instead, what we experience is that reality breaks in, and does so with almost a studied disregard for the knower's previously articulated expectations. It does break in, I argue, in person-like, undictated, response to what might be called heart dispositions—

---

31. These are Newbigin-inspired comments.

namely, trust and obedience. And thus we may and can only *invite* the real. Its gracious breaking in is akin to the descent of God.[32]

The descent of God, therefore, both underscores realism in epistemology and indicates what knowing reality will be like. We can expect it to invade and transform the knower. We can expect it to unfold an abundance of surprising future manifestations. But even more profoundly, it is appropriate, humbling, and thrilling, to explore the implication that the knower, in exercising initiative to engage the real, isn't the partner taking the first step. Reality initiates the engagement. All human knowing is response.

Newbigin offers a hauntingly beautiful analogy: to know is to ask into the darkness, "Is someone there?"[33] People who ask such a question may well have been prompted, often inexplicably, from without.

Communion/Friendship as the Goal of Knowing

The fact that the goal of covenant in Williams, as well as of knowledge of God in Frame, is communion or friendship holds an important implication if we make covenant a contour of epistemology. It implies, I believe, that a vibrant account of knowing should construe the goal of the enterprise, not as the acquisition of exhaustive, lucid information, but as the kind of knowing that one person enjoys of a close covenant partner. The dichotomies of the defective default continue to incline us to a "certainty, or bust!" attitude.

People with perfectionistic inclinations are particularly vulnerable to the misguided appeal of exhaustive knowledge. Sincere Christians can misguidedly anticipate knowing all there is to know about God and reality. So the idea of ultimate indeterminacy or mystery can sound like settling for second-best, a product, we conclude derogatorily, of our finitude—as if we were somehow hampered by finitude. That is one reason why I think it is revolutionary and altogether wonderful to cast the idea of knowing in light of the paradigm of interpersonal relationship. The very realizable, yet grace-filled and joyful, goal is communion. Communion is desire fulfilled. But persons, like all reality, are inexhaustible—and that is because they are profoundly real. They always surprise you. Seeing

---

32. Similarly, note Annie Dillard's intertwining of a muskrat sighting with God's coming in Meek, *Longing to Know*, ch. 11, n.22.

33. Newbigin, *Foolishness to the Greeks*, 94.

knowing as interpersonal helps us see that this is a wonderful situation, far better, not worse, than two-dimensional certainty.

Covenant Blessing, Covenant Curse: Knowing for Shalom

Finally, Scripture indicates that construing divine-human dealings covenantally leads us to expect that keeping covenant brings blessing, and breaking it brings curse. I have already said that human knowing as covenantal just is an expression of the cultural mandate. Where covenant is operative, results are either blessing or curse; there is no neutral result. Humans, I observe, do not have the option of opting out of the cultural mandate. It is as if we are hardwired to interact with the world, for good or for ill. We can't not shape our environment, we only can choose to bless or to curse (or some exasperating mixture of both).

Similarly, I want to argue, we should expect human knowing either to bless or to curse. One thing that this leads us to expect is that every human knowing event changes both knower and known in the process. Theologically, we should not have been surprised by findings in the sciences about the unavoidable interplay of observer and observed. Knowing is a responsible, active shaping by the knower, said Polanyi. In light of Williams' idea of covenant, knowing is an unfolding and mutual relationship. Where we behave covenantally, both knower and known should be healed, transformed, and blessed. Knowing responsibly brings blessing; knowing irresponsibly brings curse. Where humans have been made covenantally central to creation, there is a profound link between knowing the world well and knowing God; correspondingly, cursing the earth and not knowing God.

Respectfully appropriating Nicholas Wolterstorff's beautiful phrase, "educating for *shalom*," I want to speak of knowing for *shalom*.[34] This, surely, is what human knowing as part of the cultural mandate was meant to be. Yes, this side of the renewal of all things, our efforts are thwarted and poisoned. We bring curse even when we intend blessing.[35] In fact, we do this by, among other things, blindly harboring a defective epistemology. But that does not require that in our epistemology we may not live in light of the ideal.

---

34. See ch. 16.

35. Common grace means that in God's kindness we sometimes do the opposite.

Thus we see how Williams' idea of covenant accords with Polanyian epistemology and Frame's insights, and with everyday human experience. They blend together to point powerfully in the direction of covenant epistemology. Williams supplies the idea of covenant as unfolding interpersonal relationship that suggests the pattern of the interpersoned in that dynamism of coming to know, not to mention the presence of persons in the vicinity of knower and known. Covenant elucidates the reciprocity of the relationship, in particular with respect to the descent of God as the primary direction of motion in the relationship, and with respect to the goal of communion.

QUESTIONS FOR DISCUSSION

1. In what respects does Williams' portrayal of biblical Christian religion amplify your own understanding of it?

2. Does it make sense to connect the normative and the covenantal?

3. How does the motif of unfolding relationship, covenantally constituted, make helpful sense of your experiences of knowing?

4. Discuss the idea that knowing involves being known. Where in your life have you experienced this? How does it help to view this as the descent of God? What is it like to see the motion of reality as descent?

5. What does it look like to know for *shalom*?

PART FOUR

Interpersonhood

8

KNOWING AS INTERPERSONAL

Conversation with John Macmurray

So FAR IN THIS book we have given attention to three contours of covenant epistemology. The first was negative: the widely held default regarding knowledge as information, characterized by damaging dichotomies and problematic attitudes and implications, calls for another kind of knowing, one in which the personal, the interpersoned, is paradigmatic. Second, Polanyian subsidiary-focal integration positively anchors the thesis of covenant epistemology: all human knowing involves subsidiary-focal integration in a transformative knowing event. Hints of the personed, and of interpersoned reciprocity, are evident in the vicinity of knower, known, and knowing.

Hints of interpersonal reciprocity led us to inquire: given how reality responds to us in our knowing and especially to our knowing well, is it apt to think of knower and known as persons or personlike, and of knowing as an interpersonal relationship? And if so, what does this look like? And how does such a vision reform our efforts to know? This suggests the covenant epistemology vision.

Some of those telltale hints of the interpersonal are covenantal. So next we culled from Christian theology the idea of covenant as unfolding, storied interpersonal relationship. We have developed the accompanying idea of relationship as covenantally constituted. These are germinating components of covenant epistemology. We have in the process also attended to key dimensions of a theological vision of God, reality, humanness, and knowing, as well as a sophisticated, triadic, conceptual handle on them. Knowing integrally involves the normative dimension, and we have linked the normative with the covenantal.

Through this we are gaining a perspective on reality in which the proposal that human knowing is, paradigmatically at least, covenantally-constituted interpersoned relationship, makes more sense. We are building, we might also say, a palette of conceptual color rich enough that we may paint such a proposal, or paint it in such a way that signatures of the interpersoned may be seen to enrich allusively throughout.

The third positive contour of covenant epistemology is what I call interpersonhood. This made-up word of mine stands for the two-part thesis: that we should see personhood itself as interpersonal, or interpersoned; and that we should see this interpersonhood as the context and central nerve of human knowing. As I noted before, even when dealing with an epistemology as rich as Polanyi's and with an idea of covenant as rich as Frame's or Williams', our penchant persists to render knowing and being in the impersonal key. Counteracting this calls for a focused study of personhood as it pertains to human knowing.

But this is not just about correcting bad habits, it is about responsibly following the lead of our own concepts. The normative and covenantal in knowing begs the larger interpersonal context. This compels us to explore the interpersonal and endeavor to understand how it and knowing are integrally related. This will help us elucidate the telltale personal features of human knowing. And this in turn will make us better knowers and more whole persons.

As my own being-on-the-way to covenant epistemology has been unfolding, interpersonhood is the contour the apprehension of which I most lacked initially, the one most needed, and also the one most recent as a focus of my study. Thus in this section of the book I engage a number of thinkers whose work develops, or allows us to develop, the idea of personhood and its bearing on human knowing. I go over the ground of their work, indwelling the very words in which they express their proposals because I need still to hear and mull over their insights as they express them. The fact that this slow attention is needed is not due entirely to the author's personal deficiency; it is due, I believe, in good measure to the defective understanding of knowing that our cultural tradition has allowed to accrue over centuries. I trust that my more attentive mulling will aid the reader even as it is needed by the author. So on the way to fleshing out the vision of covenant epistemology, we will engage in an extended exploration of interpersonhood. I believe that we must think it through, but also that we must dwell in it in order to be reattuned by it.

With this conversation with John Macmurray, I believe that the unfolding trajectory of this book turns an important corner. Up to this point I have referenced the interpersoned repeatedly, descrying hints of it right and left. Now is the time we may finally attend to it directly. And with John Macmurray, we come on a fresh vista: we start to be able to see our way in restoring the interpersoned to personhood, then to cast knowing as interpersoned.

We will find that interpersonhood is not simply an account of personhood. It offers the very context and core of knowing that we seek. Interpersonhood explores what covenant metonymously references, and thus further elucidates the interpersonal nuances of knowing. Hitherto, we might say, we have attended to knowing, and found the interpersoned, now we attend to the interpersoned, and find knowing.

MEEK ENCOUNTERS THE PERSONAL: EYE-OPENING CONVERSATION WITH JAMES HOUSTON

In June of 2002, I participated in a colloquium that featured James Houston, a gentle octogenarian who, after thirty-five years at Oxford, founded Regent College in Vancouver, British Columbia.[1] Listening to his talks, I marveled at the vast breadth of his learning. But a throw-away comment he made caught my attention, and proved to open this entire vein of the personal to my exploration.

At first I thought I had misheard. Then I heard him say it again and was stunned. He was suggesting that we should cease to construe the human person substantivally. Instead, we should construe personhood in terms of directedness to the other. Substantivalism, you will recall from chapter 1, is the approach to reality that views things, including humans, as substance-attribute, as in, "Man is a rational animal." I have come to believe that this view contributes negatively to our defective epistemic default. But it was in this talk of Houston's that I first heard this proposed. What? I thought. Isn't that what I was supposed to overcome in middle school—you know, succumbing to peer pressure? Isn't that what directedness to the other is? He can't possibly be serious!

After his talk, I asked him about it. He surprised me with his counter-question: "Esther, where do you suppose that Polanyi got the 'person-

---

1. The colloquium, "Love of God, Love of Learning" was sponsored by the Center for Christian Study, University of Virginia, Charlottesville, VA, June 2002.

al' in *Personal Knowledge*?" Houston had been acquainted with Michael Polanyi in England. He shared his generational milieu. He referred now to Polanyi's mid-twentieth-century *magnum opus*. I, of course, counted Polanyi's work as my area of competency. Even though I had written a dissertation on Polanyi's work and a book on Polanyian epistemology, it had never occurred to me to ask that question, nor even to think about personhood as a result of the word in the title.

Dr. Houston answered his own question: "He got it from John Macmurray." Houston also alerted me to the work of John Zizioulas and Colin Gunton, trinitarian theologians whose work we will engage in a later chapter. When we parted at the end of the colloquium, he simultaneously encouraged and humbled me: "With your work in Polanyi, you have made such a wonderful beginning!" Indeed!

From this exchange you can surmise that before that time, in my own thought, the personal had not been a starting category. When I first studied the Framean triad, I was thinking of an abstract triad and abstract dimensions of Lordship, missing entirely that the whole thing was seated in intimate covenantal relationship. My dissertation on Polanyi was completed a decade and a half before I came to identify and jettison my own gut-level Cartesianism.

In 2002, when Dr. Houston so shockingly challenged my own default setting, *Longing to Know* was substantially written. What was in place in my thought, by that time, was a seminal sense of the role of covenant in knowing.[2] The idea of covenant, as we have seen, clearly implies the requisite involvement of persons, both as knower and as known. If knowing is like a marriage, then knowing is covenantal, and it is a relationship between persons. Implied in covenant is personhood, and multiple persons, or at least two. If knowing is covenantal, knowing involves the interpersonal. I had, in a footnote, already marked a place for what I coined as *covenant epistemology*, and looked forward to developing. Thus, my thought was ripe to explore the nature of personhood and its implications for knowing.

But even so, apart from Dr. Houston's tantalizing comments, this rich area might have been bypassed untapped. Instead, my sensitization to things personal has heightened, culminating now in this many-conversationed exploration of interpersonhood with reference to knowing. And my own personal oblivion at the time graphically and sadly repli-

2. Meek, *Longing to Know*, ch. 22.

cates that of an entire, historic, cultural milieu—a default epistemic setting: when it comes to knowledge and knowing, we overlook persons.

Philosopher of religion John Macmurray delivered the prestigious
Gifford Lectures (intended for work in natural religion) in 1954, thus
about the time Polanyi did. These lectures became *The Self as Agent*, and
Persons in Relation.[3] Much like Polanyi's work, Macmurray's has been
overlooked by mainstream philosophical discussion, and perhaps may
find more receptive ears now, decades later.

Now having studied Macmurray's work, I feel that, even if he did
get the *personal* in *Personal Knowledge* from Macmurray, Polanyi did
not actually do with personhood and the personal what Macmurray did.
For Polanyi, the personal in personal knowledge signifies the personal—
human, not subjective, and responsible—involvement of the knower in
knowing: he argues persistently and persuasively that we accredit the
knower's tacit, responsible commitment and active shaping of clues in
any epistemic act.[4] We will get a sense of this as we move through this
conversation.

Having discovered by now not just Macmurray's work but that
of other contemporaries of Polanyi's, I am that much more confident
that Polanyi's work nevertheless falls in line with a wider trend of ideational developments that probed the personal, unlocking profound
insights.[5] And I believe—this is central to what I am doing in covenant
epistemology—that Polanyi's subsidiary-focal integration is fraught
with intimations of the interpersoned, covenantally constituted, and so

---

3. Macmurray, *Self as Agent*; Macmurray, *Persons in Relation.*

4. Polanyi, *Personal Knowledge, passim.* What's more, I believe that Polanyi would
have thought himself to be disagreeing with Macmurray's commitment to the primacy
of the personal. Polanyi's preoccupation with emergence constitutes his attempt to explain how personhood might emerge from impersonal realities. I do not myself believe
that his own views here were consonant with his own best insights.

5. I am thinking here of Martin Buber (see ch. 9) and other theistic existentialists,
and of Max Scheler and others in the personalist tradition. See Allen, "Dialectic of
Adaptation and Assimilation Revisited," which I engage briefly in ch. 15. It may also be
noted as telling that Polanyi came from a Jewish family. Knowing, in the Hebraic tradition, has more commonly been linked to intimacy and covenant, thus, to the personal—
we will see this evidenced in others of our conversations in this book. As I will note, the
rabbinic tradition still requires masters and companions. Polanyi's maternal grandfather
was well-respected as a teacher in the Jewish community in Vilna, Lithuania. And his
mother, Cecile, attracted and anchored a lively intellectual salon in the Polanyis' home
in Budapest. Scott and Moleski, *Michael Polanyi*, ch. 1.

may be fruitfully developed in that direction. To that end, we may probe Macmurray's proposals with greater intentionality than perhaps they were by Polanyi himself.

Macmurray offers an understanding of personhood which requires and, I believe, demonstrates the necessity of casting personhood itself as fundamentally interpersonal and which advances dramatically our insight into knowing as interpersonal.

It would have been wonderful support for covenant epistemology if Macmurray had developed an account that elucidates simply the person-hood of individuals without relationship to other such persons (not that he would have thought this was even possible). But that he understands personhood itself as interpersonal dramatically underscores the propos-al that human knowing is interpersonal. After considering Macmurray's proposals, we hardly need to argue that knowing is interpersonal; we are left only to wonder how we could have thought otherwise. As over against our disembodied, impersonal, default mode, Macmurray points the way to a felt, lived, and celebrated sense of our interpersonhood in knowing and being.

KNOWLEDGE AS INFORMATION SIGNPOSTS
AN INTERPERSONAL CONTEXT

To begin with, even knowledge understood on an impersonal paradigm hints of something more. Knowledge is about statements and proofs? Information? This begs a question, it compels our deference to a larger context. Verbally articulated statements have to do with communication. Communication absolutely requires more than one person. So knowl-edge as statements and proofs requires interpersonhood and thereby witnesses to it.

Macmurray argues that the philosophers of language at the outset of the twentieth century were definitely on to something. These important thinkers worked from the assumption that language is the appropriately all-consuming focus of philosophical study. It is critical and fruitful to attend intensely to language. In attending to language, these people also found a way to bypass some of the difficult philosophical quandaries that can be associated with the defective default mode. But they over-looked the glaring point that language is a form of communication, and that communication requires persons. Macmurray's comment on the implication of the then-current philosophy of language is that it should have itself undermined the theoretical standpoint of the Thinking Self in favor of interpersonhood:

> This conclusion has clearly a positive relation to the current linguistic philosophy. Both are concerned to stress the centrality of language for philosophy. To transfer the task of logic from the analysis of thought to the analysis of language is to take a step towards the recognition of the mutuality of the personal and its implication, the primacy of action. But to rest here, to conceive philosophy as simply the logical analysis of language, is to fail to see the implications of this step, and to remain stuck in the presuppositions of the philosophical tradition from which it could release us. Language is the major vehicle of human communication. Communication is the sharing of experience. If language is fundamental to human existence, it follows that the human sphere, the field of the personal, cannot be understood through organic categories, in functional or evolutionary terms. It means, in other words, that men are not organisms.[6]

At the end of the day, language can't be all that there is. The personal is the more fundamental context for statements and proofs. The personal is the only context in light of which statements and proofs make any sense. So in order to make sense of knowing, it is important to think through the personal and the interpersonal.

THE SELF-AS-AGENT

Frank Kirkpatrick, editor of one edition of Macmurray's work, writes of him that "at the heart of all his work was his attempt to reverse modern philosophy's commitment to an 'egocentric' starting point, by which he meant the self understood primarily as thinker withdrawn from action and participation in the world."[7] Macmurray wanted to recover "the field

---

6. Macmurray, *Persons in Relation*, 12. Parker Palmer also makes this point. "An abstract idea is a word. Words are spoken by a human voice. When we study an idea we need first to treat it not as an abstraction but as a human sound. Our opening question should not be 'How logical is that thought?' but 'Whose voice is behind it? What is the personal reality from which that thought emerged? How can I enter and respond to the relation of that thinker to the world?' These questions do not exclude logic and critical intelligence, but they remind us that true knowing involves more than a disembodied intellect computing data. Knowledge of the truth requires a personal dialogue between the knower and the known, a dialogue in which the knower listens to the world with obedience" (Palmer, *To Know as We are Known*, 64).

7. Kirkpatrick, "Introduction," in Macmurray, *Persons in Relation*, x.

of the personal" and mine this reorientation of philosophy for a wide array of implications, including the Gifford Lecture's specified agenda of natural religion.

His work is complex, but difficult to access primarily because it calls for such a tremendous revamping of our thinking. It is a reorientation akin to what I envision for covenant epistemology, and thus the overall gesture of his proposals critically advances our discussion. Here I want to recapitulate these with a view to their implications for the project at hand.

In *The Self as Agent*, Macmurray argues that hitherto philosophy has construed the Self as the Self-as-Thinker, where Descartes' *cogito* is most exemplary. However, starting from the Self-as-Thinker, no account of the personal is possible, and plenty of other things go awry as well. If you start with the Self-as-Thinker, there is no way logically to get beyond that starting point. There is no way, for example, to account for epistemic engagement of the world (thus, truth and reality), to account for the personal, to account for human action, not even to account for error. This is the egocentric predicament.[8]

We need rather to construe the Self as the Self-as-Agent: we "need to transfer the centre of gravity in philosophy from thought to action." Simply put, Macmurray argues that we need to replace Descartes' "I think, therefore, I am," with "I do, therefore, I am." The justification of the reorientation lies in its result:

> The effect of transferring the centre of reference to action, and at the same time its sufficient justification, is that man recovers his body and becomes personal. When he is conceived as agent, all his activities, including his reflective activities, fall naturally into place in a functional unity. Even his emotions, instead of disturbances to the placidity of thought, take their place as necessary motives which sustain his activities, including his activity

8. On reading a draft of this chapter, my former student Andrew Colbert told me that this brought to mind Rodin's famous sculpture called, *The Thinker*. Andrew pointed out that he is just sitting, alone. He has no clothes, perhaps suggesting the ideal of pure abstraction. But, says Andrew, he has no joy, either. The notion of the Self-as-Thinker additionally calls to mind the telling assessment of Anton Pegis, in his introduction to his 1948 abridgement of St. Thomas' *Summa Theologiae*: with Descartes, man became a thinker, and thus ruined himself as a philosopher. Pegis argues masterfully that Aquinas bends his life work to combat Platonism's "flight from existence," and restores thereby the key ingredient, being in the sense of existence, without which neither life nor thought would be possible (ibid., xi–xxx).

of thinking. For our present purpose, however, the result which concerns us especially is that it ends the solitariness of the "thinking self," sets man firmly in the world which he knows, and so restores him to his proper existence as a community of persons in relation.[9]

I find especially intriguing the phrase, "man recovers his body and becomes personal"; it bodes well for connecting integrally our personed body with ourselves and our enterprises. But if this is the first time you have heard it, or even, as for me, the umpteenth, it can be either meaningless or promisingly mysterious. It takes some indwelling to begin to make sense of this idea.

Action, by definition, is modifying the world with the rational intent to do so. It is to do something, knowing what we are doing. In the following paragraph, we can see how Macmurray construes action and its essential components. "Freedom is the capacity to act, and so the capacity to determine the future. This freedom has two dimensions, the capacity to move, and the capacity to know, both of which have reference to the Other. To move is to modify the Other; to know is to apprehend the Other. To act, then, as the essential unity of these two freedoms, is to modify the Other by intention."[10] Already we can see how Macmurray's account relates to the matter of human knowing. For Macmurray, action is going to be fundamental, and knowing will be a component— one of the two dimensions of our capacity to act. Here he also indicates that knowing has a reference to the Other: to know is to apprehend the Other. And, of course, the reference to "the Other" is intriguing, we will be exploring this.

In writing *The Self as Agent*, Macmurray says, he "argued from the theoretical standpoint for the concept of action." Having done so, he is, in *Persons in Relation*, "able to take the practical standpoint and consider the Agent, not as an abstract concept, but in its concrete actuality as existent."[11] Acting is what makes us *persons*. For any agent is an existing being, and thus a person. Taking the practical standpoint is what Macmurray means by moving into "the field of the personal."[12]

9. Macmurray, *Persons in Relation*, 11, 12.

10. Ibid., 166.

11. Ibid., 24.

12. While this move, as I have tersely summarized it, is difficult to understand, I do not believe I need to replicate his entire explanation of it for my purposes here.

Macmurray describes his thesis in the second book as follows: "It is the purpose of this book to show how the personal relation of persons is constitutive of personal existence; that there can be no man until there are at least two men in communication."[13] Also: "The thesis . . . is that the Self is constituted by its relation to the Other; that it has its being in its relationship; and that this relationship is necessarily personal."[14] And again: "Any agent is an existing being, a person. Any agent is necessarily in relation to the Other. Apart from this essential relation he does not exist. But further, the Other in this constitutive relation must itself be personal. Persons, therefore, are constituted by their mutual relation to one another. 'I' exist only as one element in the complex 'You and I.'"[15] Thus, once he moves to consider the Agent from a practical standpoint, as he/she exists concretely, he finds that the Agent is constituted by his/her relation to "the Other" and has his/her being in this relationship of mutual interpersonal "You and I." The fundamental unit of existence, where "existence" is what humans alone display, is "You and I." Thus, where action is fundamental, "You and I" is fundamental as well.

MOTHER AND CHILD

I know of no other philosophy book which has, as the title of the first chapter of its argument, "Mother and Child"! This is telling, in so many ways, and Macmurray shows how. He starts his argument by attending to humans' first point of separate existence: infancy.

He suggests that substantival anthropology leads us mistakenly to construe babies as "animals" which have to develop their "rationality" as they mature. We even think this is empirical—that this is what we observe. Far from it, he argues. If you actually look at babies, what you see isn't an animal, but rather a *person*. A baby has virtually no instincts. What the baby is best at doing is crying for human care. His essential natural endowment is the impulse to communicate with another human being.[16]

Interested readers may consult Macmurray, *Self-as-Agent*, as well as how he sets up his agenda in Macmurray, *Persons in Relation*.

13. Macmurray, *Persons in Relation*, 12.

14. Ibid., 17.

15. Ibid., 24.

16. Ibid., 51.

It takes a mother—and even this term can't be interpreted merely biologically, for an array of people besides a baby's biological mother can offer this care[17]—to interpret the crying and care for the baby. Macmurray argues that a baby "is made to be cared for. He is born into a love-relationship which is inherently personal."[18] Not merely his personal development, but his very survival depends upon the maintaining of this relation. And love requires mutuality. It is not complete unless the personal Other responds. For the baby, such mutuality assures him of all the care he needs. And while this personal caregiving involves animal-like needs, such as food, because it is caregiving, the feeding comes embedded in personal relationship.

What is more, given the baby's complete physical inadequacy, personal care requires and is most extensively communicated by physical touch. Quite literally, I think it is telling, a baby is born into a human's arms—born from within the comforting environment of a person in whose body he has been wrapped. Personhood and the tactile are connected from the outset. The tactile is meaningfully set within the context of interpersonhood, and not vice versa.[19]

In this existentially primordial relationship, interpersonal communication is proceeding apace, well before actual words are learned and used. It is emphatically not the case, Macmurray argues, that communication only begins after a language is learned. Language constitutes a highly developed and specialized means of communication, not the only kind of communication.[20] I am confident that one need only spend a day with a mother and her six-month-old to have this claim corroborated. From very early on—babies can be smiling within a month—this interpersonal relationship is enjoyed and celebrated for its own sake by both mother and child. It is apparent that from an early age, a baby is comforted by and enjoys the mere physical nearness of the caregiver.

The human baby is a person, a rational being, not an animal. Macmurray points out that the baby's survival depends on action—not

17. Ibid., 50. In *Peter Pan*, it was a dog who was named *Nurse*.

18. Ibid., 48.

19. I say this in challenge to Lakoff and Johnson's thesis in Lakoff and Johnson, *Philosophy in the Flesh*. I discussed this in texture 2, as part of my foray regarding embodiment. Macmurray's position confirms mine by showing that it makes no sense to reduce the personal to the physical. Instead, the human physical is understood in the prior context of the interpersonal. Human touch is first of all interpersonal.

20. Macmurray, *Persons in Relation*, 12.

his or her own rational foresight and action, but that of the caregiver. "The reason is that his life, and even his bodily survival, depends upon intentional activity, and therefore upon knowledge. If nobody intends his survival and acts with intention to secure it, he cannot survive." The baby "cannot think for himself, yet he cannot do without thinking; so someone else must think for him."[21] Says Macmurray, "Perhaps his cry ... has no meaning for *him*, but for the mother it has ... [T]he satisfaction of motives is governed by the mother's intention."[22] Since this is what is going on, "he lives a common life as one term in a personal relation."[23]

Thus, the child's first knowledge is "the recognition of the Other," so to speak, "as the person or agent in whom we live and move and have our being."[24] The child's knowledge of the Other is practical rather than theoretical. And it is tactual before it is visual. The baby recognizes the Other as that which resists and supports the baby's intention, to which the baby him/herself is thus related. "Logically, the Other is the correlate of the Self as Agent. It is that which resists, and in resisting supports, my intention ... The form of the Self and the form of the Other must be identical ... If I am the agent, then the Other is the other agent. If my act is the realization of my intention, then the activity of the Other is the re-alization of his intention."[25] This principle—that the form of the Self and the form of the Other must be identical—is one to which Macmurray appeals more than once as an axiom in his argument.

He summarizes as follows: "In the human infant—and this is the heart of the matter—the impulse to communication is his sole adap-tation to the world into which he is born. Implicit and unconscious it may be, yet it is sufficient to constitute the mother-child relation as the basic form of human existence, as a personal mutuality, as a 'You and I' with a common life. For this reason the infant is born a person and not an animal."[26] Every functioning human being was born into someone's arms. Every functioning human being is so because he/she was moth-ered. We are born, not, fundamentally, into a physical or organic rela-tionship, but into a humanly personal one. The human being's survival

21. Ibid., 48.
22. Ibid., 51.
23. Ibid., 50.
24. Ibid., 77.
25. Ibid., 79.
26. Ibid., 60.

physically and organically, not to mention his/her normal development as a human being, presupposes an interpersonal relationship of caring. In fact, it is appropriate to say, that the mother-child relation, as "You and I," is the basic form of human existence.

The first context, the interpersonal caring relationship, into which a human being enters, constitutes human identity, shapes human being and all human action. The interpersonal relationship continues to be the fundamental context for human action. We never grow out of being persons-in-relation. As Macmurray puts it, humans don't mature and then go off by themselves and live among the trees. They go to school, and they get employment, and they serve in governmental structures, and join clubs and churches.[27] "All his subsequent experience, all the habits he forms and the skills he acquires fall within this framework, and are fitted to it." Thus "human experience is, in principle, shared experience; human life, even in its most individual elements, is a common life; and human behaviour carries always, in its inherent structure, a reference to the personal Other."[28]

Macmurray concludes, as a result, that all human life and identity displays its fundamental character of "You and I." "All this may be summed up by saying that the unit of personal existence is not the individual, but two persons in personal relation; and that we are persons not by individual right, but in virtue of our relation to one another. The personal is constituted by personal relatedness. The unit of the personal is not the 'I', but the 'You and I'."[29]

Thus the fundamental shape of humanness, Macmurray argues, is not substances with attributes, rational animals, but *persons in relation*. And the personal, to be personal, is constituted by interpersonal relationship.

HUMAN KNOWING IS INTERPERSONAL— IN ORIGIN AND INHERENT STRUCTURE

If "human experience is, in principle, shared experience; and human behaviour carries always, in its inherent structure, a reference to the personal Other," then this includes everything that comes to be in the

27. Ibid., 66.
28. Ibid., 61–62.
29. Ibid., 60–61.

way of *knowing*. The first knowledge is knowledge of the personal Other, as personal. "The first knowledge, then, is knowledge of the personal Other—the Other with whom I am in communication, who responds to my cry and cares for me. This is the starting-point of all knowledge and is presupposed at every stage of its subsequent development . . . The knowledge of the Other is the absolute presupposition of all knowledge, and as such is necessarily indemonstrable."[30] Here he calls knowledge of the personal Other the starting point of all knowledge, presupposed at every stage of subsequent development, and the absolute presupposition of all knowledge. Knowledge is interpersonal—in its original setting and in virtue of its fundamental presupposition. Every person's most original and pervasive orientation to the world is interpersonal.

It is interesting to note that the human child's first cognition is of the Other, not of him or herself. Macmurray has a recurrent motif that also appears here: the child comes to know himself secondarily, as the "negative aspect" of the Other, which, as such, is "both subordinate to and constitutive of" the Other. I am the one who is not the Other, but nevertheless foundationally connected to the Other, correlated in mutuality. In other words, what Macmurray is saying is that the infant's primordial awareness is of the personal Other, and growing out of that, of him/herself as not the Other, but the one to whom the Other responds. It's as if each person in the relationship needs the Other in view of which to make sense of her/himself. And the sense made is a communal wholeness, which makes each what she/he is.

Also, he says, "This original reference to the Other is of a definitive importance. It is the germ of rationality. For the character that distinguishes rational from non-rational experience, in all the expressions of reason, is its reference to the Other-than-myself." [31]

Rational experience, due to the original reference to the Other, is typified by this reference to the Other-than-myself. Thus human rationality, by definition, is embedded in action, and characterized by reference to the Other. As a result, the interpersonhooded "You and I" is the implicit structure of all human behavior and rational experience, including all further acts of coming to know.

Attempting to think this through, we may say that Macmurray is linking action ("I do"), the practical, and the personal, in the baby's

30. Ibid., 75.
31. Ibid., 61.

knowledge of the personal Other. Since all this is taking place in the field of the personal or practical, not in the field of the theoretical, lively interpersoned mutuality is the practical action more basic than any theoretical statement. Action, by definition, for Macmurray, is always with respect to the Other. We noted at the outset that Macmurray locates knowing as one of two integral components of action. Knowing is apprehension of the Other, without which action is not action. The knowing that is apprehension of the Other is a negative and constitutive aspect which the larger action includes and requires. But he speaks of self-awareness as a negative and constitutive aspect. And he will go on to say, as we will soon see, that the theoretical standpoint is a negative and constitutive aspect with respect to the practical standpoint.

So perhaps we may say it like this: That which we typically think of as knowledge relates as a negative and constitutive aspect to a larger, positive, personal, and interpersoned reality. This relatedness, I would like to postulate, has the same structure of metonymy that we have already identified. I think it works to say that knowing, as negative and constitutive, metonymously references the field of the personal, the way that the normative, the covenantal, metonymously references the larger interpersonal relationship that contexts and haunts it. And this recurring motif, I suggest, is itself an intrinsically human sort of dynamism that permeates human being and knowing.

THINKING IN A PERSONAL CONTEXT

So we move on to make sense of how Macmurray relates "thinking" or "reflection" to knowledge, the theoretical standpoint to the practical, and in light of this, how he views science. This in turn helps us understand what he is saying about the form of the personal.

Here is that motif again: Macmurray says that thinking and the theoretical standpoint represent a negative aspect within the positive knowing/acting, the practically apprehended form of the personal. The positive "subordinates and is constituted by" its negative. Macmurray states that "[t]he act of thinking is constituted by a purely theoretical intention. It involves a withdrawal from action, and so from all positive, practical relations with the Other."[32] When we think, we retreat into our

32. Ibid., 20. It makes me remember the signs all over my daughters' grade school which read, "Stop and Think." That was meant as a premeditative withdrawal from adversely negative relations with the Other!

own ideas and observe a methodological solipsism. We behave as sub-
jects, observers only, "unimplicated in the dynamic relatedness of real
existence." He writes: "[T]he thinking Self—the Self as Subject—is the
Agent in self-negation. In reflection we isolate ourselves from dynamic
relations with the Other; we withdraw into ourselves, adopting the attitude of spectators, not of participants. We are then out of touch with
the world, and for touch we must substitute vision; for the real contact
with the Other an imagined contact; and for real activity an activity
of imagination."[33] So Macmurray aligns the world, touch, real activity,
and real contact with the Other. He sets it over against vision, imagined
contact and activity of imagination. Here Macmurray imbues the old
cliché, "out of touch," with literal meaning. Touch is primordial. Vision,
by contrast, is the substituting sense. At another point, he calls vision
the *modus operandi* of depersonalization.[34] But it isn't vision as sense,
so much as vision as interpretively imagined as viewing from afar, and
as such a metaphor for knowing. So Macmurray is joining others we
named in chapter 1 as challenging the ocular metaphor for knowledge.
He is offering his argument to show that it is not primary. We will recur
to the notion of vision in a later discussion, in which what Macmurray
says here will also bear.[35]

One more note: Macmurray says here that science requires imagination. He means imagination, not in the good, creative sense that Loder
does, but in the not-so-good sense of solipsistic and less-than-real.[36]
Even so, his point is that the theoretical standpoint's depersonalizing,
somewhat two-dimensional artificiality, is just the sort of thing that
makes theorizing productive. And his larger point is that the theoretical
standpoint is not original and is depersonalized; it is less real—out of
touch! He is not condemning reflective activity, but rather locating it in
the context of the personal. What is real is activity in contact with the
Other—touch, over imagined vision.

33. Ibid., 16.

34. Ibid., 83.

35. See later, ch. 15.

36. Compare this with our discussion of Loder in ch. 5. It may be helpful to note that
Macmurray does not speak condemningly of *the* imagination, but of imagination—not
the human capacity, but the human misuse of the capacity, as in the phrase just prior
to this one.

It would take some work to distinguish Macmurray's and Loder's differing senses of the word, "imagination," but we should keep in mind that what Loder means by it is has more to do with the creative, dynamic, idea-producing faculty that spurs what Polanyi terms integration. We will see that for Loder this is rooted in the very depths of what it means to be human. For Loder this human dynamism that is imagination is as closely implicated in the interpersoned as being human is, in being in communion, for Macmurray. I surmise that imagination^M can be seen, on a Loderian/Polanyian account, as a product of imagination^L, one that is specific to theorizing. As we will see as we relate Polanyi and Loder in chapter 10, I do believe that Polanyi would see even the imagined visualizing of theorizing as profoundly integrative. Nevertheless, Macmurray's point stands and contributes to Polanyi's: more fundamental, and more original, than the theoretical standpoint is the interpersonal one. And the two concur in rejecting as defective the notion that the theoretical is all there is to knowing.

To return to Macmurray's discussion of the theoretical standpoint, then: he underscores that to move from the personal to the impersonal is depreciative, negative, not positive; what we do is *de*-personalization. We should not see ourselves as starting with the impersonal, and then personalizing or personifying.[37] The impersonal presupposes the personal, and never the other way round. Of course, there is no way, then, to offer an account of humans or of knowing that begins from the impersonal, either inorganic or organic.

There is no objection to this depersonalizing procedure, he says, "so long as it remains within the agency of the thinker as its negative aspect." In other words, thinking is a legitimate enterprise—more than legitimate, it constitutes, in a negatively complementary way, the personal: "in a personal relation between persons an impersonal relation is necessarily included and subordinated. The negative is for the sake of the positive."[38] Thus, Macmurray distinguishes "two types of knowledge

---

37. Macmurray, *Persons in Relation*, 221: "We should recall here an earlier conclusion, that the personal conception of the world is not the result of personifying what is first recognized as non-personal. The personal conception of the Other is original; and the conception of the impersonal is reached through a process of depersonalization, and remains always more or less ambiguous."

38. Ibid., 34. Macmurray notes, by the way, that "[t]his duality of knowledge, personal and impersonal, is the concrete statement of the antimony [sic] of freedom and determinism" (ibid., 31). This implies that an account of freedom is only possible in the field of the personal.

we possess: knowledge of persons as persons, and knowledge of persons as objects." He says that both are correct, and they are not opposed; they just don't refer to the same field.

I think it is helpful here especially to consider the concept of *reflection*, because it has about it some sort of quality of secondariness: it is a pulling back from something in order to consider. Reflection is something distinctively human—*not* something my dog does. What Macmurray adds to this, however, is the critical point that, as such, reflection, the depersonalized theoretical standpoint, cannot be construed to be original. There has to be something that it is pulling back from in order to count as reflection. This explains, he says, how we may say that all cognition is recognition.

Professionally stylized reflective activity—theorizing—occurs in the realm of science. But if you use the negative moment in personal experience philosophically to determine the nature of the Self, as Thinker, contemplation is generalized without limit and Self must be conceived as totally isolated from the Other. "[I]f we take the scientific account as a complete account—as absolute and not relative . . . then we are indeed in error. But the error is not in the scientific account. The error lies in our failure to understand the special character of scientific knowledge, and so not in our science but in our philosophy of the personal."[39] The problem with taking a theoretical standpoint is not that it is illegitimate, but that it is not original. To make it original is not an error committed within the theoretical activity, but rather an error beyond it, in the philosophy of the personal. Cartesian-inspired philosophy has mistakenly taken it to be original, a key move that has contributed to the widespread defective epistemic default.

And even in theoretical activity, in which the thinker objectifies or depersonalizes the Other—something Macmurray says ought nevertheless always to come in the context of personal relationship with the personal Other, for the sake of the Other—the "I" can never depersonalize itself. It cannot objectify its own activity of objectification.[40] This illustrates another motif in Macmurray's argumentation: science itself

39. Ibid., 38.

40. Ibid., 41. An example of depersonalizing the Other for the sake of the Other would be the sort of thing that a therapist or counsel might be seen to be doing in an appointment with a patient. Also, what teachers and coaches do for students could be so described.

cannot account for the scientist. This demonstrates that the theoretical standpoint should never be taken to be original, for it would be self-defeating to do so. I think that the defective default has indeed borne this out; despite this, it continues to prevail.

Substantival anthropology as well as the default mode infecting our subcutaneous epistemic layer are thus understood and criticized by Macmurray on this scheme. They have come about from mistaking the theoretical standpoint for the original standpoint. Philosophers professional and amateur have not understood that to do this is self-defeating. The theoretical standpoint is legitimate, but derivatively so or not at all. There is a different kind of knowing that is foundational.

KNOWING AS BASIC

There is, then, a kind of knowing that is basic, we may say. "Thought presupposes knowledge and knowledge presupposes action and exists only in action." Macmurray continues:

> The reason lies in this, that in acting I am not "over against" an object, but in contact with the Other. In acting I meet the Other, as support and resistance to my action, and in this meeting lies my existence. Consequently, I am aware of the Other and of myself as dependent upon and limited by the Other. This awareness is knowledge, for it is awareness of the existence of the Other and of my own existence in dynamic relation with the Other.[41]

The kind of knowing that is basic is personal; the other kind of knowing—the theoretical, thinking—is secondary. Basic knowledge is knowledge of an Other through personal intercourse, knowing one another as persons in personal relation. Kirkpatrick says that Macmurray called the kind of knowledge that is present in such relationships the knowledge of "immediate experience." It is "prior to theoretical knowledge and is characterized by unity, completeness, and feeling, all fused into a single whole."[42] And "since our knowledge of one another conditions all our activities, both practical and reflective, we find here the ultimate condition of all our knowing, and of all our action."[43]

41. Ibid., 209.

42. Kirkpatrick, "Introduction," xi. We will see later on that Martin Buber pans "immediate experience" as egocentric. This means that the two thinkers are evidently using the term in differing senses (see later, ch. 9).

43. Macmurray, *Persons in Relation*, 212.

Thus, basic knowledge is interpersonal. As such, it consists of mutuality. To know another person, Macmurray points out, the other person must know us: "If you do not know me, then necessarily I do not know you."[44] Thus it requires communication. Thus, also, "[a]ll knowledge of persons is by revelation." This means that the other person must self-disclose, for me to know her or him. Macmurray draws another consequence: where "I" and "You" are mutually constituted and correlative, "I know myself only as I reveal myself to you, and you know yourself only in revealing yourself to me. Thus, self-revelation is at the same time self-discovery."[45] These insights offer important implications for knowing cast in an interpersonal key.

As we may imagine, for the interpersonal relation to be, it must be characterized by love. "[A] negative personal relation between persons makes knowledge of the other and of oneself alike impossible. My knowledge of another person is a function of my love for him."[46] Thus, "[a]ll meaningful knowledge is for the sake of action, and all meaningful action for the sake of friendship."[47] So Macmurray links love, and the goal of friendship, to basic knowing.

What I hear Macmurray saying is that to understand what knowledge is, you have to get down to its most basic form. In direct opposition to the widespread default assumption that knowledge in its most basic form is impersonal bits of sense data—an implication which is the fall-out, I believe, of the modern philosophical outlook stemming from Descartes—Macmurray avers that basic knowledge is personal knowledge, relational communion with a personal Other. What is most fundamental is personal, and interpersonal, interpersoned, communal, and I will add, covenantal. It is not impersonal.

Impersonal theorizing should be seen to involve depersonalization to move from a more intentionally interpersonal situation. Impersonal theorizing, it should be glaringly evident, isn't meant to be taken as ultimate, for a person is always ever the one doing the impersonal theorizing. (She or he is also always, at least implicitly, doing it for another person, as we noted at the outset.) It is more of an artificial exercise, a two-dimensional simplifying that is thereby extremely powerful and

44. Ibid., 169.
45. Ibid., 170.
46. Ibid.
47. Macmurray, *Self as Agent*, 15.

potentially beneficial. But if we were to remove it, epistemologically, from its interpersoned context to exalt it to epistemic ultimacy, not only would that not be true, it would also be—and has been—deadly.

How you see the primordial state of knowing, it is evident, permeates how you approach all knowing. In light of basic knowledge as interpersoned, one should expect to find hints of interpersonhood through knower, known and knowing, and knowers should be able to be better at knowing for understanding its primary and basic form. These, of course, are the claims of covenant epistemology.

THE REAL AS PERSONAL

Finally, let us explore what Macmurray's account holds for us with respect to the question of whether reality, the known, is personal. In his culminating chapter, Macmurray addresses this matter. It is the question of whether God exists; however, according to him, that is the theoretical form of the question and thus wrongheaded. Existence is not the sort of thing you prove: "[T]here is no need to prove existence, since existence, and the knowledge of it, are given from the start. The 'I do' *is* existence and includes, as its negative aspect, the knowledge of existence; primarily and positively the existence of the Other; and negatively and derivatively its own existence in dependence upon the Other and limited by the Other . . . The 'I do,' then, is the primary certainty, and it is the certainty of existence."[48] The field of the personal is the field of religion; religion—in contrast to science and art—Macmurray says, is *for the sake of* the Other. The question must be expressed in the form, "Is what exists personal?" Is the universal Other personal or impersonal? "This is a real question only if it has a reference to action." And in the field of the personal, the answer is evidently, yes: we must act toward the universe as a personal universe.[49]

How does Macmurray demonstrate this? He says that its verification lies in its difference as a way of life from that of the apperception, i.e., the formative perception, that the world is impersonal.[50] In response to this, Macmurray uses three, by now familiar, arguments to exhibit the

---

48. Macmurray, *Persons in Relation*, 209.

49. Ibid., 214. There is an obvious alignment between this and Buber's I-Thou as a mode of existence different from I-It. See my next chapter.

50. Ibid., 215.

inadequacy of an impersonal conception of the world.[51] First, "the world which has to be represented is the world in which we live and to which we belong." Thus, for us ourselves to be persons, the world must be so construed as to contain the personal. An impersonal conception by nature does not do this.

Second, in an impersonal conception of the world, every thing "happens," nothing is ever "done." There is in a scientific world no place for scientists, no place for agents. I cannot raise events to actions; I can, in the context of the personal, depersonalize agents to events. "In that case we cannot know that the world is a process of events, for nothing that we say can be meaningful. And this is self-contradictory; for if it were true we could not know that it was true." But we are agents. "We must conclude, therefore, that the physical world is an imaginary world, and not the world in which we exist. A world in which there are no persons is not the real world."[52]

Macmurray's third argument recurs to his axiom that "I" and "You" are correlative. "What is given immediately in action is the existence of the self and other in practical relation. In action, I know that I exist as agent, and that the Other exists as resistance and support of my action. The rule governing the process through which I seek to determine the character of the Other is this; I must determine myself and the Other reciprocally, by means of the same categories." Thus, the Other is agent as well, and so personal. To know the world is to know it as personal Other.

We may note that basic knowledge, as we called it in the last section, takes the form, grammatically speaking, of the second person, not the third person. I know reality face to face, in a relationship in which I may say, "You." To know reality is to say "You" to it. Buber will develop this.

Macmurray sums up his argument: "There is, then, only one way in which we can think our relation to the world, and that is to think it as a personal relation, through the form of the personal. We must think that the world is one action, and that its impersonal aspect is the negative aspect of this unity of action, contained in it, subordinated within it, and necessary to its constitution. To conceive the world thus is to conceive it as the act of God, the Creator of the world, and ourselves as created

51. Ibid., 218–19.
52. Ibid., 219–20.

agents."[53] Macmurray underscores that this is not pantheistic, nor could it be. "A personal conception alone is fully theistic and fully religious."

While it is impossible from an impersonal standpoint to cast the world as personal, to prove the existence of God, or even the existence of ourselves and others, the personal standpoint is inclusive of the impersonal. The "I do," which is to say also the "I know," necessarily includes the "I think" as its negative, subordinate, constitutive, aspect. Macmurray draws implications of this for the unflagging debate between science and religion: they are not incompatible from a religious perspective. They are only incompatible from an absolutized theoretical standpoint—but that would eliminate science also. Macmurray says that "religious beliefs can be verified only by persons who are prepared to commit themselves intentionally to the way of life which they prescribe." However, science which attempts to exclude the realm of the religious denies the very ground on which it stands.

Taken as a whole, what Macmurray himself derives from his effort is a reaccreditation of religion in connection with knowledge, and also a reaccreditation, in a many-centuried atmosphere adversely sensitized about "dogmatism," of the discipline of philosophy. He has modeled both in his argument in the Gifford Lectures, a lecture series which has to do with natural theology.

WEAVING MACMURRAY'S INSIGHTS
INTO COVENANT EPISTEMOLOGY

Theoretical Knowledge: Metonymous Reference
Rather Than Opposition to the Personal

Since Polanyian epistemology forms an integral component of covenant epistemology, it helps the project to ask how what Macmurray says bears on Polanyi's claims.[54] Polanyi would dispute Macmurray's characterization of science as exclusively a theoretical standpoint. I was hinting at this earlier as I tried to distinguish what Macmurray was saying about

---

53. Ibid., 222.

54. I do not have the leisure in this project to make an extended study of this, although I have every reason to believe such a study would be immensely valuable. Note, for example, that recently a conference was convened on just this topic: "Science, Art and the Ethical: The Form of the Personal." Polanyi–Macmurray Conference, Oxford, UK, March 3, 2007.

imagination, from what Loder (and, by my inference, Polanyi) would say about it.

Polanyi actually practiced science, Macmurray did not. I think we can trust that Polanyi's proposal represents in what science, scientific research and discovery, actually consists. According to him, science actually possesses far more of the personal than the common epistemic stylization recognizes. Polanyi was exploring what I might call "portals to the personal." Passion, commitment, conviviality, apprenticeship, what Polanyi called the fiduciary programme—all these Polanyi was arguing are essential to accredit if we are to account for scientific discovery and knowledge. He was arguing that these are the features that are most critical to science, and which drive it, even in the unfortunate instances in which they are unacknowledged. Polanyi understood himself to be acknowledging that the epistemic enterprise is rich and personal—human. His very mission was to have us accredit the personal in knowing, scientific knowing in particular.

Polanyi's project and covenant epistemology share the commitment that exploring the personal from within the theoretical standpoint, we may say, is a good and helpful epistemological strategy. The overall project is consonant with Macmurray's claims, but perhaps even more consonant than Macmurray himself. It seems to me that we can overdo a separation between knowing as basic, and thinking as a different field or form (that of the impersonal). Polanyi, I believe, like myself, was endeavoring to show how the personal must necessarily come through in the impersonal. But Macmurray calls science "completely impersonal and merely objective." I do not see Polanyi saying this!

We may recur to my odd motif of metonymy. The theoretical standpoint isn't so much opposed, as truncated, with respect to the field of the personal. The same can be said about knowledge, for we remember that Macmurray used the same language of it: "negative and constitutive of the personal." Knowing does not oppose the personal, and yet cannot be entirely reduced to it. Rather, it metonymously references the larger interpersonal context. For the normative and covenantal is (negatively) constitutive of relationship. Macmurray's phrase sounds a bit like this. The whole point of covenant epistemology is that as a result the interpersoned somehow permeates it. There is no way to shut the door and keep it out. It is actually what sustains it—cores it, contexts it, paradigms it, makes sense of it. This approach of mine accords with Polanyi's stance;

and apart from comments to the effect that theoretical knowledge opposes the personal, I think it accords with Macmurray's as well. Our
conversation with Buber in an upcoming chapter will shed more light
on how we bring the personal into the impersonal.

The Personal in Knowing

On the other hand, I do not believe that Polanyi was thinking of the
personal—that is, the interpersonhoodedness of Macmurray's form of
the personal—as a kind of basic field or form, a basic normative kind of
knowing. That is why I am developing covenant epistemology and seeing
it as what Macmurray and others add to Polanyian epistemology. It is as
if Polanyi dips in halfway, and what he produced points us in the direction of wholesale immersion. The fact that Polanyi attempts to develop
an emergent evolutionary scheme is evidence of the half-way-ness—and
the misdirection—of his dip into the personal. Marjorie Grene said that
she and Polanyi agreed that "epistemology is ultrabiology."[55] He wanted
to arrive at the personal from the impersonal, albeit in a way that would
not reduce to it.[56] I do not see Macmurray saying this!

Yet we are right to discern a fundamental sympathy. I think it is
evident that Macmurray's argument for the more fundamental interpersonal context and structure of knowledge, with respect to theoretical
knowledge, corresponds with what Polanyi is saying when he argues that
there has to be more to knowledge than explicit knowledge, more to
science than the impersonally theoretical. This must be rooted in something else; for Polanyi, it is the tacit, in particular, the subsidiary—which
he designated, in the title of his book, personal. This correlation leads

---

55. Polanyi, *Personal Knowledge*, part 4, and Grene, *Knower and the Known*, part 3.

56. I find it intriguing to contrast Macmurray's interpersoned as foundational with
the common attempt to characterize any sort of metaphysical levels as ascending from
simple to complex, which locates material as basic and rationality as a highest level.
Macmurray is indicating that, of necessity, the "lowest" level is the most complex, and
it is fundamentally personal—where personal always means interpersonal. We may
construe this as Macmurray's pronouncement regarding all attempts at evolutionary
explanations of persons. As I am saying here, that means he rejects these attempts on
the part of Polanyi and Polanyian philosopher of biology, Grene. See Grene's fascinating
attempt in Grene, *Philosophical Testament*, or Polanyi's in *Personal Knowledge*, part 4.
See also part 3 of Grene, *Knower and the Known*, and my further discussion of Grene
and personhood in texture 8.

me to raise the possibility that what makes Polanyi's knowledge personal knowledge in Macmurray's sense just is the subsidiary.

Is Subsidiary-Focal Integration Personal?

My question here is this: what is the relationship of the subsidiary-focal integration and Macmurray's personal standpoint? Macmurray's theoretical standpoint sounds very much like Polanyi's notion of "destructive analysis." Polanyi says that it is helpful, in knowing, temporarily to revert in our epistemic effort to focus on what ordinarily is subsidiary—to articulate it, to examine it, to practice it. That is what we do when we study a language, practice scales, memorize a procedure or times tables. Polanyi believes, however, that the mistake of the dominant western epistemological tradition, as well as of our default, is, not to do destructive analysis, but to limit knowledge to it. This is just what Macmurray described and criticized with regard to the theoretical standpoint. I think it would be fair to say that both thinkers represent what they are describing—the theoretical standpoint or destructive analysis—as a "negative aspect," one that involves a stepping aside from the overall "main act." The main act, for Macmurray, is knowledge of the personal Other. For Polanyi, it is dynamic integration to a focal pattern that unlocks the world. Polanyi's destructive analysis and Macmurray's theoretical standpoint are not the original, nor the exclusively proper focus. And the main act does not derive from them in a linear fashion.

If the theoretical standpoint aligns with destructive analysis, is it appropriate to see an alignment between knowledge of the personal Other and integration to a reality-unlocking pattern? And does that mean that the personal standpoint aligns essentially with subsidiary awareness?

In his later writing, Polanyi attended more to the notion of subsidiary-focal integration, and saw himself as leaving behind the less helpful concepts such as personal commitment—or rather, of better articulating them.[57] This can sound as if he wanted to take back "his rash overcommitment" to the personal in his epistemology! However, I believe that he did not mean to deny the fundamental personal dimension of all knowing, but rather to specify more concretely what is happening when we know. The latter should be seen as a further development of the former, inherently of a piece with it. If so, does this not suggest that

---

57. Polanyi, *Tacit Dimension*, xviii.

Polanyi felt there was something inherently personal about subsidiary-focal integration?

Personal commitment, and thus the need for person as knower, and for persons as knower and known, continues to cry out from the language of subsidiary-focal integration. We *rely* on clues, clues that we responsibly and sometimes riskily choose and shape, to leap to engage a pattern that never reduces in a linear fashion to the clues on which we rely. This is the language of trust, of pledge, of commitment, of covenant. Only persons covenant. And as Polanyi lived to underscore, it's the active (an exclusively human sort of thing, Macmurray would say) shaping into a pattern that makes knowing happen. The subsidiary, as involving a stance of *relying*, is inherently the action of a person with a pledge, I am using Macmurray and others to argue, to the personal Other.

Starting once more from the evident coincidence of Macmurray's theoretical standpoint and Polanyi's destructive analysis, we can argue in the other direction to make the same point. Macmurray characterizes the move to the theoretical standpoint as depersonalization. By analogy, destructive analysis is depersonalization. Thus, returning to indwell the subsidiaries, to reintegrate to the pattern that unlocks the world, would be repersonalization. Think of leaving the driving range and heading for the golf course. It certainly feels more human, even as it also feels more risky.

I see the covenant epistemology project as the attempt to draw out with greater intentionality the personal that subsidiary-focal integration implicitly signposts. And Macmurray is showing the way to that amplification. I think that more can be done—and we have done so already in *Loving to Know*. We can be more intentionally personal in our exploration of the knower's subsidiary awareness—this is what we were doing when we talked about virtuosity, embodiment, and presence.[58] We have not closed that conversation; we will see in upcoming chapters that those dimensions are best, first, apprehended and felt, "face to face with the personal Other." We will see, for example, that it takes the presence in mutuality of a personal Other for me to develop these sorts of subsidiaries. And covenant epistemology works to develop the interpersoned dimensions of known and knowing, also. Macmurray contributes what is really an all-embracing notion of the interpersoned, and he shows the way to the overall task of covenant epistemology.

58. See texture 2.

Polanyi's Contribution to Macmurray

But it isn't just that Polanyi stands to benefit from Macmurray; Polanyi contributes helpfully to Macmurray. Covenant epistemology, after all, starts from subsidiary-focal integration, not from "the form or field of the personal." Polanyi's subsidiary-focal integration is a superior contribution to epistemology. If Macmurray's insights helpfully further the covenant epistemology vision, Polanyi's insights are the ones which inaugurate it. This is partly because it is easier to understand Polanyi's description of how knowing actually works. It is also because Polanyi's expertise as a scientist as well as his technical-sounding description is something we can relate to more at the beginning of our attempt to reform our epistemic default. But I believe also that Polanyi's is a more helpfully sophisticated treatment of the asymmetric relation of integration to destructive analysis.

Another thing that Polanyi's account involves, and that we will be able to develop in covenant epistemology, is that scientific practice—even the theoretical standpoint—involves the personal as much as does the baby's awareness of the personal Other. Polanyi writes to call positive attention to these personal dimensions. He does not merely argue that the theoretical standpoint, if taken as original, is self-defeating, as does Macmurray.

Polanyi actually stresses the positive impact of destructive analysis on our capacity as knowers. Seemingly mindless practice of a skill will only hurt you if you see it as information collecting and you think mistakenly that that is all there is to knowing. It impedes if you see it as intended-to-be-perennially-focal-information-and-behavior, rather than as eventually-subsidiary-person-forming-skill. If you see it as building a skill in the context of larger reciprocal relationship, it will in fact radically leverage your personal capacity and genius. Even as we identified a dynamic motion from one sector of the Framean triad to another, and back and forth, in coming to know, we move dynamically back and forth between looking from and looking at, subsidiary to focal and back. Polanyi's account pushes covenant epistemology further in the direction of taking seriously this dynamic to and fro.

I believe, therefore, that we may opt to take Polanyi's account as the more accessible expression of the knowing process—so long as we keep in view that it is the identifiable workings that can stem only from an interpersoned context. Subsidiary-focal integration is an account of human knowing that shows knowing for what it is, and shows that it is that way because it grows out of and remains fraught with a "default" of interpersoned, relational, context.

Subsidiary-focal integration, I commend, is fundamentally knowledge of the personal Other. What if we ask the other question—is knowledge of the personal Other subsidiary-focal integration? I believe that the answer is yes. Polanyi often talks about recognition of a face as a supreme example of knowing on his account.[59] To recognize a face involves relying on the clues of it, but it involves obviously so much more. He uses this to show how rich the integrative pattern is, and how leap-like must be the integration, even as the clues are integral. A baby's first smile, I believe we may say, is the integrative recognition of the face of the personal Other. It is arguably the baby's first integration. Is it the beginning of the personal and interpersonal? No—and this just underscores what we are saying—the interpersonal outruns and contexts, and has imbued the baby's awareness from the beginning, *in utero*. So the smile is the first integrative sign that he gets it. I think it is telling that the smile, as a first integrative feat, is also intrinsically a delighting. Delight involves a valued noticing, a noticing regard. It is deeply human, and deeply interpersonal. And it is powerfully epistemologically effective: delight, we will say, invites the real.

What I am doing in covenant epistemology is to link Polanyi productively with Macmurray. Perhaps we may say that we are developing a Polanyian-inspired way to maximize the positive effect of the personal on knowing, and a Macmurray-inspired way to carry it off.

Two brief notes of a different sort. There is another most intriguing alignment between these two. For Macmurray, action cannot be fact, because action involves intention, and what is intended is always future.[60] To me this suggests that wonderful aspect of the Polanyian account: that which confirms that we have made contact with reality is the intimation of unspecifiable future prospects. This means that knowing on a Polanyian account has the same open-endedness to the future that action does for Macmurray. For Macmurray, action is always personal, with reference to the personal Other. Thus, Macmurray also provides positive

59. This is where he begins his discussion in "Tacit Knowing," the first lecture in Polanyi, *Tacit Dimension*, 4.

60. Macmurray, *Persons in Relation*, 39.

grounds for my conviction that this aspect of Polanyian epistemology hints at the interpersonhood of the known as well as of the knower.

I have argued something similar with respect of Frame's triad—namely, that its three-dimensionality is uniquely personal and interpersonal. One way to do this would be to see the normative just as the interpersoned covenanting that (potentially) binds the lived bodily self more deeply in and for the world. Apart from the normative, the existential devolves into the self-thwarting Cartesian thinking subject, and the situational into things that happen (as opposed, as Macmurray says, to things that are *done*.) If so, then the triadic nature of human experience—in particular, Frame's distinctive normative—pervades and constitutes (to use that term in a manner reminiscent of Macmurray) the other dimensions. This reveals that the Framean account of human experience is one of agents acting, and thus one that implies and requires persons as persons in relation. After all, Frame professes only ever to be describing what humans do as what servants—creatures, image-bearers, stewards—do. In other words, knowing, as stewardship, is done (not, knowing *happens*) *coram Deo*. All this suggests that we may helpfully overlay not only Polanyi and Frame, but both with Macmurray. So joined, the interpersoned dimensions of human knowing continue to be amplified.

Insights for Covenant Epistemology

We can see effortlessly that Macmurray brings into the unfolding thesis of covenant epistemology nothing less than a fully developed rationale for the interpersoned relationality of human knowing. Intimate interpersonal relationship is the context of everything human, of human action, and thus of human knowing. Relationship is prior to knowing, the primordial and fundamental form of knowing that continues to contribute an inherent structure to all knowing, and to imbue all knowing with interpersoned features. The interpersonal is the default, we may say. In efforts to theorize, we depersonalize to analyze. Theorizing is laudably effective, but without its interpersonal context it is self-defeating and damaging. But with its proper interpersonal context, and with practiced intentionality with respect to the interpersoned covenantal dimensions with which it continues to be fraught, theorizing is better understood and even more successful. It is sensible to take as our paradigm, for all acts of knowing, the interpersoned covenantal relationship. This is the thesis of covenant epistemology.

Certain features of Macmurray's proposals especially underscore or develop the covenant epistemology vision. First, to realize that our entire experience as knowers and as humans begins in the mother-child relationship is to recover the obvious and find it surprisingly wonderful. Face-to-face, ten or so inches apart, caring human touch on touch, as mother holds and feeds her baby. That such care, to be care, must be covenantally constituted, is obvious as well. Caring for a baby, from conception onward, calls for covenantal pledge. Yes, there are those smiles. But there are multitudinous bouts of crying and appalling discomfort and menial service that are weathered only through self-sacrifice as the product of faithful pledge. For the child to grow safely and healthily, in full personhood, this mother must be bound to the child covenantally, faithfully discharging obligations whether it is convenient or fun for her to do so or not. That pledge alone is the child's safety and comfort and hope and future. We may justifiably add to Macmurray's account that, apart from covenant, the "You and I" is not constituted in wholeness.[61] And if knowing is relational, it is also covenantally so.

All this also makes sense of the profound role that emotional health plays in knowing. The confident knower—the knower free of the sense of personal betrayal and distrust that issues from a broken covenant in the intimate relationships we need to be who we are—is the effective knower.

Third, Macmurray allows us to draw attention to the integral relationship between knowing and the felt body, or body knowledge. Knowing with the body is the medium of interpersonal awareness, of basic knowledge. Far from the Cartesian presumption that the human body is mindlessly out of touch, it turns out instead that the Cartesian thinking self is what is mindlessly out of touch. Here we apprehend, quite concretely, the bodily rootedness of all thought. And also, what Polanyi never said: the necessarily interpersonal character of the bodily rootedness of all thought. This is a stunning realization.

61. This may be what Macmurray has in mind by intention when he says: "The unity of the personal is, then, to be sought in the community of the 'You and I,' and since persons are agents, this community is not merely matter of fact, but also matter of intention" (Macmurray, *Persons in Relation*, 27). That this point does not go without saying is underscored by the aphorism on the Dove Chocolate candy piece I opened recently: "Love without rules."

Fourth: in covenant relationship, the prior person, we may say, is not the knower. The knower is the one who has already been known. There is a sense that that Person was there before I was. The personal Other is a person prior to even the personhood of the knower. To know involves a sense that one has already been known. It is the Other who has initiated, and my knowing comes as response. We should be able quickly to sense the accord here with Frame's knowing as covenant response, as well as Williams' descent of God. Together these align in my thinking with the realist conviction that reality breaks in, generously, especially, but not necessarily, when invited. It breaks in often not as what was explicitly expected. And we may revel in the healthy reversal this brings to the cultural fallout of the Cartesian *cogito*. Basic knowledge is not, first, my knowing; it is first my *being known* by the Other.

Blending our discussion of covenant now with Macmurray's discussion, Macmurray underscores that covenant is intentional action in relationship. He says: "I can know another person *as a person* only by entering into personal relation with him. Without this I can know him only by observation and inference; only objectively."[62] Thus we may link covenant with Macmurray's form of the personal. The goal of knowing far outstrips information. The goal of knowing is interpersonal communion—friendship. And just as friendship involves information, but neither exclusively nor exhaustively information, focusing more on living and ongoing communion, the same may helpfully be said of humans knowing the real.

And finally, seeing the embracing interpersonal context and core structure of knowing, and the known as the personal Other, accords profoundly with a theological vision of the sort we have described. If God is Scripture's Lord, we should expect human knowing to be interpersoned and covenantal throughout. We should expect that the to-be-known is, ultimately, He. Macmurray's rich account shows that there is always an aura of the transcendent, personal, Other around acts of coming to know. Knowing intimates the presence of God.[63]

All this exposes the wrongheadedness of the impersonal dichotomous epistemic default that continues to prevail. It shows how that default

---

62. Macmurray, *Persons in Relation*, 28.

63. Compare George Steiner's *Real Presences*: literature intimates the presence of God. I only found this book recently. He could well have been a conversant in this book.

may have developed, and it shows the way to transform it. If knowledge is situated and grounded in the interpersonal, then identifying, accrediting, and strategically drawing on its interpersonal dimensions has a payoff. To construe the act of coming to know interpersonally, to see that thus it calls for epistemological etiquette to be practiced in inviting the real (as we will discuss directly in a later chapter), means that we revamp our idea of good knowing practices. "Analysis," for example, must be set in the larger interpersonal context—else we thwart our very efforts. My belief is that people unconsciously practice this even when they don't accredit it; how much more effective we would be as knowers, and how much more whole as persons, if we did! You have to love a frog to dissect him; this is an aphorism I have uttered for some years now as I have thought toward covenant epistemology. Macmurray's account makes profound sense of this: the impersonal for the sake of the personal.

And so we are on our way to knowing knowing—on our way to covenant epistemology.

QUESTIONS FOR DISCUSSION

1. To further your understanding, express in your own words, in a single sentence, each section of Macmurray's claims.

2. Of his claims, what do you find especially striking, and why?

3. How does a philosophical anthropology that defines persons as being-in-communion challenge the defective default and bring healing?

4. What concrete difference does it make to think of human persons this way?

5. How does interpersonhood open the way to seeing knowing as covenant epistemology claims—as, paradigmatically, covenantally constituted interpersonal relationship?

9

KNOWING AS I-YOU

Conversation with Martin Buber

M Y SEARCH FOR MORE about personhood, and knowing as interpersonal, led me back to indwell Martin Buber's *I and Thou*. Buber's influential book appeared in 1923 and was popular in the mid-twentieth century, and the terms "I-It" and "I-Thou" made their way into common parlance. Buber was, like Michael Polanyi, yet another remarkable European intellectual of Jewish descent whose life in the first half of the twentieth century must have been painfully marked by the ravages of the World Wars. Buber shared with John Macmurray a focus of philosophy of religion. His work epitomizes the attention to the personal and to personal encounter that grew out of existentialism, phenomenology, and the atrocities of twentieth-century Europe, not to mention his own religious awareness.

Buber's classic I-Thou, or I-You, underscores and contributes to the covenant epistemology project. Macmurray spoke of "You and I" as the fundamental shape of humanness, and of knowing, in its primordial instance and context, and inherent structure. Buber's account meshes with Macmurray's, but we'll find that it also takes us further along the way.[1] The paramount epistemic event is the I-Thou encounter. From Buber we will get more of a working sense of what it looks like or feels like to have our knowing shaped by commitment to the personal. We will see what it involves for the knower to mature into that, and to cultivate it. We will start to get a sense of how to live out covenant epistemology. In particular, he shows how *we* may be different and thus better knowers

---

1. I do not mean to imply that the concepts we develop in this chapter are all ones that Macmurray did not develop, rather, I mean only to say that I am using a conversation with Buber as the portal through which I may bring these insights into covenant epistemology.

and better people. Thus his work gives impetus to this book's proposal of covenantal interpersonal relationship as paradigmatic for all knowing.

I-IT

In life, Buber maintains, a human being orients to the world in one or the other of two ways. These are modes of existence or ways of being. They are two different sorts of orientation to the world. These two modes of existence are themselves the expression of two, not spoken but rather lived, word-pairs: I-It and I-You.[2] Each mode of existence "speaks" both words of the pair.[3] Either I orient toward the world, or something in the world, as an I to an It, or I orient toward the world as an I to a You. I live out a mode of existence of the I-It sort or of the I-You sort. Whichever one of these it is, it shapes the sort of being that I am. But it takes both the words in each word-pair to shape and specify that being.

I-It is a manner of relating to the world that constitutes the world as objects, goals, and projects. I-It views the It from a distance (what we sometimes call "objectively"), without a self-giving. For I-It, there are many Its, with boundaries, that border on one another, that can be categorized and expressed in terms of laws and principles, named in concepts. In I-It mode, the subjective and objective have the sense they have had in the modern western tradition. The I of I-It is the ego, which "experiences" the world. An experience, in Buber's usage, is something that the I of I-It has internally, subjectively. It actually distances the I from the It. Virtually all of what is commonly deemed knowledge—the various disciplines from science to art—is I-It. Piling up information is I-It. I suppose that writing books on epistemology might be I-It.

I-It is not at all to be despised or avoided—it is necessary to being human in the world. What is to be avoided is a life of the ever-encroaching, deadening (Buber chooses the metaphor of choking weeds) take-over of I-It that squeezes out I-You. For it is only as I-It is set within the larger and deeper relation of I-You that it remains good and fruitful, and that the I grows to full humanness and personhood, capable of self-giving.

---

2. Walter Kaufmann, in his translator's introduction, helpfully suggests that there are a couple other possible word pairs. One is the It-It: "they study without experiencing; they have no time to have a self, no subjectivity; a community of solid scholars with no room for a core." Buber, *I and Thou*, 12.

3. Ibid., 53ff.

I-It arguably coincides with Macmurray's theoretical standpoint, and with Polanyi's destructive analysis. Buber agrees with these thinkers in saying that I-It is legitimate, and even necessary to human being in the world, but only as it is located within the context of I-You. Not to be so located is to generate the damaging epistemic default we keep talking about. But now Buber adds his own graphic metaphor to it: choking weeds!

I note that Buber's use of the term, *experience*, is different from Macmurray's: while Macmurray approved its alignment with the relation of You and I, Buber consigns it to the subjectivistic I, the ego, of I-It. Buber says, "Experience is remoteness from You."[4] What Buber will commend, as over against subjectivist experience, is *encounter*. This, I feel sure, Macmurray would applaud, despite the terminological disagreement.

I-YOU

I-You, as a mode of existence, is not an ego *experience*, but a *relation* of I to a You. Where the I of I-It *has something*, the I of I-You *stands in relation*.[5] I-You, in contrast to I-It, is neither bordered nor compartmentalized: the exclusive relation fills space and time in a different sort of way. This does not mean that there can't be more than one I-You relation, but that in the I-You relation, I and You are present to one another in a way that puts all else in the background. Rather than "experiencing" the You, I behold it, encounter it, confront it, commune with it. In that encounter, I and You are present to one another in an enduring present.

I-You involves action; each acts on the other. And the action is self-giving, responsibility-taking, love. Each says You to the other. You say You with your whole being. All actual life is encounter, says Buber, thus tying both phrases—"actual life" and "encounter"—to I-You relation, and tying it all to covenant love. I believe there is an alignment between Buber's "actual" and Macmurray's "action." Macmurray linked action with what humans do, and what they do in relation. Buber says, in fact,

<hr>

4. Ibid., 59. See later, ch. 8, n.47.

5. In this book I do not work with Søren Kierkegaard's thought. That, of course, is the book's loss, but also the reader's opportunity for further development of covenant epistemology. But readers of Kierkegaard will easily detect the affinity of thought both here in Buber and elsewhere.

that in I-You, each acts on the other. It is fair to say that the two thinkers have in mind, by I and You, the same actual relation, or mode of being.

The I of I-It, the ego, says, "This is how I am." The I of I-You says, "I am."[6] I think that this characterization of it by Buber deepens our feel for the distinction. I-It is subjectivistic/objectivistic, focused on an inward self that I set over against an object which I bound, compartmentalize, set off from other items (the whole point of Aristotle's definition by genus and difference) in my description. It fosters disconnection of knower and known. If it were taken to be epistemologically ultimate, it would be our dangerous default. By contrast, I-You isn't experience so much as an active, or actual, standing in relation of each partner to the other.

For believers of the Christian (and Hebrew) Scriptures, the resonance of I-You with God's name, Yahweh, cannot be missed. In fact, theologian Mike Williams emphasizes that, when God reveals his name to his people as I Am, he is not making some dispassionate metaphysical statement.[7] Quite the contrary: he is expressing, I am the One who is present to you, and there for you. Buber's description of I-You thus accords with God as I Am. For well-meaning believers who nevertheless have misunderstood law and grace, this appropriately recasts the dynamic: it becomes possible to see and to sense that God exercises the initiative, and does so in self-exposing, self-giving revelation. This is sovereign, covenant love. Buber's translator and student, Walter Kauffmann, underscores this understanding. Of Buber's ideas he comments, "The only possible relationship with God is to address him and to be addressed by him, here and now—or, as Buber puts it, in the present. For him, the Hebrew name of God . . . means *he is present* . . . He is there . . . He is here."[8] Buber also asserts that Jesus, in calling God "Father," and teaching his disciples to do the same, is expressing, evoking, I-You.[9]

6. Buber, *I and Thou*, 113.

7. Williams, *Far as the Curse is Found*, 27–33.

8. Buber, *I and Thou*, 26.

9. Ibid., 116. This also calls to mind what C. S. Lewis refers to as joy. Joy was the I-You event he longed for and found in Christ. Lewis titled his spiritual autobiography, *Surprised by Joy*. We Christian believers can, and especially under the heavy onus of western philosophical modernism, have even gone at our Christianity wrong; we can have been prevented by well-intended I-It thinking, not to mention a sinful fear of exposure, from actually encountering God. We have encapsulated and subdued him into theological propositions, often isolating ourselves from the sweet terror of his wildly

If it were not already apparent, the I-You relation that I may stand in is covenantal. By contrast, I-It is not obviously so—unless it could be seen to be contexted by a larger, relational, component.

Buber links experience of the present, and of being present, together in the I-You encounter. "The present . . . the actual and fulfilled present—exists only insofar as presentness, encounter, and relation exist. Only as the You becomes present does presence come into being."[10] By contrast, I-It has only a past and no present. This suggests a sense of the present that is different from how we typically, arbitrarily, construe it. Says Buber: "present is not what is evanescent and passes but what confronts us, waiting and enduring." He also says that in the I-You, the You fills not only time but also space: "When I confront a human being as my You and speak the basic word I-You to him, then he is no thing among things nor does he consist of things. He is no longer He or She, . . . Neighborless and seamless, he is You and fills the firmament." There is a timelessness and a transcendence to I-You. So the I-You involves being present to one another—being there, or at home.

Buber's characterization of the Other aligns with Macmurray and Williams also in the respect that the Other exercises the initiative. "The self-giving of the Other is gracious; I can in no way dictate it, but rather only wait for it. I say You, and listen." Similarly: "The You encounters me by grace—it cannot be found by seeking. But that I speak the basic word to it is a deed of my whole being, is my essential deed."[11]

I-YOU ENCOUNTERS AND DEVELOPING THE I OF I-YOU

Buber, like Macmurray, and also Loder, sketches the development of I-You, which is a human's maturation to full humanness.[12] In the yet-to-be born and newborn baby is a natural, primitive, connectedness to a

---

fearsome presence. No doubt this was central to what Kierkegaard found loathsome about Christendom in the 1800s. But it might also be construed in a more conciliatory way: Christians who love Scripture, who faithfully study and meditate on its sentences, do so not as a substitute or to hide themselves from encounter, but precisely to put themselves in the way of it. Often there might not be much difference in how these may appear on the surface. It would be discerned only as one person sensed another's spirit indwellingly. And upon occasion the most duplicitous hypocrite finds himself stunned by the graciously invading Person of Christ.

10. Buber, *I and Thou*, 63.

11. Ibid., 62.

12. Ibid., 69–80.

You; this is the primordial and prototypic impetus that shapes the child's longing for full-fledged (self-consciously personal and interpersonal) relation to the You.

Even as Macmurray says that a person is not a person without there being another person, so Buber says that I cannot be the kind of I of an I-You word pair without the You.[13] In fact, the I-You mode of existence cannot be had without the Other. I am completely in need of the Other to actualize this lived actuality. Add to that: to be fully human, I-You must have come to center my mode of existence. To be human, fundamentally, is to stand in relation to a You.[14]

All this suggests that the I-You relation is both our original experience, thence shaping all our experience, and also a relation that, as we mature, we must look to actualize. We are both persons and also in need of full-fledged personhood. In this latter sense, not all humans are persons, or, at least, fully persons. The reality of this distinction points us in the direction of asking how we may so mature, and how such maturing affects our knowing and invites the real. Of course, to repeat, it takes a You to bring an I into full-fledged personhood. "Man becomes an I through a You."[15] Buber says that this occurs over time, occasioned by relationships.

The I-You encounter can occur in the course of our involvement of any sort with the world. For example, consider our involvement with nature. We may observe it in an I-It mode, classifying it, considering natural laws that bear on it. In this mode, "the tree remains my object and has its place and its time span." But, says Buber, "it can also happen, if will and grace are joined that as I contemplate the tree I am drawn into a relation, and the tree ceases to be an It. The power of exclusiveness has seized me."[16] Buber also says: "One may encounter the You in all spheres of life: in nature, in human interrelationships, and in relationship to God. In every sphere, through everything that becomes present to us, we gaze toward the train of the eternal You; in each we perceive a breath of

13. Ibid., 62.

14. And in contradistinction to monisms of either eastern or western secularist origin, reality is most fundamentally at least two, personal and interpersonal. Without this, we cannot be fully human. So as Macmurray said that relationship with a personal Other is essential to true religion, Buber, Macmurray, and Loder all stipulate that it is also essential to true humanness.

15. Buber, *I and Thou*, 80.

16. Ibid., 57–58.

it; in every You we address the eternal You, in every sphere according to its manner."[17] Buber says of the poet Goethe: "Goethe's I is the I of pure intercourse with nature. Nature yields to it and speaks ceaselessly with it; she reveals her mysteries to it and yet does not betray her mystery. It believes in her and says to the rose: 'So it is You'—and at once shares the same actuality with the rose."[18] The lived actuality of I-You is haveable in every corner of the universe, and in all spheres of life.

And in whatever sphere I-You is actualized, that encounter connects us to God, the eternal You. I think it is significant that Buber says that there is nothing that I must "not see" in order to see. I do not turn away from the ordinary in order to see the extraordinary. This underscores the fact that this is an ordinary, rather than ecstatic, sort of event. How mistaken to think one must turn away from the world to encounter God, he says! It isn't that one must get behind "appearances," or "beyond this world." It isn't that the You is merely the world. Yet we encounter the You where we are, in the world, in space and time. But it is a different manner of relating to what is there.[19] All this that Buber so richly and perceptively describes is neither mystical nor beyond our reach. In fact, it centers our being; it is the orientation closest to who we are.

I-You encounter incurs existential change, transformation: "[In] the moment of encounter something happens to a man. At times it is like feeling a breath and at times like a wrestling match; no matter: something happens. The man who steps out of the essential act of pure being has something more in his being . . . Man receives, and what he receives is not a content but a presence, a presence as strength."[20] Here we note that the quality that the I has about itself, having sustained the I-You relation, is presence. Buber links this, as I do in other places in *Loving*

17. Ibid., 57, 150. Note here the same metaphor that Annie Dillard expressed: the hem of God's robe, here, the train of the eternal You. These allude to the Scripture passages in Isaiah 6, Luke 12, and Exodus 32. To have grasped even the hem of God's garment is to be transformed, and to know that it is entirely his gracious self-giving that has permitted it.

18. Buber, *I and Thou*, 116–17.

19. I feel confident that Buber's distinction is essentially the same as Kierkegaard's delineation of subjectivity and objectivity as different modes of engaging the world. (Kierkegaard, "Truth is Subjectivity") Both assert that proving God's existence is fundamentally wrongheaded. God, as we confront one another, can only be addressed, not asserted (Buber, *I and Thou*, 129).

20. Buber, *I and Thou*, 57–58.

to Know, both to "being at home," and to differentiation, which I will introduce in a subsequent conversation. Buber writes: "The spirit is truly 'at home with itself' when it can confront the world that is opened up to it, give itself to the world, and redeem it and, through the world, also itself . . . the essence of the spirit: being able to say You."[21] And further: "Between you and it there is a reciprocity of giving: you say You to it and give yourself to it; it says You to you and gives itself to you. You cannot come to an understanding about it with others; you are lonely without it; but it teaches you to encounter others and to stand your ground in such encounters; and through the grace of its advents and the melancholy of its departures it leads you to that You in which the lines of relation, though parallel, intersect . . ."[22] These two passages indicate that the I of I-You has come to the maturity of a self-awareness that is at home with itself, can confront the world and stand its ground in the encounter, while consenting to the being of the Other. I will talk more about this later as I connect Buber's I-You with the knowing event.

Personal maturity issues in covenant love. "Among humans, the action on what confronts us is love. Love occurs. Exclusiveness comes into being miraculously again and again—and now one can act, help, heal, educate, raise, redeem. Love is responsibility of an I for a You; in this consists what cannot consist in any feeling—the equality of all lovers." And while responsible obligation is involved, it is always situated within the context of the relationship: "Of course, whoever steps before the countenance has soared way beyond duty and obligation—but not because he has moved away from the world; rather because he has come truly close to it."[23] Thus, covenant love brings us truly close to the world.

I-You is meant to center all of our life and knowing, as we can bring the I of I-You to characterize us in all of our I-It experience. I-You encounters change us. Having once or more actualized this mutual encounter, we can bring the I-ness distinctive of I-You to all our relating to the world. Having become the I of I-You, we may be that I even in the I-It mode of existence. That is a way of saying that I-You, which is central to our full personhood, also makes us better at everything that we seek to know and do.

21. Ibid., 100.
22. Ibid., 84.
23. Ibid., 156–57.

The I-You event continues to seed and center subsequent I-It events. Using a great analogy of a lamp remaining lit, Buber says: "But the I that steps out of the event of the relation into detachment and the self-consciousness accompanying that, does not lose its actuality. Participation remains in it as a living potentiality. To use words that originally refer to the highest relation but may also be applied to all others: the seed remains in him."[24] I-You encounters change us. They do not leave us as we were. And we are far better at knowing for it, and so are the objects of our efforts. This, says Buber, is how we and they are redeemed and transfigured.[25]

I-YOU AND ACTS OF COMING TO KNOW

If there is a profound sense in which I-You should pervade our lives, there is another sense in which a specific I-You encounter is not meant to last. I-You encounters are never permanently sustained, but are meant to contain the seeds of their own demise. This has to do with two things, the first of which is the mutuality of action by which I and You serve each other. Buber says that the You of the relation needs the I.

Buber interprets the artistic experience, and invention and discovery, as being fundamentally I-You encounters. In these encounters, it's as if the You asks the I to lead it across (*traduceo*) into the world. It asks for concretion (my word), at the inevitable risk of depersonalization. Yet that work of art, that invention or discovery, ever contains within it the potential of confronting the I again and again.

> This is the eternal origin of art that a human being confronts a form that wants to become a work through him . . . What is required is a deed that a man does with his whole being: if he commits it and speaks with his being the basic word to the form that appears, then the creative power is released and the work comes into being.
>
> The deed involves a sacrifice and a risk . . . whoever commits himself may not hold back part of himself; and the work does not permit me, as a tree or man might, to seek relaxation in the It-world; it is imperious: if I do not serve it properly, it breaks, or it breaks me.

24. Ibid., 113.
25. Ibid., 119.

The form that confronts me I cannot experience nor describe; I can only actualize it . . . And it is an actual relation: it acts on me as I act on it.

Such work is creation, inventing is finding. Forming is discovery. As I actualize, I uncover. I lead the form across—into the world . . . The created work is a thing among things . . . But the receptive beholder may be bodily confronted now and again.[26]

Encounters are supposed to be led over into I-It understanding. As an author, I say You and listen for the encounter of insight. It comes as I sit here and key sentence after sentence of my unfolding thought into this computer. But this event is the living edge of the mollusk, somehow the point at which the ossified shell is concreting into a thing. What I want, and what the You wants, is the publication of a book.

I know from having had this experience before that giving birth to a book is giving birth to an object that is then public and that is independent of you. It inevitably must be catalogued and categorized and marketed and shelved and bought or passed over. It is a funny feeling to see your book—as it were a piece of your soul—on a remainder book shelf priced at 80 percent off.

Yet just because it is a book, an object, for those who come to it with the readiness of the I of I-You, the I that says You and listens, the book readily returns to life in the lived actuality of relation. And that, as an author, is something I live for: a reader's transformation as a result of encounter with a book on epistemology.

Polanyi, Loder, and I would concur with Buber that there is a fundamental kinship between the artistic creation and scientific discovery. I think it is especially profound to align all the distinctive things Polanyi the discoverer says of the experience with what Buber says here. We will return to consider the implications of the fact that the act of coming to know involves an I-You encounter.

The other reason that the I-You encounter is not meant to last is that what is developing is a relationship characterized by a rhythmical reciprocity. "Relation is reciprocity. My You acts on me as I act on it. Our students teach us, our works form us . . . How are we educated by children, by animals! Inscrutably involved, we live in the currents of universal reciprocity."[27]

26. Ibid., 60.
27. Ibid., 67–68.

> This, however, is the sublime melancholy of our lot that every
> You must become an It in our world . . . The actualization of the
> work involves a loss of actuality. Genuine contemplation never
> lasts long; the natural being that only now revealed itself to me in
> the mystery of reciprocity has again become describable, analyz-
> able, classifiable—the point at which manifold systems of laws
> intersect. And even love cannot persist in direct relation; it en-
> dures, but only in the alternation of actuality and latency. . . Only
> it is not only as if these states took turns so neatly; often it is an
> intricately entangled series of events that is tortuously dual.

Love itself endures, not in a direct relation, but in the alternation
of actuality and latency. "Every individual You must disappear into the
chrysalis of the It in order to grow wings again. In the pure relationship, however, latency is merely actuality drawing a deep breath during
which the You remains present."[28] This description of Buber's helps us
get a better sense of what a lifetime of the sort he has in mind would
look like: an unfolding relationship, studded (as diamonds might stud
a black velvet cape) with I-You encounters, which matures the knower
and binds her or him ever more deeply—in self-giving, covenant love
and faithfulness—to a world to which it might be said, at any place and
time: "So, it is You!"

WEAVING BUBER'S INSIGHTS
INTO COVENANT EPISTEMOLOGY

Given that Buber associates the I-You encounter with discovery, it makes
sense to bring its dimensions into our deepening vision of knowing. And
his work may be taken to underscore the reciprocity—overture, response,
the unfolding relationship of covenant love, that pertains in knowing.

I think we are right to interpret the act of coming to know as having
this same wonder-full dynamic. Polanyi insightfully underscores that an
act of coming to know is something that unfolds over time. A scientific
discovery reveals this extended being-on-the-wayness of knowing. The
trajectory unfolds as the aspiring knower, guided by his/her creative
intuition and its sense of increasing proximity to the solution, in the
function of his/her creative imagination gropes and scrabbles to arrange
possible pieces of the puzzle in a way that may align with and allow the

---

28. Ibid., 147–48.

nevertheless surprising inbreaking of the discovery.[29] I have always been intrigued by Polanyi's astounding claim at one point that the essence of knowing is "the kind of knowledge that the scientist has of an *approaching* discovery"![30]—That is, the very being-on-the-way to I-You encounter: the overtures, the dance, the "courtship" of knower and known. The actual Oh-I-See-It! moment of insight, of recognition, is a living I-You encounter, an interchange between knower and known that is mutually transformative. Efforts to articulate the vision are both compelled by the vision and are nevertheless fraught with the risk and sacrifice of a two-dimensionalizing, a thingifying, that exposes the encounter to misunderstanding and rejection, but nevertheless is the only way to enshrine it for posterity. But that articulation retains the potential, as does every corner of the real, to occasion other I-You encounters.

Buber expresses what anyone involved in live acts of knowing can feel, that there is an asymmetry between the knowledge we articulate and the lived engagement it aspires to voice.[31] To put words on the I-You is to take it into the I-It. We have, in the western tradition, long been enamored of the account of language that views words and sentences as representing reality. Others have come to reject this as fundamentally flawed. This rejection has often led to an antirealist stance, a surrendering of hope regarding any way to accord independent status to the real. But acknowledging this asymmetry as Buber does, and as we experience it in the transformative quality of Polanyian integration, accomplishes two things: it displays the wrongheadedness of our western attempts to align words and world without remainder, and it does so while in the same act underscoring the surpassing objectivity of reality. Reality, as Buber says of God, is not to be asserted so much as addressed as You. And true objectivity—no wonder we have struggled to pin it down in the I-It mode. True objectivity is the You encountered in actual relation.[32]

You may wonder, as you hear me say this, if I have forsaken my earlier commitment to the biblical understanding of God as transcendent Creator, distinct from his creation. No! God is not in his creation in a pantheistic way. I do not believe that one can espouse a panentheism,

29. Polanyi, "Creative Imagination," 88–89.

30. Polanyi, *Tacit Dimension*, 25.

31. Buber, *I and Thou*, 76, 89, 150, 153–54, 160.

32. Buber avers that the I of I-It is actually worldless! No wonder we have had problems! (Ibid., 142)

either, to affirm the creative richness and mystery of reality created by an infinitely rich and mysterious God.[33] Of course, such a reality is so rich that sometimes our words fall short of doing it justice. Of course, it is so rich that it reveals God. And, of course, what I am saying here is that acts of coming to know have about them the aura of I-You encounter. But we can affirm all these things without making created reality God.

While vast reaches of articulated knowledge and information lie at our fingertips, literally, in this age of the internet, while it is right and healthy to struggle to systematize claims rationally, and articulate systematic justification, a humanly healthful epistemology must profess that this is not all there is to knowledge. There is a living encounter that centers both human being and knowing and that must be the heart of knowing, else we die to human being and to knowing well. Sadly, we have not been taught in our epistemology, or even in our pedagogy, to cultivate I-You, let alone to see it as foundational. How can we do epistemology before we properly identify the character of true knowing? The I-You of Martin Buber puts us on the track of the central living nerve of truly human knowing.

The I-You that centers knowing cannot be exhaustively reduced to articulation. A manual cannot be written for teaching it or guaranteeing it. Rather, the I-You is something modeled, or conveyed from master to apprentice tacitly, as Polanyi said. Walter Kauffman divulges a telling recollection of the man, Martin Buber: Buber's friends tried to keep him from lecturing, wanting rather just to be involved with him in discussions, which were—I infer—I-You incarnated.[34] And also, tellingly, Kauffman says that one of the most important things to learn from Buber is how to read: one must learn to feel addressed by the book.[35] This too indicates that the aspiring knower must become a knower, one who invites an I-You encounter, who says, You, and listens.

To know well, one must become a knower, one who invites the real, as I shall say. Buber calls the word "I" the true shibboleth of humanity— a clear indicator of a person's mode of existence. "Listen to it!" Socrates' "I," for example, Buber says, is "the I of infinite conversation, and the air

---

33. *Pantheism* is generally taken to describe a view that identifies God and the world: the world is "all God." *Panentheism* involves the perhaps more complex claim that the world is "all in God," and/or that God is in all the world.

34. Buber, *I and Thou*, 22.

35. Ibid., 38.

of conversation is present in all its ways, even before his judges, even in the final hour in prison. This 'I' lived in that relation to man which is embodied in conversation. It believed in the actuality of men and went out toward them; thus it stood together with them in actuality and was never severed from it. Even solitude cannot spell forsakenness, and when the human world falls silent for him, he hears his *daimonion* say You."[36] I love how Buber speaks of Socrates' I of I-You as that which lives in that relation to man which is embodied in conversation. This adds impetus to my approach to this work as so many conversations, between me and thinkers, between me and you, between you and others over the book. It suggests that covenant epistemology, as it unfolds through these conversations, seeks and involves I-You encounter. To "believe in the actuality of men and to go out toward them, to stand together with them in actuality"—that is the I-You as embodied fittingly in conversation. Conversation, this confirms, is highly appropriate as a medium for an epistemology that centers on I-You. And you, the reader, will have appropriated this book, not when you have identified its concepts, but when, in the conversation, you are led to respond as an I to a You.

The knowing event, the active shaping of particulars transformatively into a deeply coherent whole that compels our submission to reality, an insight that has been sought for, longed for, waited for, cultivated in apprenticeship and anticipative obedience, but which nevertheless comes graciously and surprisingly, in these respects shares the contours of an I-You encounter. Its manifestation in any particular knowing event, depending on its location in the unfolding trajectory of our lives, may be anticipative and prototypical, or, as we have had more I-You encounters, and as Loder will argue, ultimately the centering I-You encounter of convictional knowing, the I-You mode of existence will pervade and quicken the most mundane acts of knowing.

To put ourselves in the way of knowing, what Buber would have us do is to say "You"—and listen. This is just what I will expound as inviting the real, in chapter 15. And what we need to do—for our epistemology, for our knowing, for our human flourishing—is cultivate a different kind of looking. I-You constitutes a different kind of looking—a beholding—or as I will characterize it, a seeing rather than a looking.[37] It is an encoun-

36. Ibid., 115–16.

37. We will see that Robert Farrar Capon speaks of "looking the world back to grace." See ch. 15.

ter, an apprehension that is a mutual encounter. We will recognize this as it comes to expression in Simone Weil's thought. It is what Kauffman, we saw, described as learning to be addressed by a book. I think that the inviting the real that I describe in later chapters just is the cultivation of this different kind of looking. Inviting the real is composing oneself to wait for, putting oneself in the way of, the surprising, gracious, inbreaking of the You. We will talk more of this.

However, Buber adds two helpful insights that qualify our proper longing for encounter. One is that I-You is not expected to last. Rather, it studs and advances a developing relationship of overture and response: I-You, I-It, I-You, I-It . . . inhale, exhale . . . But what we are meant to do is bring the I of I-You into all our I-Its. The aura of encounter must imbue all knowing—else we are choked by the weeds of I-It. We contrasted Polanyi's outlook on science with Macmurray's: Macmurray seems to oppose theoretical knowledge to the form of the personal; Polanyi seems rather to seek portals of the personal in science. Buber's insights make sense of the latter.

In conclusion, we may say that, for the sake of deep humanness, one must see knowledge as fundamentally and centrally I-You. Knowing is interpersonal—we must take it to be so—or else we and our efforts are thwarted deeply. The aspiring knower who labors in the absence of the formative I-You encounter is relegated to I-It information and fundamental absence of understanding. But the good news is that, with the reorientation of epistemological therapy, we can learn to tap into the I-You knowing event to grow and center our humanness.

We are able to see that the epistemic act, the knowing event, taps deeply into and voices the central constitutive relationship of human life. Knowledge, before it can properly be accounted for and understood, must be redefined to be, not centrally the I-It of information and categories and statements and proofs, but rather the far richer, personally defining, relational encounter with the You. Buber has contributed this perspective to the covenant epistemology project, showing us as well how we may live as knowers in light of it.

Yet Buber's account suggests that I-You is not all there is to knowing. We could not sustain such high-powered face-to-face intimacy. This suggests a rhythm of apart and together, drawing a deep breath between encounters, all in the context of an unfolding relationship. In those breaths of I-It, we bring the I of I-You into the I-It. Encounter as the central event of knowing transforms us to be better collectors of data, so to speak. But freeing space between encounters seems to fuel them. How this is so we will begin to address in chapter 11.

QUESTIONS FOR DISCUSSION

1. Discuss together Buber's description of I-It and I-You modes of being. Give examples from your own experience.

2. Talk more about the I-You encounter. What does it involve? How does it center knowing and being?

3. Discuss the capacity to "take the I of I-You into the I-It." What does this look like? How does this make us more effective knowers, able to know for *shalom*?

FRIENDSHIP AND LEARNING

All Knowing is Knowing With

NATE AND JONAS HAVE been learning together for years, since they were in high school together. I had them as students in a June-term at seminary a few years ago. Jonas was a full-time student; Nate, a youth pastor, traveled there just to take the class with his friend. Upon finishing high school, I learned, they had chosen different colleges, but this did not prevent their long-distance discussion of what each was learning. Friendship and learning have gone on, for Nate and Jonas, for more than a decade.

Kalyn and Anna, students a few years back at my college, might as well be twins. When I first had them as students, I learned that they talk in tandem sometimes, and when they are both raising their hands to respond one might pull the other's hand down—which they called an "arms race"!

Friendship and learning have gone on, for Anna and Kalyn, for their entire college career. Now that they have moved on to graduate schools and work, they continue to pursue inquiries informally together.

Let me tell you about my dear book club of twelve years when I lived in St. Louis. Together roughly ten of us read over forty books. We all came to feel that we couldn't read any book without discussing it with the others. We came to appreciate the signature contribution of each member. The books we read turned into events of journeying together in learning.

Then there is my colleague in philosophy at Geneva, Dr. Robert Frazier. From the outset of what are now several years as colleagues, Bob insisted that we be friends also. Friendship and co-scholarship have grown in tandem. We seek to model this for our philosophy students as part of the packaging of philosophical living. Each of us serves as a first reader of the other's work. He amplifies my own insights by adding his own. His insights have turned up in my work, and mine in his, as we have shaped one-another's thought. We abet and celebrate each other's "exploits." But more than that, as a friend Bob sees and comments on me as well as my work. I have come to know myself better for seeing myself in the mirror of Bob's gentle and healing seeing of me. I am truly a better knower for knowing in the presence of, and knowing with, Bob.

Obviously blending friendship and learning is a good thing. But covenant epistemology suggests that "knowing *with*," or *"in the presence of,"* is integral to all knowing. I want to argue that, for learning (coming to know) to occur, friendship must have pertained at least in some measure. Friendship is necessary to learning. And friendship, because it taps into the fundamental structure of all epistemic acts, strategically betters efforts to know.

Covenant epistemology involves the claim that person-like features permeate knower,

known, and knowing, strongly suggesting the pattern of interpersoned covenant relationship. It is only natural that this epistemic state of affairs should come to expression in it being more than a chance occurrence that friendship enhances learning. But I want to suggest that there may be implied, not two persons, but three.

Covenant epistemology argues for the knower as person, the known as personed, and the knowing as that interpersoned covenant relationship in which the two persons encounter one another as I-You. But perhaps there is a third person as well. The contours of covenant epistemology are not two-personed, but three-personed. When we take a look at the knowing event, we find that the knowing event implicitly involves, not two, but three—persons. It takes a triad: the knower, the known, and the known for or with whom. Knowing implies another person, in the presence of and with whom the knower is knowing. All knowing is *knowing with* or *in the presence of.*

This is easy to get at from covenant epistemology. We have talked extensively of the infant mother relationship, and that as a prototype of the human-divine relationship which is its ultimate context and goal. But both the mother and the Holy (Loder's term, we will see) are involved in a person's knowing, at one or another point, not directly as "the whom," the personed reality known, but also as "the with whom," the comrade alongside in the knowing. Worship, for example, is communion directly with God; exploring his world is *coram Deo*—before the gaze of God. You can imagine God as a beaming parent watching a baby play on the floor nearby. An infant's smile, shared with her mom, is that which prototypes communion with the personed Other, the act that continues to be central for the covenant epistemology vision. But Mom is also first witness and teacher in every respect. The baby encounters the world, and God, *coram maternae*. If first knowledge is *knowledge of* the personal Other, second knowledge is *knowledge with* the personal Other.

From the outset, all formative experience of reality is encountered, interpreted, and mediated, in the context of life-giving mother-child relationship. We do everything, including our primitive knowing, in the presence of another. Nor is the face before which a baby learns indifferent or expressionless. It must be the face transformed with delight and care, the face of one is never unmoved by our cries nor our delights, who welcomes being known all the while knowing intimately.

Personed, covenant love is the requisite context for coming to know, learning, everything that we learn. Structurally it shapes and enables the knowing journey of our entire lives. The precovenanting "Other" provides life and love. He or she also serves as authoritative guide. The caregiver names and thereby guides the child to see and rightly interpret the world. I actually think that this delightful interpreting is prerequisite to the seeing. Dad says, "ball!" and baby visually picks out the ball, loves the ball, throws the ball, says "ball!", loves Dad, and is loved into personhood by Dad. Parenting is perhaps the most profoundly philosophical occupation there is. Walker Percy has made this point with regard to language: we label and describe things as speaking to another person. We are, in his lovely phrase, "cocelebrants of what is." We name something for the other, for mutual acknowledgement of the other.[1] The mere fact that we express knowledge in words presupposes the presence of one to or for whom we express it. Percy's apt terms say more: the tenor of the agreement is delight, communion, on the way to worship.

My intentional appropriation of Frame's triad led me, when I wrote *Longing to Know,* to discover the normative dimension of subsidiary clues, and subsequently to think through the role of authoritative guides in knowing.[2] One way the normative dimension comes to expression in any kind of knowing, then, is in the key role that such guides play in our acts of coming to know. Coaches, teachers, parents, and any other authoritative guides to whom we submit in our endeavors, teach us to see what is there. One nontraditional student I had in a class, a retired jet pilot, later emphatically corroborated my claim by saying that there was simply no way to learn to fly a fighter jet apart from an authoritative guide.

In *Loving to Know,* I have pushed a little further to identify personal features of the normative dimension, and thus to amplify it in the direction of covenant epistemology. The calculus professor, piano teacher, or skating coach trains us to see ourselves and our world as we submit in trust to their efforts. We have to trust them even to interpret ourselves to ourselves. They see us better than we see ourselves, at least with respect to the subject in view. But the involvement of parents, coaches, and teachers is more than authoritative guidance with respect to normative directions. These things come effectively embedded in the semi-formal covenantal interpersonal relationship that the student has with these directors. Thus we learn under the guiding gaze of a covenanted authority. All knowing is knowing with or in the presence of another in covenant relationship.

1. Our own personal enjoyment of a discovery can I think be seen as nevertheless triadic, in the sense that a celebration or a reflection involves setting ourselves off from the matter and regarding our regarding it. Also, as Polanyi and Loder argued, the discoverer is compelled passionately to persuade others to share the vision. But what I am arguing here is that the threefold relationship is implicitly prior.

2. Meek, "Learning to See."

Primordial and defining relationships—with our caregivers and with God—are just what give impetus not only to the involvement of teachers and mentors in learning, but also to the involvement of good friends with whom we learn well. Our personal friend in learning is the concrete embodiment of the Other before whom we come to know, the co-celebrant of what is, to and with whom we are interpreting the world. She or he is the authoritative guide to whom we submit to see ourselves and the world.

All knowing is knowing from myself, a self so close as to be almost impossible to see, from a self about which we can be grossly mistaken, toward a world which we mistakenly think just passively registers on our awareness the way this computer takes the hits of my key punching. Solitary and passive objectifying of the world is inherently flawed. An Other knowing us into self-awareness, and a sensitive indwelling communion-with that invites the surprising self-disclosure of the world—that is the knowing that engages the real.

Serious study should be seen to be not the insular, solitary practice sadly common to so many doctoral dissertations, but instead like that of the Rabbinic tradition. "Make thee a master, and get thee a companion and judge," says *Pirke Aboth*, the sayings of the fathers.[3] Both the authoritative master guide, as well as the companion learners are needed, with whom one may both learn the ways of the tradition and continually shape new contributions within it.[4] And if learning is transformation more than it is information, persons with whom you are united in learning catalyze that transformation.

How antithetical this approach to knowing is to the solitary Cartesian self, standing alone, and over against an impersonal world which passively appears to his scrutiny. Philosopher Marjorie Grene writes that Descartes' *cogito* is "one of the great falsehoods

3. *Pirke Aboth,* Tractates I, no. 6; 23.

4. I have this from more than one student of Hebrew among my colleagues and students, but specifically from Andrew Colbert. Andrew, looking back on his college years, which have only just come to a close, cherishes the hearty debate and discussion among friends in the context of living together in the dorms, as some of the best times of learning. Also he values times "living life on life," alongside mentors and professors.

of philosophy."[5] Knowing our-selves, and all by ourselves, is what we are worst at, not best at. A great work of lit-erature, Dostoyevsky's *Crime and Punishment*, graphically depicts how "knowing alone" goes awry. Young Raskolnikov, sitting day in and day out in the stifling solitariness of his coffin-like apartment, draws unsupported and damaging conclusions that, had they been held up to the light of friendly scrutiny, would have been exposed for their limita-tions. It is the gentle challenge and witness of another, Sonya, walking as she does before the gaze of God, which points him beyond his sick solitary reason-ing to himself, and to redemp-tion and hope.

Where is such a friendship to be had? Indeed, if you are reading this, you have already had many such friendships. Probably there are a few that stand out as especially impor-tant in your life. Your mother, father, siblings, extended fam-ily members, all in at least some measure, with respect to some avenue of learning. Your school teachers can be numbered among such friends, from kin-dergarten to graduate school.

5. Grene, *Knower and the Known*, 86.

To realize this may take revising our estimate of them in light of what I have described here. We can tend thoughtlessly to have dismissed teachers as impas-sive fact-dumpers. And then classmates, some always more significant than others, those rare and precious comrades in knowing with whom you en-joy a covenantal solidarity and trust that unleashes. It includes marriage partners, who are also often our dearest co-knowers, and colleagues, with whom some of us are privileged to share collaboration in learning as their job.

All knowing is knowing *with*, knowing *in the presence of*, implicitly *before the face of*, knowing *under the caring guid-ance of*—a covenant friend. There is present an implicit interpersonhood that we may be intentional in acknowledg-ing and developing, in the cov-enant epistemological vision, and in direct challenge to our culturally ingrained tendency to depersonalize knowing. Recognizing the triadic inter-personhood of all coming to know (learning) is a critical first step to being intentional in cul-tivating and practicing it.

This conviction is also what motivates my seeing

this book—my writing it, your reading it—as conversations (among covenanted friends) on the way to knowing. It is, for me most assuredly, a knowing *in the presence of*, my teachers, such as Michael Polanyi and John Frame, my colleagues, such as Mike Williams and Bob Frazier, and the conversation partners whose work I have indwelled. It is also knowing in the presence of, with a view to the watchful care of and the reciprocal insight of, my readers. It is a knowing that longs to invite others into the vision.

I think it is appropriate to generalize this. If you do, what you have is a tradition. Michael Polanyi was perhaps the first epistemologist in the wake of Descartes' isolationism to argue for the reinstatement and reaccreditation of apprenticeship in a tradition as critical to the formation of experts in a field. Knowing with whom comes to expression even more widely, in the wider community of our knowing. Not only does the community and the tradition shape the very things we come to know. Also the relevant community plays a critical role in the public confirmation of all our claims to know. This is a wider covenantally interpersoned context.

The shape of this epistemic camaraderie, we will see, is dynamic, rhythmical, dance-like, a gracious overture-response. The idea that all knowing is also knowing in the presence of another, we can surmise, suggests the Holy Trinity. An upcoming conversation will align the motion of the dynamism with the *perichoresis* of the Trinity.

Scripture says, "Now we see but a poor reflection as in a mirror; then we shall see face to face. Now I know in part; then I shall know fully, even as I am fully known."[6] This verse is often quoted to prooftext our fallible and finite knowledge (as information) that some (mistakenly) infer will be one day infallible and infinite. But I believe whether now or later, human knowing is face-to-face, as well as face-by-face, a knowing and being known. Covenanted interpersonal knowing is what we humans were made for, and that for which we hope. And it is also our glory to practice it now, even as we know "in part."

6. 1 Cor 13:12.

QUESTIONS FOR DISCUSSION

1. Make a list of your significant authoritative guides. Make a list of the friends with whom you learn together.

2. Choose one of each to describe to the group. Tell how that person exemplifies "knowing with whom or in the presence of."

3. What concrete strategies of learning does this dimension of covenant epistemology indicate?

$$\approx 10$$

KNOWING BEFORE THE FACE OF THE HOLY

Second Conversation with James Loder

MARTIN BUBER'S I-YOU, ALONG with John Macmurray's form of the personal, has plunged our epistemology deeply into the well of interpersonhood. It is becoming evident that the most important thing about knowledge is that interpersonal root. It is the relationship of reciprocity in which human knowing is embedded that centers and enlivens and lends its contours to it. And that reciprocity aspires to being communion, interpersonal communion, a being-there before the face of the Other. But now James Loder bats clean-up, as they say in baseball of the fourth hitter in the line-up. Loder gives us the fullest and most helpful account of the central interpersonhoodedness of knowing, one which draws together and moves beyond all that we have explored thus far in this respect.

We have already engaged Loder's account of knowing as transformation, making the case that it aligns with Polanyi's subsidiary-focal integration, lends credence to it, and elucidates it.[1] I noted that this is only the beginning of what he is up to in *The Transforming Moment*. We also saw that Loder repeatedly affirms the personlike reciprocity of the knowing event between knower and known. He says that knowing implies a mutual indwelling of the knower and the known, both before and after the imaginative crux—the Aha! moment—of the event. "Knowing *anything* is to indwell it and to reconstruct it in one's own terms without losing the essence of what is being indwelt." In this mutual indwelling of subject and object lies true objectivity. Knower and known "mutually create each other in face to face relationships." This reciprocity is not heavy-handed or controlling: Loder hints that the character of being is the inherently dynamic "letting flourish." And the knower comes

1. See ch. 5.

to know him- or herself "in the face of the other." He suggests that the knowing event, in which the knower is more fully herself or himself than ever before, also compels the knower to "reopen the whole question of reality." Now in this chapter we can explore these tantalizing hints.

The contours of Loder's overall thesis are as follows: that human knowing, which he construes along Polanyian lines, has the power that it does, and unfolds the way it does, on the one hand, because it taps into our humanness, and on the other hand, because it is ultimately anticipative of a species of the gracious being known by God as he is described in the Judeo-Christian Scriptures. All this he does to offer an account of convictional knowing, by which he designates existential experiences that a person has of the Holy Spirit, of the convicting presence of God.

First he makes the case that the knowing event has the transformative power it does because it taps in to the four dimensions of humanness, the fundamental nature of the human spirit. Second, he develops the profound claim that all human knowing, understood transformatively, prefigures and anticipates and ultimately is itself transformed as the Holy Spirit co-opts a human knowing event to bring the knower into face-to-face encounter with the Holy. This existence-centering encounter is most succinctly and ceremonially epitomized in the Eucharist. Third, he shows how both of these connect with human development, offering an account that accords with Buber's and Macmurray's, with the helpful addition of his consideration of the face of the Other. Because the epistemic model in question is in effect the Polanyian one, we may take this multi-directional alignment as powerful explication of subsidiary-focal integration that confirms the interpersonal root of human knowing.

Loder traces four unfolding sequences: the knowing event, the four dimensions of humanness, convictional knowing, and human development. As our conversation proceeds, I will add lines to a chart I have devised that shows how I believe he means these sequences to align. A distinctive feature of Loder's thought is its systematized, multilayered comprehensiveness. As I have with our other conversants, I am adapting his work away from his particular agenda to the end of covenant epistemology, while nevertheless allowing his agenda to remain as enriching background. I am attending to those features of his work which demonstrate why human knowing is fundamentally interpersonal, and also why it is that we humans are so passionate to be on the way to knowing.

The first line of my chart gives us a quick summary of Loder's account of the transformative knowing event. In this chart, I have grouped Loder's five stages into four, in order later to show their alignment with the other trajectories he describes.

Knowing event	1Context	Conflict, 2Scanning	3Aha, 4Release	5Interpretation

ROOTING KNOWING IN THE DYNAMIC OF FOUR-DIMENSIONAL HUMANNESS

Following his opening account of human knowing as the transformative event, Loder proceeds to show "how the whole matter of transformation [is] connected to the essence of being human, and indeed, to being itself."[2] Knowing has the trajectory that it does, and the power that it does, and the transformative quality that it does precisely because it taps into the dynamic of what it is to be fully human. What is more, although he does not exactly say it this way, developing as a human is itself a trajectory of knowing that involves knowing the self in the knowing of the Other.

I do not find that he makes further reference to the fact that he has titled his chapter on the four dimensions of humanness, not, "The Four Dimensions of Humanness," but "The Fourfold Knowing Event."[3] But the fact that this is the chapter's title indicates that knowing and being human are integrally of a piece. If to know is to be human, to be human is also to know. As it turns out, it is not just any kind of knowing that is fully human. The act of coming to be four-dimensionally human is a layering on of knowings that ultimately transform all that one is and knows.

Giving a kind of existentialist account, Loder asserts that there are four dimensions of humanness. Once we see what these four dimensions are, I think we will be able also to affirm that four-dimensional humanness exists prototypically in the experience of the infant, but that full-fledged four-dimensionality is something that must be developed, and will be developed as part of maturing through a lifetime. And that means that it is possible for the process to be thwarted and truncated.

2. Loder, *Transforming Moment*, 67.
3. Ibid., ch. 3.

It is possible both to be human and be not yet fully human. The kind of personhood that is interpersonhood and is paradigmatic for excellent human knowing is full humanness. What is more, a remarkable implication of what Loder will be saying is that to be fully human, a human needs both an experience of the void and an experience of the Holy.

The first dimension of humanness is embodiment in a composed environment. Loder calls this the world, but it includes our embodied situatedness in it—the lived world. The second dimension, which he calls the self, is both in this environment and transcends it, ever recomposing its world in a way that coherently accords with the self.

It is possible—in fact, it is our common expectation and attempt in this secularized western society—to live as two-dimensional humans. As I listen to Loder describe two-dimensionality, what comes to mind immediately is high school commencement speeches: life is about success in careers, marriage, and having two kids. You can throw in personal fitness training, weekend fun, and the American Dream. We actually do all we can to screen ourselves from the void, and take coping with our environment to be normalcy for humans. This is not to say that these first two dimensions of humanness are bad. They are bad only if they are all that characterize us. They are two-dimensional.

Of world and self-as-ego, the first two dimensions of humanness, Loder says, "both these dimensions of human being are weak with respect to the third: the possibility of annihilation, the potential and eventually inevitable absence of one's being." This is "the void." About this grim prospect, he says: "Void is the ultimate aim of all proximate forms of nothingness; the implicit aim of conflict, absence, loneliness, and death is void."[4] The void is the threat of non-being.

In other words, the void is any experience of having your nose rubbed in your contingency—the fact that you might not be here, and the fact that you are depends on a plethora of factors far outside your control. Near-death experiences, affliction, fears and doubts, mid- and quarter-life crises are experiences of the void. There can for some of us be a myriad of times in which we feel as if we look down at our feet and find we are standing on thin air. Some of us, of the commencement speech frame of mind, could use to experience the void more often. Some people try to live as if the void is not either inevitable or necessary to our full humanness.

4. Ibid., 81.

Sadly, the young are not spared either. At a high school commencement I attended recently, success wasn't the only topic; they also commemorated the death of a loved classmate on an icy highway in January, and the continued comatose state of a second one, that had mashed the faces of those eighteen-year-olds into the third-dimension of humanness, the void.

The way the void aligns with the five-step sequence of the knowing event is that "void is implicit the moment the lived 'world' is ruptured and the process of transformational knowing begins." Void is the conflict in the context that initiates the struggle to know. The struggle to know, to reintegrate one's life and world, is at first at least the attempt to address the void. Because the rupture of our world is an experience of the void, and because experience of the void is an essential dimension of our being human, the knowing event has the power it does, the centrality to who we are. And most centrally, experience of the void is the threshold for the untransformed self to develop. For, says Loder, "the nothingness . . . is not merely 'out there,' it is embedded in the very heart of the untransformed self." Relating all this to human knowing: there comes a time when we can no longer say that ignorance is bliss. The fact that we do not know something becomes a problem. That is how the void drives our longing to know.

Aligning four-fold humanness with the five-fold sequence of the knowing event, the world is the situation in which occurs the rupture that begins the knowing event. The self tries to recompose the world in response. Thus, I begin to align this sequence with the fivefold knowing event, as follows:

Knowing event	1Context	Conflict, 2Scanning	3Aha, 4Release	5Interpretation
Dimensions of Humanness	1World, 2Ego	3Void	4Holy	→

The chart, in a simplistic way, suggests Loder's point: that knowing as the fivefold transformative event draws its intense dynamism from its fundamental rootedness in and correspondence with four-dimensional humanness. Eventually it will be evident that the actualizing of the self for Loder is akin, in substance and consequence, to Buber's I-You encounter. Thus we may infer that the growth of the self to fullness is intermingled with the move to four-dimensionality in humanness. So though, in my chart, I place self, as ego, in the first of the four consecutive boxes, somehow we need to think of self, in its dynamic unfolding, as permeating all four. For the self is always embodied and situated in the world; and for the self to move to fullness, it must have undergone the third and fourth dimensions. This permeation characterizes the third dimension, and that means that the hope is that the fourth dimension will transformatively invade all dimensions as well. So the chart's linearity can be misleading. But we have only to keep in mind, as we will see, the supervening transformative quality of the event of the third column.

If you want to diagram Loder's four dimensions, use a cross, as follows:

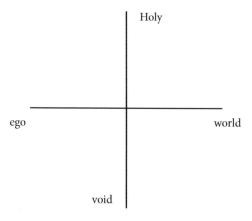

When I first read Loder's account of the void, I wondered if he was saying that evil is necessary to humanness. I came to conclude that he isn't. The void isn't evil *per se*, but that which evil, in our bentness, is sometimes the only circumstance capable of bringing us to understand. Evil and unfortunate circumstances often most effectively reveal our contingency, our ontological dependence on something beyond ourselves—the fact that we might not exist. And of course, it is one thing to affirm our contingency, and quite another to experience it existentially! Experience of the void is that existential version.

We began our conversation with John Frame by speaking of the Creator-creature distinction. I propose that the experience of the void so central to Loder's account is fundamentally an existential apprehension of this metaphysical reality. Implicated integrally in confessing that God is God, Lord, King, Creator, Sustainer, Savior, what have you, is confessing that *I* am not. It is confessing my ontological dependence on him—my contingency. This, I believe, is worship.

But if contingency and experience of it is essential to humanness, and if that is also essential to worship and enjoyment of God, this should be a delightful and freeing experience (though we can never be complacent about it). Whence the terror, then, of the void—the sense of *threat* to nonbeing?[5] I think that the biblical story affirms that this is the result of human rebellion and part of the world's current brokenness. There is so obviously an angst about contingency in our everyday experience. I can be doing the speed limit and patrol car lights flashing in my rear view mirror send a pang of terror through my body. I remember as a child a time my mother picked me up out of bed to carry me downstairs. I was terrified that she would fall and drop me. And she did. To be restored one day, as Scripture promises, will be to shed the terror. Human contingency will be simply and joyfully once more a matter of delightful confidence in God.

In the interim of the already-not yet, as theologians call our times between Christ's advents, in existential experience of our contingency, there is a choice: will we draw the lid over the void and continue to deny it, or reach out to embrace it in some way we cannot at that point understand? And may we, as we mature, come to relate well to our contingency—may we learn to dance on the void?

We will see that Loder makes the courageous claim that the prevailing notions of "normal human development" restrict their account to the first two dimensions and thus short-circuit, in a damaging way, the opportunity of being fully human. For in order for full humanness, the self must experience the fact that in itself it cannot ever ultimately be victorious over nothingness, the possibility of nonbeing, and "surrender" to the gracious gift of new being from a personal other.[6]

Loder moves on to ask: In the face of the void, why do we continue to live? And he responds:

> the answer, like the question, is intrinsic to our selfhood. We continue to live precisely because in the center of the self, for all of its potential perversity, we experience again and again the reversal of those influences that invite despair and drive toward the void.

5. I owe this insight to Andrew Colbert. Personal conversation.
6. Loder, *Transforming Moment*, 157–69.

Kierkegaard repeatedly insisted with bewildering brilliance that
the faces of the void become the faces of God.

. . . The reason we do not cease to live is the deep sense that
we are not merely three-dimensional creatures . . . we witness to
another reality . . . the Holy.[7]

On the verge of the yawning chasm of the void, we experience again
and again a gracious reversal of its undertow, and we find that the face of
the void becomes the face of God. Transformation to four-dimensional
humanness requires something, some Other, beyond the human ego,
only capable of disclosure once the void has been acknowledged—one
may say, *in* the void—to let-be flourishingly, and in whose gaze the self
may be transformed.

The Holy is "the manifest Presence of being-itself transforming and
restoring human being in a way that is approximated by the imaginative image as it recomposes the 'world' in the course of transformational
knowing. As the Presence of being-itself, the Holy is both within and
beyond people, but always it retains its essential character as *mysterium
tremendum fascinans.*"[8] To experience the Holy is to gain a sense of "self
anchored on the Rock." It is to experience the power of being-itself to
bring forth new being. The experience of the void proves graciously to
be a pathway to centeredness in the Holy. Far beyond humanness being
adaptive, as per a two-dimensionally human psychology, it is transformational, and the self becomes truly itself for the first time. It is within
us, but it is always something that has laid hold of us from beyond us.
Notice in this passage that Loder aligns the experience of the Holy with
the moment of insight in the five-fold knowing event.

Is this talk of third and fourth dimensions, the void and the Holy,
true to human experience? It can sound like a religious conversion.
In fact, conversion is an instance of it. But not all people experience
religious conversions. How are we to understand this and to see it in
our lives?

First let's remember that many people live in denial of the void as
long as they can—longer than they ought to, certainly. Midlife crisis is
midlife—and that stands in judgment on the stubborn denial that has
kept us from figuring life out sooner. The fact that younger people experience *quarter*-life crises is in this respect to their credit. But sooner or

7. Ibid., 85.
8. Ibid., 91.

later we face our own unavoidable death. At the point that we face it, it is only apparently more imminent than it has been all along. So what seems to make for our experience of the void is that we actually acknowledge the pervading reality of our contingency and inadequacy. We get it.

Second, this happens to everybody. Contingency is true of all humans, our pretensions notwithstanding. So the void characterizes all people, and the question is only at what point someone takes this to heart. Recently I saw for the first time a film called, *Grand Canyon*, which depicts some people who live in Los Angeles coming to terms with the awfulness of life, trying to make sense of the fact that life isn't the way it is supposed to be. This is the void: life sucks, always has, always will. There is no mention in the film of God, except in profanity; yet the main characters come to the point of speaking of miracles, things that they were meant to be and do that are truly good. For example: the female lead, despite having already moved beyond the years of young child-raising, when she discovers a discarded baby, she decides to adopt her. This is, I believe, an implicit form of what Loder identifies as the Holy, the fourth dimension of humanness. In contrast, another main character has a palpable experience of the void and the Holy, only to dismiss it as temporary insanity! His loss!—the film itself suggests the viability of that assessment.

But third, and this really is our point in the context of the contours of human knowing, Loder confirms explicitly that every act of coming to know is at least prototypically, maybe more, essentially a grappling with the third dimension of humanness and an embracing of the fourth. "Even those who would not agree that being is gracious implicitly live by that premise with every affirmation of scientific discovery, esthetic intuition, or therapeutic success. The central turning point in the transformational knowing event, the imaginative vision, is an eruption of new being in the presence of imminent void; it is a manifestation of the abundance with which being-itself supplies the deepest needs of human being . . . the power of being-itself to bring forth new being."[9]

All human knowing must be seen to tap into and share the contours of the pull to full four-dimensional humanness that in turn reflects the character of reality itself. For "at the center of transformational knowing in science, esthetics, or therapy the imaginative, constructive insight or

9. Ibid., 87.

vision is an undoing of nothingness."[10] Loder's account of the human spirit and of the knowing event as embedded in it explains the longing humans have to know which carries them into and through, time and again, risky efforts to know. The Oh-I-See-It! moment, every time it occurs—every time we actively rely on clues to shape a pattern that unlocks the world—implicitly displays this dynamic, shaping the knower toward four-dimensional humanness, as well as testifying to the Holy, to the graciousness of being. This is how knowing is transformation, not mere information: it taps deeply into the reservoir of who we are and what reality is, and draws these into profound accord.

Imagine, then, the damage done by an epistemological account that, like a psychological account of "normal development," fails to include all four dimensions of human knowing! How defacing, depersonalizing, dehumanizing, if it is not understood that knowing is a transformative event. As we concluded the conversation with Buber, we must revise our epistemology to exhibit contours consistent with this kind of knowing that transforms us by centering us in the presence of the Other—or else we are doomed. Loder expresses this implication: "This situation calls for not just a dialogue or a synthesis but for a new understanding of knowing commensurate with the nature of convictional experience . . . Knowing as event."[11] Revising our epistemology, we may thus fully anticipate, will heal knowers in the direction of wholeness, even as it also holds prospect for thus restoring both knowing and the known. Additionally, this means that once we are aware of this underlying dynamic, we can be that much more intentional about four-dimensionality in being human, centering our selves in the Holy, in all our acts of coming to know. And that, I argue in this book, will make us better knowers.

CONVICTIONAL KNOWING

As I said before, Loder offers a dynamic rationale for the knowing event in multiple directions. We have looked at the first, how the knowing event has about it the contours and powerful impetus of four-dimensional humanness. Now a brief look at the second, how the Holy Spirit, in gracious complementarity with the human spirit, often takes knowing events—they are his medium—and transforms the transforming into

10. Ibid., 70.
11. Ibid., 21.

convictional knowing events. "Central to the Christian faith is that human transformations must themselves be transformed. All transformations are forms of knowing that reflect, in respect to the character of each context, that decisive transformation by which we come to know Christ. This is only possible through redeemed knowledge of him, but the others are proximate forms and participate "sacramentally" insofar as they are visible forms of that infinite and invisible truth." Thus, says Loder, "I will eventually argue that all transformational knowing participates in the knowledge of Christ as its norm and paradigm."[12]

"At the center of a knowing event is a nonrational intrusion of a convincing insight," says Loder, as we noted before: "This is the central common feature that makes every convictional event an act of knowing and every act of knowing an event." The transformational undoing of nothingness which is the knowing event "is a proximate form of the ultimate manifestation of 'the Holy' in revelation. That which is unique, set apart and manifest as new being, reversing and overcoming annihilation, expresses the graciousness of being-itself." The knowing event is a prototype of knowing God. Transformational logic is a proximate norm of convictional knowing. In this, Loder's work offers a nuanced account for Frame's pronouncement that all knowing is knowing God.

This transformative knowledge of Christ is epitomized and experienced repeatedly in the Christian celebration of the Eucharist. For in Jesus Christ's abandonment, death, bodily resurrection, and accession to kingship, he has plunged into the abyss, the void, and filled it with his being. From the standpoint of Christian conviction, Loder says, we do not have to be afraid of plunging in ourselves, for he is there, and has changed reality.[13] In that event, we experience intimacy with Christ.

	1	2	3	4
Convictional knowing (the Eucharist)	I am in the world	I need rescue from sin and death	Jesus plunges in and undoes Void with his fullness	I respond and enjoy intimate communion with Christ
Knowing event	1Context	Conflict, 2Scanning	3Aha, 4Release	5Interpretation
Dimensions of Humanness	1World, 2Ego	3Void	4Holy	→

12. Ibid., 33.
13. Ibid., 121.

I add this third line to my chart on the topside. For the knowing event is seen to anticipate or prototype it. We may thus sense about the chart in its current form that the knowing event taproots down into our humanness and signposts upward to communion with Christ.

Two fabulous discussions occur in Loder's chapter on convictional knowing. He shows, first, how convictional knowing cannot be what is envisioned or attainable in eastern religions.[14] For the end result is the intimate communion of two persons, not one, and not none. Buber and Macmurray, we have seen, affirm the same. The consummate Christian experience, I believe, is not God *is* us, but God *with* us—Emmanuel. Milking the alignments of knowing and interpersonal relationship which we are developing in this work, it is exclusively a Christian experience that uniquely expresses and empowers the essential nerve of human knowing.

Second, as I have done in *Longing to Know*, Loder employs the New Testament account of the resurrection day road to Emmaus event, in which the disciples unknowingly encounter the risen Jesus, experience his explaining the seemingly tragic events of the weekend in light of the Old Testament, and only subsequently recognize him as Jesus breaks the bread. Loder, in a powerful annotation of the story, shows how this convictional knowing event draws on all four dimensions of humanness.[15] He links the Emmaus event strategically to the Eucharist; after all, it is in the breaking of the bread at Emmaus, this side of his resurrection, that Jesus comes and his disciples recognize him. In *Longing to Know*, I described the Emmaus encounter to make the point that "knowing God is like knowing your auto mechanic," that it is an ordinary act of knowing. My agenda in this book shares a commonality with Loder's own, as I now argue the converse: that knowing your auto mechanic is like knowing God. For Loder, the Emmaus event is the central act of coming to know, the coming to know Christ, who will, if we welcome him, invade all our knowing and our persons, to center us in the Holy, to make us

---

14. Ibid., 94–97.

15. I am in particular tantalized by Loder's comment that at the moment the disciples' eyes are opened, Jesus disappears from view. He suggests that they are no longer looking *at* him, but rather are looking *through* him at everything else. I find uncanny and thrilling the resemblance here to the language of subsidiary-focal integration. Once again, it suggests an alignment of the Polanyian account with knowing God. Loder, *Transforming Moment*, 97–120.

fully human, and—oh yes, by the way—to make us better knowers. To know Christ is to have one's being primed for knowing.[16]

It is Loder's central and valuable purpose in his book to offer an account of convictional knowing, and thereby to give vision and means for convictional knowing to a Protestant church largely absent of these, reticent to accredit or even acknowledge convictional knowing. That is not my purpose here; my purpose, in contrast to his, appears much more modest. Nevertheless, for the very reason that knowing can align with experience of God, and must do so for us to invite the real that is God and God's, my task of epistemological therapy, though modest with respect to Loder's, is critical. We must remove the deadening blinders of a false paradigm of knowing if we are ever to be able to see and experience the human knowing event as prototype of, proximate norm of, and participatory in an encounter of intimacy with the living Christ. And this will be good, not just for our souls, but also for our bodies, our science, our art, our business, our counseling, our pedagogy—I could go on.

Loder shows us the way that we may see our relationship with God as central to our epistemology—something I promised at the outset. This move both requires and effects the important and positive challenge to a damagingly defective epistemic default that will issue in epistemic health and effective knowing. And for the Christian believer, it makes wonderful sense of the centrality of that relationship which, despite the wrongheadedness of the default that we have only known to concede, we have maintained must be the most important thing about us. Now we can see that it is, and how it is, central to human knowing and being.

THE FACE OF THE OTHER

At this juncture in an engagement with Loder, the reader can have the sense that the matter is complex enough; we cannot take in any more. But Loder persists to give us yet another parallel trajectory, that of human development. Since we have encountered a similar account in Macmurray and in Buber, here I want to show only three things about it.

First, as I have hinted previously, Loder the psychologist challenges the very assumptions that shape typical accounts of "normal human

---

16. The reader should now link this thought back to what I said in texture 2, about Christian academics. This begins to suggest more effectively just why construing Bible courses as content so tragically eclipses the epistemic value proper to the gospel.

development": that human development involves only the first two dimensions of humanness. Normal humanness, they believe, is healthy adaptation to one's environment. For Loder this is radically, damagingly, false. Human development requires an experience of the void and of the Holy. "What's wrong with normal development is its inherent loss of the Face, hence its denial of person-centeredness," says Loder.[17]

Second, Loder's account of human development is yet another trajectory which aligns with and thus embeds and empowers human knowing. It is yet another line on the chart, as follows:

	1	2	3	4
Convictional knowing	I am in the world	I need rescue from sin and death	Jesus plunges in and undoes Void with his fullness	I respond and enjoy intimate communion with Christ
Knowing event	1Context	Conflict, 2Scanning	3Aha, 4Release	5Interpretation
Dimensions of Humanness	1World, 2Ego	3Void	4Holy	→
Human development	Face of mother; "normal development"	Sense of the absence of the Face	Recentering personality in Face of Other	→ (the self that gives love)

So Loder's account of human development also partakes of and shares contours with human knowing, the fourfold knowing event of humanness, and the convictional knowing event.

Loder's account, just like Macmurray's and Buber's, features preoccupation with the child and the mother, moving to a communion with the personal Other as the transformed and fully developed self. The shaping contours of this centering act of coming to know once again are interpersonal and covenantal. But Loder's account showcases the *face* of the Other. I will give this third distinctive my attention.

He shows how the infant in the earliest months of life, in responding to the presence of a human face by giving a smile, seeks and finds in this interpersonal facial mirroring "the primary organizer of the personality." He calls this a nucleus of trust. "The face, then, is the personal center that is innately sought by a child and the focus of the earliest sense of one's

17. Ibid., 174.

humanity. The smiling response focuses primal wholeness . . . the undifferentiated 'cosmos' of the child becomes personal and interpersonal, focusing on the face."[18]

Through life, this primal longing persists "for the face that will not go away . . . for a loving other to address the whole person (as before), including the differentiated ego with all its competencies, and to set that whole-differentiated person into the cosmos as self-affirmed and beloved."[19] What should happen is that in person-person relationships the child grows by experiencing being known by another Person, in whose gaze the child comes to be fully her- or himself, a self capable of giving love. Loder speaks of "face-to-face relationships in which two people mutually create each other."[20] Loder sees this recentering of the personality as the miraculous transformation of the ego into a self that gives love. The ego takes on the character of being, itself graciously letting being flourish.[21] It is important to see that such ego transformation does not destroy the ego but rather recenters it decisively around a transcendental reality that points to the invisible God. "The net effect actually enhances ego functioning, because the ego has less need to control or limit perceptions or understandings of self, world, or others . . . [O]nce the center is invested with God's Presence, the ego's anguish at absence and abandonment is dissipated, and its defensive energies can be poured into its competencies . . . [D]ecentering the ego liberates and empowers its functioning . . . because it is no longer the presumed center of the personality."[22] In the process of human development, there is danger on

18. Ibid., 162–63.

19. Ibid., 166.

20. Ibid., 63.

21. Ibid., 78–80. Thanks to my friend and colleague, Dr. Shirley Kilpatrick, for pointing me to Jonathan Edwards understanding of beauty as "cordial consent to being" (Delattre, "Jonathan Edwards and the Recovery of Aesthetics," 282). This phrase accords with Loder's idea of letting being flourish. Similarly, in *Captivating*, the Eldredges define beauty as conveying the message, "All will be well."(135) See texture 6, for my fullest discussion of personal beauty and its connection to knowing and being.

22. Loder, *Transforming Moment*, 167. Dooyeweerd emphasizes that a face-to-face relationship with Yahweh defines our identity as humans. He cites the opening phrases of Psalm 139: "O LORD, you have searched me and you know me." According to Scripture, to be human is to stand in the presence of the world-making, world-redeeming, covenantally-loving, gaze of the sovereign Lord. Human rebellion bends us to want to run and hide. But even the running and hiding proclaims the intimacy of

every side: on one side, real abandonment, or a lecherous or some other sort of gaze that induces shame, and on the other side, devolvement into idolatry, in which the person tries to make the other person into the missing Face of God. In our bentness, any number of things can go wrong, and it takes many years to find recovery and healing. But when healing comes, I believe that what Loder describes is ever the shape that it takes.

In the texture after this chapter I will connect this experience to a person's sense of personal beauty. A sense of personal beauty comes, I believe, only in the generous, self-giving gaze, the noticing regard, of another person. I will argue that such a sense invites the real.

It is telling to lay this incredible claim of Loder's alongside Descartes' culture-shaping move to install the *cogito*—the "I think"—as the ultimate anchor of human knowing. If Loder is right, Descartes thereby contributed to the disempowerment of human knowing and being. For the ego as *cogito* had "need to control and limit perceptions and understanding of self, world, or others," experiencing "anguish and abandonment," as it poured its energies into them and not into "competencies." One can only imagine what western culture might have accomplished if Descartes hadn't so installed the *cogito*! We need the face of the Holy, the personal Other—we need it as the decentering and recentering of who we are, to be well, and to know well.

Loder aligns his description of human development with the other trajectories we have discussed: "The face of the loving parent is prototypical of the Face of God; the early sense of absence is prototypical of the ultimate void, 'outer darkness' and abandonment of God."[23] This relates the dynamics of human development prototypically to basic Christian theological concepts; the dynamics of human development are a deficient form of the ultimate categories of meaning.

> I suggest that what is established in the original face-to-face interaction is the child's sense of personhood and a universal prototype of the Divine Presence. In the face-to-face interaction (whether actualized or remaining an innate potential), the child seeks a *cosmic, self-confirming impact from the presence of*

---

the face-to-face standing. The gaze embraced makes us fully the humans we are meant to be, and extends outward and embraces all of reality with in God's dominion and humans' stewardship. See Dooyeweerd, *In the Twilight of Western Thought*, 189.

23. Loder, *Transforming Moment*, 174.

> *a loving other . . .* [I]n Christian context, the self-understanding
> of the convicted person combines the sense of personal presence
> and transcendent order. Thus the primal experience of the face
> as actual presence and in its significance as symbolic expression
> provides a prototype for the convicting Presence of God.[24]

Along with Buber, Loder indicates that, once a person has met God
in this formative encounter, all ordinary knowing events, from then on,
do not merely anticipate it prototypically, but actually are imbued with
his presence. In Buber's categories, the I-ness of the I-Thou pervades
even I-It events. Loder concludes:

> Yes—there is an inevitable and decisive shift somewhere in every
> act of creation and discovery from the active to the passive mode:
> in the moment of insight the knower is being known; the self is
> caught in the act of knowing. From such experiences where we
> discover the unreasonable workability of mathematics as well as
> the incomprehensible realization that we have been fully com-
> prehended by a loving Other, we sense deeply within ourselves
> that under the right conditions and because of how we are made
> and in spite of how we have come to our present state, we have
> access to that higher intelligibility which directly or indirectly
> has addressed us.[25]

Knowing events as events are, generally speaking, transformative
and wonderful.[26] Knowing events undergone in the wake of a convic-

24. Ibid., 163. Dr. Terri Williams, psychology professor at Geneva College, has propounded the thesis that there is a link between the health of a six- to twelve-month-old
child's relationship with her/his caregiver, and the child's likelihood later in life to have
a relationship with God (Williams, "Faith Development"). Her claims offer support to
Loder's account.

25. Loder, *Transforming Moment*, 217.

26. I have in mind here the fact that the tree, in the biblical story of Adam and
Eve (Gen 3), from which they were not to eat and nevertheless did—the first and all-
impacting human rebelling—was called the tree of the knowledge of good and evil.
How are we to understand this text in light of the account of knowing I am developing
here? Two things can be said. First: this account of knowing makes far better sense of
knowing evil having such adverse, deeply personal, covenant breaking consequences.
For on this account, knowing evil could be said to *be* covenant rebellion. Second: if
all knowing events are good and transformative, does this mean that we cannot know
evil things? Take, for example, the horrifying discovery of genocide, such as occurred
in the wake of World War II. An Oh-I-See-It! moment such as this is good because the
truth is disclosed; and transformative in that it radically changes me, deepening, albeit
painfully, my understanding. In fact, it is an instance of encountering the void; into this,
graciously, may come the Holy—the possibility of new being.

tional encounter are transformed transformations, incrementally wonderful concomitant beholdings of the face of God. In effect, you can't do knowing *a la* Loder, without it being convictional knowing. Simone Weil, as we have already noted, gives us the thesis that things such as friendship and love of neighbor are "forms of the implicit love of God." We may on the basis of Loder's account maintain that all acts of knowing are forms of the implicit love of God. And centering, recentering the personality, in the gaze of the loving Other, which for the Christian believer is the self-giving face of Jesus Christ, is the critical to-be-known that both constitutes us and makes us better knowers.

Tying together all the transformational developmental trajectories that Loder aligns, the whole is shot through with what one author has called the "Beloved Invader." One whose face forms us in personhood, who is flourishing being-itself, subsisting beyond and before us—all dimensions of our knowing and being beg for his descent. Though my schematic capacities fall far short, this suggests my addition of an all-enveloping final column to our chart. Also in it I allude to the phrases of the Scriptures' Aaronic Benediction: "The Lord bless you and keep you; The Lord make his face to shine upon you and give you peace; The Lord lift his countenance upon and be gracious to you."[27]

	1	2	3	4	
Convictional knowing	I am in the world	I need rescue from sin and death	Jesus plunges in and undoes Void with his fullness	I respond and enjoy intimate communion with Christ	Yahweh knowing (forming) humans— "making his face shine upon them"
Knowing event	1Context	Conflict, 2Scanning	3Aha, 4Release	5Interpretation	
Dimensions of Humanness	1World, 2Ego	3Void	4Holy	→	
Human development	Face of mother; "normal development"	Sense of the absence of the Face	Recentering personality in Face of Other	→	

27. Num 6.

The contours of human knowing, we may justifiably conclude, just are the contours of interpersonal relationship. A dynamic, gracious, deliverance to restorative relationship centers knowing, shaping all epistemic acts at least implicitly. As a result, all epistemic acts at least prototype anticipatively that central relational core of knowing and being. And for those who are blessed to embrace this: the deliverer, the personal Other, is the uniquely personal Lord of Christianity.

WEAVING LODER'S INSIGHTS
INTO COVENANT EPISTEMOLOGY

Hardly any need remains to weave Loder's insights into covenant epistemology, for the correspondence of the two has been patently evident throughout our conversation with Loder. Loder *is* talking about human knowing, even as he is talking about all the other trajectories he so admirably develops and aligns with it. Those trajectories infuse human knowing with interpersoned overtones; and Loder's account affords insight regarding how they do. We have noted this all along in our account. And you, the reader, by this point, are well attuned to recognizing it.

Specifically, Loder contributes to I-You encounter with the personal Other the important constitutive contribution of the face. In this transformative encounter we see how knowing prototypes it and thus is imbued with the personal. We see what the paradigmatic act of knowing should be: transformative encounter of the personal Other. Loder adds to our covenant epistemology project the well-supported claim that convictional knowing—experience of the gracious presence of God, as emblemized in the celebration of the Eucharist—is that in which all acts of knowing participate, and that which they all prototype. Knowing is a form of the implicit love of God. We also see corroborated the motion of the descent of God, as I continue to refer to the gracious, surprising, and transformative inbreaking of the real at our invitation or cry for help, and thus in support of a hearty realism.

The Transformational Logic of the Covenant Drama of Redemption

But I do want to point out two, further, fruitful connections. We can connect Loder's work with the idea of covenant relationship with God which is the substance of the Scriptures. Along the way in the rich density of his presentation, Loder drops what for me is a most intriguing comment.

He says that he would like to see someone explore transformational logic as a key to biblical narrative.[28] While it may be that he has in mind that there are plenty of accounts in Scripture of individuals' acts of coming to know that display the features of transformational logic—the Emmaus event is just one, as are the "conversions" of Paul, Thomas, Samson's father, Job, and Nathaniel—I think Loder's desire finds fulfillment in the overall story of the Bible, what Mike Williams in his title refers to as the biblical drama of redemption. In reformational circles, the components of this story are expressed as: Creation, Fall, Redemption, and Restoration (or consummation). Indeed, I think we can add another row to the chart.

	1	2	3	4	
Bib. Narrative	Creation	Fall	Redemption	Restoration	Yahweh knowing (forming) humans— "making his face shine upon them"
Convictional knowing	I am in the world	I need rescue from my sin	Jesus plunges in and undoes Void with his fullness	I respond and enjoy intimate communion with Christ	
Knowing event	1Context	Conflict, 2Scanning	3Aha, 4Release	5Interpretation	
Dimensions of Humanness	1World, 2Ego	3Void	4Holy	→	
Human development	Face of mother; "normal development"	Sense of the absence of the Face	Recentering personality in Face of Other	→	

As we have seen, the story of the Bible is the story of the unfolding relationship between Yahweh and his chosen people. As Williams unpacks the story, he speaks of the Exodus as the Old Testament deliverance which sets the pattern so that God's people will recognize his coming and redemption in Christ.[29] I want to talk about the Exodus briefly here.

One of the best examples I know of, of Loder's void, is that of the people of Israel on the near side of the Red Sea. On the heels of God's powerful revelation and devastation of Egypt in the plagues, Pharaoh

28. Loder, *Transforming Moment*, 97.

29. Williams, *Far as the Curse is Found*, 20–25.

demands their immediate departure, and the Egyptians are so desperate to have them leave that they actually throw their jewels at them. The people depart, and subsequently Pharaoh changes his mind. He pursues them with his chariot-driving army, and pins the fleeing Israelite people up against the impassable Red Sea. I cannot imagine a better case of the void: I can imagine them wailing in terror, "We're doomed!"—as, indeed, they were.

	1	2	3	4	
Biblical Narrative	Creation	Fall	Redemption	Restoration	
Exodus Narrative	1 Egyptian slavery, 2 Hebrew slaves	First caught in slavery, then between Pharoah and the Sea	God's deliverance and self-disclosure	People respond in the relationship that the law structures	Yahweh knowing (forming) humans— "making his face shine upon them"
Convictional knowing	I am in the world	I need rescue from my sin	Jesus plunges in and undoes Void with his fullness	I respond and enjoy intimate communion with Christ	
Knowing event	1Context	Conflict, 2Scanning	3Aha, 4Release	5Interpretation	
Dimensions of Humanness	1World, 2Ego	3Void	4Holy	→	
Human development	Face of mother; "normal development"	Sense of the absence of the Face	Recentering personality in Face of Other	→	

Loder speaks beautifully of God as the One who always comes from the other side of ultimate human emptiness, transformatively superseding all human efforts for knowledge and redemption.[30] It is true that God's deliverance is sovereignly initiated. But it comes in the moment of their greatest need. In delivering the Hebrews through to the other side of the Sea, Yahweh frees them in such a way that they actually have a choice to respond to him in love. Loder's analysis has included

---

30. Loder, *Transforming Moment*, 8.

features that I have not described here that also pertain to the Exodus deliverance, namely, a summons to a new reality, and an authorization in history.

The alignment of the Exodus deliverance with the experience of the void enables us to see more graphically the act of coming to know as an invitation into relationship that is also a summons to a new reality and obedience to it.

I think it also interesting to note that, when Williams refers to it as God setting the pattern of redemption, he means that God is giving his people a prototype of what his signature moves will always look like, and what one specific, central, for-all-time action of redemption—namely, Christ's coming—will look like. So Williams' account displays the same dynamic of anticipative, prototypic, implicit knowledge that Loder's does, and which brings both in line with Polanyian epistemology.

To become a Christian is to be welcomed into this larger story of God's people.[31] What happens with us as individuals with God happens because it is a part of a larger, corporate, cosmic relationship. Christians speak of this time now, between Christ's first coming and his second coming (the consummation), as the "already-not yet." That phrase speaks of void, longing, and the beginning of transformation. Scripture indicates that we cannot yet see what that renewed reality will be like. Thus we are in the middle of the story of the relationship.

People have said, parodying the "It's turtles all the way down" cosmogony, such things as, "It's interpretation all the way down." What we are saying here is that it is relationship all the way down—and all the way along.

The Normative Dimension and the Void-Holy Dynamic

Secondly, I want to suggest that we align Loder's four dimensions of humanness with John Frame's triad of the situational, the existential, and the normative. The alignment provides warrant for claims I have offered tentatively already. It shows the way to embedding the Framean triad in the interpersoned.

---

31. Meek, "My Father, My People, My Story."

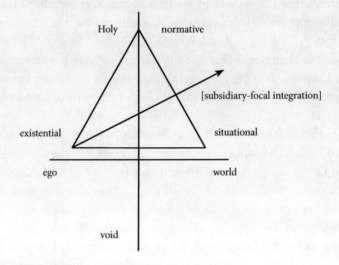

It is reasonable to align Frame's situational and existential with Loder's first and second dimensions of humanness. The first dimension, we saw, is the world, meaning our embodied situatedness in it—the lived world. Loder calls the second dimension "the self." The self is both in this environment and transcends it. It always is recomposing its world in a way that coherently accords with the self.

This alignment makes sense because Frame, in a manner similar to Loder's agenda, is using the triad to identify dimensions of humanness that result from our creaturely relationship to the Lordship of God. Both are saying of their proposals that these features are essential to being human. Laying Loder's account alongside Frame's starts to give Frame's a dynamism, a more three-dimensional sense of how the triad plays out in our lives.

For Loder (in telling contrast, by the way, to Descartes' *cogito*), the situational is prior, and the self starts to distinguish itself from the situational, but always within the situational. What "happens next," according to Loder, is an experience of the void, a threatening sense of potential or actual non-being. This sets up what can only be initiated from outside of me—an inbreaking experience of the Holy as a Personal Other who delivers, graciously according new being. If Frame's lower two corners of the triad align with Loder's first and second dimensions, what happens if we align the third, the normative, with Loder's transformative void-Holy dynamic? I think that this gives us the way to see that, in fact, the normative is embedded in transformative interpersoned relationship. With respect to that relationship, the normative just is the constitutive covenantal structure, as I distinguished it in my conversation with Mike Williams. Frame's reference to the normative and its critical role as third component of human knowing and engagement is something we can see to be a metonymous reference to an overarching interpersoned relationship. Metonymy, as we said, involves a reference to the part that is meant to stand for the whole. By way of metonymy, the interpersonal relationship is implicit in the normative.

	1	2	3	4	
Biblical Narrative	Creation	Fall	Redemption	Restoration	
Exodus Narrative	1 Egyptian slavery, 2 Hebrew slaves	First caught in slavery, then between Pharoah and the Sea	God's deliverance and self-disclosure	People respond in the relationship that the law structures	
Framean triad	Situational, Existential	(need)	(deliverance)	Normative (covenantal constitution) as metonymous, for interpersoned relationship with God.	Yahweh knowing (forming) humans— "making his face shine upon them"
Convictional knowing	I am in the world	I need rescue from my sin	Jesus plunges in and undoes Void with his fullness	I respond and enjoy intimate communion with Christ	
Knowing event	1Context	Conflict, 2Scanning	3Aha, 4Release	5Interpretation	
Dimensions of Humanness	1World, 2Ego	3Void	4Holy	→	
Human development	Face of mother; "normal development"	Sense of the absence of the Face	Recentering personality in Face of Other	→	

Further, to add the void-Holy dynamism—the I-You encounter—to the triad is a little like adding water to one of those flattened sponges: the effect transformatively supersedes the original. I have been uncertain regarding whether the personal may be aligned with the normative, or whether we should view it as the larger context of the entire triad. This shows why and how both are true. Just as Loder says that experience of the void and of the Holy eclipses the first two dimensions of humanness, and transforms them, so the relationship for which the normative acts as a metonymous reference eclipses, transforms, and thereby contexts, the existential and the situational—in fact, the entire triad. James Loder voices the wonder of this realization: "[I]n the end we will not be able to imagine the depth and magnitude of the reality to which even the best images of the most profound minds are pointing us. All understanding and models must finally become transparent and vanish. Then, in death to all else, each one may appear face to face before the One who always comes from the other side of ultimate human emptiness."[32] Knowing need not be exclusively the being known graciously by the Holy Other nevertheless to be fraught transformatively by it. In anticipation of the encounter, we search for the face that will go away. Being known transforms us as knowers. Part of this, I will argue in the next texture, is a healing self-knowing that may appropriately be understood as a sense of personal beauty. Recentered in the gaze of the Holy, we take the I of I-You into all our I-Its. We respond by freely binding ourselves to covenant response. Knowing is that response. And the whole becomes the unfolding relationship of life, that is knowing God.

QUESTIONS FOR DISCUSSION

1. Draw your own diagram or the four dimensions of humanness, locating the four on the points of a cross: world and self at the ends of the horizontal line, void at the bottom of the vertical, Holy at the top.

2. How does your own life experience converge with this account? In particular, what has been your experience of the void (the threat of nonbeing) and of the Holy (the possibility of new being)?

3. For you, whose has been the face that constituted you as a person?

---

32. Loder, *Transforming Moment*, 8.

4. Does it make sense to align the void-Holy dynamism with the normative dimension of the triad, allowing for the dynamism to transform and context the whole? Why or why not?

5. Do you think that Loder successfully enables us to make sense of the claim that all knowing is, (at least prototypically) knowing God?

A SENSE OF PERSONAL BEAUTY

ODD AS IT MAY sound at the outset, I want to offer an account of personal, bodily, beauty that ties it integrally with covenant epistemology. That covenant epistemology supports such an account shows how it concretely makes us better knowers and better persons.[1]

I will speak of a sense of personal beauty. Beauty, I believe, is not about "personal appearance." While "personal beauty" is a term we associate more with females than males, and while the matter plays out distinctively for women, what I have in mind applies equally to both genders. I will argue that a sense of personal beauty is a kind of self-knowledge. It results from a certain kind of successful knowing event. I also want to suggest that a sense of personal beauty is available to all human beings, both as human beings in relationship and especially for those who have been redemptively known by God. In chapter 15, I will argue further that a sense of personal beauty enhances effectiveness in knowing. It invites reality, prompting further knowing. You rightly may guess that I will be challenging the commonly held opposition of intelligence and beauty. I will be arguing that beauty is essential to intelligence.

At this juncture—having explored Macmurray, Buber, and Loder—we have built into covenant epistemology the structures we need to make profound and helpful sense of

1. This texture originated as part of a copresentation with my daughter, Starr Meek, as "Personal Beauty and Epistemology," the epistemological counterpart of her "Made for Glory." Meek argued that the goodness of personal beauty accords with the biblical vision, by locating it in its theological context. This surprising claim challenges the prevailing workaday theology of most believers, which dissociates concern for bodily beauty from all things "spiritual." Our co-presentation occurred at Covenant Seminary's Friday Nights at the Francis Schaeffer Institute Series (Kaldi's Coffee House, St. Louis, August 2007).

this important idea. We are now in a position to relate the I-You encounter to a person's sense of personal beauty. A sense of personal beauty comes, I believe, only in the generous, self-giving gaze, the noticing regard, of another person.

As I have sketched the claims of Buber and especially Loder, you may have also noticed the connection between knowing and a sense of personal beauty that they imply. Loder explicitly links beauty with the experience of convictional knowing. He speaks of "the gift of God's beauty within the attender [the one who pays attention to the Holy], a gift that may be described as a quality of completeness, or a sense of no lack. Such a sense within allows renewed perception of every proximate form of beauty without. Then, too, the proximate forms of beauty without are often enabled to initiate the inner attending of the Holy . . . This beauty and the Holy are inextricably related."[2] And in an exposition of the Holy One as the Knower and transformation as coming to

be known, to be addressed in the four dimensions of one's humanness, Loder says that the knowing, among its many effects within the one known, "brings beauty out of chaos."[3] Plus, we have seen that he says that as the person is constituted in the gaze of the other, the person "takes on the character of being," which is fundamentally that which "lets being flourish." This description accords with two definitions of beauty, which I noted in the last chapter: beauty is consent to being; and beauty says, "all will be well."[4] It speaks of a wholeness within that blesses surrounding people and environs with the same privilege.

I want to argue that a sense of personal beauty is a kind of self-knowing that develops within the gaze of another person. Here I make my point by telling you of the personal experience which led my thought in this direction. I grew up in a family of people all much older than myself, all of whom were, as I often say, "grandly good or grandly bad." I was not noticed, and I found safety from personal attack in

2. Loder, *Transforming Moment*, 109. This supports Starr's point that beauty aligns with holiness (Starr Meek, "Made for Glory," 10).

3. Loder, *Transforming Moment*, 179–80.

4. See, ch. 10, n.20.

keeping my head down and not being noticed, all the while craving that notice. I realized neither of these consciously at the time. I only know I grew into adulthood and toward middle age with the feeling that inside me, if I ever turned my eyes there, was—nothing—a big hole of non-existence. I did not feel I knew myself; I did not feel there was anybody there to know. I do not mean to say that my family never noticed me, or was unkind; but I can say that somehow I didn't take their notice to heart. Perhaps, out of fear, I was blocking the gaze. Add to this, that I think it was very easy in my church culture, as a woman, to not be expected to think or to be heard.

But with the publication of my book, *Longing to Know*, I was given a voice. And that occasioned the marching into my life of new friends who all seemed to have taken to themselves a mission to help me know what I knew—if you know what I mean!—and to do so for me as a person. The first of these, actually, had nothing to do with the book, other than the providence of God: it was the tiny wild cedar waxwing, which grew back to flying health

that summer of 2003 sitting on my shoulder.[5] He wanted nothing more than to gaze at and be near my face. He wanted me always in his sight. He would fall asleep with his chest and bill gently touching my cheek. I learned that cedar waxwings are birds that dwell in groups. I was Bandit's "group." Bandit taught me that I may so gaze, even in my brokenness, at the life- and love-giving face of my Heavenly Father. Bandit was teaching me, you can see, Loder and covenant epistemology.

Freshly graced with that understanding, I found myself apprehended by human friends who noticed me. In the case of one of them, a pastor with training in both philosophy and counseling (who continually preached to his congregation about the importance of epistemology), it was the astounded and enthralled gaze of someone who had just discovered the embodiment of all that he thought was important but that nobody else seemed to understand.[6]

5. See Introduction.

6. In subsequent months, as I got to know this pastor's congregation, I saw that all of them seemed to *glow*. After our presentation of this topic, a couple came up to me, grinning from ear to ear. "We go to Russell's church!" they said. "And

I termed this *noticing regard*. The notice I had commonly experienced had made me feel shame at myself. Notice, I realized, could be a bad thing, or it could be a good thing. This was a good thing—regard.

I felt immediately that in the gaze of my friends I was seeing the gaze of God. It closed the loop of what Bandit had shown me, for now I was seeing what Bandit must have been seeing in my face, and what I was meant to see in the face of God. I felt that *this* was what the woman at the well in Samaria must have seen, in the face of Jesus, and what understandably lit her fire. His look of noticing regard conferred dignity.[7] It was the noticing regard, not the naming of her sins, which impelled her excited race to bring her antagonists to Christ. In the context of his noticing regard, the sense of her sins she received from the Savior was something more along the lines of: "That dress doesn't do you justice; here, let me replace it with something more becoming."

you are right!" To know Russell Louden, I concluded, was to have experienced noticing regard.

7. John 4.

This noticing regard, it was my palpable, bodily, experience, began to fill in the hole of nonexistence inside me. I felt, as if for the first time, that I was there, present to myself. I thought at the time that if I compared my life to a tooth with a gaping cavity, and Jesus' redemption to the soft filling material, these friends with their noticing regard were the dental instruments God was using to pack his redemption down into the core of my being. And I felt as if the experience was retroactive, as well as indefinite in duration. It transformed me and gave me, for the first time, a fledgling sense of personal beauty and wholeness. And I felt that it made me more magnanimous, somehow, to invite the real. On the strength of that new sense, I waltzed through my interviews for a teaching position, with a sense of deep presence, and landed the job.

What is more, for the first time in my life I began to think of God knowing me with specificity. I remember one communion, as I meditated on the words, in the Bible open on my lap, "This is My body," that it was as if God was saying them to me uniquely, specifically, and somehow in real time like an instant message. I also, for the first time, began to be able to think of God's love for me as more like that of the lover in the Song of Songs, not just in terms of the metaphor of father. I actually began to feel that God delighted in me. And the Eucharist, since then, has come to be a most intimate event; often I cannot stop the tears.

Noticing regard, as I experienced it palpably, was a transformative knowing by another. It was self-knowing engendered by the face of another. It somehow composed me as a being. I felt a sense of personal beauty. I connected it to seeing the face of God. It was a simultaneously self-knowing and God-knowing in reciprocity. And it changed me to invite the yet-to-be-known disarmingly. My personal experience exemplifies the dynamic of being known transformatively which Loder helped us identify and connect with the convicting presence of God.

Others underscore the critical importance of the loving gaze of the Other to confer being and beauty. In her *I Am My Body: A Theology of Embodiment*, Moltmann-Wendel recounts the early alienation of females from their bodies, often due to the lack of a "glint" in the eye of a father in which a girl may see her body as beautiful and desirable. "From then on too much emptiness and a longing for fullness dog girls' lives, and that can become the drama of their lives . . . Where a 'glint' is provoked—by men or women—security grows. Where insecurity prevails, women allow judgments to be foisted on them which are not their own."[8] Thus, this author links a sense of personal beauty to a certain kind of gaze of an Other—not indifference, not any old gaze, not a bland one, not a lecherous one, but noticing regard that includes seeing that girl as beautiful and saying so, verbally and with the facial expression of delight. According to Moltmann-Wendel, this is a distinctly female need only because little boys are more likely to receive that "glint" from their mothers. She suggests that the modern father is often away from home. I suggest that, in our two-dimensionally over-sexualized society, fathers are often not helped to distin-

8. Moltmann-Wendel, *I Am My Body*, 10–11.

guish delight in bodily beauty from inappropriate lust; thus conflicted, they refrain from what the little girl most deeply needs. However, the point here is that being composed in the gaze of the loving Other, the sort of thing that issues in a sense of personal beauty, is needed by all humans.

Similarly, John and Staci Eldredge argue that every little girl asks a haunting question: "Am I lovely?" From her father in particular, for the sake of her life-time wholeness, she needs an affirmative response to her question.[9]

Both Moltmann-Wendell and the Eldredges suggest that a sense of personal beauty is something meant to grow in the context of the loving notice of parents from a child's earliest days. That it took me until I was almost fifty reveals the abnormality of my situation and my misperception. Sadly, my abnormal situation is very common, as both authors write to address. It is never too late for an I-You encounter that re-centers a life.

Other writers testify to the reflexivity of a sense of personal beauty. Hannah Coulter, in Wendell Berry's novel with that title, describes this self-understanding of beauty in the gaze of the other. "I was beautiful in those days myself, as I believe I can admit now that it no longer matters. A woman doesn't learn she is beautiful by looking in a mirror, which about any woman is apt to do from time to time, but that is only wishing. She learns it so that she actually knows it from men. The way they look at her makes a sort of glimmer she walks in. That tells her. It changes the way she walks too. But now I was a mother and a widow. It had been a longish while since I had thought of being beautiful, but Nathan's looks were reminding me that I was."[10] Robert Farrar Capon, in *The Supper of the Lamb*, offers a defense of amateurs as the lovers the world needs. Capon is an Episcopal priest and a cook, and he is telling why we need another cookbook. This passage does two things. It confirms what I am saying about noticing regard and a sense of personal beauty; but in talking about amateurs in the world, it underscores the epistemic dimension of both. He writes:

9. Eldredges, *Captivating*, 46.

10. Berry, *Hannah Coulter*, 65.

The world . . . needs all the lovers—amateurs—it can get. It is a gorgeous old place, full of clownish graces and beautiful drolleries, and it has enough textures, tastes, and smells to keep us intrigued for more time than we have. Unfortunately, however, our response to its loveliness is not always delight; it is, far more often than it should be, boredom. And that is not only odd, it is tragic; for boredom is not neutral—it is the fertilizing principle of unloveliness. In such a situation, the amateur—the lover, the man who thinks heedlessness is a sin and boredom a heresy—is just the man you need . . . The real world is indeed the mother of loveliness, the womb and matrix in which it is conceived and nurtured; but the loving eye . . . is the father of it. The graces of the world are the looks of a woman in love; without the woman they could not be there at all; but without her lover, they would not quicken into loveliness. There, then, is the role of the amateur: to look the world back to grace . . . Man's real work is to look at the things of the world and to love them for what they are. That is, after all, what God does, and man was not made in God's image for nothing. The fruits of his attention can be seen in all the arts, crafts, and sciences.[11]

Capon takes as given that the lover's delighting look quickens the looks of a loved woman to loveliness. He expands this to epitomize the way we are to come at the world: "looking the world back to grace." One might well take this as a motto for all efforts to come to know! It fits well with what I will say about inviting the real.

Noticing regard actually constitutes a person. Simone Weil offers a must-read account of the critical act of creative attention:

> Christ taught us that the supernatural love of our neighbor is the exchange of compassion and gratitude which happens in a flash between two beings, one possessing and the other deprived of human personality. One of the two is only a little piece of flesh, naked, inert, and bleeding beside a ditch; he is nameless; no one knows anything about him. Those who pass by this thing

11. Capon, *Supper of the Lamb*, selections from 3–5.

scarcely notice it, and a few minutes afterward do not even know that they saw it. Only one stops and turns his attention toward it. The actions that follow are just the automatic effect of this moment of attention. The attention is creative . . . [which] . . . will give existence to a being other than himself, who will exist independently of him . . . It is a redemptive act. [12]

Creative attention "means really giving our attention to what does not exist . . . Love sees what is invisible." "God *thought* that which did not exist, and by this thought brought it into being. At each moment we exist only because God consents to think us into being . . . Only God, present in us, can really think the human quality into the victims of affliction, can really look at them with a look differing from that we give to things, can listen to their voice as we listen to spoken words. Then they become aware that they have a voice, otherwise they would not have occasion to notice it . . . wherever the afflicted are loved for themselves alone, it is God who is present." Weil is affirming

12. Weil, *Waiting for God*, 90–93.

that in our human acts of creative attention, we image God the creator.

These authors' insights indicate that what is called for is the I-You encounter, the look of love that confers dignity and actually calls a person into existence. A delighted gaze accords value to the person in her or his embodied particularity. And this knowing and self-knowing lights the lamp of personal beauty that then may glow indefinitely, conferring life-giving dignity and beauty upon others. All these texts, when I found them, confirmed my personal experience of noticing regard.

And lest you think this is only an experience for females, I want to tell you about my philosophy student, Gregg, who manfully tackled this novel idea just as he has previously tackled two tours of duty in Iraq. He tells his own very male version of a time in boot camp when he thought he would die rather than make it to the end of a muddy course he was to traverse on his elbows and belly. Then he heard his burly sergeant yelling *his name*, telling him he had what it took. He raised his besmirched face to find the sergeant's gaze of regard directed on him! With fresh energy, Gregg elbowed his way to the finish line . . . and would happily have kept going. That is the self-knowing that comes from noticing regard and in turn bestows it to engage the world.

While I have cast much of this discussion with reference to female beauty, I underscore that this sense of personal beauty is a self-constitutive experience that all humans should have. I only need to point out that all that Macmurray, Buber, and Loder have elucidated has made no reference to one gender over the other. It is about humanness. Developing a sense of personal beauty, I am arguing, just is a concrete instantiation of the I-You encounter. It shows how such an encounter transforms us in the direction of being more fully ourselves, as well as, as we shall see in a later chapter, being more effective knowers.

Such an experience must be had by every human being, not just to be better knowers, but fundamentally in order to be whole, and in order to feel the blessings of Christ's redemption. This is because these all involve the fourth dimension of humanness, the in-

cursion of the Holy. This holds a most critical exhortation for all of us: we must grow much better at registering delight in other persons. We are too quick to be indifferent—the fertilizing principle of *unloveliness,* says Capon!—too quick to qualify our praise out of a faulty construal of spirituality, and the inability to distinguish dignity from vanity.

Scripture indicates that God intended palpable, touchable human faces and gazes in each person's life to prototype his own and most readily convey what Scripture indicates about the face of God.[13] In this broken world, however, it may be that a person does not receive this from the conventional human sources—one's parents, one's spouse, or one's friends. A sense of personal beauty is nevertheless accessible to all, in the life-giving (in both senses) noticing regard of Jesus Christ. If—when—human noticing regard fails to occur, any person may nevertheless experience it in the gaze of the Lord, in personal redemption and the celebration of the Eucharist. His alone is the face that will not go away, and his

13. Num 6:25; Pss 27:8; 105:4; 1 Cor 13:12; Rev 22:4.

alone is our highest joy. But this does not absolve any of us, mothers and fathers in particular, of the responsibility to image God in the exercise of noticing regard.[14]

The beauty that noticing regard confers involves the particulars of the human body. Any bodily particularities one has been given may sustain a sense of personal beauty. In fact, for the specific beauty of a particular person, only these particularities will do. For me to be beautiful, I require the body that I am. It is not required that my body conform to a prevailing cultural standard in order to prove beautiful.

Beauty can never be merely material. But neither can it

ever be merely immaterial. The person's actual bodily expression must be involved. I have found it helpful, actually, to apply to this the Polanyian distinction between focal and subsidiary. Beauty involves interpreted embodiment *subsidiarily*. The *focus* is not on physical appearance. On this understanding, I find it delightfully subversive to maintain, beauty is outward (and outward-oriented) rather than inward. Personal beauty involves a virtuosity of our body as subsidiary, and its focus is beyond us.

This was confirmed when I asked my Aunt Lorraine, in her eighties still a most beautiful woman, what she thought beauty is.[15] She said: "It is a feeling. And it evokes a certain feeling in others. And it's not what you have so much as what you do with it—do you use it to call attention to yourself, or do you mean its excellence to bring delight to others?" We may thus co-opt the old adage:

14. There are two very large matters that profoundly and adversely affect the whole experience of personal beauty and which need a radically corrected theological analysis similar to what Starr has done with the matter of personal beauty. One is the general propensity of Christians and people in the West generally to devalue the physical body. The other is the propensity of human societies, Christians included, to reduce female beauty to a matter of sexual attractiveness to males. It will take a continual and intentional onslaught of good philosophy, good theology, and redeemed living to counter these unbiblical, ungodly, and dehumanizing penchants. But even toward these stubborn problems, perhaps my analysis of personal beauty may offer a start.

15. Lorraine Fleming Irons, a singer and voice coach, has devoted her life to beautifying the voices (also a body part) of others, as well as conferring dignity generally. See, for example, Roy Clouser's expression of gratitude to her and my uncle Dale Fleming, in the front matter of *Myth of Religious Neutrality*.

"Beauty is as beauty senses, or feels." Beauty is a quality that graciously infills and directs one's presentation of one's lived body to the world and to society. A cultivated sense of personal beauty is a kind of virtuosity.

Beautifying the body should be understood as conferring dignity. Of course, it isn't usually understood this way. I believe that that is due in part to the damaging divorce between body and spirit that leads us to distinguish "outward" and "inner" beauty. To beautify is not a vain fixation on body appearance, but the personal care which lights the lamp of personal presence, value, and beauty.

It is especially personal care by another. An important part of this dignity conferring is the caring touch of the other. Touch speaks volumes. Redemption must be bodily apprehended as one of its dimensions. I think of African-Americans submitting to hours of caring labor on each other's corn rows. Or of myself as a band mom, laying hands on the heads of every marcher whose hair I French-braided, conferring dignity in the process. As can be seen in the movie,

Legally Blond, what goes on in a salon can and ought to be about redemptive healing through conferring dignity and unleashing beauty.[16]

A sense of personal beauty that invites the real is, in what it is and what it does, a delighting notice. All perception, and thus all knowing, involves notice. Notice involves assigning a kind of value to the particulars—picking out and foregrounding some, backgrounding others. Delight is a form of notice, one that values, enjoys and celebrates something for what it is. Delight evokes a sense of personal beauty in the one found delightful. This brings persons forth. I think it is a critical strategy for all sorts of things we long to know.

David Bentley Hart writes, "For Christian thought, then, delight is the premise of any sound epistemology: it is delight that constitutes creation, so only delight can comprehend it, see it aright, understand its grammar. Only in loving creation's beauty—only in seeing that creation is beauty—does

16. My daughter, Starr, while pursuing a degree in exegetical theology, felt it profoundly consonant to work in a beauty salon for just this reason. I learned this from her.

one apprehend what creation is."[17] While this is directly true of the knower's knowing of the known, it has a specially significant application in this more reflexive context: delight in the knower, accorded by someone else, is needed for the knower to be a better knower. For the knower is God's creation also. This hints of the "knowing in the presence of" we explored in texture 5.

I am told that someone asked prize-winning author Toni Morrison to which course of study she owed her literary prowess.[18] She replied, "Oh—no *course*! I owe it to the fact that when I was a child, whenever I walked into the room where my father was, his face lit up." Such is the transformative epistemic power of the delighted gaze of the personal other. A sense of personal beauty unleashes us to be engaging, winsome, knowers who exercise delight, noticing regard, as an effective strategy to invite the real.

17. Hart, *Beauty of the Infinite*, 253.

18. Oral illustration used by my pastor, Steve Maker (October, 2008), to welcome believers to the celebration of the Eucharist. He followed the story with this invitation: "Bask in the delighted gaze of your Heavenly Father!" An illustration well suited to the point.

QUESTIONS FOR DISCUSSION

1. When have you experienced noticing regard? Connect this with the face you named in the chapter 10 discussion.

2. Describe your own experience of the sense of personal beauty. If you are comfortable sharing this with the group, do so.

3. How might this account of personal beauty prove healing personally, societally, and epistemically?

4. Why is expressing delight to others important? How may we be better at that?

11

KNOWING AND HEALTHY INTERPERSONHOOD

Conversation with David Schnarch

IF KNOWING IS IN some key way interpersonal and relational, then it
should be the case that dynamics of healthy interpersonal relationships
should also positively impact knowing. Also, working from Macmurray,
Buber, and Loder, we can make the converse point that persons' growing
to maturity is linked in mutuality to the central knowing event. In some
respect, knowing matures a person, and a mature person knows well. The
covenant epistemology thesis, especially in view of our recent preoccupation with the interpersonhooded context, requires that we attend to
what makes such a relationship mature, or fully interpersonal.

To state the obvious, not every relationship between persons is a
healthy one. In an unhealthy one, the full personhood of one or more
of those involved is truncated. The paradigm of knowing that covenant
epistemology recommends involves covenantal interpersonhood; for
there to be true covenantal interpersonhood, the interpersonal relationship envisioned must be healthy—covenantally mature—functioning in
such a way that the persons involved may be fully persons.

Insight into the dynamics of the personal will expand our grasp
of the dynamics of knowing, of covenant epistemology. We will see that
healthy interpersonal practices suggest corresponding healthy epistemic
practices. Plus, cultivating healthy interpersonhood heightens the knower's effective agency in the epistemic act. This epistemic exploration,
therefore, additionally shows how we may valuably appropriate insights
from psychotherapy to epistemology.

In this chapter, I want to show that the psychotherapeutic concept
of differentiation, one current working hypothesis concerning interpersonal maturity, doubles as a key to effective knowing. I will sketch
the concept of differentiation as articulated by psychiatrist Dr. David

Schnarch. Then I will show how his recommendations can be construed as epistemologically sound and beneficial also. I will link this additionally to the well-known work of sociologist David Riesman.

You may well have felt that all our talk of intimacy in face-to-face encounter and communion was becoming too intense and claustrophobic. You may have been longing for space to breathe! There have been some hints of space along the way, especially Buber's comment that the I-You encounter was never meant to be sustained. Differentiation will start to give us that space. And perichoresis, in the upcoming conversation with Colin Gunton, will flesh it out further.

THE PROCESS OF DIFFERENTIATION

Differentiation is a concept that helps us get a handle on "better" in interpersonal relationships. Here follows a brief introduction from David Schnarch.[1] This introduction is quotation-heavy. But Schnarch is a great writer and, unlike me, an expert in psychology. I remain in listening mode with respect to what he says, and I believe it is important for the reader to be able to hear him directly.

Differentiation is a process of maintaining ourselves in close interpersonal relationship. Long-term interpersonal relationships in which the process pertains include, not just marriage and family, but also offices, churches, sports teams, or any other close-knit relationships.

Schnarch writes: "In a nutshell, differentiation is the process by which we become more uniquely ourselves by maintaining ourselves in relationship with those we love. It's the process of grinding off our rough edges through the normal abrasions of long-term intimate relationships

---

1. Schnarch, *Passionate Marriage*. This well-written, insightful book is not one I recommend to young single people to read, given that it concerns improving sexual relationships for couples who have been married for decades. Schnarch argues that the best kind of intimacy is "self-validated," and it makes for richer sexual encounters. He also argues that sexual encounters can be utilized to grow differentiation and self-validating intimacy. My concern here is to cash in on his superbly written description of differentiation. While Schnarch makes the application to sexual experience, I make it to covenant intimacy in epistemic experience. It is interesting to note, as an aside, that the Hebrew word for *know* is used to refer to sexual intercourse. Another book which employs the concept of differentiation, this time in connection with an array of often abusive relationships that involve women, is Harriet Lerner's *Dance of Anger*.

. . . Differentiation isn't a trait, however. It's a process—a lifelong process of taking our own 'shape.'"[2] He continues to amplify this definition:

> [D]ifferentiation is your ability to maintain your sense of self when you are emotionally and/or physically close to others—especially as they become increasingly important to you. Differentiation permits you to maintain your own course when lovers, friends, and family pressure you to agree and conform. Well-differentiated people can agree without feeling like they're "losing themselves," and can disagree without feeling alienated and embittered. They can stay connected with people who disagree with them and still know who they are. They don't have to leave the situation to hold onto their sense of self.[3]

The well-differentiated person has the ability to stay in connection without being consumed by the other person. The entire system of connected people stands to benefit immensely from maintaining differentiation in relationships.[4] "When you have a wide repertoire of possible responses, you, your business, and our species have increased versatility and adaptability. Fewer resources in well-differentiated families and marriages have to be rigidly devoted to compensate for the inability of any one member to take care of himself/herself. Conversely, there is less need for anyone to sacrifice growth or self-direction to maintain the stability of the family or marriage. Differentiation allows each person to function more independently and interdependently."[5] Differentiation must be distinguished from individuality, autonomy, and independence, where these connote absence of connection. Says Schnarch:

> It's entirely different from "individualism," which is an egocentric attempt to set ourselves apart from others. Unlike "rugged individualists" who can't sustain a relationship, differentiated folks welcome and maintain intimate connection. Highly differentiated people also behave differently than the terms *autonomy* or *inde-*

---

2. Schnarch, *Passionate Marriage*, 51.

3. Ibid., 56.

4. Differentiation is a concept embedded in family systems therapy, the thesis of which is that people in a group of close interrelationships, such as a family, function a bit like a total system. As a result, the identified patient may be so designated not because of an internal deficiency but simply by virtue of that person's location in the system.

5. Schnarch, *Passionate Marriage*, 62–63.

pendence suggest. They can be heedful of their impact on others and take their partners' needs and priorities into account.[6]

The opposite of differentiation is not, *not* being connected; it is being *poorly* connected, or "emotionally fused." According to Schnarch: "When we have little differentiation, our identity is constructed out of what's called a reflected sense of self. We need continual contact, validation, and consensus (or disagreement) from others. This leaves us unable to maintain a clear sense of who we are in shifting or uncertain circumstances. We develop a contingent identity based on a 'self-in-relationship.'"[7] Schnarch says that people whose identity is primarily dependent upon their relationship don't facilitate the development of those they love. Instead, they lose their identity when others change. Emotional bonds choke individual members' development; emotional entanglements and guilt deprive them of the choice that meaningful sacrifice involves.[8]

Seeking to develop differentiation doesn't imply selfishness: "When you have a solid core of values and beliefs, you can change without losing your identity. You can permit yourself to be influenced by others, changing as new information and shifting circumstances warrant." Nor are highly differentiated people emotionless. They have strong emotional bonds. But they can choose contact with others out of deep liking, without being compulsively driven toward them or away.[9] On the other hand, it is important not to think that emotionally fused people are exercising love. "We confuse love with emotional fusion . . . Jealousy is a form of emotional fusion. At its most severe, jealousy illustrates our intolerance for boundaries and separateness from those we love. Our desire to possess our partner is inherently frustrated by the immutable fact that we are two fundamentally separate (though interrelated) people. You can see emotional fusion in the mayhem we commit in relationships, in our inability to separate, to leave well enough alone, when we're on the edge."[10] Schnarch says, don't believe for a moment that emotionally fused relationships are examples of "loving too much." Instead they illustrate how emotional fusion increases domestic violence.

6. Ibid., 57, 67.
7. Ibid., 59.
8. Ibid., 63.
9. Ibid., 64.
10. Ibid., 64.

He explains that the source of the tenacity of emotional fusion is *borrowed functioning*. "Basically differentiation refers to your core 'solid self,' the level of development you can maintain independent of shifting circumstance in your relationship. However, you can appear more (or less) differentiated than you really are, depending on your marriage's current state. Borrowed functioning artificially inflates (or deflates) your functioning. Your 'pseudo self' can be pumped up through emotional fusion."[11]

Schnarch summarizes his exposition of differentiation by saying that it's about mutuality: "What I am describing is called mutuality. Differentiation is the key to mutuality; as a perspective, a mind-set, it offers a solution to the central struggle of any long-term relationship: going forward with your own self-development while being concerned with your partner's happiness and well-being." Schnarch argues that the process of differentiation moves forward through holding on to one's sense of self in intense emotional relationship. One's sense of self should be both solid and permeable. And Schnarch ends his discussion with an allusion to mysterious spiritual dimensions of this process: "And what if this trial by fire is the integrity-building path of differentiation? Would you, like me, begin to wonder if there was something spiritual about the process?"[12]

DIFFERENTIATION, PERSONHOOD, AND COVENANT

Everyone we have engaged who has talked of relationship has taken for granted or positively developed the idea that relational capacities grow to maturity over a lifetime, and that certain untoward relational occurrences radically thwart that normal process. It is reasonable to judge that the process of differentiation as per Schnarch's description can be expected to correspond with Macmurray, Buber, Loder, and Williams. It is interesting to note that this correspondence spans disciplines: philosophy, theology, natural religion, and psychology. It also corresponds, I feel sure, to the reader's personal experience, as it does to mine. There are better and poorer interpersonal dynamics and maturity. In connection with this, people can be less or more fully persons.

11. Ibid., 65.
12. Ibid., 74.

One might not think of there being issues of variance with regard to growth and maturity with respect to covenant. But the whole point of Williams' account of covenant as unfolding relationship is that it is a process that grows over time and through particular occasions of engagement, toward the end of deepening communion. It grows, as is the case in Williams' primary example of marriage, as the partners themselves grow and change. And yes—there are trials by fire.

But I think that the question of use or abuse of authority counts as an example of how covenantal involvement requires maturity. This is something that Mike Williams addresses in developing the biblical notion of covenant.[13] Williams feels it important to say that authority properly utilized is never authoritarianism. Authoritarianism is "Trust me, period, no matter what." Biblical authority doesn't work this way. Good authority gives, through relationship, reasons to trust it. The authoritarian is not worthy of trust and is not a proper object of commitment. That an authority is worthy of trust is the sort of thing that we pick up in part through our embodied sensing apparatus, as well as being the kind of judgment we tacitly are compelled to make with every time we are faced with believing or complying with someone else's belief or order.

Williams notes that the best authorities will appeal to us across the whole spectrum of human experience and knowing. They will be rational, testable, and practical. Of his own son, he says, "Sawyer knows that he has to obey me, but he knows it is only partly because of the formal reality of my authority. He also knows that I love him. As he matures he discovers (hopefully) reasons for his nascent trust. Similarly, in covenanting with them, God calls his people to obey, and he also gives mighty acts as empirical testimony. And he invites us to live in relationship and see the benefits of it." By contrast, in our culture, authority has been misunderstood to be identical to authoritarianism. It is thought to be mindless, requiring resigned compliance. Instead, says Williams, authority ought to be, you have to trust me, but I have given you reasons to trust me. To accredit authority as viable and responsible, and to see ourselves as responsible in trusting authority, is completely alien to the Enlightenment, rationalist mind. In epistemology, counting authority as a source of knowledge has for centuries fallen into disrepute.[14] However,

---

13. Personal conversation, and our coauthored unpublished document, "Covenant Epistemology," 9. See also Meek, *Longing to Know*, 103.

14. I have developed the interconnection between knowing and authority in Meek, "Learning to See."

we have seen that Polanyi reinstates it, Frame does too, and so does covenant epistemology.[15]

Applying the concept of differentiation to this discussion of authority, I think we can safely say that relationship characterized by authority and submission, in contrast to authoritarian behavior, is a differentiated one. The situation of "Trust me no matter what" tends toward emotional fusion, with notable absence of mutuality. This helps us see that for covenant to pertain requires that healthy interpersonhood pertain; differentiated mutuality characterizes the kind of relationships that are fully covenantal. I think it can be argued not only that where covenant relationship flourishes, differentiation is operative and gives expression to the manner in which covenant flourishes. I think the converse can justifiably be held as well: where differentiation flourishes, its key features can be expressed covenantally in the balanced dimensions of mutual trust and submission. The idea of *covenant* implies the operative presence of differentiation, in the sense that covenant presumes that parties relate in a mutuality of personal liberty and initiative, in allegiance and the fulfillment of obligations.

DIFFERENTIATION AND KNOWING

Not only can there be better and worse in personhood and covenant; there can be, as a result, better and worse in knowing. We are justified in bringing the claims in this exposition on differentiation to bear on human knowing. Consider how the phrases of the previous discussion come to expression in acts of knowing.

Differentiation is a lifelong process, with some occasions enhancing it, others setting it back. The act of coming to know is a process that evidences an unfolding reciprocity between knower and yet-to-be-known. There are likely to be many mid-course corrections that involve the knower in self-reform in anticipation of contacting the real. Take, for example, the case of Annie Dillard stalking muskrats: she had to adjust to encountering them on their terms.[16]

Well-differentiated people can agree without feeling like they're "losing themselves," and can disagree without feeling alienated and

15. Polanyi and a growing number of others have noted that science can only grow in the context of communities of tradition—these, too, are authority covenantally discharged.

16. Dillard, *Pilgrim at Tinker Creek*, ch. 11; see ch. 2 in this book.

embittered. Sometimes there are things we resist knowing because we feel threatened to lose ourselves in the grandeur of the discovery or its dissemination, or the rejection of others, or we can find change required of us by the discovery that we do not welcome. Similarly, we can be so "married" to preconceived notions that we can feel the attempt to move beyond them as alienation, a threat of loss of sense of self. Think here of the old notion of the *idée fixe*. We know that for there to be healthy growth in knowing and responsible action, we must push ourselves to "think outside the box," "get out of our comfort zone," as we say.

When we have little differentiation, our identity is constructed out of a reflected sense of self. We develop a contingent identity based on a "self-in-relationship." Continuing the thought of the last paragraph, knowers operating with a "reflected sense of self" are not able to bring to the epistemic situation the kind of solid personal presence that is comfortable with moving beyond taken-for-granted interpretations into uncharted waters, and which, we will say, invites the real. A would-be knower with a reflected sense of self would resist the vulnerability and risk that potential transformation requires.

Being differentiated, by the way, shares kinship with the sense of personal presence, of being there, which we discussed in our forays into the subsidiary.[17] The process of differentiation involves, we may say, a growing subsidiary virtuosity, a presence we indwell as we orient toward the world.

People whose identity is inappropriately dependent upon their relationship don't facilitate the development of those they love. Emotional bonds choke individual members' development, emotional entanglements and guilt deprive them of the choice that meaningful sacrifice involves. Would-be knowers can operate from an immature vested interest in obtaining certain results in the epistemic effort. We need only think of recent instances of data forging. While it is appropriate and properly formative to have something in mind of what one is looking for, and certainly to be committed to what we have yet to discover, we also know that a line between this and impropriety is easily and often unwittingly crossed.[18]

17. See texture 2.

18. See my discussion of the dwarfs, in C. S. Lewis's *Last Battle* in Meek, *Longing to Know*, ch. 23. Commitment to an as-yet undiscovered reality continually poses the question whether that commitment is justified or ridiculous. This dynamic is also

When you have a wide repertoire of possible responses, you, your business, and people working together have increased versatility and adaptability, Schnarch says. Fewer resources in well-differentiated families and marriages have to be rigidly devoted to compensate for the inability of any one member to take care of himself/herself. I should think that any employer or director of a scientific inquiry would prefer to hire such people. Interpersonal health on the part of the knower maximizes the integrity and the value of the epistemic enterprise in any profession. We may also draw a connection here to how a scholar works in a tradition, or how a Christian disciple is formed in the Scripture and liturgy: in each case, a well-differentiated individual honors the tradition by creative new interpretations and applications of it.

Differentiation allows each person to function more independently and interdependently. I feel it is critical to effective knowing that the knower exercise and invite mutual respect and trust with respect to the known and the yet-to-be-known. It involves playing by covenantal rules that preserve both knower and known from inappropriate personal violation. In the safety of this space alone, truthful knowing can grow and flourish. Where inappropriate pressure is exercised, what is "known" is no longer the thing as it is.

Highly differentiated people are not emotionless but have strong emotional bonds; but they can choose contact with others out of deep liking, without being compulsively driven toward them or away. On the other hand, it is important not to think that emotionally fused people are exercising love. Polanyi, in developing his proposals for personal knowledge, made much of the role that passion plays in discovery.[19] In this he was making his case for us to accredit the personal in knowing, as over against the prevailing paradigm which presumes that epistemic engagement, to be legitimate and profitable, must be dispassionate and impersonal. What he was defending may be deemed healthy "choosing contact out of deep liking"—the scientist must be free to pursue what interests her/him, riding the wave of that interest into sustained research. On the other hand, we can think of cases in which knowers, fictional or otherwise, evidenced emotional fusion: think, for example of

---

played out in the film, *Contact*, starring Jodi Foster. The commitment to know always involves this risk.

19. Polanyi, *Personal Knowledge*, ch. 6.

Frankenstein, or of Dr. Jekyll, or of Eve. One's "area of competence," sadly, can become a fetish.

Parker Palmer begins his formative work on education contemplating the devastation of "objectivism" in a misguided attempt at impersonal knowledge: the "Trinity" experiment that first unleashed atomic power in a bomb.[20] He distinguishes knowledge motivated by curiosity and control or power, from knowledge motivated by love. The one, in seeking to transcend morality, inevitably acts immorally; the other contains its own morality. The one incurs violence; the other brings healing. The one involves immature arrogance, and a kind of compulsion; the other involves the knower in remaining open to personal change, even sacrifice, for the sake of the known. In the end, the one alienates the knower; in the end, "a knowledge that springs from love will implicate us in the web of life; it will wrap the knower and the known in compassion, in a bond of awesome responsibility as well as transforming joy; it will call us to involvement, mutuality, accountability."[21] Palmer immerses us in the resonances between knowing, covenant, and personhood in this discussion of differentiation.

Differentiation is the key to mutuality, going forward with one's own self-development while being concerned with one's partner's happiness and well-being. Mutuality is to be distinguished from autonomy, individualism and independence. There is such a thing as healthy epistemic comportment. And epistemic health makes for better and more responsible knowing. The knower's search for the known must be specific enough that it is paying attention, not so specific that it falls short of entertaining unanticipated surprises that revamp the inquiry.

Comparing the insights of the psychological concept differentiation with ordinary knowing experiences shows how they have their counterparts in good knowing practices. This anticipates the discussion of epistemological etiquette in our inviting the real. It suggests that "etiquette" may have a connotation of it being too frivolous to represent what we have in mind. What is important is interpersonal maturity, and no bare list of rules of etiquette can ever substitute for this.

Schnarch's highly readable book ends with an entire chapter devoted to the spiritual dimensions of this process—dimensions he feels sure are there just by virtue of the wonder of the process. I make a guess

---

20. Palmer, *To Know as We Are Known*, ch. 1.

21. Ibid., 1–7, *et passim*.

that Schnarch did not think of himself or of his work, at the outset, as religious. That he ends in this place is telling. Awe, in the experience of the world's gracious self-disclosure, is often attested to. Annie Dillard, for example, artistically blends her experience stalking muskrats with Heisenberg's discovery of the Principle of Indeterminacy and with Moses' request to see God:

> And then occasionally the mountains part . . . The news, after all, is not that muskrats are wary, but that they can be seen. The hem of the robe was a Nobel Prize to Heisenberg; he did not go home in disgust. I wait on the bridges and stalk along bands for those moments I cannot predict, when a wave begins to surge under the water . . . "Surely the Lord is in this place; and I knew it not." The fleeing shreds I see, the back parts, are a gift, an abundance. When Moses came down from the cliff in Mount Sinai, the people were afraid of him: the very skin on his face shone.[22]

There is indeed a mysterious, spiritual dimension to knowing the world. This dimension is just what is accredited in the vision of covenant epistemology. All knowing has about it the aura of persons in the vicinity. Not only does knowing unfold in healthy mutuality of knower and known, it is from time to time studded and transformed by a face-to-face encounter. Both Schnarch's and Dillard's expositions allude to such an encounter.

DIFFERENTIATION AND RIESMAN'S
AUTONOMOUS PERSON

Sociologist David Riesman, writing his quickly popular *The Lonely Crowd* in the 1950s, described the distinguishable social characters he termed "inner-directed" and "other-directed."[23] These terms entered common parlance as a result of that book. In my recent first reading of it, I was surprised to see that their popular usage has contained connotations that obscure Riesman's actual message.[24] Riesman defines inner-directed societies as those whose members develop a social character whose conformity is insured by their tendency to acquire early in life an internalized set of goals. This occurs in a transitional (as opposed to

---

22. Dillard, *Pilgrim at Tinker Creek*, 205.

23. Riesman, *Lonely Crowd*.

24. This is confirmed by Wilfred McClay's 1998 article, "Fifty Years."

traditional) society. And in a society of incipient population decline, the social character members develop is one whose conformity is insured by their tendency to be sensitized to the expectations and preferences of others.[25] This social character he calls other-directed.

I suggest that we can align Riesman's categories with the thesis of differentiation, and also that this association might help us better understand his categories and his message. Riesman's autonomous person demonstrates qualities of differentiation and thus mature personhood. I maintain this despite the fact that Schnarch disapproves of autonomy and Riesman uses the term with approbation. Schnarch distinguished differentiation from autonomy. Perhaps Riesman's term choice was less than facile. But careful attention to how each thinker uses the term reveals that they are using it to mean different things, and that in spite of their terminological disagreement, their ideas converge.

Riesman notes that in his own description of these types, it is virtually impossible to keep the other-directed person from coming off looking inferior to the apparently upstanding inner-directed person. This was so especially in the 1950s, I might add. But his own conviction is that both inner- and other-directed persons share a similar dynamic and are equally and similarly flawed.[26] Riesman indicates that the inner-directed person really is other-directed, and that the other-directed person has internalized something just as much as the inner-directed person—it's just that it's a different sort of something (not a gyroscope but a radar dish). The inner-directed person is just as other-directed as the other-directed person, he/she just doesn't quite acknowledge it. The inner-directed person depends on things around him or her, just as the other-directed person does. It just has a different feel to it. I have a friend who makes this point by saying that "independence" is really "in dependence." Schnarch's account of differentiation affords us some insight regarding how this can be. The inner-directed person, Riesman is saying, is as emotionally fused as the other-directed one.

What Riesman himself advocates, in place of both the inner- and the other-directed, is the "autonomous" person, who can through self-

25. Riesman, *Lonely Crowd*, 8.

26. Ibid., 31, 159, 160, 260. McClay's brief description of Riesman's own family dynamic is telling. It also is one to which a lot of people my age (baby boomers and a bit older) resonate. That means that some of the inter-generational tensions we have all participated in either as children or as parents are understandable as tensions between inner-directed parents and other-directed children.

consciousness in the context of his/her surroundings rise above or out of either of these types.[27] In particular, Riesman explores possibilities latent in the other-directed person type that may be capitalized upon to develop autonomy.

Moving from inner-directedness to other-directedness is thus potentially a step in the *right* direction because it gets authentic about our connectedness. We can't avoid connectedness, nor should we condemn it. What we must see is that we have a choice to do it well or poorly. Doing connectedness well is what Riesman has in mind by autonomy. *Autonomy* is a heightened self-consciousness that enables a person to orient with respect to the connectedness while transcending it.[28] He connects this with freedom, or as commentator Wilfred McClay puts it helpfully, autonomy is the ability to operate *in* a social order without being *of* it.[29]

I believe that what Riesman is describing is differentiation. Differentiation, once again, is the ability to maintain one's own personhood and identity while staying connected to one's close system of vital others, such as one's family or church or office group. If you are not differentiated, then you are "emotionally fused." Codependence is a form of emotional fusion, for example. Actually physical proximity or physical distance has little to do with differentiation or emotional fusion: if we are emotionally fused, say, to our father, we may try to manage it by moving far away, but the emotional fusion remains in the very disconnecting. On the contrary, if we have a healthy relationship of differentiation with an adult child, for example, we are healthily, spiritually, connected, no matter how physically far away we may be.

These ideas confirm Riesman's. Both inner-direction and other-direction, apart from some transcendence, are emotionally fused, and also toxic. What Riesman is calling us to is differentiation. Differentiation may be attained working from either connectedness or disconnectedness, since they are two sides of each other. However, there is a sense in

27. Ibid., 242.

28. Ibid., 259.

29. McClay, "Fifty Years," 42. While McClay attributes this to Riesman's old-fashioned liberalism, I humbly suggest that Riesman's Jewishness might have something to do with it. I am sure that my colleague, Bob Frazier, would agree, arguing as he does that Jewish scholars typically demonstrate the ability to think excellently across disciplinary boundaries, and holistically. Perhaps this may stem from the Hebrew sense of the word, *to know*, which as we know, also describes sexual relations.

which understanding connectedness is an honest admission that gets people on the way to autonomy.

Riesman's concept of inner-directedness describes the character type that dominated the modernist milieu that persisted at least a decade past the 1950s. I think that that milieu was so dominant that Riesman was popularly heard to be saying that inner-directedness is superior to other-directedness. An easy reading of the text shows that this is false. In his concept of other-directedness, I believe that Riesman captures the character type that has come to predominant expression today, as opposed to the milieu in which he first wrote. We may see it as our culture having shifted from inner- to other-directed. The category aptly fits people I know in their late teens and early and mid-twenties, as well as myself, as I have come to be in a good measure as part of this current milieu. To discredit other-directedness is to miss what Riesman in 1950 had a hard time convincing us of: not only is other-directedness real, it holds some really nice possibilities for moving us to healthy autonomy. In the last forty years since he wrote, our culture has found a way *not* to disintegrate (surprise!), despite the pressure of industrialism and wealth, but rather to reclaim and celebrate a *post-industrial* humanness. Often this gets called *postmodern*.

What I observe when I am with my daughters and their friends, and with my twenty- and thirty-something student/friends, is a connectedness that is humanizing, a commitment to community, with little concern about their living in poverty minus the standard middle-class must-haves such as a stable household. Technology is taken for granted, but is pressed into service both to maintain community in easy subversion of the ravages of industrialization (email, instant messaging, cell phones, Facebook, YouTube, texting, now tweeting), but also to stay connected with and influence culture (pop music, film, business, politics). Plans do not get made far in advance, but an informal gathering can get called without much effort.

Their conversations sometimes seem shallow, but I also feel that informal, testimonial expressions of personal commitments are welcomed and heard and pondered, because mutual respect is highly valued and intact. Many have to work through together their own fall-out from broken trusts of people they should have been able to count on—including parents who have exhibited the utmost in inner-directed living. This is honesty about other-directed connectedness. It is a stage on the way to autonomy or differentiation.

Thus, the fifty-plus years between the first publication of Riesman's famous work and its reissue, are years in which the dynamics of social groups have evolved from looking more like his inner-directed person to looking more like his other-directed person. This generation is better at something other than competition in business and politics, namely, creative collaboration. And it is better at sensitivity and respect for the nonhuman world.[30] While the two—inner-directedness and other-directedness—are both inadequate with respect to a mature autonomy (differentiation), since both involve sub-par connectedness (emotional fusion), if Riesman is right, this culture registers an improvement. For the other-directed person has taken a step in the right direction to acknowledge the reality and need for interconnectedness.

So in the twenty-first century we are quite possibly better positioned to apprehend and cultivate healthy interpersonal relation. And if, as I think laying the one alongside the other makes clear, Schnarch's categories and Riesman's are of a piece, we may utilize the insights of the one to help us grow with respect to other. We are able to draw from both a sense of healthy interpersonhood that we may then press into epistemic service.

WEAVING SCHNARCH'S AND RIESMAN'S INSIGHTS INTO COVENANT EPISTEMOLOGY

To begin with Riesman: I suggest that people in the twenty-first century are positioned, better than those of the mid-twentieth, to appreciate the interpersonal in epistemology. Younger people understand that knowing isn't about truth (in the sense of propositional accord) so much as it is about trust. It is true that we all are tempted to give up on the possibility of such healthy interpersonal trust. The ravages of hurtful relationships seem to careen out of control in our current milieu. And the older ideal of truth as certain propositional information lingers "in our utopian disillusionment," as Marjorie Grene comments.[31] Thus many continue to fall prey to the false dichotomy of truth of that sort or no truth at all.

But just as inner-directed and other-directed are not the only alternatives, and not the best ones, knowing need not be seen either

---

30. These are generalizations, I realize. Yet I would argue that people my age would agree on the basis of their recollections that these other-directed virtues were not widely touted when we were twenty.

31. Grene, *Knower and the Known*, 66.

as disconnected, impersonal, information, or as personal connection without objective truth. Inner- and other-directedness, I propose, reflect the dichotomous epistemic divorce. Covenant epistemology strives to challenge this discouraging and false alternative and point the way to, not a compromise, but a full-fledged understanding of knowing that restores knower, known, and knowing to wholeness, an understanding of knowing that has trust and love—mature interpersoned relationship—at its core.

The younger generation, in contrast to earlier ones, understands connectedness, mutuality, and the importance of trust in relationships. That these are critical to knowing would be, I believe, a viable notion for them. I therefore believe that covenant epistemology is a timely proposal. It may be heard and appropriated better now.

Also in reference to the discussion of Riesman, we may note its correlation with Jim Houston's claim that we must revise our anthropology from a substantival one to an other-directed one.[32] No doubt I was scandalized by the proposal, when I initially heard it, because I was part of the generation which exalted inner-directedness as a good. This may even be why I misheard—or why the populace at large misheard—Riesman's assessment of inner-directedness—why we missed his not approving of it.

To return to the matter of differentiation: I think it justifiable to link healthy differentiation to flourishing covenantal dimensions in relationship. The idea of covenant presumes relationship. My claim that all relationships are covenantally constituted implies that parties relate covenantally in a mutuality of personal liberty and initiative, in allegiance and the fulfillment of obligations. So covenant involves differentiation. Both, we may note, have been cast as processes.

I do not believe that covenant, for all its richness, is actualized in the absence of healthy interpersonhood. Betrayal is an obvious violation of covenant boundaries that constitute a relationship. So is emotional fusion. Given that covenant involves a process of relationship that unfolds through the years, emotional fusion, as a defect in that process, is a defect in how covenant is playing out in the relationship. Emotional fusion, it is easy to see, displays features similar to what Scripture terms idolatry. Idolatry depersonalizes. Idolatry is covenant unfaithfulness. Thus, covenant faithfulness implies the operative presence of differentiation.

32. Ch. 8.

Finally, to return to this conversation's main thesis: Knowing, as paradigmatically interpersoned covenant relationship, displays a dynamic that, similar to interpersonal relationships, can be more or less healthy. Differentiation, as a process characteristic of healthy interpersonal relationship, additionally offers insight into the dynamics of knowing. Epistemic differentiation, as we may term it, makes for better knowing, better knowers, and a better-understood known. All this taken together adds momentum to the vision of covenant epistemology. It makes sense to attend to the interpersoned dimensions of knowing and to cultivate excellence with respect to them. And covenant epistemology, as we have noted, makes profound sense of the tantalizing spiritual dimension of knowing that continues to crop up.

The next chapter speaks further to this by tying the ultimate interpersoned relationship, the Holy Trinity, to healthy cultural engagement, including knowing. The persons of the Trinity, arguably, exercise mature differentiation in relationship. That sentence sounds comical precisely because the Trinity obviously is the original relationship; it sets the standard, in comparison with which the health of all human relationships may be gauged. What we will learn from Gunton will underscore what we have discussed here, as well as help us draw out its implications more concretely.

QUESTIONS FOR DISCUSSION

1. Discuss how differentiation makes sense of healthy space in close relationships. In what ways does this offer breathing room to the intensity of I-You encounter?

2. What are some real-life examples of emotional fusion and differentiation?

3. Do you agree that covenantal relationship involves interpersonal health? Why or why not?

4. Discuss the examples I give, and come up with your own, of ways that differentiation characterizes good knowing.

12

KNOWING AS DANCE

Conversation with Colin Gunton

KNOWING HAS A DYNAMISM that is interpersoned. It unfolds in covenantal relationship. And within that relationship, it seems, is some to and fro. We've talked of "triangulating" among the sectors of knowing, the world, the lived body, and the norms. My entire effort to articulate covenant epistemology has grown out of the apparent dynamic of overture and response of knower and known. We've seen that Buber commends a coming and going with respect to I-You and I-It. And Loder's void-Holy is certainly a dynamism, that of contingency, deliverance, and transformation. Schnarch's differentiation shed light on the shape of healthy interpersonal relationship as freeingly differentiated. But I believe that Colin Gunton's notion of perichoresis expresses the to and fro most concretely. I want to draw this motif into covenant epistemology to add to our growing understanding of knowing.

My conversation with James Houston in 2002 also alerted me to the work of the Trinitarian theologians, in particular, John Zizioulas and Colin Gunton.[1] These scholars espouse an interpersonal account of personhood, and especially link it with the Christian doctrine of the Trinity. The Trinity is best characterized as persons-in-relation, they argue; and if we profess the Trinity as ultimate reality, we may see that human persons, as beings-in-communion, reflect this original.

Gunton's *The One, The Three, and the Many*[2] concerns, not so much the existential experience of personal encounter that we have engaged in the work of Macmurray, Buber, and Loder, as the dynamics of the interrelationship between members of the Trinity and the involvement

---

1. Zizioulas, "Human Capacity and Incapacity." I offered a brief description of Zizioulas' claims in ch. 1. I describe the conversation with Houston at the beginning of ch. 8.

2. These are his 1992 Bampton Lectures.

of all three persons of the Godhead in creating the world, in order to offer the healing implications of this for humans' involvement with the nonhuman creation. Gunton's agenda is not just interpersonal, and not just epistemological; it is nothing less than cultural and societal healing. But the way he goes about his task accords profoundly with our other conversants in this interpersonhood discussion, yielding complementary insights for covenant epistemology.

We will draw from perichoresis not only further insight into knowing as interpersoned relationship, but also into knowing as it accords with the wider world. We will also confirm a Trinitarian backdrop for the covenant epistemology project. Our conversation with Gunton integrally links interpersonhood with knowing understood as both subsidiary-focal integration and covenantal unfolding, linking parts 2, 3, and 4 of this work. Gunton's proposed cosmic dynamism of perichoresis will help us make sense of telltale features of knowing that we keep encountering, as well as showing us a way forward in our account of knowing as interpersonal covenantal relationship. We will see additionally that covenant epistemology, as an account of knowing as perichoretic, itself implements Gunton's own mission.

Once again, I do not feel that this foray leaves the unbeliever without a ticket outside the door. For Gunton is concerned to offer theological motifs that he argues are identifiable throughout all dimensions of reality, and which helpfully redress the ravages of what I have been referring to as the default mode. Everybody in western culture has been adversely affected by defective theology, and everybody, and our world, stand to benefit from what proves to be a theological realigning of our most fundamental conceptual handles on life.

While these helpful theological motifs characterize reality, it is not as if we have, in fact, arrived at them, in the history of western thought, apart from a trinitarian conception of God. What is more, Gunton will show, not even an explicit confessional allegiance to the doctrine of the Trinity has always prompted Christendom to lay hold deeply of its resources to challenge the dominant western approach. This is because Christians have espoused a subpar understanding of the Holy Trinity, especially with respect to the members' involvement in creating the world. Gunton will argue that the philosophy of engagement that our culture needs can be had in the context of a perichoretic understanding of the triune Lord's involvement. For him, this is the Christian theologian's long-overdue, critical contribution to our cultural tradition.

GUNTON'S DIAGNOSIS OF THE BREAKDOWN OF MODERN CULTURE

Colin Gunton's project is to diagnose and address the paradoxes of modernity, which have perpetrated a breakdown especially in culture (the way humans relate to nonhuman reality). He is concerned about how people and the non-human world are so alienated from each other—the sort of thing evident in the environmental crisis. Other significant paradoxical features he identifies include how modernity can have been so committed to freedom and yet have generated the horrors of totalitarianism; how it can be that we have so much leisure and yet live at frantic pace; and how at the end of a tradition committed to certainty and truth we can have come to lose truth and meaning.[3]

I have spoken somewhat playfully of the practical need for epistemological therapy in overcoming a defective default mode, an unhealthy subcutaneous layer. Gunton, by contrast, offers a sustained analysis of the culture of modernity. But his analysis and my default mode are kin to each other. His is more general; mine has to do specifically with knowing. Knowing is a specific but widely permeating instance of humans engaging the world.

Culture is humans' relation, or lack of it, to nonhuman reality. So a crisis in culture, as Gunton's concern, involves him integrally in the question of this relationship. Gunton believes that the culprit in this alienation in cultural engagement is that we are missing any sense of humans being internally related to the rest of the world, to nonhuman reality. He argues that we have no warrant in our legacy of western thought to support any positive relationship at all. And, he says, "we shall not understand our place in the world unless we face up to the way in which we are internally related to the rest of the world. Without a philosophy of engagement we are lost."[4]

---

3. Gunton, *One, the Three, and the Many*, 7 *et passim*. Gunton explores these features of modernity in the first four chapters; each of the succeeding four chapters is paired chiasmatically to these in response. At the inception of each chapter, Gunton very helpfully recapitulates his argument to that point. So it gets easier as you read along to understand his argument.

4. Gunton, *One, the Three, and the Many*, 15.

In an extensive historical analysis, Gunton argues that certain fundamental shaping factors of modernity were holdovers from the ancient world, and the reversal that brought about modernity failed to address these latent factors. He argues that the problem is the age-old philosophical problem of "the one and the many," exacerbated through the centuries by Christian theology failing to bring its own resources to bear on the problem.[5]

The problem of the one and the many asks, what is reality *fundamentally*? Is it fundamentally a monism—everything reduces to one thing? Or is it ultimately a pluralism—nothing reduces to anything and so you have a plurality of ultimate things? Or is reality dual, with one part of it being one and the other part of it being many?

Ancient Greek philosophy posed all three of these alternatives. The Presocratic, Parmenides, said that all is one, immaterial, and rational. The Presocratic, Heraclitus, was taken to have said that all is many, and in flux. Plato proposed the dualism, saying that one part of reality—the material world—is plural and changing (and both of these because it is material), and that the other part of reality—the part accessible only to the rational intelligence—is one and unchanging (and most real, and most valuable, because it isn't material).

Some of the early Christian thinkers (not all) allowed their Platonism to shape their Christianity, rather than the other way around. As a result, the God of Scripture came to be aligned with Plato's one, and material creation was deemed to be the many. Christian theologians such as St. Augustine offered essentially a Platonic rendering of Genesis 1. God was seen to have created the world by shaping material to copy his own original ideas, the way a builder follows the blueprint.[6] As a result, Christianity came to accord little intrinsic value to plurality. It overlooked its own unique and alone effective resources to undercut the damaging dualism and to resolve the problem of the one and the many. Thus it excluded the rich resources of the Trinity's involvement with creation (both original and ongoing) from rendering valuable service to understanding and living as humans in the world.

So a key factor in the crisis of culture has been a defective Christian theology that failed to stem the tide of Greek monism or dualism. This perpetuated the ancient problem of the one and the many, rather than

5. Ibid., ch. 1.
6. Ibid., 23.

exposing "the false assumptions commonly held by both."[7] Coupled with characteristically modern developments, these factors made a bad situation worse, indeed, explosive. Coming into the modern era, it came to be widely felt that a transcendent One was devaluing and restricting the immanent many. This, Gunton says, is absolutely right: the *problem* of the one and the many is just that if you overdo the one, the many disappears, and if you overdo the many, the one disappears. Also, because the two are locked in an unstable relationship, if you save the many to the exclusion of the one, the many turns into the one. In the modern era, people rejected the one. Because of the earlier defective Christian alignment of the one with the transcendent God, what people felt they had to do in order to reject the one was to reject God, reject the transcendent. Gunton says that God was thus *displaced* in modernity.[8] He says that "much modern social and political thought can be understood as the revolt of the many against the one, and at the same time that of humanity against divinity."[9] Modernity involves an immanent monism: "the specter at the whole banquet of modernity is homogeneity"—here Gunton employs Stanley Jaki's evocative phrase.[10]

That led to the Enlightenment ascendancy of human reason: reason, the rational, came to be seen as common to all, thus uniting all, and capable of unlocking every secret of the universe. The one thus was brought into our immanent realm. This is evident in the confidence of the age in the ideal of certainty in knowing (something Gunton suggests is inappropriate for humans as creatures). But this also meant that the now-immanent one, the human mind, was set over against the many of materiality, both bodies and world. This is what Gunton refers to as *disengagement*.[11] He immediately cites Descartes' *cogito*, which sets the knower as over against the known and even against his own body.

This has led, eventually but inexorably, to a postmodern rejection of all forms of the one, immanent as well as transcendent, in an attempt to recover the many.[12] Gunton points out that this has no hope of succeeding, however, because it too is stuck in the misguided seesawing

7. Ibid., 18.
8. Ibid., 28.
9. Ibid., 27.
10. Ibid., 44. Original reference: Jaki, *God and the Cosmologists*, 37.
11. Gunton, *One, the Three, and the Many*, 13.
12. Ibid., ch. 2.

between one and many, rather than addressing underlying assumptions. Where the ancient world devalued the particular, and the modern world persisted in rejecting it—one need only think of modern empiricism's ultimately meaningless sense data—postmodernity renders it irrelevant. Homogenization remains with a vengeance, as postmodernity presumes to celebrate the individual, but in effect reduces all individuals to relatively valueless similitude: everyone is unique, just like everybody else.

Since the Enlightenment, the ideal of human reason has both endured and self-destructed, leading to the paradoxes of contemporary culture that Gunton puts forth as evidence of the problem. The ideal of certainty in objective knowledge devolves into suspicion—knowers so disengaged from the known as to be uncertain of its reality. On the one hand, knowing suspects objective materiality; on the other hand, knowing itself is reduced to the material. Either way, meaning and truth elude our grasp.

Surrounded by time-saving devices, we are busier than ever; we so live in the future that we no longer know how to be at home in the present. People and environment alike have suffered from the adversarial approach of modern industry. Freedom has disappeared repeatedly into collectivism, totalitarianism, and similarly into capitalism and democracy, with devastating results. A primary irony is that the liberation of the many from the one has devolved into fresh bondage, as the many itself has become one. People and cultures are pressed to conform to the ironic homogeneity of individualism.

And for Gunton a key evidence of the unhealth of the relation between knower and known is the dualisms, as in my daisy.[13] Most telling of the dualisms is, for him, that of appearance versus reality (or of knower and known), which leads knowers to question the connection between what is perceived and what is there. The dualisms oppose knower to known. Reality is not a trusted partner. This is just the sort of thing that must be challenged if we are to heal culture in our relationship to it.

We can locate the problem of the one and the many itself in the daisy of dichotomies. Our default mode generally believes that what is in the daisy middle is one, unified, and to be preferred. The unified center marginalizes the plural petals. But where the plural petals are valued, the daisy center is eliminated. But then what is left is all the same—petals. Where all you have is one and many, and these are opposed, there is

13. Ibid., 197.

no way to resolve the problem, and culture can be expected to seesaw between the one and the other. You see the problem.

Also we can connect Gunton's diagnosis with what we already have said about his and others' concern to reject substantival anthropology.[14] For Gunton, a substantival anthropology is a piece of a larger problem: that of the one and the many. What is at stake is a Trinitarian theological vision and its signature reflections in the cosmos. So in addressing the cosmic problem, Gunton also addresses the more specific one of what it is to be human.

Gunton's rich account exposes another damaging development in the unfolding of western culture: the exaltation of the arbitrary will. This, too, stems from a faulty, in particular, non-Trinitarian, interpretation of Genesis 1. Where the story had been rendered by early Christian philosophers in a Platonic key, medieval rejection of the reality of transcendent universals stripped the act of creation down to a matter of the arbitrary will of God, and also deprived the created world and human beings of even the, albeit defectively construed, connectedness they had hitherto enjoyed.[15] This also exposed human will as arbitrary choice, leading to the unthinkable atrocities of the recent century.

For Gunton, the problem plaguing culture, ancient and modern, is an inadequate account of relationality, how to interconnect the many and the one, and how to relate particulars in a way that does not deface, but rather accentuates, their particularity.[16] The book title suggests both the problem and the solution he will put forward: faulty assumptions that set up the false dualism of the one and the many are the problem, and he alludes to the solution by inserting "the three" between them. We may surmise correctly that Gunton believes that restoring theology in a more trinitarian direction will accomplish this.

TRINITARIAN PERICHORESIS

What is needed is an account of relationality that does not thereby devalue particularity. You have to have both, and they need to be connected to each other as mutually constitutive. That is, each, as part of the core of what it is, has to make the other more what it is. Gunton believes that

14. See chs. 1 and 8.

15. Gunton, *One, the Three, and the Many*, 57–58. Gunton lays the blame at the door of William of Ockham in particular for this decisive and damaging move. Ockham's thought contributed formatively, in a couple centuries, to the Protestant Reformation.

16. Ibid., 37.

"only where relatedness is held in tension with genuine otherness can things, both human and divine, all be given their due."[17] Genuine otherness, in this sentence, is what true particulars would have. They would have their own thisness, their unique and valued individuality. It is not possible to have an account of particularity without relation, he says; what you would have is not particularity but rather meaningless individualism—what Gunton says characterizes the current milieu. What is needed is a fundamental understanding of reality in which particulars receive their fullest expression in a freeing space accorded in their relation to one another. This dynamic is what we have in the Trinity.

A Christian view of the world holds the only hope of such an account. It is the only religion which professes an ultimate real that is three-in-one. But obviously, it is not enough to confess belief in the Holy Trinity without going to the bank on it in a certain way. You cannot have an account of particularity without a doctrine of creation that is trinitarian; that is, not just creation by God the Father, but creation as also christological (involving Christ) and pneumatological (involving the Holy Spirit). The same with an account of relationality: this "is to be derived from the one place where they can satisfactorily be based, a conception of God who is both one and three, whose being consists in a relationality that derives from the otherness-in-relation of Father, Son, and Spirit." Unlike the more influential Augustine, the ancient church father Irenaeus avers that both Son and Spirit are actively involved in the act of creation.[18]

Medieval theologians, in reflecting on God and on being in general, spoke of "transcendentals": characteristic marks of all being, both God's and creation's. They designated the transcendentals as "one," "true," "good," and "being."[19] Gunton argues that the list tellingly omits relationality and particularity, and thus offers no ground for our treating either of these with integrity. Gunton's project is to offer a way of tapping the Trinity's involvement in creation to show that these—relationality and particularity—are transcendental as well. Since creation comes about and is sustained by the involvement of both the Lord Christ and the Holy Spirit, creation can be expected to bear this mark of being.

17. Ibid., 6.
18. Ibid., 53–54, *et passim.*
19. Ibid., 139.

The question of the various assignments the different members of the Trinity carry out in the creation of the world, and in what way, is the question of economy.[20] The very idea of the economy of God also draws us to consider what that implies regarding the relationships between them as persons. There must be diversity at the same time as there is reciprocity. The action of Father, Son, and Spirit—in fact, their very being, is constituted in a relationship in which their uniqueness is a function of their relatedness. Appealing to the language of mutual indwelling in the Gospel of John, Gunton says that the Trinity is characterized by relatedness without absorption. "Trinitarian love has as much to do with respecting and constituting otherness as with unifying."[21]

The concept that evocatively captures this mutually constitutive being and diverse working is *perichoresis*—a Greek word meaning, dancing around. The fourth-century Cappodocian church fathers appropriated it to describe the Trinity. In a dance, two persons actually constitute the particularity of one another in the relationship. Within the relation each individual has space freely to be oneself, to be other, and in so doing shape and be shaped by the other in relatedness. This occurs dynamically, thus also honoring time—a dynamic unfolding of the work as part of its perfection. The motif presupposes persons in love relationship, for both love and freedom sustain, and are sustained (only) in, perichoretic relationship. Plus, Gunton also commends it as a concept heavy with spatial and temporal conceptuality: movement, recurrence, interpenetration, and interanimation.[22]

So Gunton says: "It would appear to follow that in eternity Father, Son, and Spirit share a dynamic mutual reciprocity, interpenetration and interanimation." The three Persons "do not simply enter into relationship with one another, but are constituted by one another in the relation." Perichoresis "implies an ordered but free interrelational self-formation . . . There is thus a richness and space in the divine life, in itself and as turning outwards in the creation of the dynamic universe that is relational order in space and time." The motif of perichoresis, therefore, gives us a viable picture of God, and of his/their economic creating of and ongoing involvement with the world. Gunton will argue that perichoresis is also a transcendental—a mark of all being, created being as well. He

20. Ibid., 157.
21. Ibid., 204, 206.
22. Ibid., 163.

claims centrally that the fertile concept of perichoresis "enables theology to preserve both the one and the many in dynamic interrelations."[23] In perichoresis, particularity and relatedness may both be given their due right and their due place.

How do the Persons of the Trinity collaborate in creating the world? Gunton suggests that what Christ brings to creation is a distinctive unity of things which is not at the expense of the many.[24] Christ is the Logos. How may a unity of relationality, especially one named the Logos, avoid that deadening stillness so embedded in the western tradition? Gunton reminds readers of ancient western philosophy, that Heraclitus was the philosopher who originated the idea of logos. In one of the sad ironies of western thought, he is remembered for advocating an ultimate pluralism. All is flux, he is reputed to have said. But Heraclitus' working examples, a river and a fire, reveal, not an amorphous flux, but a rather a dynamic, immanent unity—one which he calls logos. Each is continually changing, yet each is one. Similarly, Christ is not an abstract unity, an underlying rationality. He is the Person in whom all things cohere.[25] "Logos is not only the Word spoken to time from eternity, but the immanent dynamic of meaning which holds time and space together"[26]—just as a dance is an immanent union of space and time dynamically. Christ brings the dynamic unity of relationality to the perichoresis.

The Holy Spirit's contribution is twofold, Gunton gleans from Scripture. The Spirit enables boundary-crossing, that is, the openness of the one to another to be shaped by the other. "What a person is comes from outside," he says.[27] The Spirit works, secondly, to maintain, strengthen, and develop particularity.[28] But this is a particularity forged dynamically in relationship, perichoretically. Particulars are neither disparate and meaningless, nor submerged and lost to a relational homogeneity. This is relation in otherness. The Spirit gives freedom. The result is not a collective, but community. The Spirit is the source of autonomy, not homogeneity, he says. Actually, he says, the Spirit insures particularity in the heart of the very Trinity of God. So particularity in creation

23. Ibid., 164.

24. Ibid., 212.

25. Col 1:16.

26. Gunton, *One, the Three, and the Many*, 178–79.

27. Ibid., 181–84.

28. Ibid., 188–204.

is a way that being shows the marks of its Creator. Also, Gunton argues that the Spirit works to develop the particularity of things. His work is eschatological, unfolding in time.

Why does the notion of particularity, in both God and his creation, strike us as strange? Gunton tells us that it has to do with the exigencies of translation from Greek to Latin. The Greek Christian Fathers had employed the word, *hypostasis*, to signify the unique thisness of each individual thing, and of each Person of the Trinity. But the Latin *substance* misled us in the West to associate it with a homogenous underlying plenum, the true reality distinguishable from the particularity that only was apparent. [29] Particularity thus was devalued to the insubstantial.[30] Knowledge was taken to be about the universal in its oneness. Attention was diverted from the particular, even in sensation; concreteness was lost. In our homogenized society this continues to play out. No, Gunton argues: particularity, substantiality, means that things are what they are and not another thing. There is a unique thisness, what in Latin was called *haecceitas*, to each particular thing.

God is involved perichoretically with the world in another sense also: where he is one partner of the dance, and his world the other, the created world is free to be its particular self in its relatedness to God. The world has its own derivative validity. God creates neither out of necessity nor out of arbitrary, all-powerful will. Neither of these would grant particularity in relatedness to either God or creation. He creates freely out of love, and he redeems freely out of love. Love is indeed at the core of all things, says Gunton.[31]

Since its creator is a Trinity perichoretically related, and since its creation and continuance involve that perichoresis, we can expect creation to display perichoresis in some way. This is what it means to say that perichoresis is a transcendental, a mark of all being. Does reality exhibit this perichoretic dynamism? Gunton explores this "especially in areas most ill-served in recent thought": the personal world, the material world in itself and in relation to humanity, and culture (including knowledge).[32]

---

29. Gunton makes the important point that David Hume, in arguing that substance does not exist, failed, because he meant the wrong thing by substance. Would that the fallout of his argument might have also been so easily dissipated!

30. Gunton, *One, the Three, and the Many*, 190–95.

31. Ibid., 179.

32. Ibid., 168.

To demonstate perichoresis with regard to persons, Gunton cites with unqualified approval John Macmurray's ringing case for personhood as persons-in-communion.[33] His elaboration of this resonates noticeably with what we have said about differentiation and Riesman's autonomous person. He also speaks of the relationship of a person to a tradition: this is best seen perichoretically as well. A tradition forms a person even as it confers the freedom to contribute distinctively to it.

In the nonhuman world, Gunton cites physicists who affirm that the nature of real things derives from their relations and their relations derive from their nature. We live, he says, in a perichoretic universe.[34]

The relation of humans to the nonhuman world, which constitutes culture, is the area that concerns him particularly in this book. Gunton argues that fragmentation of culture is evident in the fact that major disciplines—science, art, and ethics (to which correspond truth, beauty, and goodness, as goals of these arenas)—typically oppose one another in exalting their own homogenous apprehension of reality and meaning. But perichoresis offers "a clue to the due integration of the three realms of meaning while maintaining their relative autonomy."[35] He suggests, for example, that scientific knowing often involves an assessment of beauty. Truth, beauty, and goodness should be profoundly related to each other.

My own persistent preoccupation with knowing induces me to see that knowing itself is a prime instance of humans relating to the nonhuman world. And covenant epistemology offers just this sort of interdisciplinary therapy, as we saw in an earlier texture. This convergence points in the direction of my claim that healthy knowing is perichoretic. We will speak of this further.

Gunton is arguing that perichoresis, particularity, and relationality (these last being perichoretically understood) are transcendentals: they mark all being, both God's and creation's. Although he doesn't say it this way, where things in our experience are in fact going well in human relationships with God, others, and world, the dynamism of perichoresis in which relationality and particularity create and strengthen each other, can be seen to pertain. Both Christ the Logos, and the particular-cultivating Spirit, are present.

33. Ibid., 169–70.
34. Ibid., 173.
35. Ibid., 176.

Gunton develops all this further by noting the asymmetry of perichoresis. What you have is not an even mutuality so much as what he calls the logic of gift and reception.[36] Here I note that gift-givers often forget that gift-giving is supposed to be asymmetrical! Too often we have reduced gift giving to a symmetrical gift *exchange*. But the point of a gift is that a gift is not conditioned or warranted. It should be part and parcel (!) of a gift that it surprises and transforms. This is what Gunton is getting at. Asymmetry makes sense of sacrifice, which is a costly and unreciprocatable gift. And it allows for there to be transformation.

So this rich nexus of motifs gives much to draw on: it honors both the related and the distinctively particular, and it shows, in perichoresis, the dynamic way in which this balanced honoring comes to expression. And it does all this by tapping into the Holy Trinity: creation is perichoretic because the Trinity is perichoretically related, as well as relating perichoretically to their creation.

Gunton argues, "If it is not believed that the world is the creation of God, it is hard to accept the goodness and rationality of the temporal and limited."[37] It is not possible to accord to particulars genuine value and distinctiveness apart from the doctrine of creation. One thing Gunton suggests that this means is that, for particularity to be genuine, a thing must be doubly constituted. The concrete real things of this world "are what they are by virtue of being wholes that are constituted indeed of parts but in such a way that they are more than simply the sum of the parts."[38] Also, Gunton reminds his readers, "substantiality is not fully given . . . but has to achieve its end."[39] This is a reference to the fundamental dynamism of created things, which includes their moving toward their full flourishing.

We live in a perichoretic universe, says Gunton: "everything may be what it is and not another thing, but it is also what it uniquely is by virtue of its relation to everything else."[40] Gunton emphasizes that perichoresis, properly understood, is the foe, not the agent, of homogeneity.[41] The unity of the dance is never a monism, but rather showcases the particularity

36. Ibid., 225.
37. Ibid., 202.
38. Ibid., 210.
39. Ibid., 208.
40. Ibid., 173.
41. Ibid., 172.

of each dancer, and each dance pattern that they together accomplish. "All particulars are formed by their relationship to God the creator and redeemer and to each other. Their particular being is a being in relation, each distinct and unique and yet each inseparably bound up with other, and ultimately all, particulars. Their reality consists, therefore—and this is the crucial difference from other theories of substance—not in the universals they instantiate, but in the shape of their relatedness with God and with other created hypostases. Their form is secondary to, because derivative of, their relations to the Other and to others."[42] This kind of perichoretic particularity in relatedness characterizes both humans and nonhuman creation. It allows things, cabbages, songs, stars and oceans, to be important as things, he says, and for me to relate to them as such.[43]

PERICHORETIC KNOWING

Of course, what especially interests me is the implications of all this for human knowing, and how it confirms and amplifies the covenant epistemology thesis. Knowing is a central form of human engagement with the nonhuman world, as well as with God and other humans. Plus, every act of human engagement involves knowing in some form. So Gunton's perichoresis, with its dynamic affirmation of both relationality and particularity, should pertain to our discussion. Following Gunton, for knowing to be healthy and healing, it should display this perichoretic dynamism. In addition, if it does, then from the idea of perichoresis we may glean a richer understanding of knowing.

Neither Foundationalism Nor Nonfoundationalism

Gunton had begun his response to his diagnosis by talking about the matter of the one and the many in reference to meaning and truth.[44] He said that accounts of knowing in modernity overemphasized the one—a monolithic, absolute, understanding of truth that lauds universality and devalues the particular. The postmodern reaction has been right to attempt to recover the particular, but in so doing has often lost the ability

---

42. Ibid., 207.

43. Gunton cites G. K. Chesterton as alone understanding this profoundly. (Gunton, *One, the Three, and the Many,* 204) I would like to add that Robert Farrar Capon does as well.

44. Ibid., ch. 5.

to affirm the universal. In this context, Gunton criticizes the opposing visions of knowledge known as foundationalism and nonfoundationalism; they reflect the modern monism and the postmodern pluralism, respectively. Foundationalism involves a homogeneously universal certainty; nonfoundationalism, which seeks to honor particular perspectives, often reduces knowledge to fideism.[45] Gunton says of foundationalism and antifoundationalism that they actually share the same false presuppositions—namely those characteristic of the faulty dichotomy of the one and the many.[46] Even though one apparently exalts the universal and the other the particular, both denegrate particulars, on the one hand, and result in humans' imperious ascendancy, on the other. Neither foundationalism nor antifoundationalism positively characterizes the epistemic efforts of the knower as a created person. Ultimately, both alike face an ultimately insurmountable self-immolation; both threaten truth and lead to meaninglessness.

What we need, Gunton says, is an account of knowledge that is "in its own way universal and objective, while acknowledged to be the work of fallible human minds," "a conception of the universal which does not force the particular into a procrustean bed" but rather preserves the rights of both particular and universal.[47] He says that we must seek nonfoundationalist foundations: "to find moments of truth in both the contentions, namely that particularity and universality each have their place in a reasoned approach to truth."

Specific Commendation for Polanyi

It should come as no surprise that he proceeds to offer Polanyi's epistemology as exemplary of this—indeed as the single positive example that *The One, the Three, and the Many* commends. Quoting Polanyi's famous comment in *Personal Knowledge*, that the book's purpose is "to achieve a frame of mind in which I may hold firmly to what I believe to be true, even though I know that it might conceivably be false,"[48] He says of Polanyi that "he hoped to demonstrate that the basis of knowledge is a form of particularity: not the particularity of a disembodied empiricism,

---

45. See ch. 4 for this book's fuller discussion of foundationalism and the Polanyian alternative.

46. Gunton, *One, the Three, and the Many*, 129–35.

47. Ibid., 134.

48. Ibid., 135. Original reference: Polanyi, *Personal Knowledge*, 214.

but that of an embodied mind in particular and determinate relations with the world. The personal capacity for pattern recognition and classification serves for him as a paradigm case for the form this experience takes." Gunton says: "Although he would not have put it like this, what Polanyi is seeking is a conception of created rationality rather than the divine reason aspired to in the tradition. It is a rationality appropriate to created knowers in a world with which they are continuous."

It is not hard for us to compare this favorably with Frame's conviction that human knowing must be creaturely. This means that Gunton confirms what I have believed for a long time: that Polanyian epistemology accords with the Framean mission of construing human knowing as a creaturely endeavor. Plus, I am especially gratified to note, Gunton appreciates about Polanyi's work not only that it espouses the knower's creaturely status, but that in the process it unhesitatingly professes realism. Real creatures engage the real world. Both knower and known exhibit embodied particularity, and knowers may hope to unlock the real. For Gunton, such knowing-sustaining reverence for particularity is only possible on a trinitarian theological understanding of all things.

While he does not elaborate on Polanyian epistemology, our engagement of subsidiary-focal integration will allow us later in the chapter to confirm the presence of perichoretic dynamism in it and substantiate Gunton's conviction about Polanyi's epistemic proposals. Demonstrating this will offer substantial support for my claim that knowing, in the vision of covenant epistemology, is perichoretic—knowing as dance. Knowing construed perichoretically, as Gunton believes Polanyi's epistemology construes it, creatively honors particularity in relationship. As such it taps into the marks of being that reflect a dynamic understanding of a trinitarian God. Thus, the act of knowing itself is a knowing of God.

PERICHORETIC BEING

Let's also note a little more of what Gunton says about perichoresis and nonhuman being. In doing this we set it into play in this conversation; we will tap it again in chapter 13, as we specify in what respect the real is personal.

For accessibility's sake, I have spared us the complexity that a full account of Gunton's argument would require. I have been able to extract the rich notion of perichoresis while sidestepping some tough concepts and complex development. I will be continuing this and thus only sketching Gunton's conclusions regarding non-human being. But to offer a nugget from his argument strategy: Gunton is concerned to show that his proposed concepts—perichoresis, particularity, and relationality— are transcendental, that is, marks of *all* being, whether God's, humans', or the nonhuman creation's. Some of the concepts he considers, however, fall short of characterizing all being. They are richly influential notions, but not transcendental. Economy is not a transcendental, perichoresis is, he argues. Spirit is not a transcendental; substantiality (particularity) is. Sociality is not a transcendental; relationality is.[49]

It is this last distinction which is pertinent to our conversation here. Sociality is not a transcendental, relationality is. That means that all being, including nonhuman being, is characterized by distinctively perichoretic relationality. We saw earlier that nonhuman creation does display perichoresis in the way that each thing is distinctively itself in the context of its relations with all reality. However, sociality, being in communion, which is of the essence of God and absolutely critical to human being, does not pertain to nonhuman created realities. This is because these lack a few necessary components of personal being, namely, spirit (personhood), love, and freedom. As an implication of this, Gunton remarks, he feels he cannot use the word, *covenant*, to apply to nonhuman creation. Covenant is Scripture's word for free and joyful partnership with God and so with each other.[50] Covenant should be reserved for the personal.

Let us consider this, asking how Gunton's position comports with or contrasts with what I am developing here. Even though he does not want to attribute sociality to nonhuman creation, Gunton nevertheless persists in speaking of an ontology of communion—all being as communion, being in relation—and of a personal and social metaphysic.[51] It is difficult for me to see how the terms, "communion," and "personal," may be applied where *covenant* cannot. My argument has been that "personal" and "communion" entail covenantal constitution, and that covenant metonymously references their presence.

Additionally, as we have already noted, Gunton further develops perichoretic relationality as the asymmetrical one of gift and reception. He calls this the heart of all human action as praise of our Creator. He ap-

49. Chs. 6, 7, and 8, respectively.

50. Gunton, *One, the Three, and the Many*, 222.

51. Ibid., 223, 219, 214–15.

plies the motif to the way humans engage nonhuman creation to the end of summoning each thing's particularity to its full flourishing in praise of God. In doing so, it seems that he means that humans are the givers and nonhuman creation is the recipient. He also seems to suggest that gift and reception elucidates exclusively personal relationality, or sociality.[52] Apparently the asymmetry of gift and reception functions, for Gunton, not only as the way to incorporate important notions of sacrifice into the account, but also as an account of the distinction between human and nonhuman creation especially with respect to personhood and calling as prophets and priests of the nonhuman creation before God.

But we may well ask: can covenant not also involve asymmetry in relationship? Also, is not human involvement with nonhuman creation, in the biblical account of humans as covenant mediators, essentially covenantal? And then, does not the nonhuman creation surprise us with its gracious self-disclosure? He never demonstrates that humans alone are on the giving end. But this is what covenant epistemology is especially concerned to deny. It is also what it would seem that perichoresis would serve to deny as well.

Gunton doesn't follow through the implications of this rich metaphor for the personlike character of the nonhuman. For where there is gift *and* reception, one is the giver and one the receiver. It is arguable that only persons can give and receive gifts. Both alike are personal acts: one in overture, one in response.[53] It is as personal to receive as it is to give. This is borne out by the fact that some people we know don't know how to receive. It involves a personal grace, a humility, what we might call an active passivity. The grateful recipient gives a different sort of gift. Plus, the recipient often gives a gift at a different time, or to a different person. Applying the logic of gift and reception to human-nonhuman engagement, which is giver and which is gift? It would seem that at one time it is one way, and at another it is the other. It is perichoretic. Non-human creation surely gives abundantly, both in being and in self-disclosure. But if at any point non-human creation is aptly construed as giver, that makes it personlike. We can speak of the surprising, transformative, self-disclosure of reality in the overture-response that is knowing, which comes graciously (the language of giver or gift, not of recipient) in response to covenantal self-binding on the part of the aspiring knower—

52. Ibid., 227.

53. See, for example, Philip Rolnick's case for reality as gift, in Rolnick, *Person, Grace, and God*; I will engage this in ch. 13.

this is a phenomenon Gunton could well have tapped in support of his rich thesis. Why may not the logic of gift and reception be applied to nonhuman reality, at least to describe its signature behavior, the asymmetric, perichoretic mutuality of knower and known?

On the other hand, there are a couple critical things to be said for not forcing personhood on nonhuman creation. Gunton certainly has supplied warrant to respect nonhuman things. One implication of this respect is that forcing personhood onto the nonhuman world would be to deface the very particularity, the intrinsically valuable, derivative, otherness, that a perichoretic relationship between God and the world is meant to free and honor. The other is that if reducing nonhuman creation to personhood means reducing it to God, this produces a pantheistic theology, not a Christian one.[54] We will discuss these things further later on.

Despite the distinction, as I said before, Gunton obviously remains committed to talking of ontology (study of being) as an ontology of communion, and a personal or social metaphysic (study of reality). Whatever his caution about nonhuman creation as nonpersonal, it does not stop him from characterizing *the whole* as personal. It might be argued that, even if one follows Gunton in denying sociality to nonhuman creation, two of the three sorts of beings that comprise reality (God and humanity) are in fact fully personal. And given that all the relationships between one and another member of the triad involve at least one person, it is appropriate to cast the whole nexus as personal.

For Gunton, it is the case that nonhuman, nonpersonal, creation shares with human persons trinitarian motifs of perichoretic particularity in relatedness, value, reciprocity, and an inherent status as intended for and being on the way to full flourishing particularity in relationship. Nonhuman creation itself displays perichoretic features. It is a dynamically perichoretic collaborative enterprise, with *humans* invited into the dance![55] After all, in the human-nonhuman relationship, it is not the nonhuman that needs to reform its cultural behavior, epistemic and otherwise. The partners who need to reform are indeed persons. They should be the receivers.

54. See, for example, Annie Dillard's tentative, moving, theodicy in Dillard, *For the Time Being*.

55. I have in mind here the Rublev Icon of the Old Testament Trinity: there is room at the table for you and me, and we are invited to join in.

These commonalities, Gunton stresses, justify and encourage mutuality in relationship between humans and their world. We can see that this mutuality in relationship occurs, says Gunton: take the well-known example of the invention of the internal combustion engine, which now has come so to define the contours of our lives. Cars were invented, roads and suburbs were created as a result. Now we depend on cars.[56] But the perichoretic approach envisions a symbiotic relationship of humans and nature, "of a kind of community which makes us neither wholly active and dominant nor wholly passive and receptive in relation to the rest of creation."[57] This is in distinct contrast to the kind of baldly arbitrary will that has led to wholesale dominance of humans over nature, and to their mutual deprivation.

Gunton's own most important and well-supported conclusion is that, where persons and nonhuman creation link profoundly as equally perichoretic and in perichoretic relation with God, the two are no longer opposed but may relate healingly. What he has offered is a theologically informed vision of perichoretic dynamism in the universe. In our culture-making, and thus in our knowing, we would do well to tap it intentionally and creatively, eschewing the deadening fallout of the age-old one-or-many dualism. Human beings, Gunton has argued, in order to heal both the world and our engagement with the world, must reform our most fundamental categories that we bring to all of life. Those categories must be interpersonal, a perichoretically dynamic balance of relationality and particularity, the very dynamism evidenced by the Holy Trinity, biblically understood. Covenant epistemology carries out Gunton's mission.

WEAVING GUNTON'S INSIGHTS
INTO COVENANT EPISTEMOLOGY

Covenant epistemology embraces Gunton's motif of perichoresis. It has every reason to do so: Gunton's very project has been to argue that we apply the motif to culture-making—humans' dealings with the non-human creation. Knowing is pervasively the way we deal with the world. Since knowing is a culturish relationship, Gunton's proposals apply di-

56. Gunton, *One, the Three, and the Many*, 178.
57. Ibid., 213.

rectly to epistemology. Knowing should be perichoretic. And construed perichoretically, knowing will be mutually transformative and healing.

Gunton argues that perichoresis involves an asymmetry in relation. Thus a logic of gift and reception characterizes it. This resonates profoundly with covenant epistemology's central notion of transformation and of redemptive deliverance. We may improve the covenant epistemology proposal by following Gunton's lead on this. Covenant epistemology easily affirms the notion of gift, and of sacrificial gift.

And we may follow him also in his conclusion regarding the purpose of all human action: the sacrifice of praise to the creator that, when directed toward the world, is action directed to allowing the world truly to be itself before God.[58] "Redemption means the redirection of the particular to its own end and not a re-creation."[59] These comments underscore what we have already said about the way covenant epistemology renders knowing part and parcel of the cultural mandate.

We will find many additional ways in which perichoresis deeply enriches our understanding and practice of knowing.

Polanyian Epistemology as Perichoretic

Earlier I noted that Gunton explicitly commends Polanyi's work. In the context of covenant epistemology we can be more concrete about how subsidiary-focal integration is intrinsically perichoretic, thus profoundly embodying Gunton's ideal.

In subsidiary-focal integration, do we find both relationality and particularity? Does it have a perichoretic shape? I believe that it is just its perichoretic shape that is distinctive about the Polanyian account.

Let's think again about your recognizing that a copperhead is curled up in the leaves beside your doorstep. That recognition takes an array of hitherto unrelated particulars and transforms them into a meaningful pattern. In that integration, the pattern gives meaning to the clues, even as it continues to rely on them to sustain it and give it the shape and texture that it has. Between pattern and clues is a dynamic relation. Within the integrative dynamism, over time, the exact array of particulars may be shifting, developing the focus as they do. Specifically, you the knower are dynamically relating parts to whole. The realization that you

58. Ibid., 227.
59. Ibid., 230.

are gazing at a copperhead at your feet starts to reshape you and your world. It starts even to reshape the particulars-turned-clues that you brought to the integration. Pattern and subsidiaries imbue one another meaningfully in different ways, and thus asymmetrically, in an unfolding perichoretic dynamic. Because there is no necessary linearity to which particulars shape a pattern, or what shape a pattern takes with respect to its particulars, there is space for significant mutual involvement and integrity simultaneously.[60]

Here is a different critter story that displays how the integrative dynamism perichoretically unfolds. The last evening my family and I were in our home in South Louisiana, we took a last goodbye wander around our yard among the many trees and bushes we had planted. Four-year-old Stacey gently kicked what we all thought was a clod of mulch off the grass back onto the bed at the base of a tree. Suddenly we realized that what she had kicked was no clod of mulch, but the largest tarantula I had ever seen, and the only uncaged one! It was the size of my open hand. My terrified first thought was that it was hideous; no spider should be so gargantuan. But gradually my terror gave way to fascination. I ran for a large peanut butter jar (ridiculous, I know) and a stick. As I gently prodded him, he slowly raised himself elegantly to attentive notice in response. At that moment, I lost my heart to a tarantula. He was incredibly beautiful. To this day, Stacey and I regret that we gave "Harry" to a family of delighted boys, rather than finding a way to move him with us to Missouri. That hour of encounter, I hope you see, contained a perichoretically dynamic, unfolding mutuality of pattern and clues. I was changed. So was he.

So subsidiaries and focus relate in a perichoretic dynamism. But you can also say that subsidiaries as subsidiaries are both particular and related in the focus. Particulars at Point A, prior to the Oh! I see it! moment, do not bear the relation to each other that affords their advance meaning. But particulars at Point B, as subsidiaries, have gained richer meaning (and thus Gunton's particularity) in relationship to the focal whole. The unifying whole is not meant to repress or deface them, but to showcase them as more profoundly what they are than we had realized hitherto. It should never be the case that the focal pattern so subsumes the meaningful particularity (Gunton's word) of the particulars

---

60. See my argument, at the end of ch. 4, that there is a transformative gap between clues and pattern.

(Polanyi's word) that they disappear. As I said in *Longing to Know*, you forget the particulars at your peril. Honoring particularity in the very act of relationality—honoring the many in the one and vice versa—is just what Polanyian epistemology enables us to do. There is a sense in which, after you learn to read, you don't see the words anymore. But there is a profounder sense in which it is only once you learn to read that you do see them. My thesis in an earlier texture regarding virtuosity, embodiment, and presence represent my attempts to honor the persisting particularity of subsidiary particulars.

The focal pattern achieved itself is uniquely particular. The subsidiaries that have coalesced transformatively have rendered it so. It is a unique, hitherto unspecified, union of particulars not ultimately reducible to them. But it is the subsidiaries in relationship that produces the particularity of that pattern, and sustains it as it unfolds dynamically. Again we have perichoretic particularity in relationality.

Also, as I have said before, the knower is continually dancing among the subsidiaries. We triangulate—my co-opted word for how, in an unfolding trajectory of coming to know, we move back and forth between consideration of the existential (what our body is sensing), the situational (what the world looks like), and the normative (what proposed descriptors and maxims mean). The knower repeatedly lays the one afresh alongside the other, adjusting each with respect to the other. We triangulate in our pursuit of the yet-to-be-known. This triangulation, therefore, may be construed as perichoretic.

According to Polanyi, in the unfolding trajectory of coming to know, we alternate between intuitive sensing of the pursued yet-to-be-known and imaginative scrabbling to reach it. In developing a skilled performance, we move back and forth from subsidiary to focal as well: golf lessons, driving range, and golf course, and back. All these may be seen to alternate perichoretically.

I noted that Gunton stipulates that things, to be particular, must be dually constituted. They are constituted in their relatedness to their created context, and they are specifically constituted as what they are by God. For any reader of Polanyi, Gunton's reference to parts and wholes, and to the whole needing to be more than the sum of the parts, is uncanny. The focal, in Polanyian integration, is indeed a whole that transcends the parts.[61] He drew the idea of part and whole from Gestalt theory, but

61. Polanyi, *Tacit Dimension*, 6.

stipulated additionally that the whole is actively pursued and integratively shaped—not at all a passive association of inkblots. Throughout his work, also, Polanyi attempts to articulate a correspondence between this dual structure of human knowing and real things—what he sometimes called comprehensive entities. Take, for example, a computer: composed of metal and plastic, in no way reducible to them.[62] Polanyi's ontological forays are allusive and continue to be topics of ongoing discussion and dispute among his scholarly readers.[63] But we can see it clearly in his account of knowing: all knowing involves two levels; this is what is unique about his account. And these two levels are both distinguishable and inextricably bound in a living dynamism. So Polanyi and Gunton were employing similar ways to get at something they both thought critically important to identify for the sake of the practice of human knowing.

Another notable similarity between Gunton and Polanyi is that both commend mutual indwelling. The kind of attention and self-disclosure on the part of both knower and known that allows them to listen to one another from within each other is like a gentle hospitality and not a forced entry. Parker Palmer has made much of hospitality as a posture that should characterize teacher and learner. He has drawn on Henri Nouwen's justly famous definition of hospitality as creating an inviting space into which the stranger may enter and become a friend.[64] What we should appreciate here is the welcome to open but not indifferent space and overture to reciprocity that hospitality involves. This matches all that Gunton has endeavored to cast as perichoresis.

There is another important and distinctive thesis of Polanyi's that I have yet to mention. I note it here with far less attention than it deserves, because it too evidences the perichoretic nature of Polanyi's epistemic proposals. In *Personal Knowledge*, Polanyi is especially concerned to make sense of how all knowing is, as I say, profess-sional. To say, *p* is to say, I believe *p*. All knowing, is profession. Polanyi labors to recover the critical role of personal responsibility in the holding of truth claims. A truth claim is a truth *claimed*. On the other hand, he emphatically rejects any implication that this privatizes knowledge. So he develops a very helpful approach: he speaks of our holding beliefs "responsibly,

---

62. Polanyi, "Emergence," Lecture 2 in Polanyi, *Tacit Dimension*.

63. My firsthand report from the yearly Polanyi Society meetings.

64. Nouwen, *Reaching Out*; Palmer, *To Know as We are Known*, ch. 5.

with universal intent."[65] Martin Luther's famous, "Here I stand; I cannot do otherwise," Polanyi says, exemplifies this balanced approach. We must acknowledge responsibility for our claims, while at the same time seeing that in the process of affirming them, we are committing ourselves to their truth, and to the conviction that anyone else in our position would be also be able to see that they are true. This balance, along with Polanyi's fallibilism—the propriety of holding beliefs that may prove false—affords space, within the dynamic relationship of knower, other persons, and known, to honor the particular dignity and integrity of each. This is perichoretic.

We may therefore affirm that Polanyian epistemology profoundly accords with Gunton's project. It bears the telltale marks of trinitarian perichoresis. And, therefore, it constitutes a representation of the relation of the humans to the world that is creational and healing. It thus counts as a trinitarian (according to Gunton) epistemic resolution of the problem of the one and the many. Also, Gunton's work underscores that Polanyian epistemology has about it features that align knowing with knower and known and with Creator—rhythmical and dynamic reciprocity that honors the particularity of knower, knowing, and known. In this it also vindicates the vision of covenant epistemology.

Covenant Relationship as Perichoretic: Perichoresis as Covenantally Constituted

Let us discuss further what we may draw from Gunton's work for the covenant epistemology vision, by laying his proposals alongside those of the other theologians we have engaged. First, Gunton's emphasis on dynamism in relationship accords with what Williams' notion of covenant underscores as central. Covenant is unfolding relationship of love. Covenant arguably involves asymmetry, love, freedom, and particularity in union. Williams' distinctive approach to covenant could consistently be more fully understood as perichoresis. The idea of dance injects "unfolding," in Williams' account, with rhythmical reciprocity and artistry.

The motif of covenant as interpersonal relationship also amplifies the key features that Gunton is concerned to mark as signature features in creation: relationality, particularity, and dynamism. I think this is so because covenant relationship requires healthy, that is, differentiated,

---

65. Polanyi, *Personal Knowledge*, 377, *et passim*.

interpersonhood. So if differentiated, covenanted, interpersonhood is healthy, then dancing, differentiated, covenanted interpersonhood is that much more healthy. It is artful and beautiful as well. Covenant epistemology will follow Gunton in viewing the unfolding dynamism of any interpersoned covenantally constituted relationship as, at its best, perichoretic. This is the dynamism that covenant epistemology considers paradigmatic for knowing.

Two dancers dancing are a specific form of interpersonal relationship. It is a relationship in which the covenantal features constitute a dance. And they are indeed covenantal features: I have only to recall the suppressed panic I endured one evening I watched my daughter and her swing partner practicing new aerials! Trust is required. So is conformity to certain normative standards of what constitutes a successful version of a dance.

To note another feature of dance that makes it accord with my account of covenant epistemology: for a two-personed dance to be successful, mutual trust and individual particularity must be evenly balanced. I am a devoted fan of *Dancing with the Stars*, a currently popular reality TV show in which celebrity contestants must learn dancing and dances from their professional partners, perform them, and be judged on their performance. One evening, the judge's comments on one dance and the one immediately following it reflected this balance. The judge told the first one: you need to trust your partner more. The same judge told the second one: you need to dance your own dance. In this I hear the dynamics of differentiation. A healthy dance relationship balances mutuality and particularity evenly in an artistic dynamism. And dance involves covenantal trust if it is to occur.

The way I have developed the idea of covenant as the constitutive normative structure of the relationship, adds something to Gunton's discussion. Gunton hasn't really talked about *the dance*, as over against the dancers and the dancing. In addition to the relating, and to the particularity, and to the dynamism, is the product: the certain identifiable set of steps and motions (salsa, macarena, bossa nova, Serbian dance, *pas des deux*, . . .). Thinking about the dance brings to light the covenantal or structural features that make it what it is.

Granted, Gunton has put forth perichoresis as a corrective to combat the West's penchant for the static that inclines us to depersonalize and generalize covenant, dance, reality, into impersonal objects or structures, and counting them exclusively as objects of knowledge. We might say that Plato watched dancing and only saw the form of the dance; and the western heritage follows his gaze. Gunton helps us see (and be), not just the dance, but the dancers, and the dancing. But we may take covenant, the normative, to be that structural constitution. Just as covenant never occurs apart from a dynamically unfolding, interpersonal relationship, the dance doesn't either. But it is as one-sided to emphasize relationship without covenant as it is to emphasize covenant without relationship.

Melding Frame and Gunton—with a Dash of Buber

How does Gunton's work align with Frame's? We noted that Frame's teacher, Van Til, underscored the importance of the triunity of God to the Creator-creature distinction (what Gunton refers to as transcendent otherness). Van Til also maintained that the Trinity alone holds the key to solving the philosophical problem of the one and the many, and thus the only ground for human knowledge of anything. For Van Til, this meant that the triune God is essential to all communication and meaning. Gunton's perichoresis—as an immanent dynamism—both amplifies this and makes the point more effectively.

Frame explicated the covenant lordship of God, and biblical parameters of creaturely knowing, in a triad. He did note that each aspect can be associated with a member of the Trinity. The triad thus suggests a position regarding the economy of God. Apart from that, however, in the admittedly small portion of their work that I have engaged, the Framean triad does not go to the bank on the Trinity the way Gunton does.

But the two theologians share an overarching theological vision that leads them both to make sophisticated sense of human knowing. I said that I thought Frame devised the triad in part to honor the created context of human knowers. Gunton also is concerned to modify human knowing so as to be appropriate to our created status, to link it to our situation relationally, to see perichoretic relation to our situation as a requisite dimension of particularity, and as elucidating the God-given role of humans with respect to the nonhuman creation.

I think that Frame was attempting to develop an understanding of meaning and truth that would combat homogeneity. The multidimensionality of his proposal, for example, got him in trouble with well-meaning Christian believers who thought that truth is *one*. This suggests a complementary resonance with Gunton's work.

Is it possible to line up Gunton's signature motifs of unity, particularity, and dynamism with the Framean triad? Gunton is above all concerned about human relationship to the non-human world. But this just is the existential and the situational of Frame's triad. Gunton is specifying a manner of relating one to the other that involves the normative shape of perichoresis. I want to follow the same strategy that I used in aligning Loder's proposals to Frame's triad. We have just said that perichoresis is covenantally constituted, artful relationship. So we may take the normative, the covenantally constituted, the perichoretically shaped, as metonymously referencing persons in relationship. This parallels how the normative metonymously references the void-Holy dynamism of Loder's third and fourth dimensions. If Loder's proposals add to covenant epistemology the claim that the dynamism of human-divine interpersonal relationship, specifically, sovereign deliverance and loving response, is implicit in every act of knowing, Gunton's proposals suggest that this dynamism plays out perichoretically.

Recently I heard a wedding homily that likened marriage to a great mulch pile: a lot of little deaths, little sacrifices, make it good![66] Something like this pertains here. The unfolding relationship that is communion, friendship, is so constituted. The fact that it is perichoretic means that there is a rhythmical reciprocity in the mutual, sacrificial, overtures. All this, covenant epistemology argues, characterizes human knowing.

If this is so, then covenant epistemology offers the way of connecting Frame to Gunton, as it did to Loder. Picture the Framean triad, and then augment the normative, the covenantal, with the void-Holy dynamism, perichoretically construed—this is the way I am aligning these proposals.

I did not come away from my engagement of Frame with a sense of the dynamism, the perichoresis, of either the Trinity or created reality. Perichoresis, as the shape of this dynamic, is Gunton's distinctive contribution. It only enhances Frame's, Williams', and Loder's proposals. It deepens the Christian believer's and the Christian theologian's insight and appreciation of their own belief. And it enriches covenant epistemology's account of knowing.

I do not believe that Frame and Van Til were centrally concerned to promote theological healing of culture. Their work shows a preoccupa-

---

66. Rev. Dr. Martha Giltinan, Wedding of Chloe Kuhns and Josh MacCarty, July 4, 2009, Pittsburgh, PA.

tion with the question predominant in reformed discussions at that time, of "what the unbeliever knows." Nevertheless, I have always felt that the Framean, reformational approach implies a very bullish common grace, as we discussed in texture 4. Gunton's specific project of ministering the doctrine of a perichoretic Trinity to the brokenness of cultural engagement (that infects Christian believers and unbelievers alike) elucidates the healing implicit in Frame's proposals. Common grace ought to be about, not just what the unbeliever can know, but also about how the gospel may heal all human relationship with culture. Gunton thus shows the way covenant epistemology may share and advance this commitment.

Gunton and the Conversants of Interpersonhood

Gunton's proposals embellish what we have been exploring in this part of Contours devoted to interpersonhood. Where Macmurray and Buber and Loder have worked with the all-important idea of the personal Other, the Holy, for Gunton's whole argument it is critical that this personal Other be triune, and that creation reflect the perichoretic dynamic of the Trinity.

Historically, the personal Other and the Trinity are integrally connected. Philip Rolnick, in his recent *Person, Grace, and God*, offers a well-researched history of the development of the notion of person. He argues that the very notion of person came about in conjunction with the early Christian church's efforts to articulate the doctrine of the Trinity.[67] He shows that personhood requires and entails *incommunicabilis*, an unshared ipseity, a personal particularity. Personhood and interpersonhood require a Trinity of persons. It is just the Trinitarian Persons' own perichoresis which frees the created world to its own perichoretic personal involvement with God and among its realities, human and non-human. So Gunton's advocacy of the personal Other as triune exposes a critical presupposition for the work of our other conversants in this part.

Gunton's perichoresis also advances our discussion of differentiation as healthful human interpersonhood. Differentiation incorporates a freeing space to complement the intensity of existential encounter. Perichoresis just is the dancelike dynamic of relationality and particularity, intimacy and freedom, which effectively is healthy differentiation.

---

67. Rolnick, *Person, Grace, and God*, pt. 1. See further *Loving to Know*, ch. 13.

Differentiation is a perichoretically dynamic balancing and intervolvement of relationality and particularity. As I noted at the end of the last chapter, I would dare to suggest that differentiation is a key to healthy interpersonhood because it originally characterizes the persons of the Holy Trinity in their relationship with one another. Differentiation patterns interpersonhood after the Trinity. Differentiation, we may say, is healthful because as a process it approaches the perichoresis of the love of God. Healthy human knowing must be characterized by perichoresis. In naming Christ as the Logos in whom all things dynamically cohere, Gunton underscores Schnarch's sense of the undeniable spirituality of differentiation.

I especially like how the asymmetry of perichoresis underscores the transformative character of the knowing event. If the parts have to do with our created particularity and relatedness, and the substantiality of the whole, in its situation-transcending uniqueness, is distinctively connected to God's agency, is it not entirely appropriate that integrative acts, according to Loder, prototype and anticipate the convictional encounter with the Spirit, and thus are his medium? Both Loder and Gunton—Macmurray and Buber as well—give us accounts of human knowing in which the event involves and signposts the Holy. Do we not, indeed, acknowledge this whenever we speak, in an Aha! moment, of having been *inspired?*

Our covenantal commitment that constitutes knowing is such that it must always remain open to surprising, self-transforming, developments. Where what comes from outside is akin to the Holy, this must be the case. Yes, knowing is overture, response; but it is so, never in a tit-for-tat presumptiveness. It always involves the humility, and the vision, that is openness to transformation. And the commitment always involves sacrifice for the sake of love.

I think perichoresis is also helpful in making sense of the dynamic between I-You encounters and I-It experience. Buber spoke of taking the I of I-You into I-It experience. It is helpful to see this as occurring rhythmically. Repeated returns to I-You encounter reorient all knowing to the personal context which makes it transformative, which makes us better knowers, and which blesses the world. I used the word, studded, to describe how I-You encounters graciously pepper our ordinary knowing, contexting it within, and shaping it toward, communion, growing us incrementally in that I of I-You. Growing effective skill in knowing involves aspiring to such studding encounters in perichoretic rhythm. This just is, Loder would argue, the point of the regular celebration of the Eucharist. Unbelievers have their moments of encounter also, and encourage them. Take, for example, the common injunction to stop and smell the roses. All of us know that, as members of a lightning-paced society, we desperately need this. But we also need to hear that this is central, and paradigmatically so, to our knowing well.

Covenant Epistemology: Bringing Not Just the I, But the I-You, into the I-It

Thus Gunton's theses accord profoundly with the other rich claims we have been interweaving into covenant epistemology. In covenant epistemology we are indeed championing the kinship of known and knowing to knower; and we are identifying that kinship in some way to be personal, to have person-like features such as reciprocity, self-disclosure in the context of promised covenant, unfolding and artfully rhythmical relationality, to the end of . . . *friendship*. Gunton's perichoresis strategically elucidates those features. We may now envision them perichoretically. We may conceive our epistemic efforts as characterized by the dynamic of boundary-crossing gift and reception, in a manner that will make them that much more effective.

We have spoken of overture and response as we woo the yet-to-be-known. Perichoresis describes the overture-response rhythm that we bring to engaging the real. We invite the real, and then we wait for it to disclose; then we do it again. We wait for it to open itself to us, and then we indwell it; but we also open ourselves for it to transform us. We show requisite respect for its and our own particularity in expecting that this relationship be perichoretically balanced. Thus, inviting the real, the phrase I will coin to epitomize our seeking to know, and which we will explore at length in an upcoming chapter, also epitomizes perichoresis. In all these ways, knowing—on a Polanyian account, and specifically in covenant epistemology—may be seen to occur perichoretically.

What we have been doing throughout this covenant epistemology project has been ramping up to inject more and more of the interpersonal into an account of knowing. How do we make sense of hints of the interpersoned about all our knowing? How do we make sense of the covenantal self-binding and the unfolding reciprocity that surrounds knowing, once we have understood it as subsidiary-focal integration?

Frame identifies a normative component. Williams contributes both that the normative is covenantal, and that the covenantal is dynamically unfolding interpersonal relationship. I have contributed the distinction between the covenantal constitution of the relationship and the relationship, while refusing to oppose the one to the other. Following Williams in keeping these two integrally related, with relationship foremost, leads me to this idea of metonymous reference. Covenant metonymously references the interpersonal relationship, the way studs and rafters suggest a house.

But freight travels both ways, we may say, along that metonymous link. Covenant references interpersonhood, yes; but also, interpersonhood enriches covenant. Covenant epistemology brings this dynamic into the core of knowing. So all that we have said about the interpersoned, the relational, the I-You encounter, the face of the Holy, and now about perichoresis, enriches the item which has referenced it metonymously. Knowing with normative dimension and unfolding dynamism is indeed fraught with the interpersoned, with persons in the vicinity.

Another way to say this it to draw on Buber's helpful idea of bringing the I of I-You back into all our I-Its. This, he said, readily happens after the knower has undergone the mode of being that is I-You encounter. May we not say that what this proposal of covenant epistemology is enabling us to do is bring, not just the I of I-You, but the entire I-You, in some sense, into all our I-Its?

We may see the entire endeavor of human knowing in created relatedness to God as personal and thus fraught with person-like features. And we may take the universe to be perichoretic in its covenantal constitution as well, and thus a metonym for a personed known. We will tackle this further in chapter 13. Thus, perichoresis gives us a motion of artful alternation that we can apply helpfully within our unfolding account of human knowing.

Gunton and Covenant Epistemology:
A Perichoretically Collaborative Mission

Gunton's mission and covenant epistemology share the conviction that a defective epistemic default mode is unhealthy for humans and for their world. It needs to be fixed with an approach that integrally involves the dynamics of persons in balanced relationship. Gunton makes the additional case that the defective outlook stems not just from a defective philosophical outlook, but also from defective Christian theology. A fully understood and appropriated doctrine of the Trinity and of the Trinity's involvement in creation would have been the only thing to stem the tide of the dualistic and monistic thinking that still leaves its mark on our subcutaneous epistemological layer. Gunton's mission is to correct a defective theology that has shaped our default mode.

So Gunton's work and covenant epistemology reveal profoundly overlapping diagnoses; they also share the solution. Gunton's summons our cultural engagement to perichoretic relationality; covenant epistemology reports for duty, and in turn advances Gunton's cause powerfully. Covenant epistemology shows concretely how we may know perichoretically and healingly. Covenant epistemology offers a proposal in which perichoresis is at home.

We may see Gunton's work as the wider mission of which covenant epistemology is a specific foray. But that means both that what he has offered is an over-arching rationale for covenant epistemology, and that covenant epistemology responds to his summons, applying his vision concretely to the matter of human knowing.

QUESTIONS FOR DISCUSSION

1. Supply some examples of how culture displays what Gunton is talking about. Do you agree that current emphasis on individualism is homogenizing?

2. Discuss Gunton's claims about Christ's and the Holy Spirit's involvement in the world. Where in your experience do you see this confirmed? Where do you see that it has been overlooked or resisted?

3. In what ways do you see knowing as perichoretic?

DANCE AS METAPHYSICAL THERAPY

ALL THIS RICH PHILOSOPHI-CAL exploration has a very concrete implication. You will see that this reflection draws together several of the conversations we have had thus far in *Loving to Know*. I would like to suggest, in line not only with these insights about perichoresis in knowing and universe, but also with the concrete embodiment that I argued earlier must be reverenced in knowing, that *actual dancing* may be a form of metaphysical—and theological—therapy.[1]

I was especially prompted to consider this as I watched someone very dear to me become a dancer in a spiritually dry period of her life. A growing sense of the imbalanced cerebral-ness of the Protestant church that ranked concrete care and even obedience as second to right doctrine, along with a sense that her heart-

felt questions were chalked up to "not doing quiet times and evangelism well enough," and thus dismissed, made for a long period of holding on alone in a wasteland. She had learned salsa dancing in the cramped living room of a large Ecuadorian family in Guayaquil, on a missions trip, and she built her skill at it on other trips to Hispanic countries. In college she signed up for free swing dance lessons, and worked her way to a spot on the team. The spiritually dry period eventually passed, as she was embraced by friends, teachers, and pastors who share in some measure her outlook.

Her comment on that spiritually dry period: "Dance was the one spiritual thing that kept me alive." Her comment on salsa in the context of Hispanic culture: "It redeemed my body. It made me whole." Since then, she has found that Christians who learn of her expert skill at salsa, both men

1. I cull the following from an online post I have published previously: "Dance."

and women, beg her to teach them, and start to air issues of broken self-perception in need of redemption.

Our western theological tradition has been freighted with an approach to reality that generally sees things as substances, things in themselves, with essential defining features known as attributes. And we have exalted unchangingness: things that are eternal and still, over things in flux. Our theology might be: God is a Spirit (a substance): infinite, eternal, and unchangeable in his being, wisdom, power, holiness, justice, and truth.[2] "I Am That I Am" is taken to affirm God's eternal and unchanging substance.[3] Heaven is eternal stasis. Thus, our anthropology might be: man is a rational (attribute) animal (substance). We strive for *self*-actualization, or actualization of God's image in our *selves*. That image had often been taken to be our rationality.

A couple years ago I had the chance to hear a veteran historical theologian, Les Fairfield, effectively summarize the insights of the trinitarian theologians that we have encountered in our conversation with Colin Gunton.[4] What follows are his comments, which I have constructed from my handwritten notes:

> Father, Son, and Holy Spirit, are all terms that imply an Other, that imply relationship. And the relationship is intimate; it is one of trust, reciprocity, and cooperation. Scripture tells us of the reciprocal relationships between the Persons of the Trinity. In fact, what it is to be one of these Persons is to be in relationship. Gregory of Nazianzus talked of persons as persons in relation. Gregory of Nyssa suggested that the "cooperative relational activity" of the Trinity, active and continuous as it is, constitutes their divinity.
>
> Thus, basic reality at its heart is community— reciprocal, loving, active

2. Westminster Shorter Catechism, response to Question 4. Online: http://shortercatechism.com/resources/wsc/wsc_004.html.

3. Exodus 3. This is the name God gives for himself to Moses. See my discussion of Williams, both in ch 7 and toward the end of ch 10.

4. Dr. Leslie Fairfield, Emeritus Professor of Church History, Trinity School for Ministry, Ambridge, PA, speaking in a Sunday School class at Ascension Episcopal Church in Pittsburgh, Lent, 2007.

community. There is no life without community, no human nature without reciprocity. A child not nurtured in personal relationship cannot even survive. The West, with its substantival approach, has had it all wrong.

In the early 700s, John of Damascus described the interrelationship of the Persons of the Trinity with the term, *perichoresis*—"dancing around." Contrast this to the static, clunky western idea.[5]

It was when Dr. Fairfield said, "clunky," that I remembered the apparent healing quality of dance in my dear dancer's life.

But our theological tradition has exalted God's immutability, his eternality. He has been said to be impassive, meaning, not subject to emotional change. I raised this in a question: in light of perichoresis, how are we to understand God's unchangingness? Les responded: "There are two kinds of unchangingness. One is to be motionless. The other has to do with faithfulness—God's character is utterly faithful.

God selects this or that action in this or that circumstance, but his character is always the same. The western tradition, with its Platonic legacy, plus the Roman legal context from which *persona* and *substantia* were first drawn, picks up on the first kind of unchangingness. Contrast the Father as he is represented in the story of the Prodigal Son: he *runs* to his son! He rejoices *passionately* over him! He throws a party." I could see the implications for dance: in a dance, two (or more!) people respond to each other in artistic communion. There is continual movement, an unfolding reciprocity. There is unchanging centering even as there is continual overture and response. I was recalling many things my dear young dancer has told me of the experience. There is no way, in a dance, that either partner has greater significance. The two are mutually interdependent. It would be impossible for "clunky," "static" substances ever to dance!—Or if they succeeded in dancing, they would no longer be clunky, static, substances. They would be persons in relation, perichoresis.

5. At this point in the talk, I began singing in my head the last line of the musical, *Les Miserables*: "To love another person is to see the face of God."

Dr. Fairfield offered a couple additional comments in conclusion:

If God is Relationship-in-Action, then the image of God must be relational. If, as in the West, you take human reason to be the way in which we image God, then the *imago Dei* is something that an individual possesses. But when you see that the image of God must be relational, Genesis 1:27 jumps off the page: "male and female he created them!" A single individual cannot embody the image of God; it takes at least two. Adam and Eve were different but alike.

Finally, in Christ God is setting about restoring the reciprocity, overcoming the isolation, and ultimately the death, that the Fall brought into relationships. God comes down to rescue the rebellious spouse, the daughter of Zion. The bridegroom comes in the flesh to welcome and restore his bride, the church. The times are consummated with the Marriage Supper of the Lamb.

A highly skilled couples' dance, such as swing or salsa, linking in a team one male and one female, especially evokes the "different but alike" dimension. Thus, it is not solo dancing that especially captures "the religious."[6] It's not about dance as channeling some divine in-breaking, some mystical force. It's about, in the body, achieving the most Trinity-likeness, transcribing the way of being of reality at its heart: particular persons in interpersonal communion. Partners in mutual trust wordlessly invite and respond to each other's moves to the end of lively communion. There is no absorption of the one into the other, but mutual enhancement: each shows the other off to advantage. It takes at least two to embody the image of God. The better your skills, the better the dance.

Our bodies know things, in their embodying, that may never have been worded by us. I do not think that any body knowledge on its own is incorrigible. In fact, I think the static clunkiness of the West, the disconnectedness of mind from body that often unwittingly infects our churches and our self-perceptions, is itself a case of body falsehood. But

6. Not even, as Lynn, Les's witty wife, sitting next to me, noted to me in a whisper with a grimace, what is known as liturgical dance!

364

even so, a body change can somehow put us in the way of knowing. To see Jupiter through a telescope, for example, you have to put your body in position with your eye to the eyepiece, at the right time on a cloudless night. To stand a prayer of a chance of fielding a fly ball, you have to position your body to receive it, not to mentions years of practice. To learn to touch type, you have to practice. My young dancer put herself and her partners in position to experience the communion that images the Triune perichoresis. And while dancing by itself could not have saved her, it put her in the way of redemptive healing. She grew in embodying the doctrine as her body tacitly reoriented its metaphysical stance.

This alignment of metaphysics and dance calls to mind a provocative comment by Elizabeth Moltmann-Wendel that I reported in an earlier chapter. "Despite [an alienation from our bodies brought on by the imposition of Descartes' Cogito, ergo sum], the need to live in today's world creates islands of dance, physical work, experiences of the body which explode theory."[7] Islands of dance—or other physical activity, such as athletics—body knowledge in action may explode the imposition of theory.

Where a disembodied, disconnected, static clunkiness still pervasively operates pretheoretically even (or especially) in circles of good-hearted, well-meaning Christians, it is reasonably likely that the outlook will be most effectively reshaped by something operating on the pretheoretical level. In particular, may not the very activity from which trinitarian theologians over centuries have drawn a picture of ultimate reality, if actually practiced by us in our bodies, move us toward an embodied apprehension of reality—and toward redemptive healing? And may it not also make us better knowers?

7. Moltmann-Wendel, *I Am My Body*, 11.

QUESTIONS FOR DISCUSSION

1. Share your thoughts about my claim that dancing may be metaphysically and theologically therapeutic.

2. Are there other human activities that work like this? What activities, and how do they offer this therapy?

~~~ 13

REALITY AS GIFT

Conversation with Philip Rolnick

COVENANT EPISTEMOLOGY SUGGESTS THAT the known is in some way personal. Here at the end of my exposition of interpersonhood, I want to address this matter directly, drawing together several threads only partially explored thus far. In a significant sense, this discussion forms a final link in the exposition of covenant epistemology.

The question is this: what must be the case about the real for it to lend itself so favorably to interpersoned covenantally constituted efforts to know? If it is so healingly effective to engage it as one engages a person one wishes to know personally, in what sense may we say that reality is personed or interpersoned? This fleshes out a metaphysical backdrop that itself warrants covenant epistemology: it shows why it makes sense to see knowing as relationally, interpersonally, covenantally constituted.

My goal is to specify in what respect reality is personal. That should come with an obvious qualification: specifying how anything is personal, even how we are ourselves personal, is an elusive affair. For all that, we use "personal" confidently, helpfully, to describe ourselves. But it is appropriate to expect of this exposition a result that is no less mysterious than is personhood itself.

Let us begin by revisiting a few of our conversants who have suggested that the known is personal. We can then work from this pool to clarify the matter. Additionally, we will deal in the claim of theologian and Polanyian Philip Rolnick that reality is gift.

THE REAL AS PERSONAL: PARKER PALMER

First let us mark again what Parker Palmer emphasized about the truth being personal:

I not only pursue truth but truth pursues me. I not only grasp truth but truth grasps me. I not only know truth but truth knows me. Ultimately, I do not master truth but truth masters me. Here, the one-way movement of objectivism, in which the active knower tracks down the inert object of knowledge, becomes the two-way movement of persons in search of each other. Here, we know even as we are known. To speak this way about knowing is not "merely poetic" (as if poetry could ever be mere!). Images such as these are faithful to our moments of deep knowing.[1]

Palmer, after quoting Polanyi to say that knowing proceeds by a kind of love, writes:

Polanyi's insights are obviously allied to the view that truth is personal. But by Christian understanding we must go one step further—and it is a critical step. Not only do I invest my own personhood in truth and the quest for truth, but truth invests itself personally in me and the quest for me. "Truth is personal" means not only that the knower's person becomes part of the equation, but that the personhood of the known enters the relation as well. The known seeks to know me even as I seek to know it; such is the logic of love.[2]

Palmer himself develops a case for the real as personal, as the all-important backdrop to knowing and impetus to teaching.

Searching for a model for the kind of community he feels is integral to knowing, Palmer concludes that reality itself offers the model. For reality itself is communal.[3] How we knowers historically have viewed nature has adversely impacted both nature and ourselves, and it needs to change. Following Ian Barbour,[4] Palmer says that current science supports the claim that reality is communal. "But today, our images of biological reality have been transformed. Ecological studies offer a picture of nature less focused on the terrors of combat than on the dance of communal collaboration, a picture of the great web of being."[5] Not only biology, but also physics suggests the communal nature of things. Palmer quotes Henry Stapp: "an elementary particle

1. Palmer, *To Know as We Are Known*, 59.
2. Ibid., 58.
3. Palmer, *Courage to Teach*, ch. 4.
4. Palmer quotes Barbour, *Religion in an Age of Science*.
5. Palmer, *The Courage to Teach*, 96.

is not an independently-existing, unanalyzable entity. It is, in essence, a set of relationships that reach outward to other things." Modern physics, Palmer avers, "had debunked the notion that knowing requires, or even allows, a separation of the knower from the known." Thus, "reality is a web of communal relationships, and we can know reality only by being in community with it." [6]

This shows Palmer the way to the kind of pedagogy he advocates.[7] He recommends that we to refer to the target of our inquiry, not as object, but as subject. "A subject is available for relationship; an object is not."[8] To treat the yet-to-be-known as subject rather than object is "to give it the respect and authority that we normally give only to human beings." We treat it like Nobel Prize-winning geneticist Barbara McClintock treated the ear of corn, "acknowledging its unique identity and integrity." Palmer cites McClintock's approach to genetic studies "by connecting with the world, not by disconnecting from it."[9] Her biographer quotes McClintock as saying that the key to her success was this: "Over and over again she tells us one must have the time to look, the patience to 'hear what the material has to say to you,' the openness to 'let it come to you.' Above all, one must have 'a feeling for the organism.'"[10] McClintock achieved, in her relation to ears of corn, "the highest form of love, love that allows for intimacy without annihilation of difference."

Palmer writes: "The center of our attention is a subject that continually calls us deeper into its secret, a subject that refuses to be reduced to our conclusions about it." According to Palmer, reality so treated responds.

> We say that knowing begins in our intrigue about some subject, but that intrigue is the result of the subject's action upon us: geologists are people who hear rocks speak, historians are people who hear the voices of the long dead, writers are people who hear

6. Ibid., 97. Palmer cites, for this quote, Zukav, *Dancing Wu Li Masters*, 94.

7. Palmer is blunt: On the objectivist "myth," he says, truth is a set of propositions about objects; education is a system for delivering those propositions to students; and an educated person is one who can remember and repeat the experts' propositions. Palmer's response: "There are only two problems with this myth: it falsely portrays how we know, and it has profoundly deformed the way we educate" (ibid., 101).

8. Palmer, *Courage to Teach*, 102.

9. Ibid., 54–55.

10. Palmer quotes from Keller, *Feeling for the Organism*, 198. I engage this text more fully in ch. 15.

the music of words. The things of the world call to us, and we are drawn to them—each of us to different things, as each is drawn to different friends. Once we have heard that call and responded, the subject calls us out of ourselves and into its own selfhood.[11]

This profound reciprocity in knowing and in pedagogy, Palmer underscores, is to be distinguished positively and radically both from absolutism (objectivism) and relativism (subjectivism).[12] Reciprocity in knowing and learning stems not from there being no objective reality, but from reality's far deeper objectivity, objectivity deeper than our depersonalizing epistemology has ever liberated us to recognize and celebrate. Reality is not two-dimensional; and it is not therewith non-existent. Reality is personal, interpersonally responsive.

Palmer draws a parallel between knowing and the spiritual discipline of contemplative prayer, deriving insights concerning the former from the latter:

> Prayer is opening myself to the fact that as I reach for that connecting center, the center is reaching for me. As I move toward the heart of reality, reality is moving toward my heart . . . In prayer, I not only address the love at the core of all things; I listen as that love addresses me . . . In prayer, I begin to realize that I not only know but am known. Here is the insight most central to spiritual experience: we are known in detail and depth by the love that created and sustains us . . . Yet, as love, it does not seek to confine or manipulate us. Instead, it offers us the constant grace of self-knowledge and acceptance that can liberate us to live a larger love.[13]

A view of reality that speaks of love at the core of all things, which I address and which addresses me, affirms the primacy of the covenantally-shaped personal in both knowing and in being. The accord between these phrases and what we have appropriated especially from Buber is evident. Referring to the verse of Scripture from which he has aptly drawn the title of his book, Palmer says:

> then we shall see face to face . . . This is the personal knowledge toward which Christian spirituality calls us, a knowledge that does

11. Palmer, *Courage to Teach*, 105.

12. Both relativism and absolutism, we may note along a Guntonian line, devolve schizophrenically into both monism and meaningless particularity.

13. Palmer, *To Know as We Are Known*, 11–12.

not distance us from the world but brings us into community, face to face. A knowledge that heals and makes whole will come as we look creation in the eyes and allow it to look back, not only searching nature but allowing it to search us as well. This will be perfect knowledge, Paul says, for "then I shall know as fully as I am known." The "objects" of knowledge will no longer be objects but beings with personal faces, related to us in a community of being, calling us into mutuality and accountability. It will be as the poet Rilke says, ". . . There is no place at all that isn't looking at you—you must change your life."[14]

Palmer evidently feels it critically important to underscore that there is something personlike about the invitation and agency of the real that is the subject of our attention. It is looking for us, looking to be known.

So according to Palmer, the real is communal, and the real is subject. The real exercises agency in entering dynamically into relationship with the knower. Yet it remains difficult to specify wherein reality is personal. How may we move further on to specify in what sense the real is personal, such that it lends itself so favorably to covenantal knowing?

THE PERSONAL IN THE REAL RECAPPED: MACMURRAY AND GUNTON

I first raised the possibility of the real as personal in connection with Polanyian subsidiary-focal integration: real is that which may manifest itself inexhaustively, surprisingly, transformatively. Where there are hints of surprising reciprocal response to our efforts to know, it suggests that somebody is there.

The theological vision to which we have returned repeatedly professes first of all a transcendent Person as the ultimate real. And any effort to develop an epistemology that would accommodate knowing such a Person finds the epistemological effort dramatically redrawn on the terms of that Person. If he is infinite, independent Person, it is only reasonable that all knowing is in some way knowing him. We are servant thinkers, stewarding a world that is his.

But also we have dwelt in the presence of several philosophers of religion who describe the central nerve of being and knowing as responsive encounter to the personal Other. That Other is, at first, our caregiver,

---

14. Palmer, *To Know as We Are Known*, 16.

but then also the world, and ultimately (and originally, in a theological vision), One who comes in gracious deliverance from outside ourselves and our situation. Working more phenomenologically than theologically, like Palmer they have described knowing as engagement with the personal.

Two of these conversation partners directly addressed the question of whether reality is personal: Macmurray and Gunton. Macmurray argues that the question, "Does God exist?," needs to be moved "from the field of the theoretical into the field of the personal," the field of action, of I do. The question thus becomes, is the real personal? The answer may be shown by contrasting the way of life engendered by an apperception, or formative perception, of the world as personal, and the way of life engendered by an apperception of the world as impersonal. There are two ways of apperceiving the world. Which, when thus contrasted, proves adequate? And which is wider, allowing the other?

He offers three arguments, we noted in chapter 8. First, the world contains us knowers as persons. To apperceive it impersonally, therefore, is fundamentally wrongheaded. Second, it is also absurd. For in an impersonal world, by definition, there can be no action. Everything happens; nothing is *done*. But that means we cannot meaningfully say that everything happens and nothing is done, because that itself is to do something significant. Thus, a non-personal world is imagined, not real. Third, Macmurray reminds us of the correlativity of I and the Other in the relation of action. In action, I am agent, the Other is agent as well, and thus personal.

Macmurray strives to locate the whole discussion in the field of action rather than reflection, but does so by reflecting! But the words nevertheless enable us to sense wordlessly that domain of action in which knower and known engage one another in personal reciprocity. Basic knowing is tacit, lived tactually. And to us persons, the Other comes, in knowing and action, underneath and around thinking, as personal. So to the question, is what exists personal, Macmurray responds in the affirmative. Fundamental, basic knowledge is in the field of action, and it is personal and interpersonal. In that field of action, of basic knowledge, reality is the personal Other.

We depersonalize in order to reflect; the field of the personal supports the theoretical. But not vice versa: the field of the theoretical delegitimates the field of the personal. That is, it does so if taken to be the sole domain of knowledge, the epistemic paradigm. We need only examine our culture's defective default to confirm what Macmurray is saying: an epistemology of knowledge as theoretical has indeed marginalized the personal as non-epistemic. In contradistinction to Macmurray, I suggested that theoretical nevertheless metonymously references the personal. However, on both construals the field of the personal is logically prior to the field of the theoretical. This too confirms that reality is the personal Other.

We saw that Gunton ascribes perichoretic relationality to the non-personal creation. But he states that it is not personal because it is not spirit, and it is not characterized by freedom. On the other hand, the state of affairs as he perceives it is such that he underscores that his is an ontology of communion, a social metaphysic. He shies away from the word, covenant, but lights on the asymmetry of gift and reception. We noted that gift and reception is something that, like covenant, only persons may enact.

Here, too, I suggested the tack of understanding the real's perichoretic, covenantal normativity—its systematically inexhaustive and surprising reciprocity—as metonymously referencing the presence of persons in relationship. The normative references the covenantal, and the covenantal references the interpersoned. A metonymous reference is a literary device precisely because the larger whole imbues or haunts the metonym with its fuller reality. Of course, we truncate something larger when we focus on the perichoresis, or on the covenant, or on the normative. But part of understanding them metonymously is keeping in view their necessary larger interpersonal context: persons are in the vicinity.

I introduce Rolnick's work at this point to help flesh out this idea of metonymous reference. Rolnick's notion of reality as gift offers a way to clarify a response to the question, in what sense is reality personal, and elucidate what these other conversation partners are saying. He will argue for the primacy of the personal, offering the motif of reality as gift.

THE PRIMACY OF THE PERSONAL:
NATURE IS NOT ENOUGH

Theologian Philip Rolnick's book, *Person, Grace, and God,* is an extended exposition of the concept of personhood as it must inform every Christian doctrine, and as it offers positive response to a secular age. He begins with a rich account of the historical development of the idea of personhood.[15] The ancient Christian concept of *incommunicabilis*, personal particularity—"the ipseity of the I"—requires that the thing that makes a person a person be unique to that person.[16] Central in understanding human personhood are the facts that person distinguishes, person unifies, and person is inherently relational.[17] Incommunicability means that each person knows her- or himself to be a center of relation, freedom, thought, and action that can only be her- or himself; she or he cannot become another center.[18] Without personal uniqueness to be a function of, the ultimate value of human life would make no sense, nor would communion with God.[19] "Ultimately," Rolnick claims, "to be a human person means that the totality of who we are is open-textured to the presence and power of God. Being drawn into relation with God secures who we are and recasts human nature in the light of divine parentage. This securing of identity and recasting of nature is personal."[20]

Rolnick makes it clear that nature "is not enough" to offer an account of personhood. Nature—genus and species and difference—is not enough. Aristotelian primary substance, in the case of human persons, must not be merely numerically specific.[21] Person is always something more than nature. "Nature is different from person, but it is a necessary correlate."[22]

Emphasizing this point, Rolnick takes an extended look at a neo-Darwinian understanding of evolutionary biology, which "so strongly develops an understanding of nature that person is called into question. If everything important about us can be explained naturalistically, then

15. Rolnick, *Person, Grace, and God*, pt 1.

16. Ibid., 4ff.

17. Ibid., 10.

18. Ibid., 54.

19. Ibid., 41.

20. Ibid., 9.

21. Rolnick shows that sustained development of the concept of the person came in the Christian tradition as it worked out the doctrine of the Trinitarian being of God—which you would expect if personhood has its origin with God (ibid., 15ff). The Cappadocian Fathers make crucial distinction between person and nature (ibid., 17ff). Augustine opens the question of redoing the Aristotelian quality of relation when speaking of God. Aquinas articulates this with finality (ibid., 24ff).

22. Ibid., 57. Rolnick continues: "We can imagine a nature without a person, e.g., a tree, fish, or stone, but we cannot imagine a person without a nature, whether human, angelic, or divine. In the human case, the natural origin of individuals is indisputable, the spiritual origin of human persons is a question of faith, whose articulation requires an account of nature, person, and their interrelationship."

person becomes a fictional excess."[23] He describes remarkable neo-Darwinian theories of kinship selection, reciprocal altruism, and the selfish gene. He shows that origins do not tell the whole story: these theories can neither avoid self-refutation nor account for the activity of persons.[24] "The very act of investigating genes indicates that we have to some degree transcended genes, for genes did not discover genetics . . . Accounts of human endeavor, not only in ethics and religion, but also in science, become unsustainable if we do not allow for human personhood and its quest for truth—a quest that transcends living for bread alone or genetic advantage."[25] The best and remarkable reductionist developments of evolutionary biology thus fall short of accounting for personhood. Rolnick rejects a claim by sociobiologist, E. O. Wilson that the species lacks any goal external to its own biological nature, calling it "a dogmatic claim that is no longer limited to biology but has instead become a metaphysical assertion about the ultimate nature of reality."[26] In point of fact, he says, "why should we accept the premise, that evolution rules out transcendence? . . . [T]he kind of consciousness that can discuss evolution, even in those who deny transcendence, actually indicates a relationship between evolution and transcendence . . . Attempting to explain the human person in terms of the lower levels is a strange use of the higher faculty—one that is being exercised in the very act of its denial."[27] He concludes: "The development of personal life is always undertaken within nature as it simultaneously rises above nature. As an explanation of nature, some theory of evolution is valid; as a denial of grace, it is unnecessary and unpersuasive . . . Except by the most tendentious sorts of arguments, Darwinism cannot adequately explain the full range

23. Ibid., 57. He continues: "In responding to these challenges it will become clear how much belief in that which transcends us and the concept of person are intertwined. Person is a concept rooted in faith, and such faith is itself a deeply personal act."

24. Ibid., 63–90.

25. Ibid., 75–76. Rolnick's criticism also includes contextualizing biological evolution in the even larger question of the evolution of forces and particles, as well as questioning evolution's ability to account for personal unity within complexity. He also shows that, while some theses in evolutionary biology signpost Christian virtues—Jesus' two-fold greatest commands, the enjoyment of God, self-love, and loving enemies for example—they nevertheless fall way short of explaining them (ibid., 77–90).

26. Ibid., 77.

27. Ibid., 77, 78.

of human love."[28] Rolnick is saying here that humans (thus humans as knowers) being persons is irreducible to natural explanation. There is no way to account for humans being persons if we work in Darwinian fashion from nature.[29] Rather, personhood is realized, not in violation of physical or biological law, but as a more-than, an "inherent excess."

This conclusion launches Rolnick's argument into "the realm in which the generosity of grace does not obviate the efforts of nature, but exceeds them." We will see presently that he will move from this account of personhood as irreducible to nature to speak of the primacy of the personal in all of reality.

The specific way that Rolnick is unfolding his argument brings to the fore the realization that the question of the real being personal and of the knower being personal are essentially linked. Knowers are embodied and situated. So this raises the question whether knower and knowing *reduce to* the embodied and situated. So far in covenant epistemology I have gently presumed that most people think of themselves, the knowers, as persons. But where nature has been presumed to be impersonal, it is important to affirm that the knower is irreducibly personal, and that seeing this is essential to a vibrant and healthful account of human knowing. Covenant epistemology requires human knowers to be persons. I will address this further in texture 8.

Our concern in this chapter is whether the real, as the object of knowledge, is personal. But in a reality in which humans exist, demonstrating that human personhood is irreducible to nature also provides an important piece of the argument that reality in general is personal. There is something about it that is irreducible to nature. With a view to our purposes here, this is a corollary of Rolnick's argument.

REALITY AS GIFT

In his argument for the primacy of the personal, Rolnick takes a further step to argue that the personal is intertwined essentially with *gift*. Working from an immensely rich theological understanding, Rolnick

28. Ibid., 90. Rolnick, the theologian, draws on Aquinas a good deal and finds his work helpful: Aquinas does not reject nature but works within it to show that the ultimate purpose of a rational creature exceeds the capacity of its own nature. Aquinas is one philosopher whom Marjorie Grene (I say this with a view to the upcoming texture's engagement of her theses in contrast to Rolnick's) never seems to engage.

29. Rolnick devotes another section of his argument to another popular challenge to personhood: the postmodern stance that the self is a fiction. (ibid., 91–189). This is right on, and makes his book a rich package.

proposes that person and gift are mutually constitutive. A gift, to be a gift, must be given by a person. And a world in which a gift cannot be given will also be a world in which personhood cannot appear.[30] Gift names that which is irreducible to nature, holding nature open to the interpersonal.

Here are other claims that he makes concerning personhood and gift: A gift is a new actualization of the good for the other.[31] Its highest form is self-giving.[32] A gift is only good, and thus a gift, as it actualizes the "absolute reference points, the true, the good, and the beautiful."[33] The true, good, and beautiful are thus the correlative of the personal. And friendship is gift sustained in relationship, where the gift is the continual freshness of the other in mutual self-giving.[34] So "in this continual quest for the more than, biology is utterly surpassed."[35]

Personhood thus requires two persons, Rolnick agrees. Persons cannot be persons in isolation.[36] Like Loder, Rolnick mines the additional *sine qua non* of an embodied face of the Other. He does so by engaging the work of Emmanuel Levinas. "Through his use of *face*, Levinas presents an embodied encounter with beings who cannot be subsumed under a concept," says Rolnick. "Face is a trope that focalizes much of the thought about personhood."[37] The face of the other is constitutive of us as persons. The face provokes generosity, gift, and it is the window of the freshness of the Other.

Gift, the freshness of the other, divine excess, are characteristic, Rolnick says, of all being. This is reminiscent of Loder's conviction of being as a dynamic letting-flourish. ("Letting," or consenting, is similar to giving in that it is an act that only a person can perform.) Indeed, it is being as fundamentally gift that the biblical doctrine of creation reveals. "Christian incarnational spirituality embraces the material realm from the vantage point of its relationship to God; in doing so, it

30. Ibid., 167, 164.

31. Ibid., 174.

32. Rolnick recurs repeatedly to Jesus' dictum that whoever will save his life must lose it, as a key to understanding the nexus of gift and personhood.

33. Ibid., 167–68.

34. Ibid., 182.

35. Ibid., 184.

36. Ibid., 51.

37. Ibid., 178. Rolnick works from Levinas' *Totality and Infinity*.

simultaneously values the material world and transcends it."[38] If creation is gift, then, logically, created persons are receivers and reciprocators in relationship, ultimately relationship with God. Gift and grace are only soteriological because they are first ontological, Rolnick affirms. That we are what we are by gift is apparent from our very birth, he argues: our very being is given, and we exist through choices of people other than ourselves. Gift and personhood are mutually implicative.[39] Gift-giving presupposes persons in relation. Interpersonhood intrinsically implies or involves gift, Rolnick is saying.

So Rolnick is affirming several of the motifs covenant epistemology has embraced—persons in communion, the face of the Other, and how it constitutes us as persons. He is linking them all to his own chosen motif of gift. Rolnick's notion of gift supplies another, perhaps fuller, way to get at the manner in which reality is personal, in which reality comports itself so favorably to a covenant epistemology.

GIFT, COVENANT, AND GIVER

Stop and think about what is involved in giving a gift. This highly sophisticated act, to be successful, involves all kinds of stipulations. For starters, a person must be in relation to another person, if not prior to the gift, certainly in the act of it. So Rolnick is correct to say that the notion of gift requires and implies this larger context. Further, a good gift strategically reflects both the unique giver and the unique recipient and the unique relationship the two have. The gift must match the nature of the covenant that constitutes the relationship—one should give a gift that is appropriate with respect to this covenant. Also, a gift must have no strings attached—else it is no longer a gift. So the giver has to have a sort of hands-off policy. The giver takes a risk that the gift might be rejected, and even that the giver's self might be rejected. On the other hand, its recipient should exercise a courtesy toward the giver that means that she can't do anything she wants with the gift—ignore it, destroy it, criticize it, presume about it, be ungrateful. Another thing: you can neither

---

38. Rolnick, *Person, Grace, and God,* 168.

39. I heartily concur with Rolnick, as over against some things that Jacques Derrida concludes in his deconstruction of gift, that giving a gift is a highly sophisticated human act that involves both the giver's and the recipient's knowing that a gift has been given. Rolnick, *Person, Grace and God,* 161–67. Rolnick cites Derrida's Villa Nova Roundtable discussion hosted by John Caputo, *Deconstruction in a Nutshell.*

give nor receive a gift without understanding that that is what you have done. Treating something as a gift involves, unavoidably, referencing its interpersonal context—else it isn't a gift. The recipient must recognize that it is a gift, or the action misfires, downed by cluelessness. And another thing: sometimes the gift is such that the giver himself invades and supersedes it—the giver shows up, eclipsing the gift. In that moment it is clear that it isn't about the gift so much as the giver. The gift is not the person him or herself, usually, but it could be—as in the case of sacrifice or other expressions of self-giving love. The recipient must cherish the giver more than the gift, and sometimes the giver as the gift.

All of these normative stipulations are themselves covenant-like, and they also show that a gift is fraught with the interpersoned. But it does not reduce to the interpersoned, nor does the interpersoned reduce to it. A gift requires a person as giver and one as recipient. The gift is neither the giver nor the recipient. But the act is so allusively complex that sometimes gift and giver blur together. One need only think of the gift of an engagement or wedding ring! It's proper to treat the gift with the honor due the giver, but you have to never love the gift as you would the giver.

To say that reality is gift says that reality isn't the Person/giver, generally, but that the Person/giver, and the recipient's relationship to that Person/giver, is integrally involved and near. And occasionally the Person/giver himself self-discloses, and the event comes to be about communion with him. It is that contexting interrelationship that constitutes the gift as gift. Gift, giver, and recipient are deeply implicated in mutuality, yet there must be a differentiated freedom, a perichoretic balancing of relationality and particularity, among these three.

The idea of gift sits well within the nexus of relationship and covenant that this book has labored to develop. Gift, like covenant, is a highly sophisticated interpersonal, normed, act. Only persons give; only persons covenant. Conversely, being a person involves gift and being a knower integrally involves covenant. More so than the motif of covenant, the motif of gift references the relational and the grace of the personal initiative and response. While we have had to emphasize that covenant is about graciousness in relationship rather than legal contract, no such effort is necessary with the motif of gift. (Or is it? Do we not often feel inappropriately obligated to reciprocate?) Gift captures the asymmetry of the relationship of gift and reception. It also accords with the notion of the gracious descent of God, of the surprising deliverance of the Holy, which more than restores us, which transforms us the recipients. Gift is divine excess, the flourishing of new being. And a good gift keeps on giving: it issues in future possibilities that, at the time we receive it, we can only sense. I like very much that Rolnick calls friendship "gift sustained in relationship," where the gift is the continual freshness of the other in mutual self-giving. Gift, like covenant, has as its ultimate aspiration interpersonal communion.

Rolnick's notion of gift thus accords with what Gunton has striven to argue about reality as perichoretically relational but not that nonhuman creation is person. We commit a *faux pas* if we mistake the gift for the giver. Yet the gift is profoundly imbued with the distinctiveness of the person who gives it. And gift is such a richly personally prescribed enactment that it is highly appropriate to speak of a wider ontology of communion: God in interpersonal, trinitarian, communion; human persons, so constituted in the gaze of the Personal Other; reality as gift—not itself person, but involved unavoidably in the interpersoned.

Also, the idea of gift, and of a giver who frequently comes and eclipses the gift, suggests what we have seen about the transformative moment of the I-You encounter. The face is the window of the freshness of the Other. To encounter the person, Buber said, involves a different mode of existence. Macmurray wrote that it involves the field of the personal. Both were suggesting that human knowing comes in two sorts. One sort is the personal, prior both in time and in eternity, central and transformative to all knowing and to knower. In that mode of existence we do not experience, so much as stand in relation to, the Other. That experience occurs in our engagement of the real—in the Oh-I-see-it! epiphany, in the Eucharist (the "good gift"!), in a seeing of the real that says, "So it is you!" It perichoretically studs our unfolding relationships with the yet-to-be-known. In that seeing, the real is Person, the Giver.

Ultimately, my theological vision inclines me to profess, that Person is Yahweh. Where we experience Person—although, of course, we may be only partly enlightened regarding whom we experience—the Person is God, the giver of the gift of the created real. Thankfulness, and covenant obligation, is superseded by communion. Then, taking the I of I-You into all of our subsequent I-Its aligns with an ongoing reverence which we feel toward the giver and in that person's honor accord to the gift.

And is it possible to receive a gift and have the gift lead you to the giver? Of course. Suppose someone gives you a gift anonymously. Aren't you both grateful and, by virtue of its generosity and your implied obligation, curious? Suppose, further, that you did not even at first know that what you were looking at was a gift . . . except that there was something curious and lavish about it that made you wonder if someone was behind it. Even in that state of unknowing, might not you determine to live in light of it having the status of a gift, and start to seek to understand it better, and start to seek the giver? This analogy thus accords with all that covenant epistemology emphasizes regarding how we go about knowing well.

Could reality *en toto* be Person, and not gift? In other words, could everything there is be a single Person—by default, God? That would mean that you and I, are him, are each other, are the world . . . I think. Or could reality *en toto* be impersonal—including ourselves? Or could God be nature—a pantheism? Could the known, nonhuman nature, be the person of God?

One premise that covenant epistemology's conversation partners have professed and argued strenuously is that person, to be person, takes more than one person—persons-in-communion. Interpersonal relationship must be such that each person is who they are only in relationship. Communion is not mutual absorption. It holds, in dynamic perichoretic relationship, relationality and particularity. The persons involved remain themselves and actually become more uniquely themselves. It is this rich interpersonal dynamism the telltale indicators of which permeate knowing as we attend to it. I believe that all the alternatives I specified in the last paragraph reduce ultimately to an incoherent yet depersonalizing monism. But even if this were not logically entailed, persons-in-communion is that state of affairs which human knowing signposts.

I, as a person, am never absorbed into God. This reflects the Christian vision into which, according to Rolnick, the notion of personhood was born. Its climactic hope is not, God *is* us, but rather, God *with* us—Emmanuel.[40] One way to see this is that God himself, as Person, is covenantally bound to accord us persons perichoretic space for constitutive particularity, within the relationality that also constitutes us. Thus, we knowers are never God. For the same reasons, the nonhuman creation isn't God either.

40. Meek, "'With'—the Most Christian Word."

THE SIGNATURE ASYMMETRY OF THE PERSONAL

Throughout this study we have encountered pairs related in an odd way that might well be called asymmetric. Asymmetry, with a distinctive kind of mutuality, is a conceptual relationship that recurs. One member of the pair is truncated with respect to the other. It could never entail or reduce the other. But it always suggests the other. I spoke at the outset about how neither focal nor subsidiary can be construed as necessary for the other, except in the actual relation of transformation in which they are so creatively joined. The relationship of subsidiary to focal is that of part to whole—when the item is construed subsidiarily—looked *from* rather than looked *at*. I have argued that this distinctive Polanyian epistemology instantiates perichoresis.

I spoke of my gradual conclusion that truth actually must nest in a larger box—covenant, and covenant, in turn, in interpersonal relationship. The normative is covenantal, and the two constitute the structure of interpersonal relationship. But relationship never must be seen to reduce to the normative.

We have seen several of our conversation partners endeavor to articulate this asymmetry. Macmurray's field of the personal, as over against the theoretical, stakes out an all-encompassing domain implied by but not reduceable to the theoretical. Buber distinguished two modes of being, I-It and I-Thou. Newbigin talked of "another kind of knowing" that is intimately interpersonal. Gunton has distinguished perichoretically relational from interpersonally social, arguing for the asymmetry of gift and reception. Rolnick opts for gift. Several of these have been attempts to specify wherein the real is person.

I have attempted to speak of the one as being metonymous with respect to the other. The normative and the covenantal metonymously reference interpersoned relationship. I have suggested that Frame's triad bespeaks the personal the way Williams' covenant does. Theoretical knowledge metonymously references basic knowledge, the communion of the knower interpersonally with the known. The idea of metonymy contrasts to Macmurray's apparent effort to oppose theoretical knowledge to basic knowledge and thus to delegitimate theoretical knowledge. But it accords with Buber's description of how all our I-Its may be imbued with the I of I-You. And it accords with Gunton and with Rolnick. Like the normative and the covenantal, perichoresis is distinctively interpersoned without being the persons in view. The same may be said of gift. Also, we may apply Rolnick's talk of more-than, of nature not being enough, to this asymmetry. Were you to reduce the whole to the metonym, it would no longer be either the metonym or the whole.

My own analysis now trembles on the edge of inscrutability as I suggest that perichoresis itself is perichoretic. For what the metonymous behavior of the metonym does is leave room for the other, the whole, to be itself. It is a relationship that accords space for particularity. This suggests the profound inference that this signature asymmetric mutuality which I have repeatedly called metonymy is itself uniquely the dynamism of the personal. The more-than is uniquely, exclusively, personal.

May we not settle, in light of this discussion, for saying that reality, specifically nonhuman creation beyond myself, is metonymously personal? And does this not imply that it would actually be inappropriate violation of the boundaries of perichoresis to "reduce" it to being person? Yet, precisely because it is metonymously personal, we may expect our knowing engagement of it to be studded by definitive moments of I-Thou encounter. Sometimes the Giver accompanies the gift and transforms it into himself.

The characteristic manner in which reality is personal displays this sophisticated signature. Reality—the known, the object of knowledge—is metonymously personal—or the Person himself. The idea of gift, I believe, gathers up my efforts to speak of the asymmetry, the metonymic relationship, which has recurred repeatedly in this exploration. There is a sense in which the nonhuman real is not interchangeable with a person, yet it all is so pervasively imbued with the Giver that we may encounter him, anticipatively, prototypically, implicitly, or in full awareness of who he is, in any corner of his world. Reality as gift is such that sometimes the Giver shows up. And when he does, that's the main act.

Thus I specify my answer regarding the sense in which the real is personal: The real is gift. It is characterized by more-than, divine excess, the continual freshness of the Other. Gift is metonymously personal: it is fraught with the personal, imbued with the dynamic interpersonal relationship which contexts it, yet freely distinct from Giver and recipient.

And this sense of reality is something we would do well to cultivate in our epistemic comportment. We should love to know. We should exercise an epistemic behavior suited to the personal features of the real, with the continual anticipation the we may also be apprehended in encounter by the personal Other it signposts. The world is personal in that it becomes itself in response to personal, covenantal love. The claim of covenant epistemology, that we take the covenantally constituted, interpersonal relationship as a paradigm of all knowing, involves the claim that knowing is metonymously interpersonal as well. As such, it is a form of the implicit love of God. This implies and is implied by "our moments of deepest knowing."

Our defective epistemic default has woefully and despicably underrepresented a lively, systematically inexhaustive, reality, along with a perichoretically dynamic knowing. It is time for reorientation. Covenant epistemology gives us every reason to reorient to the personal. For whether we go at it phenomenologically or from a theological profession, we are led to construe the known as metonymously personal in its generous, ever surprising, dynamism. Reality as we know it is metonymously personal. Person, persons, and interpersonal relation, are in the vicinity.

QUESTIONS FOR DISCUSSION

1. In your own words express the claims of this chapter regarding how the real is personal.

2. What do you like about the idea that reality is gift? How does it affect the way we engage the world? How would this be healing?

3. How does this view of reality confirm covenant epistemology?

Texture 8

STOPPING SHORT OF PERSONHOOD

Inadvertent Insights from Marjorie Grene

KNOWERS ARE EMBODIED AND situated. I noted in the last chapter that this raises the question whether knower and knowing *reduce to* the embodied and situated. I have not thus far directly responded to this so much as gently presumed that most people think of themselves, the knowers, as persons. But where nature has been presumed to be impersonal, it is important to affirm that the knower is irreducibly personal, and that seeing this is essential to a vibrant and healthful account of human knowing. Covenant epistemology requires human knowers to be persons.

Our concern in the last chapter was whether the real, as the object of knowledge, is personal. But in a reality in which humans exist, demonstrating that human personhood is irreducible to nature also provides an important piece of the argument that reality in general is personal. This is the corollary of Rolnick's argument strategy, as I sketched it.

I want to underscore his point that nature is not enough to make sense of personhood, and thus not enough to make sense of nature itself. I want to do this by listening to veteran philosopher Marjorie Grene and her extended argument concerning what it is to be human—what it is that makes humans persons.[1] I think that her argument lends support to Rolnick's argument in a way that she did not intend.[2]

1. This argument encompasses the entirety of her wonderful *Philosophical Testament*, written when she was in her nineties.

2. I cull the argument of this texture from my "Marjorie Grene at Fifty." In it I set Rolnick's theses, as well as Loder's, alongside Grene's for the sake of comparison and contrast.

"Was wär' ich ohne meine Umwelt?" Grene reports, was her reaction in her first college philosophy class, in which the professor was trying to make his students into Cartesian disembodied minds.[3] She suggests this as the unifying, ever-present thrust of her maverick career.[4] *Testament,* her most recent subtotaling of decades of evolving thought[5] categorically bears out her commitment to challenging what elsewhere she has called one of the greatest falsehoods of philosophy: the *cogito.*[6]

Grene's *cogito*-challenging *Umwelt* has been, from her undergraduate days as a zoology major, the biological environment characterized by evolving life. Thus, her response has been to develop philosophy of biology along with continuing attention to epistemology and perception. The driving question of *Testament* is, "What makes us humans the odd kind of animal that we are?" And what, in the end, makes us *persons*? That this latter question is central to the book only becomes apparent at its end. Grene notes, with a slightly puzzled and disappointed air, that she had intended to name the book, *Persons.* But, having reached its end, she feels that her venture has fallen short of the mark even though this effort has been perhaps her best shot. What intrigues me is that the set of responses Grene develops to her question, despite growing out of her unwavering commitment to a biological, evolutionarily developing *Umwelt,* nevertheless are uncannily personal, in the manner in which we have been developing that. They are insightful as well. As necessary conditions, which she calls them, her distinctives of human animals do get us a long way down the road toward personhood. But I believe that her wistfulness regarding the

3. That is, "Where would I be without my environment/surroundings/situation/surrounding world?" This is my guess at its meaning; I will keep to using the German, *Umwelt,* throughout. Grene, "Intellectual Autobiography," 4.

4. This is especially apt because "maverick" also includes years of farming, sheep care, and child raising. She mentions, for example, having a difficult time believing the constitutive role of the Kantian mind when alongside Kitty, her grey Percheron mare! (Grene, *Philosophical Testament,* 35) (This blend is philosophy at its richest, though not one even accredited by most practitioners of the discipline.)

5. Think of it—she studied with Heidegger, Jaspers, and Carnap!

6. Grene, *Knower and the Known,* 88.

success of her project is well-founded, for an account of personhood must in the end take a logical leap beyond the *Umwelt*, to acknowledge persons, and, I believe, Person. So Grene's effort, inadvertently, supports Rolnick's claim.

What makes us humans the odd sort of animals we are? Here is a brief summary of Grene's theses. *Humans distinctively make knowledge claims.* Given that rescuing the *Umwelt* from the *cogito* is a central concern, what it means to know requires recasting along lines consonant with Polanyi's insights. This is the worthy mission to which Grene has devoted her career.[7] What is more, humans are, thanks to Merleau-Pontyean *Dasein*, *cogitos* with thickness in spatiality—*Umwelten* and duration—"Most fundamentally . . . *I am a history*."[8] Then, thanks to nature being Darwinian, *a human is a biological individual capable of becoming a responsible person* through participation in culture (which is cultivated nature).[9] Our biological natures, she says, set limits to what we can achieve as knowers and to the ways in which we can achieve it. These limits are not such as would engender materialism, reductivism, or cognitive science, Grene scornfully insists; but on the other hand, she says just as scornfully, they are such as would exclude God or any appeal to such a Being with a view to ethics or personal mortality, and presumably personhood.[10] Fourth,

10. Ibid., 109–12. Atheism as an assumptive parameter is evident throughout her work. In what I have read of her work, she never engages the alternative head-on. She believes that Darwinism, whatever else it has accomplished, rules out the possibility of theism. "[O]nce we find ourselves as natural beings at home in a Darwinian nature, fundamentalist Christianity or any other literal and dogmatic belief in a Transcendent, All-Powerful Maker and Lawgiver with a Mind somehow analogous to ours (or to which ours is somehow analogous) must wither away" (Grene, *Philosophical Testament*, 111–12). Grene continues on to distinguish and even countenance "religiosity at its best," which would be "a sense of the vastness and vast variety of nature that must have impelled the work of natural historians like Darwin and still drives the efforts of many working biologists . . . " to the end of denying "the crude Provinian thesis: Darwin in, religion out." It seems that perhaps her main objection to theism is modern philosophy's problem of the incompatibility of determinism and free will, which she articulates in its seventeenth-century garb, and as the desperate situation which Darwin betters: "It removes the One Transcendent

7. Grene, *Philosophical Testament*, chs. 1–3.

8. Ibid., 85 (ch. 4). Italics mine.

9. Ibid., 107 (ch. 5).

humans are beings in a world, where the world is where we are and therefore who we are as human animals—thus, the primacy of the real.[11]

Opening a section she calls, *Coping,* Grene sketches an account of perception which she feels is the account that Polanyi and Merleau-Ponty themselves lacked to ground their insights. She acquires it from Eleanor and James Gibson, and it involves replacing the modernist sensation-perception one-two with a flow, an array, in which the animal is always immersed, situated, and in which it discriminates invariants and affordances.[12] Perception is "raising certain invariants to the level of affordances." What happens is that an animal, say, a squirrel, sees the world in terms of nuts and places to squirrel them; the squirrel sees some of the array's invariants as affordances. Invariants are the constancies of the world; affordances are species-selected ones of those that are significant because they afford the animal what the animal wants or needs.

Humans are distinct from other animals in that they possess the potential for limitless variety in raising invariants to the level of affordances. We only have to stop and contrast the people we know and the diversity of things they notice and cultivate. Humans have an exceptional capacity to do this, and in so doing make culture.[13] Here Grene aligns "raising invariants to the level of affordances" with Polanyi's epistemology: this is taking what is normally subsidiary and making it focal.[14] Her proposal

Source of All Being and so eliminates the problem in its radical form" (Grene, *Philosophical Testament,* 98). (It would be easy to bring Gunton's historical analysis of the cultural fallout of the problem of the one and the many to bear on Grene's stated assumption.) In Meek, "Grene at Fifty," I argue that it perhaps should have occurred to her that, if there was such a horrific problem with the Cartesian *cogito,* large enough to devote a lifetime to its redress, that its ideational fallout also might have fostered widespread misperceptions of God. Her aversion to his existence both causes and is caused by her own unexamined modernist preconception of him. Grene repudiates Cartesianism, but her atheism, in particular her view of freedom, still reflects it.

11. Grene, *Philosophical Testament,* 115 (ch. 6).

12. Ibid., 138.

13. Ibid., 147–48.

14. Admittedly, I am still working to understand the Gibsonian approach, but I am a bit puzzled why she does not also note that to move in integration from particulars to pattern is also to lower affordances to the level of invariants. In which case, the Gibsonian phrase aligns with the reverse Polanyian sequence that

emphasizes continuity, not discontinuity, between humans and other animals: our making culture, using tools, language, and pictures, is of a piece with animal perception, thus rooting us in our *Umwelt.*

But now, what makes us odd? And what conditions point in the direction of personhood? Our odd way of coping involves *symboling*, of which language is a massive piece or manifestation, but so is certainly distinctly human behavior such as ritual and even etiquette. Symboling is enacting and enforcing the system of symbols and of symbolic activities that makes a particular people group the group that it is. The purpose of all of this is not primarily communication; the purpose is rather the construction of a cultural world.[15]

But even this, apparently, does not set humans apart from some animals, sending Grene in search of additional features. In view of the evolu-

tion of our higher capacities that actually leave us with greater flexibility, what must evolve for our coping is a sense of purpose, and the ability for individuals and groups to make and keep promises and commitments. *Humankind are the promising primates, in both senses.*[16] Promising is indicating in the now what will be or what must not be, the power to bring together what is and what is not. And these become a new necessity, "obligations we take to ourselves to fulfill demands made on us by something that both defines and transcends our particular selves."[17] Promising is integral to symboling, as it is to all language. And promising is as essential to making a knowledge claim as it is to every other dimension of human life. For

16. Ibid., 16ff.

17. Ibid., 169. Grene proceeds to answer the possible charge of relativism with Polanyi's paradox of self-set standards; but in the other direction, she believes that the Polanyian stance rules out as improper any further appeal to "our founding fathers' budget of self-evident truths," despite the precariousness of the paradox. My surmise is that Grene would lump with inappropriate regressions, such as Polanyi's own "treacherous footnote," talk of a transcendent God that presumes to cut itself loose from responsible profession or *Umwelt*ish roots.

just is integration itself: transformation of what is focal (attended to) into what is subsidiary (attended from). It raises the question whether the Gibsonian account of perception does after all supply what Polanyi lacked.

15. Ibid., 156ff. All of this, by the way, puts me in mind of the Derridean claim that everything is text.

humans to be knowers, they must be promisers. They are distinct from other animals in this respect.

Yet symboling and promising are apparently not yet *it,* for Grene writes another and final chapter, in which she attempts directly to specify that which makes us persons.[18] What actually happens in the chapter is that, amidst a good deal of wing-flapping (no disrespect intended), it seems, she lights on a perch. That perch is that *human persons and personhood are/is "a center of responsibility to principles, ends, causes, something beyond myself to which I owe allegiance."*[19] She quotes with approval Augustine's statement: "This is my freedom, that I am subject to this truth." "To act freely," she continues, "as a responsible center of decision and performance, is in some sense to give oneself, of one's own accord to some principle or task or standard that obliges one's obedience or one's assent." It may be a precarious balance, she admits; but she is sure as she can be that persons are not just nervous systems. Nature is not enough.

She lights on a second perch. The final, highest, quality of personhood that she identifies is one that, in fact, not all humans achieve. It is *authenticity:* some few "live their lives out of a center that is truly theirs."[20] Here she cites a few students she has known who had endured the severe suffering of the First World War, "who had somehow transcended that early disfigurement, who were in some extraordinary fashion *really* themselves." It is an achieving of a kind of integration, a gathering of their lives into one. Here she illustrates by telling the story of the illiterate tumbler of Our Lady. The rare authentic person lives her/his life out of a center that is not self-centered. And finally, Grene links this to knowledge and to persons as knowers: "perhaps one could reasonably maintain that the honest making of a knowledge claim does

18. Grene titles the chapter, "On Our Own Recognizances." "Recognizance" is not a word she actually employs in the text. Dictionaries define it as a formal avowal, a bond, pledge, token, or acknowledgment. This does not help me completely to grasp her choice of the title. Obviously it alludes to her immediately prior discussion of humans as promisers. It may suggest that she herself means to follow through on what she has promised to do.

19. Ibid., 178ff. Italics mine.

20. Ibid., 185ff.

exemplify in a limited sphere the kind of commitment characteristic, more globally, of the authentic individual singled out now and then."[21]

Thus, in *Testament*, offering a response to the question, what sets humans apart as unique with respect to other animals, Grene proposes profound concepts such as a Polanyian "raising invariants to the status of affordances," symboling, purpose, promise, responsibly self-giving (note the *gift* here!) commitment, and centering, all of which she feels are essential to what makes humans distinct from other animals, and essential to understand human knowing, which is her primary agenda. These are telling. As a set, they accord profoundly with what covenant epistemology identifies as parameters of a responsible account of human knowing. They are what covenant epistemology has argued are irreducibly personal, as well as being essential to human knowing.

Why does Grene remain dissatisfied with her own account of necessary conditions of humanness, such that she cannot bring herself to title the

book, *Persons?* Is it perhaps that these last features—promising, responsible commitment, and authenticity—those she deems most central to humanness, are only "precariously," to use her own descriptor, supported by a studied reference to the natural? Is it that the entire enterprise of offering general *differentiae* of personhood inevitably falls short, that concrete personhood is ultimately irreducible to generalities of nature? Grene's findings inadvertently underscore the irreducibility of the interpersonal along with the necessity of the personal for humanness and human knowing. This is surprising and perhaps that much more telling because they grow out of her commitment to Darwinian nature. If, for her, promising, commitment, and authenticity remain rooted in an ecological *Umwelt*, so much the better. But an exclusively ecological *Umwelt* alone cannot complete the picture of personhood. Grene's philosophical testament signposts something—someone—more.

A comparison of Grene's and Rolnick's identified features of personhood reveals some overlap and, I feel, a fundamental resonance, but also

21. Ibid., 188.

390

a remarkable and profound difference. Rolnick has challenged the necessity of a connection between Darwinism and atheism. He thus makes it possible for a theistic rounding out of personhood to be profoundly consistent with Grene's remarkable *Umwelt*-respectful findings. Perhaps as Aristotle is to Aquinas is Grene's account to Rolnick's. Only with the needless and unsupported assumption that celebrating animals responding in their habitats excludes the possibility of God can Grene's great insights be made out to exclude Rolnick's. In fact, when we remove that disputable assumption, Grene's insights receive the rich rounding out that "the primacy of the personal" can give them. Persons in relation symbol, promise, commit, and become authentic. Persons are indeed centers of incommunicability and agency, only ever constituted as such in the loving gaze of the Other.

Rolnick's account is in fundamental accordance with the philosophical complexity that is the genius and the challenge of Polanyi's subsidiary-focal relationship. In fact, I believe that Rolnick's thesis more consistently lives out the balanced implications—implications which Polanyi in some fashion did glimpse—than Grene, ever the champion of Polanyi's epistemological insights, but ever the atheist, is able to do. For Rolnick's continual talk of the inherent excess and the freshness of the finite suggest a transforming and transformative dimension of reality as well as of human knowing. What catalyzes transformation, I believe, is person, the face of the Other, paradigmatically.

And Grene's *Umwelt*, which in career-long defiance of the *cogito* she has cherished and oriented by, is, if you grant Rolnick's outlook, itself *gift*.[22] Thus Grene is right, for more reasons than biological or epistemological, to cherish it.

A final note: Grene's work exemplifies what I have been maintaining all along—that Christian unbelievers doing profitable epistemology will offer proposals consonant with covenant epistemology, or profit from covenant epistemology; and Christian unbelievers knowing well can be said to be prototyping knowing God. Knowing is a form of the implicit love of God.

22. Rolnick, *Person, Grace, and God*, 216.

QUESTIONS FOR DISCUSSION

1. What do you find surprising about Marjorie Grene's philosophical testament?

2. Do you agree with this texture's thesis that personhood is irreducible to nature? Why or why not?

3. In what ways are humans promising primates? How does promise—covenant—anchor all that we are?

PART FIVE

Covenant Epistemology

CONTOURS OF COVENANT EPISTEMOLOGY

LET US PICTURE OURSELVES, having made numerous daylong hikes, as emerging from the forested and clefted pathways and having reached the top of the peak that was our destination. From here we may gaze back over where we have come, take stock of where we are and of the significance of our achievement, and of what we need to go from here.

Here is an all-inclusive sketch of my argument for the claim that we take as a paradigm of all knowing the interpersonal, covenantally constituted, relationship.

1. We in the West have a defective epistemic default that has wrought havoc and needs reorientation. Covenant epistemology and its epistemological therapy distinctively supply that healthful reorientation.

2. Knowing is subsidiary-focal integration. It is a transformative event. As such, knowing can be seen to be fraught with the personed. Part of this is identifiable covenantal dimensions.

3. Knowing has a normative dimension.

4. Knowing's normative dimension is covenantal.

5. Covenant is the structural constitution of interpersonal relationship. So covenant metonymously references interpersonal relationship. Interpersonal relationship unfolds dynamically and thus is profoundly akin to knowing as subsidiary-focal integration.

6. Interpersonhood involves persons as beings-in-communion, I-You encounters, the void-Holy dynamic, the face of the Other, and perichoresis. All these in turn imply interpersoned dimensions of all knowing. Knowing's context is interpersoned, and knowing's central event is I-You encounter. Perichoresis describes the unfolding rhythm of relationship.

7. The real is metonymously personal. As such it is especially suited to being known by a knowing that is fraught with the interpersoned. This too supports the covenant epistemology thesis.

8. Taken together, all these dimensions enrich the epistemic act the way the whole enriches the part in a metonymy. We have augmented knowing to accredit the interpersoned which haunts it.

9. In this chapter I will show that covenant epistemology compares favorably to standard accounts. This confirms covenant epistemology

10. In the final chapters I will argue in effect that this approach yields a strategy that makes us better knowers and heals the world. This confirms covenant epistemology.

11. Hence, we should take covenantally constituted interpersonal relationship as our paradigm of all acts of knowing.

In this last part I will summarize covenant epistemology using a taxonomy common to standard discussions of epistemology. Also in this chapter I will specify how covenant epistemology challenges and heals the defective epistemic default which thwarts our efforts as knowers. Then I will turn to what is perhaps my favorite discussion in this entire discourse, explicating how we may invite the real. In the last chapter, I sum our achievement in a way that will encourage us all for our respective journeys ahead.

Standard introductions to epistemology state positions regarding the objects, source, nature, and justification of knowledge.[1] I propose to do that in this chapter. There is an important qualification to be made. The standard strategy itself reflects commitment to the epistemological paradigm that covenant epistemology challenges. Standard epistemologies often do not challenge deeply enough our fundamental outlook on knowing. It is difficult even to utter the word, "knowledge," let alone go on to articulate its objects, sources, nature, and justification, without presuming that knowledge consists exclusively of statements with a positive truth value, disconnected from any embodied root, and tested in a

---

1. I am drawing on my own awareness of the discipline in general. Standard reference works in epistemology, as well as standard texts and anthologies, testify to my general claims about epistemology in shaping this chapter. See, for example, Dancy and Sosa, eds., *Companion to Epistemology*; and Greco and Sosa, eds., *Blackwell Guide to Epistemology*.

way that calls into question their very engagement with the world and ourselves the knowers. I believe that standard epistemology also presumes that knowledge is distinct from belief and from value, that faith and reason are opposed, and that theory (knowledge) is distinct from and precedes application or action—the daisy of dichotomies. I believe that that is what readers of standard epistemologies hear and only find confirmed in the reading. Covenant epistemology disputes all of these claims, offering a model that redraws the playing field, so to speak. So long as this mismatch is kept in mind, however, to sketch its position with respect to standard categories is a valuable exercise for distinguishing covenant epistemology from more common approaches.

Also in contrast to standard presentations, this book has attempted a pattern of engagement which reflects the message of covenant epistemology: knowing as evolving via conversations on the way. I have wanted the effect to be one of layering, insights pieced together from a plurality of voices and disciplines, with occasional lateral forays, meant to paradigm and to evoke, more than to describe exhaustively and systematically. I have wanted to do it this way also, in part, in order to invite you, the reader, into the conversation. Also, this book chronicles my own journey of developing covenant epistemology. Finally, I have laid the book out this way because reorienting one's default epistemic mode involves prolonged meditation to the end of transformation, more so than information and argumentation stripped of an interpersonal context. But this chapter, in dealing with the standard questions, draws from the conversations but presents the position of covenant epistemology more systematically.

THE OBJECTS OF KNOWLEDGE: COVENANT REALISM, COVENANT ONTOLOGY

The question of the objects of human knowledge is as follows: In our knowing, what are the proper objects of knowing? For knowledge to be knowledge, what things must you access in your knowing? For ancient Platonic philosophers, for example, the question of the objects of knowledge was the most important question. Your knowing is only legitimate and reliable knowing if you are cognizing with respect to the right objects. For Platonists, those proper objects are the transcendent Forms, the objective essence/standards—piety, justice, horseness, etc.—in which individual things "participate." The individual instances of those things themselves—a pious or just act, an individual horse, etc.—are not the proper objects of knowledge for a Platonist.

To talk about the objects of knowledge is, in a way, to do metaphysics from the vantage point of, or from within, epistemology. For you are making some claims about the reality that we are knowing, the features it has that render it knowable. Talking about metaphysics (what is real?) or ontology (what is being?) is talking about reality in itself. But the interface between epistemology and metaphysics is glaringly evident: you can't talk about knowing without presuming something about what you know (the nature of the object of knowledge), and you can't talk about reality without presuming that you are knowing it.

For me, one of the most important questions regarding knowing—important enough for me to write a dissertation on it—has always been whether, in our knowing, we access the real. If the answer to this is no, it has always seemed to me, then what I am doing isn't knowing and it isn't worth the effort. But how to justify a yes has always seemed problematic. Answering yes is what is known as epistemic realism; answering no, epistemic anti-realism. We have already seen that covenant epistemology affords a fresh way to espouse epistemic realism.

But many people hold the anti-realist position, arguing that our epistemic efforts do not access an independently existing, objective world. Some argue that this is because our epistemic efforts are always shaped by our interpretation. This is a *non sequitur*, we have seen throughout this book: just because your knowing is an interpretive, embodied, situated, traditioned, viewpoint does not mean it does not engage the world. Just because your knowing is so shaped does not mean that these factors detract from your knowing and that we should seek to eliminate them. I have argued that it is precisely *because of* our viewpoint-beachhead that we do access the world. The view from Mt. Washington is Pittsburgh at its best. Having acknowledged that we *view* the world, of course we can talk about the *world* we view. That's the advantage of Polanyi's idea of subsidiary knowledge: subsidiary and focal, we have seen, within the integration, each flesh out and transform the other.

Some anti-realists go even further, to a point of extreme subjectivism (I know *only* my subjective viewpoint), relativism (What I take to be true is only relative to my, or my group's, situation), and skepticism (What I "know" isn't really knowledge, just opinion.) This state of affairs can be assessed negatively: I don't know anything at all; but some people find it liberating: I can be and do and think whatever I want.

A popular realist stance is known as critical realism. In the wake of Immanuel Kant's famous *Critiques* (ca. 1800), which brought to the fore for the first time the immense active contribution that the mind makes to knowledge, it was generally understood that it was no longer appropriate for anyone to be a direct, or naïve, realist. Such an unfortunate person would think that he/she passively perceived things in the world the way those things "really are." A critical realism, in contrast, is more sophisticated and virtuous, it is implied, naming the contributions of the human mind, of the knower's hermeneutic bent, of social setting, and what have you, and issuing regular and extensive qualifications concerning what we can't really know of what reality in itself is. This is a greatly oversimplified caricature, but not an unfair one. I do not mean to say that no good comes from critical realist studies. However, the emphasis remains on what keeps you from knowing the world, and what you need to try to diminish in order to know it better.

In contrast to anti-realist claims, Polanyian epistemology has shown the way to be realists, having creatively reoriented the dichotomous default that opposes knowledge and belief, mind and body, etc. And also because of that creative reorientation, it is possible to take a stand that need not share the negative outlook of critical realism either. Polanyi shows how we indwell the subsidiaries, many of which are unspecifiable, to unlock the objective world. And we know we have made contact with reality precisely because it is fraught with unspecifiable future prospects, precisely because it reshapes us reciprocally. An exact representational correspondence of knowledge to reality would be possible only if the world were two-dimensionally wooden—actually, *less* real. That this is not possible is nothing to regret. That this is not possible is not a concession to skepticism, it is to affirm the magnificently greater three-dimensionality of the real. It is to affirm situational and temporal dynamism of the sort, I believe, that only the personed and the interpersoned describes. Reality is far deeper and richer, as personal, than we have given it the credit of being.

Marjorie Grene, who shares Polanyi's fundamental epistemic commitments, speaks of "the primacy of the real."[2] She says that she toyed with calling herself a naïve realist—that so-deemed unfortunate term!—

2. Grene, *Philosophical Testament*, ch. 6.

in her Polanyian rejection of the modernist legacy that drives *critical* realism. A colleague counseled her that that would be inadvisable, and so she settles for the phrase, the primacy of the real. The term aptly expresses the realism of covenant epistemology. It suggests that the real, not a disembodied-mind knower, is in the driver's seat.

Covenant Realism

In studied contrast to critical realism, I want to propose *covenant* realism. Covenant realism, I believe, grows out of Polanyian epistemology, hand-in-hand with covenant epistemology. Covenant realism consists of the following theses: In our knowing, we access the real, in fact, the real has transformative primacy in our knowing. Our knowing relationship with the real displays covenantal features, which by definition pertain in interpersoned relationship. Thus, good knowing practices involve covenantally interpersonal excellence. Also, because knowing is covenantal, humans' epistemic relationship with the real is, in an important sense, as prescriptive as it is descriptive, and about mutual transformation rather than exclusively about information collecting. The goal of human exchange with the world is not exhaustive certainty but dynamic, mutually healing, communion. And finally, reality itself is such that it responds favorably to covenantally appropriate overtures. The real is metonymously personal.

The relative superiority of covenant realism to critical realism is important to grasp: reality responds better and more transformatively, not to criticism, but to covenant faithfulness. An over-arching critical posture itself inhibits the disclosure of the real.[3] By contrast, great lovers make great knowers. Covenant realism exhibits the proper, horse-before-the-cart, approach.

This is a book about knowing, and about what we need to bring to efforts to know that will make us great knowers. What we need to bring is the comportment of great lovers. Covenant realism professes with conviction that the real is there, and that there is something compellingly, hauntingly personal about it, especially if you treat it that way. You need to behave covenantally, starting with the love part. And when you do, the personlike known self-discloses lavishly. Personal objectivity is a deeper objectivity than impersonal objectivity. Covenant realism asks,

3. George Steiner argues this emphatically about criticism of art in the present culture. See Steiner, *Real Presences*, 21, passim.

to co-opt Newbigin's poignant expression, Is someone there? Covenant epistemology and covenant realism both involve seeking the real as one seeks a person. All that we have considered thus far as we have developed covenant epistemology counts as justification for covenant realism, since the two go hand-in-hand.

The Real as Covenantally Constituted: Covenant Ontology

I coin the term, covenant ontology, as that which covenant realism and covenant epistemology obviously imply. Everything that exists is covenantally charactered: it has certain defining features which we must uncover and live covenantally on the terms of in order to know it and bless it and us in the process. This is the distinctive implication of a biblical vision of creation. But it also describes our everyday dwelling in and alongside the world. Real things are charactered. Our ordinary experience, of the you-better-water-those-trees-you-just-planted-or-they'll-die sort, evidences the covenantal nature of the real. To know a thing requires that we honor, covenantally, its covenantal constitution. And in this we are fundamentally engaged in love, care, and friendship. The world requires of would-be knowers the promise of fidelity prior to responsive personal disclosure, a pledge of faithfulness in the face of future surprising revelations. And it responds to covenantal overtures.

Every real thing is covenantally constituted, continually sustained, the biblical vision makes clear, in covenant relationship to its Creator. Yet every real thing is itself and not another thing. It has its own integral particularity, thanks to the asymmetric perichoresis that reflects the Holy Trinity.

Reality never fails to surprise. This is a signature feature. Real things are charactered covenantally, but they are personlike in their inexhaustive uniqueness. To invite the real is to unlock a door through which reality of a surprising nature might enter. Far from there being no truth, what we find sometimes is more truth than we were prepared for. We thought it was about our *coming to know*. We can find instead that it is about our *coming to be known*. We are not lone seekers in a meaningless void. Somebody Else besides us is home in the universe. Knowing proves to be a conversation. It has about it the reciprocity of the interpersonal.

Covenant ontology thus also describes reality as everywhere capable of occasioning I-You encounter. There is no corner where a recalcitrant knower may hide from this possibility. "There is nowhere that is not looking for you; you must change your life," as Rilke said. Goethe's hailing the rosebush—"So! It is You!"—indicates this penchant of the real to gracious self-disclosure. The real wants to be known.

On a biblical schema, the transcendent Other, the Somebody Else, is Yahweh, the triune God. Reality is God and God's personalized (in both senses) handiwork. God is the One, ultimately, who, when we have sought him we find he was seeking us. Jesus, the Word of God, says that he is the Truth. *Of course*, his world has the tough, responsive, characted, surprising many-sidedness about it that it does. It has the personal about it. In this world we are surrounded by God's personal effects—or better, personal gifts.

THE NATURE OF HUMAN KNOWLEDGE

In this systemization of covenant epistemology along the lines of standard accounts, what remain are the matters of the nature, sources, and justification of knowledge. As for the first of these, the entire conversation that is *Loving to Know* has concerned the nature of knowledge. Here I will only briefly summarize our findings, attending more carefully to a few further implications that grow out of these findings taken together. My consideration of the sources and justification of knowledge, in covenant epistemology, also will be selective.

All Knowing is Fraught with the Interpersoned

The central claim of this conversation has been that human knowing is fraught with covenantally constituted interpersoned relationship, a claim that is richly allusive and important to honor in all our epistemic efforts. Here is a summary of these telltale features according to knower, known, and knowing.

Knower

Far from being a disembodied *cogito*, passively recording information, the knower is irreducible person, bodily indwelling subsidiaries which themselves may be cultivated in virtuosity, embodiment, and presence. That subsidiaries may be so cultivated is fraught with the personal. The knower as person, in the relationship of knowing, and especially in transformative moments of insight and the regarding gaze of the personal Other, may grow into fuller personhood and profounder epistemic love and power.

Known

Far from being an impersonal information bank, the real is gift, the gracious flourishing excess of being created by the One whose character it reflects. The real is charactered, covenantally constituted, such that it responds to personal treatment with self-disclosure. In fact, the real exercises primacy, in the knowing relationship, as only a person would do. In moments of our deepest knowing, the real is the personal Other, the You who seeks us, initiating our transformative deliverance from the void and inviting us into communion.

Knowing

I have embedded knowing as subsidiary-focal integration in a nest of larger contexts which metonymously signpost the largest context, the interpersonal relationship. Knowing connects knower and known via a normative constituting, which in turn bespeaks a covenantal context. Covenant presupposes persons in relationship, a dynamically unfolding relationship whose goal is the mutuality of ongoing communion. And in this unfolding relationship, periodically (perichoretically), I-You, face-to-face, transformative moments graciously occur, studding and moving the relationship along toward communion, making us better knowers, healing the world, and prototyping the convictional presence of the Holy.

So covenant epistemology's central claim is one that concerns the nature of knowledge: human knowledge is fraught with the interpersoned, standing in asymmetric mutuality with the interpersonal relationship which is its fundamental context and transformative core.

Knowing is Variably Personal

I use this odd descriptor to synthesize something that we have seen from more than one conversation partner: knowing seems to come in two forms, in which the knower orients differently. One is explicitly interpersonal, a standing in relation with one who is standing in relation with me, thus, I-You. The other is I-It, not so explicitly interpersonal, even though it is fraught with the personed. It is what I have been calling metonymously personal, even though it is I-It. Not every instance (or perhaps better, in*stant*) of knowing is I-You encounter, to recur to Buber; not every instance of knowing is in the field of the personal, according to Macmurray. But sometimes the giver himself shows up, and that, and not the gift, is the main act.

But in speaking of knowing as variably personal, I voice my own creative synthesis of these two within an unfolding interpersonal relationship. Such an unfolding relationship, I have said, is studded with I-You transformative moments, each richer than the next. These moments, we have seen, grow us as persons and as knowers. The studding encounters, over time, move the whole unfolding trajectory toward deep communion—and toward deepening wisdom. I have proposed that we see the variation from one mode to the other as perichoretically rhythmical.

The knowing trajectory is constituted by faithful covenant over time. This covenantal constitution of the unfolding relationship that is knowing affords the context which both invites and protects moments of encounter. Buber mentioned that the I-It is the chrysalis for the I-You; one may hear anticipative covenantal protection and nurture in this metaphor. The trajectory is, in the words of the title of a well-known Eugene Peterson meditation on the psalms of ascent, a long obedience in the same direction.[4]

This synthesis almost seems to require that many, perhaps most, of the moments in the trajectory are not I-You encounters. But one need not sustain the I-You encounter for it nevertheless to be definitive. In fact, one cannot sustain the I-You encounter for there to be rhythmical reciprocity in unfolding relationship. On the one hand, we live for the I-You encounters; on the other, though we do not sustain them, we nevertheless grow personally and epistemically as a result of them.

Every integrative, Oh-I-See-It! moment is, at least prototypically, an I-You encounter. Each integration is one of those studs in the unfolding relationship. Perhaps it might be better to call the transforming moment, Oh-I-See-You! and Oh-You-See-Me! Each such integration both climaxes a covenantal unfolding, and is embedded in a much larger one.

It is important to acknowledge knowing as variably personal as we discuss the nature of knowledge on the covenant epistemology paradigm. This variability itself reveals knowing as interpersonal. Relationship unfolds perichoretically, in artful overture and response. This variability

4. Peterson, *A Long Obedience*.

may be seen to be the very dynamic of conferring space for particularity in the context of relationality.

Variability is what makes talking of knowing as interpersonal, and specifying the respects in which it is, a most elusive enterprise. The I-You encounters are such that I have often felt that in order to offer a satisfactory account to knowing, one must first redefine knowing, or identify a different specimen as knowing. In the I-You encounter, knowing seems fundamentally different from the rest of knowing.

Thus we may see the I-You encounter as special, paradigmatic, contexting, and centering all knowing, while at the same time, of necessity, being not exhaustively, homogeneously, the presenting character of all of it. So as we talk, we must keep this in mind.

All Knowing is Coming to Know

Knowing is an unfolding, covenantally constituted, perichoretically rhythmical, mutually transformative interpersonal relationship with a personal real. I will state briefly each of these dimensions in turn.

In contrast to impersonal knowledge, knowledge as about statements and proof, knowing includes and incorporates the process. The knower moves from situated roots in situation and history toward the world and the future. It involves the knower in reaching beyond her or his current situation and self, a vectoring from oneself toward the world. Situated roots, and vectoring outward, must be construed as subsidiary-focal integration.

All knowing is coming to know, a trajectory, a being on the way to truth. It is an unfolding story. This involves the knower in risk and plenty of not-yet-knowing. Along the way, knowing may be anticipative and implicit, hinting unspecifiably of more, surprising, and deeper dimensions, from the beginning to the end.

All knowing is thus open-ended to the future. In a way, it is not possible to write the final book on anything that is real. But far from being a defect of knowing, this is its signature and its glory. For "real" is that which may manifest itself indeterminately in the future, in the words of Polanyi. It is characteristic of being to be abundantly giving and letting-flourish. In this way, knowing has about it the quality of the real.

The trajectory of coming to know is an unfolding interpersonal relationship. The driving dynamism is love. Both partners are covenantally constituted, and the whole manifests itself in perichoretic reciprocity.

Even communion, once the relationship attains it, opens out onto a joyously anticipated future of indeterminate possibilities.

Knowing is Covenantally Constituted

The dynamically unfolding relationship that is knowing is covenantally constituted. That means that it has, as its defining boundaries and structure, self-binding pledge that honors or respects both partners and sustains the relationship through time. Knowing thus involves or is action, and the shape of the action is pledge and obligatory response. Truth is troth. Knowing is a covenant pledge. Covenant derives moral force from its personal context, a definitive interpersonal relationship whose existence covenant metonymically implies.

Knowing thus has about it a normativity that characterizes all human action, which makes it, not passive receptivity, but active and shaping overtures that invite reciprocally shaping self-disclosure of the real in response. Actively, knowing is normative and covenantal, involving the human knower in responsible stewardship of the known, finite instances of norming things into existence, creaturely "let there be"s. Receptively, the knower is obligated to knowing that is risky, responsible decision. The knower binds her- or himself in the epistemic endeavor, exercising love, respect, humility, patience, obedient submission to the real, as the sort of candidacy that invites the real's self-disclosure. To claim that something is true is to profess it responsibly but with universal intent, as Polanyi insists.

The opposite of knowing is not ignorance so much as it is rebellion, or at least a damaging inauthenticity. I have spoken little of failed knowing in this discourse. But we may see that by implication, where knowing is covenantally constituted, and situated in interpersonal relationship, one must develop an understanding of knowing's opposite as a kind of moral and interpersonal failure.[5] On the other hand, however, given the covenantally unfolding character of coming to know, ignorance may also

---

5. I must add quickly that it is important, when we gauge such matters, to take into account that we are neither solitary knowers, nor mere drops in the bucket of a Collective knower/knowing. We must be perichoretic here as well. We are persons related to other persons as knowers, giving honoring space for diverse interests and capacities. To use the language of calling: I personally am not called to cancer research; I personally am called to epistemological therapy. Thus I am accountable indirectly for the first and directly for the second. But together with others in perichoretic creativity, the effect of our jointly diverse efforts always add up to far more than the sum of the parts.

be not-yet-knowing, on-the-way-to-knowing—even when it is marked by rebellion. Rebellion displays, in some way, covenantal intimacy.

Knowing is Perichoretically Rhythmical

The dynamism of the trajectory of the knowing relationship is perichoretically rhythmical in contour. The relationship unfolds in a rhythmic to and fro over time. More than one pair is perichoretically balanced, as we have seen: relationality and particularity, love and covenant, knower and known, overture and response, attending to and from and to and from, situation and self and norm, I-You and I-It. The balance is akin to well-differentiated persons in communion. The union makes the particular participants more themselves, and the particularity of the participants makes the union more what it is.

Even as a dance is an artfully dynamic union of complementary elements unfolding over a period of time, the knowing event is characterized by this perichoresis. Knower and known are genuinely other—different from one another—but nevertheless are joined and akin in a way that makes the relationship of knowing as perichoretic the natural and normative thing to be expected. This suggests an even balance in the give and take between knower and known, and also a joint project of interdependence that exceeds the contribution of either. Knowing well involves giving the yet-to-be-known space to be itself even as we seek to indwell it understandingly. It involves consenting "spaciously" to its being.

Knowing is Subsidiary-focal Transformative Integration

Knowing is the profoundly human struggle to rely on clues to focus on a pattern which we submit to as a token of reality. All knowing can be seen to display subsidiary and focal joined integratively. Integration is such that it deserves the additional descriptors, "event," and "transformation." Michael Polanyi's elegant and concrete description of how we know forms the anchor of covenant epistemology. For it so characterizes knowing that we begin to see that knowing is fraught with personlike, covenantal reciprocity.

Knowing Transforms the Known and the Knower

All knowing unfolds according to the Polanyian schema of subsidiary-focal integration that as such is transformative of the knower. The knower's transformation is an undoing of nothingness engendered by the possibility of new being. Construing knowing in this way helps us better grasp the shape of our rootedness in our bodies and our situation: we integrate from them as meaningful, though unspecifiable, subsidiaries, rather than attending to them as specified, meaningless, particulars. The transformative focal pattern we achieve remains distinctively fraught with the clues on which it relies. Our action is simultaneously rooted and free, immanent and transcendent. And it is new being embraced above the potential non-being, the risky leap from attending-to to attending-from.

We may underscore that this subsidiary awareness that binds us to ourselves and to the surrounding world is apprehended especially via bodily human touch—fraught with personal and interpersonal meaning as it is.

The knowing event also transforms the known. One of the ways it does this is by voicing its transformative self-disclosure, characterizing it, channeling it into the known world. The goal is to bless the known, making it more fully itself for the knowing event. Blessing and voicing especially occur to the extent that we come at the epistemic enterprise with the wider, more holistic, and more allusive, relational posture that is the initiative of whole persons inviting relationship.

The wider and more personed the knower perceives both the task and her- or himself, the more the known is unleashed to be and to reciprocate distinctively in wholeness. Thus, the unfolding trajectory of knowing is this way because of the symbiotic, mutual healing of knower by known and vice versa. In this life, although it is flawed, we know even as we are known.

Corollaries of Covenant Epistemology

Knowing is Knowing God, Knowing the World, Knowing Self

All acts of coming to know are simultaneously, though no doubt in varying respects, knowing God, knowing the world, and knowing oneself. Whatever a person may believe concerning the existence of God and what he is like, every knowing event opens out to admit the ingression of new and flourishing being. For those who already confess God's reality, this experience, in oneself and when observed in others, implicitly signposts him.

Insight about reality and about oneself is a kind of knowing God. Covenantal submission to the engaged real, both in anticipation of and subsequent to the discovery, to some extent is submission to God, both with respect to the world and with respect to oneself. Obedience is lived truth. Here we may note Palmer's rich statement: "In the Christian tradition, truth is not a concept that 'works,' but an incarnation that lives."[6]

The fact that these three coextend in acts of coming to know indicates another manner in which the knowing event is transformative. One may not know God and avoid existential change. Similarly, contact with reality brings mutual transformation for knower and known.

This intertwined complexity of knowing, especially with its signature feature of undoing nothingness and the coming of the Holy, means that that actual I-You encounter with God, regularly ritualized in the Eucharist, serves as a paradigm for all acts of coming to know. There is something normative, in the sense of paradigmatic, for all knowing, about knowing God. Thus, the converse of the aphoristic analogy that drives *Longing to Know* is also true: knowing your auto mechanic, as an epistemic act, is like knowing God.[7]

All Knowing is Knowing With

Perichoretic relationality between knower, known, God, and human others seems to support the claim that all knowing is also knowing *with whom*. No knowing venture and event is utterly bereft of the significant other person. Significant other persons serve as the proximate, centering face that constitutes us as knowers, the authoritative guides who teach us to see and name what is there, the audience—the cloud of witnesses—who accord interpretive value to our efforts. Together we are "co-celebrants of what is."

Human Knowing is Creaturely Knowing

Theologically speaking, covenant epistemology casts knowing in such a way that makes it clear that the human knower differs from the divine Knower by reason of being created and dependent metaphysically—

6. Palmer, *To Know as We Are Known*, 14.

7. Okay, Jeff, don't let it go to your head!

creature rather than Creator. Thus it offers a viable construal of creature-ly knowing, or servant thinking. The human knower, within covenant relationship, differs from God, who is Truth Himself, and is so by dint of being Lord. Human knowing is creationally situated. We are rooted in metaphysically contingent, historied, locations. We are integrally embodied and encultured.

Human knowing thus includes no ultimate or absolute anchor of certainty (in contrast to the modernist ideal) but nevertheless (actually, not *nevertheless*, but *for this reason*) involves and is capable of responsible stewardship of the real. Human knowing is thus integrally interpretive, interpretive "all the way down."

Polanyi, however, lends the critical epistemic insight that our embodiment, history, and situatedness are all subsidiarily indwelt. Thus while they are inarticulable as indubitably certain statements, they afford a palpable base for knowing—for orienting winsomely and knowingly toward the world. This base is markedly superior to certain propositions. So subsidiary knowledge makes epistemic sense of our creatureliness.

Our creaturely situatedness is not a flaw or shortcoming, but rather what it is to be human. It is what locates us before God as creatures before Creator, but also quite specially as stewards, and in this respect reflective of him in our cultural engagement. This means that our efforts to know are fallible but also quite capable, *coram Deo* and in God's world, of leading us to truth. Our humanness serves as a beachhead within reality. Also, it is quite appropriate to attend well to what it is that we are actually doing when we know, as we go about writing epistemologies, and to attend carefully to the world, in covenant love, to come to understanding. On the one hand, as contingent creatures, we may not exalt to ultimate epistemic status a bedrock of certainty or a surefire method; on the other hand, our rootedness affords confidence as we vector toward reality. Our creaturely rootedness—including our very selves—displays its characteristic glory as it remains ever revisable and transformable in light of subsequent insight.

All this is consistent with affirming God as definitive Lord in knowing—Truth himself. In fact, his Lordship supplies confidence and delight, if not a talisman, in all our efforts to engage the world.

All this is not to deny what Christians call the noetic effects of sin. Indeed, our bentness negatively impacts our knowing. The point is that situatedness is not, intrinsically, either bentness or limitation.

That it has been so construed has itself been an instance of the noetic effects of sin.

Knowing is Stewardship

Following the Christian Scripture, we may say that human knowing is part and parcel of what God made and designated humans to do as stewards in his palace. We are "compelled to culturing"—hardwired to shape our surroundings, for good or ill.[8] Thus, our hard-wiring, we may say, matches the cultural mandate—God's formative command to care for and develop the earth. In carrying this out well, we reflect God. Given the active shaping that is knowing, human knowing may be knowing for *shalom*. Thus, knowing may be mutually therapeutic, making the world, and ourselves, more fully what we are. In knowing, we are thus to be exercising responsible care of the known.

HEALING THE DEFAULT DAISY OF DICHOTOMIES

It is time to return to the plethora of epistemological challenges we raised in the first chapter. How does covenant epistemology challenge the default epistemic mode that features fragmenting dichotomies, preoccupation with information, certainty, objectivism, the ocular metaphor, and substantivalism, and that seems to thwart wisdom? Here I want to sketch one-sentence responses that covenant epistemology enables us to suggest to each of these features of the default mode. Each one of these could be more fully and helpfully developed.

One thing to keep in mind that affects our view of many of the dichotomies is that the Polanyian schema of subsidiary-focal shows the way to make sense of the relationship between the pairs. It allows us to honor a duality, rather than a reductivism on the one hand and a dualism on the other. The shape of the duality is from-to—subsidiary-focal. Add to this that the subsidiary not only roots, supports, and flavors the focal, but it also outruns and contexts it—keep in mind, here, all that Macmurray said about interpersonal knowing contexting reflective thinking. Finally, remember that motion from "from" to "to" features the dynamism and reciprocity of love.

Now to the list.

---

8. Meek, "Compelled to Culturing."

- *Knowledge and belief:* Belief just is the epistemic act, the risky, responsible, inspired act of coming to know.

- *Knowledge and opinion:* To the extent that a distinction between responsible and irresponsible knowing is envisioned, we are indeed called to stewardly, wholistically expert, knowing for *shalom.*

- *Fact and value:* Apart from value, the responsible interpretive commitments of the knower, and the ·knower's noticing which assigns value to certain clues, there are no facts.

- *Fact and interpretation:* The same. However, this is not to say that the knower is thereby cut off from reality. Value and interpretation is the very thing that launches us toward the real and unlocks it.

- *Reason and faith:* Covenant epistemology recasts reason to involve integrally responsible submission to the yet-to-be-fully-known. This is faith. All acts of coming to know are acts of faith. By the same token, all acts of faith have about them assumptions and articulations and anticipations of rationality. Rationality always comes to be in the medium of faith.

- *Reason and emotion:* While we have not discussed emotion per se, we have implied passion—longing, desire, love—as constitutively driving efforts to know, and we have located knowing in the context of both the body and interpersonal relationships. Covenant epistemology thus integrally intertwines reason and emotion.

- *Science and art:* Where the knowing event is recognized to be transformational, scientific acts of discovery and artistic acts of creativity are in substance the same. Also, where knowing involves integrating subsidiaries from a range of fields in submission to the yet-to-be-discovered real, experiences in the one field must be drawn on to shape experiences in the other.

- *Objective and subjective:* The objective has been seen to be more than we thought, because it is personal, flourishing in its excess. The subjective has received a healing overhaul: we see it as the palpably felt and significant subsidiarily lived. This is not to say that we don't ever get it wrong, and don't ever exhibit an inappropriate bias. But a robust subsidiary involvement is the very thing the enables us to access the world. The objective, for covenant epistemology, is far richer than the daisy gave it credit—so rich that our insights can get a piece of it right and still be surprised to learn what we thought we had grasped.

- *Theory and practice:* knowing is action; theory is always embedded in responsible, active, interpersonal context, and only makes sense in that context. "Truth" unlived is not truth. All truth is bodily lived. Thus, practice, in hope of transformation, both embodies and invites truth; theory makes sense in the context.

- *Mind and body:* The primary phenomenon of human persons is the lived body. This phrase reflects the Polanyian schema, enabling us quite helpfully to cast body knowledge as subsidiary and thus fraught with the transcending, personally particular, meaningful awareness, not to mention the presence, that others perceive as myself. Others thus know my mind and myself.

- *Appearance and reality:* Covenant epistemology conflates and re-casts this pair. Where all knowing is interpretation and also accesses the real, we may say that what appears is real—not meaning thereby that there is no reality, nor that all that appears is real. And this is not to deny the primacy of the knower's (and knowers') capacity for and necessity of distinguishing false from true. We may be mistaken, or mistaken for a time, or partially mistaken; these epistemic situations would have no meaning were it not possible to be right, and were we not able eventually to "get it" in a way that signals the inbreaking of the objective real. Additionally, there is a sense in which, in sub-sidiary-focal integration, particulars looked *at* are appearance, and the transformative pattern emerging from the particulars looked *through* is reality. But what counts as particulars and what counts as pattern shifts according to how the act of knowing is construed.

- *Male and female:* Covenant epistemology affirms relationality and particularity in perichoretic relation. I can't imagine a better way, not to annul gender differences, but to optimize them, as in mu-tuality in joint epistemic ventures. Men and women must exercise companionship on the way to knowing, with the full expectation that their equal complementarity strategically suits them for per-ichoretic partnership in knowing.

- *Knowledge as information:* Knowing is transformation. Information is the tip of the iceberg. It becomes deceptive and damaging if we restrict our account of knowing to that tip. The most precise information is attainable and accredited and understood as it is rooted in the subsidiary that outruns it.

- *Boredom, hopelessness, and betrayal:* When knowing is cast as desire, as adventurous journey, boredom evaporates. Where knowing is about openness to the surprising self-disclosure of the real, hopelessness evaporates. Betrayal of trust is, in covenant epistemology, seen to be a factor profoundly critical to knowing. It is not "just" "about relationships." It has to do with the heart of living and being and knowing, and thus must be treated with priority and gentle perseverance. Also, we have reason to hope that knowing, involving transformation and mutuality with flourishing being as it does, may contribute to the healing of the knower who has experienced betrayal in the past.

- *Nobody's home:* The personal is everywhere in human knowing.

- *It's all about me:* Epistemic arrogance is ruled out of court; replaced by delighted and free stewardship, mutuality, and the practices of inviting the real.

- *Deadening knowing:* Where knowledge is seen to supersede information, to involve transformation integrally; where knowing is seen to involve covenant love, and the I of I-You, wisdom is finally in view. To know is to be on the way to being wise. Practically speaking, innovators, discoverers, artists, students, are all strategically helped in their task where the transformative character of knowing is understood and embraced. A sense of knowing along the lines developed in covenant epistemology itself contributes strategically to wisdom as well as expediting its growth. Also, subsidiary-focal integration's way of honoring the meaningful particularity of particulars-turned-clues effectively combats the meaninglessness of information that has generated cluelessness.

- *Certainty:* Certainty loses its appeal as the dangling carrot of two-dimensional, impersonal, informational epistemology. Lived confidence that comes to expression in virtuosity and responsible engagement of the real is superior. Formalized justification of findings is critical and valuable, and that much more effective when it is,

not exalted exclusively as the paradigm of knowledge, but rather contexted in a supportive role in a larger interpersonal communion.

- *Objectivism:* Objectivism depersonalizes known and knower into
  objects. Covenant epistemology views this as entirely uncalled
  for and incredibly damaging to knower, known, and knowing.
  Objectivism also misses the fact that personally construed reality
  is far more objective, in the better sense, than reality impersonally
  construed: open-ended, dynamic particularity that issues in interpersonal communion of perichoretic reciprocity, makes for a three-
  dimensionality that objectivism has actually obscured and thus
  endangered.

- *The ocular metaphor:* Covenant epistemology commends the tactile
  metaphor instead, even for more effective seeing. The tactile (subsidiarily experienced) is the primitive and fundamentally personed
  medium of transformative interpersonal communion.

- *Substantivalism:* Substantival anthropology is superseded by perichoretic relationality that enhances particularity rather than
  generality.

Therefore, covenant epistemology, as we embody it, effectively dissi-
pates the fragmenting and damaging distortions of our default epistemic
mode. It brings healing to knower and knowing, and thus to known. It
unleashes us to be the lovers that make better knowers.

THE SOURCES OF HUMAN KNOWLEDGE

Typical introductions to epistemology list the sources of human knowledge as primarily being reason (rationalism), sense perception (empiricism), and sometimes, taking a different approach, utility (pragmatism).
Testimony has often received a dismissive nod, as a legitimate source
of knowledge only in childhood, meant to be superseded by the others
in adulthood. *Rationalism* claims that we derive knowledge of a definitive sort from our minds. It cites as key examples of *a priori* knowledge
(claims of a caliber that cannot be drawn from sense experience)—mathematical and logical axioms—and universality in empirical generaliza-
tion (on which induction depends). *Empiricism* represents the claim that
all knowing of the external world has as its source sense perception.

These two major claims developed in opposition to each other during the era known as modern philosophy, beginning in the 1500s with Descartes. Both rejected testimony as a legitimate source of knowledge. With the growing realization that pretheoretical factors profoundly shape what we take to be reasonable and what we think we perceive, the two-sided debate of modern philosophy has been thrown into disarray. Sadly, people still operating out of a modernist stance can read this as the end of objective knowledge, rather than as the reinstatement of it. Both rationalism and empiricism, we can see from the point of view of covenant epistemology, presupposed the defective default shaped especially by Descartes. Covenant epistemology thoroughly redefines the rational and the empirical, and in a manner profoundly consonant with testimony.

Perhaps this is testimony having the last laugh. I contend that modern epistemology, in rejecting authoritative testimony as illegitimate (I have in mind Kant's ringing *Sapere aude!* of the Enlightenment), so disfigured knowing as to render it destructive, and to bind knowers to a model that cuts them off from their most strategic resources. We have seen that authoritative tradition may be perichoretically construed—and must be, in order to confer free space that abets the knower. Also, as I go on to say here, in an account of knowing as having a normative dimension, testimony must be accredited as a key source of knowledge.

"Sources"—World, Lived Body, the Normative

We may acknowledge a rough correspondence between the three dimensions of the normative, the world, and the lived body, and the triad of testimony, empiricism, and rationalism. Covenant epistemology installs testimony from the outset. But covenant epistemology transforms and integrates these three so as to be profoundly a different sort of collaborative enterprise.

Thus, covenant epistemology offers the three dimensions as sources of knowledge. As we have seen previously, cultivating the subsidiaries in every dimension, and specifically in the lived body, is conducive to knowing. Deeply indwelling the normative claims of authoritative guides unlocks understanding, as does a kind of deep perceiving, an attentive communion with the real, that is more on the level of the subsidiary, the tactile, the field of the active personal.

But covenant epistemology puts appeal to these three sources of knowing in a larger context, in which they are seen to be, not ultimate sources, not surefire sources, but proximal ones that we steward rather than summon as arbitrary philosophical oracles. Polanyian epistemology reveals that these sources are such only as we relate to them subsidiarily. And we must do this in advance of our having attained the focus to which they are subsidiary, if ever we are to attain it. The three dimensions are not sources in the sense of sufficient conditions or efficient causes, for knowing is never linear or guaranteed. There is a real sense in which the focal pattern is the gracious, transformative source of knowledge, and thus somehow the anchor of our epistemic enterprise. We steward what we have, humbly groping in the direction of the longed-for integration. But when it comes, it comes from "outside."

This phenomenon leads me to suggest that when you get right down to it, the sources of knowledge are two, of a different sort, which relate in mutuality to cut across our stewardly and responsible efforts to indwell proximal word, world, and body clues. I term them *candidacy* and *the intrusion of the Other*.

Candidacy

Our stewardly and creative efforts to indwell bodily clues, authoritative words, and features that the world presents are efforts to put ourselves "in the way of knowing," as I will call it—to locate ourselves strategically so that we are where it may be apprehended, where we may see it when it discloses. I will argue extensively in the next chapter that we may "invite the real," through covenantal behavior. Knowledge is not to be derived from sources, so much as graciously disclosed in response to covenantal candidacy. Here again we see how covenant epistemology transforms the very categories of epistemology. The question is not, where do I get knowledge, but how do I comport myself to invite it? *Source* is a word ill-fitted to express knowing that is construed as fundamentally transformation rather than information, as being apprehended rather than comprehending.

The Intrusion of the Other

Another way of saying it is to say that there is in fact something in the dynamism of human knowing to which the word *source* applies radically, but it isn't the knower. The transformative aspect of knowing, as experienced by the knower, leaves the sense that the knower did not instigate the knowing event in anything other than a stewardly way. It leaves the unspecifiable but palpable sense that the source was an Other beyond the knower. Returning to Loder here, the source of knowing is the gracious intrusion of the Other. He writes: "Implicitly, we seem to know . . . that knowing itself must yield to a higher intelligibility because knowing cannot be its own reason for being. Thus, it is from beyond such boundaries that insight—sometimes of revolutionary proportions— *comes upon us.*" And also: "Yes—there is an inevitable and decisive shift somewhere in every act of creation and discovery from the active to the passive mode: in the moment of insight the knower is being known; the self is caught in the act of knowing."[9] Quite profoundly, Loder aphorizes: "the truth always exceeds the proof."[10]

How can our efforts be even taken as efforts in knowing, if we cannot control it by tapping into its sources? I think this is just to offer an account of knowing that actually accords with our experience of it, and which suits it theologically to be called creaturely knowing. And far from despairing of knowing, this approach leaves us far better off. There is, on the one hand, plenty we can do. It takes the form of covenantal self-binding. We may invite the real. We may re-envision our whole lives as people who invite the real. It leaves us in a position epistemologically, with a healthy epistemological default setting, which itself invites the real.

On the other hand, just because we are inviting the real, the real comes in spades. Reality self-discloses lavishly. At this point, one may cease to be concerned with questions about sources! Loder states that the purpose of his book is not so much to describe the transformative knowing event as to evoke it. And that is as it should be. For:

> in the end we will not be able to imagine the depth and mag-nitude of the reality to which even the best images of the most profound minds are pointing us. All understanding and models must finally become transparent and vanish. Then, in death to all else, each one may appear face to face before the One who always comes from the other side of ultimate human emptiness.

9. Loder, *Transforming Moment*, 216–17.
10. Ibid., 216.

Sometimes one must be thrown into such a confrontation, and here is where the book begins.[11]

There is nothing like a transformative incursion of the Other to put the question of the sources of knowledge in perspective.

THE JUSTIFICATION OF HUMAN KNOWLEDGE

Finally we turn to the area of epistemology known as justification. This has been the most prominent and all-encompassing pursuit of epistemologists in the contemporary analytic tradition. It taps into the construal and heavy emphasis, in our default epistemological mode, of knowledge as statements and proofs. It reflects the general contexting of knowledge as explanation, rather than as discovery, as information rather than transformation. It also implies that personal allegiance to truth claims is to be withheld pending thorough justification.

Covenant epistemology directly challenges some of these assumptions that are often deeper than even epistemologists dig to examine. It radically reconstrues what knowledge is. We will see that the interpersoned epistemic paradigm contexts justification, even as it placed the question of sources in a larger context. Covenant epistemology qualifies rather than exalts justification. In this, it is messier, but also truer to human life.

Justification of knowledge concerns the ways that it is appropriate that we accredit a claim as knowledge. It involves asking what sorts of reasons are appropriate for taking a truth claim to be knowledge. Philosophers explore correspondence, coherence, and pragmatic responses: justification requires evidential support, coherence with other knowledge claims, or workability, respectively. Another discussion raises the question whether or not the knower must experience internal conviction as a necessary ingredient of justification—or whether the matter of justification involves externalities, such as having one's knowing equipment in functioning order, and the conditions of the event conducive to it. Philosophers now explore virtue, and also social support, to elucidate the role of these factors in epistemic justification.

Covenant epistemology rules none of these out of court but rather fundamentally qualifies all of them. In the covenant epistemology context, all of them actually receive a humanizing breath of life. Justification,

11. Ibid., 8.

on a Polanyian scheme, is inherently an informal and thus ultimately not fully specifiable process—again more of a responsible stewardship in submission to the real.

Covenant epistemology, following Polanyian epistemology, and in a way consonant with the Christian profession that human knowers are creatures, is fallibilist, as it is commonly called. Fallibilism affirms that what we at one point take to be true may possibly be either false or in need of revision. Knowing involves inherently a risk, just because it is a responsible commitment. Having reconfigured knowing as such, fallibilism is no shame, but courage enacted. And it is not the case that the impossibility of infallible knowledge leaves us in a void of skepticism. Rather, we are unleashed responsibly to engage the world.

In this work we talk of knowing as an unfolding story. Where knowing is so construed, the knower is ever in the middle of it, and as such proceeds with half-understanding. Also, as I showed in *Longing to Know*, it is true to life that we can make a discovery and only half understand what it is that we have discovered. I need only utter, by way of example, "Columbus discovered America," to make the point. Knowing is like this, I believe, not because of the absence of reality or because of our distance from it, but rather precisely because reality is so rich, systematically inexhaustive, full of gracious surprises. Where our sentences conform to reality about as well as a yardstick wraps around a basketball, we can be guilty of misplaced enthusiasm if we are too preoccupied with formal justification.

Allegiance and Obligation are Prior to and Throughout Justification

We can begin by noting that, in covenant epistemology, covenantal allegiance and obligation provide the prior context for justification. Rather than knowing in order to love, we love in order to know.[12] This is the radical opposite of the reigning paradigm in western epistemology. Obedience, especially obedience in the anticipative dark before the dawn of insight, precedes understanding, and not vice versa.

It is not that our allegiance may not be recast, that it is somehow sacrosanct and incorrigible. The fact is, however, that no knowing is to be had apart from it, even if it is to be revised continually in light of our un-

---

12. See my discussion of R. T. Allen's challenge to Leonardo da Vinci's claim in ch. 15. Leonardo averred that "every great love is the daughter of a great cognition." Allen argues against that and for the converse.

folding apprehension of the real. But where knowing is, at its root, *credo*, prior to commitment there is no knowing whatsoever. In this respect, covenant epistemology is not simply a viable alternative epistemology; it is the only alternative.

Discovery is Prior to Justification

I said already that the young Polanyi astounded a dissertation supervisor with his comment that one reaches the conclusion before one is able to articulate the premises. The transformative moment of insight is the thing without which all prefatory clues not only do not make sense, but cannot even be designated as clues. Discovery must in some respect be prior to justification.

Justification, as it is typically envisioned in western epistemology, is part of what Polanyi called destructive analysis. It is a reflective return to focus on that which, only when we rely on it, prompts the integrative transformation. As such it must be seen to make sense only in light of a return to the larger integration, and to be temporary. It also must be seen that its result bears in a tangential way (I do not at all mean to say it is irrelevant) on the focus. Destructive analysis, in bike-riding, would be memorizing the physics formula that describes how we keep balance on a bike. The relationship between this memorization and the actual balancing is not at all one of linear, passive, representation.

This is not to say that destructive analysis, a careful and methodical exploration of justification, is irresponsible. Far from it; it will, in fact, if interpreted aright and itself indwelled as a tool that invites the real, enhance our grasp on reality. Whatever formal efforts we employ in justification draw life-giving sustenance from their informal context and our personal commitment, and their outcomes must be gauged informally in light of it. But the most damaging thing we can do, and that which engenders the western default, is to restrict knowledge, in a timeless focus, to the disembodied explicit result of such destructive analysis.

Contact with Reality

In my dissertation, *Contact With Reality*, I distil the richness of Polanyi's phrases which claim that we can know we have made contact with reality, into two criteria of reality, as I called them. These criteria are evident in *Longing to Know*, although in that setting I do not use this jargonish language. With the onset of a transformative apprehension of a pattern, there are two indicators that affirm that we have made contact with reality. The first is retrospective: we sense the profundity of the pattern we have just attained. Whatever the collection of questions and clues we had hitherto amassed are radically shown to be superseded in depth and profundity by the pattern now attained. The insight more than explains our questions; it reshapes the questions. The pattern is more profound than anything our meager efforts hitherto envisioned. The insight is out of the league of our efforts to anticipate or provoke it.

The second criterion is prospective or anticipative. Discovery, the onset of the focal pattern, is accompanied and attested to by the intimation of the possibility of wide range of as yet unspecifiable prospects. I have often thought that it is not so much what we can articulate as what we can't articulate, don't even know yet how to name, that confirms the reality of our discovery.

Justification is Informally Assessed

Both of these criteria are informally gauged. And all justification is ultimately, at its root, informal. Whatever measures we use in the name of justification, even the most sophisticated and carefully developed, are informally applied and assessed. And this is no flaw; it is as it should be. At the end of justificatory efforts, as it has been both prior to discovery and throughout it, a knowledge claim must be personally, responsibly, espoused. Again, this is not to minimize the value and role of explicit and methodical efforts at justification. It is rather to identify the ultimately personal and informal context that gives even the most excellent explicit and methodical efforts their life and effectiveness.

As these criteria of reality are engaged, they resonate according to the three Framean dimensions of the clues. Thus, the truth claim is seen to unlock and engage the real, to open it up. It is seen to accord in a way that we can feel bodily (as in Gendlin's focusing) with body clues well beyond what we are able to articulate. And it seems to more than make sense of words and maxims we have heard before.

Contact with the real should issue in gradually deepening *shalom* and healing of the world, cognitive rest, wisdom, even as it opens us and the world to the future and to others in a public way.[13] It should deepen our love for and communion with the real, as we are on the way to knowing. This implies that knowing should abide within the covenantal parameters of the reality of both ourselves and the world. These all are fundamentally unformalizable indicators. Yet we rely on them continually in justification as we continually navigate forward in our efforts to know. In all this, it must be remembered that human knowing unfolds in a journeyed trajectory.

Justification, precisely because it is informally gauged, involves an artful skill that may and must be trained. Never do we substitute a technical manual for critical verification. So we must build our wise capacity for informal assessment.

Then, we must see that we hold all truth claims as professions. To say something is true is to back it, as we would our signature on a check. It is to say, Here I stand. It is a claim in vouching for which we must exercise personal responsibility. But it is also to say, I cannot do otherwise. It is to profess the claim with universal intent, to employ Polanyi's account—meaning that we believe that its objective truth is accessible to anyone in a position to see it.[14]

With this we reach the conclusion of my attempt to articulate the contours of covenant epistemology in line with standard areas of discussion in epistemology. The effect, I believe, is to locate covenant epistemology with regard to the general discussion, and to showcase its distinctiveness and superiority. We have seen repeatedly that covenant epistemology reconfigures epistemology, helpfully reshaping its very categories and discussions. In this way, covenant epistemology itself is provocative and potentially fruitful with respect to reality, to humanness, and to future exploration.

---

13. Frame, in his own analysis of the justification of knowledge, offers his term, cognitive rest, which he defines as a godly sense of satisfaction (*Doctrine of the Knowledge of God*, ch. 5). Loder, at the end of *Transforming Moment*, offers a catalog of criteria of convictional knowing which I believe might be helpfully adapted to the question of the justification of human knowing. I hint at both of these discussions in my brief sketch here.

14. Polanyi, *Personal Knowledge*, ch. 10.

QUESTIONS FOR DISCUSSION

1. This is a systematic summary of covenant epistemology. In what ways does it consolidate your understanding?

2. What does this systematization suggest to you about covenant epistemology?

3. Has covenant epistemology delivered the promised reorientation of our epistemic default? Share your response to its treatment of the daisy's dichotomies and other aspects of the diseased default.

4. Discuss covenant realism and covenant ontology. In what respects are these credible and helpful philosophical approaches?

〰 15

INVITING THE REAL

An Epistemological Etiquette

THIS CHAPTER IS THE one I have most longed to write. I have savored the delightful prospect for as long as I have conceived of covenant epistemology. Early on, I thought that the book just might be called *Inviting the Real*. At each turning, it has seemed, there have developed important preliminaries to address, postponing the moment I would be free to express the notion of inviting the real. Throughout the process, my sense of this has remained unchanged. If there is something like deep joy around intimate communion about the covenant epistemology vision, as I deeply hope that there is, that joy, in my thinking, is concentrated around this chapter. As text, this etiquette is distinctive because it is at once a meditation and a catechesis to form aspiring covenantal knowers.

I intend the phrase, "inviting the real," to suggest that the best human efforts to know should conform to this description. *Inviting* is something that only a person does. Also, the act of inviting implies the freely-initiated response of someone else. It also challenges the impersonal coercion of the real that has characterized traditional western thought and culture, implying that such behavior is entirely inappropriate and unhelpful. And it implies that what may not be taken might yet in grace be given.

Inviting the real implies that the real is there, and self-discloses. The self-disclosure is something that is beyond anything that we have imagined, sometimes, and yet we can have a sense of recognizing it. "Surprising recognition," a phenomenon that all of us have experienced, is one for which there is no account in traditional epistemology; it takes Polanyian epistemology to make sense of it. It was this feature about Polanyi's thought, the fact that contact with reality brings with it its signature sense of the possibility of indeterminate future manifestations, which tantalized and excited me from the outset. That excitement continues, and extends now to inviting the real.

To talk of inviting the real is to cash in on covenant epistemology, to identify concrete and practical guidelines to coming to know. These guidelines are eye-catchingly not the sort of guidelines we have been programmed in our default setting to expect. But I believe that they ring truer to who we are as humans, and they express more aptly what it is we are doing when we are knowing well. As I hinted once before, the default mode we have inherited in the western tradition is actually not our most fundamental default setting. Being human is—knowing humanly.

Ascertaining what it is to be human, and what we as humans are and do most naturally, is itself an act of coming to know, interpretive throughout, and capable thereby of missing or accessing the real. In asking how humans know, what goes on in knowing, and in challenging the reigning default mode, we are seeking to move beyond restrictive and wrongheaded preconceived notions to attend more sensitively—to invite the real—with respect to how we actually go about knowing.

The practices we consider in this chapter accord with the kind of knowing that covenant epistemology describes. They accord with I-You encounter, but as such they also preface, context, and imbue all effective formalized endeavors. They bring not only the I of I-You into I-It, but also the entire I-You. The fact that "analysis" or "data collection" are not listed here does not mean that these are never to be practiced. It means that necessarily the dynamic core of analysis, that by which the analyst engages and moves toward insight, is more aptly described in the practices listed here. We will be better at data collection and analysis when we properly context them and honor that about the event that drives it. What drives it is our aspiration to interpersonal communion.

In identifying these unconventional practices of knowing, we also show once again how covenant epistemology's inherently cross-disciplinary vision allows us to draw rich resources from all over human life. Texts previously deemed "unepistemic" become rich pastures for epistemic grazing.

My list of practices of inviting the real is not intended to be exhaustive. Readers, knowers all, will be able to add additional criteria, or specific instantiations. I expect that each knower can identify personality-relative practices of inviting the real, even as each is usually characterized by personality-relative dimensions of reality that intrigue and invite careful attention. Hopefully my catalog primes the pump.

One thing that will happen, as you read, is that you will find that you already have been doing plenty of inviting of the real. You may have been calling it by a different name, or you may not have been encouraged to notice it or interpret it as profoundly epistemic. Years of piano practice, for example, translates into what I call covenantal living on the terms of the yet-to-be-known, or putting oneself in position to know. So what moving through this discussion should do is help to reorient your default epistemological setting to a covenant epistemological stance. It thus counts as what I call epistemological therapy.

Understanding that aspiring knowers are to invite the real will make us better knowers. No longer fixated deadeningly on information, we will know what it is to move through it and beyond it, in hope of being met by grace, to wisdom, to discovery, to insight, to innovation, to artistry, to healing, to communion—and to see the face of God. We will be better knowers; we will also be better at living as we live this practice.

Finally, in talking of inviting the real, I believe we are making yet another powerful case for the viability of covenant epistemology. Here we see what it looks like for us concretely, how it translates into knowing and living, and thus are able to test its mettle. Effective knowing behavior can be cast as inviting the real, and vice versa.

My mode of presentation itself models inviting the real, as opposed to reflective critique. While I have waited to write this chapter, I have indwelt and savored the array of quotations that I present here. I continue to listen to them, not holding them at a distance to scrutinize them so much as trying to insert myself inside them and try on their phrases. Thus I bring you to the texts themselves in the hope that you may do the same. Such listening, such indwelling, invites the real. It does not exclude reflective scrutiny, but reflective scrutiny often excludes the kind of indwelling that invites the real.

The inference that drives inviting the real is as follows: The real behaves like a person. Treat it personally, and it will respond personally. So practice epistemological etiquette. Specifically, invite it hospitably. Healthy knowing involves a perichoretic consent to "letting flourish" that is appropriate to evoking persons' gracious self-disclosure. My hope is that reading this chapter may catch you up into the passion of the adventure of knowing.

In what follows, I have arranged the practices I have identified in five loci: desire, composure, comportment, strategy, and culmination. The taxonomy is neither sacred nor exact. I do think it is helpful, because it shows how these practices each highlight the contours of interpersonal relationship and of knowing that covenant epistemology has been concerned to elucidate. We should not view the categories as distinct from each other; rather, they overlap, transmute, and generally merge into a single, personal, effort to invite the real. Also, you will find that we at least named several of these already in the course of our study. So this exploration should come as further consolidation of your grasp on the whole.

DESIRE

Desire, as a locus of strategies to invite the real, encompasses longing and love. While these are closely related, perhaps they suggest a passive and an active dimension of what it is that invites the real. Longing would be the passive, love the active. Longing calls for the other to give; love actively gives oneself for the sake of the other.

Together as passive and active, longing and love in a way say it all. If knowing is, as covenant epistemology proposes, interpersonal covenantal relationship, then (as the Beatles sang) love is all you need: it envelops all the succeeding strategies, and no difference exists between inviting the real and knowing itself. If anything is the core of inviting the real, and of the act of coming to know, this is it.

The central and shaping motive of knowing is love. To know *is* to love, says Parker Palmer.

> But I have come to see that knowledge contains its own morality, that it begins not in a neutrality but in a place of passion within the human soul . . . [K]nowledge originates in compassion, or love . . . [T]he goal of a knowledge arising from love is the reunification and reconstruction of broken selves and worlds . . . [It] aims at reconciling the world to itself. The mind motivated by compassion reaches out to know as the heart reaches out to love. Here, the act of knowing *is* an act of love, the act of entering and embracing the reality of the other, or allowing the other to enter and embrace our own."[1]

Here we hear the mutuality of love, both active and passive.

1. Palmer, *To Know as We Are Known*, 7.

Contrast this, Palmer continues, with the objectivist ideal of knowledge and we will find that this inviting the real can be dauntingly invasive but full of potential for deep joy:

> This love is not a soft and sentimental virtue, not a fuzzy feeling or romance. The love [that is] the connective tissue of reality is "tough love"—and we flee from it because we fear its claims on our lives. Curiosity and control create a knowledge that distances us from each other and the world, allowing us to use what we know as a plaything and to play the game by our own self-serving rules. But a knowledge that springs from love will implicate us in the web of life; it will wrap the knower and known in compassion, in a bond of awesome responsibility as well as transforming joy; it will call us to involvement, mutuality, accountability . . . A knowledge that springs from love may require us to change, even sacrifice, for the sake of what we know.[2]

Palmer's "bond of awesome responsibility" is covenant language. Here we hear both covenant and relationship. In our exposition of covenant epistemology, we saw that relational intimacy and covenantal structures or boundaries form counterparts that together constitute the relationship. Intimacy is union, covenant preserves otherness, we may say. Both are requisite for differentiation. In this duality, love emphasizes relational intimacy; we attend to covenant pledge in a few paragraphs.

Philosopher and Polanyian R. T. Allen argues that knowing is an expression of love. He argues that Polanyi's approach to knowing uniquely abets a Christian epistemology in a proper designation of its own distinctive features.[3] Specifically, a Christian epistemology rightly affirms that love is prior to knowing. This is something that key influential philosopher-Christians, such as St. Thomas, missed in their over-concession to a Greek approach. "At first sight, it seems nonsensical to state that knowing is a function or expression of love, for, apart from conventional beliefs that love is blind or distorts our knowing, surely one must know something or someone first before one can love it or him. Yet . . . Max Scheler . . . reverses these assumptions." Here Allen describes Scheler's argument in his essay on love and knowing. Scheler quotes Goethe: "One

---

2. Ibid., 9.

3. Allen, "Dialectic Revisited," 41. Allen's work complements covenant epistemology, offering a sophisticated articulation of Polanyi's work, Max Scheler's, John Macmurray's and others. Much of Allen's work has been devoted to developing the role of emotion in reason.

can get to know only that which one loves and the deeper and fuller the knowledge is to become, the stronger, more forceful and livelier must the love, indeed the passion, be." Scheler then contrasts this with a claim from Leonardo da Vinci: "Every great love is the daughter of a great cognition." Allen continues:

> Scheler's main argument is that the former represents the Christian relationship and the latter the Greek (and to some extent the Indian), but that, except for Augustine and some later followers such as Malebranche and Pascal, Christian thinking has submerged what should be its great insight and has assimilated itself too much to the Greek view, in which love is a desire and striving for something yet to be attained—from the lower to the higher, from "not being" to "being," from man to God (and hence Socrates' "love of wisdom" instead of "(possession of) wisdom"), which must disappear once its object, e.g. knowledge, is attained. This is opposed to the Christian view that love is a movement downwards from God to man, who first loved us.[4]

Allen puts his finger on what is perhaps the most fundamental shift that must transpire if persons plagued by a defective epistemic default are ever to be restored to wholeness as knowers. It isn't enough to talk about how important it is for love to lead us to knowing—and then deposit us at the doorstep, so to speak. We must see, Allen is saying, that knowing begins with love and is the expression of love through and through. He confirms that this is the heart of the distortion of much of the western philosophical tradition, and is the deeply embedded cancer that must be radically removed.

If knowing is an expression of love, the implications of this for epistemological etiquette are obvious. Even in our most careful and rigorous research, the drive that actualizes that research is a contexting, coring, paradigmatic love of the yet-to-be-known. Seen this way, love leads to the utmost covenantal care that careful research evidences. We must see that the kind of love that invites the real is the kind that is the heartbeat of the knowing itself. Thus love invites because it calls out to apprehend, and be apprehended by, its own.

4. Ibid., 42–43.

Longing

I have mentioned to you already the pastor who conferred on me noticing regard. Early on in our book-occasioned friendship, Russell Louden interrogated me in a booming voice: "Esther! Do you know the most important word in the title of your book?" "Know?" I answered, not at all entertaining that it might be either of the other two. "No!" he replied. "It is *longing*. Desire is the most important thing." In this he was putting his finger confidently on the heart of the matter.

I make an arbitrary distinction between love and longing, only to make the case that there appears to be both an active and a passive involvement. Longing, I will say, alludes to the passive side of desire.

Simone Weil writes, "Love is the soul's looking. It means that we have stopped for an instant to wait and to listen."[5] Ever the mystic who enjoins waiting, emptied, here she has just that in mind. She is describing love in its passive sense. "Any human being, even though practically devoid of natural faculties, can penetrate to the kingdom of truth reserved for genius, if only he longs for truth and perpetually concentrates all his attention upon its attainment."[6] And, "In the period of preparation the soul loves in emptiness. It does not know whether anything real answers its love . . . The soul knows for certain only that it is hungry. The important thing is that it announces its hunger by crying . . . The danger is not lest the soul should doubt whether there is any bread, but lest, by a lie, it should persuade itself that it is not hungry."[7] Passive longing is nevertheless actively anticipative. Weil speaks of passive activity.[8] In this it invites the real. She writes of developing attention as that passive activity, "the greatest of all efforts, but a negative effort."[9] "Attention consists of suspending our thought, leaving it detached, empty, and ready to be penetrated by the object."[10] She says that "we do not obtain the most precious gifts by going in search of them but by waiting for them. Man cannot discover them by his own powers, and if he sets out to seek for them he will find in their place counterfeits of which he will be unable to discern the falsity." Indeed, Weil blames wrong translations, clumsi-

5. Weil, *Waiting for God*, 140.
6. Ibid., 23.
7. Ibid., 138.
8. Ibid., 126.
9. Ibid., 61.
10. Ibid., 62.

ness of style, faulty concatenations of ideas, and so on, on having seized too hastily on some idea and thus prematurely blocking the truth. Weil argues that the right use of studies is to develop the kind of attention that invites God.[11]

In this we can also glimpse the covenantal self-binding of longing, which also involves the expectation that the real must exercise the initiative to self-disclose. We are humbly at its mercy. We have spoken frequently of the incoming of the real as bound allusively to the descent of God. Weil makes this connection as well.

Similarly, Abraham Joshua Heschel said that, while the Greeks learn in order to comprehend, the Hebrews learn in order to be apprehended.[12] Scripture's book of Psalms voices the cry of longing for God: "O God! You are my God, earnestly I seek you; my soul thirsts for you, my body longs for you, in a dry and weary land where there is no water."[13] Such passive longing to be apprehended is no mere longing for information. It is longing for transformation, longing for interpersonal communion. I suggest that longing for information, in a sense, is oxymoronic.

There is another way that longing comes to expression. It is in a sense of wonder or adventure. It is right to distinguish this, as Palmer does, from selfish curiosity: this is a longing for the real that implies my readiness to engage it, and that for its own sake, and for the sake of the wonder of what will transpire when knower and known meet in creative communion. Palmer says that "knowledge contains its own morality, that it begins not in a neutrality but in a place of passion within the human soul."[14] Indeed, to rekindle the longing to know is thus to invite the real. But now this starts to lean toward the active side of desire.

Love

I talked, in texture 1, about "blowing on the coals of your care." Caring, as I said, invites the real. In fact, I suggested that caring is its own justification. It is of a piece with being human. Not to care is to be dead.

---

11. In *Waiting for God*, this essay's title is, "Reflections on the Right Use of School Studies with a View to the Love of God" (57).

12. I have this statement synopsis from my colleague, Robert Frazier.

13. Ps 63:1.

14. Palmer, *To Know as We are Known*, 7. He distinguishes longing, on the other side, from control.

Steve Garber, guru of mentoring in higher education, himself mentor to celebrities as well as to ordinary people, writes: "To have knowledge of means to have responsibility to, means to have care for. If one knows, one cares; if one does not care, one does not know. It is personal knowledge, but not private or subjective, the differences are decisive. Rather it is rooted in the deepest realities of God's nature and character, and of our bearing His image, called to care for the world in imitation of Christ . . . The biblical vision is clear: to know is to love. Simply said."[15] Garber shares by name the vision of covenant epistemology, having come to the term and his version of the concept in a time frame similar to my own.[16] Understanding this is something he feels is critical for the sake of living and learning, for the sake of keeping intact what he designates "the fabric of faithfulness"—living with integrity as Christians in all dimensions of our lives.[17] It is evident here that care, for him, is active, responsible, love.

Here are examples of two forms this can take. In her philosophical analysis of love, Caroline Simon defines it as "imagining someone's destiny truly."[18] She makes the very astute distinction between love and "fiction making," which would be a false imagining of someone's future. To define love in terms of imagining future possibilities suggests the respect in which love is active and deeply attentive to the other. It also suggests that such love summons reality to rise to its full flourishing, even as a friend calls us, sometimes, to be more ourselves than we are being.[19]

Priest-cook-author of *The Supper of the Lamb: A Culinary Reflection*, Robert Farrar Capon, as part of his justification for his book enjoins all of us to "look the world back to grace"—a powerful phrase that could be our motto for life. In an earlier texture, we considered a lengthy passage of his, noting his claim about the looks of a woman in love being quickened to loveliness in the gaze of her lover. Here we heed his central point. It is the amateur, the lover, who is best positioned to look the world back

15. Garber, "Loving, Mourning, Knowing," 7, 15.

16. Personal conversation.

17. Garber, *Fabric of Faithfulness*.

18. Simon, *Disciplined Heart*.

19. This, by the way, underscores my earlier point that what we know, though flourishingly dynamic and indeterminate, is nevertheless charactered in its openness to the future. It is decisively telling that we may distinguish imagining destiny truly from fiction making.

to grace, and such action is what we are called to. Such love makes the world into what it is meant to be.[20] Having coached the reader through an hour of communion with an onion—yes, you read that correctly!— a "man-onion event," Capon continues: "I shall give my case for paying attention. Man's real work is to look at the things of the world and to love them for what they are. That is, after all, what God does, and man was not made in God's image for nothing . . . Things must be met for themselves. To take them only for their meaning is to convert them into gods—to make them too important, and therefore to make *them* unimportant altogether. Idolatry has two faults. It is not only a slur on the true God; it is also an insult to true things . . . One real thing is closer to God than all the diagrams in the world."[21] Capon not only voices the power of love to invite the real, he displays intuitive grasp of the entire vision of covenant epistemology. These phrases additionally share Colin Gunton's concern for the particularity of the world, accurately, I think, casting it in opposition to idolatry. They indicate the reciprocity of knowing, its therapeutic healing properties. And, of course, what he says aligns, because he assumes it as an analogue, with a sense of personal beauty as that which is called forth by the gaze of one who loves. Capon commends this loving as the calling of humans in the world.

It is love that makes us knowers. Palmer writes: "In the words of Abraham Joshua Heschel (another Jew who, like Buber, has a profound understanding of personal truth), 'It is impossible to find Truth without being in love.' In the words of St. Gregory, 'Love itself is knowledge; the more one loves the more one knows.'"[22]

Annie Dillard pronounces: "The lover can see, and the knowledgeable." She makes this comment in a chapter she calls, "Seeing," in her *Pilgrim at Tinker Creek*. She herself models it, *par excellence*, throughout the book—she helps her readers to see. She had told the story of being a guest at a dude ranch, and feeling her obvious inferiority in horsemanship, contrasted to the ranch hands.[23] She thought to herself—but I bet I can *sketch* a horse better than they can. She put it to the test. But she lost that match as well: the ranch hands drew horses far better than her own, for all her artistic training. The lover can see, and the knowledgeable.

20. Capon, *Supper of the Lamb*, 3–5.
21. Ibid., 19–21.
22. Palmer, *To Know as We are Known*, 57–58.
23. Dillard, *Pilgrim at Tinker Creek*, 20.

Love, not indifference, invites the real. In Capon's astute phrase, indifference is the fertilizing principle of unloveliness. Love presumes that the real is lovely or loveable or worth loving. Then it turns out that we see things about what we love that we would not have seen in indifference. What this is arguing is that love is what enables us to see things as they are and as they are meant to be. Love invites the real, because indifference invites falsehood.

But haven't we been told that love is *blind*? I would say yes. But the question is, what is it blind *to*, in a particular epistemic situation? To know is to be involved in subsidiary-focal integrative pattern-shaping. This inherently involves assigning significance interpretively—without which, one knows nothing at all. To assign significance involves saying, this (and not that) is part of the pattern. Remember also Buber's claim that I-You encounter fills all of time and space. Especially in those moments of our deepest knowing, all else pales.

Love must operate in advance of knowing. As a fledgling trajectory of coming to know unfolds, the aspiring knower accords value in advance of confirmation that his or her judgment is well-placed. This risk of love invites the self-disclosure of the real that is sought. Such a "Here I stand, I cannot do otherwise" indeed is both a self-binding and a self-blinding to that which threatens to thwart the eventual communion of insight that discovery promises.

It is also the case that the perspectival nature of our knowing requires and expects that knowers *together* apprehend multiple aspects of a very rich real, and are meant to contribute this complementarity to the epistemic community. In collegial love and solidarity, we invite the real.

Can our love adversely blind us to reality? Can it get in the way of our knowing? Yes. In our bentness, we are idol-makers. But arguably we might no longer want to term this, love. As part of our epistemological etiquette, I will say later that we must also exercise the humility to listen beyond the categories, our preconceived notions.

Someone may ask: where is the place for criticism? For calling evil evil? For being truthful about ugliness? A little thought leads us to realize that it's a matter of context. In the context of love, one may say, to return to an earlier example, "That dress doesn't do you justice." Especially in the context of a biblical theological vision, good (not evil) is both original and ultimate. Evil is distortion of the good, and the whole point of redemption is to remove the distortion. Of course, a doctor must say truthfully to a patient, "You have cancer." But that is a truthfulness about evil that is an act of love and thus invites the real.

Finally, it is intriguing to align with this account familiar descriptors drawn from "the Love chapter" in Scripture: "Love is patient, love is kind. It does not envy, it does not boast, it is not proud. It is not rude, it is not self-seeking, it is not easily angered, it keeps no record of wrongs. Love does not delight in evil but rejoices with the truth. It always protects, always trusts, always hopes, always perseveres. Love never fails."[24] Additionally, the writer is contrasting love to great gifts of knowledge. I suggest that he is casting the point forensically. Love and knowledge are not meant to oppose each other. The opposition is between "knowledge" that is not rooted in love and knowledge that is. It may be new to those familiar with this text to read these practices epistemically. But in fact there is a high degree of correspondence between them and my list of practices that invite the real.

And we have noted elsewhere the chapter-ending claim: "then I shall know even as I am fully known." The chapter suggests the inter-relationality of knower and known. I believe we are to take this, not just to describe knowing after the renewal of all things, but ever the character of knowing to which we as humans, this side of glory also, aspire.[25]

Reality self-discloses to those who bring to it the patient attentiveness, the covenant faithfulness, the un-self-serving passion to know, of love. Thus love encompasses many other facets to inviting the real.

COMPOSURE

One key inviter of the real is ourselves—more specifically, our selves having become most fully ourselves, composed as ourselves. I am saving "I-You" for the strategy category, choosing at that point to emphasize the "saying You." But we need only recall how Buber talked about becoming the I of I-You, and bringing that to all of our knowing. That is the sort of thing I have in mind by the locus I am calling composure.

24. 1 Cor 13.

25. Obviously, Palmer shares this approach—hence his using this phrase to name his book.

Before God

Loder showed that, to be ourselves fully, four-dimensionally, we must have been composed, recentered radically, in the loving gaze of the Other. For those who have been known by God, the Other, whatever or whoever else it may be, is God. Thus I list first composure before, in presence of, within the gaze of, God. Following Loder, we can also entertain that any act of coming to know serves as a prototype of this existential encounter, as does human development in infancy. What we take into ourselves from such acts of coming to know, and from our human development, as prototypically before the face of God, composes us, and more and more over a lifetime makes us better at inviting the real.

Thus we learn from John Calvin that the knowledge of God and that of ourselves is connected. Or Clement of Alexandria: "If one knows himself, he will know God." Or St. Augustine: "Let me know myself, let me know thee."[26] And from John Frame: All knowledge is knowledge of God.[27]

I am well aware that the bentness of humans, as I have said before, turns knowing topsy-turvy, such that it seems that believers and unbelievers stand equal chances of getting things right about the world, or even about God. In no way do I mean to condone any so-called spiritual shortcuts to insight. What is more, I am very hesitant to draw inferences from awareness of Scripture to the rectitude of its readers' conclusions. Even so, there are a few things that can be said that suggest that knowing God invites the real.

The first one is obvious, and the most important. To know God is to invite *him*. And he is real. So to know God is, therein, to invite the real. As a believer, I confess to humbled awe with every realization that I have, in fact, gotten it wrong about him, and yet receive his assurance that I may feel confident of his continual advent. This is part of what is going on in repentance and the grace of forgiveness.

Mike Williams regularly asks his students: "How many doctrines— and which ones—do we have to get right about God to be a Christian?"

---

26. McNeill, editor of Calvin's *Institutes*, lists the quotations from Augustine and Clement of Alexandria in the footnote to Calvin's revolutionary opening claim of the work, that knowledge of God and of self are the two aspects of sound wisdom, and which is prior is not easy to say (ibid., 35–36).

27. See ch. 6.

His own answer: "Not very many."[28] That is in no way a statement of presumption or permissiveness. Instead, it underscores that God is the initiator in covenant and redemption. God, the ultimate reality, self-discloses. He responds to my seeking, it seems; but then I will most likely learn afterward that he was seeking me first. Here we see what Williams said about the direction of the movement of things spiritual—that is, real: not ascent, but descent.

The last chapter of *Longing to Know* chronicles stories from Scripture of the sweet terror people feel when they seek God (so they think), and then God shows up. It leads us to ask the question I pose again in a few more paragraphs: how badly do I really want to know? Longing to know, it appears, is not always something we honestly embrace. When God shows up, sometimes it makes our word, "invite," appear laughable. Either he exposes our true motives, or he eclipses them.

To return to knowing God as inviting the real: Jesus said, not, "I have the truth," but "I am the Truth." God is Truth. To affirm covenant epistemology is only to make the barest dent into the richness of that claim. However, at least it calls to mind the insights of Buber and the others: the mode of existence, I-You, is not, as he termed it, a subjective experience; it is to stand in relation. To know Jesus the Truth is not to come away with information, except in a comparatively superficial sense. It is to be radically and forever changed. Not only does knowing God invite the real; knowing God changes radically what it was we thought we were inviting, and us the inviters in the process. Knowing is, fundamentally, transformation. "My Lord and my God!" Thomas bursts forth, signaling not so much critical verification as decisive, transformative, personal recentering.

A third thing. The whole point of the biblical drama of redemption is that Jesus' incarnation, life, death, and resurrection are together the central event of history that inexorably will lead to the renewal of all things. To believe him is to receive a downpayment, so to speak. In principle, knowing Jesus redemptively should help us be better knowers. Given the ravages of brokenness in our lives, the move to wholeness seems to proceed at a glacial pace. For all that, where we see true understanding resulting from lived relationship with the triune God, we may credit the work of the Holy Spirit. For example: when we see broken

---

28. I attended Williams' *Covenant Theology* class at Covenant Theological Seminary, Fall 2002, as I was revising his text for publication as *Far as the Curse is Found*.

relationships restored out of submission to the Lord, that should count as an instance of knowing God inviting the real. Scripture is emphatic: love of neighbor and love of God stand or fall together. To the extent that loving a neighbor involves knowing him or her truly, we may say that knowing God invites the real.

And it must be said, working from this theological vision, that Jesus' redemptive act is the one act of God to restore all that was broken by human rebellion. That includes human knowing. While we continue in the "already-not yet" of that unfolding redemption, we must see believers and unbelievers as similarly "on the way" epistemically. But it is the case that those who know Christ know him who is the key to epistemic health and stewardship—even if they do not yet know him as such. We may affirm this as true, and seek to treat it with intentionality, as we are doing here in covenant epistemology, even as we affirm that such health will only come to fruition in the "not-yet."

Fourth, Scripture indicates that many entries on my list of good epistemological etiquette are the fruit of knowing God. That does not mean that people may not evidence them in advance of explicit relationship to him. But take, for example, humility. Or take, for that matter, the very sort of covenantal pledge to the as-yet-undiscovered real that invites it. Are these not practices we might reasonably expect of one who has surrendered to God? I am simply arguing pragmatically here: it would seem that the quality would be eminently transferrable.

Finally, there is this. On the Christian theological vision, all reality is either God, or God's personal effects. I recall one time I had the chance to stay overnight with a dear former student who now lived in a town I was visiting to give a talk. I arrived there before she made it home from work. Never having been in her home before, I sat and soaked in the knickknacks, the furniture, the wall hangings, the colors. I saw how much I could see of her, both what I had already known, and what was new. I experienced both recognition and surprise.

I think of that experience when I think of reality being either God or his personal effects. We dwell in his beautifully appointed palace. May we not infer that in knowing the one, we will be knowing something of the other? May we not infer that it will delight the host who feels our love to share what he loves more fully with us—the artist, his work? May we not expect a moment of symbiotic mutual admiration—I don't quite know how to express this—to transpire when he arrives? In this way, knowing God gives us rich entrée into knowing both him and his world. It invites the real.

Hearkening back to our conversation about reality: it is his gift. The gift betokens the giver, and the giver shows up.

Being at Home (Presence)

We have already talked about presence, or being there, or being at home, in the context of our discussion of being intentional with respect to subsidiary knowledge. At the point that we began that discussion, we had not yet engaged the theorists of interpersonhood. In retrospect we are able to add more to that discussion.

Being at home is a kind of self-knowledge, or self-awareness. I have argued that it is a kind of subsidiary composure, a recentering that one being known may acquire within the noticing regard of the Other. It is subsidiarily embodied and lived. Yet we may exercise intentionality with respect to subsidiary dimensions. Doing this invites the real.

Developmental psychologist Blythe Clinchy says, "[One] who is essentially a stranger to himself is unlikely to forge an affective connection to someone else . . . Without self-knowledge we cannot preserve the otherness of the other."[29] To the extent that the real is personal, what pertains to relationships between persons pertains to knowing in general. So being at home invites the real.

Palmer tells us that the teacher teaches, not a lecture, but him- or herself. "We teach who we are . . . [A]t home in our own souls, we become more at home with each other . . . The more familiar we are with our inner terrain, the more surefooted our teaching—and living—becomes."[30] Palmer has listened to many people talk about their own favorite teachers: "But in every story I have heard, good teachers share one trait: a strong sense of personal identity infuses their work . . . Such a self, inwardly integrated, is able to make the outward connections on which good teaching depends."[31] In fact, Palmer subtitles a section in this portion of his argument, "Mentors who evoked us."[32] Where the knower is the teacher, and the known is ourselves, the students, good teachers, working

---

29. Clinchy, "Connected Knowing."
30. Palmer, *The Courage to Teach*, 2, 5.
31. Ibid., 10, 15.
32. Ibid., 21.

from inward integration, evoke *us*. Palmer thus reverses the common notions that grow out of a defective presumption concerning knowledge as information rather than transformation, that what the mentor does is impart a stream of knowledge top-down. Inward integration, being at home, invites the real.

Differentiation

Thus, the capacity of inward integration that is presence is closely related to differentiation. David Schnarch defined it as "the process by which we become more uniquely ourselves by maintaining ourselves in relationship with those we love."[33] Differentiation is the key to mutuality. It is a reasonable surmise that what Palmer is enjoining teachers to cultivate is differentiation. Even as we saw that differentiation makes for better knowing, so we may say that it invites the real.

I have already said that perichoresis in knowing involves conferring or consenting to the flourishing of the reality and particularity of the yet-to-be-known. Being at home through healthy self-definition affords reality the hospitable space in which it may move from guest to friend.

Personal Beauty

This leads us to return once again to the sense of personal beauty. This sense is a kind of self-knowing, and I have argued that it forms in the loving gaze of the Other. It itself is a real having been invited or evoked, as Capon says of the looks of a woman quickened to loveliness as she is loved, and as Moltmann-Wendel talked of the glint in a parent's eye so crucial to the wholeness of the child. I compared the effect to lighting a kerosene lamp that then proceeds to glow. In other words, a sense of personal beauty, in turn, invites the real. I link the sense of personal beauty with the personal state of being at home. Our culture, Christendom in particular, seems ever to set in opposition personal beauty and knowing. Covenant epistemology challenges this: a sense of personal beauty invites the real.

In my own experience of this, I linked the sense of personal beauty to the Gospel story of Jesus' encounter with the woman at the well. My daughter, Starr, connects it to Jesus' encounter with the frenzied man

33. Ch. 11.

among the tombs.[34] He was possessed by so many demons that the demons told Jesus their name was Legion. After Jesus drove them out (into a herd of pigs, for a humorous twist) and the townspeople came to check out the situation, the text says that they found the man sitting, clothed, and in his right mind, at the feet (meaning he had become a student) of Jesus. This is composure indeed! And it is beauty that invites the real.[35]

Where something that we may call a sense of personal beauty has developed in the aspiring knower, reality has its being "consented to" and thus may flourish and self-disclose in response. Thus it invites the real.

Embodiment

Closely linked with presence, as in our earlier discussion, are embodiment and a felt body sense. "Disembodiment is lovelessness," we saw that Moltmann-Wendel avers.[36] Lovelessness, we may surmise, adversely affects knowing. In the following comment she links embodiment with apprehending God:

> The senses are nearer to God than ideas, says meditation culture. I believe that we cannot separate thinking of God and grasping God with the senses. In beginning to think with the body, to live with the senses, we can also attempt to think in a believing way with the senses . . . In the end there is no barrier between sense and thought, any more than there is between faith and life.[37]

Even a modest effort at coherent interpretation of this passage indicates that she is not talking about passive sense perception, nor of neurons firing and eye muscles orienting. Thinking with the body involves what I have described as a virtuoso-like, felt, subsidiary awareness.

Felt Body Sense

Also, we saw that Eugene Gendlin actually identified a body event, a shift in felt body sense, which we can learn to identify to confirm the aptness of a descriptor word we try on for size. Real change is about identify-

---

34. Luke 8.

35. Although, come to think of it, the townspeople were not in the mood to invite it: they demanded that Jesus leave the region. Heaven only knows how they treated the man.

36. Moltmann-Wendel, *I Am My Body*, 104.

37. Ibid., 97.

ing your felt body sense, trying out words on it, and paying attention to when your body responds. I noted that Michael Parmenter the New Zealand dance artist believes that Gendlin is also aptly describing the artistic experience. Analogously, we may expect that it describes an act of coming to know. Especially in instances where the trajectory of knowing is inaugurated in the lived body, to the extent that we are attuned to and are able to interpret that sense aright, this invites the real. Often our body awareness is a kind of anticipative knowing. "Did not our hearts burn within in us . . . ?"

Fidelity

"Truth is a fidelity rather than a conformity," states Palmer. He quotes Leslie Dewart: "Conformity is a relation towards another which is owing to another by reason of the other's nature. Fidelity is a relation towards another which one owes to oneself by reason of one's own nature. Conformity obligates from the outside. Fidelity . . . obligates from within. In the personal mode of knowing and teaching we must always be aware of the other's nature. But that nature—which is sometimes darkened by ignorance or prejudice or greed—is not the final arbiter of our response. We must respond to the other not in conformity to what he or she wants, but in fidelity or obedience to the truth within us."[38] This passage accords significantly with Gendlin's thesis, and also with the idea of inward integration, authenticity, and differentiation.

The word *true* has an array of meanings. One of them is the one we have in mind when we think of a plumbline or a wall: things coming into perfect alignment. On an epistemic model that portrays the knower as passively registering data, nothing like this sense of true, or Dewart's sense of fidelity, is bodily experienced. Yet we do have that sense, even in the moment of transformation.

While fidelity here sounds like felt body sense, perhaps it is negative rather than positive: it invites the real by rejecting what is false, untrue, to who we ourselves are. Thus, growing in the area of fidelity may be similar to the boundary setting that is part of differentiation. This suggests further that there can well be a time frame before which we are not ready to hear and apprehend, and another during which we are. This accords well with an account of knowing as a being on the way.

38. Palmer, *To Know as We Are Known*, 90. Palmer quotes Dewart, *Future of Belief*, 96.

Additionally, fidelity as boundary setting is covenantal. It is covenantal self-definition. It involves saying what I am, and what I am not,
and maintaining that integrity before the yet-to-be-known. Seeing fidelity as an aspect of covenant relationship brings it in line with differentiation as healthy composure that invites the real.

Openness

Finally, I list a couple of practices that are not so much stances with
respect to God or ourselves as they are stances with respect to the yet-
to-be-known. In this they incline in the direction of the next locus,
comportment. They involve the knower's own disposition, which she or
he cultivates within. The first is openness. We have to be open to what
inviting the real will bring into our lives. "A knowledge that springs from
love may require us to change, even sacrifice, for the sake of what we
know," says Palmer. But, he says, "When we allow ourselves to be known
in truth, we are able to see and hear and feel more of the world's reality
than we could before we were known."[39] Thus, openness invites the real.

Take, for example, the commonly desired blessing of making
friends. The old maxim is that to have friends you must show yourself
friendly. There is a kind of openness about a person that is inviting. On
the other hand, some people—and we ourselves—sometimes signal and
maintain closedness. This example shows in retrospect how fidelity can
operate helpfully. Fidelity requires that openness is to be wisely practiced. Knowing isn't just information, but leads to personal existential
change—for better or for worse. Not all instances of enlightenment
bring wholeness.

Openness is a willingness, in the knowing, to be known in turn.
Even in healthful and trust-secured situations this is risky business. It
is perhaps the thing that most prevents us from inviting the real. Our
bentness as humans means that we are more likely to run from knowing
rather than loving to know. "When academics speak of 'the pursuit of
truth,' they rightly imply that a gap exists between ourselves and truth.
But there is a conceit hidden in that image, the conceit that we can close
the gap as we track truth down. In Christian understanding, the gap exists not so much because truth is hidden and evasive but because we are.
We hide from the transforming power of truth, we evade truth's quest for

---

39. Palmer, *To Know as We Are Known*, 60.

us."[40] Who is hiding? Often it isn't the real; it is the knower. Palmer links openness to having a strong sense of self. "The courage to teach" that is the focus of Palmer's book is the courage to remain open that comes only from that inward integration, that strong sense of self, that he has described.[41]

Embracing Pain

Finally I list pain, a practice closely akin to openness. I have this from therapist Dan Allender, whose book, *The Healing Path: How the Hurts in Your Past Can Lead You to a More Abundant Life,* describes the often painful, always courageous, journey we must embrace as part of our moving to wholeness in whatever part of our lives has been broken. This calls for embracing pain. You don't have to wonder or worry *whether* you will have to embrace pain. You can be assured that at some point you will have to. Allender says: "Embracing a person or reality requires openness . . . Openness involves a hunger for life . . . In opening our arms to another, we put out a welcome sign that implies we have made room for them ourselves . . . For that reason, to the degree we open our arms, we are changed . . . Pain enables us to discover ourselves."[42]

In my own experience, I have found that pain did prove an entrée into insight and reality. I underwent a lengthy period of deep grieving— not anything I chose for the sake of therapeutic healing, but something I was thrust into by the circumstances of my life. I said earlier that there was a time that I underwent a kind of conversion from Cartesianism to being in my body. It was this experience of grief that led to that conversion. In the pain, for the first time, I began to sense my body—and, I began to know the palpable presence of God. Reality seemed to walk in through the door of my pain, changing me in the direction of wholeness. It also connected me more empathetically—more knowingly—with others in their suffering.

Moltmann-Wendel explicitly confirms this. In talking of women and their bodies, she says that "sick people can more credibly speak of their sickness as a journey on which they have unsuspected experiences with their bodies." She reports the testimony of one woman who first

40. Ibid., 59–60.
41. Palmer, *Courage to Teach*, 11.
42. Allender, *Healing Path*, 37.

grieves her mutilated body just after her cancer surgery, but comes in six months' time to a different view: "'And when life is cruel to you, don't grumble, don't cry, but hold on and wait patiently until something good happens to you. How will you become a human being without pain? It seems to me that at that moment God is nearer to me than to you. You may perhaps want to grasp him with the head, through the understanding, but he shows himself to you in quite a different way . . . Words do not express approximately what I feel is happening to me. But I am just beginning to live.'"[43]

Marjorie Grene, we saw, linked authenticity with intense suffering. Simone Weil offers a sustained reflection on affliction. "Through joy," she says, "the beauty of the world penetrates our soul. Through suffering it penetrates our body. We could no more become friends of God through joy alone than one becomes a ship's captain by studying books on navigation. The body plays a part in all apprenticeships."[44] In this testimony to the role of pain, we may also hear her affirm both the inadequacy of explicit knowledge and the covenantal binding of true knowing.

Is it only in interpersonal relationships that pain invites the real? Of course, I have been arguing persistently that we see all knowing as interpersonal relationship. But Alain de Botton, writing of our appreciation of art and architecture, says something effectively the same: "We may need to have made an indelible mark on our lives, to have married the wrong person, pursued an unfulfilling career into middle age or lost a loved one before architecture can begin to have any perceptible impact on us, for when we speak of being 'moved' by a building, we allude to a bitter-sweet feeling of contrast between the noble qualities written into a structure and the sadder wider reality within which we know them to exist."[45] It may be that pain softens us, thus producing additionally some qualities of comportment and strategies that invite the real.

COMPORTMENT

Comportment, as a locus of practices that invite the real, identifies qualities of relating to the yet-to-be-known. In a way these are akin to moral

43. Moltmann-Wendel, *I Am My Body*, 24. She draws her citation from Maxie Wander, *Guten Morgen, du Schöne*, 163.

44. Weil, *Waiting for God*, 79.

45. de Botton, *Architecture of Happiness*, 22.

virtues. But I head the list with covenant, which, of course, definitively constitutes knowing on the covenant epistemology model.

Pledge, Covenant

Covenant involves virtue—keeping one's promises. But making a pledge—covenanting—is what is known as an illocutionary act. The very saying of it is an action—a speech act. Both making and sustaining pledge is the comportment, with respect to its object, that is central to and constitutive of love.

Let us listen again to a key passage from Palmer's work that we first encountered in chapter 2. Having worked extensively through both covenant and personhood, we will now clearly recognize these elements in this text. Parker Palmer speaks of truth as troth:

> To know something or someone in truth is to enter troth with the known, to rejoin with new knowing what our minds have put asunder. To know is to become betrothed, to engage the known with one's whole self, an engagement one enters with attentiveness, care, and good will. To know in truth is to allow one's self to be known as well, to be vulnerable to the challenges and changes any true relationship brings. To know in truth is to enter into the life of that which we know and to allow it to enter into ours. Truthful knowing weds the knower and the known; even in separation, the two become part of each other's life and fate . . . Rather, truth involves entering a relationship with someone or something genuinely other than us, but with whom we are intimately bound . . . Truth requires the knower to become interdependent with the known. Both parties have their own integrity and otherness, and one party cannot be collapsed into the other . . . We find truth by pledging our troth, and knowing becomes a reunion of separated beings whose primary bond is not of logic but of love.[46]

Foremost in this text is the idea of pledge, or covenant. Palmer confirms that intimate reciprocal, perichoretic, relationship is integral to this. And he says that this invites the real: we find truth by pledging our troth; thus knowing becomes the love-, not logic-, based reunion of separated beings.

What does it look like to pledge love to the yet-to-be-known? This is how I began to envision the covenant epistemology project. Annie

---

46. Palmer, *To Know as We Are Known*, 31–32.

Dillard was modeling, in her stalking of muskrats, covenanting love.[47] To covenant with the yet-to-be-known is, accepting its guidance, to bind yourself to behaviors that position you strategically to be there when it shows up, and even to evoke it. I spoke early on about the fact that, even if we do not fully know the thing we long for, we must also begin to live our lives on its terms. We must show our readiness to obey the yet-to-be-known, to live in light of its only partially revealed reality. Many of us can list courses of study and of training in which we have invested years of our lives and thousands of dollars. Take, for example, the training it would take to contribute significantly to the search for a cure for cancer. That is what I have in mind by covenanting comportment that invites the real. Of course, sadly, we can spend the money and the time and yet register only a very uncovenantal indifference. Many of us can confess to squandering periods of our college years, for example. We often say: "you have to want it." But this just shows that, as love to be love must be covenantal, so covenant to be covenant must be the constitutive embodiment of love.

Covenantal living life on the terms of the yet-to-be-known involves a person intrinsically in the other practices of comportment.

Trust

In his 1989 book, *Real Presences*, George Steiner argues that making sense of art and its meaningfulness requires the presence of a transcendent other. He too collects motifs of the interpersoned to elucidate the artistic experience, motifs that resonate profoundly with my epistemological etiquette. Since I see the artistic experience to be of a piece with all acts of coming to know, I find it easy to appropriate his claims.

Steiner points out that the mysterious presence of the Other is both consoling and harsh.[48] We both long for the Other and feel threatened by the Other. Steiner describes us as "monads haunted by communion."[49] He then raises the fact that meeting with the other is an event that is surrounded, in most societies, by much attention to decorum, etiquette that is often quasi-religious. It has to do with welcome, with courtesy, and

---

47. See ch. 2.
48. Steiner, *Real Presences*, 137.
49. Ibid., 140.

with tact.[50] Welcome offers a wonderful parallel to my notion of inviting the real. Steiner mines these rich words to describe how we should encounter a poem or other work of art, as well as to express what that encounter involves. "Great poetry is animate with the rites of recognition," he says. He speaks of the "rendezvous of the human psyche with absolute otherness, with the strangeness of evil or the deeper strangeness of grace."[51] He talks of how we lay a clean cloth on the table when we hear a guest at our threshold, how we light the lamp in the window, and how these are both domestic and sacramental. He calls these, quite profoundly, impulses known in immediacy; they cannot be formalized or "proved"—"(no significant act of spirit can be)." But, he says, they are of the essence, or essential.[52]

Steiner makes the point that welcome requires an act of trust. For "the implicit impulses in such acts are precisely those in which the yearning towards and fear of the other, the motions of feeling and of thought which would, at the same time, guard and open outward their particular, individual dwelling, come together." He continues:

> Face to face with the presence of offered meaning which we call a text (or a painting or a symphony), we seek to hear its language. As we would that of the elect stranger coming towards us. There is in this endeavour . . . an ultimately unprovable hope and presupposition of sense, a presumption that intelligibility is conceivable and, indeed, realizable. Such a presupposition is always susceptible of refutation . . . In short, the movement towards reception and apprehension does embody an initial, fundamental act of trust. It entails the risk of disappointment or worse. As we shall note, the guest may turn despotic or venomous. But without the gamble on welcome, no door can be opened when freedom knocks.[53]

Inviting the real requires a fundamental act of trust. We have spoken of risk, and of openness to it. These closely intertwine.

The medievals' well-known *credo ut intelligam*—I believe in order to understand—assumes fresh meaning in this context. I trust as an overture to invite the real. We do not yet know fully who stands at the

---

50. Ibid., 146–49.
51. Ibid., 147.
52. Ibid., 149.
53. Ibid., 156.

door as we open it. In that not-yet-knowing, we must act or the knowing never comes to fruition.

Obedience

I have hinted that, if knowing involves covenant, we should expect "trust and obey"[54] to be sound epistemic practice. For covenant is not transfer of information; it is transaction. What makes sense in the context of transaction is language of actively responsive compliance. Thus, obedience invites the real. Here we see that confirmed in Palmer's rich work: "Learning the truth requires that we enter into personal relationship with what the words reveal. To know truth we must follow it with our lives . . . Obedience requires the discerning ear, the ear that listens for the reality of the situation, a listening that allows the hearer to respond to that reality, whatever it may be."[55] Additionally, he says, "Knowledge of the truth requires a personal dialogue between the knower and the known, a dialogue in which the knower listens to the world with obedience." The root of the word, understanding, according to Palmer, means not only to listen, but "to listen from below." "Both obedience and understanding [standing under something] imply submitting ourselves to something larger than any one of us, something on which we all depend." Referring to objectivism as "a domineering mentality," "a white, middle-class male version of 'truth,'" Palmer concludes that the view that truth is personal succeeds in moving us beyond this to a dialogue in which all parties subject themselves to the bonds of communal troth in what is more likely to be a way of knowing that heals us and our broken world.[56]

Returning to Dillard and the muskrats, we may see that her complying with what the muskrats themselves "stipulated" about stalking is a kind of obedience. Obedience just is covenantal binding.

Elsewhere I have spoken of obedience as subsidiarily lived truth. And I have spoken, in reference to knowing God, of obedience thus effectively inducing our knowing him.[57] In the case of God, obedience does invite the real. Jesus threw down the challenge to his critics: "If any-

---

54. This phrase is the name of a still-popular old gospel hymn. The hymn avers that there is no other way to be happy in Jesus, I am suggesting that there is no other way to know—which, of course, is profoundly connected, I believe, to being happy in Jesus.

55. Palmer, *To Know as We Are Known*, 65–68.

56. Ibid., 68.

57. Meek, *Longing to Know*, ch. 22.

one chooses to do God's will, he will find out whether my teaching comes from God or whether I speak on my own."[58] This is the text John Frame would cite to make the case that epistemology is a subset of ethics.

Humility

We may easily infer that humility is intimately involved in such covenantal behavior. Also, it is not difficult to think of instances in our lives where it was our stance of humility that invited the real. What comes to my mind is the moment, after a class, that a student came to me and said, "I want to know more of this—*please*." Early in the semester as it was, quite honestly I had yet to notice him. Nor did I as he began to speak to me, until he said, please. This was no perfunctory politeness. I heard the deep and urgent humility in his voice. In that instant I felt myself bound into covenant with him in knowing. Humility invites the real's self-disclosure.

David Dark, in his *Everyday Apocalypse*, puts forward the thesis that our lives are full of opportunities for revelation—for the self-disclosure of God. Apocalypse is everyday. As the best of high-school literature teachers, Dark himself models and encourages us to practice listening to the likes of Flannery O'Connor, the Simpsons, the Coen brothers, and Radiohead—voices whose message is not always pleasant to apprehend. His point that the potential for apocalypse is everywhere, if only we develop the sensitivity to identify it, I believe describes all acts of coming to know.[59] Dark is describing and modeling ways to invite the real's self-disclosure. And, of course, this hints of God's revelation.

Here is what Dark says that prompts me to list humility among dimensions of real-inviting comportment: "Unfortunately, the humility that is marked by a genuine readiness to know and acknowledge our own weaknesses and fears comes no more naturally to us than it does to the characters on The Simpsons. Yet without this humility of mind, no story, no art, and no apocalyptic can do its work on us. We walk through life unaffected, unmoved, and forever consigned to an invincible ignorance."[60] Dark links humility with genuine readiness to know, and names this a *sine qua non* for everyday apocalypse. Saying it

---

58. John 7:17.

59. Meek, "Response to David Dark."

60. Dark, *Everyday Apocalypse*, 44–45.

positively, humility invites the real. And if Dark is right, it profoundly enriches every corner, every day, of our lives. Life becomes a bounteous table of insights and transformation.

Patience

Another obvious dimension to covenantal comportment is patience. Where our epistemic task is construed as inviting the real and knowing as a whole unfolding trajectory, the knower must sustain the pledge over what can be a lengthy period of time. Another word for this is waiting, which Dillard was practicing on the bridge. Simone Weil titles her book, *Waiting for God*. She does so because she feels that this is *the* way to invite him. "We do not obtain the most precious gifts by going in search of them but by waiting for them . . . Only this waiting, this attention, can move the master to treat his slave with such amazing tenderness."[61] This negative withholding over time signals covenant love, and induces the response of the real.

Saying "You," and Listening

To finish off this locus of the practices of comportment, let us add saying "You" to reality. Really, this one belongs anywhere and everywhere. It is arguably just the active love of the first locus. It involves the I of the second. I am listing it here under comportment. But it also bleeds naturally into strategy; it is especially akin to noticing regard, and a special kind of seeing. And given that it invokes the actualization of intimate communion, which needs no justification, saying "You" to reality belongs in the fifth locus, consummation.

We saw that Buber says that the I of I-You says or speaks "You" and listens. I would like to stop writing at this point, and just leave the rest of the page blank, to surround this profound statement with the silence it deserves, but also not to detract from it by adding two-dimensionalizing attempts to develop it. Nevertheless—

To say "You" and to listen is effectively to personalize the world anticipatively. By way of analogy, think of how we sometimes say that if we treat a child like an adult, the child will behave like an adult. I heard something like this expressed in a radio commentary recently concerning the fictional character, Auntie Mame, in the book and the musical

---

61. Weil, *Waiting for God*, 63.

whose title references her, and by analogy concerning the commentator's own real Aunt Vivian. The commentator noted how Auntie Mame treated her young nephew as the grown-up he was yet to become, and how that was a signature, real-inviting, virtue of hers.[62] Similarly, Buber calls us to practice the very thesis of covenant epistemology, to treat the world as personal. His work underscores that this is to invite it, to find that it rewards such construal.

This is no impersonal technique. This is the self-exposing, self-giving, offer of friendship. It alone invites the disclosure of the personal dimensions of the real. It is a readiness to see the real in its excellence that believes and accepts nothing less.

As part of a longing I have to see the healing of brokenness in my own home town of Aliquippa, PA, I helped orchestrate a mission trip of students from the college where I teach to Uncommongrounds Café, a zesty mission of the Episcopal Church Army, staffed unforgettably by Captain John Stanley. I had come to know and admire John; I anticipated and coveted his working with students I also care about. I expected them to flourish by being alongside him in his work. My investment paid dividends well beyond what I had been able to conceive. As I worked at a table at the Cafe, doing some writing for John during that week, I witnessed John invite the students into shared ownership of the vision and unleash them to dream and actualize their dream. I watched students set free to attempt and carry out amazing things, well beyond what they thought they could accomplish. They surprised and delighted themselves in the process. John knows how to invite the real by saying "You" and listening. In fact, as an evangelist, he is committed to the practice of what he calls, listening evangelism. As you listen, people tell their stories of brokenness, and the Spirit opens their eyes to find Christ.[63]

STRATEGY

I label the next locus of practices, strategy, because they involve active investment, along with the potential to be carried out strategically with planning and artistry. They are techniques that also make good business sense.

62. Bob Mondello, "Auntie Mame."

63. Meek, "Nurturing a Mustard Seed." Also see the Café website, www.uncommon groundscafe.org.

Being in the Way of Knowing

By this phrase I do not mean planting opposition in the path of knowing. I mean, rather, planting yourself in the path of knowing. Also, it doesn't mean the same thing as being *on* the way to knowing. Being in the way of knowing means putting yourself in position, in the place where you expect something to show up. Meteor showers occur with regularity around the middle of August. You might, as I have and will, take a blanket out to a treeless yard after dark and lie on it and start watching the sky. Sometimes it is the simplest, deepest humility, just to show up.[64]

In our lives, our professions, our study, we grow and value a sense of where to find insight, counsel, innovation. This includes texts, authoritative guides, and settings conducive to our own discovery. For example, before I had read Parker Palmer's later work, *The Courage to Teach*, I knew to expect great reward. To read his work is to plant myself in the way of knowing. All I have to do is show up. I can expect a deluge of joyous insight.

People who want to buy and sell tickets plant themselves in close proximity to the flow of pedestrians toward the stadium. That's what I have in mind. Being in the way of knowing is not so much about the preparation that we talked about in connection with covenant pledge. It is more about the strategy and timing of placement. Being in the way of knowing invites the real.

Noticing Regard

The Gospel story that I have already linked to this next practice starts with a great example of being in the way. Jesus, it says, "had to go through Samaria . . . [H]e sat down by the well."[65] It is common knowledge that no Jew ever saw himself as "having" to go to Samaria! Samaria was full of half-breeds left over from the Assyrian occupation and, prior to that, the "sin of Jeroboam," the man who by setting up idols to worship in the northern part of Israel precipitated the division of north and south, Israel and Judaea, and the apostasy of Israel. Traveling to and fro between Galilee and Jerusalem, good Jews always circumvented Samaria. And the more religiously pure they saw themselves, the more they did so. Add to

---

64. In *Teaching a Stone to Talk*, Dillard describes the effort to put herself in the path of seeing a total solar eclipse (ibid., 85).

65. John 4.

that—and I am not sure of this—but I don't think a self-respecting rabbi would ever have sat himself down by the well midday: *women* draw from the well, and "bad" women do it in the heat of the day when everyone will leave them alone. Jesus evidently was up to something.

I offered my own experience of noticing regard at the end of chapter 9. Here are some other things that led me to develop that term. The concept first came to me when I was co-presenting a talk on hospitality. In a preparatory discussion with my co-presenter, I was disputing his claim that letting someone borrow your house when you are away is hospitality. I felt strongly that it wasn't. The host has to be there. On the other hand, a good host hits a happy medium between offering no attention and offering too much attention to the guest. Henri Nouwen has famously defined hospitality as "the creation of a free space where the stranger can enter and become a friend. Hospitality is not to change people, but to offer them space where change can take place."[66] Palmer adapts this fertile notion of space to cast teaching in terms of it. He envisions us inviting the real both of the student and of the subject of truth: to teach is to create a space in which the community of truth is practiced.[67] Reflecting on this and on my discomfort with my friend's proposal, I developed the idea of noticing regard. The host, graciously, while sharing the space and granting freedom, notices the guest with regard.

Not all notice is kind. It can be damning. To notice a person in regard, to have been so noticed, is personally powerful. It can constitute the very person. And noticing regard is often graciously and artfully done. One of the most provocative sentences of Scripture is what Jesus actually said to greet the woman who came to the well: "Will you give me a drink?" In it he put himself and her on the same level, inviting her initiative in response to his own need.

This, we saw, is Simone Weil's "creative attention." In talking of the Good Samaritan, one of Jesus's parables, she says, "Only one stops and turns his attention toward [the nameless bleeding lump of flesh in the ditch] . . . The attention is creative . . . not extending his own power but giving existence to a being other than himself."[68] "Creative attention means really giving our attention to what does not exist," she says. "Love

66. Nouwen, *Reaching Out*, 71.

67. Palmer, *Courage to Teach*, 90.

68. Weil, *Waiting for God*, 90.

sees what is invisible."[69] Weil is claiming for creative attention the most profound inviting of the real. Noticing regard confers dignity, assigning the value to the noticed that is an integrative epistemic event, and simultaneously invites the known to be itself freely.

Since knowers need first to be composed, to be reconstituted as the I of I-You, noticing regard serves the critical function of inviting the reality, the very humanity, of other knowers. But noticing also invites reality other than humans. Noticing is active perception. The idea of noticing underscores Polanyi's point that the simplest act of sensation is an active and personal shaping of a pattern. When Mom says to the baby, "Eye," and points first to hers and then to the baby's, she is catalyzing that picking out of the pattern that is noticing. For us to observe, we must first have noticed. And there are people who fulfill strategic roles of helping us notice certain things: homeless people, sex trafficking, genocide, Africa, sunsets, public transportation, fabrics, aromas, features of an excellent ski jump, even as I notice dimensions of the personal in knowing and being. All knowing is noticing, we may say, the assigning of value or significance that constitutes the pattern. Noticing, and noticing regard, thus invites the real.

Active Listening

As part of Gene Gendlin's practice of focusing, other people may be involved as active listeners. Active listeners, people who listen well and can prompt our own focusing by asking well-placed and well-attuned questions, can play a key role in the focusing. When I first met Gendlin, I heard him give a lecture the thesis of which was this: People don't have a story until you hear it. Literally, the story comes about in response to the active listener.[70] Clearly, active listening thus invites the real.

Similarly, Palmer references Nellie Morton saying that "one of the great tasks of our time is to 'hear people to speech.'" He asks, "What does it mean to listen to a voice before it is spoken? It means making space for the other, being aware of the other, paying attention to the other,

---

69. Weil, *Waiting for God*, 92. Consider also Weil's application of this to God's acts of creating and sustaining: "God *thought* that which did not exist, and by this thought brought it into being. At each moment we exist only because God consents to think us into being" (ibid., 92). This resonates profoundly with the covenantally normed relational love that *Loving to Know* follows Scripture in crediting with creation.

70. Gendlin, "Tacit/Implicit in a New Kind of Thinking."

honoring the other. It means not rushing to fill our students' silences with fearful speech of our own and not trying to coerce them into saying the things that we want to hear. It means entering empathetically into the student's world so that he or she perceives you as someone who has the promise of being able to hear another person's truth."[71]

Listening Beyond the Categories

Active listening involves something difficult for everyone, simply as a result of the way we are made. We generally—and this is a good thing—learn to put words on the world, and then we experience the world along the lines of the words we have put on it. However, this is the very thing that can impede our moving beyond our concepts to apprehend new insights. Thus, we have to find intrinsically informal ways to practice what I call "listening beyond the categories."

Learning to listen to apocalyptic, David Dark claims, will help us listen beyond the categories. "Apocalyptic shows us what we're not seeing ... By announcing a new world of unrealized possibility, it serves to invest the details of the everyday with cosmic significance while awakening its audience to the presence of marginalizing forces otherwise unnamed and unchallenged."[72] And Palmer writes: "To practice obedience to truth we must start to hear what the subject is saying about itself beyond all our interpretations . . . [W]hen we interview the subject instead of just viewing it, then we find the subject speaking back to us in ways surprisingly independent of our own preconceptions. In this 'otherness' of the subject we are drawn out of our isolated knowing into the community of troth; we are drawn out of merely knowing into being known."[73] Palmer suggests specific ways we may listen beyond the categories. One is simply by being silent: "In silence more than in argument our mind-made-world falls away and we are opened to the truth that seeks us. If our speech is to become more truthful it must emerge from and be corrected by the silence that is its source."[74]

Another he calls "thinking the world together"—as opposed to thinking the world apart. The latter he associates with the dichotomous

71. Palmer, *Courage to Teach*, 46.
72. Dark, *Everyday Apocalypse*, 10.
73. Palmer, *To Know as We Are Known*, 98–99.
74. Ibid., 80.

thinking I connected with the daisy diagram, the either-ors of our default epistemological setting. But he also has in mind the either-ors that result inevitably from our conceptualizing. What he encourages his readers to is "paradoxical thinking": "Paradoxical thinking requires that we embrace a view of the world in which opposites are joined, so that we can see the world clearly and see it whole."[75] We must hold opposites in tension if we are to uncover "the hidden wholeness" that is real. —In other words, invite the real.

Polanyi's integration of subsidiaries into a transcendent pattern does just this, by the way. He notes that the particulars which come to serve subsidiarily in shaping the pattern often include sets hitherto viewed, when looked at, rather than through, as mutually contradictory. The would-be discoverer, therefore, in anticipation of the discovery and as a way to invoke it, must subsidiarily shift her/his manner of relating to the clues to move beyond the apparent contradiction to the whole that makes transformative sense of them. This just is listening beyond the categories to invite the real.

Palmer mentions, as an evocative image, "practicing soft eyes."[76] He says that the Japanese self-defense art of aikido teaches students to counter the automatic narrowing of eyes produced by the fight or flight mechanism by widening their eyes, widening their peripheral vision, to take in more of the world. When our eyes can be wide with wonder, we may take in "the greatness of the world and the grace of great things." This activity prompts something akin to listening beyond the categories.

Finally, listening beyond the categories is something which may occur perichoretically in overture and response. I try one word, I receive partial response. Later, I move beyond that word to try another and receive fuller response. Knowing comes to us in stages, and those stages often are the fresh categories was try on for size.

Indwelling

The culminating strategy for inviting the real is indwelling. This concept Polanyi himself gave us as part and parcel of what is involved in the subsidiary-focal integrative process. It displays many signature features of a Polanyian construal of knowing. Indwelling refers to the way the

75. Palmer, *Courage to Teach*, 66.
76. Ibid., 113.

lived body extends itself through the skilled use of tools—the tool user both indwells and interiorizes the tools. It refers to the inherent unspecifiability of tacit knowledge, such that apprentice or student must indwell master or teacher in order to come away with knowledge that is more than the teacher is able to specify and more than the student is able to specify also. Indwelling refers to what one tries to do in order to shift one's manner of relating to the particulars so as to relate to them as clues and evoke the solution. I have spoken at times of needing to "climb into the clues," that is indwelling.

Returning to the idea of indwelling the teacher, we may now note other people's claims that underscore the need for this sort of empathetic involvement in the yet-to-be-known. For example, we noted that James Loder says, "Knowing *anything* is to indwell it and to reconstruct it in one's own terms without losing the essence of what is being indwelt."[77] "In the mutual indwelling of subject and object lies true objectivity."[78] With respect to pedagogy, Palmer argues: "If we dare to move beyond fear, to practice knowing as a form of love, we might abandon our illusion of control and enter a partnership with the otherness of the world. By finding our place in the ecosystem of reality, we might see more clearly which actions are life-giving and which are not—and in the process participate more fully in our own destinies, and the destiny of the world, than we do in our drive for control. This relational way of knowing—in which love takes away fear and co-creation replaces control—is a way of knowing that can help us reclaim the capacity for connectedness on which good teaching depends."[79] This capacity for connectedness, I am inferring, is indwelling. Overall, the passage suggests that indwelling just is the strategy where knowing is a form of love. Thus, it is the strategy of covenant epistemology.

Both Palmer and Moltmann-Wendel commend as exemplary the work of Nobel Prize-winning biologist, Barbara McClintock. Moltman-Wendel promotes embodiment, meaning, by it, in this context, something akin to indwelling. "Embodiment can be understood as a 'basic epistemological concept' which escapes the separation of reality into subject and object, into analytical thought and the intuition of feeling . . . [Scientist Barbara McClintock is known for] a respectful and sympathetic

77. Loder, *Transforming Moment*, 25.
78. Ibid., 30.
79. Palmer, *Courage to Teach*, 56.

approach. Respectful, because respect for difference is a basic condition of our interest in others. Sympathetic, because this is the highest form of love, which allows intimacy without doing away with the otherness."[80] She calls McClintock's approach sympathetic, and describes it in phrases patently suggestive of covenant epistemology: intimacy without doing away with otherness. Obviously this is a critical point: one might imagine a sort of indwelling that effaced boundaries of distinctiveness. This corresponds to Schnarch's emotional fusion. It would not be love, and it would not thus invite the real. It would not issue in transformation, only in absorption. It would attempt relationality at the expense of particularity, Gunton would say, and in the process lose both.

Palmer relates some of McClintock's telling descriptions of her work, drawing from Evelyn Fox Keller's biography (entitled, *A Feeling for the Organism*): "McClintock approached genetic material on the assumption that it could best be understood as a communal phenomenon"—in fact, that genetic material operates communally was the insight for which she received the Nobel Prize. But "it became clear that the communal premise of McClintock's work went well beyond the relationship among genes: it included the relationship between the genes and the scientist who studied them." Here he begins by quoting Keller:

> Over and over again she tells us one must have the time to look, the patience to "hear what the material has to say to you," the openness to "let it come to you." Above all, one must have "a feeling for the organism.'"... As one commentator puts it, McClintock "gained valuable knowledge by empathizing with her corn plants, submerging herself in their world and dissolving the boundary between object and observer." . . . Keller sums up McClintock's genius, and the genius of all great knowing, in a single, luminous sentence: McClintock, in her relation to ears of corn, achieved "the highest form of love, love that allows for intimacy without the annihilation of difference." [These words] describe a way of knowing and living that has moved beyond fear of the other into respect for, even a need for, its otherness.[81]

This passage refers to listening, to inviting, to lived body feel, and above all to an intimacy that is perichoretic. Indwelling, we see, just is the

---

80. Moltmann-Wendel, *I Am My Body*, 86.
81. Palmer, *Courage to Teach*, 55–56.

intimacy that is the relationality of perichoresis in knowing. Integral as it is to knowing, indwelling thus invites the real.

Recently I read Robert Pirsig's classic, *Zen and the Art of Motorcycle Maintenance*. Perhaps a bit put off by the title, I had never read this book that was first published the year I turned twenty-one, in the height of the ferment of the sixties. I found that what Pirsig was doing in it resonates with the proposals of this book. He was struggling to put two sides of a familiar dichotomy together: science and art. He was also trying to make sense of how people and technology should go together. And he uses do-it-yourself motorcycle-maintenance as a paradigm. The key prerequisite for motorcycle maintenance, he argues, is *peace of mind!*[82] And when he describes his care of his own motorcycle, what he describes is the kind of indwelling that is an empathetic seeing. It displays all the qualities that I list here as inviting the real. The art of motorcycle maintenance involves epistemological etiquette.

Connected Knowing

Blythe Clinchy is a developmental psychologist who contributed as a co-author to *Women's Ways of Knowing*. In a subsequent collection of essays related to that project, she develops the idea of "connected knowing." She distinguishes it as a practice or strategy of knowing, on the one hand in contrast to "separate knowing," and on the other hand, in contrast to pure subjectivism. Clinchy's notion of connected knowing resembles the idea of indwelling.[83]

Here are some of the ways she describes connected knowing.[84] In contrast to separate knowing, which is a doubting procedure, connected knowing is a believing procedure. She characterizes separate knowing graphically as "patriot missile epistemology." By contrast, connected knowing asks, "What do you see?" Connected knowing looks to understand, not challenge. It looks for what is "right" even in positions that seem initially wrong. In fact, feeling is essential to thinking, the connection must be felt viscerally.

---

82. Pirsig, *Zen and the Art of Motorcycle Maintenance*, 294–97; also chs. 6 and 7.

83. The Polanyi Society invited Ms. Clinchy to a roundtable session to explore the resonances between her connected knowing and Polanyi's work. For these papers see *Tradition and Discovery: The Polanyi Society Periodical* 34.1 (2007–2008). They include my own "Response to Blythe Clinchy" (ibid., 40–48).

84. The following is my synopsis of Clinchy's "Connected and Separate Knowing."

Clinchy makes comments that show how connected knowing is indwelling. How does one read a book? You "try to become" the author. She references Martin Buber saying, "Make the other present," and his speaking of "a bold swinging into the life of the other." In answer to the charge that connected knowing absorbs the other in an unhealthy and mutually depersonalizing way, she uses another graphic analogy: connected knowing involves the knower "becoming mentally pregnant" with the other.

Connected knowing takes effort and practice. It is neither easy nor natural, but strenuous. It involves an imaginative "rummaging" to find a template that makes sense of what one is hearing—this sounds much like Polanyi's construal of the scrabbling of creative imagination. Connected knowing invites surprise. Connected knowing does not necessarily issue ultimately in agreement with the views the speaker is putting forth.

Connected knowing thus uses the self to understand the other. The other can be personal or non-personal. We do not practice connected knowing on only persons. She cites someone who, in trying to fix a motor, "became a gear." This calls to mind the famous line about golf from the movie, *Caddyshack:* you have to be the ball. Thus, according to Clinchy, knowing of other and of self is reciprocal, not oppositional. Both parties should be maximally transformed.

Clinchy's connected knowing both accords with and amplifies the notion of indwelling. In this synopsis are touchpoints of commonality especially to the covenant epistemology project.

Indwelling, therefore, is the intimate relationality of interpersonal communion in knowing in which we penetrate, and view from within, the yet-to-be-known, to the extent that we are able. It is a felt body empathy. It invites the real. And if Loder and Buber are correct, the real seeks and needs the mutuality of indwelling if it is to gain voice and legs in the world.

Seeing vs. Looking

A final note—and this as not so much an additional practice as it is a different way of summing what we have been talking about. I would like to propose a distinction between "looking," and "seeing," and then I want to recommend seeing as inviting the real.[85] I am also recommending

85. I don't have much invested in the terms themselves—they could be switched, for all it matters—but rather in the distinction. Capon, for example, commends looking

that we need to redeem or revise what we think seeing is. Recall that one of the factors in the default mode was "the ocular metaphor." On the ocular metaphor, what is envisioned by the visual is what here I will call, looking. I believe that redrawing the playing field epistemologically should additionally have the potential to revise, redeem, our seeing. It would seem that our presumption about the visual is most obviously in need of this!

This is what I have in mind. *Looking* is passive, across a space, non-interactive. It is "disembodied"—that should be a clue that something is amiss! It is objectifying scrutiny. It operates consistently with the false dichotomy of theory and practice: it presumes observing and then using. Looking is in no way an aesthetic event, intrinsically valuable. Nor is it ever an agent of healing of the known. This is the default preconception concerning the visual. We might even use the word, voyeuristic. We are sensitized to the reality that looking, passed off as passive, can actually be a misuse of power.

By contrast, *seeing* is active and interactive, a kind of interpenetration. It is embodied. Recalling what some of our authors have said about touch and the interpersonal, and of vision as the agent of depersonalization, I want to suggest that there is a kind of visual activity that is touch-like—for example, what we think of when we think of a loving gaze, or noticing regard. Yes, that describes how a physiognomy looks to me the recipient; but I think it rightly can be taken to suggest an understanding of what we may do when, how we think of what we are doing when, we are using our eyes. May we not touch with our eyes? May we not feel with our eyes?

Seeing is a phenomenon of love, or reveling. It attends, gazes, and soaks in. I sometimes think of it as eating with my eyes.[86] We talk of drinking in a sight. That is what I mean by seeing. To see is to anticipate delight, and thus to delight in the interpersonal encounter that transpires between seer and seen. It is to indwell, to view from within the object of our gaze. It has intimacy about it. However, it is neither possessive nor voyeuristic. That is because it gives space by waiting for permission to enter.

---

the world back to grace. What I have in mind by seeing is just that, and just what I have been describing in this section.

86. Meek "Eating with My Eyes."

Do you think that God looks at us, or sees us? Or put it this way: would you rather be seen by him or looked at by him? Scripture, for example, records one person who said to God, "You see me"—and that was a good thing. But the Psalmist at one point asks God to look away from him, so that he (the Psalmist) can have a little relief from trouble!

Or, to suggest another line of thought, I wonder if part of what is going on with humans' mistreatment of one another, specifically men of women, and in the propensity of all to lustful looking, is, in part, not the lust, but the looking. Jesus describes it as "looking at a woman to lust after her." May this perhaps suggest an alternative way of seeing that does not lend itself to lust after her? Could it possibly be that some temptation to misbehavior, disrespectful and mercenary thought concerning another's body, could be averted by practicing seeing rather than looking? And on the assumption of the alignment of intimacy with seeing rather than looking, this would mean that some physical and sexual acts are the opposite of intimacy, the perpetrators of alienation. Obviously, all embodied human gestures are highly nuanced, interpreted acts. One can rarely simply call a spade a spade. But this does suggest that there may be something we can do to redeem our visual engagement.[87] To see—to appreciate and appropriate the whole-personed beauty of another—should not be thought to shunt automatically into lust. And if it does, you haven't—seen, that is. Lust is not intimacy, it is idolatry. But I am suggesting here that a way to correct it is, not, negatively, to not look at another, but, positively, to see another. I am also suggesting that the currently out-of-hand proportions of sexual impropriety may have an epistemological factor: they, too, may stem from our defective epistemic default.

To see is to delight, and to co-delight with God. I think this is our primary calling as humans. And it is to reflect his practice: Jesus' story of the prodigal son speaks volumes about how God sees his children. The father sees his returning son from a distance and runs to him, robes undignifyingly hiked up. He does not wait for the exact wording of confession; he starts shouting for servants to bring robes and ring of honor.

---

87. A close friend and his wife, who had spent years living abroad, testified that it was most uncomfortable to get off the plane back in the U.S. It had to do with how people here look you over. It's as if they avoid seeing you, but nevertheless manage to scrutinize you critically. This does not happen in other countries in which they have lived. Presumably, there they felt seen rather than looked at.

Apparently he does not look at the grime—the son is unclean in every sense of the word. But he sees the son.

Indeed, delight counts as its own strategy, critical to inviting the real. It is a delighted notice that drives that very act of coming to know. Integration functions by assigning value to the clues that transform it into a pattern. To delight is to assign value. Polanyi shows how delight is intrinsic to the knowing event.

David Bentley Hart writes, "For Christian thought, then, delight is the premise of any sound epistemology: it is delight that constitutes creation, so only delight can comprehend it, see it aright, understand its grammar. Only in loving creation's beauty—only in seeing that creation is beauty—does one apprehend what creation is."[88] What I have said here makes good sense of his comment. I am suggesting that seeing, as opposed to looking, is the look of delight. Seeing thus corresponds with all the other strategies for inviting the real.

CONSUMMATION

Consummation sounds like the end, the culmination of a process. How can the culmination of knowing itself count as an important strategy to invite the real? It can, where knowing has been cast as a relationship. Persons, and the personal real, continually, inexhaustibly, develop. Relationships unfold into an open-ended dynamism of living communion. The established covenant relationship that is knowing invites and catalyzes this development. Friendship and communion thus count as strategies to invite the real.

Friendship and Communion

John Frame said, "Knowledge designates the friendship between ourselves and God, and obedience designates our activity within that relation." Similarly, Mike Williams speaks of the goal of covenant, the unfolding, historied, relationship typified by mutual promises and obligations, as friendship, the richest of personal relationships, in which persons are persons to the full, as the communion between them. In this we reflect trinitarian communion and even enter into it. And John Macmurray makes the powerful claim, "All meaningful knowledge is for the sake of action, and all meaningful action for the sake of friendship."

88. Hart, *Beauty of the Infinite*, 253.

Friendship is the consummation of knowing. Or, we may—and have repeatedly done so—describe the culmination of relational knowing as communion. Palmer says: "In personal knowing, the relation of the knower and the known does not conform to the stiff protocol of observer and observed. It is more like the resonance of two persons. When we know something truly and well, that which we know does not feel like a separate object to be manipulated and mastered. Instead, we feel inwardly related to it; knowing it means that we have somehow entered into its life, and it into ours. Such knowledge is a relationship of personal care and fidelity, grounded in troth."[89] The image of friendship as the culminating ideal of knowing reminds us that the entire trajectory of coming to know is the unfolding covenantal relationship which just is a friendship. Friendship is relationship growing over time, a dynamic overture, response, a rhythmical perichoresis of particularity heightening in deepening relationality.

Friendship has the signature open-ended dynamism of the real. It is its own justification and reward. Friendship, we may say, is more than "the logic" of gift and reception, it *is* the gift and reception. Friendship is gift over an open-ended period of time, says Philip Rolnick. It is the ongoing freshness of the Other. If we follow Rolnick, the real is gift, friendship is gift over time. It is appropriate to draw from his conversation that the knowing relationship between knower and known is friendship.

Friendship is knowing and being known. It is the fully actualized, self-differentiated, perichoretic, reflection of the Trinity. To be so blessed as to be in communion in knowing is to be a person who is continually transformed and transforming. One may only imagine the richness and blessing of this. I will talk more of this in the last chapter. But we are not left only to imagine it, we are invited to practice it, to cultivate our skill at it, to delight ever more deeply in its fruit. In knowing, the consummation itself invites the further real.

The Eucharist

One last practice for inviting the real: the Eucharist. In an epistemology which takes as paradigm, context, and core the interpersoned dynamism of void and Holy that is integrative transformation, consummated in communion, the Christian church's regular practice of celebrating the

89. Palmer, *To Know as We Are Known*, 57.

Eucharist may be accorded its central epistemic role. As a sacrament, the Lord's Supper forms us as Christian believers, giving us the good gift that grows us in Christ. It also enacts communion with the present Christ—who gives his body and blood, the new covenant in his blood—and with fellow believers with whom he, in the event, binds us.

It is hard to say this with the emphasis and profundity it deserves: the Eucharist itself is both the concrete paradigm of knowing as described by covenant epistemology, and it is, I want to suggest here, the most strategic primer of the pump of human knowing. Properly understood, and with all the philosophical groundwork we have laid, it is the most effective epistemological therapy and strategy.

For the Eucharist enacts a microcosm of the creation-fall-redemption-restoration drama of biblical redemption, and of Christ the Holy entering the void to deliver us to the gracious possibility of new being, recentering us to self-giving love. Christ invites us to his table to eat with him, to eat what he provides. The point of the celebration of the Eucharist is that God himself comes and gives himself. In the Eucharist, the actual descent of God, as part of saving us and nourishing us spiritually, equips us profoundly for knowing by modeling knowing, and by forming us to be in the way of knowing. [90]

Just as we put ourselves in the way of knowing, I believe that when we understand knowing along the lines of the covenant epistemology paradigm, we may put ourselves in the way of the descent of God, the gracious invasion of the real, by enacting what is the case at the core of our being and of the world.

May we be more specific about how we put ourselves in the way of knowing in receiving the Eucharist? To partake, you must . . . *eat and drink*. Talk about embodied intimacy! This is also obviously mutual indwelling. You ingest the Person who is Truth descended, you invite the Real sacrificed for you. And the appropriate posture is to *kneel* to eat and

---

90. The language of "spiritual presence" reflects a Reformed middle position between the Roman (transubstantiation) and the Baptist (memorialism) views of communion. My experience has been that people have not understood how "presence" pertains, and the Reformed position has lapsed into the Baptist one. At least one aspect of the debate between a memorial and a more sacramental understanding is epistemology: if knowledge is information, then remembering information is what the Lord's Supper involves. But if knowing is transformation, this makes better sense of an understanding of the Lord's Supper, or worship, and of Scripture reading, as enactment, in which he comes to be really present.

drink. You signify the honored role of the Giver, your need for his generosity, and your readiness for the gift. It is no small stretch to say that this invites the real—the deepest real. That celebratory ritual forms us in that posture. And it shapes us also for the communion of knowing.

To realize this cannot help but make us better knowers. Celebrating the Eucharist is rightfully the most strategic way to invite the real, one we may be intentional about practicing faithfully. It invites God and enacts his descent. We meet him on our knees and partake the gracious Gift. All this renders the celebration of the Eucharist, and to the gospel of Jesus Christ, rightful centrality in knowing and life.

There are two reasons why the thought might be alien to you that the Eucharist is paradigmatic and a best practice for the art of knowing. Only one is epistemological. The other is a matter of Christian discipleship and theological understanding. It may be that a Christian hasn't experienced God coming, hasn't had her nose rubbed in the void and experienced the deliverance of God; nor has she experienced the Eucharist in this way. It helps to realize that an important part of getting your epistemology to resonate with the Christian faith is understanding and experiencing that Christian faith. The interface between the one and the other is complex and dynamic.

To invite the real is to practice covenant epistemology. From desire, through composure and comportment, exercising strategies distinct to the cultivation of an interpersoned dynamism, to the end of communion of knower and known—that is the best sort of knowing. Covenant epistemology offers its philosophical warrant and explication. The practice also confirms covenant epistemology. Covenant epistemology as expressed in inviting the real subverts and heals our epistemic default and makes us better knowers.

QUESTIONS FOR DISCUSSION

1. Discuss the practice or practices you find most appealing. What do you like about them? Where do you see them in your own life?

2. Do you yourself have distinctive ways of inviting the real? Describe these, and identify which of the loci they belong to. How do they accord with your personality?

3. In what areas of your life might you implement this epistemological etiquette? What would the change look like?

4. How does inviting the real happen in your discipline?

16

KNOWING FOR *SHALOM*

THE RESPONSE OF THE reader to covenant epistemology, if the book has most successfully accomplished its task, is not mere receipt of information, but existential transformation. That is a tall order, but it also implies that in such transformation, the book would only be one operative factor. You may guess the others. Nor would such transformation necessarily be sudden. It may be a step along the journey.

The last word regarding covenant epistemology, in one sense, will not be said here. I hope that this is only the beginning of the very sort of trajectory of relationally unfolding coming to know that covenant epistemology envisions. I have confidence that by now you are able to say, "I know how to go on." In fact, I have surrendered this book to publication only by overcoming a palpable sense of its defects, able to do so because of my confidence that its readers will likely see more in it and through it and beyond it than I myself am able to see at this point. Covenant epistemology itself promises this.

I want to leave you with some summative maxims for living and knowing that both synthesize what has been said and summon us to a life—an eternity—of good knowing.

A VISION FOR LIFE

Covenant epistemology's central commitments offer a full-orbed holistic vision, not only of knowing, but by implication, of life. To know well involves living in a certain way. For covenant epistemology, this is integral. No false disjunction between "theory" and "practice" can remain. Knowing takes, as whole persons, our whole lives—in both senses.

This understanding of knowing puts together all the dimensions of our lives. In all dimensions, knowing involves the same transformative event. Plus, a powerful integrative pattern draws from multiple dimensions of life.

Covenantal knowing brings the knower to recentered wholeness. And the event is a coming to be known that woos us graciously toward the Holy. It holds the potential of pointing us in the direction of looking for God. It is anticipatively open to his descent.

The integrality that this calls for is daunting, on the one hand. As Blythe Clinchy said of connected knowing, it takes hard work. It also takes risky whole-personed personal investment. Risking the exposure that intimacy requires is not always comfortable. Yet knowing's perichoretic space for liberty, for differentiated particularity, renders the yoke easy and the burden light.[1]

Knowing holds the prospect of our perichoretic overtures restoring us to the world, and the world to us. The manner of living and knowing that covenant epistemology forms is good for the known even as it is good for the knower. Thus, covenant epistemology offers a vision for all of life.

TAKE OFF YOUR TWO-DIMENSIONAL GLASSES!

A critical implication of covenant epistemology is the correction of our defective epistemological presumptions. Although I believe that reading this book helps, this is something that we must exercise some responsibility to bring about. It takes intentionally persistent effort, first to identify, and then to overcome, a defective outlook. It is similar to correcting a bad habit. It's harder to the extent that everyone around you sees neither it nor the need to address it. You are in many ways fighting upstream.[2]

One aphoristic way I express what we have to do is this: take off your two-dimensional glasses! I derive this from Loder's account of the eikonic eclipse—that about our default mode that prevents us from seeing the central transformative role of the imagination in rationality. Three-dimensional glasses are sometimes issued in film screenings: they enable us to see the two-dimensional film three-dimensionally. People in

---

1. Matt 11:28–29. It is no mistake that the promise of this text begins with, "Come to me . . ."

2. True to my hopeful conviction about common grace—and knowing, for that matter—we can choose to see the cup half-full even in this. Yes, we are fighting upstream with regard to culture, but we are coasting downstream with regard to humanness. I am convinced that every human being, in some part of her or his living and knowing, already displays what covenant epistemology strives to identify and optimize. So for me it is a challenge I love and accept to find that point of living tissue, so to speak, and set it free. "Blow on the coals of their care." See texture 1.

the western tradition come with a pair of two-dimensional glasses, not only issued, but plastered to our faces. What two-dimensional glasses do is block out the three-dimensionality that is there.

In a culture acclimated to two-dimensional glasses, three-dimensionality, while it is always operative, certainly has atrophied, like muscles only sparingly used. In our lives and surroundings, having now identified overlooked features of human knowing, we may start to attend to them and explore ways to activate them. As we do, we will be more fully human, and better knowers.

This is a colorful way of saying that we must cultivate the practice of identifying and accrediting the transformative dynamism that is the engine of all knowing. Covenant epistemology additionally identifies the personal perichoresis of knower, knowing, and known, as three-dimensionality that must be identified and accredited. We must cultivate our attentiveness to the hints of the interpersoned with which knowing is fraught.

After reading *Longing to Know,* a Nashville recording engineer wrote me: "Because of this book, I do my job better, faster, and have more fun!" A perfectionist, he had been laboring under the presumption that if he perfected every track, when he put them together the product would thereby be perfect. What he learned was that he needed to indwell the tracks subsidiarily, creatively synthesize them within the indwelling, while he was focusing on the yet to be actualized pattern he held before him. Similarly, an analyst of "serial innovators" in corporate engineering has informed me that the Polanyian account makes better sense of what these consistent producers of great solutions appear to be doing.[3]

It is not easy to articulate what it looks like to go to the bank on covenant epistemology, particularly, as in these cases, on subsidiary awareness. For all that, as the case of the recording engineer shows, what cannot be said can nevertheless be lived. But that, of course, is what the account stipulates. In *Loving to Know,* one way in which I have done it has been to explore body knowledge; another way has been to catalog epistemological etiquette. Both are ways we have been intentional about the implications of covenant epistemology—helping us remove the two-dimensional glasses that keep us from seeing, and then strengthening to virtuosity, what is there.

---

3. Personal email and phone conversation and consultation.

PILGRIMAGE: BEING ON THE WAY

To take seriously that all knowing is coming-to-know, that it is an unfolding relationship, means that we see ourselves as pilgrims, so to speak—on the way. Indeed, this has been suggested from the outset by the subtitle of this book. It means that we are, as Newbigin has put it, in the middle of the story.

Half-understanding and not-yet-understanding are epistemic phenomena that no other epistemology addresses. Yet they are real. As Polanyi showed, if we do not accredit them, no discovery would ever happen. Covenant epistemology calls us positively to accredit them. But this is not to say that these stations are comfortable. Half-understanding and not-yet-understanding quite naturally engender distress, impatience, apprehension—or a sense of adventure or anticipation. I experience this often as I write, trying to think things through. It is an ingression of the void.

But to see that we are pilgrims on the way is to suggest a perspective on ourselves and our knowing that enjoins patience with ourselves as we learn to dwell graciously with half-understanding. Grace offsets a misplaced sense of failure at being short of knowing. The idea of pilgrimage also calls us to joy, and to hope. Joy—a kind of delighted savoring of the already-not yet of our knowing, as well as in our companions, both the yet-to-be-known and co-knowers, and in the conversations that mark the stages of our progress. Hope—both of our eventual success and of the eventually deeper profundity of our insight, with its indeterminate future manifestations; hope of transformation, hope of ever-deepening communion.

To say that knowing is being-on-the-way-to-knowing is to accredit the journey as itself epistemic. In our journeying, there is a sense in which we are already living life on the terms of the yet-to-be-known. We are involved in the dance-like overture response in which we woo the as yet-undisclosed reality, and it woos us. This is to be human. It is to be person in a world fraught with the personal, and personally involved with it.

As the Hebrews sang the psalms of ascent on their joyful, familied, mounting pilgrimages to Jerusalem, so may we sing on the way. There is blessing for the pilgrim:

Blessed are those whose strength is in you,
>who have set their hearts on pilgrimage [literally, in whose
hearts are the highways].
As they pass through the valley of tears, they make it a place of
springs;
>The autumn rains also cover it with pools.
They go from strength to strength,
>till each appears before God in Zion.[4]

This passage hints of healing seeing, the descent of God, the consummation of the journey, and of inviting the real.

SEMPER TRANSFORMANDA

Echoing, with due respect, one of the cries of the Protestant Refomation, *semper reformanda*, I coin this maxim: *semper transformanda*—always transforming. The one who "gets" covenant epistemology is one who has therein been transformed. Even as the loving gaze lights a lamp of personal beauty in a person, who then enduringly gives off the light, so the one who is transformed epistemologically becomes, we may say, a transformer. That person comes alive to continually transforming and continually catalyzing transformation in what or who she or he knows. There will be an ongoing newness about their thought and life and work. Delight and excited anticipation will be characteristic of the demeanor they bring to forays into the unknown. They will be the I of I-You, bringing that to all I-It. And it will extend to catch up other I's in its purview: children, students, friends, colleagues. It will be a blowing on the coals of other people's care.

KNOWING FOR *SHALOM*[5]

Shalom means peace. But it contains rich hints of redeemed restoration to health, safety, rest, completeness, wholeness, welfare, perfection, blessing, harmony. Seeking the *shalom* of the world is what we have always been called to do. I have said this repeatedly: knowing should heal—both the knower and the known. It should bless, bring *shalom*, rather than curse.

---

4. Ps 84:5–7.

5. Recall that earlier I credited—and mean to honor—Nicholas Wolterstorff and his legacy in this allusion to his great phrase and contribution.

The pattern that results from subsidiary-focal integration actively and creatively shapes a whole. It creatively harmonizes what had hitherto been perceived to be at odds. It restores what John Frame calls cognitive rest. Contrast the destructive consequences of our legacy of depersonalized, disembodied, linear epistemology.

One thing that this maxim alludes to is that the knower is involved in active shaping, rather than passive reception. Knowing is action, said Macmurray. Action ought to be, according to him, for the sake of friendship—or, we may say, for healing *shalom*.

The maxim also suggests that, where the knower-known relationship is cast interpersonally and perichoretically, the growth is not one-sided. Not only the knower is on a trajectory, so is the yet-to-be-known. It is as if knower and known rise to intercept one another, down the road toward each other, and toward a new thing, from where each had started. In knowing, what comes to be known is a new thing.

Recalling Buber's claims, the You needs the I to bring it over into the I-It. Transformative "Oh-I-see-it"s restore the known to be more fully itself than it has hitherto been permitted to be. Consider bloodletting, that all-too-common, tragically misinformed, medical practice of earlier centuries: people knew blood was important; they had yet fully to understand how. (Indeed, *we* may not, either.) Surely human patients, as the known, have collectively sighed, thank you, for blood given rather than blood taken. Thus transformatively integrative patterned insight heals the world.

This brings knowing in line with all that is enjoined in the cultural mandate, which calls all humans to covenant mediation, stewardly action in the world to bring it to its full flourishing in presentation to God. The known should be blessed, rather than cursed, by the knower in the knowing.

It can be difficult to be specific about what this looks like—although never more difficult than our actual experience of coming to know. Is Palmer right that the development of nuclear power resulted from unloving objectivist curiosity? What does this imply about human gene research? Or global warming? The answers are as complex on the model of covenant epistemology as they are apart from it.

But surely there is positive value for the known if the knower construes his or her effort as a respectful covenanting. And surely we see plenty of examples of stewardly knowing. Consider something that continues to amaze me: that engineers are actually *building* wetlands, to clean up ground water. Surely it is covenantal reciprocity to develop that which gives back more and better than what it takes. And surely that is a practice that makes practical sense in our ordinary lives, day in and day out. In any situation, we face a set of options. We are often able, in covenantal knowing, to sense which ones accord more truly to the integrity of the object. Ordinarily we may call this wisdom, good sense, or good stewardship, or doing the right thing. What covenant epistemology is saying is that it is epistemic, and that it helps to see it that way. Knowing, therefore, should be seen to heal the known. It also heals the knower, this is just what transformation is. This knowing, we have seen, even constitutes us.

Finally, covenant epistemology heals the knowing itself. It heals it from the ravages of the two-dimensionalizing default epistemic mode. Part of the noetic effects of sin, as Christians in the reformational tradition have called the impact that human brokenness has on our knowledge, is the distortion of our very view of knowing. Covenant epistemology hopes to provide a healing corrective to this.

FRIENDSHIP WITH THE TRUTH

Friendship with the truth is a phrase that speaks volumes of the manner in which covenant epistemology has cast knowing, knower, and known. Truth and friendship are intrinsic goods; covenant epistemology envisions an interface of the two that enhances both. Friendship with the truth could thus well be a model for living and knowing. We may savor this prospect, submitting to its motivating call. For it is the good that we seek. And to the extent that we attain it.

To be presumptuous about this—to suggest that we are somehow the guardians that truth can't do without, or that we condescend to it when we bless the truth with our friendship—is by the very covenantal nature of friendship, not to mention of truth, ruled entirely out of court. In fact, what is rather the case is that we find ourselves held to personal authenticity. Also, we bear a cross. Leading the I-You over into the I-It can call for personal sacrifice and pain. But friendship is the continual freshness of the Other. And that is deep joy.

THE DESCENT OF GOD

Theologian Mike Williams is alive and well. A former competitive weightlifter and paratrooper, he is, additionally, strong. But when we were speaking of my teaching his work to college students and he said to me, "Tell them about the descent of God," it was as if he was speaking from beyond the grave. It had about it the gravity of last words. Thus I return to it in this last chapter, as I did in the last chapter of *Longing to Know*.

There is something more important than understanding covenant epistemology and knowing well. It is being known by God. So this statement puts the whole covenant epistemology project in perspective in a way that is integral to its nature. To know well is to put oneself in the way of knowing, as we have spoken of it. It is to learn in order not merely to comprehend but *to be apprehended*. It is to say "You," and listen. It is to have one's epistemic efforts give way to the coming of the Other. Such is the necessary corollary of any account that is transformative at heart.

The fact that knowing is interpersonal suggests, as Newbigin said, that the ultimate object of knowledge is the Person, namely, God.[6] There is a sense in which anyone who embraces covenant epistemology opens him- or herself to the sweet terror of being known by him. It is definitely to expose one's flank, one's most vital parts. There is a risk of transformation.

This is the epistemic dimension of longing: the one who longs will know and be known. By the descent of God, I have in mind also the metaphysical dimension. God, and his world, comes. The real comes unbidden, with fecundity. Real *happens,* we may say, redeeming a crass but common aphorism.[7] The real is gift. Gift, by definition, comes unbidden, unrequested, unanticipated, unmerited. While we may be blessed to cultivate practices of inviting the real, these must be placed in the larger context where the movement, the prevailing winds, are in the opposite direction. The prodigal son in a small way invited the father. But to think that way is to miss the glaringly, savingly, obvious.[8]

Thus, to enjoin people to remember the descent of God is to call them to cast away scales of blindness to see what is there. The Episcopal

6. See below.

7. Actually perhaps more appropriately, Real *is done*. I have Macmurray's comments in mind here. See ch. 8.

8. Luke 15.

prayer book's Prayer of General Thanksgiving leads us to pray: "Give us that due sense of all Thy mercies that our hearts may be unfeignedly thankful." Being unfeignedly thankful is a speech act, as well as a life orientation, that embodies our need for the Other, God and his works. Enacting thankfulness opens our eyes to see what is going on under our nose. It is being in the way of knowing. Thankfulness is a due and continual appreciation that references the void and the Holy that are the third and fourth dimensions of our humanness. Thankfulness makes us what we are. But this, too, is the descent of God.

The point of the celebration of the Eucharist is that God himself comes and gives himself. The Eucharist enacts the story of the actual descent of God into our void to effect our deliverance. In the Eucharist, Christ is really, spiritually present. He comes. This is the heart of the regular assembly of Christian believers—to invoke the Lord's coming, and to find that he does.[9] All worship is response to this.

The descent of God, like our friendship with the Truth, is our highest good.

"SO, IT IS YOU!"

I personally have grown through this exploration that is now *Loving to Know*. I am deeply grateful for it all. But this sentence of Buber's is perhaps my favorite. Buber records this comment that Goethe the poet addressed to a rose, to typify, define, the I-You encounter. It holds the promise that we may at any moment in any place come face to face with the Other who centers us and transforms us. It prompts me to long for such encounter.

C. S. Lewis cast his spiritual autobiography as the story of how he was "surprised by joy."[10] Throughout his younger life, at times there came unbidden a bittersweet sense of joy. These moments captured his heart and haunted him, but he did not know what they were. When he met God, it was as if—and this is my interpretation of it—he was able to say, "So, it is You!"

All of our knowings, our discoveries, our insights, prototype this. But some, as Loder says, occasion the inbreaking of the Spirit of God. I want to tell you the story of my "surprised by joy" experience. I was sur-

9. Meek, "Why I Go to Church."
10. Lewis, *Surprised by Joy.*

prised by reality. It was my turn to say, in a life-transforming moment, "So, it is You!"

I have told you how, when I read Polanyi's work for the first times, I began to note and then be tantalized by his recurring promise that "we know we have made contact with reality when we have a sense of indeterminate future manifestations." "Real is that which we expect indeterminately to manifest itself." And so on. These excited me, first, because as a *de facto* Cartesian I had long felt that the one main problem was to prove that there was a material world outside my head; that not to succeed would call into question all knowing and being, and be an unconscionable act of inauthenticity. The idea of contact was just what my disembodied mind and mindless body craved to prove.

I also was tantalized by the excitement of it. "Indeterminate future prospects" sounds pretty much like Christmas to me—delightfully anticipating presents. I loved thinking that reality just is like that, that that is its signature. This not only made sense of reality to me, but it also tantalized me into longing for it. It tantalized me into a dissertation, too.

That was in 1979, perhaps. In 1983 I finished the dissertation and shelved it, turning my attention to my young family. In a phone chat in 1998, my old college philosophy professor asked if I had read Lesslie Newbigin's *Proper Confidence*. I was not acquainted personally with his work, and I set out to rectify that as soon as I could. Newbigin, the missiologist, I soon saw, had drunk deeply at the well of Michael Polanyi. He worked with accuracy and sensitivity to the broad sweep of Polanyi's contributions. Newbigin, for example, appropriates both Polanyi's critique and his proposals regarding the defects of the western tradition. Newbigin moves beyond Polanyi to put these to missiological use: if one is to proclaim the gospel in the West, one must first challenge what I have here been calling the default mode if one expects the gospel even to be heard.

Reading along on page 62 and following, I followed Newbigin's presentation of Polanyi as it turned to my favorite Polanyi sentence. Please indulge me as I quote that passage extensively here:

> Polanyi's explanation [of the Meno Dilemma, the problem of how coming to knowledge is even possible] is to acknowledge the power of the human mind to recognize "intimations of things hidden which we may yet discover" (*The Tacit Dimension*, pp. 21–23). The immediate implication which Polanyi draws is that,

if all our knowledge is to be of the kind sought by Descartes, namely, certain knowledge capable of explicit formulation in precise terms, then scientific discovery will be forever impossible. But is it not legitimate to suggest a further implication? Polanyi depicts scientists . . . [in such a way that they] must be seen as people drawn by a reality beyond themselves. Is it not reasonable, then, to think of this reality as something more than a lifeless, impersonal "something"? Scientists, and indeed all serious scholars, speak often of the love of truth. But can love be finally satisfied with an impersonal "something"? Have we, perhaps, failed to draw out the full meaning of the words spoken by the apostle Paul to the scholars and debaters of Athens when he said that "the God who made the world and everything in it . . . did this so that men would seek him and perhaps reach out for him and find him, though he is not far from each one of us" (Acts 17:24, 27)?

Here I can only answer that question by speaking of the fundamental affirmation of the gospel, namely, that the ultimate reality which is the object of all our search for truth has been made present in history in the person and work of Jesus Christ . . . If that is true, then it must define the nature of all our search for truth, including our searches for truth in the world of impersonal entities.

What I heard was Newbigin linking reality *a la* Polanyi, characterized by intimations of hidden things we may yet discover, to . . . *God*. That sentence that had so tantalized me that I wrote an entire dissertation on it, that signature tantalizing feature of reality that made me long for it, that knife that cut the Gordian knot of my Cartesianism, that sentence that grew with me through subsequent decades of living—that sentence itself had been, all along, the prompting of God, and it now became his door of overwhelming ingress. Of course!—reality is like that because God himself is behind and in it. Of course, it caught my heart, because it was the Lord wooing me, all along. I felt as if I had finally found out what had drawn me in that sentence, and it had been, all along, God.

Hot on the heels of my realization, somehow, *he came.* I had been sitting on my bed, reading. Never in my life was I on my knees so fast, so convulsed with tears of love and joy. "So, it is You!"

That was ten years ago. As I have written the concluding passages of *Loving to Know* I have once again remembered that event. Now I see that it was pointing, not only backward to my love affair with contact with reality, but forward to covenant epistemology. You may remember that

Newbigin was one of the first whose work prompted me to think about the known and the knowing as personal.

To love to know is to anticipate the I-You encounter that is the descent of God, the transformative moment in which we find ourselves surprised with his healing gaze in a moment of timeless communion. The moment we long for is the one in which we find the these words spring to our lips: "So, it is You!"

It is quite possible to be prohibitively impatient. But "love is patient." Friendship, Simone Weil teaches us, is "the miracle by which a person consents to view from a certain distance, and without coming any nearer, the very being who is necessary to him as food."[11] Seeing the love that invites the real as the patient journey of whatever length of time, the sacrifice of effort, the costly gift of creative attentiveness that it takes—that is knowing indeed.

QUESTIONS FOR DISCUSSION

1. Discuss the claims of this final chapter. Which do you especially like and why?

2. Has covenant epistemology enabled you to understand and live out these injunctions? How does doing so reshape your epistemic efforts and your life?

PUTTING TOGETHER *LOVING TO KNOW*

1. Sketch the argument of this book, making a diagram if you can.

2. What do you think are the most critical premises that support the covenant epistemology vision?

3. Compile a list of the ways we have seen in *Loving to Know* that knowing is healing or that covenant epistemology is therapeutic?

4. Describe knowing in your professional discipline. Show how it exemplifies the claims of covenant epistemology.

5. Does *Loving to Know* successfully deliver on its claim to render knowing God the central paradigm for all knowing?

6. How does *Loving to Know* reorient your Christian discipleship?

7. How might *Loving to Know* contribute to healthy cultural change?

11. Weil, *Waiting for God*, 135.

Bibliography

Allen, R. T. "The Dialectic of Adaptation and Assimilation Revisited." In *Michael Polanyi and Christian Theology*. Edited by Murray Rae. Eugene, OR: Cascade, forthcoming.

Allender, Dan B. *The Healing Path: How the Hurts in Your Past Can Lead You to a More Abundant Life*. Colorado Springs: Waterbrook, 2000.

———. *To Be Told: Know Your Story, Shape Your Future*. Colorado Springs: Waterbrook, 2005.

Apczynski, John. "The Relevance of Personal Knowledge: Reflections on the Practices of Some Contemporary Philosophers." Paper for Polanyi Society's "*Personal Knowledge* at Fifty" Conference, Loyola University, Chicago, June 2008.

Aquinas, Thomas. *Summa Theologica*. Introduction and abridgement by Anton Pegis. New York: Modern Library, 1948.

Barash, David P. "Believing is Seeing." *The Chronicle of Higher Education* (June 27, 2003). No pages. Online: http://chronicle.com/article/Believing-Is-Seeing/11865.

Bartholomew, Craig, et. al., editors. *After Pentecost: Language and Biblical Interpretation*. Scripture and Hermeneutics Series, vol. 2. Grand Rapids: Zondervan, 2001.

Berry, Wendell. *Hannah Coulter: A Novel*. Berkeley, CA: Shoemaker and Hoard, 2004.

———. *Jayber Crow*. New York: Counterpoint, 2000.

———. *Remembering*. Berkeley, CA: Counterpoint, 2008.

Booth, Wayne C., et al. *The Craft of Research*. 2nd ed. Chicago: University of Chicago Press, 2003.

Botton, Alain, de. *The Architecture of Happiness*. New York: Vintage, 2006.

Buber, Martin. *I and Thou*. Translated by Walter Kaufmann. New York: Scribner's, 1970.

Calvin, John. *Institutes of the Christian Religion*. Translated by Ford Lewis Battles. Edited by John T. McNeill. Library of Christian Classics, 2 vols. Philadelphia: Westminster, 1960.

Capon, Robert Farrar. *The Supper of the Lamb: A Culinary Reflection*. New York: Harcourt Brace, 1967.

Caputo, John. *Deconstruction in a Nutshell: A Conversation with Jacques Derrida*. New York: Fordham University Press, 1997.

Chisholm, Roderick. *Theory of Knowledge*. Englewood Cliffs, NJ: Prentice-Hall, 1966.

Clinchy, Blythe McVicker. "Connected and Separate Knowing: Toward a Marriage of Two Minds." In *Knowledge, Difference and Power: Essays Inspired by Women's Ways of Knowing*, edited by Mary Field Belenky, et. al., 205–47. New York: Basic, 1996.

Cowan, Steven B., editor. *Five Views on Apologetics*. Grand Rapids: Zondervan, 2000.

Dancy, Jonathan, and Ernest Sosa, editors. *A Companion to Epistemology*. Blackwell Companions to Philosophy Series. Oxford: Blackwell, 1992.

Dark, David. *Everyday Apocalypse: The Sacred Revealed in Radiohead, The Simpsons, and Other Pop Culture Icons*. Grand Rapids: Brazos, 2002.

Delattre, Roland. "Jonathan Edwards and the Recovery of Aesthetics for Religious Ethics." *Journal of Religious Ethics* 31.2 (2003) 277–97.

Dillard, Annie. *For the Time Being*. New York: Vintage, 1999.

———. *Pilgrim at Tinker Creek*. New York: HarperCollins, 1974.

————. *Teaching a Stone to Talk: Expeditions and Encounters.* New York: Harper & Row, 1985.

Dooyeweerd, Herman. *In the Twilight of Western Thought.* Nutley, NJ: Craig, 1980.

Eldredge, John, and Staci Eldredge. *Captivating: Unveiling the Mystery of a Woman's Soul.* Nashville: Nelson, 2005.

Frame, John. *Cornelius Van Til: An Analysis of His Thought.* Phillipsburg, NJ: P & R, 1995.

————. *The Doctrine of the Knowledge of God.* Phillipsburg, NJ: P & R, 1987.

Frazier, Robert M. "Considering the Tie That Binds: The Scottish Presbyterian and Neocalvinism Divide." Paper for Board of Trustees, Geneva College, 2006.

Garber, Steve. *The Fabric of Faithfulness: Weaving Together Belief and Behavior during the University Years.* Downers Grove, IL: InterVarsity, 1996.

————. "Loving, Mourning, Knowing." *Discernment: A Newsletter for the Center for Applied Christian Ethics, Wheaton College* 9.2/3 (2004) 6–7, 15.

Gendlin, Eugene T. "The Tacit/Implicit Actually Employed in a New Kind of Thinking." Paper for Polanyi Society Conference, *Polanyi's Post-Critical Thought and the Rebirth of Meaning,* Loyola University, Chicago, IL, June 8–10, 2001.

————. *Focusing.* New York: Bantam, 1979.

Greco, John, and Ernest Sosa, editors. *The Blackwell Guide to Epistemology.* Blackwell Philosophy Guides Series. Oxford: Blackwell, 1999.

Grene, Marjorie. "Intellectual Autobiography." In *The Philosophy of Marjorie Grene.* Library of Living Philosophers, vol. 29, edited by Randall E. Auxier and Lewis Edwin Hahn, 3–28. Carbondale: Open Court, 2002.

————. *The Knower and the Known.* Berkeley: University of California Press, 1974.

————. *A Philosophical Testament.* Chicago: Open Court, 1995.

————. "Tacit Knowing: Grounds for a Revolution in Philosophy." *Journal of the British Society for Phenomenology* 8 (Oct 1977) 164–71.

Gunton, Colin. *Enlightenment and Alienation: An Essay towards a Trinitarian Theology* Grand Rapids: Eerdmans, 1985.

————. *The One, the Three, and the Many: God, Creation, and the Culture of Modernity.* Cambridge: Cambridge University Press, 1993.

Harris, John, and Dennis Sansom. *Discerning is More Than Counting: Higher Education and Assessment.* Occasional Papers in Liberal Education #3. The American Academy for Liberal Education. Online: http://www.aale.org/pdf/harris-sansom.pdf.

Hart, David Bentley. *The Beauty of the Infinite: The Aesthetics of Christian Truth.* Grand Rapids: Eerdmans, 2003.

Heidegger, Martin. *Being and Time.* Translated by John Macquarrie and Edward Robinson. New York: Harper & Row, 1962.

Horton, Michael. *God of Promise: Introducing Covenant Theology.* Grand Rapids: Baker, 2006.

Hurley, Patrick. *A Concise Introduction to Logic.* 10th ed. Florence, KY: Wadsworth, 2008.

Jones, David C. *Biblical Christian Ethics.* Grand Rapids: Baker, 1994.

Keller, Evelyn Fox. *A Feeling for the Organism: The Life and Work of Barbara McClintock.* New York: Freeman, 1983.

Kierkegaard, Søren. "Subjective Truth, Inwardness; Truth is Subjectivity." In *Concluding Unscientific Postscript to* Philosophical Fragments, vol. 1, edited and translated by

Howard V. Hong and Edna H. Hong, 189–250. Princeton: Princeton University Press, 1992.

Kline, Meredith. *By Oath Consigned: A Reinterpretation of the Covenant Signs of Circumcision and Baptism.* Grand Rapids: Eerdmans, 1968.

Kuhn, Thomas S. *The Structure of Scientific Revolutions.* Chicago: University of Chicago Press, 1962.

Kuyper, Abraham. *Lectures on Calvinism.* Grand Rapids: Eerdmans, 1931.

Lakoff, George, and Mark Johnson. *Philosophy in the Flesh: The Embodied Mind and its Challenge to Western Thought.* New York: Basic, 1999.

Lerner, Harriet. *The Dance of Anger: A Woman's Guide to Changing the Pattern of Intimate Relationships.* New York: HarperCollins, 1997.

Levinas, Emmanuel. *Totality and Infinity: An Essay On Exteriority.* Translated by Alphonso Lingis. Pittsburgh: Duquesne University Press, 1969.

Lewis, C. S. *The Last Battle.* Chronicles of Narnia, vol. 7. New York: Macmillan, 1956.

———. *Surprised by Joy: The Shape of My Early Life.* New York: Harcourt Brace, 1955.

Loder, James E. *The Transforming Moment.* 2nd ed. Colorado Springs: Helmers & Howard, 1989.

Lyotard, Jean-Francois. *The Postmodern Condition: A Report on Knowledge.* Translated by Geoff Bennington and Brian Massumi. Theory and History of Literature, vol. 10. Minneapolis: University of Minnesota Press, 1984.

MacLaren, Brian D. *A New Kind of Christian: A Tale of Two Friends on a Spiritual Journey.* San Francisco: Jossey-Bass, 2001.

Macmurray, John. *Persons in Relation.* Introduction by Frank G. Kirkpatrick. Atlantic Highlands, NJ: Humanities, 1991.

———. *The Self as Agent.* Introduction by Stanley M. Harrison. Atlantic Highlands, NJ: Humanities, 1991.

McClay, Wilfred. "Fifty Years of *The Lonely Crowd.*" *The Wilson Quarterly* 22 (1998) 34–42.

Meek, Esther Lightcap, "Common Grace: An Irenic Proposal." Online: http://common groundsonline.typepad.com/common_grounds_online/2006/04/common_grace_ an.html.

———. "Compelled to Culturing." Online: http://commongroundsonline.typepad.com/ common_grounds_online/2008/03/esther-l-meek-f.html.

———. *Contact with Reality: An Examination of Realism in the Thought of Michael Polanyi.* PhD diss., Temple University, 1983.

———. "Covenant Epistemology for the 21st Century." Paper for "Calvinism for the 21st Century" Conference, Dordt College, Sioux Center, IA, April 8–10, 2010.

———. "Cultivating Connected Knowing in the Classroom: Response to Blythe Clinchy." *Tradition and Discovery: The Polanyi Society Periodical* 34.1 (2007–8) 40–48.

———. "Dance: Metaphysical and Theological Therapy," *Commongroundsonline.* http://commongroundsonline.typepad.com/common_grounds_online/2007/04/ esther_l_meek_d.html#more.

———. "Eating with My Eyes." Online: http://commongroundsonline.typepad.com/ common_grounds_online/2007/01/eating_with_my_.html.

———. "The Epistemology and the Realism of David Dark's Apocalyptic: Response to David Dark." Paper for the Christian Reflections on Contemporary Culture Conference, Missouri Baptist University, June 19, 2005.

———. "Learning to See: The Role of Authoritative Guides in Knowing." *Tradition and Discovery: The Polanyi Society Periodical* 23.2 (2005–6) 38–49.

———. "Knowledge as ~~Information~~ Transformation." Presentation for Geneva College Faculty, Geneva College, Beaver Falls, PA, November 7, 2007.

———. *Longing to Know: The Philosophy of Knowledge for Ordinary People.* Grand Rapids: Brazos, 2003.

———. "Making the Most of College: Learning With Friends." *Comment Magazine.* Online: http://www.wrf.ca/wrf-rd.cfm?linkID=137.

———. "Marjorie Grene at Fifty: Stopping Short of Personhood?" Paper for "*Personal Knowledge* at Fifty" Polanyi Conference, Loyola University, Chicago, IL, June 13, 2008.

———. "Michael Polanyi and Alvin Plantinga: Reinforcements from Beyond the Walls." Paper for Evangelical Philosophical Society, Atlanta, GA, November 18, 2010.

———. "My Father, My People, My Story: You and the Bible and Mike Williams' *Far as the Curse is Found.*" Online: http://commongroundsonline.typepad.com/common_grounds_online/theological_reflection/index.html.

———. "Nurturing a Mustard Seed in Aliquippa." *Geneva Magazine* Spring-Summer 2008, Geneva College, Beaver Falls, PA, 2008.

———. "A Polanyian Interpretation of Calvin's *Sensus Divinitatis.*" *Presbyterion* 23 (1997) 8–24.

———. "Proposing Covenant Epistemology: Response to Frazier's 'Considering the Tie that Binds.'" Paper for Board of Trustees, Geneva College, Beaver Falls, PA, April 26, 2006.

———. "'Recalled to Life': Contact with Reality." *Tradition and Discovery: The Polanyi Society Journal* 26:3 (1999–2000) 72–83.

———. "Servant Thinking: Polanyian Workings of the Framean Triad." In *Speaking the Truth in Love: The Theology of John M. Frame*, edited by John J. Hughes, 611–27. Phillipsburg, NJ: P & R, 2009.

———. "Take Off Your Two-Dimensional Glasses." Online: http://commongroundsonline.typepad.com/common_grounds_online/2007/12/esther-l-meek-t.html.

———. "Why I Go to Church." Online: http://www.commongroundsonline.org/content/why-i-go-church.

———. "'With'—the Most Christian Word." Online: http://commongroundsonline.typepad.com/common_grounds_online/2009/09/esther-l-meek-withthe-most-christian-word.html.

———. "Working Implications of the Subsidiary Nature of Worldviews: Response to David Naugle's *Worldview: The History of a Concept.*" Paper for Midwest Regional Evangelical Theological Society Conference, Lincoln Christian College, March 19, 2004.

Meek, Esther L., and Michael D. Williams. "Covenant Epistemology." Document for *Epistemology* class, Covenant Theological Seminary, 2002.

Meek, Allison Starr. "Made for Glory: Toward a Biblical Vision of Personal Beauty." Paper assignment, *Ethics* class, Covenant Theological Seminary, Spring 2007.

Mendenhall, G. E. "Covenant Forms in Israelite Traditions." *Biblical Archaeologist* 17 (1954) 25–53.

Merleau-Ponty, Maurice. "Cezanne's Doubt." In *The Merleau-Ponty Reader*, edited by Ted Toadvine and Leonard Lawlor, 69–85. Chicago: Northwestern University Press, 2007.

————. *Phenomenology of Perception.* Translated by Colin Smith. London: Routledge, 1962.

Moleski, Martin X., S.J. *Personal Catholicism: The Theological Epistemologies of John Henry Newman and Michael Polanyi.* Washington, DC: Catholic University of America Press, 2000.

Moltmann-Wendel, Elisabeth. *I Am My Body: A Theology of Embodiment.* New York: Continuum, 1995.

Mondello, Bob. "Auntie Mame: An Antidote to Social Caution." In *Character: The Origin and Impact of American Fictional Characters* (radio series). National Public Radio, July 31, 2008.

Mouw, Richard. *He Shines In All That's Fair.* Grand Rapids: Eerdmans, 2001.

Mullins, Phil."On Persons and Knowledge." In *The Philosophy of Marjorie Grene,* edited by Randal E. Auxier and Lewis Edwin Hahn, 37–38. Library of Living Philosophers, vol. 29. Chicago: Open Court, 2002.

Myers, Ken. *Tacit Knowing, Truthful Knowing: The Life and Thought of Michael Polanyi.* Mars Hill Audio Report #2. Online: http://marshillaudio.org/catalog/reports.asp.

Naugle, David. *Worldview: The History of a Concept.* Grand Rapids: Eerdmans, 2002.

Newbigin, Lesslie. *Foolishness to the Greeks: The Gospel and Western Culture.* Grand Rapids: Eerdmans, 1986.

————. *The Gospel in a Pluralist Society.* Grand Rapids: Eerdmans, 1989.

————. *Proper Confidence: Faith, Doubt and Certainty in Christian Discipleship.* Grand Rapids: Eerdmans, 1995.

Niebuhr, H. Richard. *Christ and Culture.* New York: Harper & Row, 1951.

Noll, Mark A. *The Scandal of the Evangelical Mind.* Grand Rapids: Eerdmans, 1994.

Nouwen, Henri J. M. *Reaching Out: The Three Movements of the Spiritual Life.* New York: Doubleday, 1975.

Palmer, Parker J. *To Know as We Are Known: Education as a Spiritual Journey.* San Francisco: HarperSanFrancisco, 1966.

————. *The Courage to Teach: Exploring the Inner Landscape of a Teacher's Life.* San Francisco: Jossey-Bass, 1998.

Penner, Myron B., editor. *Christianity and the Postmodern Turn: Six Views.* Grand Rapids: Brazos, 2005.

Percy, Walker. *Lost In The Cosmos: The Last Self-Help Book.* New York: Farrar, Straus, and Giroux, 1983.

————. "Naming and Being." In *Signposts in a Strange Land,* 131–38. New York: Farrar, Straus, and Giroux, 1991.

Peterson, Eugene H. *A Long Obedience in the Same Direction: Discipleship in an Instant Society.* Downers Grove, IL: InterVarsity, 2000.

Pirsig, Robert M. *Zen and the Art of Motorcycle Maintenance: An Inquiry into Values.* New York: Morrow, 1974.

Plantinga, Alvin, and Nicholas Wolterstorff, editors. *Faith and Rationality: Reason and Belief in God.* Notre Dame: University of Notre Dame Press, 1983.

Polanyi, Michael. "The Creative Imagination." *Chemical and Engineering News* 44 (April 25, 1966) 85–93.

————. *Knowing and Being: Essays by Michael Polanyi.* Edited by Marjorie Grene. Chicago: University of Chicago Press, 1969.

————. *Personal Knowledge: Towards a Post-Critical Philosophy.* Corrected ed. Chicago: University of Chicago Press, 1962.

————. "Science and Reality." *British Journal for the Philosophy of Science* 18 (1967) 177–96.

————. *Science, Faith and Society*. Chicago: University of Chicago Press, 1946.

————. *The Tacit Dimension*. Foreword by Amartya Sen. Chicago: University Press, 2009.

Quine, Willard Van Orman. "Epistemology Naturalized." In *Ontological Relativity and Other Essays*, 69–90. New York: Columbia University Press, 1969.

Ridderbos, Herman. *Redemptive History and the New Testament Scriptures*. Phillipsburg, NJ: P & R, 1968.

Riesman, David, with Nathan Glazer and Reuel Denney. *The Lonely Crowd: A Study of the Changing American Character*. Hartford: Yale University Press, 2001.

Rolnick, Philip A. *Person, Grace, and God*. Grand Rapids: Eerdmans, 2007.

Schnarch, David. *Passionate Marriage: Keeping Love and Intimacy Alive in Committed Relationships*. New York: Henry Holt, 1997.

Scott, Drusilla. *Everyman Revived: The Common Sense of Michael Polanyi*. Grand Rapids: Eerdmans, 1985.

Scott, William Taussig, and Martin X. Moleski, S.J. *Michael Polanyi: Scientist and Philosopher*. New York: Oxford University Press, 2005.

Sennett, James F., editor. *The Analytic Theist: An Alvin Plantinga Reader*. Grand Rapids: Eerdmans, 1998.

Simon, Caroline. *The Disciplined Heart: Love, Destiny, and Imagination*. Grand Rapids: Eerdmans, 1997.

Smith, James K. A. "Biblical Studies across the Disciplines," Geneva College Faculty Development Workshop, May 21–24, 2007.

————. *Desiring the Kingdom: Worship, Worldview, and Cultural Formation*. Grand Rapids: Baker, 2009.

————. *The Fall of Interpretation: Philosophical Foundations for a Creational Hermeneutic*. Downers Grove, IL: InterVarsity, 2000.

————. "A Little Story About Metanarratives: Lyotard, Religion, and Postmodernism Revisited." In *Christianity and the Postmodern Turn: Six Views*, edited by Myron Penner, 124–40. Grand Rapids: Brazos, 2005.

————. *Radical Orthodoxy: Mapping a Post-Secular Theology*. Grand Rapids: Baker, 2004.

Snell, R. J. "Following Tiresias: How Evangelical Discussions of Postmodernity Go Wrong (and Thus Go On Forever)." Paper for Evangelical Philosophical Society, Washington, DC, November 2006.

————. *Through a Glass Darkly: On Knowing Without a Gods-Eye View*. Marquette Studies in Philosophy, no. 45. Milwaukee: Marquette University Press, 2006.

Sosa, Ernest. "The Raft and the Pyramid." *Midwest Studies in Philosophy* 5 (1980) 3–25.

Spencer, Stephen R. "Between Faith and Criticism: Evangelicals, Scholarship, and the Bible in America." *Bibliotheca Sacra* 150 (July–Sept. 1993) 378–79.

Steiner, George. *Real Presences*. Chicago: University of Chicago Press, 1989.

Vanhoozer, Kevin J. *The Drama of Doctrine: A Canonical-Linguistic Approach to Christian Theology*. Louisville: Westminster John Knox, 2005.

Van Til, Cornelius. *The Defense of the Faith*. Phillipsburg, NJ: P & R, 1955.

Weil, Simone. *Waiting for God*. Translated by Emma Craufurd. New York: HarperCollins, 2001.

Williams, Michael D. *Far as the Curse is Found: The Biblical Drama of Redemption.* Phillipsburg, NJ: P & R, 2005.

Williams, Terri Robinson. "Faith Development, Attachment, and the *Sensus Divinitatis.*" Faculty tenure paper, Geneva College, Beaver Falls, PA, Fall 2006.

Wittgenstein, Ludwig. *Philosophical Investigations.* 3rd ed. Translated by G. E. M Anscombe. New York: MacMillan, 1968.

Wolterstorff, Nicholas. *Educating for Shalom: Essays on Christian Higher Education,* edited by Clarence W. Joldersma and Gloria Goris Stronks. Grand Rapids: Eerdmans, 2004.

———. *Reason Within the Bounds of Religion.* 2nd ed. Grand Rapids: Eerdmans, 1984.

———. *Thomas Reid and the Story of Epistemology.* Cambridge: Cambridge University Press, 2004.

Zizioulas, John D. "Human Capacity and Incapacity: A Theological Exploration of Personhood." *Scottish Journal of Theology* 28 (1975) 401–48.

abandonment, 172n, 204, 282, 286–87
absolute, -ism, 11, 12n, 62, 157, 160,
    163, 206, 340, 368
academia, academic, xii, 10, 55–56, 86,
    131–42, 284n, 444
action, active, activity, act, 27, 43, 105–
    6, 109, 112, 178, 199, 221, 223,
    225–30, 233–36, 241, 243–44,
    246, 250, 317, 335, 347, 362–64,
    370, 372–73, 375–78, 397, 406,
    413, 418, 428, 431–34, 447, 450,
    452–53, 456, 463, 465, 474
    active listening, 456–57
    active passivity, 113, 344
    agents, 224, 226, 236–37, 244–45,
    390
    self as agent, 221–24, 226, 230
actual, actuality, 27, 98, 223, 250–54,
    257–58, 261, 276, 287, 325, 361,
    375, 430, 452–53, 466, 471
aha! moment. See Oh! I see it! moment
aletheia, 128
alienation, 26, 302, 317, 329, 364, 464
anticipation, 85, 118, 125, 208, 296,
    316, 381, 409, 412, 458, 472–73,
    478
anticipative, anticipative knowing,
    22, 33, 85–86, 88, 107, 118,
    120, 125, 137–38, 147, 174–76,
    184–91, 259, 261, 273, 290, 293,
    381, 404–5, 417, 420, 422, 431,
    443, 452, 463, 470
anti-realism, 14, 54, 57, 59, 91–92, 157,
    259, 398
antithesis, 61, 184–86
apocalyptic, 451, 457
apologetics, 86
    evidentialist, 56–57

presuppositional, 57–58
    un-, 59
apprehend, 22–23, 47, 91, 97, 135–36,
    207, 223, 229, 241, 245, 308, 324,
    430, 435, 442–43, 451, 457, 465
    be apprehended by, 137, 300, 378,
    381, 408, 417, 430–32, 476
apprenticeship, 79, 95, 109, 166, 208,
    238, 261, 270, 446
art, artistic experience, 23, 121, 175,
    235, 256–57, 304, 320, 338, 352,
    400n, 412, 443, 446, 448–49
articulation, 80, 146, 198, 259–60,
    372n, 412, 422, 429n
asymmetric, -y, 90, 242, 259, 339,
    344–45, 347–48, 351, 356, 371,
    377, 380–82, 401, 403
atheist, -ism, 18, 55, 177, 385–86, 390
attend, attention, -ive, -iveness, 32–33,
    40, 42, 47, 60, 67, 69–71, 77, 104,
    107–8, 115, 120, 139, 164, 170,
    172, 201, 205, 215–17, 220, 242,
    248, 299, 304–5, 310, 321, 337,
    367, 369, 379, 384, 386n, 402,
    407–8, 410, 416, 426–27, 429,
    431, 433, 436, 443, 447, 452,
    455–57, 463, 471, 478
    creative, 304–5, 455–56
authentic, -ity, 115, 120, 191, 322,
    388–90, 406, 443, 446, 475, 478
authoritative guides, 71, 79, 82–84, 106,
    137, 141, 147, 160, 166, 205–6,
    219, 266–68, 409, 416–17, 454.
    See also directions

beauty, 18, 176, 308, 338, 375, 446,
    464–65

beauty (*cont.*)
  personal, sense of, 115, 118–19,
      286–87, 296, **298–309,** 434,
      441–42, 473
  being, 26, 29, 55, 80, 159, 202, 249, 369,
      375, 380, 467
    as gracious, 273, 280–82, 286,
        402–3
    at home, 114–16, 252, 255, **440–41**
    composing, conferring or constitut-
        ing, 299, 302–3
    consent to 116, 286n, 299, 305, 407,
        427, 441–42
    excess of, 403, 412
    here, present, **114–16,** 251–53, 317
    in communion, 157, 231, 343.
        See also persons, as beings in
        communion
    -itself, 279–80, 282, 289
    letting flourish, flourishing, 129,
        272, 279, 286, 289, 299, 344,
        375, 378, 403, 405, 409, 412, 414,
        427, 433, 441–42, 453, 474
    mark, -s of. *See* transcendental, -s
    new, possibility of new, 278–80,
        282, 288n, 296, 378, 408, 467
    nonhuman. *See* world, nonhuman
    on the way to knowing. *See* know-
        ing, being on the way to
    perichoretic, **342–46**
    possibility of non-, 275, 294, 408–9.
        See also void
belief, 57–58, 60, 88–89, 141, 157, 167,
    170, 174, 185, 206–7, 313, 351,
    355, 373n, 385, 397, 399, 412,
    429
  as the epistemic act, 88, 170, 207,
      412
  commitment, fundamental, 57, 79,
      141, 185
  control, 58, 185n
  religious, 58, 60, 237
better knowers. *See* knower, -s, better
betrayal, 12–14, 204, 245, 325, 414
bias, 10, 14, 22, 90, 412.

body, 76, 89, 284, 307, 362–64, 412–13,
    422. *See also* embodiment
  as object/subject, 77–78, 89, 107,
      109–10, 112, 119,
  as interpreted, 117, 119
  care, 118–19, 308
  felt body sense, 70, 106, 112–13,
      120, 125, 245, 412, **442–43,** 445
  knowledge, 77, **104–22,** 245, 413
  lived, 70, 76, **77–78,** 82, 89, 105–6,
      117, 119, 121, 124, 147, 167–69,
      244, 308, 327, 412–13, **416–17,**
      443, 459, 460
  rootedness of all thought, 78, 120,
      205, 245, 408
boredom, 12–13, 31–32, 132, 304, 414
borrowed functioning, 314
boundaries, 29, 202, 249, 313, 322n,
    325, 381, 406, 418, 429, 460

Calvinism, 61, 146–47, 160, 185n
  Neo-Calvinian philosophy, **57,** 58
candidacy, 406, **417.** *See also* knowing,
    being in the way of
care, xv, 31–33, 40, 42, 73, 111, 118–20,
    124, 176, 189, 199–200, **207,**
    224–25, 228, 245, 266, 308, 360,
    401, 411, 430, 432–33, 447, 466,
    473
Cartesian, Cartesian tradition, 17n, 19,
    77, 89, 91, 96, 104, 110–12, 117,
    157, 218, 232, 244–46, 268, 384,
    386, 445, 478–79
center, recenter, 8–9, 12–13, 15, 87–88,
    90, 97, 114, 127, 131, **135–36,**
    138–40, 208, 253–56, 260–63,
    272–73, 278–83, 285–87,
    289–92, 295–96, 303, 332, 362,
    367–68, 372, 388–89, 391, 405,
    409, 437–38, 440, 467, 470, 477
certainty, 13, 18, 20–22, 29, 39, 54, 56,
    69, 73, 88, 91, 92–93, 125, 138,
    140, 166n, 209–10, 235, 329,
    341, 400, 410–11, **414–15**
Christ. *See* Jesus Christ

Christian, -s, -ity, xiv, xv, 6, 7n, 11–12, 18–20, 29n, 38–39, 43–44, 49, 54n, 55, 57–64, 86, 90n, 94, 123, 131, 133, 135–40, 146–51, 157n, 160n, 162–63, 167, 169–70, 172n, 175–77, 182, 184, 186, 188–89, 193–95, 197, 200, 206, 209, 215, 251, 273, 282–84, 287–90, 293, 307–8, 318, 327–31, 333–34, 337, 345, 353–55, 359–60, 363–64, 366, 368, 371–73, 375, 379, 385n, 390, 409–11, 420, 429–30, 433, 437, 439, 444, 465–68, 475, 477
  discipleship, xiv, 40, 44, 62–63, 139, 154, 318
  scholarship, 56, 131–52, 185, 187, 202,
cluelessness, 15–17, 78, 98, 132, 139, 377, 414.
clues, 45–46, 51, 67, 69–73, 85, 88, 101–2, 106–9, 133, 137, 147, 170, 173, 219, 241, 243, 281, 348n, 407–8, 414, 421, 458–59
  assigning value to, 79, 111, 166, 266, 308, 347–48, 386,412, 465
  climbing inside the, 78–79, 125, 399, 459. *See also* indwelling
  triad of, 74, 76–84, 93, 104, 124–25, 267, 327, 417, 422. *See also* Framean triad
cocelebrants of what is, 80, 267–68, 409
cogito,19, 112, 222, 237, 246, 268, 287, 294, 331, 364, 384–86, 402
cognitive rest, 422–23, 474
coherence, -ntism, 46, 52, 54, 92–93, 107, 124, 126, 419
coming to know, acts of. *See* know, coming to
commitment, 6, 15, 20–23, 38, 56–60, 69, 72, 79, 85, 88, 91, 94–95, 117, 133, 141, 147–48, 166, 169–71, 185, 202, 207, 219, 221, 238,

240–41, 248, 259, 323, 351, 355–56, 384, 387, 389–90, 399, 412, 420–21, 469
  to as-yet-undiscovered reality, 41, 175, 207, 256, 317
common grace, 61, 174–76, 184–86, 190, 205, 210n, 355, 390, 437, 439, 470n
communion, xv, 17n, 28–29, 36, 38, 41, 47, 63, 115, 131, 138, 147, 157, 178, 198, 202, 204, 209, 211, 231, 238, 241, 266–68, 282–85, 289–92, 295, 301, 311, 315, 327, 338, 357, 371–72, 377, 387, 388–90, 395, 400, 403–4, 406–7, 414, 416, 423, 425, 427, 432, 434–35, 448, 452, 460, 465–68, 472, 480
  interpersonal, 116, 155, 165, 228, 234, 246, 272, 363, 378, 380, 415, 426, 432, 462.
  ontology of, 343, 345, 354, 356, 378
communication, 26, 113, 220–21, 224–28, 234, 353, 387
community, 13, 42, 85–86, 95, 160, 188, 206, 219, 223, 245n, 249n, 270, 323, 336, 346, 361–62, 366–67, 369, 435 , 455, 457
compartmentalization, 52, 55, 132, 134, 251
comportment, 189, 319, 381, 400, 428, 444, 446–53, 468
composure, 428, 436–46, 452, 456
confidence, 68, 78, 83, 88, 93, 138, 151, 170, 278, 331, 410, 414
connected knowing. *See* knowing, connected
consummation, 291, 293, 452, 465–68, 473
contact with reality, 25, 36, 74–76, 92, 97, 99, 168, 175, 208, 243, 316, 399, 409, 421–22, 425, 478–79
contingent, -cy, 152, 275, 277–78, 280, 313, 317, 327, 410

convention, -alism, 54, 105, 140–41, 163

conversation, -s, ix, x, xii, xiii, xv, 4, 5, 35–36, 40, 46–47, 58–61, 64, 141, 187, 218, 260–61, 270, 323, 397, 401

convictional knowing, 123, 127–28, 261, 273, **281–84**, 285, 289–90, 299, 302, 356, 423n

conviviality, 95, 189, 238

coping, 32, 73, 101, 275, 386–87

correspondence, 54, 75, 159, 276, 290, 314, 350, 399, 416, 419, 436

covenant, 33, 196–97, 218, 241, 245, 343–44, **376–79**, 380, 407, 446, 465

  and biblical story, 44, 194–95, 205

  and differentiation, **314–16**, 319, 325

  and faithfulness, 34, 153, 157, 197, 203, 400

  and law, 197, 203

  and love, 153–54, 197–98, 203, 258, 266

  and obligation, 197, 378–79

  as contract, **198**, 203, 377

  as gracious, 197, 377

  as historical, 195, **196–97**

  as interpersonal relationship, as constitutive of relationship 33–34, 45, 47, 67, 80–81, 84, 102, 138–39, 156, 162, 164, 174, 177, 182, **193–211**, **195–96**, **202–5**, 244, 295, 315, 380, 403, 406

  as pledge, **207**, 439, **447–48**, 452

  as unfolding, 162n, 181, 193–95, 215, 315

  blessing, curse, **210–11**

  breaking, rebellion, 155, 204, 245, 288

  love, 382, 414, 452, 456n

  mutuality in, **196**

  of redemption, **290–93**

  ontology. *See* ontology, covenant

realism. *See* realism, covenant

relationship, 129, 153, 155–56, 162n, 179, 181, **351–53**

response, 139, 154–57, 177–79

solidarity, 154, 269

covenantal, xiv, 140–41, 229, 238, 244–46, 429–30, 443

  behavior, 37, 42, 201, 207, 417

  care, **207**, 245

  self-binding, 37, 41, 181, 203, 205, 207, 316, 344, 357, 406, 418, 432, 435, 446–47, 450

covenant epistemology, xiv, xv, 17n, 35–36, 39, 43, **44–47**, **49–64**, 76, 80–81, **87–103**, 104, 111, 113, 123, 129, 131, 145–48, 154, **164–82**, 174, **176–77**, 179, **201–10**, 211, 218, 235, **237–47**, **244–47**, 248, 260, **263–68**, 269, **290-96**, 298, 300, 310, 320, **324–26**, 327–28, 338, 340, 344, **346–59**, 365, 374, 376, 381, 389, **395–423**, 425, 453

  value of, 46–47, 55–56, **131–42**, 176–77, 184, 193, 383, 439

creation, 57, 257, 288, 291–92, 295, 308–9, 369, 378, 418, 455–56, 459, 465, 467

  and covenant, 153–57, 197, **199**, 200, 202, 207, 210, 401

  and situatedness, 163, 168, **205–7**, 410. *See also* situatedness

  as normatively effected, 152–53, 159, 456n. *See also* "let there be"

  as metaphysically dependent, 152

  doctrine of, 206, 339, 375–76, 401

  goodness of, 188

  nonhuman. *See* world, nonhuman

  Trinitarian, 328, 330, 333–36, 339, 351, 355, 359

creator-creature distinction, **151–53**, 154–55, 157n, 177, 259–60, 277, 353, 410

Credo ut intelligam, 449

critical, criticism, 24, 139, 179, 182, 399–400, 435

culture, cultural, xii, 4, 50, 55, 94, 184–88, 205–6, 245–47, 287, 323–26, 328, **329–33**, 333–38, 354–55, 359, 385–87, 410–11, 470–71. *See also* humans, engaging the world
    mandate, 17, 156, 169, 199, 207, 210, 411, 474

curriculum, academic, **133–35**, **135–36**, 138–40

cynicism, 23, 31

dance, 38, 51, 82, 98, 100, 119, 121, 204, 259, 270, 278, **327–59, 360–64**, 366, 407, 443, 472

data, 14–15, 22, 43, 91, 134, 136, 161, 221n, 234, 263, 317, 332, 426, 443

deconstruction, 90–91, 140–41, 376n

deduction, 70, 127

default, epistemic, 3–7, 22, 29, 359
    healthy, 7, 284, 310, 319, 418
    impact of, 6, 11, 12–14, 19, 131–32

default, epistemic, defective, 12–16, 27, 29, 31–33, 39, 49–50, 63, 93, 107, 112, 117, 123, 128, 131, **132–33**, 136, 210, 216, 219–20, 229, 242, 250–51, 284, 358, 382, 395–96, 416, 421, 426–27, 430, 444, 464, 478–79
    as disembodied, 220–21, 384, 443, 446, 474, 478
    as impersonal, 216, 220, 246–47, 425, 479
    as objectivist/objectifying, 429, 463. *See also* objectivism
    as two-dimensional, **470–71**, 475
    challenging the, 16, 67, 131–32, 158, 160, 179, 185, 188, 284, 329, **411–15**
    impact of, 61–62, 64, 134–36, 139, 367n, 429–30

delight, 49, 63–64, 69, 78, 243, 266–67, 278, 302, 304–6, 308, 410, 463–66, 473, 478

depersonalizing, -ation, 39, 87, 100, 132, 178, 180, 230–32, 234, 236, 241, 244, 256, 269, 281, 325, 352, 368, 370, 379, 415, 462–63, 474

descent of God, 138, **200**, 209, 211, 246, 289–90, 292, 296, 313, 370, 378, 412, 428, 430–32, 437, 445–46, 467–68, 470, 473, **476–77**, 477, 479–80

desire, 33, 208–9, 291, 313, 412, 414, **428–36**, 468

destructive analysis, 108, 168, 240–42, 250, 421

dichotomies, epistemic, 8, 18, 27, 86, 146, 155, 457–58
    challenging/healing the, 53–54, 67, 86, **87–95, 411–15**
    in academics, 10–11, 131–33

dichotomies, epistemic, instances of
    classroom/extracurriculum, 133
    fact/interpretation, 8, 160–61, 412
    facts/morals, 8
    fact/opinion, 8, 412
    fact/value, 8, 88, 160, 164, 397, 412
    knowledge/belief, 8, 88, 397, 399, 412
    male/female, 9–10, 413
    mind/body, 9–12, 18–19, 27n, 32, 61–62, 77–78, 89, 104, 110, 167, 308, 342, 363, 396, 399–400, 413
    mind/reality, 9, 91
    objective/subjective, 8, 103, 128–29, 249, 251, 412, 459
    one/many, 332. *See also* one, the, and the many, problem of
    public/private, 9–10
    reality/appearance, 9–10, 332, 413
    reason/emotion, 8, 10, 87, 412, 459, 461
    reason/faith, 8, 10, 62, 94, 397, 412
    science/art, 8, 10, 88, 257, 412, 461

dichotomies, epistemic, instances of
  (*cont.*)
  science/authority, 8, 88
  science/imagination, 8, 88, 126–28,
    132
  sciences/humanities, 88, **133–34**
  science/religion, 8, 10, 88, **94–95**,
    237
  theology/personal relationship
    with Christ, 139, 186–87
  theory/action, 8, 88, 132, 397
  theory/application, 8, 10, 62, 88,
    132–33, 397
  theory/practice, 88, 179, 413, 463,
    469
differentiation, 46, 255, 310, **311–26**,
  327, 338, 352–53, 355–56, 363,
  367, 377, 407, 429, **441**, 443–44,
  466, 470
dignity, 37, 119, 203, 351, 456
  conferring, 301, 305–6, 308
directions, 71, 76, **79–81**, 93, 104, 147,
  267. *See also* normative
discover, -y, 23, 32–33, 68, 72, 79, 85,
  91, 94–95, 97, 100, 126, 166n,
  171, 175, 238, 256–59, 280, 288,
  317, 412, 419, **421**, 422, 427,
  435, 454, 458, 472, 479
disembodiment, 112, 442
disengagement, 331–32
dualism, metaphysical, 89, 110–11,
  330, 332–33, 346, 359, 411
Dutch Reformed tradition, 60–61, 166
dynamism, dynamic, xv, 4, 29n, 38–39,
  88, 101, 107, 123, 126, 128–29,
  134, 136, 145, 162n, 174, 182,
  187, 193, 211, 229–30, 242, 270,
  272, 274, 276–77, 281, 294, 310,
  321, 327, 335–37, 339, 346,
  348–49, 351–54, 369, 375, 379,
  381–82, 395, 399–400, 403,
  405–7, 411, 415, 417, 426, 433,
  465–66, 468, 471

Eastern religion, 17n, 253n, 283
education, 6, 10, 16, 117, 149, **131–42**,
  254, 367
  Christian higher, 55, 133, **134–36**
  higher, 131–32, 433
  theological, **138–40**, 429–30
ego, 233, 249–51, 275–77, 279, 282,
  285–87, 289, 291–92, 294–95
  -centric predicament, 27, 221–22,
    312
eikonic eclipse, **126–28**, 133–34, 470
embodiment, 25, 32, 83, 105, **109–14**,
  116, 141, 159–60, 168, 181n,
  225n, 241, 268, 275, 300, 307,
  315, 342, 349, 360, 363–64, 375,
  398, 402, 410, **442**, 448, 459,
  463–64, 467
Emmaus, 208, 283, 291
emotion, -al, 9–10, 12–13, 28, 85,
  87–88, 222, 245, 317, 362, 429n
  fusion, 312–14, 316, 318, 321–22,
    324–25, 363, 460
empathy, 24, 42, 124–25, 459–62
empiricism, 42, 82, 107, 332, 341,
  415–16
encounter, 141, 248, 250, 252, **252–56**,
  257, 260, 262, 273, 283–84, 288,
  348, 355–56, 358, 369–70, 375,
  437, 441, 463. *See also* I-You
  as studding unfolding relationship,
    258, 262, 320, 356–57, 403–4
  I-You, 258–59, 265, 276, 290, 296,
    299, 303, 305–6, 311, 356, 378,
    395, 401–2, 404–5, 409, 426,
    435, 477, 480. *See also* I-You
Enlightenment, 24, 26, 58, 90, 140, 150,
  157n, 315, 331–32, 416, 444
epistemic, -ological
  etiquette, 38, 41, 247, 319, **425–68**,
    471
  realism. *See* realism, epistemic
  strategy, 238, 246, 467

epistemic, -ological (*cont.*)
   therapy, 3–30, 67, 132, 135, 138,
     157n, 160, 165, 262, 281, 284,
     329, 395, 406n, 427, 467
   vision, 5, 6, 36, 39, 44, 73, 90, 145,
     165, 269
epistemology, xi, 3–4, 33, 159–60,
     164–65, 240, 308, 369, 384, 390,
     398, 425, 451
   Polanyian, 44, 59, 67–103, 105, **169,**
     185, 193, 206, 218–19, 237–41,
     242–44, 293, 341–42, **347–51,**
     365, 369, 380, 386, 387n, 390,
     400, 417, 419, 425, 429, 458,
     462, 465, 471–72, 478
   Reformed, **58**
   social, 54, 419
   standard, 396–97
   virtue, 54, 419
ethics, 159–60, 164–65, 338, 373, 385,
     451
Eucharist, 273, 282–83, 290, 301–2,
     306, 309n, 357, 378, 409, **466–
     68,** 477
evil, 185, 188, 206, 277, 288, 435–36,
     449
evolution, evolutionary, 53, 209, 221,
     239, 372–73, 384, 387
excess, divine, 375, 378, 381, 390
existence, 51, 112, 141, 152–53, 155,
     159, 178, 181, 199–201, 221–24,
     226–27, 230, 233, 235–37,
     249–50, 253–55, 260–61, 273,
     300, 305, 378, 385n, 406, 408,
     438, 455
existential dimension, 147, 158–59,
     169–70, 244, 293–94, 354
existentialism, 16n, 248
experience, 249–53, 255–57
explanation, 68–69, 171, 223n, 239n,
     373–74, 419, 478
explicit, 16, 20, 50, 55–56, 58, 70,
     73–75, 78, 83, 85–86, 92–93,
     102, 124, 133–34, 186, 188, 239,

259–60, 267, 328, 421–22, 439,
     446, 479
externalism, 54, 419

face, 129, 243, 266, 301, 409
   of God, 278–79, 287, 289, 301–2,
     306, 362n, 427, 437
   of the Holy, **272–96,** 358
   of the other, 125, 129, 243, 269,
     272–73, **284–90,** 302, 375–76,
     390, 395
   -to-face, 111n, 129, 147, 236, 245,
     262, 270, 273, 286, 287, 311, 320,
     368–69, 375–76, 378, 390, 403
facts, 7, 13–14, 39, 42, 75, 88, 109n, 161,
     185, 372
faith, 7, 10, 13, 20, 23, 42, 62, 94, 133,
     139, 162n, 167, **169–71,** 175,
     189, 282, 288n, 372n, 373n, 397,
     412, 442
faithfulness, 34, 153, 157, 199, 201, 203,
     258, 325, 362, 400–401, 433, 436
fallibilism, 92, 122, 270, 341, 351, 410,
     420
fideism, 341
fidelity, 42, 201, 401, **443–44,** 466
focal, 45–46, 53–54, 70, 73–75, 78, 82,
     84–86, 88–91, 94, 96–97, 101–2,
     104, 106–7, 109, 116, 118, 141,
     147, 160, 164, 170, 172, 240, 242,
     307, 348–49, 375, 380, 386–87,
     398, 407–8, 411, 417, 422
formation, 40, 47, 63, 135, 137, 141,
     194, 270, 318, 355
form of the implicit love of God. *See*
     knowing, as form of the im-
     plicit love of God
foundationalism, nonfoundationalism,
     54, **56–57,** 58, 61, 91, **92–93,**
     122, 157, 163, **340–41,** 410
Framean triad, 46, **76–83,** 147, 155,
     158–64, 165, **171–74,** 176, 178,
     180, 182, 218, 242, 244, 267, 293,
     295, 349, 353–54, 407, 422.

Framean triad (*cont.*)
    See also normative; existential;
    situational
free, -dom, 29, 37, 50, 96, 114, 127n,
    138, 203–4, 223, 231n, 245, 278,
    292, 318, 322, 329, 332, 335–38,
    343, 345, 351–52, 355, 371–72,
    377, 385–86, 388, 408, 416, 449,
    453, 455, 470n
from-to, 70, 172–73, 242, 380, 407–8,
    411. *See also* subsidiary-focal
    integration
friendship, 41, 140, 154, 176, 178–79,
    181, 194, **198**, 203–4, **209**, 234,
    246, **264–70**, 289, 354, 357, 375,
    378, 401, 431, 453, **465–66**, 474,
    475, 477, 480
future
    manifestations, indeterminate, 36,
        75, 77, 97, 99, 125, 169, 175,
        208–9, 399, 405–6, 422, 426,
        433, 472, 478–79
    possibilities, intimations of, 46, 92,
        174, 243, 378, 422
    prospects, 97, 101–2, 134, 138, 189,
        243, 399, 405, 422, 478

gaze, 27, 79, 115, 120, 155, 172n, 253,
    266–67, 269, 279, 286–87, 289,
    296, 299–303, 305–6, 309, 353,
    378, 390, 395, 402, 433–34, 437,
    441, 463, 473, 480. *See also* face
generosity, 114, 374–75, 379, 382, 468
gift, 33, 39, 99, 102, 115–16, 278, 299,
    320, 339, 344, 347, 357, 375,
    376–79, 380–81, 389, 390, 402–
    4, 431, 436, 440, 452, 466–68,
    476, 480. *See also* reality, as gift
    and reception, logic of, 339, 343–45,
        347, 357, 377–78, 380, 466
    giver, 339, **376–79**, 381, 404
God, 154, 235, 251, 254, 361–62, 368,
    379, 385–86, 389, 433–34, 445,
    464

and creation, 337, 368, 403. *See also*
    creation, Trinitarian
as covenant Lord, 17, **153–56**,
    157–60, 163, 185–86, 196–97,
    199, 246, 353, 410
as Creator, 236, 368, 378, 385n
as Emmanuel, 283, 375, 379
as Person, 358, 377–79, 381–82, 385
as the One who comes from the
    other side of our emptiness,
    292, 296
as the Other, 246, 378–79, 381–82,
    385, 402, 477
authority of, 154, 158
before God, 156, 344, 347, 410,
    437–40
being known by, 33–34, 273, 464,
    476
communion with, 63, 178, 372,
    377–78. *See also* communion
control of, 154, 158
descent of. *See* descent of God
face of. *See* face, of God
imaging, image of, 304–5, 307, 363,
    385n, 434
knowing, 33–34, 63, 71, 94, 139–40,
    145–46, 148, 150, 154–55, 160,
    162–63, **174–76**, 177, 182n, 184,
    205, 210, 282–83, 296, 302, 369,
    390, 408–9, 437–40, 442, 446,
    450, 465, 480
knowledge of, and ordinary know-
    ing, 57, 135, 146, 150, 154,
    156–58, 193, 209, 282, 284, 302,
    437
law of, 158, 385n
love of, 118, 176, 251, 289–90, 356,
    382, 390, 439
power of, 154, 372, 385n
presence of, 154, 158, 246, 273, 288,
    290, 302, 305, 372, 445
relationship with, 20, 61, 63,
    154–56, 193, 251, 266, 284,
    288n, 290, 295, 346, 354, 372,
    375–76

God (*cont.*)
 transcendence/immanence of, 154,
  385n, 387n
 Trinity. *See* Trinity
 wanting to be known, 201–2. *See
  also* revelation
gnosis, 128, 132
gospel, 11, 39, 56, 63, **135–36,** 139–40,
  197, 200, 284n, 335, 355, 441,
  450n, 454, 468, 478–79
 as castrated by defective epistemic
  default, 61, 64, 135–36
 as epistemic paradigm, 17, 25, 44,
  50, 63, 69, **134–36,** 371, 419
grace, gracious, 37, 40, 56n, 97, 115–16,
  123, 139, 150, 175, 184, 189,
  191, 196–97, 205, 209, 251–55,
  261–62, 270, 273, 278–82, 286,
  288n, 289–90, 294, 296, 300,
  304, 308, 320, 344, 356, 368, 370,
  373–74, 376–78, 402–3, 417–18,
  420, 425, 427, 433–34, 437, 449,
  455, 458, 463n, 467–68, 470, 472

heal, healing, xiii, xiv, 4, 22, 25, 33, 40,
  47, 49, 51, 94, 112, 127, 131, 140,
  148, 179, 204n, 210, 254–55,
  265, 281, 287, 296, 308, 319, 328,
  332, 340, 346–47, 351, 354–55,
  359, 362, 364–65, 369, 396, 400,
  403, 408, 411–12, 414–15, 422,
  427, 434, 445, 450, 453, 463,
  468, 473–75, 480
heart, 57, 61, 161, 163, 166, 168, 184,
  191, 208, 428n, 443, 473, 477
hermeneutics, 91, 105n, 140–41. *See
  also* interpretation
 philosophical, 60
history, ed, 53, 128, 140–41, 149, 151n,
  157n, 163, 166n, 177, 195,
  196–97, 202, 205–6, 219, 293,
  328, 330, 355, 361, 385, 405,
  410, 438, 465, 479

Holy, the, 266, **272–96,** 299, 306,
  355–56, 358, 378, 403, 409, 467,
  470, 477
Holy Spirit, 159, 182n, 273, 281–82,
  334, 336, 338, 356, 359, 361, 438
homogeneity, 331–32, 336–37, 339–41,
  353
hope, 6, 13, 32, 35, 38, 41, 87, 131, 147,
  200, 208, 245, 259, 269, 277,
  436, 449, 472
hopelessness, 12–13, 15, 32, 414
hospitable, -lity, 131, 137, 350, 427, 441,
  448–49, 455
human, -s, 225–27, 229, 231–32, 241,
  243–45, 362, 367, 374–76, 385,
  387, 389, 472
 as covenant mediator, **199–200,** 207
 as creatures, 244, 331
 as imaging God, 159, 186, 244,
  410–11
 as knowers, 270, 374, 378, 383–84,
  388
 as persons, 266, 378, 383–84, 388,
  414
 as situated in the world, 32, 163,
  277, 386, 410
 development, 123, 273–75, 278,
  284–90, 291–92, 295, 311, 314,
  437
 engaging the world, 50, 73, 160–62,
  168, 187, 199, 329, 342, 344–47,
  351, 353–54, 398, 410, 420. *See
  also* culture
 spirit, 126, 128, 273, 281
humanness, 7, 12–13, 26–27, 31, 46,
  50, 113, 123, 127, 186, 227, 249,
  252, 262, 273, 306, 323, 372, 387,
  389, 410, 419, 423, 426, 470n
 and I-You, 253–54, 262
 and knowing, 215, 248, 274–75
 four dimensions of, 46, 273, **274–
  81,** 282–83, 285, 289, 291–92,
  293–96, 299, 306, 477

humility, 33, 38, 41, 207, 344, 356, 406,
　　435, 439, **451–52,** 454

idolatry, 150, 287, 325, 434–35, 464
I-It, 235n, 248, **249–50,** 251–53,
　　255–59, 262, 288, 296, 327,
　　356–57, 403, 407
imagination, 125, 127–28, 132, 134,
　　230–31, 237–38, 470
　　creative, 72, 106, 124, 134, 231, 258,
　　349, 462
impersonal, 14–15, 21–22, 24, 39–40,
　　42–44, 49, 75, 85, 89, 96–97,
　　100, 129, 152, 180, 216, 219–20,
　　231, 234–39, 246–47, 268,
　　318–19, 325, 352, 370, 374, 379,
　　383, 400, 403, 405, 414–15, 425,
　　453, 479
implicit, 14, 61, 85, 120–21, 129, 133,
　　145, 164, 175, 181, 186, 188,
　　203, 226, 228, 241, 265, 275–76,
　　280, 293, 295, 354–55, 381, 405,
　　409, 418, 449
Incarnation, -al, 39, 159, 200, 375, 409,
　　438
incommensurability, 167
incommunicability, 372, 390
individualism, -ity, 52, 79, 312, 319,
　　332, 334
induction, 127, 415
indwelling, ix, xiii, 6, 24, 33, 63, 68, 70,
　　76, 79, 82, 87–88, 95, 124, 131,
　　137, 141, 168–70, 172, 201, 216,
　　223, 241, 252, 268, 270, 272, 317,
　　357, 402, 410, 416–17, 421, 427,
　　457, **458–61,** 462–63, 467, 471,
　　mutual, 128–29, 272, 335, 350, 459,
　　466
information. *See* knowledge, as
　　information
insight, 24, 26, 60–61, 69, 73–75, 88,
　　97, 119, 125, 127, 145, 207, 257,
　　259–60, 279, 282, 288, 402, 418,

420–22, 427, 435, 445, 452, 454,
　　457, 474
integration, -tive, 46–47, 54, 67, 69–71,
　　72–73, 74–78, 82, 88–89, 96–97,
　　101–2, 106–8, 117–18, 125,
　　131, 134, 147, 170, 189–90, 231,
　　240, 242–43, 259, 338, 347–50,
　　356, 386n, 388, 398, 404, 407,
　　412, 416–17, 421, 440–41, 443,
　　445, 456, 458, 465–66, 469,
　　474. *See also* subsidiary-focal
　　integration
intention, -ality, 6, 20, 50, 87, 104, 108,
　　119, 126n, 137, 172, 204, 207,
　　220, 223, 226, 229, 241, 243–46,
　　439, 468
internalism 54, 419, 440
interpersonhood, -ed, -al, xiii, xiv, xv,
　　28, 34, 40–47, 49–51, 55, 63,
　　67, 80–81, 87–88, 111–12, 116,
　　123, 129, 131, 133, 136, 138–41,
　　147, 155–56, 165, 169, 176–77,
　　178, 180–81, 187, 191, 193–94,
　　198, 204–5, 210–11, **215–47,**
　　248, 253, 262, 269–70, 272–73,
　　275, 285–86, 290, 293, **310–26,**
　　327–28, 346, 352–53, **355–57,**
　　358, 363, 365, 368, 370–71,
　　375–80, 382, 389, 395–97,
　　399–401, **402–403,** 404–6, 408,
　　411, 413, 415, 419, 426, 432,
　　440, 448, 462–63, 466, 468, 471,
　　474, 476
　　hints of, 47, 87, **95–103,** 179,
　　193–94, 357
　　role in pedagogy, **136–37**
interpersonal relationship. *See* rela-
　　tionship, interpersonal
interpretation, 8, 10, 15, 90–91, 93,
　　109–10, 126, 157, 160–61, 173,
　　274, 276, 282, 285, 289, 291–93,
　　295, 317–18, 333, 398, 412–13,
　　442, 457, 477

interpretive framework, 45, 88, 141, 167, 398. *See also* worldview
intimacy, 111n, 125, 155, 197–98, 203–5, 219, 262, 266, 282, 284, 286n, 311, 355, 361, 367, 407, 429, 460–61, 463–64, 467, 470
intuition, creative, 72, 93, 124–25, 258, 349
invention, 11, 91, 256–57, 346
inviting the real, 33, 38, 41, 50–51, 119, 137, 207, 209, 243, 246–47, 260–62, 284, 287, 298–99, 302, 304, 308–9, 317, 319, 357, 406, 414–18, 421, **425–68**, 473, 476, 480
I-You, I-Thou, 46, 224, 228, 232, 234–36, 245, **248–63, 250–58,** 265, 272, 276, 288, 290, 296, 299, 303, 305–6, 311, 327, 356–58, 378, 380–81, 395, 401, 403–5, 407, 409, 414, 426, 435–36, 438, 452, 456, 473, 475, 477, 480. *See also* encounter
  as central to knowing, 260, 262, 272, 403
  taking the I of I-You into I-It, 259, 262, 288, 296, 356, 378, 380
  taking the I-You of I-You into I-It, **357–58**
  the I of 250–51, **252–56,** 257, 260–62, 288, 296, 356, 358, 378, 380, 414, 426, 436, 452, 456, 473

Jesus Christ, 6n, 11, 18, 39, 44, 62–63, 128n, 139–40, 159, 179, 186–89, 191, 196–97, 200, 206, 208, 251, 278, 282–85, 289, 291–93, 295, 301, 304, 306, 334, 336, 338, 356, 363, 373, 375n, 402, 433, 438, 439, 441–42, 450, 453–55, 464, 467–68, 479
  the Truth, 39, 44, 63, 156–57, 402, 438, 467, 479

joy, ix, 80, 186, 202, 222n, 251, 307, 319, 425, 429, 446, 454, 472, 475, 477, 479
justification, 20–21, 43, 58, 68, 92, 159, 179, 207, 222, 260, 401, 414, 432–33, 452, 466. *See also* knowledge, justification of
  allegiance and obligation as prior to, 207, **420–21**
  as informally assessed, **422–23**
  discovery as prior to, **421**

know
  coming to, xii-xiv, 33, 53, 55, 60, **68–69,** 70–71, 75–76, 81–82, 84–85, 96, 99–100, 117, 121, 124, 129, 134, 171, 173, 175–76, 182, 188, 204n, 208, 211, 228, 242, 246–47, **256–58,** 260, 265–69, 280–81, 283, 285, 291, 293, 304, 316, 349, 401, **405–6,** 408–9, 412, 426, 428, 435, 437, 443, 448, 451, 465–66, 469, 472, 474, 478
  coming to, as coming to be known, 33, 100, 401, 414, 470
  longing to, **12–14,** 31–32, 71, 73, 138, 260, 275–76, 281, 308, 417, 432, 438
  loving to. *See* love, in order to know
  rekindling the longing to, 16, **31–34,** 138
  knower, -s, 14–15, **95–96,** 157, 245–46, 366, 379, 385, 388, **402–3,** 435, 444, 456
  as being known. *See* being known
  as changed by knowing, 84, 100, 117, 158, 216, 377–78, 414
  as embodied, 374, 383
  as person, 95, 246, 265, 366, 383, 402
  better, 28, 43, 47, 50, 63, 85, 100, 122–23, 184, 216, 235, 245, 247–48, 265, 281, 284, 289, 298,

knower, better (*cont.*)
　306, 309–10, 326, 356, 364, 396,
　403–4, 414–15, 427, 438, 468,
　471. *See also* knowing, better
　personal contribution of, 20, 90,
　127, 159, 166, 474
knower and known, 26, 33, 38, 50, 95,
　99–100, 128–29, 160, 174, 215,
　221n, 234, 241, 327, 342, 351,
　357, 366, 370, 380, 403, 407,
　408, 409, 415, 440, 468, 473
　disconnect of, 19, 251, 332, 367
　mutuality of, 210, 259, 272, 318,
　320, 345, 350, 368–69
　relationship of, 41–42, 87, 259, 316,
　351, 366, 369, 429, 432, 436,
　447, 450, 460, 463, 466, 470–71,
　474–75
knowing, 185, 238, 244, 367–68, 379
　aesthetic, 126, 128
　and being known, 33, 62–63, 246,
　270, 288, 366, 408, 418, 466
　and cultural mandate, 199, 347
　and differentiation, **316–20**
　and God's Lordship, 150, 157–58,
　176
　and healthy interpersonhood,
　310–26
　anticipative. *See* anticipative
　knowing
　as active shaping of particulars into
　a pattern, 69, 261, 386n. *See also*
　pattern, active shaping of
　as basic, 40, **233–35**, 236, 238–39,
　245–46, 380, 405
　as belief, 88, 157, 170, 421
　as care, 31, 33, 124, 430, 433, 466
　as coming to know. *See* knowing,
　coming to
　as covenantal, -ly constituted, **36**,
　37, 41, 50–51, 138, 155, 161,
　201–2, 210, 218–19, 267, 328,
　369, 395, 400, 403, **406–7**,
　465–66

as covenant response, 157, **177–82**,
　246, 296
as creaturely, 153, 155, 160, 187–88,
　194n, 205, 342, 353, **409–11**,
　418, 420
as cultural engagement, 338, 340,
　347
as embodied, 6, 11, 18n, 32, 374,
　383
as form of the implicit love of God,
　176, 289–90, 382, 390
as healing, 51, 127, 347, 365, 368,
　403, 408, 411, 414, 427, 434,
　438, 445, 450, 473–75
as interpretive, 410, 413
as journey, 445, 472, 480
as knowing God, 63, 139–40, 145,
　148, 150, 154–55, 160, 162–63,
　174–76, 177, 182n, 184, 205,
　210, 296, 342, 369, **408–9**,
　437–38, 439–40, 450. *See also*
　knowing, as prototyping know-
　ing God
as knowing whom, 41, 137, 180–81
as knowing with whom, 180–81,
　261, **264–70, 409**
as negative and constitutive, 229,
　238
as perichoretic, **340–42**, 347, 382
as personed, interpersoned or per-
　sonal, interpersonal, 34, 39, 41,
　45, 49, 51, 67, 88, **100–103**, 113,
　129, 147, 155, 164, **177–82**, 186,
　215–47, 265, 270, 273, 289, 325,
　365, 378–80, 382, 395–96, 400,
　402–3, 403–5, 428, 432, 443,
　446, 448, 471, 474, 476
as perspectival, 435
as prototyping knowing God, 33,
　282–84, 288–90, 390, 403
as relationship, 155, 179, 186, 402
as servant thinking, 153, 163, 369,
　410

knowing (*cont.*)
as situated, **205–7**, 374, 383. *See also* situated
as skill, 73, 78
as stewardship, **145–83**, **169**, 194n, 200, 207, 244, 406, 410, **411**, 412, 420, 474. *See also* stewardship
as subsidiary-focal integration, 13, 134, 241–43, 471. *See also* subsidiary-focal integration
as trajectory, 78, 81, 96, 102, 124, 182, 189, 258, 274, 349, 404–5, 407–8, 423, 435, 443, 452, 466, 474
as transformation, **123–30**, 272, 400, 414, 466, 469, 471, 474–75, 480
as transformation, not information, 63, **131–42**, 281, 397, 413–14, 417, 432, 438, 441, 443–44, 450, 467n
as transformative, transformational, 70, 88, 208, 279–80, 288, 302, 309, 347–48, 356, 378, 390, 395, 408, 412
as unfolding, 36, 82, 174, 208, 258, 316, 403, 420, 423, 435, 452, 466, 472
as unfolding covenant relationship, **193–211**, **207–8**, 328, 404–5, 466
being in the way of, 38, 118–19, 207, 261–62, 364, **454**, 467, 476–77
being on the way to, 36, 40, 47, 85, 138, 147, 175, 184, 188–89, 207, 216, 258–59, 273, 345, 405–6, 423, 443, 454, **472–73**. *See also* anticipative knowing
better, 17, 20, 41, 113, 254, 281, 316, 318–19, 326, 441. *See also* knowers, better
central dynamic of, 158, 168, 254, 260

connected, **461–62**, 470
convictional. *See* convictional knowing
correlativities between knowing God, world, self, 160–63
evil, 288n
examples of, xv-xvi, 3, 16, 46, 69–71, **83–84**, 86, 98, 106, 109, 125, 166–68, 175, 243, 267, 427, 434, 439, 445–46, 451–56, 462, 464n, 471–73
for shalom. *See* shalom, knowing for
God. *See* God, knowing
half-understood, 41, 117, 175, 188, 420
in the presence of, 265–67, 269–70, 309
"moments of our deepest," 382, 403, 435
more than we can tell, 44n, 188
not-yet-. *See* anticipative knowing
relational, 49, 187, 218, 244–45, 365, 372, 459, 465–66
relationship with God central to, 61, 282, 284
role of Christ, Christian belief in, 177, 186, 189
self. *See* self, knowing
therapeutic, 126–29, 434, 445
knowing event, 7, 75, 79, 95, 100, 106, 118, **124–26**, 127–29, 138, 145, 210, 215, 255, 260–62, 265, 272–74, 276, 279–85, 288–89, 291–92, 295, 298, 310, 356, 395, 407–9, 412, 418, 465, 469
five-step sequence of the. *See* transformation, five-step sequence of
knowledge, 5, 6, 16, 41, 45, 82–83, 97n, 141, 152, 157n, 199, 231, 233, 238, 292, 337, 341, 465, 475, 478
as exhaustive, 20, 75, 77, 132, 147, 209, 397

knowledge (*cont.*)
  as explicit, 16, 20, 50, 55–56, 70,
    73–75, 86, 133–34, 239, 259–60,
    267, 446, 479. *See also* explicit
  as information, facts, statements
    and proof, 7–8, 10, 12–15, 43,
    49–50, 58, 62, 69–70, 73–75,
    85–89, 94, 105, 132–35, 140,
    152, 160, 209, 215, **220–21**, 229,
    234, 242, 246, 249, 260, 262, 270,
    324–25, 396, 405, 411, 413–14,
    419, 427, 432, 441, 444, 467n
  as impersonal, 24, 43, 87, 100, 129,
    220, 231n, 319, 405. *See also*
    impersonal
  justification of, 68, 92–93, 396,
    402, 414–15, **419–23**. *See also*
    justification
  nature of, 54, 396, **402–4**
  objects of, 159, 353, 366, 369, 374,
    381, 383, 396, **397–402, 476**
  sources of, 315, 396, **415–19**
known, ix, xi, 4, **14–15**, 75, 77, 246,
    379, **403**, 456. *See also* reality;
    creation
  as God and his effects, 181, 201
  as personed or personlike, 41, 45,
    95, **96–100,** 103, 128, 137, 141,
    215, 234, **235–37**, 244, 265,
    272, 344, 358, 365–66, 369, 382,
    400–401, 452–53, 476
  as subject, not object, 367–69
  being, 33, 62, 97, 176, 246, 265–67,
    270, 273, 286, 288, 296, 302, 309,
    396, 418, 440, 457, 466, 476
  living on the terms of the yet-to-be,
    33, 38, 201, 317, 401, 427
  yet-to-be-, 32–33, 38, 71, 137, 170,
    175, 246, 289, 302, 316, 318,
    349, 357, 367, 378, 381, 407,
    412, 427, 430, 441, 444, 446–48,
    459, 462, 472, 474

language, xi, xii, 4, 33, 38, 52, 54, 76, 79,
    107, 206, 220–21, 225, 240, 259,
    266, 387
  games, 80–81, 140–41
learning, xiii, xiv, 14, 33, 69–70, 72–74,
    78, 81, 105, 109, 131–38, 170,
    264–70, 368, 433, 450. *See also*
    pedagogy
legalism, 139
"let there be," 141, 152–53, 161, 199,
    406. *See also* creation
linear, -ity, xiii, 14, 35, 47, 70, 73, 126,
    160, 164, 208, 240–41, 277, 348,
    417, 421, 474
listening, xiii, 35–36, 51, 311, 427, 450,
    452–53, 460
  beyond categories, 41, **457–58**
liturgy, liturgical formation, liturgical
    practice, 62–63, 141, 162n, 318,
    363n
logos, 336, 338, 356
longing, 21, 32–33, 208, 293, 412, 428,
    431–32, 438, 476, 478
  to know. *See* know, longing to
Longing to Know, ix, x, xiv, xv, 36n, 38,
    67–69, 76n, 86, 94, 97, 99–100,
    102, 106, 125, 147, 187n, 199n,
    209n, 218, 267, 283, 300, 315n,
    317n, 349, 409, 420–21, 438,
    450n, 471, 476
love, 18n, 23, 33, 37, 41–43, 103, 113,
    118, 128–29, 139, 153, 155n,
    169, 176–77, 179, 197–98, 203,
    225, 234, 245n, 247, 250–51,
    254–55, 258, 266, 285–86, 289,
    292, 302, 304–5, 308, 311, 313,
    315, 317–19, 325, 335, 337, 343,
    351–52, 356, 362n, 366–68,
    373–74, 377, 381–82, 390, 400–
    401, 403, 405–7, 410–12, 414,
    420, 423, 428–31, **432–36,** 439,
    441, 444, 447–48, 452, 455–56,
    459–60, 463, 467, 479–80

love (*cont.*)
  in order to know, 33, 141, 234, 319,
    366, 400, 403, 405–6, 411–12,
    420, 429–30, 434–35, 444
  lovelessness, 112, 442

material, 18–19, 97, 239, 301, 307, 330,
    332, 337, 367, 375–76, 460, 478
materialism, 332, 385
maxim, -s, 73n, 79, 206, 243, 349, 422,
    444, 469, 473–74
meaning, 7, 13–14, 19, 70, 74, 76n,
    77–79, 91, 106, 110, 112–13,
    125–26, 150n, 226, 230, 259,
    287, 329, 332, 336, 338, 340–41,
    347–48, 353, 362, 384n, 408,
    413, 434, 443, 449, 459, 479
Meno dilemma, 53, 85, 170, 174
metanarrative, 157n, 185
metaphysics, 159–60, 259, 364, 398
metonymy, -ous, 180, 217, 229, **237–39**,
    295–96, 343, 354, 358, 371,
    380–82, 395–96, 400, 403, 406
mistake, -s, -en, 13, 19n, 20, 24n, 62,
    73, 86, 93, 109n, 122, 132, 165n,
    177, 188, 197, 224, 232, 240, 242,
    254, 268, 270, 378, 406, 413, 470
modernism, 19, 54, 60–61, **89–91**, 94,
    146–47, 157, 161, 163, 165n,
    185, 251n, 323, 331–32, 385–86,
    416
modernity, 185, 329–31, 340
monism, 89, 253n, 330–31, 339–41,
    359, 368n, 379
mother-child. *See* relationship,
    mother-child
mutual, -ity, xiii, xvi, 26, 29n, 33, 41–42,
    47, 92, 98, 101, 119, **128**, 129,
    131, 137, 140, 162, 188, 194,
    196, 197, 204, 210, 221, 224–26,
    228–29, 234, 241, 255–56, 259,
    262, 267, 272, 286, 310, 314,
    316, 318–20, 323, 325, 333, 335,
    339, 345–48, 350, 352, 354,

362–63, 369, 375–81, 400, 403,
    405, 408–9, 411, 413–14, 417,
    428–29, 439, 441, 458–59, 462,
    465, 467
mystery, 37, 89, 98, 180, 209, 254, 258,
    260, 365

naturalism, 89
  epistemic, 54, **88–89**, 109–10
nature, 36–37, 43, 152, 163, 173,
    253–54, 346, 366, 368, **371–74**,
    375, 379, 381, 383, 385, 388–89.
    See also real
neutral, -ity, 8–9, 59, 161, 185, 189, 191,
    210, 304, 428
normative, 76, 141, 152–53, 156, 159,
    161–62, 164–65, 169–73, 199,
    202, 204, 207, 229, 238–39, 294,
    349, 352–54, 358, 371, 377, 403,
    406–7, 409, 416
  and covenant, 178, 180, 194, 216,
    238, 358, 380, 395, 406
  and interpersonal relationship, 178,
    180–82, 194, 197, 380
  dimension, **79–81**, 124, 145, 147,
    158, 160, **164–66**, 174, 178, 194,
    202, 205, 215, 244, 267, **293–96**,
    358, 395, 416. *See also* direc-
    tions; word
notice, -ing, 79, 82, 97, 299, 303, 305,
    308, 348, 386, 412, 427, 455–56,
    465. *See also* clues, assigning
    value to
noticing regard, 115, 136, 243, 287,
    299–307, 309, 402, 431, 440,
    452, **454–56**, 463, 465

obedience, 33, 43, 139, 155, 177–79,
    197, 207, 209, 221n, 261, 293,
    360, 388, 404, 406, 443, **450–51**,
    457, 465
  as lived truth, 207, 409, 412
  as preceding truth, 207, 260, 420

objectivity, objective, 6, 8–9, 14–15, 21, 23–24, 54, 56, 74, 92, 97n, 103, 127–29, 199, 238, 246, 249, 254, 259, 272, 325, 332, 341, 368, 397–400, 412–13, 415–16, 423, 459

objectivism, 20, 22–24, 29, 38–40, 52, 54, 146–47, 157n, 164–66, 268, 319, 365, 368, 411, 415, 429, 450

ocular metaphor, 20, 24–26, 29, 230, 411, 415, 463

Oh! I see it! moment, 69–70, 125, 259, 281–82, 288n, 348, 356, 378, 404, 474

one, the, and the many, 330–33, 336, 340, 346, 351, 353, 386n

ontology, 26, 160, 197, 201, 343, 345, 371, 376, 378, 398

    covenant, **397–402**

openness, 28, 32, 41, 131, 148, 336, 356–57, 367, 413–14, 433, **444–45**, 449, 457, 460

orient, orientation, xii, xiii, 20, 31, 36, 44, 82, 84, 86, 88, 95, 134, 136, 138, 140–41, 146, 161, 171–73, 184, 186, 188, 206, 222, 228, 249, 254, 262, 307, 317, 322, 356, 364, 382, 391, 395, 397, 399, 403, 410, 427, 442, 477

other, the, 129, 223, 228–30, 252–53, 268, 273, 279, 281, 290, 302–3, 340, 355, 375, 378, 380, 428, 440, 443, 456, 462

    personal, 224–25, 227–30, 232–36, 240–43, 246, 253n, 266, 278, 285, 287, 290, 294, 299, 309, 355, 369–71, 378, 381, 402–3

    freshness of, 375, 378, 381, 390, 466, 475

    intrusion of, **417–19**

    self as constituted by/form of, 224, 226–27, 232–33, 236

    self as negative aspect of, 228–29, 235

transcendent, 246

otherness, 41, 334–36, 340, 345, 353, 429, 440, 447, 449, 457, 459–60

overture, response, 33, 38, 99–100, **196**, 258–59, 262, 270, 327, 344, 350, 354, 356–57, 362–63, 400–1, 404, 406–7, 449, 458, 466, 470, 472. *See also* reciprocity, rhythmical

pain, -ful, 3, 13, 101, 115, 120, 204, 248, 288n, 475

    embracing, **445–46**

pantheism, 152, 260n, 345, 379

paradigm, paradigmatic, xii, xv, 15, 17, 22–23, 25, 38–41, 43–45, 50, 63, 67–69, 75, 86, 95, 99–100, 112, 117, 128–29, 131–32, **134–36**, 175, 179, 181, 193–94, 196, 209, 215, 220, 238, 244, 247, 249, 259, 275, 282, 284, 290, 310, 318, 326, 342, 352, 357, 371, 382, 390, 395–97, 404–5, 409, 415, 419–20, 430, 461, 466–68

particularity, xiii, 29, 187–88, 205, 305, 333–49, 351–57, 368, 372, 377, 379, 381, 401, 405, 407, 413–15, 434, 441, 460, 466, 470

passion, -s, -ate, 4, 9, 13, 17, 21, 23, 33, 126, 128, 136, 139, 193, 238, 267n, 273, 318, 362, 412, 427, 428, 430, 432, 436

    persuasive, 126

passivity, 112, 132, 160, 344, 428, 431–32, 443, 463

patience, 33, 38, 41, 138, 189, 207, 367, 406, **452**, 460, 472, 480

pattern, 5, 36, 45–47, 67, 69–76, 79, 100–102, 104, 106–8, 118, 125–28, 147, 153, 166, 169–70, 178, 196, 200, 207–8, 211, 240–41, 243, 265, 281, 291, 293, 340, 342, 347–49, 356, 367, 386, 397, 407–8, 413, 417, 422, 435,

pattern (*cont.*)
  452, 456, 458, 460, 465, 469,
    471–72, 474, 480
  active shaping of, 79, 207, 261, 348.
    See also knowing, as active
    shaping of clues to form a
    pattern
pedagogy, 5, 10–11, 40, 49, 55, 131,
    136–38, 260, 284, 367–68, 459
  as hospitality, 137–38, 350
perception, sense perception, 14, 24,
    26, 41, 69, 79, 82, 104, 107, 125,
    152n, 235, 286–87, 299, 308,
    361, 363, 370, 384, 386–87, 415,
    442, 456
perichoresis, perichoretic, 29, 46, 100n,
    270, 311, 327–28, 333–46,
    347–51, 352–55, 357–60, 362,
    364, 371, 377–82, 395, 403–6,
    407, 409, 413, 415–16, 427, 441,
    447, 458, 460–61, 466, 470–71,
    474
  asymmetry of, 339, 343, 356,
    380–81, 401
person, -s, 42, 55, 209, 223–26, 236,
    239, 241, 253, 310, 345, 355,
    366, 372, 375–78, 380–82,
    384–85, 389
  as being in communion, 285, 338,
    395
  autonymous, 320–24, 338
  as constituted in the gaze of
    another, 115, 120, 299, 304–5,
    375–76, 378, 390
  in communion, 36, 165, 227, 231,
    407
  In relation, 223–24, 227, 231, 233,
    244, 246, 376, 390
  in relationship, 41, 112
  inner- and other-directed, 320–25
  in the vicinity, 45, 102, 191, 205,
    211, 215, 230, 320, 358, 371, 382
  more or less fully, 314, 404
  self disclosure of, 234, 377

personal, 11, 23, 38, 43–46, 67, 74,
    95–96, 102–3, 105, 113, 127,
    140–41, 147, 164–65, 173–74,
    179–80, 205, 215, 217–20,
    221–25, 227–38, 239–40,
    241–46, 248, 253–54, 262, 266,
    272, 286, 290, 296, 298, 310,
    318, 342–45, 357–58, 365–66,
    368–70, 375–76, 378, 381–84,
    389, 396, 399–400, 402, 404–5,
    408, 412, 414, 416, 422, 440,
    444, 453, 456, 462, 472, 480
  asymmetry of the, 380–82
  beauty. *See* beauty, sense of
    personal
  context, 43, 148, 164, 180, 229–33,
    356, 406
  field/form of the, 46, 221, 223, 229,
    231n, 235–36, 238–39, 242, 246,
    262, 272, 370–71, 378, 380, 404
  primacy of the, 219n, 368, 371–74,
    378, 390
personhood, 28–29, 55, 89, 96, 100,
    103, 111, 122, 135, 216, 218–20,
    248, 253, 255, 266, 275, 287,
    289, 310, 314–16, 319, 321–22,
    327, 338, 343–45, 355, 365–66,
    371–76, 379, 383–90, 403, 447
perspective, -al, -ism, 10, 13, 58, 76, 91,
    107, 125, 127, 135, 158–59, 160,
    162–65, 169, 171–73, 179–80,
    185n, 215, 237, 262, 314, 341,
    419, 435, 472, 476. *See also*
    Framean triad
  and subsidiary-focal, 164, 171–74
phenomenology, ical, 16n, 44–45,
    105n, 126n, 248, 370, 382
philosophy, xi, xii, 6n, 16, 18–20, 43–
    44, 50–51, 53, 57, 59–61, 63, 68,
    89, 91, 110–11, 113, 117, 137n,
    149–50, 152, 154n, 157n, 159,
    163, 165–67, 171, 185, 220–22,
    224, 232, 237, 248, 265, 269,
    300, 305, 307n, 314, 328–30,
    336, 384–85, 416, 478

philosophy (*cont.*)
  analytic, 52, 55–56, 58, 147, 164,
    419, 459
  Continental, 59
  importance of, xi, xii, 17–18
  of biology, 384
  Thomist, **60–61**
  value of covenant epistemology for,
    51–55
physical, 18, 25, 27, 78, 88–89, 106,
    109n, 111–12, 117, 119, 206,
    225–27, 236, 307n, 312, 322,
    364, 374, 464
pilgrimage, **472–73**
place, 71, 91, 105n, 113, 115n, 136, 141,
    253, 258, 304, 428, 432
Platonic, -ism, 18, 330, 333, 362, 397
pledge, 33, 40–41, 72, 155, 195, 197,
    199, 201–4, **207**, 241, 245, 388n,
    401, 406, 429, 439, **447–48**, 452,
    454
pluralism, 330, 336, 340–41
Point A, -B, 70, **71–74**, 75–78, 83, 126,
    348
Polanyian epistemology. *See* episte-
    mology, Polanyian
possibilities, 26, 46, 75, 77, 84, 96, 97,
    176–77, 322–23, 378, 406, 433
Postmodern, -ism, -ity, postmodern
    thought, 54, 56n, **58–59**, **89–91**,
    140–41, 147, 157n. 161, 163,
    165–66, 323, 331–32, 340–41,
    374n
power, 11, 13, 20, 22–23, 25, 85, 121,
    140–41, 155, 253, 256, 273–74,
    276, 279–80, 309, 319, 361, 372,
    387, 403, 429, 431, 434, 444,
    455, 463, 474, 478
practical, 9, 96, 121, 133, 223–24, 226,
    228–29, 233, 236, 315, 329, 370,
    414, 426, 431, 475
pragmatic, -ism, 56, 89, 415, 419
prescriptive, prescriptivity, 81, 85, 141,
    152–53, 202, 204, 400

presence, 22, 25–27, 72, 75, 81, **114–16**,
    118–20, 128n, 155, 158–59, 164,
    178, 181n, 211, 241, 246, 252,
    254, 258, 265–67, 269–70, 273,
    279–81, 285–88, 290, 301–2,
    308–9, 316–17, 325, 342–43,
    349, 369, 371–72, 400, 402–3,
    413, 437, **440–41**, 442, 445,
    448–49, 457, 467n. *See also* be-
    ing present
presupposition, -s, -al, -alism, **57–58**,
    61, 140–41, 157n, 161, 163,
    165–68, 173, 176–77, 185, 221,
    228, 341, 355, 449
pretheoretical factors in knowledge,
    56, 85, 105, 416
profess, profession. *See* truth, as
    profession
promise, 25, 37, 41, 141, 145, 147, 155,
    195, **197–98**, 199, 201, 208, 278,
    357, 387–90, 401, 435, 447, 457,
    465, 469–70, 477–78
purpose, 184, 347, 374n, 387, 389

Radical Orthodoxy, **58–59**
rationalism, 82, 415–16
rationality, rational, xii, 7, 10–11, 18,
    20, 22, 26–28, 32, 42, 58, 60–62,
    68, 79, 85, 98, 107, 127–28, 149,
    154n, 168, 185, 217, 223–28,
    239n, 315, 330–31, 336, 339,
    342, 361, 374n, 412, 416, 470
real, reality, 42, 129, 222, 230, 246, 330,
    332, 334, 363–64, 368, 373, 398,
    410, 412–13, **425–68**. *See also*
    being; known; world
  accessing the, 42, 51, 90, 188–89,
    398, 400, 413–14, 426
  as communal, 366–67
  as gift, 344n, **365–82**, 402–3, 440,
    466–68, 476. *See also* gift
  as God and God's effects, 379, 402,
    433, 437–39, 452, 467, 476,
    478–79

real, reality (*cont.*)

as gracious, 205, 261, 290, 320, 344, 402, 420, 427, 468. *See also* grace; being, as gracious

as impersonal, 14–15, 21, 22-24, 379

as independent of knower, 259. *See also* realism, epistemic

as inexhaustible, 209, 369, 382, 405, 420

as personed, personlike, personal, 23, 100, 137, 221n, 229, 234, **235–37**, 344–45, **365–71**, 374, 376, 378, 380-83, 399–400, 402-3, 415, 427, 440, 452-53, 465, 472, 478

as responsive to covenantal, personal treatment, 201, 403

as rich, 75, **87**, 119, 188, 259–60, 368, 399, 420, 435

as surprising, 33, 51, 75, 77, 84, 87, 205, 208-9, 261, 290, 344, 369, 382, 401, 414, 420

as systematically inexhaustive, 84, 208, 369, 371, 382, 401, 420

breaks in, 208, 246, 290, 367, 432, 445, 467

contact with. *See* contact with reality

covenantal dimensions of, 33, 155, **201-2, 401-2**

criteria of, 74-76, 96, 421-22

indeterminate bearing of truth on, 75, 88, 146

primacy of, 386, 399–400, 403

self-disclosure of, 33, 37, 51, 57, 87, 97–98, 196, 201, 205, 208, 254, 268, 292, 295, 320, 344, 350, 357, 367-69, 400, 402-3, 406, 408, 414, 418, 425, 427, 432, 435, 437, 442, 451-53

submission to, 55, 69, 74–75, 90, 95, 141, 169, 184, 201, 205, 207, 261, 406, 409, 412, 420, 439

token of, 67, 69, 74–75, 407

transforms knower, 100, 209, 344, 400

yet-to-be-discovered, 32–33, 37, 72, 75, 100, 207, 378, 412, 439

realism, 138, 175n

anti- *vs.* anti-. *See* anti-realism

covenant, **397–402**

critical, 399–400

epistemic, 15, 54, 56, 61, 75, 90, **91–92**, 168, **208-9**, 259, 267, 290, 342, 398

reason, 8–9, 11, 18, 27–28, 41–42, 58, 62, 82, 87, 90, 94, 110, 115, 127, 170, 228, 331–32, 342, 363, 397, 409, 412, 415, 429n, 443

rebellion, 155, 180, 184–88, 191, 200, 206–7, 278, 286n, 288, 406-7, 439

reciprocity, 25–26, 29, 34, 67, 87, **95–103**, 106, 123, **128**, 129, 204, 211, 215, 236, 242, 254–55, 257–58, 272, 302, 316, 335, 345, 350–52, 354, 357, 361–63, 368–71, 401, 404–5, 407, 411, 415, 434, 447, 452, 475

rhythmical, 100, 257, 351, 354, 358, 399, 404, 411

redemption, redeem, 26, 57, 139, 152, 177, 186, 188–89, 206, 254–56, 262, 269, 282, 286n, **290–96**, 298, 301, 305–8, 337, 340, 347, 360–61, 364, 405, 416, 435, 439, 463–64, 467, 473, 476

Biblical drama, **59–60**, 61, 195–96, 291, 438

Biblical pattern of, 200, 208, 291, 293

reductionism, -ivism, 89, 110–12, 141, 373, 385

relation, 4–5, 27–29, 38, 42, 80, 102–3, 149, 159n, 204n, 221, 223–27, 229–30, 233–34, 236, 242–44, 246, 249–59, 261, 327, 329, 332,

relation (*cont.*)
334–40, 342–43, 346–48, 351, 353, 361–62, 366–67, 370, 372, 376–80, 382, 390, 403, 413, 438, 443, 446, 460, 465–66

relational, 28–29, 36, 49, 113, 131, 133, 138, 187, 197–98, 201, 203, 207, 234, 243, 245, 252, 262, 290, 310, 314, 335–36, 353, 358, 361, 363, 365, 372, 377–78, 380, 408, 429, 456, 459, 462, 466, 469

relationality, 244, 333–34, 336, 338, 340–41, 343–44, 346–47, 349, 351, 355–57, 359, 371, 377, 379, 405, 407, 409, 413, 415, 436, 460, 461, 466

relationship, interpersonal relationship, xii, 18n, 27, 42, 45, 64, 81, 84, 88, 95, 100, 111, 155, 174, 178–79, 181–82, 194, **195–96**, 197–98, 201, 204–6, 209, 211, 215–16, 224–25, 227, 229, 236, 238, 242–45, 249, 253–54, 258, 265, 267, 283, 290, 295, 310–11, 324–28, 351–54, 358, 361, 367, 377–82, 395–96, 400, 402–6, 412, 414, 428–29, 440–41, 446–47, 465

as covenantally constituted, 67, 174, 265, 358, 380, 382, 395, 404

as paradigm of knowing, 63, 67, 209, 249, 382

as ultimate context for knowing and being, 206, 361, 403

as unfolding, 258, 262, 352, 378, 395, 404

giver/receiver, 376–77, 380–81

healthy, **310–26**, 338

mother-child, **224–27**, 245, 265–66, 285, 288n, 362

space, in 263, 279, 311, 334–35, 355, 379, 381, 405–6, 416, 463

relativism, 11, 21, 61–62, 90, 157, 368, 387n, 398

renewal of all things, 186, 188–89, 200, 206, 210, 436, 438

respect, 15, 33, 38, 42–43, 51, 56, 75, 100, 115, 187–89, 207, 315, 318, 323–24, 335, 342, 345, 357, 367, 390, 405–6, 433, 459–60, 474

responsible, -ility, 6, 12n, 15, 17, 18n, 20–21, 23, 32, 38–39, 46, 49, 58, 69, 70, 72, 74, 88, 91–93, 95, 104, 110, 115, 132–34, 138, 145–46, 148–50, 156, 161, 166–67, 169, 175, 177, 179, 197, 199, 205, 207, 210, 216, 219, 241, 250, 254–55, 307, 315, 317, 319, 350–51, 385, 387–89, 406, 410–14, 417, 419–23, 429, 433, 450, 470

revelation, 11, 152, 173, 201, 234, 251, 282, 291, 377, 401, 451

rhythm, -ic, -ical, xiv, 82, 100, 204, 257, 262, 270, 351, 354, 356–57, 395, 404–5, 407, 466. *See also* reciprocity, rhythmical

risk, 20–21, 32–33, 46, 69, 72, 78, 92–93, 95, 134, 138, 169, 207–8, 241, 256, 259, 281, 317n, 376, 405–6, 408, 412, 420, 435, 444, 447, 449, 470, 476

sacrament, -al, 62–63, 282, 449, 466–67

sacrifice, 91, 245, 256, 259, 312–13, 317, 319, 339, 344, 347, 354, 356, 375, 429, 444, 467, 475, 480

say "You" and listen. *See* You, say "You" and listen

scholarship, xiv, 63–64, 94, 134, 149, 153, 157, 185, 188–89, 191, 264, 367n

Christian, 44, **56–61**, 134, 139, 185, 187, 202

value of covenant epistemology for, **51–55, 131–52**, 184

science, -tific, 8–10, 14, 23, 52, 55–56, 60, 79, 88–89, 91, 94–95, 107, 109–10, 112, 131, 133–34, 140,

science, -tific (*cont.*)
  149, 152, 166–67, 171, 210,
    229–30, 232–33, 235–39, 242,
    249, 258–59, 262, 284, 304,
    316n, 318, 338, 366, 373, 385,
    412, 461
  method, 127, 136
  discovery. *See* discovery
  knowing, 23, 126–28, 170, 175, 238,
    338
  knowledge, 56, 109n, 175, 232
Scripture, 20, 36, 57, **59–60**, 61, 63, 83,
    123, 133, 139, 146–47, 150–53,
    155–57, 159, 161–63, 165, 170,
    193–99, 201–3, 205, 208, 210,
    246, 251–52, 254n, 270, 273,
    278, 286n, 289–90, 293, 306,
    318, 325, 330, 336, 343, 361,
    368, 432, 436–39, 441, 455–6,
    464, 467n
seeing, 226, 230–31, 378, 452, 463
  as seeing-as, 158
  vs. looking, 261–62, 305, **462–65**
  what is there, 266–67
self, 27n, 230, 234, 236, 275, 294, 374n,
    376, 413, 437, 440, 443–45, 462
  -giving, 115, 249–52, 254, 258, 287,
    289, 299, 375, 377–78, 388–89,
    453, 467
  knowing, 115, 120, 127n, 161–63,
    189, 204n, 267–68, 296, 298–99,
    302–3, 305–6, 361, **408–9**, 441
  reflected sense of, 313–14, 317
  role of other persons in knowing,
    206, **264–70**, 268, 273, 279
  sense of, 113, 312–14, 317, 445
semper transformanda, ix, 136, 473
sense of increasing proximity to the
    solution, 124–25, 175, 258
sensus divinitatis, sense of deity, 58,
    149n
sense of personal beauty. *See* beauty,
    sense of personal
servant thinking, 147, 153, **156–58**,
    159, 163, 181, 205, 410

shalom, 116, 197
  knowing for, 51, 136, 210, 408,
    411–12, 422, **469–80**
silence, 114, 452, 457
sin, 155n, 155, 185, 200, 282, 285, 289,
    291–92, 295, 304, 454. *See also*
    rebellion
  noetic effects of, 60, 188, 210,
    410–11, 475
situation, situational, 4, 15, 31–32, 49,
    76, 87, 101, 112, 121, 124–25,
    134, 158–63, 165n, 169, 171–74,
    180, 187, **205–7**, 208, 210, 234,
    276, 281, 294–96, 303–4, 312,
    316–17, 331, 349, 353, 356, 370,
    398–99, 405, 407–8, 410–11,
    413, 435, 442, 444, 450, 475
  dimension, 147, 158, 244, 293, 354,
    384–85. *See also Umwelt;* world
situatedness, 32, 84, 160, 163, 168, 187,
    205–6, 275, 294, 410
skepticism, 11–13, 21, 39, 90, 92–93,
    132, 157, 398–99, 420
speech acts, 140, 447, 477
spirituality, 19, 62, 133, 306, 356, 368,
    375
"starbucking," 36, 204. *See also* friend-
    ship; intimacy; communion
stewardship, 51, 88, **145–83**, 188, 200,
    205, 244, 287, 369, 406, 410,
    411, 414, 417, 420, 439, 475. *See
    also* knowing, as stewardship
story, storied, 36, 59, 81, 162–63, 168,
    181–82, 193, 196, 201, 204n,
    215, 410, 440–41, 451, 454, 456,
    464, 472, 477
  biblical, 139, 195, 200, 205, 278,
    288n, 291, 293
  in the middle of a, 207–8, 293. *See
    also* knowing, being on the way
  unfolding, 405, 420
strategy, 51, 121, 131, 171, 179, 238,
    308–9, 343, 354, 383, 396, 428,
    436, 452, **453–65**, 467

subjective, -ivity, 8, 11, 13, 23, 103, 112, 128, 159, 168, 219, 249, 250–51, 254n, 412, 433, 438

subjectivism, 11, 52, 54, 61, 82, 90, 157, 165n, 368, 398, 461

submit, submission, xiii, 33, 55, 67, 69, 74–75, 90, 95, 131, 137, 141, 155, 163, 169, 184, 201, 205, 207, 261, 267, 268, 308, 316, 406–7, 409, 412, 420, 439, 450, 475

subsidiary, -ies, 22, 45–46, 70–72, 74, 77–78, 81–82, 84–93, 96, 100–101, **104–22**, 134, 137, 140–41, 145, 147, 159, 164, 167–70, 172–73, 175, 206, 239–42, 267, 307, 317, 348–49, 380, 386–87, 399, 402, 408, 410–17, 440, 442, 450, 458, 471

subsidiary-focal integration, 46, 53–54, **67–103**, 104, 111, 123–24, 132, 134, 138–39, 145, 158, 169, **171–74**, 181, 188, 215, 219–20, **240–42**, 243, 272–73 283, 294, 328, 342, 347, 357, 369, 380, 386–87, 390, 395, 398, 403, 405, **407**, 408, 411, 413–14, 435, 458, 474

substance, 27–28, 110, 127, 202, 217, 227, 276, 290, 337, 340, 361–62, 372, 412
  ontology, 26

substantiality. *See* particularity

substantivalism, -al anthropology, 20, 26–30, 162n, 193n, 217, 224, 233, 251, 325, 333, 337, 362, 411, 415

surprise, -ing, 33, 35n, 51, 74, 75–77, 84, 87, 102, 110n, 125n, 201, 205, 209–10, 251, 259, 261–62, 268, 290, 298n, 319–20, 339, 341, 344, 356, 369, 371, 378, 382, 389, 401–2, 405, 413–14, 420, 439, 453, 457, 462, 477, 480
  recognition, 176, 208, 425

symboling, 80, 178, 387–90

tacit, 4, 6, 22, 50, 56, 69–70, 74n, 76, **85**, 86, 89, 92–93, 95, 107, 110, 120, 133, 137, 139, 168, 172, 174, 185, 202–3, 219, 239, 260, 315, 364, 370, 459

teacher, 6, 79, 131–32, 136–38, 151, 219n, 232n, 266–70, 350, 360, 440–41, 451, 459. *See also* authoritative guides

testimony, 315, 415–16, 445–46

thankfulness, 378, 477

theism, theistic, 18, 182n, 219n, 237, 385n, 390

theological, xv, 6, 59–60, 94, 145–46, 148, 150, 154, 164, 176, 179, 181–82, 186, 188, 193–94, **201–2**, 207, 210, 215, 246, 251n, 287, 298n, 307n, 333, 342, 346, 353–54, 360–62, 409, 418, 435, 439, 468
  education. *See* education, theological
  method, 131, 140–41
  motifs, 44, **148**, 328
  posture, 139, 382
  study, 138–39, 149

theology, 7n, 10–11, 20, 29n, 59, 61, 63, 123, 134, 139, 149–50, 155, 157, 162–63, 166, 193–94, 206, 237, 298, 302, 307–8, 314, 328, 333, 336, 345, 359, 361
  and philosophy, 44, 147, 149
  biblical, 146, 435, 438–39, 467
  biblical vision of, xv, 146, 369–70, 374, 378

theoretical, theory, theorizing, 8–9, 16, 23, 27, 45, 52, 54, 62, 88, 91, 112, 133, 179, 221, 223, 226, 229–35, **237–39**, 240–42, 244, 250, 262, 340, 349, 364, 370–71, 373, 380, 397, 413, 416, 440, 463, 469

theoretical, theory, theorizing (*cont.*)
as metonymous reference, 229,
237–39, 295–96, 358, 371. *See also* metonymy
personal dimensions of, 229, 242, 244
standpoint, 221, 223, 229–33, 237–38, 240–42, 250
thinking, thought, 6n, 8, 15, 17–18, 27, 32, 44, 49, 52n, 54–55, 57–58, 62, 84, 110–12, 127, 146–47, 152, 168, 172, 176, 184, 189, 202, 205, 221–23, 226, 229–31, 233, 238, 244–46, 250–51, 257, 265, 273, 308, 328–29, 331, 333, 336–37, 359, 370, 372, 375, 384, 411, 425, 430–31, 435, 442, 449, 457–59, 461, 464, 473
bodily rootedness of all. *See* body, rootedness of all thought
in a personal context, **229–33**
thisness. *See* particularity
touch, tactile, tactual, 24–26, 111–12, 119, 225–26, 230, 245, 308, 370, 408, 415–16, 463
tradition, 17, 23–25, 35, 39, 43, 52, 55, 58–61, 79, 85, 95, 105, 107, 141, 146n, 150–51, 166, 170, 176, 184–86, 206, 216, 219n, 221, 240, 249, 259, 268, 270, 316n, 318, 329, 336, 338, 342, 361–62, 398, 409, 416, 419, 425–26, 430, 471, 475, 478
transcendental, -s, 286, 334–35, 337–38, 343
transformation, 6, 16, 33, 63, 72, 77, 82–83, **123–30**, 254, 257, 268, 272, 279–82, 286, 289, 299, 306, 317, 327, 339, 347, 356, 369, 378, 380, 387n, 390, 400, 407–9, 412–14, 419, 421, 429, 445, 452, 460, 462, 466–67, 469, **472, 473**, 475–78

knowing as. *See* knowing, as transformation
logic of, five-step sequence of, 124–27, 274, 276, 279, 282, **290–93**
triangulating, **81–83**, 84, 124, 173–74, 242, 327, 349
Trinity, 29n, 140, 151–52, 159, 198, 201–2, 270, 319, 326–28, 330, **333–40**, 342, 345–46, 351–56, 359, 361–64, 372n, 378, 401, 465–66
trust, 13–14, 21–22, 43, 83, 155, 169, 177–79, 207, 209, 241, 267, 269, 285, 315–16, 318, 323–25, 352, 361, 363, 414, 436, 444, **448–49**, 450
truth, 11–13, 17, 21, 23, 32, 39, 43–44, 54, 56, 88, 95, 112, 120, 127–28, 140, 164–65, 167n, 169, 175, 179, 186, 189, 207, 221–22, 282, 288n, 324–25, 329, 332, 338, 341, 351, 353, 361, 367, 373, 375, 380, 387–88, 396, 401, 405, 409, 412–13, 418, 422, 431–32, 436, 438, 443–44, 455, **475–77**, 479
absolute, 11–12, 157, 160n, 163, 340
and God, 156–57, 402, 410, 467
as personal, 23, 43, 103, 365–66, 434, 450
as profession, 63, 74, 88, 92, 157, 176, 350, 406, 423
as propositions, 62, 367
as troth, 13–14, **40**, 41–42, 157, 406, 447, 450, 457, 466
claims, 7, 21, 41, 54, 57, 63, 68–70, 75, 92–93, 121, 134, 161, 169, 174, 177, 260, 270, 350–51, 385, 387–88, 406, 416, 419, 422–23
held responsibly with universal intent. *See* universal intent
Jesus the. *See* Jesus, the Truth

Umwelt, 384–85, 387, 389–90

unbeliever, 56–58, 148–49, 155, 176, 184–89, 191, 205, 328, 355, 357, 390, 437, 439

understanding, 5, 12n, 15–16, 18, 23–30, 37, 42–43, 47, 54, 59, 70, 72, 81, 88, 90, 100–101, 103, 109, 119, 149, 163, 168, 170, 176, 185, 187, 193–95, 200, 204, 207, 220, 235, 251, 255, 257, 259, 262, 281, 286–87, 296, 300, 307, 323, 325, 327–28, 330, 334, 340, 342, 347, 353, 366, 371–72, 374, 377, 406, 410, 416, 418, 420, 427, 433–34, 438, 444, 446, 450, 463, 467n, 468, 476

unfolding, 35, 38, 61, 84, 87, 98, 100, 123, 163, 175, 182, 216–17, 244, 257–58, 260–62, 273, 277, 291, 296, 333, 335, 337, 348–49, 351–54, 357–58, 362, 374, 378, 395, 406–8, 420, 439, 465, 469
covenant relationship. *See* covenant, as unfolding relationship; knowing, as unfolding covenant relationship

universal intent, 12n, 95, 177, 350–51, 406, 423

unspecifiable, 74–76, 91–93, 96–97, 99, 107, 138, 243, 399, 408, 418, 420, 422

vector, vectoring, 32, 72–74, 81–82, 84, 158–60, 172, 174, 208, 405, 410. *See also* subsidiary-focal integration; intentionality

virtue, 29, 38, 56, 85, 93, 153, 155, 159, 199, 205, 227, 228, 312n, 319, 324n, 339, 373n, 379, 419, 429, 446–47, 453
epistemology. *See* epistemology, virtue

virtuosity, 6, 105, **108–9**, 114, 116, 119, 181n, 241, 307–8, 317, 349, 402, 414, 442, 471

void, 275–80, 282, 285, 287–89, 291–95, 401, 403, 420, 466–68, 472, 477
-holy dynamic, -ism **293–96**, 327, 354, 395, 403

waiting, 33, 97, 120, 252, 262, 305, 357, 367, 431, 452, 463

Western tradition of ideas and culture, 6–7, 13, 17–20, 24, 26, 29, 55–56, 79, 85–86, 170, 249, 259, 328–29, **329–33**, 336, 361–62, 420–21, 426, 471, 478

wholeness, ix, 47, 113, 118, 147, 158, 228, 245, 247, 281, 286, 299, 301, 303, 325, 368, 381, 408, 430, 438, 441, 444–45, 458, 470, 473

will, 40, 333, 337, 345–46, 447

wisdom, 9–10, 15–16, 50, 104–5, 121, 131, **133**, 137, 139, 361, 404, 411, 414, 422, 427, 429–30, 437n, 475

wonder, 9, 27, 31–32, 171, 220, 258–59, 296, 314, 319, 432, 458

world, 5, 9, 12–13, 18–19, 22, 24, 28, 30, **76–77**, 158, 160, 199, 208, 221–23, 230, 240, 244, 249, 268, 303–4, 306, 329, 367, 379, 384n, 416, 457, 459, 463n, 467. *See also* reality; creation; situation; known
accessing the, 15, 31, 329, 399, 412
and I-You encounter, 253–54, 256–58
as impersonal, 14, 235–36, 268, 370, 383
as personal, 23, 236–37, 337, 370, 381–82, 453
engaging the. *See* humans, engaging the world
knowing, correlative with knowing God, 160, 162n, **408–9**
lived, 275–76, 293–94

world (*cont.*)
  looking the world back to grace,
    261, 304
  nonhuman, 156n, 324, 329, 338,
    340, 342–43, 345
  orienting to the, 31–32, 84, 249,
    317, 378–79, 381
worldview, 57, 79, 135, 140–41, 154,
    163, 167–68, 200
worship, 62–63, 94, 131, 138–39, 200,
    266–67, 277–78, 454, 467n, 477

You, 234, 250–54, 258–59, 262, 403
  say "You" and listen, 236, 252, 257,
    260, **452–53**, 476
  "so it is You," 254, 258, 378, 402,
    477–80

NAME INDEX

Aaron, 289
Adams, Richard, xiv-n
Allen, R. T., 219n, 420n, 429–30
Allender, Dan, 204n, 445
Apczynski, John, 52n
Aquinas, Thomas, 28n, 60, 149, 152n, 222, 372, 374n, 390
Aristotle, 26, 28n, 171, 251, 372, 390
Augustine of Hippo, 59, 149, 205, 330, 334, 372n, 388, 430, 437

Barash, David, 24n
Barbour, Ian, 366
Bartholomew, Craig, 60n
Belkina, Marija, 113n
Berry, Wendell, 111n, 114–16, 303
Blackburn, Simon, 157n
Booth, Wayne, 16n
Botton, Alain de, 446
Brentano, Franz, 172
Buber, Martin, 17n, 43, 46, 129n, 219n, 233n, 235–36, 239, 248–62, 272–73, 276, 281, 283–85, 288, 290, 299, 306, 310–11, 314, 327, 353, 355–56, 358, 368, 378, 380, 404, 434–36, 438, 452–53, 462, 474, 477

Calvin, John, 57–58, 61, 146–47, 149n, 151, 155–56, 161–62, 165, 177, 185n, 437
Capon, Robert Farrar, 261n, 303–4, 306, 340n, 433–35, 441, 462n
Caputo, John, 376n
Chesterton, G. K., 340n
Chisholm, Roderick, 92n
Clark, Tony, 94n
Clement of Alexandria, 437

Clinchy, Blythe, 440, 461–62, 470
Clouser, Roy, 307n
Colbert, Andrew, 202n, 222n, 268n, 278
Columbus, Christopher, 420
Copernicus, Nicolaus, 36n, 91
Cowan, Steven, 56n
Craig, William Lane, 56n

Dancy, Jonathan, 396n
Dark, David, 451, 457
Darwin, Charles, 372–74, 385, 389–90
da Vinci, Leonardo, 420n, 430
Derrida, Jacques, 9n, 376n, 387n
Descartes, Rene, 17–19, 27, 77, 89, 91, 96, 104, 110–12, 117, 157, 168, 218, 222, 232, 234, 244–46, 268, 270, 287, 294, 331, 364, 384, 386n, 416, 445, 478–79
Dewart, Leslie, 443
Dewey, John, 127
Dillard, Annie, 35–37, 43, 176, 209n, 264n, 316, 320, 345n, 434, 448, 450, 452, 454n
Dilthey, Wilhelm, 57, 166
Dooyeweerd, Hermann, 57, 149n, 286–87
Dostoyevsky, Fyodor, 269

Edwards, Jonathan, 286n
Eldredge, John and Staci, 286n, 303

Fairfield, Leslie, 361–63
Fenelon, Francois, 113, 307n
Fleming, Dale and Lorraine, 307n
Frame, John, 36, 45–46, 51n, 57, 76, 81, 88, 145–47, 149–51, 153–56, 158–82, 184–85, 188, 193–95,

Frame, John (*cont.*), 198–201, 205–7,
    209, 211, 216, 218, 242, 244, 246,
    267, 270, 277, 282, 293–95, 316,
    342, 353–55, 358, 380, 422–23,
    437, 451, 465, 474
Frazier, Robert, ix, 56n, 137n, 264, 270,
    322n, 432n

Garber, Steve, 433
Geivett, Douglas, 56n
Gelwick, Richard, 94n
Gendlin, Eugene, 120–21, 125, 422,
    442–43, 456
Gibson, Eleanor and James, 386–87
Giltinan, Martha, 354n
Gladwell, Malcom, 121
God *See* Subject Index
Goethe, Johann Wolfgang von, 254,
    402, 429, 477
Goldman, Alvin, 89n
Greco, John, 396n
Gregory, Saint, 43, 434
Gregory of Nazianzus, 361
Grene, Marjorie, 19n, 53, 68n, 80–81,
    84–85, 92, 105n, 110n, 120,
    172n, 178, 239, 268–69, 324,
    374n, 383–90, 399, 446
Grier, James M., 199n
Gunton, Colin, 17n, 24–26, 28–29, 46,
    100n, 182, 218, 311, 326–59,
    361, 368n, 370–71, 378, 380,
    386n, 434, 460
Guthrie, David, ix
Guthrie, Donald, 10n

Harris, John, 16n
Hart, David Bentley, 308, 465
Hegel, G. W. F., 16n, 157
Heidegger, Martin, 7n, 26n, 53, 59,
    384n
Heisenberg, Werner von, 37, 320
Heraclitus, 330, 336
Heschel, Abraham Joshua, 43, 137, 139,
    432, 434

Homer, xiv-n
Horton, Michael, 59
Houston, James, 217–18, 325, 327
Hughes, John J., 146n
Hume, David, 337n

Irenaeus of Lyons, 334

Jaki, Stanley, 331
Jesus Christ *See* Subject Index
Job, 291
Johnson, Mark, 110, 112, 225n
Jones, David, 159n

Kant, Immanuel, 384, 399, 416
Kaufmann, Walter, 249
Keller, Evelyn Fox, 367n, 460
Kierkegaard, Søren, 16n, 250n, 252n,
    254n, 279
Kilpatrick, Shirley, 286n
Kirkpatrick, Frank, 221, 233
Kepler, Johannes, 36n
Kline, Meredith, 153n
Koestler, Arthur, 125n
Kuhn, Thomas S., 52, 167
Kuyper, Abraham, 57, 185n

Lakoff, George, 110, 112, 225
Lerner, Harriet, 311n
Levinas, Emmanuel, 375
Lewis, C. S., xiv-n, 251n, 317n, 477
Locke, John, 24
Loder, James, 17n, 46, 123–29, 134,
    182, 230–31, 238, 252–53,
    257, 261, 266–67, 272–94, 296,
    298–99, 300, 302, 306, 310, 314,
    327, 354–57, 375, 383n, 418,
    423n, 437, 459, 462, 470, 477
Lonergan, Bernard, 60, 145n
Louden, Russell, ix, 300–301, 431
Luther, Martin, 28n, 169, 351
Lyotard, Jean Francois, 7n, 157n, 185

MacIntyre, Alasdair, 52

Macmurray, John, 46, 215, 217–48, 250,
    252–53, 262, 272–73, 283–85,
    298, 306, 310, 314, 327, 338,
    355–56, 369–71, 378, 380, 404,
    411, 429n, 465, 474, 476n
Maker, Steve, 309n
Malebranche, Nicolas, 430
McClay, Wilfred, 320–22
McClintock, Barbara, 367, 459–60
McCoy, Charles, 94n
MacLaren, Brian, 90n
McNeill, John T., 437n
Meek, Starr, 298–99, 307–8, 441n
Mendenhall, G. E., 194n
Merleau-Ponty, Maurice, 26n, 53,
    77–78, 107, 110n, 385–86
Moleski, Martin, 52n, 60–61, 73n, 94n,
    166n, 219n
Moltmann-Wendel, Elizabeth, 25,
    112–13, 120, 302–3, 364,
    441–42, 445–46, 459–60
Mondello, Bob, 453n
Moreland, J. P., 56
Morrison, Toni, 309
Morton, Nellie, 456
Moses, 37, 320, 361n
Mouw, Richard, 185n

Nathaniel, the Apostle, 291
Naugle, David, 105n, 166–67
Niebuhr, Richard, 206
Nietzsche, Friedrich, 7n, 16n
Newbigin, Lesslie, 35–36, 38–40, 43,
    94n, 102–3, 135n, 151n, 175n,
    179, 202n, 208–9, 380, 401, 472,
    476, 478–79
Newman, John Henry, 61
Noll, Mark, 19n, 135
Nouwen, Henri, 350, 455

Ockham, William, 333n

Pascal, Blaise, 430

Palmer, Parker, 4–5, 22–23, 35, 40–43,
    97n, 102–3, 137n, 198, 221n,
    319, 350, 365–70, 409, 428–29,
    432, 434, 436n, 440–41, 443–45,
    447, 450, 454–60, 466, 474
Parmenter, Michael, 121, 443
Parry, Robin, 63n
Parish, Peggy and Herman, 4n
Paul, the Apostle, 202, 291, 369, 479
Pegis, Anton, 222n
Peirce, Charles Sanders, 178
Percy, Walker, 80, 178, 266–67
Peterson, Eugene, 404
Pharoah of Egypt, 292, 295
Pirsig, Robert, 461
Plantinga, Alvin, 58, 149, 150
Plato, 6n, 17–18, 21, 24, 53, 80, 170,
    222n, 330, 333, 353, 362, 397–98
Plessner, Helmuth, 172n
Polanyi, Michael, 7n, 12n, 16n,
    21–25, 35–36, 44–47, 51–54,
    57–61, 67–79, 81, 84–91, 93–97,
    99–100, 102–3, 105–11, 117,
    120–29, 134, 141, 145–47, 149n,
    151n, 158–59, 161n, 163–64,
    166–77, 179, 181–82, 184, 187–
    88, 193, 205–8, 210–11, 215–20,
    231, 237–45, 248, 250, 257–60,
    262, 267n, 270, 272–73, 283n,
    293, 307, 316, 318, 341–42,
    347, 349–51, 357, 365–66, 369,
    380, 385–87, 389–90, 398–400,
    405–8, 410–11, 413, 417,
    420–21, 423, 425, 429, 456, 458,
    461–62, 465, 471–72, 478–79
Poteat, William, 94n

Quine, W. V. O., 88–89

Ridderbos, Herman, 151n
Rilke, Rainer Marie, 369, 402
Riesman, David, 27n, 311, 320–25, 338
Robertson, O. Palmer, 198

Rolnick, Philip, 344, 355, 365, 371–76, 378–81, 383, 385, 389–90, 466
Rorty, Richard, 24n
Ryle, Gilbert, 88–89

Samson, 291
Sanders, Andy, 94n, 178
Schaeffer, Francis, 60, 298n
Scheler, Max, 219n, 429, 430
Schnarch, David, 46, 310–14, 318–21, 324, 327, 356, 441, 460
Scott, William, 52, 73, 93, 166, 219
Scott, Drusilla, 93
Sennett, James, 58n
Simon, Caroline, 42, 118, 177, 433
Smith, James K. A., 58–59, 157, 188
Smith, R. Scott, 56n
Snell, R. J., 24n
Sosa, Ernest, 92, 396n
Spencer, Stephen, 135n
Stanley, John, 453
Stapp, Henry, 366
Steiner, George, 246n, 400n, 448–49
Stump, Eleonore, 60n
Taylor, Charles, 52
Tertullian of Carthage, 149
Thomas, the Apostle, 291, 438
Tolkien, J. R. R., xiv-n
Torrance, Thomas, 94n

Vanhoozer, Kevin, 59
Van Til, Cornelius, 57–58, 151–54, 161, 173, 184, 353–54

Wander, Maxie, 446n
Weil, Simone, 118, 176, 204, 262, 289, 304–5, 431–32, 446, 452, 455–56, 480
Weinerth, Roger, 115
Williams, Mike, 36, 46, 59, 145, 150n, 153, 162n, 182, 193–211, 216, 246, 251–52, 270, 291, 293, 295, 314–15, 351, 354, 358, 361n, 380, 437–38, 465, 476
Williams, Terri, 288n
Wilson, E. O., 373
Wittgenstein, Ludwig, xiii, 16n, 53, 80–81, 150n, 159
Wolterstorff, Nicholas, 58, 135n, 149–50, 185n, 210, 473n

Zizioulas, John, 28–29, 218, 327
Zukav, Gary, 367n